PLACE IN RETURN BOX to remove this checkout from your record.
TO AVOID FINES return on or before date due.

DATE DUE	DATE DUE	DATE DUE
853 JAN 24 199	46 043 JUL 19 1998	MAY 0 8 2006
9 1996 69	113	03 12 07 MAR 1 2 2007
MAY 0 2 JUL 15 183	345 NOV 2 7 1998	FEB 08 2010
NOV 289 FEB 0 5 1997	DEC 0 1 2001	
FEB 2 4 1997 54	JAN 2 8 2002	
MAR 3 1 90	JAN 0 6 2003	
MAY 6 1997	OCT 0 0 2003	

A Biographical History of
Blacks in America Since 1528

A BIOGRAPHICAL HISTORY OF
BLACKS
IN AMERICA
SINCE 1528

by Edgar A. Toppin

This book is based on a series of articles that appeared weekly in The Christian Science Monitor, *March 6 to June 12, 1969.*

DAVID McKAY COMPANY, INC.   NEW YORK

A BIOGRAPHICAL HISTORY OF BLACKS IN AMERICA SINCE 1528

This book is dedicated to my mother, the former MAUD CATHE-RINE JOELL of Bermuda, in hopes that it helps fulfill the quest that brought her to the United States half a century ago in search of better opportunity for herself and her descendants.

Acknowledgments

This book grew out of an educational television course the writer taught and a series of newspaper articles he wrote. He is indebted to Mary Anne Franklin, vice president and program director of Central Virginia Educational Television Corporation in Richmond, for suggesting the 30-lesson e.t.v. course, "Americans from Africa: A History," and to Robert C. Nelson, American news editor of *The Christian Science Monitor* in Boston, Massachusetts, for proposing the fifteen-part newspaper series, "Blacks in America: Then and Now."

For their donations that financed the preparation of the television scripts, the writer is grateful to Thomas C. Boushall, a bank founder and staunch supporter of educational television, and four of his fellow Richmonders: a publisher; a department store scion; the board chairman of a bank; and a senior partner in a leading law firm. Actual production was made possible by a grant from The Old Dominion Foundation to the television station, for which the writer is thankful. Many persons contributed their time, talents, and thoughts in the making of the television lessons, the newspaper articles, and this book, but a special thanks is owed to television director Wilbert Keys, *Monitor* editorial staffer Stanley Hall, and David McKay Company's editorial vice president, Elliott Schryver, all three of whom exhibited patience beyond the call of duty. The writer is also thankful to the administrator of Virginia State College in Petersburg for permitting him to take leave to work on these projects.

Both the television lessons and the newspaper series had unexpected ripples. Produced at the e.t.v. station in Richmond and first telecast over its channels 23 (WCVE-TV) and 57 (WCVW-TV) in the fall of 1968, the lessons were redistributed by the Great Plains National Instructional Television Library, located at the University of Nebraska in Lincoln, Nebraska, and were being used before the end of 1969 by e.t.v. stations and closed circuit educacational systems from coast to coast. After the newspaper articles, based on the thirty television lessons, appeared in *The Christian Science Monitor* in fifteen weekly installments, March 6 to June 12, 1969, they were redistributed by the Copley News Service of San Diego, California, running in many other newspapers from *The Newark* (N.J.) *News* to *The Seattle* (Wash.) *Times*. Moreover, the series received additional circulation as one of the first booklets in the *Monitor*'s reprint series.

In preparing this greatly expanded version and in adding an extensive biographical section not found in the original series, the writer received assistance from many persons. He particularly wishes to thank Mrs. Sadie Richie and the other reference librarians at Virginia State College as well as at the State Library and Virginia Union University library, both in Richmond. He is grateful to Miss Ernestine Coleman and Mrs. Rose Bland for typing the manuscript. Finally, he was blessed to have a devoted wife, son, and daughters who proved so understanding during many lost evenings and weekends preempted by the book and who cooperated in doing some of the chores connected with the book.

Needless to say, none of the persons cited above can be held in any way responsible for the views expressed by the writer in the television series, the newspaper articles, or this book. Their counsel was always appreciated even when the imperatives of marching to the drum he heard caused the writer not to heed it.

Contents

Acknowledgments   vii

1   African Background   1
    Prehistory to 1591

2   The Slave Trade and Latin American Slavery   17
    1441-1565

3   Slavery in the British Colonies   34
    1619-1763

4   Afro-Americans in the Revolutionary Era   48
    1763-1800

5   Cotton Kingdom and Plantation Slavery   64
    1791-1860

6   Slave Life and Revolts   79
    1800-1860

7   North of Slavery and Black Abolitionists   92
    1800-1860

8   Slavery Issue and the Civil War   105
    1850-1865

9   Freedmen and Carpetbag Regimes   120
    1865-1877

10   Atlanta Compromise, Disfranchisement, and Jim Crow   134
    1877-1900

11   Northward Migration and Turn-of-the-Century Achievers   148
    1880-1910

12   The Niagara Movement, NAACP, and World War I   162
    1905-1921

13   UNIA, Harlem Renaissance, and the New Deal   175
    1920-1940

14   Era of Progress: World War II Through
    Desegregation Decision   188
    1941-1955

15   Civil Rights Revolution and New Militancy   202
    1955–1971

Suggestions for Additional Reading (by Chapter)   222
Biographies of Notable Black Americans   241
Index   485

A Biographical History of
Blacks in America Since 1528

1

African Background

Prehistory to 1591

As Mansa Musa stepped into the palace yard, he had more on his mind than the customary audiences. Soon he would be leaving on the hajj. He was anxious to resume preparations for this journey, but his subjects awaited him.

He stepped from a door in the corner of his palace, wearing a golden skullcap and a "velvety red tunic, made of the European fabrics called *mutanfas.*" Preceding him as he strode across the courtyard were his musicians, carrying "gold and silver *guimbris* [two-stringed guitars], and behind him come three hundred armed slaves." The procession moved toward the *pempi*, or *bembe*, a triple-tiered platform under a tree. As described by the Arab traveler, Ibn Batuta, in his book, *Travels in Asia and Africa, 1325–1354*, the *pempi* "is carpeted with silk and has cushions placed on it." Above the platform "is raised the umbrella, which is a sort of pavillion made of silk, surmounted by a bird in gold, about the size of a falcon." As Mansa Musa took his seat on the *pempi*, the drums, trumpets, and bugles sounded.

As the emperor listened to his people, his thoughts kept turning to his trip. Finally, the audiences were over. Mansa Musa could concentrate again on the Hajj, the pilgrimage to Mecca that Moslems undertake at least once in their lifetime. He would not be the first ruler of Mali to make the journey, but he planned on a more lavish display than any of his predecessors. He wished to make an impression on his subjects as he visited many parts of his far-flung empire on the way to Mecca; he wanted to impress his fellow Moslems of the Middle East and also the whole world.

His preparations completed, Mansa Musa set forth in the year

1

1324 from his capital city of Kangaba. In his history of Afro-Americans, entitled *From Slavery to Freedom*, Professor John Hope Franklin of the University of Chicago states that Mansa Musa's

> entourage was composed of 60,000 persons, a large portion of which constituted a military escort. No less than 12,000 were servants, 500 of whom marched ahead of their king, each bearing a staff of pure gold. Books, baggage men, and royal secretaries there were in abundance. To finance the pilgrimage, the king carried eighty camels to bear his more than 24,000 pounds of gold.

Altogether, Mansa Musa had $5,000,000 worth of gold with him to make princely presents, sometimes as grandiose as mosques.

Thus he rode out of West Africa in golden splendor on this historic journey eastward. He spent so much money in the Middle East that he depressed the price of gold in the great commercial center of Cairo. But the anger of the gold merchants was assuaged when he subsequently borrowed huge sums, at handsome rates, after running low on cash. Years later, people still spoke and wrote with awe of the impact of this wealthy ruler's visit.

The ripples from his journey spread beyond the Middle East. He literally put his country on the map. Fourteenth-century European cartographers added drawings of this fabulous monarch to their maps, labeling him "Rex Melle, King of the Gold Mines." Melle, Mellestine, and Mandingoland were other names for Mali, an empire of the Sudanic blacks in West Africa.

Of what significance in 1971 is this journey made 647 years ago by Mansa Musa (also known as Gonga Musa)? It is symbolic of the efforts of black people, then and now, to write a proud record on the pages of history. African emperors, like Mansa Musa, ruled realms larger than non-Russian Europe, at a time when there were no rapid communications or transportation. In wealth and power, these black states were comparable to the medieval European kingdoms of their day. Africans had developed complex politico-economic systems and a humane social order stressing, through the extended family, responsibility for one's fellow man. Furthermore, these blacks of West Africa possessed a highly sophisticated art of great power and beauty.

Nonetheless, writers in modern Europe and America have often dismissed Africa as a dark continent where no significant progress ever occurred. They have considered Africans inferior and primitive people.

Despite his pompous display on the pilgrimage of 1324, Mansa Musa made no lasting impact on the consciousness of the Western world. His failure was duplicated many times in Africa, Latin America, and the United States. No matter what the accomplishments of black men, little was ever heard of them as long as books were written by whites from a point of view that regarded Africans as backward people who only made progress when colonized by European powers. Hence the appalling ignorance of the average American today concerning the role played by blacks in their nation's past. This ignorance begins with misconceptions about Africa, the continent whence blacks came.

Raised on a diet of Tarzan stories, movies, and telecasts, many Americans believe Africa to be a land of hot, steamy jungle. But Africa is more savanna than anything else. Of the continent's 11,600,000 square miles (three and a half times the size of the United States—including Alaska and Hawaii), 5,600,000 square miles consists of savanna. Savannas are grassy, mostly treeless, regions with little rainfall, similar to, but a little warmer and drier than, the American prairie from Texas to the Dakotas. Next to the savanna grasslands, the terrain found most often in Africa is desert. The continent has 4,000,000 square miles of desert, the Sahara in the north and the Kalahari in the southwest. The remaining 2,000,-000 square miles of Africa is divided evenly between two quite dissimilar regions: a million square miles of mountainous areas and of coastal strips with Mediterranean-type climates, and a million square miles of the tropical rain forests popularly called "jungles." Comprising less than ten percent of all Africa, the jungles are located primarily on sections of the Guinea coast, in the Niger River delta, and astride the equator stretching inland along the middle Congo River to the highlands of East Africa, and only one-fourth of this jungle region has more average annual rainfall than occurs in a spot like Mobile, Alabama. Only about two percent of the entire continent comprises the wet, steamy jungle popularly thought of in connection with Africa.

Misinformation about Africa's terrain is matched by misinformation about Africa's past. Most people regard Africa as the last continent to show any signs of progress. But Paul Bohannon, Professor of Anthropology at Northwestern University, contended in his book, *Africa and Africans*, that "Africa seems to have been the home not merely of mankind but also, and obviously, of human culture." In 1959, Dr. Louis S. B. Leakey and his wife, Mary, discovered at Olduvai Gorge near Lake Tanganyika in East Africa the fossil remains of Zinjanthropus, a toolmaker who lived a million and a half years ago. He existed so long before other known fossil remains—such as Peking Man of 350,000 years ago—that it seems safe to assume that Africa was the birthplace of man. Also, toolmaking, a basic step in man's evolution from lower life, apparently first occurred on the black man's continent. Similarly, the earliest known pottery was made in Africa in the Paleolithic (Old Stone) Age, more than thirty thousand years ago.

There were other signs of early development in Africa. Black men of West Africa were among the first to learn to farm. They practiced agriculture in the Niger River valley over six thousand years ago, apart from its origins in the Jordan River valley of Asia four thousand years previously. Moreover, Africans were among the first, if not the first, men to make iron tools and weapons. As Dr. Leakey pointed out in his book, *The Progress and Evolution of Man in Africa*, "Africa was in the forefront of all world progress [playing] the dominant role . . . for something like 600,000 years."

The fact that a higher civilization developed in Egypt posed a dilemma for Western men who regarded Africa as "the dark continent." This complex civilization and other evidences of progress in Africa were explained, however, by attributing them to white men who came to Africa from elsewhere. In his recent book, *The Image of Africa*, Professor Philip Curtin of the University of Wisconsin told of one nineteenth-century writer who

> claimed that the Negro people of the Western Sudan were not really Negroes at all. They were physically like other Negro peoples, but their "state of comparative civilization" . . . showed they had reached heights impossible for the "inferior" Negro race.

Fortunately, scholars increasingly recognize that civilization is not the exclusive province of any race. Racial mixing was too extensive in some parts of Africa, especially the northeastern portion, to permit objective standards by which achievements can be racially apportioned. In other areas, especially the southern and western, black men were undoubtedly responsible for all progress that occurred.

The dynastic civilization that began in the Nile River valley more than five thousand years ago was founded by people of mixed stock who settled there: Mediterraneans from southern Europe, Semites from southwest Asia, and Negroid people from the upper Nile. Professor John Hope Franklin contends that "before the culture and civilization of Egypt took shape there had come into being a new group of people, neither basically Mediterranean, Semite, nor Ethiopian, but Egyptian—the sum total of the intermingling." Pharaoh Ra Nahesi, who ruled about 3000 B.C., was described as a black man. The Egyptians engaged in commerce along the Nile River with the land to the south (the Upper Nile) dominated by darker peoples, the Nubians or Kushites (often called, inaccurately, Ethiopians). Many of these darker people moved into Egypt, adding to the racial mixture there. When the Hyksos of Asia Minor (called Shepherd Kings in the Bible) invaded Egypt, many Egyptians fled up the Nile, settling among and intermingling for several centuries with the Nubians of Kush.

Egypt and Kush were frequently at war. Finally, Kush conquered Egypt and established a black dynasty of pharaohs. The five Kushite rulers who composed the Twenty-fifth Dynasty were Piankhi, Shabaka, Shabataka, Tarhaqa, and Tanutamon. They ruled Egypt from 725 B.C. to 656 B.C. There was a cultural revival under these men who ruled from their capital at Napata in Kush. In the article on Egypt in the *Encyclopaedia Britannica*, Egyptologist Margaret S. Drower says of these black pharaohs:

> New vigour was breathed into the failing talents of Egypt's artists under the encouragement of the Napatan pharaohs. Themselves enthusiasts for the great days of the past, they sought to revive the ancient skills and recapture the old inspiration. . . .

Shabaka built a chapel at Karnak and restored the temple of Thebes. Tarhaqa tried to revive the religion and restore texts; he began the massive temple at Karnak. Fierce Assyrians drove out

these black pharaohs and subdued Egypt. Another dynasty followed the Assyrians and five dynasties ruled during the Persian
conquest, before Egypt finally fell to the Greeks under Alexander
the Great in 332 B.C.

Although Egypt fell, the Nubian kingdom of Kush continued for
seven more centuries. Nubian civilizations had existed south of
Egypt as early as 3000 B.C., but Egyptian attacks had disrupted
them. Kashta founded the kingdom of Kush in 750 B.C., three centuries before the Golden Age of Greece. His successors conquered
Egypt, forming the Twenty-fifth Dynasty. Ruins of pyramids and
temples stand along the Nile at the sites of the Kush capitals:
Napata (750–590 B.C.) and Meroe (590 B.C.-A.D. 350).

When the ruins at Meroe are fully excavated and when scholars
are able to decipher Meroitic inscriptions, we shall know more
about the accomplishments of this important civilization. Meroe
was one of the world's great centers for the iron industry. Huge slag
heaps from the smelting of iron at Meroe still tower near the ruins
of the city. Other imposing ruins of Meroitic Kush are the temple at
Naga and the great enclosure at Musawarat as-Safra.

Although Kush flourished for a thousand years, it dropped from
sight after its destruction by conquering armies three and a half
centuries after Christ. The excavations at Meroitic centers in recent
times brought this lost civilization to light again. Ancient and modern writers often confused Kush, the land of the Nubians, with
Ethiopia. For example, in the eighth chapter of the Book of the
Acts of the Apostles, the Evangelist Philip, one of the original seven
deacons, is depicted as converting a eunuch on the road to Gaza.
This eunuch is described (Acts, 8:27) as an envoy of Queen
Candace of Ethiopia, but we now know that he was really from the
Meroitic civilization of Kush.

The kingdom of Kush corresponded roughly to the modern nation of Sudan. To the east and south of Kush on the plateau over-
looking the Somalia seacoast was the kingdom of Aksum, which is
Ethiopia today. Aksumites traced descent from the people of Saba,
a kingdom across the Red Sea in the southwestern corner of the
Arabian Peninsula. Saba is now the modern nation of Yemen. The
Queen of Saba (Sheba in the Bible) visited King Solomon in Jerusalem, lending a basis for the Ethiopian legend that the Queen of

Sheba had a son by Solomon, named Menelik, founder of the dynasty of the Lions of Judah, whose latest representative is Ethiopia's current emperor, Haile Selassie. Aksum, however, was not founded as a kingdom until about 700 B.C., several centuries after the Queen's visit to Jerusalem.

Aksumites carried on extensive trade with Arabia, Greece, Egypt, and India, especially through their port city of Adulis on the Red Sea. Under King Ezana, the Aksumites waged war on and destroyed the civilization of the Nubians at Meroe about A.D. 350.

In A.D. 333, Frumentius, who was appointed Bishop of the new Ethiopian Church by the Patriarch of Alexandria, Athanasius, converted King Ezana to Christianity. From that time to the present, the Aksumites or Ethiopians have remained steadfast to the Coptic monophysite Christianity of the Alexandrian Church. Because of its resistance to the spreading Moslem religion that overwhelmed its neighbors several centuries later, Ethiopia is able to boast today of being the world's oldest continuous Christian nation.

Aksumites built decorative, obelisk-like stelae. The seventy-foot-high stela still standing at the ancient capital city of Aksum in northern Ethiopia is a reminder of the grandeur attained by this civilization. Excavations at such places as Haulti, Melaso, and Hawile-Assaraw have unearthed statuettes and altars that shed further light on the Aksumites.

Some writers term the Egyptians, Nubians, and Ethiopians "white" because they and the Berbers of North Africa speak Hamito-Semitic (Afro-Asiatic) languages. Labeling Semitic-speaking people white, however, confuses language with race. Black Semites include the Chadic and Kushite branches of the Afro-Asiatic language grouping. Herodotus and other ancient writers called the Nubians black. The Arabs termed their land Bilad-as-Sudan, meaning "Land of the Black Men." And the name Ethiopia derives from a Greek expression for "burned-faces." Obviously, Egypt, Kush, and Aksum were civilizations of mixed stocks, including many blacks.

There were other civilizations in southeastern and southwestern Africa that were developed by blacks, such as Kilwa, Zimbabwe, and Kongo. These civilizations demonstrated the progress that could be achieved by blacks without the aid of whites.

South of Kush and Aksum, on the east coast of Africa from Somalia to Tanganyika, a group of trading cities developed. The Arabs called this area the Land of Zanj, hence today's Zanzibar and Tanzania. It included such thriving cities as Mogadishu, Malindi, Mombassa, Kilwa, and Sofala. A lively trade with Arabia, India, the East Indies, and China was carried on across the Indian Ocean taking advantage of the alternating monsoon winds. Gold and ivory of Africa and spices, cotton cloth, and cowrie shells of the East were the staples in this trade which continued from the first to the nineteenth centuries. As archaeologists uncover the ruins of these once prosperous cities, we learn that they had a well-developed civilization.

The people who developed these flourishing trading cities in the Land of Zanj were undoubtedly influenced to some degree by the Arab merchants, by traders from the Orient, and by the Portuguese who seized these cities after Vasco da Gama's voyage of 1497-1498 and dominated them in the sixteenth and seventeenth centuries. But basically the Land of Zanj was a land of black men, and they developed its culture. Medieval geographers referred to its people as Negroes. The Arab traveler, Ibn Batuta, upon visiting the east coast of Africa in the fourteenth century, "describes Kilwa as a beautiful and well constructed city," writes Gervase Matthew in *The Dawn of African History*, edited by Roland Oliver, "but he also noted that its inhabitants were jet black." The basic language in this area, especially in the later centuries, was the Swahili branch of the Bantu-Negro language group. The ruins of the great mosque at Kilwa, two hundred miles south of Zanzibar, remain, but the flourishing port declined in the aftermath of attacks by Portuguese warships.

Inland from the southernmost of the trading cities, Sofala, there are the impressive stone ruins of another lost civilization, Zim- babwe. Located south of the Zambesi River and north of the Limpopo River in what is now Rhodesia, Zimbabwe existed some- time between the eleventh and seventeenth centuries. Nothing is left of it now except the great stone ruins and the fragments of porcelain, pottery, and beads that prove it traded with India or Malaya.

The hill-fort, the huge elliptical enclosure, and the solid conical tower, all made out of stone, astounded European explorers when they encountered them at Zimbabwe in the nineteenth century. The British historian, Professor Roland Oliver, reported their reaction, stating that these explorers "were convinced that such things could never have been constructed by Africans. . . . [thus] they attributed Zimbabwe to Phoenician gold-traders of the millennium before Christ." Scholars now know better. Professor Oliver points out that "modern opinion is coming increasingly surely to the view that the builders themselves were Africans."

Closer study showed that the Zimbabwe ruins were simply a translation of the basic mud-and-thatch construction of African architecture to stone. Also, analysis of the accounts by sixteenth-century Portuguese travelers who visited Zimbabwe in its declining days revealed that its basic customs and institutions were similar to those found elsewhere in Africa. One example was the respect shown the King by groveling and by imitating him. When the King coughed, all the royal court coughed, and when he twisted an ankle, all limped. Zimbabwe is still a mystery; further excavation may shed more light on its past greatness.

Another interesting African kingdom was Kongo in the region south of the Congo River that today is mainly Portuguese Angola and partially the Republic of Congo. When Portuguese explorers came upon this kingdom in the late fifteenth century, they found that its Bantu Negro people had an efficient government divided into six provinces ruled by governors who administered their areas for the king. These Bantu blacks used cowrie sea shells from the Orient for currency, knew how to work iron and copper, and were skillful in pottery and weaving.

King Dom Affonso I, ruler of the Kingdom of Kongo from 1506 to 1543, was an enthusiastic convert to Christianity who built a cathedral in his capital city of Mbanza Congo. He set out aggressively to have his people adopt Western ways, bringing in European missionaries, craftsmen, printing presses, and advisers. He sent his sons to schools and colleges in Portugal. The Portuguese found the

Bantu blacks of Kongo to be very intelligent and cooperative, learning Portuguese fluently. But the experiment in westernization failed. One of the main reasons for failure was the souring of the relations between Portugal and Kongo when the Portuguese insisted on pursuing the harmful slave trade. King Dom Affonso of Kongo wrote a long series of letters to Portugal's King John III (1521–1557) discussing the relations of the two kingdoms and protesting the slave trade. These letters, mostly written in Latin, are preserved in the Portuguese archives and are being translated and published by such scholars as Professor Asa Davis of San Francisco State College.

Portuguese slavers carried many Bantus to Brazil. Most Afro-Americans in the United States, however, are descendants of the Sudanic blacks of West Africa. Sudanic-speaking blacks and Bantu-speaking blacks form the Niger-Congo language grouping, which makes up the bulk of Africa's people. Other language stocks found in Africa include the Afro-Asiatic-speaking people of North Africa and northeastern Africa and the short-statured Bush and Pygmy stocks.

The Bushmen and Pygmies once occupied most of Africa south of the equator. Primarily hunters and food-gatherers, they were pushed aside by the expansion of the Bantu people, so that today Pygmies are mainly found deep in the rain forests of central Africa and Bushmen in dry and desert regions of southwestern Africa.

The Bantu originated in West Africa. They formerly occupied the northern fringes of the equatorial rain forests, but, about two thousand years ago, set out southward in a remarkable expansion that swept them into control of sub-equatorial Africa. Armed with iron weapons and equipped with iron tools for farming, they easily subdued the land and peoples (Bush and Pygmy) they encountered. There may have been only one Bantu tongue at first, but during the course of the dispersion, 82 Bantu languages developed.

The Sudanic-speaking blacks occupied most of Africa above the equator, including the Sahara, where they probably originated and where they engaged in farming when the Sahara was greener. They speak 264 languages that may be grouped into two major categories, geographically separated by Lake Chad, the Eastern Sudanic or Adamwa languages and the Western Sudanic or Mande languages.

To most Americans, the black men of Africa are people with no experience in government above the tribal and village level. But great African empires ruled by powerful black monarchs existed in the Western Sudan (whence came the ancestors of black Americans). These empires were at their height from the eleventh through the sixteenth centuries, with Ghana dominating the area from 1000 to 1240, Mali from 1240 to 1473, and Songhay from 1473 to 1591. They were of varying geographical extent, with the last and largest, Songhay, occupying almost the entire region. Black governments successfully administered an area that sprawled twenty-eight hundred miles from east to west (Atlantic Ocean to Lake Chad) and twelve hundred miles from north to south (Sahara to Gulf of Guinea), an area that would cover almost all the continental United States. The prosperity and power of these empires arose from: (1) their agricultural base in the Niger River valley; (2) their control of trade as middlemen between the Arabs of North Africa, the Saharan salt mines, and the gold mines of the Guinea forest; (3) their existence on the open savanna, which their foot and horse soldiers could traverse rapidly to hold the empire together; and (4) their monarchs' adoption of the Islamic faith, giving them aid, allies, and smoother trade with Moslems of North Africa and the Middle East.

There were numerous kingdoms among the Sudanic-speaking blacks of West Africa, including Kanem-Bornu, the Mossi states, and the Hausa states. None of these achieved the extent, prestige, or power of the three great successive empires, Ghana, Mali, and Songhay. These three great West African empires each originated as a small, peaceful kingdom, but eventually expanded to dominate the area. Ghana's existence as a small kingdom goes back to the time of Christ, Mali originated in the seventh century, and Songhay began in the eighth century.

Farming existed among the Sudanic blacks of West Africa as early as 4000 B.C., when crops were grown in the Niger River valley. Sudanic blacks farmed in the savanna, the rain forests of the Guinea coast south of the savanna, and the Sahara north of the savanna. Until about 2000 B.C., much of what is now the Sahara was fertile land. Cattle were still grazed there until 1000 B.C. Gradually, the Sahara desiccated, spreading into some of the savanna and pushing out the Sahara's former inhabitants, the Berbers and the Sudanic blacks. The Berbers, a mixed stock, moved north toward the Mediterranean coast; the Sudanic blacks moved southward into what remained of the savanna.

Despite the growing Sahara barrier, there was continuous trade between the Western Sudan and the rest of the world. This trade was carried on through the inhabitants of North Africa, the original Berbers and Libyans, and the subsequent conquerors of North Africa: the Phoenicians (who built Carthage), the Greeks, the Romans (who crushed Carthage in the Punic Wars), the Byzantines, and the Arabs. The Romans introduced the camel into Africa from central Asia about 46 B.C. so that the trade between North Africa and the Western Sudan could be carried on as the growing desert made horse and oxen travel more difficult. In 622 in Arabia, Mohammed founded the Islamic faith; in the seventh and eighth centuries, the Arabs took over North Africa, bringing this faith with them. Arab missionaries now penetrated the Western Sudan, and their Islamic religion proved an important vitalizing force in the development of the black empires of West Africa.

Ghana was the first West African empire to emerge. Its inhabitants were mostly black Soninke people whose language belonged to the Mande branch of the Sudanic language group. Ghana was a confederacy of agricultural people living in villages but also carrying on trade from their chief commercial center at Koumbi (Kumbi). The center of Ghana was then located in the savanna region between the upper Senegal and the upper Niger rivers, hundreds of miles northwest of the modern nation of Ghana. The people of Ghana were middlemen in the trade between North and West Africa. They obtained gold from the black gold miners of Wangara in the forest region just to the south of Ghana, exchanging it for salt from the Sahara salt mines to the north controlled by the desert people, first the Berbers and later the Arabs. Since salt was scarce in the Sudan and gold plentiful, salt was highly valued and readily bartered for gold. The government of Ghana taxed all caravans, merchants, and commercial transactions, increasing the kingdom's wealth. Ghana also traded West African ivory and slaves for textiles and beads brought in from North Africa.

Islamic influence stimulated military expansion. By the eleventh century, Ghana's boundaries extended from the Senegal River to the middle Niger River and well into the desert where the salt mines lay. For several centuries the empire flourished, levying tribute from subject peoples brought under its control as it extended its boundaries.

Much of our knowledge of Ghana at its peak comes from the Arab geographer al-Bakri, who wrote a book in 1067 entitled *Description of North Africa*. Al-Bakri, who lived in Spain, based his accounts on the reports of Arab traders who visited or lived in Ghana. Writing one year after Duke William of Normandy conquered England with only 20,000 men, al-Bakri reported: "The king of Ghana can raise 200,000 warriors, 40,000 of them being armed with bows and arrows." Al-Bakri also explained how the king of Ghana, Tenkhamenin, controlled the amount of gold in circulation in order to keep an oversupply of gold from driving down the price: "All the gold nuggets found in the mines belong to the king; but he leaves to his people the gold dust, with which everybody is familiar." According to al-Bakri, the houses in the capital city were made of stone and wood.

Religious strife late in the eleventh century weakened Ghana, and drought in the twelfth century added to its decline. It survived, but as a medium-sized kingdom rather than a large and powerful empire. Various former subject kingdoms of the empire, such as Kaniaga (the Sosso people) and Mali (the Mandingo people) vied to replace Ghana as the dominant power of West Africa. Mali won out under the leadership of Sundiata Keita, who defeated King Sumanguru of Kaniaga in the battle of Karina in 1235, going on to subdue Ghana in 1240.

The people of Mali were Sudanic-speaking blacks. The word for the great Western Sudanic language grouping, Mande, is a variant of their word, Mali, which means "where the king lives." Their word Mandingo means "the people of Mali." Mali was a powerful and prosperous empire, with its capital city of Niani (or Mali, as it is better known) on the Niger River. The emperor administered the realm through appointive local officials, including *ferbas* (governors) of provinces and *mochrifs* (mayors or inspectors) of important towns. A standing army of 100,000 upheld the emperor's authority, and he made periodic tours to inspect his possessions. Mali reached its height under Mansa Musa (1307–1332), who made the pilgrimage of 1324.

The Arab traveler, Ibn-Batuta, who visited all the Moslem lands in the fourteenth century, commented in his book, *Travels in Asia and Africa,* on the law and order that prevailed in Mali:

> The negroes possess some admirable qualities. They are seldom unjust, and have a greater abhorrence of injustice than any other people. . . . There is complete security in their country. Neither traveller nor inhabitant in it has anything to fear from robbers or men of violence.

Few kingdoms of medieval Europe then could match Mali in that regard.

Mali gradually declined, and Songhay rose to supplant it. Under the Sunni dynasty, established in 1335, Songhay emerged as a rival of Mali for supremacy in Western Sudan, neither able to subdue the other for a century and a half. Songhay finally won out under King Sunni Ali Ber who reigned from 1464 to 1492, passing away the year Columbus discovered America. Using a river navy, Sunni Ali captured Timbuktu in 1468 and took the independent city of Jenne, which had withstood Mali's assaults, in 1473. Now Songhay was dominant.

Sunni Ali's son was overthrown by one of his father's generals, Askia Muhammad Touré, who established the Askia dynasty. He was a much more devout Moslem than Sunni Ali. Ruling from 1493 to 1528, Askia extended the boundaries of Songhay to take in the salt mines of the Sahara, the Hausa states of the Lake Chad region, and the Mossi people of the Volta River region.

Askia Muhammad was the greatest of the emperors of West Africa. He not only ruled through appointive local officials, but also established efficient, centralized ministries to administer the affairs of the vast empire. On his great pilgrimage to Mecca, from 1495 to 1497, Askia took along fewer soldiers and less wealth than Mansa Musa, but he spent his money more carefully, bringing back numerous learned scholars and doctors for the imposing University of Sankore at Timbuktu, for the university at Jenne, and for the other intellectual centers of his empire.

An Arab traveler named al-Hasan ibn Muhammad visited West Africa from 1513 to 1515 while the empire of Songhay was at its peak under Askia Muhammad. Better known by the name of Leo Africanus, this traveler published in 1526 his famous *History and Description of Africa,* in which he described the Songhay city of Timbuktu thus:

> all the houses are cottages built of chalke, and covered with thatch. Howbeit there is a most stately temple to be seen, the walls whereof are made of stone and lime; and a princely palace also built by a most excellent workman of Granada. Here are many shops of artificers, and merchants. . . . The inhabitants, and especially strangers there residing, are exceeding rich. . . . The rich King of Tombuto [Timbuktu] hath many plates and scepters of gold, some whereof weigh 1300 pounds; and he keeps a magnificent and well furnished court. . . . He hath always three thousand horsemen, and a great number of footmen that shoot poisoned arrows, attending upon him. . . . Here are great store of doctors, judges, priests, and other learned men, that are bountifully maintained at the king's cost and charges. And hither are brought divers manuscripts or written books out of Barbary [North Africa], which are sold for more money than any other merchandise.

After the golden age of Askia Muhammad's reign, decline set in. His sons deposed the aging emperor in 1528. He lived another decade while warfare over the succession disrupted the empire. Order was restored under Askia Ishak I (1539–1549) and Askia Daud (1549–1582), but the efficient, centralized rule of the great Askia Muhammad could not be established everywhere. In 1590, an army of invaders from Morocco led by Judar Pasha managed to cross the desert with cannon and gunpowder, encountering the Songhay army of Ishak II in the fateful battle of Tondibi near the old Songhay capital of Gao at the Niger bend in 1591. Though the Songhay army was much larger, its spears, arrows, and swords were no match for the Moroccan guns. Thus, sixteen years before the founding of Jamestown, the last of the great Sudanic black empires of West Africa fell.

Mali rose from the shambles of Ghana, and Songhay from the wreckage of Mali, but no subsequent Sudanic empire rose in Songhay's place. The salt and gold trade across the Sahara that enabled these empires to flourish dwindled because world trading interests now focused on the gold, silver, tobacco, and sugar of North and South America and on the new all-water routes to the Far East. The rise of the slave trade to America caused a great increase in warfare among the people of West Africa, disrupting life there. And Europeans now began trading directly with the coastal peoples of the Gulf of Guinea, bypassing the peoples of the savanna who had served as intermediaries in that trade.

These coastal peoples were also Sudanic blacks. The flourishing kingdoms that developed among them during the heyday of the slave trade constitute an interesting byproduct of that otherwise nefarious commerce in human beings.

2

The Slave Trade and
Latin American Slavery

1441–1565

Captain Antam Gonçalvez of Portugal was ambitious. Prince Henry the Navigator had sent him to get skins and oils in West Africa, but this youthful captain sought to do more.

His men hesitated, fearing that their brash leader might cause trouble by exceeding orders. Sensing their uncertainty, Captain Gonçalvez pleaded with them, as recorded by Azurara, the chronicler of Portuguese exploration: "O how fair a thing it would be if we who have come to this land for a cargo of such petty merchandise, were to meet with the good luck to bring the first captives before the face of our Prince."

Stirred by his zeal and by prospects of obtaining glory and gold, the men agreed. He selected nine of them and went ashore below Cape Bojador (now in Spanish Sahara, one hundred fifty miles south of the Canary Islands), looking for human cargo.

After traveling a dozen miles, they encountered an African following a runaway camel. He fought bravely with his spear, but surrendered after being wounded by a Portuguese javelin. Then they captured a black Moorish woman who had strayed from a group of Africans to whom she was a slave.

The next night, reinforced by men from Captain Nuño Tristam's ship, the Portuguese made a surprise attack on the band of forty Africans from which the first two captives came. Four Africans were killed, ten were captured, and the rest escaped.

The dozen captives Captain Gonçalvez took to Portugal in 1441 marked the beginning of direct European involvement in the African slave trade. Previously, European trade with West Africa was through North Africa intermediaries. Arab caravans traveled overland, exchanging European fabrics and other goods for African gold, ivory, and slaves.

Now Portuguese ships were questing along the coast of West Africa. The driving force behind them was Prince Henry the Navigator (1394–1460), younger son of a Portuguese monarch. From 1415 until he passed away, Henry sent forth ships during the reigns of his father (John I), his elder brother (Edward I), and his nephew (Afonso V).

Prince Henry was seeking a direct, all-water route to the Far East that would bypass the Italian city-states and the Arab lands of the Middle East. Italian merchants skimmed the cream of profits from the Far East trade and Arab rulers laid heavy taxes on the caravans. Henry also sought to find the legendary Christian kingdom of Prester John.

Each ship Henry sent ventured farther than its predecessor before returning. By 1448, the Portuguese had reached the mouth of the Senegal River on the Guinea coast. Guinea was a European word for the Berber expression "land of the black man." By then, the slave trade had begun, with the first three slaving voyages, from 1441 to 1444, netting forty-nine slaves, the first trickle of what would be a mighty river of commerce in human flesh.

By the time Henry passed away in 1460, the Portuguese had reached what is today Sierra Leone. The portion of the African coast from the Senegal River to Sierra Leone was labeled Upper Guinea by the Europeans. The region from Sierra Leone to Nigeria was termed Lower Guinea. It was divided into four coasts from west to east: the Grain Coast (for the grains of Malagueta pepper), equivalent to Liberia; the Ivory Coast, equivalent to the modern nation of the same name; the Gold Coast, equivalent to modern Ghana; and the Slave Coast, equivalent to Togo, Dahomey, and western Nigeria. The Portuguese voyages of exploration kept on after Prince Henry's death. By 1475, the Portuguese had passed the Niger River delta, which lay to the east of the Slave Coast. This delta was called the Oil Rivers because of the palm oil produced there. In 1482, the Portuguese reached the Congo River in subequatorial Africa. In 1487, Bartolomeu Dias rounded the Cape of Good Hope at the tip of Africa. And in 1498, Vasco da Gama reached India after sailing around Africa. Portugal's search for a direct route to the Far East had ended.

Portugal had also uncovered a very profitable trade in Africans, bypassing Arab slave traders. The Portuguese generally approached the blacks as commodities to be used and exploited, rather than regarding them as human beings from whom the Portuguese might learn something about dignity, respect, and considerate treatment of one's fellow men.

A man named Lançarote received in 1444 the first license to trade in blacks issued by Prince Henry. When Lançarote returned with forty-six captives, the chronicler Azurara was at the Portuguese port where they were brought ashore. He was deeply touched on seeing "their heads low and their faces bathed in tears." When they divided up these captives, Afonso V was at the port to receive his share of the cargo, one-fifth. Azurara described how the partitioning separated families:

> as often as they had placed them in one part the sons, seeing their fathers in another, rose with great energy and rushed over to them; the mothers clasped their other children in their arms, and threw themselves flat on the ground with them, receiving blows with little pity for their own flesh, if only they might not be torn from them.

Among the throng of onlookers, Azurara noted only a few weeping at this pitiful spectacle.

Despite such cruelty as that witnessed by Azurara, African slaves carried to Europe were generally treated better than those Africans subsequently carried to the Americas. Blacks were not needed in Europe as workers to amass wealth there for Europeans. Europe already had a surplus of labor. The African slaves in Europe tended to be curiosities, baubles of the rich. They were a luxury, a visible means to display how wealthy a person was, rather than a tool of production to help a person become wealthy. Thus, African slaves in Europe sometimes were pampered and indulged, unlike African slaves in the Americas where there was a shortage of labor and where these black workers were needed to produce wealth for their masters.

Accordingly, some Africans in Europe were given a chance to develop their talents. Some of their descendants went on to fame and glory. The greatest Russian poet, Alexander Pushkin, was of African descent, as was one of France's most beloved novelists, Alexander Dumas. The Polish violinist George Augustus Polgreen Bridgetower was a friend of Beethoven's, for whom Beethoven composed one of his most famous works, a violin sonata. But Beethoven, who had a towering temper, fell out with his black friend Bridgetower and renamed the work the "Kreutzer Sonata."

Such outstanding blacks in Europe were indicative of the latent abilities that Africans possessed and could develop if given a chance. Similarly, the blacks of West Africa displayed advancement in many ways, but Europeans paid little heed. Although apologists for slavery claimed that Africans were rescued from savagery and taught to be civilized under Western tutelage, most of Africa had gone far beyond the primitive level of existence that characterized some parts of Africa up to the present and that too many Europeans and Americans associate with all of Africa. In fact, long before Europeans entered, Africans had developed a way of life that was much more complex and highly developed than most Europeans suspected.

The existence of the kingdoms and empires in West Africa shows that political life went well beyond the tribal and village level of development. A rather sophisticated political process developed in West Africa, the ancestral home of most black Americans. This process combined the best features of hereditary rule and elective choice. The eighteenth-century Arab traveler, El Hage, described one version of this innovation as he saw it among the Hausa; his account is given in his book, *Timbuctoo and Hausa*:

> If the king has children, the eldest, if a man of sense and good character, suceeds; otherwise, one of the others is elected. The grandees of the court are the electors. . . . the choice of the council must be unanimous, and if no person of the royal line be the object of their choice, they may elect one of their own body.

More typically, this system provided in most West African states for three hereditary families: the royal, electing, and enthroning families. The monarch came from the hereditary royal family, thus providing stability. But, the hereditary electing family selected the best member of the royal family, not simply the deceased king's eldest son. As a final check, the hereditary enthroning family had to confirm the choice by installing the new ruler. Many African kingdoms, small and large, used this system.

In agriculture, Africans combined private enterprise and communitarianism. In the economic life of West Africa, agriculture ranked first. Land belonged collectively to the descendants of the first occupant. It was parceled out for use by individual descendants, but when active cultivation was abandoned, the land reverted to the collective domain. In any given region, the administrator of the soil was the Master of the Ground, invariably the oldest living male descendant of the first occupant. He settled all disputes on ownership, boundaries, and usage. In El Hage's account, *Timbuctoo and Hausa*, there appears an account of some such official: "They have a class of men whose peculiar business it is to adjust all disputes concerning land; the office is hereditary; the *offender* pays the compensation, and also the fees of these officers; the *innocent* pays nothing."

Next to farming, the most prestigious occupations were herding, hunting, fishing, construction, navigation, commerce, gold mining, and manufacturing (of soap, oil, beer), in descending order. Numerous artisans devoted their time to such crafts as basketry, pottery, woodwork, metallurgy, and textile weaving. Different villages specialized in different lines of economic activity, facilitating trade between villages. Women traders controlled much of the local commerce, but kings controlled external trade, charging fees for granting persons the privilege to trade in certain items, especially gold, European imports, and slaves.

African social organization centered in the extended family. It consisted of several generations of adults descended from a common ancestor, together with their spouses and children, all sharing a residential compound. Any needy member of an extended family could call on his relatives for support. Welfare was unnecessary because even persons lacking genealogical ties would be taken in and cared for in return for performing servile labor for the extended family. But even such a servant was treated considerately as an adopted member of the family. The oldest living descendant of the common ancestor in an extended family served not only as the Master of the Ground, but also as the local priest of the pagan, animistic worship that stressed propitiating the spirits of the ancestors.

The many different spoken languages proved a barrier to written literature; most writing was done in Arabic. But there was an abundant oral literature, including tales, fables, and sagas of the past. Griots (storytellers) who collected and recited tales for a living developed in fourteenth-century Africa. Africa was rich in music, with singing including work chants, lullabies, festive tunes, and sacred songs. Musical instruments used included the xylophone, violin, guitar, zither, harp, and flute. Dancing was used considerably in Africa for many ritual, religious, and recreational occasions.

Africans developed a great art that had an important influence on modern artists such as Picasso, Matisse, Klee, and Modigliani. An aesthetic sense was deeply embedded in African life. Everyday objects such as pulleys, latches, shuttles, weights, cookware, and eating utensils were beautifully made with a lavish design and decoration that lifted them from the utilitarian to art. Ceremonial masks, fertility dolls, statuettes, and ivory tusks were elaborately carved by artists. African art tended to be non-representational, distorting natural shapes, such as the human figure, with marvelous plasticity to achieve a truer artistic reality. Several great periods of art existed before the coming of the Europeans, especially the Nok culture period of northern Nigeria (300 B.C. to A.D. 200) and the Ife art of western Nigeria (1000–1400).

Scholars disagree as to the impact of the African heritage on American blacks. The outstanding black sociologist, E. Franklin Frazier, in his classic study, *The Negro Family in the United States* (1939), contended that the traits of black Americans developed out of the New World experience and the contact with Western ways. He may have been influenced by the prevalent tendency of American blacks then to try to blend into the American melting pot, thus deemphasizing an African heritage that would set blacks apart from Americans of European ancestry. The white anthropologist, Melville Herskovits, insisted that many African traits survive in America, identifying many of them in his book, *The Myth of the*

Negro Past. Herskovits pointed to such matters as matriarchal patterns of family life, folk tales, and emphasis on the devil and on rivers in religion, citing counterparts in West African life. Frazier, however, cited New World experiences to account for such matters. African survivals seem stronger in Latin America, where Herskovits found much of his evidence. Evidently the great ability of Africans in music and the dance carried over to their descendants in North and South America. Whatever the final verdict of scholars, American blacks today tend to be much prouder of, and to search for, African roots.

Knowing that slavery existed in Africa and thinking that Africa was a barbaric land, Europeans rationalized that they were doing Africans a favor by carrying them into enslavement under "civilized" European masters. But slavery in Africa, as in the ancient world, was different from modern New World slavery.

It is not surprising that slavery existed in Africa before the coming of Europeans. Slavery is one of mankind's oldest institutions. It existed universally in the ancient world, without respect to race, religion, or nationality. Victorious Greek city-states enslaved Greeks of defeated city-states. The Romans enslaved barbarous Gauls, including Franks, Goths, Celts, and Saxons, ancestors of the French, Germans, Irish, and English. Egyptians made slaves of Hebrews, and the Israelites in turn held slaves. Christians sold Moslem captives into slavery, and the Moslem pirates of Barbary enslaved Christians captured on the Mediterranean. The modern word slave is derived from the word Slav and originated from the Germans capturing and placing in bondage eastern European Slavs, a stock that includes Bulgars, Croats, Czechs, Poles, Russians, Serbs, and Slovaks.

Slavery became the universal means of disposing of prisoners of war once man advanced into a more settled, pastoral existence and stopped slaughtering the vanquished, as nomadic people often found it necessary to do. Slavery was also used to settle debts, to punish criminals, or to secure a master who would protect and support one in return for free labor. Just as in Asia and Europe, slavery existed in Africa. But, throughout the ancient world, the slave, even when cruelly treated, was still generally regarded as a human being who happened to be a slave. Anyone might be a slave.

Yesterday's king might be today's slave. And today's slave might be tomorrow's poet. Slaves everywhere were looked down upon as degraded persons because they were slaves, not because slavery was their natural condition. In the ancient world and in African slavery, the slave and free man often worked at the same tasks, slaves might rise to supervisory positions over free men, and slaves might be teachers of the children of free men. Very often, slavery stopped with the slave; his children did not always automatically inherit his status.

The slave in Africa was respected as a person. He was regarded as a member of the family, but one without the proper genealogy. He lacked the privileges of those who could trace their descent, but this proved no barrier to his advancement to positions of trust. Hence, slavery in Africa was far more humane than the slavery that developed in the Americas in modern times, a slavery that regarded black men as inferior, as fit only for slavery, and as objects to exploit for the sake of making money.

African rulers had been accustomed to selling surplus slaves, generally prisoners taken in warfare, to Arab slave traders. Such slaves were valued in the Middle East as harem guards, soldiers, and household servants. Hence it was a simple matter to sell such slaves to European traders. The Africans did not learn until too late of the way these slaves were cruelly used in the New World.

Until 1481, European trade with West Africa had been indirect, passing through the hands of Berber or Arab traders of North Africa. In 1481, the Portuguese built Elmina Castle on the Gold Coast to tap the gold trade of the mines of the Ashanti people in the forests behind the coasts. At that time, the bulk of gold, slaves, and other products of West Africa were traded by the Sudanic empire of Songhay to the Arabs of North Africa. Elmina Castle marked the beginning of the European effort to bypass the Arabs and trade directly with the coastal peoples of West Africa for their ivory, gold, pepper, and palm oil, but above all, eventually, for their slaves. Not only did Europe bypass the Arabs, however, they bypassed the black Sudanic empires of the savanna.

Now, the black people of the coastal and forest regions of the Gulf of Guinea, previously the outlanders who traded only through the empires of the savanna, found themselves at center stage, dealing directly with Europeans. These coastal and forest blacks of West Africa were also Sudanic-speaking blacks. Now they received the guns, goods, and prosperity to rise to dominate their region. As they rose, the Sudanic empires of the savanna that lay to the north and east of these emerging states lost their economic base. Kingdoms still existed in the savanna, but another empire did not rise to replace Songhay after it fell in 1591.

Initially, the Portuguese ventured inland, as did Captain Gonçalvez, to seize Africans. They soon abandoned this because of suspicions and hostilities aroused. Instead, they found it more expedient and less hazardous to purchase slaves from African rulers who were accustomed to selling their surplus slaves to Arab traders.

Europeans usually stayed in forts and posts along the African coast. The forts were built primarily along the coast of Upper Guinea and in the Gold Coast region of Lower Guinea. The Gold Coast had many good harbors, unlike the dangerous and stormy Grain and Ivory coasts. Not only the Portuguese, but the Dutch, French, and English had forts along the African coast.

To the east of the Gold Coast, trade was carried on in the Slave Coast and Oil River regions, but usually without the great forts. Along the Slave Coast, generally, merchants built factories, so named because the agent of a merchant was called a factor. The factory was simply the building in which the factor gathered the slaves to await the merchant's ship. Unlike the Gold Coast forts, which permitted Europeans to dominate the trade, the factories were more under the dominance of the local African rulers. Along the Oil Rivers (Niger delta), slaves were generally assembled in floating hulks, called *barracoons*, to await the coming of the slave ships.

When a factor first arrived at a Gold Coast fort or Slave Coast factory, he had to carry favor of the local African king with presents. The king's agent designated to supervise the trade on the king's behalf had the title of *caboceer*. Not only did the Europeans have to pay the African rulers for the privilege of engaging in the slave trade, they had to pay bribes, called "dash," in order to get anything done. In some parts of Africa, "dash" is still a fact of life if one hopes to get action from soldiers, customs officials, and governmental clerks. A French slave trader, John Barbot, reported that it was

> usual for the Europeans to give the king the value of fifty slaves in goods, for his permission to trade, and customs, for each ship, and the king's son the value of two slaves, for the privilege of watering; and of four slaves for wooding.

Sharp dealing was prevalent on both sides. The Europeans wanted healthy, vigorous slaves in their young adulthood. The Africans palmed off what they could. The Africans desired in return woolen goods made in Europe, fine cotton goods from India, iron bars, guns and gunpowder, pots and pans, and jewelry. The Europeans tried to pass off shoddy goods whenever possible. Knowing that the European traders were anxious to get a full shipload and sail because of the mounting expenses of ships and crews tied up on the coast, the African rulers and *caboceers* deliberately haggled and drew out the negotiations to get better prices. Captain Thomas Phillips of the English ship, the *Hannibal*, while slave trading at Wydah along the Slave Coast, wrote in his log on May 21, 1694, that "Capt. Clay and I had agreed to go to . . . buy the slaves by turns . . . that we might have no . . . disagreements in our trade, as often happens when there are here more ships than one, and the commanders . . . outbidding each other, . . . the blacks well knowing how to make the best use of such opportunities . . . endeavor to create . . . jealousies between commanders, it turning to their great account in the disposal of their slaves." In this same log entry, Captain Phillips said of the slaves they purchased:

> our surgeon examin'd them well in limb, making them jump, stretch out their arms swiftly, looking in their mouths to judge of their age; for the cappasheirs are so cunning, that they shave them all close before we see them, so that let them be never so old we can see no grey hairs in their heads or beards; and then having liquor'd them well and sleek with palm oil, 'tis no easy matter to know an old one from a middle-aged one, but by the teeths decay. . . .

African slave labor and the slave trade from Africa to America played an important role in the development of the modern world. Like Portugal, Spain searched for a new route to the Far East, accidentally discovering the Americas, half a century after Captain Gonçalvez first captured slaves in Africa. Africans solved the New World labor problem so well that Europeans concentrated on buying slaves, slighting the other African products (gold, ivory, peppers, nuts, and palm oil) for which the Arabs, and the Europeans initially, had traded as well as for slaves.

To prevent quarrels between Spain and Portugal over the newfound lands, Pope Alexander VI divided all unclaimed lands between Spain and Portugal. The demarcation line he drew in 1493 was modified by a treaty between those two powers in 1494, the Treaty of Tordesillas. As a result, the Americas, except for the eastern bulge of South America that is now Brazil, were assigned to Spain. Brazil, Africa, and most of the East Indies were assigned to Portugal. Since Spain was excluded from Africa, the Spanish colonies in the New World had to rely on Portugal or other nations to bring African slaves across the Atlantic. The license issued by the King of Spain granting the privilege to carry slaves to the Spanish colonies for sale was known as the *asiento*. This license was so lucrative and so much sought after that, as Daniel Mannix and Malcolm Cowley point out in *Black Cargoes*, "For more than two centuries the Asiento was to be a prize in European wars. Thousands of Dutchmen, Frenchmen, and Englishmen would die so that each of their nations in turn could possess that valuable piece of paper."

From the outset, other European nations objected to all the world being divided between Spain and Portugal. The King of France commented that "the sun shines for me as for others. I should like very much to see the clause in Adam's will that excludes me from a share of the world." A famous Elizabethan sea dog, John Hawkins, made a celebrated voyage in 1563 that challenged Portuguese control of Africa and Spanish control of America. Hawkins secured slaves in West Africa and forced Spanish officials in the West Indies to let him sell his human cargo to the Spanish colonies. The Dutch, French, and English pushed their way into Africa and America, setting up New World colonies and securing the vitally needed labor from Africa.

Many capitalist fortunes were built on the slave trade. The port of Liverpool owed its eminence and prosperity to this trade. Triangular trades developed that fitted well with the Commercial Revolution and Mercantilism.

In one triangular trade, ships from Europe carried manufactured goods, including guns and textiles, to Africa. By providing a market for their products, the slave trade aided the rise of such manufacturing centers as Manchester and Birmingham. In Africa, the goods were exchanged for slaves. On the second leg, called the Middle Passage, the slaves were carried to the West Indies and sold at great profit. Some of the proceeds were used to purchase tropical goods, such as sugar, tobacco, and coffee, to carry back to Europe.

There were several other triangular trade routes. One of these involved ships from New England carrying rum and other products to Africa. After exchanging these for slaves, the cargo of blacks would be carried to the West Indies and sold. Part of the profit was used to buy sugar and molasses, which were carried back to New England to manufacture into more rum.

To increase profits, captains packed as many slaves as possible into the holds on the Middle Passage. On a voyage of several months' duration, slaves were chained together below deck day and night, with only a brief daily exercise period on deck. The overcrowding resulted in filth, stench, and epidemics of disease, making the Middle Passage a voyage of horrors.

On a typical slaving vessel, the *Brookes*, each adult male slave had a space six feet long, sixteen inches wide, and two feet seven inches high, with proportionately smaller spaces alloted slave women, boys, and girls. The holds of slave ships were divided by building decks between decks and by building extra shelves along the walls. The Reverend John Newton, a reformer who had formerly been a slave-ship captain himself, described what the slaves had to endure, as quoted in *Black Cargoes*:

> The cargo of a vessel of a hundred tons or a little more is calculated to purchase from 220 to 250 slaves. . . . the slaves lie in two rows, one above the other, on each side of the ship, close to each other like books upon a shelf. I have known them so close that the shelf would not easily contain one more.
>
> The poor creatures, thus cramped, are likewise in irons for the most part which makes it difficult for them to turn or move or attempt to rise or to lie down without hurting themselves or each

other. Every morning, perhaps, more instances than one are found of the living and the dead fastened together.

Similarly, a slave-ship's surgeon, Dr. Alexander Falconbridge, noted that the slaves were so tightly wedged in that "They had not so much room as a man in his coffin either in length or breadth."

Some slave-ship captians were "loose packers," carrying fewer slaves in hope of deriving more profits by cutting down the chances of disease and death. Others were "tight packers" who believed that many would die anyway and thus carried as many as possible to make up for those lost on the way. About twelve percent of the slaves taken on board never reached the journey's end. Their bodies were simply thrown overboard, to the benefit of the sharks that trailed each slave ship across the Atlantic.

Scholars disagree as to how many blacks were carried away from West Africa during the years of the slave trade. Most estimates cite about ten to twenty million people, most of them Sudanic blacks. Millions of others were killed in slaving wars or while resisting enslavement.

Despite these losses, several kingdoms flourished in West Africa in the coastal forest regions from which most of the slaves were taken. These kingdoms developed and reached their peaks while the slave trade was at its height. Chief among them were Oyo, Benin, Dahomey, and Ashanti. The first three were in the forests behind the Slave Coast and the Oil Rivers and would correspond to modern Dahomey and western Nigeria. Ashanti was in the forests behind the Gold Coast and corresponds to modern Ghana. The Sudanic blacks who predominated in these states were the Yorubas in Oyo and Benin, the Fons in Dahomey, and the Akan in Ashanti. Euorpean goods and guns procured in the slave trade provided much of the impetus for the rise of these kingdoms. They were also stimulated by the cultural tradition inherited from the Nok of northern Nigeria and the Ife of western Nigeria. Some of the greatest art of West Africa flourished in these kingdoms, free of the restrictions imposed on art by the Islamic religion in the great savanna empires that preceded these forest kingdoms.

Aside from the rise of these kingdoms, the slave trade from Africa to America was generally ruinous for West Africa. It accentuated African autocracy because the wealth gained from the slave trade tended to concentrate in the hands of African rulers. Their control of the trade enriched the kings and made them more powerful as they secured guns and as goods piled up in their warehouses.

Wars, insecurity, and economic blight were other byproducts of the slave trade. At first, African rulers sold the surplus slaves that they had on hand from wars that arose from legitimate causes. Anxious to continue receiving European goods, they turned to raids and wars for the sake of securing captives to sell. Once the process started, there seemed no way to stop it. If a king refused to procure slaves, the slave traders simply went elsewhere on the coast, where other kings would provide slaves in order to get the European goods. Soon, it became a matter of hunt or be hunted. If a king refused to engage in the slave trade any more, as some did, he found it impossible to get guns and gunpowder. Monarchs of rival African tribes or kingdoms secured the guns and waged war on the pacifist-minded in order to procure slaves to sell. In self-defense, a king had to get guns, which could only be secured by waging war to get captives to trade. A vicious cycle developed and trapped the people of West Africa. They would not unite to halt the slave trade because they were as fragmented in their loyalties to their own tribes and kingdoms as the twentieth-century Balkan states.

Constant warfare made life insecure in West Africa and retarded progress. People saw little use in building or toiling or planning for the future. The incentive to develop and produce declined, and some of Africa's old skills were lost. West African economy was ruined by the fact that traffic in human beings was a non-productive basis for trade, and this one-sided traffic had taken the place of a balanced trade involving Africa's many products. Europeans assumed that the resulting turmoil, chaos, and decline they observed were the normal state of affairs in what they regarded as a backward continent. Actually, they were seeing the accumulated impact of the slave trade. Contact with Europe had disrupted Africa's way of life and set it on the path to decline from its earlier age of great empires.

African slaves became the chief source of labor during the colonial period of Latin American history, particularly on the rich sugar islands of the Caribbean. Within five years after the Spaniards founded the first permanent European settlement in the New World (Santo Domingo in 1496), African slaves were toiling for them. As the Spaniards brutally attacked and wiped out the gentle Carib Indians, native to the islands, more and more blacks were brought in. The first Africans were living in the Spanish colonies as early as 1501. Fears of too many blacks being brought in caused Spanish authorities to place restrictions on their importation. In 1517 Bartholomew Las Casas helped to persuade King Charles I to lift the restrictions so that African labor could substitute for the sorely pressed Indians. In 1518 there began the large scale admission of "bozal" Negroes, those fresh from Africa, as contrasted to the earlier imports who had been initially carried to Europe and converted to Christianity.

Some blacks participated in explorations. On Columbus's last voyage, which set out in July, 1502, a black named Diego el Negro was a crew member on the caravel *Capitana*. When Balboa set out in 1513 to cross Panama and become the first European to see the Pacific Ocean, an African named Nuflo de Olano was in his party. And when Balboa made preparations to explore the new-found ocean three years later, thirty black men were among those carrying the timbers across mountains and jungles for his ships. The first highway built from ocean to ocean, under the direction of Balboa's successor, was constructed by Indian and Negro laborers. Conquistadores such as Hernán Cortés and Francisco Pizzaro took blacks along on their expeditions. The Indians were so astonished on encountering the slave accompanying one Spaniard that they had him wash his face repeatedly to see if the black would come off.

The greatest black explorer was Estevanico. He was on the ill-fated Narvaez expedition that left Spain in 1527 to explore the western coast of the Gulf of Mexico. Blown off course, the ships landed far to the east, at Tampa Bay, Florida, in 1528. Traveling onward by land and boat, the expedition shipwrecked on Galveston Island off Texas. Only four men survived the ordeals they encountered, Cabeza de Vaca, Alonzo del Castillo, Andres Dorantes, and the latter's slave Estevanico (or Esteban). This slave was a black man from the town of Azamor on the west coast of Morocco. These four did not return to civilization for eight years, and when they did they had crossed the continent to the Gulf of California.

At first held as slaves by the Indians, the four men later escaped and attracted a following of Indians by practicing healing. With their help, they trekked westward. In the report that he wrote after returning to civilization, Cabeza de Vaca said of Estevanico: "The negro was in constant conversation [with the Indians]; he informed himself about the ways we wished to take, of the towns there were, and the matters we desired to know." Finally, they reached the Gulf of California in 1536.

When these four explorers reached Mexico City, they excited the officials there with accounts the Indians had given them of seven golden cities of Cibola somewhere to the northwest. Francisco Coronado was assigned to conquer Cibola. In 1539 he sent an advance party led by Friar Marcos, but guided by Estevanico. Marcos sent Estevanico ahead and this black man became the discoverer of Arizona and New Mexico. The Zuñi Indians of Cibola killed him, and the rest of his party retreated. When Coronado reached Cibola (near Gallup, New Mexico) in 1540, he found only cliff dwellings that appeared golden from a distance.

Although he passed away sixty-eight years before the founding of Jamestown in 1607, Estevanico had already explored in Florida, Texas, Arizona, and New Mexico. Even in those early times, other blacks were already in other areas that were to become part of the United States. In 1526, Lucas Vasquez de Ayllon established the short-lived colony of San Miguel de Gualdape at the mouth of the Pee Dee River in South Carolina. African slaves were in his party. Another Spaniard, Menendez de Aviles, founded the city of St. Augustine, Florida, on September 8, 1565, making it the first permanent settlement in what is now the United States. A French official of a rival Huguenot colony in Florida that was soon destroyed by Menendez reported that "the Spaniards in great numbers were gone on shore [taking] possession of the houses of Seloy [an Indian village on the site] in the most part whereof they had placed their negroes, which they had brought to labor." Thus, forty-two years before the founding of Jamestown and fifty-five years before the *Mayflower* set sail, blacks were already living in St. Augustine, Florida.

Most of the blacks in Latin America worked on the great plantations of the West Indian islands in the Caribbean Sea. They grew and processed tobacco, cocoa, and coffee, but mainly sugar. The plantation system made it impossible for small-scale white farmers to compete, so that the rural population became confined primarily to white planters, white overseers, and African slaves. Slaves were driven at a furious pace. Some planters calculated that it was more profitable to drive a slave to the utmost for eight to fifteen years until his health was ruined or he passed away and then to discard him and purchase a new slave than to treat him well over a longer lifespan.

In the mainland colonies of Spain and Portugal on the American continents, Africans were used mainly in the mines and in the cattle ranches. Since relatively few Spaniards and Portuguese came to settle in the Americas, Africans (slave and free) performed a great variety of tasks, both skilled and unskilled, in Caribbean and mainland colonies.

Fear of slave revolts led to harsh slave codes, severe punishments, and cruel treatment. Many slaves ran away. Many of these runaways, called Maroons, congregated in camps of fugitive slaves. Such camps were called *quilombos*. From these camps, the escaped slaves would raid nearby plantations and communities for food and other supplies. The largest *quilombo* was Palmares, in the northeastern section of Brazil, in Pernambuco Province. From 1630 to 1697, a succession of three republics of runaway slaves existed at Palmares. At its height, Palmares had twenty thousand residents, an elected king, laws, and government. It carried on agriculture and trade. When an invading army finally broke through their fortifications, the leaders jumped off a cliff rather than return to enslavement.

Meanwhile, slavery was developing in the English colonies to the north.

3

Slavery in the British Colonies

1619–1763

Anthony Johnson was furious because Samuel Goldsmith and Robert and George Parker had deprived him of the services of John Casor. Johnson filed suit in Northampton County Court in 1654.

Casor, a black, resident in Virginia since 1640, told the court that "he came unto Virginia for seven or eight years of Indenture, yet . . . Anthony Johnson his Master . . . had kept him his servant seven years longer than he should or ought." Johnson claimed that he had never seen Casor's indenture papers, insisting that "he had the Negro for his life."

The litigation originated in November, 1653, when Goldsmith visited Johnson and Casor sought Goldsmith's help. Goldsmith brought in the Parkers, who backed Casor's story saying that "they knew that the said Negro had an Indenture." Johnson still refused to release Casor. Goldsmith and the Parkers warned that Casor could be awarded Johnson's cows for damages. Thereupon, yielding to the pleas of his fearful wife, sons, and son-in-law, Johnson released Casor.

What made him angry was that Casor then indentured himself to Robert Parker. Johnson brought suit against Parker claiming that "he detains one John Casor a Negro the plaintiff's servant under pretense the said John Casor is a free man."

In March, 1655, came the judgment: "The court . . . do find that . . . Robert Parker most unrightly keeps the said Negro John Casor from his right Master Anthony Johnson. . . . Be it . . . ordered that . . . Casor . . . shall forthwith return into the service of his said Master Anthony Johnson. . . ." The court made Parker pay all expenses of the suit.

This historic decision was the first civil case in which a Virginia court made a black indentured servant a slave. Casor was returned on the terms on which Johnson brought suit, that Casor was his servant for life.

The strangest thing of all about this case was that Anthony Johnson, the master, was himself a black man. Goldsmith and the Parkers were white, but Robert Parker lost the case.

Although he is properly obscure, Johnson symbolizes a neglected aspect of life among Negroes in colonial Virginia: some were free citizens. Johnson came to Jamestown, Virginia, in 1621 as an indentured servant but became a free man and a land owner upon completing his term. He married another black, Mary, who had entered on the ship *Margarett and John* in 1622. In 1651, Johnson imported five indentured servants and was granted 250 acres of land along the Pungoteague River in Northampton County as head-rights (50 acres per person) on them. Other free Negroes settled nearby, forming the first black community in America.

Early the next year a disastrous fire impoverished the Johnsons, and they petitioned the county court for tax relief. Accordingly, on February 28, 1652, the court issued an order that in "consideration . . . of their hard labor & honored service" as county residents for thirty years, the Johnsons "be disengaged and freed from payment of Taxes and levies in Northampton County for public use." Grateful for this but embittered by his financial reverses, Johnson was in a mood to defend his ownership of Casor, thus winning the suit that made Casor his slave.

When Johnson sued Parker in 1654, blacks had been living in Virginia for thirty-five years. Writing in January, 1620, to Sir Edwin Sandys, Treasurer of the London Company that established Jamestown, John Rolfe (husband of Pocahontas) reported that

> About the latter end of August, a Dutch man of War with the burden of 160 tons arrived at Point Comfort, the commander's name, Captain Jope, his pilot to the West Indies, one Mr. Marmaduke, an Englishman. They met with the *Treasurer* in the West Indies and determined to hold consort ship hitherward, but in their passage lost one the other. He brought not anything but twenty and odd negroes, which the Governor in Cape Marchant bought for Victuals, (whereof he was in great need, as he pretended) at the best and easiest rates they could. He had a large commission

from his Excellency, to arrange and take purchase in the West Indies.

There are some misconceptions about these Africans who entered in August, 1619, twelve years after the founding of Jamestown. First, many people assume that these were the earliest blacks in the New World, but as has been shown earlier, the history of blacks in North and South America began more than a hundred years before.

Second, some people assume that the Africans who came to Virginia in 1619 were slaves. Although John Rolfe's letter stated that the colonists bought some twenty Africans, this is no certain indication that they were made slaves. Such words as "sold," "bought," and "servant" were utilized in the Jamestown colony to apply to almost all individuals who were not in the status of officers of the company. Most of the colonists were servants of the company, and these twenty-odd Africans imported in 1619 might have been in the same status. Some writers argue that these blacks were indentured servants, because Virginia lacked laws on slavery before 1660. Others have argued that they were slaves almost from the outset, that the attitudes and outlook of the colonists reduced blacks to a distinctly inferior status, below that of all other inhabitants.

The ship *Treasurer*, mentioned in the letter of Rolfe to Sandys, dropped off some Africans in Bermuda before coming to Jamestown later in the year 1619 to drop off still one more African. In the next few years, other ships brought in several more Africans. In the temporary census of 1624–1625 taken in the Colony of Virginia, the twenty-three Negroes then residing there were listed as servants, not as slaves. Evidently some, if not all of them, were treated as indentured servants, who served a limited term and then became free, as in the case of Anthony Johnson.

Although the first statutory recognition of slavery in Virginia did not take place until 1660, there were many indications that slavery was developing prior to that time. From 1619 to 1640, there were some black indentured servants, but, apparently, also some being held as slaves. In the period from 1640 to 1660, slavery was becoming increasingly the status of black Virginians. From 1660 to 1682, laws gradually evolved that gave legal sanction to slavery, making all blacks who entered after 1682 slaves. Nonetheless, there was always a class of free Negroes in Virginia. Those blacks who were free before the basic slave codes were enacted between 1660 and 1682 generally remained free. Others were set free by their masters after slavery became the law of the land in Virginia. Consequently, from the 1620s to the end of slavery in 1865, there were always some blacks in Virginia who were free men.

The first recorded case of enslavement in Virginia came in a criminal case in 1640. Three indentured servants, two white and one black, had run away. The three runaways were captured and put on trial for the crime of deserting their lawful masters who had bought their contracts and were entitled to the full period of service that the indentures had contracted for. As punishment, the General Court, in which the cases were tried, added four years to the terms of each of the two white runaways. But the court then ruled that "the third, being a negro named John Punch shall serve his said master or his assigns for the time of his natural life. . . ." Thus, the black man, John Punch, became a slave unlike the two white indentured servants who merely had to serve a longer term. This was the first known case in Virginia involving slavery. The 1654–1655 case involving John Casor and Anthony Johnson was the first known civil case enslaving a man in Virginia. The fact that such casual mention was made of the General Court's making John Punch a slave in the 1640 criminal case would seem to indicate that enslavement of blacks was not a startling new departure from the existent practices in Virginia. It is this criminal case of 1640 that causes some scholars to assume that slavery existed in practice in Virginia long before the passage of slave laws.

There were other indications of slavery in Virginia before 1660. County records of the 1640s indicate that some Negroes were being sold for life indentures. Thus, slavery began to develop covertly as black indentured servants had their terms lengthened to life. Also, records of estates probated in the 1640s and 1650s indicate frequently that black indentured servants were listed as being of much greater value than white indentured servants. For example, a young male white indentured servant with six years' service remaining was listed in one probated estate at half the value of an old Negro woman indenture who could not possibly have been as productive as the young white man. She must have been listed at twice his value only because she was a servant for life, in effect a slave, while he had a limited term to serve. Thus, as early as the 1640s, there were blacks in Virginia living in virtual slavery, even in the absence of slave legislation. Yet it is also important to note that there were blacks in Virginia as late as the 1670s and 1680s who were bringing suits that limited their indentures or won their freedom.

Slavery in Virginia evidently antedated slave laws. In 1660, law caught up with custom. Virginia passed a law then stating "That in case any English servant shall run away in company with any negroes who are incapable of making satisfaction by addition of time . . . the English so running away . . . shall serve for the time of the said negroes absence as they are to do for their own. . . ." This law recognized that there were Negroes who could not be punished for running away by being forced to serve more time because they were already serving lifetime indentures, or in other words were slaves. Another step toward legalizing slavery came in 1662 when the General Assembly of Virginia passed a law stating that "all children born in this country shall be held bond or free only according to the condition of the mother. . . ." In England under the common law, by contrast, the child took the status of the father. But in Virginia a child born of a slave woman by her master or any other white man remained a slave.

In 1667 the colonial legislature passed a law that would encourage slave-owners to convert their slaves to Christianity without fear that the newly baptized Christian brother would therefore cease to be a slave. This statute enacted by the General Assembly stated that "the conferring of baptism does not alter the condition of the person as to his bondage or freedom; that divers masters, freed from this doubt, may more carefully endeavor the propagation of christianity. . . ." In contrast to Christianity, the practice among Moslems was to emancipate any slave who converted to the Islamic faith. Moslems would not hold their coreligionists as slaves, as Christians did.

These laws of the 1660s paved the way for the statutes passed by the Virginia legislature in 1670 and 1682 that enslaved all blacks coming to the colony. The law of 1670 provided that "all servants not being christians imported into this colony by shipping" were to be slaves for life. The phrase "all servants not being christians" referred to blacks imported from Africa, almost all of whom were pagans or Moslems. This law had a loophole, however, in that such persons who entered Virginia by land from neighboring colonies were to "serve, if boys and girls until thirty years of age, if men or women, twelve years and no longer." Another loophole arose because some Africans were converted to Christianity before reaching Virginia and thus, under the terms of the law of 1670, had to be limited to a service of thirty years if children or twelve years if adults. As a result, the General Assembly, in 1682, repealed the law of 1670 and passed a new law closing both loopholes. The act of 1682 made slaves of all persons of non-Christian nationalities (which meant persons from Africa) coming into Virginia, whether they came by land or by sea, and whether or not they had been converted to the Christian faith after being captured in their homeland.

A final step in this process of degrading the black man was taken in 1705. In that year, the General Assembly of Virginia passed a law that stated: "all negro, mulatto, and Indian slaves, in all courts of judicature, and other places, within this dominion, shall be held, taken, and adjudged to be real estate. . . ." Thus, a slave became chattel, a piece of property, losing his inherent dignity and value as a human being.

Which came first, prejudice or slavery? Were whites initially prejudiced against blacks, therefore enslaving them? Or did prejudice develop gradually after whites observed blacks living in slavery? Historians disagree. Carl Degler and Wesley Frank Craven adopt the view that whites were prejudiced against blacks from the outset because of their color, therefore regarding them as different and inferior, hastening the process by which blacks were pushed into slavery. Oscar and Mary Handlin and Kenneth Stampp have argued that the English colonists were not prejudiced initially, but that prejudices developed as they observed blacks serving as slaves.

In his recent Pulitzer Prize-winning book, *White Over Black,* historian Winthrop Jordan takes a middle ground between the Degler-Craven and the Handlin-Stampp points of view. Jordan cites many evidences that whites in the English colonies had prejudices even before slavery was fully developed and legally sanctioned. He points to the fact that restrictions were placed on the right of blacks to bear arms, that black female indentured servants customarily worked in the fields while white female indentured servants generally were not required to do so, that strenuous efforts were made by laws and criminal court cases to prevent cohabitation of blacks and whites, and that more severe penalties were meted out to blacks than to whites for committing identical offenses. Therefore, Jordan concluded that:

> Rather than slavery causing "prejudice" or vice versa, they seem rather to have generated each other. Both were, after all, twin aspects of a general debasement of the Negro. Slavery and "prejudice" may have been equally cause and effect, continuously reacting upon each other, dynamically joining hands to hustle the Negro down the road to complete degradation.

Slavery developed only gradually in Virginia, evolving almost absentmindedly, Professor Jordan observed. In Virginia, as in Latin America, efforts were first made to use Indian slaves to solve the New World's problem of a shortage of labor. But the Indians proved unsatisfactory because they were not skilled farmers as were the Africans; the Indian braves had concentrated on hunting and fighting, leaving farming to the squaws. Unaccustomed to the hard, laborious drudgery involved in mining and farming and used to a more carefree existence, many Indians succumbed in slavery.

White indentured servants could have solved the New World's labor problem in the English colonies as they did in Australia, if there had been enough of them. But although Europe scraped the bottom of the jails and brothels, and although kidnappers worked feverishly to seize children and adults, there were never enough to fill the needs of employers. Moreover, as capitalists in England and other European countries realized the need for surplus labor there in order to hold down wages in the rising domestic industries of nascent capitalism and the forthcoming factories of full-fledged capitalism, they saw to it that brakes were applied to retard the draining off of white labor. Laws passed in England late in the seventeenth century, for example, made kidnapping of persons for indentured servitude much more difficult. As the supply of white indentured servants dwindled accordingly, the competition for their labor increased. This resulted in their contracts being sold for shorter terms and for higher "freedom dues" at the end of their service. Freedom dues were the grants in land, goods, and money provided an indentured servant at the end of his term, under the specifications of his contract. The rising expenses, therefore, made white indentures more costly and thus less desirable.

Africa, with a vast supply of slaves to offer, became vital to development of the New World. Since a slave served for life, with his children also being slaves, African slavery proved far more profitable than European indentures. Also, black slaves could be more easily detected and apprehended on running away than white indentures who could melt into the general population. Being black and pagans, Africans could be disciplined (whipped) with fewer pangs of conscience than white Christian servants.

In 1649, Virginia's population was estimated to be 15,000 whites and only 349 blacks. By 1671, despite the slave laws of the 1660s and 1670, white indentures outnumbered black slaves three to one, or 6,000 to 2,000. As late as 1683, there were about 12,000 indentured servants to 2,700 slaves. Thereafter, slavery increased rapidly. One reason slavery now outstripped indentured servitude was the passage of the laws in England hampering kidnapping of persons for indentures noted above. Another was the formation of the Royal African Company in England in 1672. Granted a monopoly by King Charles II, this company vigorously pushed the slave trade. When Virginia colonists became alarmed at the great increase in the slave population, by 1772 this company had used its influence to get the king to veto some twenty-three laws that the Virginia assembly passed from time to time to discourage the slave trade. So, with the aid of the Royal African Company, slavery grew in Virginia. In 1708, there were 12,000 slaves to 18,000 whites. In 1756, the 120,000 blacks (less than 3,000 of whom were free) constituted 41 percent of the total population in Virginia of 293,000.

African slaves were a vital labor force on the tobacco farms and plantations of Virginia and of the neighboring colony of Maryland. Maryland was unlike Virginia in that the blacks who entered soon after the colony's founding in 1634 were apparently regarded as slaves from the outset. Yet, as in Virginia, the first law in Maryland recognizing slavery did not come until later, in 1664. This law of 1664 in Maryland stated that

> All negroes or other slaves already within the province and all negroes and other slaves to be hereafter imported into the province shall serve during their lives and all children born of any negro or other slave shall be slaves as their fathers were for the term of their lives, and forasmuch as several freeborn English women forgetful of their free condition and to the disgrace of our nation do intermarry with negro slaves . . . be it further enacted . . . that all the issue of such free-born women so married shall be slaves as their fathers were.

By 1750, the colony of Maryland had 40,000 black residents, or 29 percent of the total population of 140,000.

Settled about 1654 by poorer migrants coming out of Virginia, the colony of North Carolina had the smallest percentage of blacks among Southern colonies. More of North Carolina's people tended to be small, independent farmers than in the neighboring colonies of Virginia and South Carolina. Thus, there were fewer large plantations and fewer slaves. In 1760, the 16,000 blacks in North Carolina constituted only 17 percent of that colony's total population of 93,000.

Throughout the colonial period and on until the end of the Civil War, Virginia had a larger number of Negroes in its population, in absolute figures, than any other colony or state. South Carolina, however, was the only colony with a black majority. In 1763, a century after it was chartered, South Carolina had a population of 70,000 blacks and 30,000 whites, making Afro-Americans 70 percent of the total population.

Slavery was sanctioned in South Carolina from the start. The eight proprietors who received a charter from King Charles II in 1663 selected John Locke to draft a constitution for their colony. The man who was to become the famed political theorist of the doctrine of human liberty provided in Article 110 of The Fundamental Constitutions of Carolina that "Every freeman of Carolina, shall have absolute power and authority over his negro slaves. . . ." However, this constitution of 1669 was too elaborate and feudalistic in nature, and was not put into effect.

The first settlement in the colony was established at Charleston in 1670. The cultivation of rice was introduced in 1694. The colony had a great need for slave labor on its extensive rice plantations. Since four of the eight proprietors were also directors of the Royal African Company formed in 1672 to monopolize the slave trade, they had a vested interest in pushing the institution of slavery in their colony.

Fears developed, however, because of the large number of blacks in the population. Laws were passed to keep the slaves under control. These laws, similar to slave codes in other English colonies and in Latin America, placed restrictions on the movements of slaves, sought to prevent them from assembling and plotting, denied them the right to possess weapons, and provided severe penalties for any insubordination. For example, the South Carolina Slave Code of 1712 provided that "every master . . . shall cause all his negro houses to be searched diligently and effectually once every fourteen days for fugitive and runaway slaves, guns, swords, clubs, and any other mischievous weapons." This code also provided:

> That if any negroes or other slaves shall make mutiny or insurrection, or rise in rebellion against the authority and government of this Province, or shall make preparation of arms powder, bullets or offensive weapons, in order to carry on such mutiny or insurrection, or shall hold any counsel or conspiracy for raising such mutiny, insurrection or rebellion, the offenders shall be tried by two justices of the peace and three freeholders . . . who are hereby empowered and required to try the said slaves so offending, and inflict death, or any other punishment, upon the offenders. . . .

The passage of such a severe slave code, however, did not stop the Negroes from rebelling. One such insurrection was the Cato Conspiracy that took place in 1739 at a plantation called Stono some twenty miles from Charleston. According to one account: "A number of negroes having assembled together at Stono first surprised and killed two young men in a warehouse, and then plundered it of guns and ammunition. Being thus provided with arms, they elected one of their number captain . . . marching towards the south-west with colours flying and drums beating. . . . In their way they plundered and burnt every house." These blacks were marching toward freedom in Florida where the Spaniards provided liberty for slaves fleeing from the English colonists. Militia forces caught up with them, however, stopping them before they could make good their escape. They had marched some twelve miles before being halted. Some thirty whites were killed by the black rebels, and some forty-four blacks perished in the fighting or were executed after trials.

James E. Oglethorpe (1696–1785) founded Georgia in 1733 to give worthwhile imprisoned debtors a new start in life. He planned to have his colonists concentrate on products that England had to import from tropical countries, including silk, oranges, grapes, and olives. He and his fellow proprietors forbade slavery and black residents; prohibited rum, brandy, and other strong drinks; and restricted landholding.

Oglethorpe was not opposed to slavery; he was a director of the Royal African Company formed in 1672 to monopolize English slave-trading. But blacks and slavery had no place in his utopia. Slavery would lead to dissension and inequality among white settlers. Slaves would have to be guarded, diminishing Georgia's role as a military buffer for Carolina against attacks from Spanish Florida. Without a staple crop like tobacco or rice or sugar, slave labor was not needed; even women and children could tend the silkworms and mulberry trees. And if Georgia had no Negro residents, runaway slaves from South Carolina could be more easily detected.

From the outset, the colonists complained about these restrictions and petitioned for their removal. They evaded them by smuggling in strong "spirits" and by hiring blacks from South Carolina for 100-year terms. Oglethorpe relented, ending his experiment: alcohol was permitted in 1742, slave-holding in 1749, and unrestricted land ownership in 1750. By 1760, one-third of Georgia's 9,000 residents were black.

Southerners felt that they needed slaves; some New Englanders also yearned for them. In 1645, Emanuel Downing of the Massachusetts Bay Colony wrote to his brother-in-law, John Winthrop, who was the Governor of Massachusetts:

> I do not see how we can thrive until we get in a stock of slaves sufficient to do all our business, for our children's children will

hardly see this great Continent filled with people, so that our [white indentured] servants will still desire freedom to plant for themselves, and not stay but for very great wages. And I suppose you will very well see how we shall maintain 20 moors [Negro slaves] cheaper than one English servant.

All of the New England colonies had slaves, Massachusetts as early as 1638. The Puritans rationalized that heathen blacks would learn from Christian masters. Most of the slaves in New England were household servants, dockworkers, or urban laborers. Rhode Island had the most Negroes among the four New England colonies: by 1760, blacks were 12 percent of the population of Rhode Island (4,700 blacks to 36,000 whites), 3 percent in Connecticut (3,600 blacks to 128,000 whites), 2 percent in Massachusetts (4,500 blacks to 195,000 whites), and only 1 percent in New Hampshire (633 blacks to 52,000 whites).

The New England colonies, especially Rhode Island, were involved in the slave trade. Vessels returning with unsold Africans added to Rhode Island's black population. The Brown brothers of Providence, Rhode Island, Nicholas and Moses, were merchants and manufacturers who at one time engaged in the slave trade. Moses Brown (1738–1836) was a partner in America's first factory, set up in Pawtucket, Rhode Island, in 1790. By then, he had become a Quaker, had stopped participating in the slave trade, and had helped establish an abolition society. As a result of the generosity of Nicholas Brown and other members of his family, Rhode Island College was moved from Warren to Providence and was later renamed Brown University.

Slavery was much milder in New England than in the other colonies. Nonetheless, slave plots and insurrections took place there also at such places as Hartford, Connecticut, in 1658, and Charlestown, Massachusetts, in 1741.

New York had the largest black population among Middle Atlantic colonies. In 1756, its 13,500 blacks constituted 14 percent of the 96,500 residents. New Jersey, with 4,700 Negroes and 57,000 whites, was 8 percent black in 1745. Afro-Americans were only 2 percent of Pennsylvania's population: 10,300 blacks to 424,000 whites in 1790.

Delaware may be classified with either the Middle Atlantic or the

Southern colonies. Geographically and politically, it belonged with the Middle Atlantic colonies. Founded by the Swedes in 1638, seized by the Dutch in 1655, and taken over by the English in 1664, Delaware was granted to William Penn in 1682, making it part of the colony of Pennsylvania. In 1701, Delaware was granted a separate legislature, but it continued to have the same governor as Pennsylvania until 1776, when it became completely separated. But its climate and its tobacco economy made Delaware a Southern colony. Hence, it is no surprise that Delaware developed a large slave population. By 1790, Delaware was 22 percent black, with 12,800 Negroes to 46,000 Caucasians.

When New York was the Dutch colony of New Netherland, from 1624 to 1664, "half-freedom" grants elevated some slaves to a contractual status. This is described in *A History of Negro Slavery in New York*, by Dr. Edgar McManus, Professor of History at Queens College of the City University of New York. Professor McManus pointed out that

> the system of half-freedom under which slaves were conditionally released from bondage . . . was introduced into New Netherland by the [Dutch] West India Company as a means of rewarding slaves for long meritorious service. Slaves who enjoyed half-freedom enjoyed full personal liberty in return for an annual tribute to the Company and a promise to perform labor at certain times. . . . the half-freedmen were given passes which certified them to be free and at liberty on the same footing as other free people.

The system, he continued, "enabled slave owners to be free of the cost and petty nuisances of slave holding while reserving the right to specific labor from their former bondsman." The system worked because it was provided in the half-freedom passes "that freedmen who defaulted" by failing to live up to the terms of the agreement "lost their freedom and returned back into the said Company's slavery." The system was convenient for the masters and was popular among the slaves because "Half-freedom was better than no freedom, and there were few slaves indeed who did not prefer it to absolute servitude." This pragmatic and flexible form of slavery showed that there were alternatives to slavery as it developed among the thirteen English mainland colonies and the United

States. The English, when they gained control of the Dutch colony in 1664, dropped this interesting experiment that blurred the line between freedom and slavery and that converted slavery into a contractual obligation.

New Yorkers feared slave plots. In 1712, rebellious slaves set a fire on the outskirts of New York City and then ambushed whites racing to the scene. Although the revolt was crushed and twenty-one slaves executed, panic prevailed. In 1741, a robbery investigation led to a white tavern owner, John Hughson, who included blacks among his patrons and who evidently helped black burglars dispose of their stolen goods. Hughson's Irish indentured servant, Mary Burton, told investigators of plots being hatched in the tavern to overthrow the government of New York, with Hughson to become king and a black named Caesar to become governor.

The authorities believed her incredible tale, especially because of mysterious fires that broke out in various parts of the city at this time. They arrested persons she named. These cooperated, accusing others to save themselves. After trials in an atmosphere of hysteria, without any defense lawyers to assist the defendants overcome the unfair and prejudicial prosecution tactics, thirty-five persons were executed, including Hughson and his wife. Of those given the extreme penalty, eighteen blacks and four whites were hanged and thirteen blacks were burned alive. Another seventy blacks were deported from the colony. Far fewer persons were executed in the well-known Salem witch trials of 1692 than in this New York panic of 1741. At Salem, only twenty were executed, nineteen by hanging and one by being pressed to death. Officials finally realized that Mary Burton was lying when she began to accuse prominent persons who could not possibly have been involved. To save face, however, the city council passed a resolution thanking her for saving the city from this slave plot. Moreover, when she stepped forward to claim the reward that had been offered, they had to give it to her to prevent their gullibility from being revealed.

But, although English colonists became fearful of the mass of blacks in the thirteen colonies after adopting African slavery as the most profitable solution to their labor problem, in the revolutionary atmosphere of the last third of the eighteenth century, whites would develop a new appreciation for individual blacks.

4

Afro-Americans
in the Revolutionary Era
1763–1800

Tension ran high in Boston as two regiments of British infantry disembarked on October 1, 1768. Having forced Britain to repeal the Stamp Act of 1765, colonists now demonstrated against the "unjust" Townshend duties of 1767. Stirred by the protests of such agitators as Samuel Adams, John Dickinson, Patrick Henry, and James Otis, the colonists fought British "oppression" by boycotting certain British goods. In June, 1768, mobs in Boston assaulted customs officials, forcing them to flee to Castle William in the harbor and to appeal for military aid. The Governor, Sir Francis Bernard, said that the British regulars that landed in October were needed "to rescue the Government from the hands of a trained mob."

The presence of these redcoats, or "lobsterbacks," as the colonists derisively termed them, inflamed Bostonians. There were daily confrontations between townspeople and troops. The people hurled insults, taunts, profanity, and even missiles at the soldiers. Bloodshed seemed imminent, but was averted for seventeen months. Then, on March 5, 1770, the British shot into a crowd of demonstrators, killing five men, including Crispus Attucks.

Attucks was a runaway slave from Framingham, Massachusetts, who had fled from his master two decades before. In 1750, his owner, William Brown of Framingham, advertised in the *Boston Gazette* for the fugitive, describing him as "a mulatto fellow, about 27 years of age, named Crispus, 6 feet 2 inches high . . ." As a fugitive slave who could be seized and returned to his owner at any time, Attucks quietly worked in Boston, remaining in obscurity until the events of Monday, March 5, 1770.

About 9 P.M. on the tragic day, a British sentry posted on King Street near the State House called for help against a hostile mob that pressed around him. Captain Thomas Preston rushed to his rescue with a squad of men from the 29th Regiment. Words were exchanged, blows were struck, and the beleaguered soldiers fired into the crowd, hitting eleven persons; three were killed instantly, two passed away later. On March 8, Bostonians turned out in great numbers for a public funeral for the first four to pass away. The *Boston Gazette* reported that "Last Thursday . . . were carried to their grave in succession the bodies of Samuel Gray, Samuel Maverick, James Caldwell, and Crispus Attucks, the unhappy victims who fell in the bloody massacre of the Monday evening preceding. . . . The bodies were deposited in one vault in the middle burying ground."

The American Revolution, which began at Lexington and Concord in 1775, could have started five years earlier over this "Boston Massacre." A widening of hostilities in March, 1770, was averted when Lieutenant Governor Thomas Hutchinson eased the tense situation by removing the British regiments to harbor islands.

When Captain Preston and his men went on trial in a colonial court, their defense lawyers were John Adams and Josiah Quincy. Adams tried to belittle the incident, calling the five slain men (Patrick Carr was the fifth to pass away) "the most obscure and inconsiderable that could have been found upon the continent." He argued that the rioters were not patriots for whose passing retribution should be exacted. Instead, he called them an unruly mob of ruffians led by a black man "whose very looks was enough to terrify any person." Attucks, said Adams, "appears to have undertaken to be the hero of the night; and to lead this army with banners, to form them in the first place in Dock Square, and march them up to King Street with their clubs." Hence, he concluded, "the dreadful carnage of that night is chiefly to be ascribed" to the black man, Attucks.

The sworn testimony of Oliver Wendell's slave, Andrew, agreed with Adams's designation of Attucks as the ringleader. Andrew testified that "a stout man with a long cordwood stick, threw himself in, and made a blow at the officer, . . . the stout man then turned round, and struck the grenadier's gun at the captain's right hand . . .

and struck him over the head. . . . This stout man held the bayonet with his left hand, and twitched it and cried kill the dogs, knock them over . . ." Andrew then continued: "I turned to go off, when I heard the word fire; . . . I saw the same grenadier swing his gun, and immediately he discharged it." When Andrew was asked, "Do you know who this stout man was, that fell in and struck the grenadier?" he replied, "I thought and still think, it was the Mulatto [Attucks] who was shot." Addressing the jury, John Adams likewise asserted that Attucks "with one hand took hold of a bayonet, and with the other knocked the man down."

By downgrading the "Massacre," Adams succeeded in getting all but two of the British acquitted. These two were convicted of manslaughter and branded on their hands. Nonetheless, colonial agitators used the "Boston Massacre" to stir emotions and fan revolutionary embers, making martyrs of the slain men.

The trial established the prominent role of Attucks. Adams labeled him merely a troublemaker. Patriotic propagandists asserted that Attucks and his fellow victims were heroes protesting British oppression. Historians do not know whether Attucks was just seeking excitement or consciously demonstrating against unjust treatment of the colonists. It is significant that a black man, himself not free, would be in the forefront of the mob and the first to fall.

Meanwhile, Britain repealed the Townshend Acts except for the duty on tea. The next outburst came in December, 1773, when colonists dumped tea in Boston Harbor, protesting a new Tea Act that favored English over colonial merchants. Outraged at this destruction of property, Britain closed the port and sent additional troops under General Thomas Gage.

On April 19, 1775, Gage sent seven hundred men under Lieutenant Colonel Francis Smith to seize colonial leaders and arms at Lexington and Concord. When the British advance party under Major John Pitcairn reached Lexington, they were met by a seventy-member militia company led by Captain Jonas Parker. One of the Minutemen in this company was a black man, Prince Esterbrooks of West Lexington. Pitcairn ordered the colonists to drop their weapons and to disperse. The colonists filed off toward a stone wall but retained their guns. Suddenly, shots rang out; eight colonists lay dead, ten wounded. The British pressed on to Concord, where they destroyed colonial military supplies. Forewarned by such riders as Paul Revere and Will Dawes, the leading agitators who were to be arrested, Samuel Adams and John Hancock, escaped.

By now, thousands of Minutemen were rushing to battle. Some were black, including Cuff Whittemore, Cato Wood, Pomp Blackman, Peter Salem, and Lemuel Haynes. In the fighting at Lexington and Concord on April 19, British casualties outnumbered American, 273 to 95. One of the patriots wounded at Concord was the black Minuteman who had fought at Lexington, Esterbrooks.

After fighting at Concord, Peter Salem became a hero at the Battle of Bunker Hill (fought on Breed's Hill). His career typifies service of blacks in the War for Independence.

Peter was born in Framingham, Massachusetts, about 1750, the slave of Jeremiah Belknap, who came from Salem. Later, Belknap sold him to Major Lawson Buckminster. Although laws excluded blacks from the militia, some were admitted of necessity because of manpower shortages. Hence blacks, including Salem, were enrolled in militia and Minuteman companies. Customarily, those who were slaves gained their freedom upon enrollment in the military. Thus, Salem became a free man on enlisting.

On the opening day of the Revolution, April 19, Peter Salem was a member of a Minuteman company in Framingham, led by Captain Simon Edgell. This company rushed to Concord to join in the fighting. On April 24, Salem enlisted in Captain Thomas Drury's company of Colonel John Nixon's 5th Massachusetts Regiment. Salem was usually the only Negro in his company and one of only about a score in his regiment.

On June 16, 1775, General Artemas Ward, commander of the colonial forces besieging the British in Boston, sent various regiments to occupy Charlestown Peninsula on Boston's northwest side. This move was to counter British plans he had learned of, to fortify Dorchester Heights on the southeast side of the city. Led by Colonel William Prescott, the Americans fortified Breed's Hill on the peninsula, with Bunker Hill as a secondary line of defense. When the British, under General William Howe, landed on the peninsula on June 17 to dislodge the Americans, reinforcements were sent in, including Colonel Nixon's regiment.

In the battle of Bunker Hill (June 17, 1775), one British charge was led by Major John Pitcairn, who had commanded the redcoat vanguard at Lexington on April 19. One of the earliest accounts of the battle, an account written by Samuel Swett that was later published in 1818, in a biography of one of the patriot leaders in the battle, General Putnam, stated that "the gallant Major Pitcairn . . . exultingly cried 'the day is ours,' when a black soldier named Salem, shot him through and he fell." In a report to the Massachusetts Historical Society in August, 1862, historian George Livermore stated that "Pitcairn . . . it is well known, fell just as he mounted the redoubt. . . . The shot which laid him low was fired by Peter Salem." At the dedication of a statue of General Warren at the Bunker Hill Monument in 1857, orator Edward Everett said of the great obelisk at the monument: "No name adorns the shaft. . . . It is the monument . . . of all the brave men . . .—alike of Prescott and Putnam and Warren,—the chiefs of the day, and the colored man, Salem, who is reported to have shot the gallant Pitcairn as he mounted the parapet." In a footnote to his "Historical and Topographical Sketch of Bunker Hill Battle," Swett commented about Peter Salem: "A contribution was made in the army for this soldier, and he was presented to Washington as having performed this feat." Although some writers question whether Peter Salem was the hero that fired the shot that stemmed this British charge led by Pitcairn, most seem to agree that he was the marksman and that he was a hero of the day.

Finally, the British broke through, forcing the Americans to retreat across Charlestown Neck to Cambridge where General Ward had his headquarters. The Americans were jubilant because raw militia withstood several charges of redcoat veterans and because American casualties were only 397 compared to 1,054 for the enemy.

Whatever Peter Salem's role at Bunker Hill, another black unquestionably distinguished himself there. Fourteen officers, commissioned and non-commissioned, including Colonel Prescott, signed a petition and sent it to the Massachusetts legislature on December 5, 1775, stating:

> The subscribers beg leave to report to your Honorable House . . .
> that, under our own observation, we declare that a negro man

called Salem Poor, of Col. Frye's regiment, Capt. Ames' company, in the late battle at Charlestown [Bunker Hill], behaved like an experienced officer, as well as an excellent soldier. . . . in the person of this said negro centres a brave and gallant soldier. The reward due to so great and distinguished a character, we submit to the Congress.

Peter Salem had joined Colonel Nixon's regiment on April 24, 1775, as an eight-month volunteer. He was eager to reenlist, but opposition was developing. To ensure wider support for a conflict that was being fought in its first three months primarily in Massachusetts and New York, the Continental Congress chose a wealthy tobacco planter and slave-owner from Virginia, George Washington, to command the Continental Army. Washington arrived in Massachusetts early in July, 1775, to take command of the forces opposing the British under General Howe. Washington was reluctant to employ black soldiers. On July 10, he issued instructions to his recruiting officers that they were not to enlist any more Negroes. Those already serving, like Peter Salem, could finish out their terms. A Southern delegate in Congress, Edward Rutledge of South Carolina, offered a resolution to bar blacks who had enlisted prior to Washington's July 10 order, but Congress refused. In meetings during October with his officers and with such civilian advisers as Benjamin Franklin, General Washington received support for his policy of excluding blacks from the new army that would be raised when current enlistments expired that December. Accordingly, on November 12, 1775, Washington issued orders that barred blacks from serving, whether new volunteers or those trying to reenlist when their current terms expired.

The British, however, were willing to utilize blacks. On November 7, 1775, the royal governor of Virginia, John Murray, Earl of Dunmore, proclaimed all blacks "free, that are able and willing to bear arms, they joining his Majesty's Troops as soon as may be . . ." With the British actively recruiting Negroes and offering freedom to slaves who deserted their masters and enlisted in the British forces, Washington had a change of heart. He became alarmed as slaves in Virginia flocked to the British side.

On December 30, 1775, therefore, General Washington ordered recruiting officers to enlist free Negroes. The next day, he wrote to John Hancock, president of the Continental Congress, telling him that the free black soldiers were displeased at being excluded, hence he was reenlisting them but would stop if Congress ordered. Congress assented, however, approving on January 16, 1776, the reenlisting of free Negroes. Wartime pressures and a dearth of white volunteers liberalized the recruitment policy so that slaves as well as free blacks came to be accepted. Rhode Island began enlisting slaves in 1778 at General Washington's request; Massachusetts was the second state to enlist slaves, doing so later that year. Black soldiers served with Washington throughout the Revolution, at Valley Forge, in the crossing of the Delaware, and in the final triumph at Yorktown.

Peter Salem reenlisted in January, 1776, and served until the end of the war. Most of his service was in the Massachusetts regiment, commanded by Colonel John Nixon until the summer of 1776 and by his brother, Colonel Thomas Nixon, thereafter. The Sons of the American Revolution erected over his grave in Framingham a memorial that reads:

PETER SALEM
A Soldier of the Revolution
Concord
Bunker Hill
Saratoga
Died, August 16th, 1816

About five thousand blacks served in the Continental Army, in the regiments of all states except Georgia and South Carolina. Those two Southern states refused to enlist blacks, although North Carolina, Virginia, and Maryland accepted them as soldiers. Negroes were welcomed in the navy from the start. The two thousand black sailors were a tenth of the naval forces; blacks formed only a sixtieth of the army. In both army and navy they served in integrated units; there were only three or four all-black units involving only a few hundred men.

More than twenty thousand slaves fled their masters to gain freedom on the British side. Most served the British as military laborers; some served as soldiers. Fearing for the safety of these blacks who had abandoned their masters and borne arms against them, the British carried many of them with them as their regiments left the

United States. The redcoats took at least nineteen thousand with them to such places as Jamaica in the West Indies, Halifax in Canada, and London. Problems developed, however, with these American freedmen. In Jamaica, they set a bad example for the many blacks toiling in slavery on sugar and tobacco plantations. In London, they sometimes were involved in brawling and other disturbances. And in Halifax, some of them found the climate too severe. Accordingly, Britain established in 1787 the colony of Sierra Leone on the west coast of Africa for these former slaves. This was the first major effort to restore to Africa blacks who had lived in what had been the English mainland colonies.

As a result of the Revolutionary War atmosphere, opposition to slavery intensified and awareness of the unjust treatment of black Americans increased. The earliest known protest against slavery had been registered on February 18, 1688, by a religious group in Germantown, a suburb of Philadelphia, Pennsylvania. These Mennonites were members of one of the group of German pietistic sects whose ideas of pacifism, equality, and brotherhood were similar to those of the Quakers. At their monthly meeting in February, 1688, these Germantown Mennonites stated their opposition to slavery and the slave trade, resolving:

> These are the reasons why we are against the traffic of menbody, as followeth: Is there any that would be done or handled at this manner? viz., to be sold or made a slave for all the time of his life? . . . Now, though they are black, we cannot conceive there is more liberty to have them slaves, as it is to have other white ones. There is a saying, that we should do to all men like as we will be done ourselves; making no difference of what generation, descent, or colour they are. And those who steal or rob men, and those who buy or purchase them, are they not all alike? . . . But to bring men hither, or to rob and sell them against their will, we stand against. . . . Pray, what thing in the world can be done worse towards us, than if men should rob or steal us away, and sell us for slaves to strange countries; separating husbands from their wives and children. . . . And such men ought to be delivered out of the hands of the robbers, and set free. . . . Or, have these poor negers not as much right to fight for their freedom, as you have to keep them slaves?

For many decades, most Americans ignored such antislavery protest. The struggle against British oppression, however, opened many eyes to the paradox of Americans demanding more freedom from Britain while denying freedom to the blacks in their midst. More and more, anti-British protest came to be coupled with anti-slavery protest. In 1764, James Otis of Massachusetts, in his pamphlet, *The Rights of the British Colonies Asserted and Proved*, not only denounced British oppression, but spoke up for Negro rights as well. Abigail Adams wrote to her husband, John, on September 22, 1774: "It always appeared a most iniquitous scheme to me to fight ourselves for what we are daily robbing and plundering from those who have as good a right to freedom as we have."

Slaves petitioned for freedom, often stating their claims in the Revolutionary rhetoric of natural rights to life and liberty. These ideas had been expounded by John Locke in England to justify the Glorious Revolution of 1688–1689, by which the Parliament's actions rejected the divine right of kingship and asserted the right of the people to overturn an unjust government. These ideas expressed in Locke's *Second Treatise on Government* inspired the colonists as they struggled against what they regarded as unjust British rule. But these ideas also inspired slaves who turned these doctrines of liberty against the institution of human bondage. Typical of this approach was the petition sent to the Massachusetts legislature by a group of slaves in May, 1774, two years before Jefferson's Declaration of Independence. The slaves stated: "we have in common with all other men a natural right to our freedoms . . . as we are a freeborn people and have never forfeited this blessing by any compact. . . . But we were unjustly dragged . . . hither to be made slaves for life in a Christian land."

In the Revolutionary War generation, more concerted efforts were made against slavery than ever before in America. Antislavery societies were formed, the earliest in the United States being organized by Quakers in 1775. After the American Revolution, antislavery groups were formed by other Americans, beginning in 1785 with the New York Society for Promoting Manumission, which had John Jay as its president. By 1792, there were such societies in every state from Massachusetts to Virginia. Northern states took steps to end slavery. Massachussetts ended slavery abruptly in 1783 with a decision of the Massachussetts Supreme Court that the new state constitution of 1780 did not permit slavery to continue there. For the other Northern states, beginning with Pennsylvania in 1780 and ending with New Jersey in 1786, legislation that instituted a gradual abolition of slavery, extending over many years in some cases, achieved the same eventual result as in Massachusetts. Southern states, meanwhile, passed laws making it easier to manumit (set free) slaves and also laws restricting the slave trade.

As royal colonies, the Southerners had been prevented from limiting the slave trade by vetoes. In his original draft of the Declaration of Independence, Thomas Jefferson, though a Virginia planter and slave-owner himself, denounced King George III for waging "cruel war against human nature itself, violating its most sacred rights of life & liberty in the persons of a distant people who never offended him, captivating & carrying them into slavery . . . suppressing every legislative attempt to prohibit or to restrain this execrable commerce. . . ." Jefferson's denunciation of the slave trade went too far, however, by bitterly assailing slavery itself. This passage was deleted during debate in the Continental Congress and thus was not a part of the final Declaration.

The peak of the antislavery movement was reached in the Northwest Ordinance of 1787 that proclaimed: "There shall be neither slavery nor involuntary servitude in the said territory. . . ." This Northwest area, which later became the states of Ohio, Indiana, Illinois, Michigan, and Wisconsin, stretched from the Ohio River to the Great Lakes and from the Appalachian Mountains to the Mississippi River.

But the Federal constitution drafted later in 1787 recognized slavery in three ways: (1) counting five slaves as three persons for determing taxes and representation; (2) restricting Congressional interference with the African slave trade for two decades; and (3) providing for the return of fugitive slaves. Without ever using such words as slave or African or black or Negro, the Constitution provided an unequal status for black Americans. Article I, section 2 of the Constitution provided that: "Representatives and direct Taxes shall be apportioned among the several States which may be included within this Union, according to their respective Numbers, which shall be determined by adding to the whole Number of free Persons, including those bound to service for a Term of Years, and excluding Indians not taxed, three fifths of all other Persons." Section 9 of this first article stated that "The Migration or Importation of such Persons as any of the States now existing shall think proper to admit, shall not be prohibited by the Congress prior to the Year one thousand eight hundred and eight, but a Tax or duty may be imposed on such Importation, not exceeding ten dollars for each Person." And Article IV, section 2 stipulated that "No person held to Service or Labour in one State, under the Laws thereof, escaping into another, shall, in Consequence of any Law or Regulation therein, be discharged from such Service of Labour, but shall be delivered up on Claim of the Party to whom such Service or Labour may be due."

During the Revolutionary era, Americans began to pay more heed to the talented blacks among them. More Negroes accordingly received opportunities to make fuller use of their abilities, to secure training, and to make meaningful achievements.

Some of these achievers remain anonymous. They were the slave craftsmen who did much of the labor, whether crude or skilled, especially in the South. Slaves built the homes, constructed the furniture, wove cloth and made garments, and produced the pottery, utensils, and ornaments in many Southern plantations and homes. Visitors admire the beautiful wrought-iron work found in such places as New Orleans, Mobile, and Charleston. Much of this beautiful, decorative work on balconies, lampposts, gates, and doors was done by slave craftsmen.

Other achievers came to be known. Some blacks became writers, such as the slave poets, Lucy Terry in Deerfield, Massachusetts, and Jupiter Hammond in Long Island, New York. A Philadelphia slave named James Derham secured training from a British army doctor and went on to become a free man and the first black physician in America. The renowned early American doctor Benjamin Rush attested that Derham was so skilled that he was able to learn some things from him. Prince Hall founded the first social organization among black Americans, establishing Masonic lodges. Joshua Johnston was an early portrait painter who did portraits of some of the most prominent families in Baltimore. Jean Baptiste Pointe de

Sable was a western pioneer who is considered the founder of Chicago. He had a substantial trading post near Lake Michigan where he lived with his Indian wife and daughter from the 1770s to 1800. The city of Chicago grew up around the thriving establishment of this first permanent resident of the Windy City. Bill Richmond was one of the nation's first professional fighters, having been assisted by a British regiment that secured fights for him in Europe. Other blacks, though their names are unknown, were the leading jockeys at race tracks in Saratoga and Charleston.

Of all the early black achievers, however, none were more prominent than Phillis Wheatley (1753–1784), Benjamin Banneker (1731–1806), and Richard Allen (1760–1831).

Born in Africa, Phillis came to America in a slave ship in 1761. Purchased by John and Susanna Wheatley of Boston, Phillis proved adept at learning to speak, read, and write English. She composed poems in the style of Alexander Pope, publishing a book, *Poems on Various Subjects, Religious and Moral*, in 1773. The book was published in England while she was on a visit there.

Phillis was hailed as a sensation and as proof of what blacks could accomplish. Her poetry, however, was generally stilted, classical, and imitative. She did not display much race consciousness, saying very little about the plight of blacks held in slavery and discriminated against when free. One of the very few times in which she said anything about the problems of black Americans was in the last four lines of her eight-line poem "On Being Brought from Africa to America," published in the 1773 collection. This poem read:

> 'Twas mercy brought me from my *Pagan* land
> Taught my benighted soul to understand
> That there's a God, that there's a *Savior* too;
> Once I redemption neither sought nor knew,
> Some view our sable race with scornful eye,
> "Their color is a diabolic die."
> Remember, *Christians, Negroes,* black as *Cain,*
> May be refined, and join th' angelic train.

In a poem written in 1775 entitled "His Excellency Gen. Washington," Miss Wheatley praised the commander of the colonial forces. The poem refers to the United States as Columbia in four places, as in the lines that went: "When *Gallic* powers *Columbia's* fury found; / And so may you, Whoever dares disgrace / The land of freedom's heaven defended race! / Fix'd are the eyes of the nations on the scales, / For in their hopes *Columbia's* arm prevails." Her use of Columbia for this nation is apparently the earliest such usage. In this same poem she says of General Washington, "Thee, first in peace and honours, —we demand / The grace and glory of thy martial band, / Fam'd for thy valour, for thy virtues more, / Hear every tongue thy guardian aid implore!" Similarly, this is the first known time that any one referred to Washington as first in peace, a phrase immortalized at a later time into "first in war, first in peace, and first in the hearts of his countrymen."

Phillis sent the poem to Washington in a letter of October 26, 1775, in which she said, "I have taken the freedom to address your Excellency in the enclosed poem, and entreat your acceptance . . ." Washington responded in a letter of February 28, 1776, saying in part: "I thank you most sincerely for your polite notice of me, in the elegant Lines you enclosed; and however undeserving I may be of such encomium and panegyrick, the style and manner exhibit a striking proof of your great poetical Talents." He apologized for the lateness of his response and indicated that only modesty prevented him from publishing the poem, which would display her talent to the world, but also lay him open to charges of vanity. He closed by inviting her to visit him, saying, "If you should ever come to Cambridge, or near Head Quarters, I shall be happy to see a person so favoured by the Muses . . ." At the time, Phillis was staying in Providence, Rhode Island, and sent the letter and poem to him from there. According to historian Benson J. Lossing, Phillis Wheatley visited Washington in March, 1776: "She passed half an hour with the commander-in-chief, from whom and his officers she received marked attention."

Benjamin Banneker was born a free person in the slave colony of Maryland and attended an integrated school taught by a Quaker there. He showed great ability in mathematics, devising mathematical puzzles that stumped some of the best mathematicians in the colonies. In 1761, he made a clock out of wooden parts, the first clock made wholly in America. In his late fifties, he studied and mastered astronomy. He began issuing annual almanacs in 1791.

Early in 1791, Banneker was appointed by President George Washington to serve, along with a French Major Pierre-Charles L'Enfant and with Andrew Ellicott III, to help lay out the new Federal capital in the District of Columbia. Banneker was the first black appointed to a post by a President of the United States. Although the Secretary of State, Thomas Jefferson, had recommended Banneker to President Washington, Banneker addressed a militant letter to Jefferson on August 19, 1791. Along with the letter, he sent a copy of his first yearly almanac. Banneker chastised Jefferson for the views expressed in Jefferson's only book, *Notes on Virginia* (1785). In that book, Jefferson had cast doubt on the intellectual ability of blacks. In his letter, Banneker pointed out that blacks "are looked upon with an eye of contempt; and considered rather as brutish than human, and scarcely capable of mental endowments." Knowing that Jefferson expressed sentiments of that sort in his book, Banneker went on to state, "I hope . . . that you are a man far less inflexible in sentiments of this nature, than many others. . . ." Banneker stated his own beliefs on the subject firmly, saying: "One universal Father hath given being to us all . . . endowed us with the same faculties . . . we are all of the same family. . . ." Banneker then reminded Jefferson of the liberal views Jefferson expressed in the original draft of the Declaration of Independence. He then denounced Jefferson, who was a slave-owner, as an apostate to his own creed:

> how pitiable it is to reflect that although you were so fully convinced of the benevolence of the Father of Mankind and of his equal and impartial distribution of these rights and privileges which he hath conferred upon them, that you should at the same time counteract his mercies, in detaining by fraud and violence, so numerous a part of my brethren under groaning captivity and cruel oppression, that you should at the same time be found guilty of that most criminal act, which you professedly detested in others, with respect to yourselves.

Pointing to his enclosed almanac as proof of what Negroes could do when given a chance, Banneker urged Jefferson "and all others, to wean yourselves from those narrow prejudices which you have imbibed with respect to" blacks. Jefferson replied on August 30, 1791, saying, "Nobody wishes more than I do to see such proofs as you exhibit, that nature has given to our black brethren, talents equal to those of the other colors of men, and that the appearance of a want of them is owing merely to the degraded condition of their existence, both in Africa and America."

Like Banneker, Richard Allen was a militant fighter for the rights and dignity of black Americans. Born a slave in Philadelphia, he and his parents and siblings were sold by their lawyer-owner to a planter in Delaware. Here, Allen became a convert and a devout Methodist. He converted his owner, who then allowed Allen and his brother to buy their freedom in 1777. Continuing his religious work, Allen held various jobs while traveling around as an unlicensed itinerant minister. Bishop Francis Asbury praised his work and wanted Allen to accompany him on missionary trips through the South. Allen preferred to work in the Middle Atlantic states, however, where there was less danger of inconvenience, insults, and being resold into slavery.

Eventually, Allen settled in Philadelphia, where he worked among black residents, bringing many of them into a white church, St. George's Methodist Episcopal Church, where he was allowed to preach to them at odd hours. He felt the need for a separate church where blacks could develop their own leadership and talent free of domination by whites. In 1787, along with Absalom Jones, he founded the Free African Society dedicated to improving the lot of blacks. Encountering discrimination in St. George's Church later in 1787, Allen and Jones and their followers pulled out. In the early 1790s, Jones founded a black Episcopal church, Allen a black Methodist church. Each acquired a building and both churches were dedicated in July, 1794, Jones's St. Thomas African Episcopal Church, which was the beginning of Negro congregations in the Episcopal denomination, and Allen's Bethel African Methodist Episcopal Church.

At first Bethel retained its ties with the white Methodists. Bishop Asbury ordained Allen a deacon and a minister. The officials at St. George's Church tried to run the affairs of the black Bethel Church. It took a court judgment handed down early in 1816 to prevent further interference by white Methodists in the operation of Bethel. Meanwhile, African Methodist Episcopal (A.M.E.) churches were set up in various other cities. In 1816, a national convention was attended by official delegates from these churches. At that convention, the A.M.E. denomination was organized, the first separate religious denomination among black Americans. Richard Allen was consecrated and served as the first bishop of the new denomination.

Allen may be considered a pioneer leader of black Americans. His Free African Society was the first organization of black Americans. His A.M.E. denomination was the first denomination among Negroes. And he was a leader in setting up the first national organization of Afro-Americans. This was the Convention of 1830, the first of a series of national conventions at which blacks gathered to air their grievances and state their hopes and aspirations. Allen was instrumental in helping call this first meeting, and he was the chairman at its sessions. This Convention of 1830 took a strong stand against the idea of recolonizing blacks in Africa, a leadership position that Richard Allen had long espoused.

Thus, during and after the American Revolution, talented blacks began proving their ability and also protesting injustice.

5

Cotton Kingdom
and Plantation Slavery

1791–1860

Every eye in the room turned toward the tall Yankee. He had said little during the conversation at Mulberry Grove that winter evening. Could he, as Mrs. Greene hinted, solve their problem? The visitors to her plantation near Savannah surveyed the scholarly guest whom the charming hostess described as a mechanical genius. Was it possible that this dignified young man from Yale could find a way to turn their useless green-seed crop into a golden harvest of boundless prosperity?

If so, Georgia's generosity to General Greene would be unexpectedly requited. Phineas Miller, manager of Mulberry Grove Plantation, recalled the chance encounter he and Mrs. Greene had had with the young man on the boat to Savannah late in 1792. How fortunate for them that his original employer had found another tutor, leaving him free to accept Mrs. Greene's invitation to be a guest at Mulberry Grove. Out of gratitude and in spare time from his study of law, the Yale graduate made and repaired things about the plantation. In displaying the mechanical ability he had developed by working in the shop on his father's farm in Westboro, Massachusetts, he had greatly impressed Mrs. Greene.

How strange it would be, mused the visitors, if a Yankee sojourning on a transplanted Yankee's plantation would devise a solution that had escaped many inventive minds in the South. They remembered the Yankee general who had rescued the South during the Revolution. After participating in the siege of Boston and aiding Washington at Trenton and Germantown, Major General Nathanael Greene, who was a Rhode Island Quaker, had been placed in command of the Southern forces. In battles at Cowpens, Guilford Court House, and Eutaw Springs, he and his subordinate, Francis "Swamp Fox" Marion, had disrupted British ascendancy in the South. A grateful state of Georgia had given General Greene the plantation upon which he lived until he passed away in 1786. Now his vivacious widow, Catherine Littleton Greene, was about to repay the South for the gift of Mulberry Grove.

Responding to the challenge, Eli Whitney set to work in the plantation shops. He called on the knowledge he had acquired during the years 1780 to 1783, when he manufactured nails and hatpins in his father's shop in Westboro, and during the years 1789 to 1792, when he worked his way through Yale repairing apparatus and equipment about the campus. A carpenter there had remarked, "There was one good mechanic spoiled when you went to college." But Whitney retained his mechanical bent. Upon graduating from Yale in the autumn of 1792, he accepted an offer to serve as a tutor on a Southern plantation, so that he could study law and earn his way at the same time. Now by solving the problem of the green-seed cotton mechanically. Of the many varieties of cotton, two when the tutoring job failed to materialize, leaving him stranded.

Urged on by Mrs. Greene and her plantation manager Miller, Whitney took only ten days to come up with a device to clean green-seed cotton mechanically. Of the many varieties of cotton, two major categories grew in the Southern states, sea-island (long staple) and upland (short staple). Sea-island cotton had a glossy black seed and silky two-inch lint that could be separated from the seed easily. Upland cotton had a fuzzy greenish seed to which its one-inch lint adhered tightly, making it extremely difficult to clean by hand. Neither type was grown commercially in the United States before the end of the American Revolution. Throughout the colonial period, blacks cultivated primarily tobacco, rice, sugar, and indigo. The union of slavery and cotton was a product of the 1800s; for the 1600s and 1700s, it was slavery and tobacco that went hand in hand.

The green-seed short-staple upland cotton had been known to Jamestown's early settlers. A slave working all day, however, could only clean (separate from the seed) a single pound of this cotton's fiber; it would cost more to feed him for the day than the one pound of cotton would sell for. Thus, it was uneconomical as a commercial crop. Yet it grew easily in the warm southern regions, where two hundred frost-free days a year and at least twenty-three inches of annual rainfall were not uncommon. Prior to 1793 it was grown for home use only. Housewives cleaned a few ounces a day in their spare time, subsequently spun it into yarn on their wheels and wove it into cloth on their household looms, a laborious process that helped the time pass in isolated Southern farmhouses.

The long-staple black-seed cotton was introduced into the United States in 1786 when a Loyalist living in the Bahama Islands sent some seeds to a friend in Georgia. This type could make a commercial crop, but it grew only in a few places along the coasts of Georgia and South Carolina, especially such sea islands as Edisto, St. Helena, and Hilton Head. This cotton was used to make the finest cloth, such as lace and cambric.

Since long-staple cotton grew only in restricted locales, the South's problem was to find a way to make the short-staple type profitable. The Industrial Revolution supplied the motive. During the 1760s, 1770s, and 1780s, such machines as the spinning jenny, water frame, spinning mule, and power loom, invented by James Hargreaves, Richard Arkwright, Samuel Crompton, and Edmund Cartwright, respectively, transformed the textile industry. English factories needed great quantities of cotton. A machine that would clean green-seed cotton would meet the demand and enrich the South.

Whitney's cotton engine (slurred in Southern speech to cotton "gin") solved the problem. The machine was basically simple, as historian Clement Eaton explains in his book, *The Growth of Southern Civilization, 1790–1860*, "consisting of a roller equipped with wire teeth which tore the fiber from the seed as the spikes revolved between the slats of a hopper." By April, 1793, Whitney had a larger, improved machine. The next month, he formed a partnership with Mrs. Greene's manager, Phineas Miller. Miller put up the money to back Whitney in a venture to monopolize cotton ginning by patenting the process and manufacturing the machines in New Haven, Connecticut. All the South would have to bring its cotton to their gins for cleaning. The machine was so simple, however, that many others simply copied it and infringed on the patent Whitney obtained on March 14, 1794.

A Southern mechanic, Hodgen Holmes of Augusta, Georgia, patented a gin in 1796 that utilized circular saws instead of wire teeth. The saw-toothed gin became the standard process in the industry and still is today. The firm of Whitney & Miller became so entangled in expensive patent suits that Miller was a disappointed man when he passed away in 1803. Whitney received a favorable verdict in 1807. Several Southern states agreed to make payments to him, but he never realized the vast profits that so important and lucrative an invention should have yielded.

Some writers have claimed that Whitney borrowed the idea for the cotton engine from a home-made device that he had observed used by a mechanically-minded slave on a plantation. Whether or not that is true, Whitney gave ample proof throughout his life of his abilities as an inventive and innovative manufacturer. While his cotton engine patents were tied up in litigation, he went on to develop the mass-production system of using interchangeable parts. He first applied it in 1798 in the manufacture of firearms for the United States Government. Prior to Whitney's pioneering techniques, each gun was an individual, hand-crafted piece, which would have to go back to the original gunsmith for repair. Parts from two guns of the same make, made the same day, at the same gun factory could not be substituted one for the other, for no two guns were exactly alike. With Whitney's directing genius, the manufacturing process was changed to provide for standardized parts that could be interchanged. This became the basic technique in American mass production. After arduous struggle, Whitney finally achieved success, spending his last decade as a prosperous manufacturer in New Haven, Connecticut. He passed away there in January, 1825, a month after his fifty-ninth birthday.

Few inventions have ever had the impact of Whitney's cotton gin. It transformed the South. Constant growing of tobacco had so exhausted the soil that many Southerners were contemplating switching from that great staple crop to diversified farming. Some coupled this with thoughts of abandoning slavery (with the owners compensated, of course) and recolonizing the blacks in Africa. With the advent of cotton growing, such ideas had much less appeal. Cotton became such an obsession that Senator James H. Hammond of South Carolina boasted in the United States Senate in

1858: "What would happen if no cotton was furnished for three years . . . England would topple headlong and carry the whole civilized world with her save the South. No, you dare not make war on cotton. No power on earth dares to make war on it. Cotton is king."

With the cotton gin, far more slaves were needed than ever before. The gin cleaned the cotton, but slaves were needed to plant, tend, and pick it, to transport it, to operate the gins, and to press it into bales (of about 500 pounds each). Cotton cultivation was especially suited to the use of the gang system preferred for handling slaves. The slave population increased greatly. In 1790, when the first census of the United States was taken, nearly 698,000 slaves lived in the United States, but in 1860 there were 3,953,000 slaves. In 1790, the 757,000 blacks (59,000 of whom were free) constituted 19 percent of the nation's total population of 3,929,000; one out of every five Americans was a Negro then. Interestingly, in 1790, more free blacks lived in the South (32,000) than in the North (27,000) and the North had more slaves (40,000) than free blacks. The gradual emancipation provided for by law in most Northern states in the 1780s had not yet removed enough Negroes from bondage to have the free black population outnumber the slave population above the Mason-Dixon line.

Cotton-growing also increased dramatically. In 1792, the United States exported 138,000 pounds of cotton, in 1794 (the year the gin was patented) 1,601,000 pounds were exported, in 1795, 6,276,000 pounds, and in 1800 exports had risen to 17,790,000 pounds. In 1792 all of the cotton exported from the United States was sea-island cotton. By 1810, however, ten times more upland cotton was exported than the sea-island variety. As early as 1803, cotton surpassed tobacco in value as the nation's leading export. Total cotton production (in bales) leaped forward from 3,000 bales in 1790 to 335,000 bales in 1820, to nearly 2,000,0000 bales in the 1840 census, and 5,300,000 bales in the 1860 census. By 1860, three-fourths of the world's supply of cotton came from the Southern states.

Much of the cotton was grown increasingly in the trans-Appalachian South extending from western Georgia to Texas. This region became known as the Cotton Kingdom.

The older Southern states along the Atlantic seaboard had grown cotton year after year without rotation of crops. Farmers and planters had so much invested in land, equipment, and slave labor that they could not afford to let the land lie fallow for a year, or switch to another crop from time to time, to allow the nutrients to be restored to the soil. Instead, they simply replanted the big money crops (tobacco or rice or sugar) every year, because only these staple crops brought in sufficient cash profits to enable them to repay their debts, realize a return on their investments, and expand by acquiring more land and slaves. Ignoring the advice of soil specialists, Southerners grew these commercial crops constantly, exhausting the soil and reducing its fertility.

To meet the great world demands for the raw material of cotton, virgin lands had to be opened, lands that had not previously been exhausted by many decades of growing tobacco or other staple crops. The best hope for such land lay in the area across the Appalachian Mountains. There, the fertile soil of the Gulf states region beckoned, the states of Alabama, Mississippi, Tennessee, Arkansas, Louisiana, and Texas. By 1830, the six states of this Gulf region produced more cotton than the Atlantic coastal states (Florida, Georgia, South Carolina, North Carolina, and Virginia). By 1860, three out of every four bales of cotton were produced in the Gulf states.

The trans-Appalachian South was not able to assume this position of prominence as soon as the world demand for cotton arose in the 1780s and Whitney's gin in the 1790s made the growing of upland cotton economically feasible. Cotton growers were anxious to move into these fertile western lands drained by the Mississippi, Red, Yazoo, Tennessee, Tombigbee, Alabama, and Pearl rivers. Their westward migration was impeded, however, by the presence of hostile Indians, such as the Creeks, Cherokees, Chickasaws, and Choctaws, who opposed the encroachment of the white settlers on their lands. Spanish and British agents in the area intrigued against the westward expansion of the United States, instigating and abetting Indian attacks on the settlers. The great Shawnee Indian chief in Ohio, Tecumseh, visited the Creek Indians of Alabama in 1811, encouraging them to resist the advance of the whites who sought to take their lands. Two years later, the Creeks, in one of the major assaults on white settlements in the trans-Appalachian South, attacked 550 persons huddled in Fort Mims on the Alabama River thirty-five miles above Mobile. Most of the whites were wiped out in this Fort Mims Massacre. The War of 1812 was caused not only by demands for freedom of the seas, but also by the eagerness of Westerners to end the intriguing of foreign agents, especially the British, with the Indians along the western frontiers.

Since militia laws in the new nation generally excluded blacks, fewer Negro soldiers served in this war than in the American Revolution. Blacks did participate freely in the navy, and on an integrated basis. Afro-American sailors shared the same posts (seamen, gunners, etc.) as white sailors, and lived and ate in the same quarters with them. In fact, that was the practice in the navy through all of America's early wars, up to and including the Spanish-American War. It was not until World War I, with a Southern-oriented administration in power, that the United States Navy became a segregated institution.

Many black sailors served with Commodore Oliver Perry in the Battle of Lake Erie on September 10, 1813, helping the United States win its greatest naval victory of the war. Commander Nathaniel Shaler, in a letter of January 1, 1813, described the heroism of two black sailors, John Johnson and John Davis, who were mortally wounded during a naval encounter on the Atlantic Ocean. He wrote of Johnson, who lay in severe pain: "the poor brave fellow . . . several times exclaimed to his shipmates, 'Fire away my boys, no haul a color down.'" Davis, who fell near the captain, "several times requested to be thrown overboard, saying, he was only in the way of others."

Blacks served with General Andrew Jackson in the Battle of New Orleans on January 8, 1815. Facing General Edward Pakenham's attacking force of 5,300 veterans, Jackson had 5,000 men, including two volunteer battalions (totaling 430 men) of free blacks of Louisiana. These two battalions were led by black officers: Major Pierre Lacoste, Major Louis Daquin, and Captain Joseph Savary, who took over for Daquin when he was wounded. Suffering 2,036 casualties to only 21 American casualties and demoralized by the loss of Pakenham, the British surrendered. In a letter to Napoleon Bonaparte of France, Jackson said that in the second assault, the British "were led by General Pakenham in person. . . . I heard a single rifle-shot . . . and a moment thereafter I saw Pakenham reel and pitch out of his saddle. I have always believed he fell from the bullet of a free man of color, who was a famous rifle-shot . . ." The marksman apparently was one of Savary's men. The letters of Commander Shaler and General Jackson were included in William L. Katz's documentary collection, *Eyewitness: The Negro in American History.*

The War of 1812 removed the Indian menace and cleared the way for unfettered westward advancement into the Gulf states region. General Jackson accomplished this objective when he defeated the Creek Indians and their Cherokee Indian allies in March, 1814, in the Battle of Horseshoe Bend. This victory along the Tallapoosa River in central Alabama not only avenged the Fort Mims Massacre, but resulted in the Creek Indians signing the Treaty of Ft. Jackson in August, 1814. In this treaty they surrendered two-thirds of Creek lands to the United States, an area almost half the size of the present state of Alabama. Cotton growers were now free to trek westward. Entire plantation households moved along the road with furniture, livestock, and slaves, as slave-owners sought the fertile lands of the Gulf states.

Although they had solved the problem of available soil for the Cotton Kingdom, Southerners had to surmount another difficulty, the labor supply. From the time the first Africans were brought to Jamestown by the Dutch ship in 1619, a steady stream of migrants from Africa had been arriving in chains to do much of the labor of building America, especially in the South. Fearful that this endless flow of workers might be closed off, some Southern delegates to the Constitutional Convention of 1787 had opposed giving the Federal government control over commerce except by a two-thirds vote, which would give Southern Congressmen a virtual veto on trade measures. The Commerce Compromise had settled this issue by providing that: (1) Congress could not tax exports, thus freeing the South of fears that the movement of its great export crops, such as tobacco, would be impeded; (2) Congress could pass laws regulating commerce and trade by a simple majority, thus keeping the North from being hampered by a virtual Southern veto on trade measures; and (3) Congress could not interfere with the slave trade from Africa prior to 1808 and could not tax slave-trade cargoes until then at a rate higher than $10 per person imported.

As the twenty-year grace period (1787–1807) for the slave trade drew near its close, the President of the United States was a Southern planter and slave-owner, Thomas Jefferson, who had been elected to his second successive term in 1804, a term lasting from 1805 to 1809. In his annual message to Congress on December 2, 1806, Jefferson recommended action be taken to cut off the slave trade completely. Jefferson sent this message because he had inaugurated the practice of sending his State of the Union Message to the Congress in writing to be read by a clerk, rather than going to the Capitol to address the assembled Congress in person. He wrote: "I congratulate you, fellow-citizens, on the approach of the period at which you may interpose your authority constitutionally to withdraw the citizens of the United States from all further participation in those violations of human rights which have been so long continued on the unoffending inhabitants of Africa." Here spoke the Jefferson of the original draft of the Declaration of Independence in which he denounced the slave trade as a "cruel war" that violated "sacred rights" of an unoffending people and that constituted an "execrable commerce."

There were other motives, however, than the genuine dislike of the brutalities of the slave trade, a horrible business that would have proved offensive to any sensitive person. There had always been fears of the numbers of blacks that were inundating areas where slavery flourished. The Spanish authorities in the early 1500s had restricted the African slave trade because of apprehensions that the settlers and the colonial garrisons would be unable to keep the slaves under control where the black population was growing so rapidly. A number of the English mainland colonies had experienced similar fears. Their efforts to curb the trade through laws passed by eighteenth-century colonial legislatures had been blocked, however. The powerful influence exerted by slave traders, especially the Royal African Company, resulted in such laws being vetoed by authorities in England. After the War for Independence removed English interference, several Southern states in the 1790s took steps to curb the slave trade.

In addition to this fear of being inundated by blacks, there was also the matter of the increment in value of the slaves. By reducing the influx of slaves, slave-owners were able to realize an increase in value for the slaves they possessed. Hence, varied motives operated in support of a cessation of the African slave trade.

Responding to Jefferson's recommendation, Congress passed a law on March 2, 1807, to prohibit the importation of slaves from Africa. This statute provided that: "from and after the first day of January, one thousand eight hundred and eight, it shall not be lawful to import or bring into the United States or the territories thereof from any foreign kingdom, place, or country, any negro, mulatto, or person of colour, as a slave, or to be held to service or labour." The law provided penalties, including fines of $5,000 for persons engaging in the slave trade and $800 for any person knowingly buying a slave smuggled in contrary to the law. It also declared that ships carrying slaves from Africa or other places would be seized by United States naval vessels and would be forfeited to the United States government, thus subjecting owners of ships that ventured to carry slaves to the risk of losing their vessels.

The slave trade continued, however, particularly because of the failure of the United States to cooperate fully with Great Britain in the suppression of this horrible traffic in human beings. Major Western nations were turning against slavery about this time. Denmark was the first to abolish the slave trade, doing so in 1792. In February, 1794, the radical extremists in power during the second stage of the French Revolution abolished slavery in the French colonies. The permanence of this reform was in doubt, however, as France underwent successive changes in government: the Directory government in the third stage of the Revolution, the Napoleonic era, and the Bourbon restoration. The reform was finally accomplished when France abolished the slave trade in 1818 and abolished slavery in 1848. Meanwhile, in England, a reformer, William Wilberforce (1759–1833), led a drive against the slave trade and then against slavery. Success came with the English law of March 25, 1807, that abolished the slave trade and the emancipation law of August 28, 1833. The slave trade was abolished by the other major European powers also: Sweden in 1813, Holland in 1814, Spain in 1820, and Portugal in 1830.

Despite the nearly universal ban on the slave trade by the maritime powers, slaves continued to be brought out of Africa. The profits to be realized by bringing slaves to labor-hungry New World planters made traders willing to risk the fines and forfeitures provided under the laws of various Western nations. Britain worked vigorously for international cooperation to stop the slave trade. In November, 1814, at the Congress of Vienna that was trying to set Europe in order following the initial overthrow of Napoleon, Britain got the powers to agree to the principle that the slave trade should be abolished. Subsequently, she signed bilateral treaties with most of the European powers by which they agreed to permit each other's merchant ships to be stopped, searched, and seized in an effort to curb the slave trade. Since Britain had the world's greatest navy by far, it would be the British who could most effectively enforce the prohibition on the slave trade.

Only one major power refused to cooperate with the British, and that was the United States. Americans were sensitive over the issue of freedom of the seas. They feared British interference with their commerce. They were suspicious that Britain might enforce the treaty provisions in a zealous manner that would cause loss of American property. The treaties generally provided that a ship could be seized if it carried equipment that the inspecting vessel deemed was on board for the purpose of carrying out slave-trade activities. Americans did not mind a ship being seized where actual evidence of its carrying slaves, such as the presence of slaves on board, could be established. But they were reluctant to permit their ships the risk of seizure on flimsy grounds. Finally, there was the highly emotional issue of impressment of seamen who had deserted. Americans feared that granting Britain blanket permission to stop and search American merchant ships might result in impressment of men Britain claimed as deserters. Since Britain would not surrender its right of impressment or ensure against violation of freedom of the seas as Americans interpreted it, the two nations could not agree on a treaty for mutual search of suspected slavers flying the other's flag.

The result was that slave ships kept an American flag handy to run up whenever a British warship on slave patrol duty came in view. Naturally, the United States did not condone foreign ships flying the American flag illegally. Therefore, the United States did not object to Britain stopping and seizing any vessel that it knew or strongly suspected was flying the American flag without really being a vessel registered in the United States. The hitch, however, was that we reserved the right to prosecute for damages in case Britain made a mistake and stopped a vessel that was entitled to fly the American flag. Unwilling to face the risk of having a claim made against him, a British naval captain would seldom stop a vessel flying the American flag. As a consequence, the slave trade kept on, despite the fact that the European powers, as well as most Latin American nations, had outlawed it. The American flag became a refuge for persons engaging in the traffic that Jefferson had denounced as this "execrable commerce."

The United States realized that its own law of 1807 banning the slave trade as well as Britain's efforts to suppress such traffic were ineffective largely because of the traders who hid behind the American flag. America began to take steps, accordingly, to make the prohibition more effective. In March, 1819, Congress passed a law to pay informers $50 for each illegal African slave import rescued as a result of the informer's tip. The fact that such a law was passed in 1819, eleven years after the slave trade was banned, is indicative of the fact that slaves continued to be smuggled in. In May, 1820, another Congressional law declared those participating in the slave trade to be pirates and decreed the death penalty for any American citizen caught in the act. That did not deter Americans from carrying on the illegal traffic. It is estimated that about 250,000 African slaves were smuggled into the United States between 1808 and 1860, despite the laws against it and the extreme penalty provided.

Part of the problem was that the Federal government neither took effective action to patrol the seas against slave traders nor agreed to cooperate with Britain's efforts to serve as the world's policeman on this problem. American warships patrolled against slave traders only fitfully. It was not until 1842 that the United States made provision for a regular patrolling of the sea lanes traversed by slave traders. This was done in the Webster-Ashburton Treaty (August 9, 1842), in which the United States and Britain settled many outstanding issues between them, primarily boundary questions, but also including effective patrolling to stop slave traders. Article VIII of this treaty provided that "each shall prepare, equip, and maintain in service, on the coast of Africa, a sufficient and adequate squadron, or naval force of vessels . . . to enforce, separately and respectively, the laws, rights, and obligations, of each of the two countries, for the suppression of the slave trade. . . ." The two squadrons were to be separate, but were to cooperate. Since the United States continued to refuse to grant the right of mutual search and seizure, this action was still limited. Consequently, the smuggling kept on.

Meanwhile, incidents of slave mutiny began to occur on slave ships. In 1839, a group of slaves on a Spanish slave ship, the *Amistad*, revolted and slew their captors. Their leader was Joseph Cinque, who had been a prince in Africa. The revolt took place off the coast of Cuba. Cinque and his fellow mutineers sailed the ship northward into the Atlantic Ocean off Long Island, New York, where a United States naval vessel seized the *Amistad* and brought the black mutineers into port at New London, Connecticut, charging them with piracy. President Martin Van Buren, a Democrat, and his administration wished to return the men to their Spanish masters, which would have meant certain death for them. Former President John Quincy Adams, who, after his single frustrating term in the White House (1825–1829), served in the House of Representatives from 1831 until he passed away in 1848, defended Cinque and his fellow blacks. Congressman Adams argued their case before the United States Supreme Court in 1841. The Court agreed with him that the men had been kidnapped illegally in view of the international prohibitions against the slave trade. Hence the Court held that they were free men and they were allowed to return to freedom in Africa.

Another case involved an American slave ship, the brig *Creole* that engaged in the coastwise slave trade. On November 7, 1841, slaves who were being transported from Hampton Roads, Virginia, to New Orleans mutinied, killed an officer, and took the ship to Nassau in the British Bahamas. The British authorities tried and hanged those responsible for the murder, but were inclined to grant freedom to the others. Naturally, the British who had ended their slave trade and slavery felt little sympathy for the ship's owner and crew. Southerners were incensed with this deprivation of property rights and with the condoning of mutiny, especially that involving black slaves rising against their white lords and masters. The President then was John Tyler, a Virginia slave-owner himself. Tyler and his Secretary of State, Daniel Webster, vigorously protested the refusal of the British to return the cargo of slaves from *The Creole* to their American owners. The issue was finally settled by submitting it to an Anglo-American mixed claims commission under an agreement of 1853. In 1855, the umpire decided that Britain should pay the United States the sum of $110,330 in compensation for the slave property lost by Britain's freeing of the *Creole* mutineers.

The attitude of the United States toward the nineteenth-century slave trade from Africa was ambivalent because of national politics. On the one hand, the United States was one of the first nations to ban the slave trade. At the same time, however, it was the least cooperative in international efforts to enforce the ban. Furthermore, it was one of the last Western nations to end slavery. The humanitarian drive against slavery had ended it almost everywhere in the Western world by 1863 except the Spanish colony of Cuba, the Latin American nation of Brazil, and the United States. While the whole world was moving toward this humanitarian goal, the United States was facing in the other direction. As the century progressed, particularly from the 1830s on, the South became more determined not only to protect slavery but to expand the institution into new areas. The South became a closed section insofar as discussion of slavery was concerned. In the North, abolitionists were generally considered meddling busybodies and fanatics and were often attacked by mobs in Northern cities.

Except for the twelve years in office of the one National Republican administration (J. Q. Adams, 1825–1829) and of the two Whig administrations (Harrison–Tyler, 1841–1845 and Polk–Fillmore, 1845–1849), the Democrats were in power from 1801 to 1861. Since that party tended to be dominated by its Southern wing in this period, the Federal government was generally in the hands of persons sympathetic to the South's viewpoint on slavery. Increasingly, influential Southerners spoke out in favor of reopening the African slave trade. Every Southern commercial convention in the period between 1854 and 1860 passed resolutions calling for Congress to drop its ban on the slave trade. Fortunately, even pro-Southern Democratic administrations refused to take that step, a move which would have had little Northern support. At the same time, however, these pro-South administrations took little action toward making the slave-trade ban really effective.

It was not until after the Southern states seceded and the national government was in the hands of a Republican administration which was oriented toward Northern interests that effective action was taken against the slave trade. In February, 1862, for the first time, a slave trader was hanged in the United States. Despite the almost open smuggling that had gone on since the 1820 law decreed the death penalty for the "piratical" slave trade, the nation had to wait forty-two years for the extreme penalty to be applied. Two months later, on April 7, 1862, the United States finally signed an agreement with Great Britain empowering mutual search and seizure. With that agreement, the death knell was sounded for the Atlantic slave trade. No longer could slavers flout the law, gaining impunity by running up an American flag to avoid searches by patrolling British naval vessels. At last, the "execrable commerce" could be stopped.

Despite all the smuggling and the violations of the slave-trade ban, the Cotton Kingdom could not get enough hands for its cotton plantations by the illicit Atlantic slave trade. Instead, much of the labor for the Gulf state cotton plantations was secured by the domestic slave trade in which slaves from the older Atlantic Coast tobacco states were sold to the newer Gulf Coast cotton states. This domestic slave trade brought in its train some of the most serious evils of the entire institution of slavery.

6

Slave Life and Revolts

1800–1860

Josiah Henson's mother dreaded the pending auction. She shuddered at the announcement that Dr. Josiah McPherson's property would have to be sold in order to divide the proceeds among his heirs.

Although he was only a child of five then, Henson remembered that McPherson "was far kinder to his slaves than the planters generally were, never suffering them to be struck by any one." He was "a man of good, kind impulses, liberal, jovial, hearty," but he accidentally drowned in a shallow stream on his plantation in Charles County, Maryland, while returning intoxicated from a party. As was often the case, a slave-owner's passing was grievous to his friends, but calamitous to his slaves, for few things were more detested than the auction sometimes required to settle an estate.

Much later, when Henson (1789–1883) wrote his autobiography, *Father Henson's Story of His Own Life* (1858), he recalled the auction vividly. "My brothers and sisters were bid off first, and one by one, while my mother, paralyzed by grief held me by the hand. Her turn came, and she was bought by Isaac Riley of Montgomery County. Then I was offered to the assembled purchasers." Henson was the youngest of the six children. The other five had been sold to buyers other than Riley.

"My mother, half distracted with the thought of parting forever from all her children, pushed through the crowd while the bidding for me was going on, to the spot where Riley was standing. She fell at his feet, and clung to his knees, entreating him in tones that a mother only could command to buy her *baby* as well as herself, and spare to her one, at least, of her little ones." Not only did Riley turn "a deaf ear to her supplication," Henson related, he shook her loose "with such violent blows and kicks, as to reduce her to the necessity of creeping out of his reach . . . mingling the groan of bodily suffering with the sob of a breaking heart. . . ." Threescore years later, Henson (who was bought by a tavern owner named Robb) stated, "I seem to see and hear my poor weeping mother now." Henson's case had a happier ending than most such auctions; the forsaken lad became so sick that within a month Robb sold him to Riley cheaply, reuniting mother and son.

Apologists for the South questioned the stories of family separation that appeared so regularly in narratives of former slaves. Many of the slaves who escaped to the North were illiterate because the South made no provision for educating slaves and often passed laws to prevent their learning to read and write. Accordingly, most of the autobiographies, memoirs, reminiscences, and other personal accounts of fugitive slaves had to be written for them by Northern whites who sympathized with their efforts to inform the world about conditions under slavery. The slave would dictate from his memory of life under slavery to the white ghostwriter who would write down the slave's account and prepare it for publication. Usually, the person serving as "editor" or "ghostwriter" for these slave narratives was an abolitionist, since runaway slaves received support from abolitionist societies in Northern communities. As abolitionists hated slavery and detested slave-owners, they did not always serve as completely objective reporters in preparing the slaves' narratives for publication. Concerned primarily with striking a blow at the hated institution of slavery, they sometimes used these narratives as propaganda vehicles to put slavery in the worst possible light. The abolitionists aimed to turn public opinion against slavery and did not mind stretching the truth in order to do so. But in spite of the exaggeration that crept into some narratives, these accounts by slaves provide an important source of knowledge about slavery, if read with caution. Who would know better what slavery was like than the man who had worked under it and had felt the sting of the lash? Moreover, a number of narratives were written by slaves who educated themselves and did not need the aid of abolitionist editors or ghostwriters. Josiah Henson and Frederick Douglass are among the slaves who were literate and therefore wrote their own stories.

Essentially they tell the same things about slavery, including separation of families, as are told in the ghostwritten accounts.

Although the repetitious recital in slave narratives of heart-rending separations leads to suspicions of exaggeration, it might just as well indicate that such separations occurred frequently. Southern whites, themselves, attested to these tragic scenes. In his book, *The Growth of Southern Civilization 1790–1860*, a leading historian, who is also a Southerner, Professor Clement Eaton, quoted from the manuscript journal of an itinerant merchant. This white merchant, William Reynolds, witnessed the sale of twenty-three slaves at an auction in Memphis. Reynolds stated in his journal: "One yellow [light-skinned] woman was sold who had two children. She begged and implored her new master on her knees to buy her children also, but it had no effect, he would not do it. She then begged him to buy her little girl (about 5 years old) but all to no purpose, it was truly heart rending to hear her cries when they were taking her away." Professor Eaton pointed out that "Only Louisiana, and Alabama after 1852, prohibited the sale of a child under ten years of age from its mother."

Settling estates was one reason for selling slaves. The domestic slave trade was another. With the African slave trade abolished in 1808, the surplus slaves of the tobacco states were eagerly bought by planters in the cotton states. This led to a shift of the black population from its overwhelming concentration in the South Atlantic states (Maryland, Virginia, the Carolinas, Georgia, and Florida). More and more blacks came to live in the Gulf states (Alabama, Mississippi, Louisiana, Texas, Arkansas, Tennessee, and Kentucky). In 1800, 860,000 Southern blacks lived in the Atlantic Coast states, fifteen times the 59,000 blacks then living in the Gulf states. In 1830, however, nearly a third of Southern Negroes lived in the Gulf states, 630,000, contrasted to 1,500,000 of them in the Atlantic Coast states. In 1860, the regions were nearly equal, with 2,058,000 Southern blacks (slave and free) in the Atlantic states and 2,038,000 in the Gulf states. Thus, not only cotton growing expanded into the Cotton Kingdom (Gulf states region) as a result of Whitney's invention of the cotton engine, the black population began shifting in that direction also. Slaves were desperately needed for the cotton plantations established on the virgin soils of the Gulf states, particularly after the Indian problem was reduced by the War of 1812.

Many businessmen were attracted to the lucrative slave trading. In 1860, a prime field hand (young male, 18–25 years old) could be bought for $1,250 in Virginia, but sold for $1,800 in New Orleans. The variance in price was a result of the cutting off of the legal slave trade from Africa coupled with the great demand for slaves in the Deep South's Cotton Kingdom. Dealers traveled throughout the Upper South buying surplus slaves from planters, purchasing them at auctions of estates and bankruptcies, or buying slaves convicted of crimes and banished from their localities. Many of these slave traders were cruel, coarse, dishonest men, scorned by gentlemen. Others were of better standing, shunning the term slave traders and calling themselves agents, auctioners, brokers, and commission merchants. In the 1850s, Richmond had sixty-nine dealers, Charleston more than fifty, Montgomery about a hundred, and New Orleans nearly three hundred.

A leading firm in the 1830s was Franklin & Armfield, founded in 1828 by Isaac Franklin and John Armfield. The latter collected slaves in the company's pens in a three-story building on Duke Street in Alexandria, Virginia. They had agents in other cities such as Richmond and Baltimore. Franklin resided in New Orleans, selling the slaves in the Deep South markets of Natchez, Mississippi, and New Orleans, Louisiana. By 1834, this respected firm was shipping a thousand to twelve hundred slaves a year to the Southwest. They owned four ships (the *Isaac Franklin, Tribune, Uncas,* and *United States*) that transported their slaves and the slaves of other traders from the Atlantic Coast to the Gulf of Mexico. Armfield made $500,000 by 1834 and Franklin amassed an even greater fortune eventually.

When selling slaves who had long been in the family, planters often arranged the deal late at night and then rode off early in the morning. That way they avoided witnessing the mournful scene when the trader carried off slaves who had no foreknowledge of being parted from home and loved ones. Sometimes, such slaves sold away from the plantation were the planter's own children, the products of his illicit relations with slave women. When a planter passed away, his widow would sometimes avenge his infidelity by selling his slave mistress to the Deep South. The long-suffering widow would also sell away the slave children whose resemblance to her own would remind her painfully of her husband's midnight forays to the slave cabins. The phrase, "sold down the river," synonymous with betrayal, originated to express the attitude the slaves had toward going down the Mississippi to the Cotton Kingdom. Planters used the threat of "selling down the river" to keep slaves in line, exporting to the Deep South those who were defiant or who frequently tried to run away.

Coffles (gangs of slaves fastened together) traveled from the border and Atlantic states to the Gulf states by several routes. They made the journey by coastal shipping or by railroad or by steamboat on the Ohio and Mississippi rivers or by walking overland. Travelers frequently saw coffles of ten to three hundred slaves on the way to Deep South markets. Thomas Hamilton, who observed a coffle on a Mississippi steamboat, commented that the men "loaded with chains . . . were in an especially wretched and disgusting condition, for their chains prevented their performing the ordinary functions of cleanliness." Summarizing contemporary accounts, historian Frederic Bancroft, in his book, *Slave Trading in the Old South*, reported on a coffle of 51 (32 men, 19 woman) walking from Maryland in 1805: "The women were tied together with a rope about their necks, like a halter, while the men wore iron collars, fastened to a chain about one hundred feet long, and were also handcuffed. . . . At the end of the day all, without being relieved of their collars, handcuffs, chains or ropes, lay down on the bare floor. . . ."

More disgusting than auctions or coffles was the breeding of slaves. Frederick Law Olmsted discussed this phase of life in the South. Olmsted (1822–1903) was America's pioneer landscape architect and the designer of many parks, including New York City's Central Park. He made three trips through the South and is generally regarded as the most reliable observer of living conditions in the South before the Civil War. Olmsted noted that Southern gentlemen "denied, with feeling, that slaves are often reared . . . with the intention of selling them to the traders." But Olmsted concluded that slaves were deliberately bred for market. He quoted a slave-holder who wrote to him that "as much attention is paid to the breeding and growth of negroes as to that of horses and mules. . . . Planters command their girls and women (married or unmarried) to have children; and I have known a great many negro girls to be sold off, because they did not have children." Another planter boasted to Olmsted that "his women were uncommonly good breeders; . . . he never heard of babies coming so fast as they did on his plantation; . . . and every one of them, in his estimation, was worth two hundred dollars, as negroes were selling now, the moment it drew breath."

Professor Bancroft, on the basis of his detailed study of the records, made estimates as to the number of slaves exported each year from states of the Upper South to those of the Deep South. The leading exporter was Virginia, the state that had more Negroes than any other from the colonial period to the Civil War. Virginia had more slaves than it needed for its tobacco plantations. Instead of the surplus slaves becoming a drain on the economy of Virginia, however, they became an asset as the state exported its surplus blacks to the Deep South Cotton Kingdom where the shortage of labor brought good prices for these products of the domestic slave trade. Bancroft estimated that in the thirty-year period from 1830 to 1860, Virginia shipped out 281,142 slaves, an average of 9,371 exported annually. Professor Thomas R. Dew of William and Mary College in Williamsburg, Virginia, commented on the role of the state as a "Negro raising" area, showing the importance of this activity to the state's economy. Dew made his comments in 1832. Four years later, he became the president of William and Mary College. In 1832, he stated that "Virginia is, in fact, a negro raising State for other States; she produces enough for her own supply, and six thousand for sale." He explained that "slaves in Virginia multiply more rapidly than in most of the Southern States" because the slave-owners took good care of slave women and children in Virginia. Thus, "the Virginians can raise" slaves, Dew continued, "cheaper than they can buy; in fact, it [raising slaves] is one of their greatest sources of profit."

Some Southern whites criticized the institution of slavery. Most of them, however, supported the South's "peculiar institution" even though most of them were not directly involved in slavery through ownership of slaves. Of the 8,000,000 Southern whites in 1860, only 384,000 were slave-holders. There were, of course, many white women and children whose husbands or fathers were slave-owners. Census statistics for that era assumed an average of five persons per family in the United States. The 384,000 slave-owners, multiplied by five, yields a figure of 1,920,000 Southern whites living in slave-owning families. This was only 24 percent of the 8,000,000 whites in the Southern states. A few of the slave-owners were black, mostly because the increasing legal difficulties of manumitting slaves in some states made it advisable for blacks who bought the freedom of their wives, children, or other relatives to continue listing them legally as "slaves" in order to prevent their being seized and sold into real slavery. Some 6,000,000 (75 percent) Southern whites were independent, non-slave-owning yeomen farmers, artisans, shopkeepers, and laborers. About 100,000 (1 percent) were marginal whites (called by their contemporaries such names as "poor white trash," "crackers," "clayeaters," "hillbillies," and "rednecks") who were barely subsisting on the poorest lands and in remote backwoods and hill country. Many of the yeomen hoped to move into the slave-owning class; they worked hard to accumulate enough capital to invest in their first slave, thereby, many felt, rising in the social order. Marginal whites, however, could barely scratch out a living on their unproductive soils, and many of them, it was learned subsequently, suffered from dietary deficiencies, disease, and parasites such as hookworm that incapacitated them for hard-driving, energetic work to move ahead, causing most unknowing observers to dismiss these people contemptuously as "shiftless" and "lazy." Many of these marginal whites were put in their plight by the unfair competition of slave-owning planters and farmers, forcing them onto the poorest lands. Nonetheless, many marginal whites supported the institution of slavery even though they had virtually no prospect of ever rising enough in the economic order to become slave-owners themselves. They supported the institution because as long as slavery existed, blacks would be at the bottom of society. No matter how low a marginal white sank in the socio-economic order, he could always glory in being "free and white." Although slavery did him economic harm, it gave him the psychological lift of having someone to look down upon. One-third of all Southerners in 1860 were blacks, some 4,000,000 of them being counted by the census enumerators.

Most of the slaves lived on plantations. Only a few of the slaveholders, however, fell into the planter category. Of the 384,000 slave-owners, more than half, 200,000 (52 percent), owned only 1 to 5 slaves. Another 139,000 slave-holders, or 36 percent of the total slave-owners, possessed only 6 to 19 slaves. In order to be considered a planter, one had to own at least 20 slaves. Yet 88 percent (339,000) of the slave-owners owned only 1 to 19 slaves apiece, so were not planters. Only 45,000 (12 percent) of the slaveholders could be classified as planters. Of these, 11 percent (42,000) were small planters who owned from 20–99 slaves apiece. Only 3,000, or 1 percent of all slave-holders, were great planters, owning 100 or more slaves. The romanticized picture of antebellum Southern life as seen in *Gone With the Wind* would lead people to think of the typical plantation as being a place like Tara with hundreds of slaves thereon. Actually, the census figures for 1860 showed that there were only 11 slave-owners in the entire South who owned as many as 500 slaves apiece. Although 88 percent of the slave-owners were not planters, the 12 percent (45,000) who were owned more than half of the 3,953,000 slaves in the United States in 1860. The planters dominated the economic and social order in the South, setting the tone for Southern life and philosophy. In a region that had more pretensions to an aristocracy than any other section of the nation, the planter class provided the bulk of the leadership. Despite the opposition of some Southern whites (less and less vocally expressed from the 1830s onward) the interests of the planter class generally dictated the Southern position and stand on issues of local and national policy.

Living conditions for slaves varied considerably. Conditions varied according to whether the slave lived on a small farm or large plantation, whether he was in the Upper South or Deep South, whether he lived in a rural area or urban environment, whether he worked on a tobacco, rice, sugar, or cotton plantation, and whether he was a house servant, skilled craftsman, or field hand. Most important of all, conditions varied according to the temperament and attitude of the individual slave-owner. Slavery took as many forms in its interpersonal relations as there were individual slave-owners to mold the institution in their particular sphere. Generally, food, clothing, and quarters were crude, the work was long and arduous, and the lash of the whip was frequently felt. And, no matter how pleasant a rare, kindly disposed owner might try to make living conditions, the inescapable fact always remained that one was a slave, almost completely at the mercy and sufferance of the slave-owner who was generally free to do with his slave as he wished with little interference from or restraint by society.

Josiah Henson, who had been a field hand, remembered that:

> The principal food . . . consisted of corn-meal, and salt herrings. . . . we had two regular meals in a day:—breakfast at twelve o'clock, after laboring from daylight, and supper when the work of the remainder of the day was over. . . . Our dress was of tow-cloth . . . and a pair of coarse shoes once a year. We lodged in log huts. . . . Wooden floors were an unknown luxury. In a single room were huddled, like cattle, ten or a dozen persons, men, women and children. . . . There were neither bedsteads, nor furniture. . . . Our beds were collections of straw and old rags, thrown down in the corner. . . . The wind whistled and the rain and snow blew in through the cracks, and the damp earth soaked in the moisture till the floor was miry as a pig-sty.

House-servants would, to be sure, have lived under much better conditions than those described by Henson.

But, Henson continued, "I have no desire to represent the life of slavery as an experience of nothing but misery." He also had memories of "extra meat at holiday times, midnight visits to apple orchards, broiling stray chickens, and first rate tricks to dodge work."

Historians disagreed concerning the life of the slave and the nature of plantation slavery. The two major histories of slavery in America—*American Negro Slavery*, written by Ulrich B. Phillips in 1918, and *The Peculiar Institution*, written by Kenneth M. Stampp in 1956—demonstrate this. Each book reflects its times and its author's outlook.

Phillips was a Southerner, born and reared in Georgia, who, although he spent decades teaching in leading Northern universities, remained a dedicated apologist for the South all his life. He felt that Northerners neither understood Southern Negroes nor the relationships between whites and blacks in the South. Phillips spent more years doing research in the sources on Southern slavery than any other historian, but his research and writings were colored by his preconceptions about the nature of blacks and of slave-owners. For long, his writings dominated the textbook, general, and popular writings on slavery, teaching generations of Americans that slavery was not as horrible an institution as some might think.

Knowing little of the true background of the African, Phillips wrote confidently of Africa as a place where blacks could pluck food without having to work hard. He asserted concerning blacks that "Impulsive and inconstant, sociable and amorous, voluble, dilatory, and negligent, but robust, amiable, obedient and contented, they have been the world's premium slaves." He insisted that blacks generally "were by racial quality submissive . . . lighthearted . . . amiable" and that these "very defects invited paternalism rather than repression." Phillips grew up in close proximity to Southern blacks and associated with them in the typical paternalistic pattern of Southern whites accustomed to having blacks tell them what they (the whites) wanted to hear and never really finding out what blacks really felt and thought. Most Southern blacks were in no position in a society so thoroughly dominated by oppressive whites who were their employers as well as the police, judges, and jurors really to speak their true sentiments. Accordingly, Southern whites, like Phillips, assumed they knew "their" blacks and what was best for them.

Phillips insisted that "Negroes had a healthy human repugnance toward overwork." He doubted that blacks could be worked to the point of harm, saying "anyone who has had experience with negro labor may reasonably be skeptical when told that healthy, well fed negroes, whether slave or free, can by any routine insistence of the employer be driven beyond the point at which fatigue begins to be injurious."

Phillips contended that slavery benefitted the blacks by civilizing them:

> Every plantation of the standard Southern type was, in fact, a school constantly training and controlling pupils who were in a backward state of civilization. . . . This, rudimentary as it necessarily was, was in fact just what the bulk of the negroes most needed. They were in an alien land, in an essentially slow process of transition from barbarism to civilization. . . . On the whole

plantations were the best schools yet invented for the mass training of that sort of inert and backward people which the bulk of the American negroes represented.

Phillips did most of his research in the journals, record books, diaries, and correspondence of the large planters and in Southern newspapers. He ignored the slave narratives, holding that they were propaganda shaped by anti-Southern abolitionists. Thus, his view of slavery and its benefits stems from the outlook of the Southern planter class and its allies, with little cognizance of the outlook of the slaves as expressed in accounts by fugitive slaves. He also showed little awareness of the real background of Africans.

Stampp's book, *The Peculiar Institution*, was written while the civil rights movement was in progress and reflected a determinedly liberal approach to the black man and his past. Writing nearly four decades after Phillips, Stampp was aware of the new researches that were uncovering much of the African past that Phillips knew little of. In addition, Stampp is a Northerner trained in a Midwestern university, who is on the faculty of the University of California. Concerning the African background, Stampp rebutted Phillips by averring that "to describe these people as savages who led an animal-like existence is a serious distortion. Long before the seventeenth century they had evolved their own intricate cultures." In contrast to Phillips's notion that blacks were childish people ideally suited to be slaves, Stampp pointed out that "Modern biologists, psychologists, sociologists, and anthropologists offer an impressive accumulation of evidence that Negroes and whites have approximately the same intellectual potentialities." Thus, Stampp rejected Phillips's notion that all blacks were alike and on a different and lower plane than whites. Stampp contended instead that "One fact is established beyond any reasonable doubt. This is the fact that variations in the capacities and personalities of individuals within each race are as great as the variations in their physical traits. Therefore it is impossible to make valid generalizations about races as such. Negroes as a race were no more psychically fitted for slavery than were white men as a race."

Stampp did not view the plantation as a school preparing Africans for civilized living, as did Phillips. Stampp asserted:

Unquestionably when adult Negroes were imported from Africa they had trouble learning to live in a strange environment and to understand unfamiliar social institutions. But the idea that Negroes needed to be civilized by a slow evolutionary process, during which they would gradually acquire and transmit to their descendants the white man's pattern of social behavior, contains . . . fallacies. . . . Actually, the first generation of Negroes born in America in the seventeenth century was just as well prepared for freedom as the generation that was emancipated in the 1860's. The adaptation to the white man's culture involved a process of education, not one of biological evolution. The only way that Negroes ever learned how to live in America as responsible free men was by experience—by *starting* to live as free men. The plantation school never accomplished this: its aim was merely to train them to be slaves.

Stampp did include the slave narratives in his research, thus taking into account the sentiments of the slaves themselves toward the institution of slavery.

The treatment of the slaves in the Southern slave codes would seem to buttress Stampp's view that plantation slavery only trained the slave to be a slave rather than to support Phillips's thesis that the plantation was a school preparing blacks for civilization. Slave codes made it a crime to teach slaves to read or write; prevented their testimony against whites; denied them property rights; left them virtually defenseless against physical or sexual aggression by whites; and gave their marriages no legal standing. By contrast, slaves in Latin America, according to Professors Frank Tannenbaum and Herbert Klein, had legal rights (to own property, sue and testify, marry, and purchase freedom on installments), training them for freedom.

Slaves resisted, most dramatically by rebelling. Early in 1800, Gabriel (slave of Thomas Prosser of Henrico County, Virginia) and Jack Bowler organized several thousand slaves—making swords, bayonets, and bullets—to attack Richmond on August 30. Although two slaves informed on the plot that afternoon and Governor James Monroe organized defenders, many of the plotters, according to some accounts, gathered six miles outside Richmond. Their plans were disrupted by a great storm that washed out bridges and blocked roads. Many were arrested, more than thirty were executed, but none informed on his fellows, showing "contempt for danger," wrote John Randolph, one of Virginia's leading states-men, who represented the state in Congress.

A remarkable free black named Denmark Vesey organized some ten thousand slaves for an assault on Charleston in July, 1822. Informers and spies alerted authorities who executed thirty-five and deported forty-two plotters. Most heeded a slave leader, Peter Poyas, who urged: "Do not open your lips! Die silent, as you shall see me do."

A slave preacher in Southampton County, Virginia, Nat Turner, confessed to having visions, saying "the Spirit instantly appeared to me and said . . . Christ had laid down the yoke . . . and that I should take it on and fight. . . ." On August 21, 1831, Turner and six confederates gathered, feasted, and "quickly agreed we should commence at home" (his master's) and that initially "neither age nor sex was to be spared." Within twenty-four hours, proceeding from house to house, they killed sixty whites, secured guns and horses, and gained fifty followers. Soldiers and militia stopped them, slaughtering innocent blacks with them. Twenty, including Turner, were tried and executed.

Less spectacular, but involving many more blacks, was day by day resistance: sabotage, slow-down, runaway, self-maiming, sui-cide, arson, and murder of masters. One entrepreneur told Olmsted that slaves "will not labor at all except to avoid punishment, and they will never do more than just enough to save themselves from being punished." Dr. Samuel Cartwright of Louisiana told him that slaves had a disease, *Dysathesia Aethiopica*, a "stupidness of mind" that made them "break, waste, and destroy everything they handle —abuse horses and cattle—tear, burn . . . steal . . . wander about at night, and keep in a half nodding state by day . . . slight their work—cut up corn, cotton, and tobacco, when hoeing it, as if for pure mischief." Similar "stupidness" caused slaves to break ordi-nary hoes so rapidly that special, heavy, cumbersome, unproductive "Negro hoes" were invented. Observing field hands slaving under a whip-wielding overseer, Olmsted noted that "as often as he visited one line of the operations, the hands at the other end would discon-tinue their labor, until he turned to ride toward them again."

Thus, slaves mastered the system. Meanwhile, free blacks over-came discrimination to achieve and joined movements to abolish slavery.

7

North of Slavery
and Black Abolitionists
1800–1860

Frederick Douglass strode down the platform at Lynn, Massachusetts, boarded the train to Newburyport, and took a seat in a luxurious car for the twenty-five-mile trip. "As usual, I had purchased a first-class ticket," he narrated in his autobiography, but "I was soon waited upon by the conductor and ordered out."

When Douglass refused to leave, the conductor recruited half a dozen men to throw him out. "They attempted to obey with an air which plainly told me they relished the job," Douglass continued, and "clutched me, head, neck, and shoulders." Anticipating their move, Douglass held on with all his might so that "in removing me I tore away two or three of the surrounding" seats, which "must have cost the company twenty-five or thirty dollars. . . ." This was possible because "I was strong and muscular, and the seats were not then so firmly attached or of as solid make as now."

What could prompt such an assault in the early 1840s on a dignified gentleman like Douglass? He explained that "on that road," identified by him as the Eastern Railroad from Boston to Portland, "as on many others, there was a mean, dirty, and uncomfortable car set apart for colored travelers called the Jim Crow car." Since he had escaped from slavery and was "determined to fight the spirit of slavery wherever I might find it," Douglass decided against riding in the Jim Crow car.

Douglass was sometimes beaten for his efforts. He also did not have the full support of all of his fellow blacks in his courageous crusade. He noted that "the colored people generally accepted the situation and complained of me as making matters worse rather than better by refusing to submit to this proscription." But Douglass had been a fighter all his life. He had early learned the lesson that change and progress come only through struggle and through persistent effort. He knew that oppressors and exploiters rarely yield to the disadvantaged merely out of the goodness of their hearts or because of the pangs of conscience. They yield when the oppressed and their supporters push them to the point of discomforting and embarrassing them, or reducing their profits. That is what Douglass continued to do in his fight against railroad segregation in New England. He was not deterred by the murmurings of those of his fellow blacks who thought conditions would automatically improve without any effort of their own.

The trouble caused the railroad by having to throw Douglass out of the cars set aside for whites embarrassed the management to the point that "Stephen A. Chase, superintendent of the road, ordered all passenger trains to pass through Lynn, where I then lived, without stopping." The entire city was inconvenienced because many residents used the road regularly for business trips to Boston and other cities. Many residents of Lynn denounced the railroad. In response to these denunciations, Douglass reported that:

> Mr. Chase made reply that a railroad corporation was neither a religious nor reformatory body, that the road was run for the accommodation of the public, and that it [the white public] required the exclusion of colored people from its cars. With an air of triumph he told us that we ought not to expect a railroad company to be better than the evangelical church, and that until the churches abolished the Negro pew we ought not to expect the railroad company to abolish the Negro car.

Douglass acknowledged that that was a telling point against the churches, which, shamefully, were discriminatory and prejudiced, but Chase's reasoning was "good for nothing as against the demands of justice and equality."

As Douglass pointed out on numerous occasions, it was not simply a matter of physical separation or of the presence of blacks being distasteful or offensive. He noted that slaves accompanying their masters rode on first-class accommodations and went with their masters into the finest hotels and restaurants. The point was that they had to be there in a clearly subordinate status as slave or

servant. Thus, black slaves and servants were present almost everywhere. But an educated, well-dressed, clean, dignified black person holding his head high and entering a hotel, theater, restaurant,
or railroad car as a free person, equal to any one present, could not
be tolerated. Whites did not want physical separation, else they
would not have blacks cook their food, serve it, draw their baths,
lay out their clothes, mind and even suckle their babies, make their
beds, tidy up their rooms and offices, wash, mend, make their garments, and drive them about. What most whites needed, Douglass
realized, was a sense of feeling superior to someone else. They
needed to take refuge in their white skins as a badge of superiority
and thus be able to look down upon those of darker skins as inferior. For many whites, then and now, the need to have a class of
people to be their "niggers" whom they can dominate and despise
and exploit indicates a basic weakness in them, not among the
blacks they excluded then and still exclude now.

Douglass was joined in his fight by a number of leading whites,
especially abolitionist-minded persons, in Lynn. One of these whites
pointed out to the railroad company that it "often allowed dogs and
monkeys to ride in first-class cars, and yet excluded a man like
Frederick Douglass!" Gradually, during the 1840s, the railroads in
New England yielded to the resistance by blacks, the pressures by
abolitionists, the public opinion that was aroused by Douglass's
crusade, and the threats of enactment of antidiscrimination statutes.
As Douglass recalled: "In a very few years this barbarous practice
was put away, and I think there have been no instances of such
exclusion during the past thirty years, and colored people now,
everywhere in New England, ride upon equal terms with other passengers."

The struggle against railroad segregation in New England serves
as a reminder of the presence, problems, and perseverance of free
blacks in the first half of the nineteenth century. Slavery so domi-
nates the antebellum period that there is a tendency to neglect the
growing free black population. At the first census in 1790, only 8
percent (59,000) of the nation's 757,000 blacks were free. At the
last slave era census, in 1860, 11 percent (488,000) of the nation's
4,441,000 blacks were free. Since blacks were found mostly in the
South, there were more free blacks there than in the North. In

1790, there were 32,000 free blacks in the South and only 27,000 in the North. In 1860, 250,000 of the free blacks were in the South and only 238,000 were in the North. Both in the North and in the South free blacks faced many barriers, but some overcame them, achieved distinction, and strove to set their brothers free.

Although the North began abandoning slavery in the Revolutionary atmosphere of the 1780s, it did not abandon long-standing prejudices. A Frenchman, Alexis de Tocqueville, on visiting America in 1831 found racial prejudice "stronger in the states that have abolished slavery than in those where it still exists. . . ." He found blacks free, but they could "share neither the rights, nor the pleasures, nor the labor" of whites. In his book, *White Over Black: American Attitudes Toward the Negro, 1550–1812,* that won the Pulitzer Prize in 1968, Professor Winthrop Jordan analyzed this racial prejudice. He explained that white Americans, North and South, feared three things: loss of identity, lack of self-control, and sexual license. They achieved peace of mind (a sense of protecting identity and purity) by cruelly suppressing and setting apart blacks, denigrating them as inferior. Thus, Jordan noted: "In fearfully hoping to escape the animal within himself the white man debased the Negro, surely, but at the same time he debased himself."

To suppress the black man, whites had to make him the great exception to their religious-political ideology of brotherhood and equality. Federal laws set the tone. In 1790 Congress passed a law barring nonwhite aliens from becoming naturalized citizens. In 1792, another Congressional measure excluded blacks from serving in the militia. And in 1810, a Federal law barred blacks from employment as postmen. The states followed suit. Some states that had let blacks vote previously later stripped them of that right. Three states that took away the Negro's vote were Connecticut, New Jersey, and Pennsylvania, all three doing so by 1840. As of 1860, only the five states of Maine, Massachusetts, New Hampshire, Rhode Island, and Vermont granted Negroes equal voting rights. The other thirteen Northern states, where 94 percent of the Northern blacks lived, except for New York, did not let blacks vote. In New York blacks could vote only if they met a special property qualification that many low-paid blacks could not satisfy, although propertyless whites of New York were entitled to vote.

Northern blacks encountered job discrimination. As a slave in his native state of Maryland, Frederick Douglass (1817–1895) had learned a skilled trade, working as a caulker on ships in Baltimore. After escaping in 1838, he settled in New Bedford, Massachusetts, where he sought work caulking and coppering a vessel being outfitted for a whaling voyage. "I was told that every white man would leave the ship in her unfinished condition if I struck a blow at my trade upon her." Working at his skill he "could have earned two dollars a day, but as a common laborer I received but one dollar." The privilege of having a skin color that entitled the white man to a job paying twice as much as the one permitted an equally qualified black person was a tremendous economic advantage that gave many whites an inducement, over and beyond their psychological needs, to perpetuate discrimination. The economics of prejudice paid and still pays all too well for whites who are on the receiving end of the benefits of job discrimination. At the same time, unfair employment practices exacted a heavy price in economic loss to blacks who for centuries have been jobless, underpaid, and denied promotion for no reason other than the color of their skins.

Douglass's experience was typical. Southern white craftsmen objected to the competition of skilled slaves, but the slave-owners, having a vested interest in the earnings of the slaves, saw to it that slave craftsmen were employed. Hence, blacks worked at many skilled tasks in the South. In fact, more of the skilled craftsmen in the South were blacks than were whites. In the North, however, white workers and their unions generally restricted blacks to menial tasks. Even a prominent abolitionist like Arthur Tappan did not hire blacks as clerks in his department store in New York City, apparently fearing the reaction of his white clerks and customers. Douglass called on abolitionists to back their antislavery principles and attacks on the South with practical demonstrations of equal employment in the North, especially in businesses that they controlled. He pointed out that a few abolitionist businessmen "might employ a colored boy as a porter or packer" but most of them "would as soon put a hod-carrier to the clerk's desk as a colored boy, ever so well educated though he be." Not only the abolitionist businessmen, but abolitionists in all lines of endeavor could do far more, Douglass insisted, toward helping blacks economically by fair hiring practices. In an editorial in his newspaper in 1853, he asked, "What boss anti-slavery mechanic will take a black boy into his wheelwright's shop, his blacksmith's shop, his joiner's shop, his cabinet shop? Here is something practical; where are the whites . . . that will respond to it?"

Some black men in the North, unable to secure work, had to depend on the earnings of their wives as maids, cooks, and laundresses. Unable to fulfill the male role of breadwinner and feeling themselves more of a burden than a help to their families, some of these men deserted their wives and children, leaving the wife to support herself and the children out of her earnings as a servant for white families. Thus, the job discrimination and prejudice in the North helped to break down the structure of some black families.

As the century progressed, the job plight of black workers worsened because of competition from newcomers, especially the Irish. In 1790, blacks were 19.3 percent of the total population, but in 1860 they were only 14.1 percent of the total population of 31,443,000. The black population had increased in absolute numbers from 757,000 in 1790 to 4,441,000 in 1860, but white population had increased more rapidly in this period. This was primarily because the ban on the slave trade as of 1808 had cut off the great numbers of Africans being brought to this nation each year (even though some continued to be smuggled in). During the 1840s and 1850s, the great waves of immigration from Ireland and Germany added considerably to the white population. In an editorial in his newspaper in 1853, Frederick Douglass lamented that "every hour sees the black man elbowed out of employment by some newly arrived emigrant, whose hunger and whose color are thought to give him a better title to the place. . . ." He listed various jobs once left to blacks that the newcomers were eagerly seizing, including porters, cooks, stewards, hod-carriers, stevedores, wood-sawyers, white-washers, barbers, and coachmen.

Douglass therefore urged blacks to become educated for better positions, such as crafts, mechanical skills, and professions, but such education was not easily obtained. Though blacks were taxed everywhere in the North, public schools were not always open to them on an equal basis. In some places, no schools were provided.

In others, only segregated schools in dilapidated buildings abandoned by white pupils, with much lower-paid teachers and shorter school terms, were furnished to blacks. Blacks brought suits for equal education. Douglass won a case for his children in Rochester, New York, where he moved in 1847 to found his newspaper, *The North Star*. In the Roberts case, brought in 1849 to desegregate schools in Boston (schools were already integrated in other cities in Massachusetts), Charles Sumner was the lawyer for the plaintiffs. The Chief Justice of Massachusetts, Lemuel Shaw, originated the "separate but equal" doctrine in his ruling that approved Boston's segregated system. Subsequently, the legislature, prodded by both black and white abolitionists, passed a law that desegregated Boston's schools in 1855. Despite dire predictions of bloodshed and turmoil, school integration in Boston took place peacefully.

Private schools suffered harassment. A Quaker schoolteacher, Prudence Crandall, admitted one black girl early in 1833 to the private school she had opened for girls two years earlier in Canterbury, Connecticut. Her neighbors objected violently to this integration, and the white parents withdrew their daughters. Thereupon, Miss Crandall opened her school to blacks only and tried to conduct classes with about twenty black girls as pupils. Townspeople reacted with insults, abuse, and ostracism. Local storekeepers refused to sell her provisions needed for the school. Mass meetings were called and petitions circulated to get rid of her school. In May, the State of Connecticut passed a "Black Law" forbidding operation of an educational institution for blacks who were nonresidents of Connecticut. Since most of Miss Crandall's pupils came from other states, she was arrested, convicted, and jailed in October, 1833. Although a higher court reversed her conviction in the summer of 1834, the violent attempts to force her out mounted. That summer her house was attacked and partially destroyed. Manure was thrown into the school's well. Unable to endure any longer, the courageous and valiant young schoolteacher (she was then 31) closed her school.

A similar incident happened in New Hampshire, a state with very few blacks. At Canaan, New Hampshire, the Noyes Academy was opened as a private school for boys. It was to open on an integrated basis, with 28 white and 14 black youths enrolled. White residents objected, claiming property values would fall if an integrated school were operated there. In 1835, accordingly, the school's opponents tied ropes and chains around the structure, hitched it up to teams of oxen, and yanked the school building completely from its foundations, forcing it to close.

Some Northerners feared that Southerners would emancipate their aged, crippled, worn-out slaves and send them North to become public wards. There were enough such occurrences to convince some Northern communities that some Southerners would squeeze all the productive labor they could out of slaves and then let the burden of caring for these slaves in their declining, unproductive years be borne by the North. Accordingly, many states in the North passed statutes, such as Ohio's Black Laws, to discourage blacks from settling there. Black newcomers to the state were forced to post bonds guaranteeing that they would not become welfare cases; white newcomers faced no such handicap, but were free simply to move in. Throughout the North, most hotels, theaters, restaurants, and other public accommodations barred blacks. Mobs often attacked blacks, invading their neighborhoods and burning down their homes. Such riots occurred in many places, including Cincinnati in 1829, New York in 1834, and Philadelphia in 1842. The white mob that rioted against blacks in Cincinnati did so at a time when there were increasing demands to enforce the Black Laws against the many fugitive slaves who had fled across the Ohio River to freedom in Cincinnati without posting bonds. Half the city's black population moved away to Canada as a result of the mob attacks and this drive to enforce the Black Laws.

In defense of slavery, Southerners cited such Northern oppression. But Southerners ignored the fact that Northern blacks were free to speak out, organize, and fight back, and also that many white allies aided them in their quest for equality. Southern free blacks, by contrast, were treated as outcasts and increasingly restricted. The South feared that their presence might make slaves discontented by reminding them that all blacks were not owned by white men. Also, Southern whites suspected that the free blacks in their midst aided, encouraged, and abetted slave insurrections, as some of them did. Neither white person nor black person, from the early 1830s onward, could openly oppose the South's way of life and expect to live safely there.

To their credit, many Northern and Southern blacks did well in spite of all adversity. In almost every field imaginable, there were some blacks who overcame obstacles to make notable achievements.

The phrase "black capitalism" became fashionable under President Richard Nixon in the late 1960s as a possible solution to the economic problems of black Americans. But there have always been some blacks who did well in business. Some were successful in business before the Civil War. Such success, however, did not lessen the need for an end to the job discrimination that then and now deprives most black Americans of a chance for a decent and satisfying livelihood. William Leidesdorff was a light-skinned Negro from the West Indies who settled in San Francisco. There he became a merchant and the owner of 35,000 acres near Sutter's Mill. He served on the city council. When he passed away, he left an estate of $1,500,000. A street in downtown San Francisco is named after him. In New Orleans, Thomy Lafon amassed a fortune of $500,-000 in real estate, moneylending, and merchandising. On his passing he left his wealth to charities irrespective of race. Still another who succeeded in business was James Forten. He began as an employee of a sailmaking business in Philadelphia owned by a white man. He went on to become foreman and later the owner of the business. Employing forty blacks and whites in his sail loft, he accumulated a fortune of $100,000. Paul Cuffe began as a sailor, but rose to become a ship captain and the owner of a fleet of vessels that engaged in coastal and in transatlantic commerce. His fleet included a 268-ton ship, a 162-ton bark (three-masted), a 109-ton brig (two-masted), two schooners (of 69 and 42 tons), and several smaller boats. These ships journeyed to Canada, Europe, Africa, and the South. In 1816, Cuffe, out of his own resources, carried the first load of blacks (38 of them) from the United States to colonize in Africa, establishing them in the British colony of Sierra Leone.

An outstanding black inventor was Norbert Rillieux (1806–1894). He was born in New Orleans, the son of a French engineer-inventor and a light-skinned, free black woman. Rillieux developed an improved industrial process for the refining of sugar. He invented the first practical multiple-effect vacuum chamber evaporator. As described in the patent he took out in 1846

> A series of vacuum pans, or partial vacuum pans, have been so combined together as to make use of the vapor of the evaporation of the juice in the first, to heat the juice in the second and the vapor from this to heat the juice in the third, which latter is in connection with a condenser, the degree of pressure in each successive one being less. . . .

As George P. Meade explained in an article entitled "A Negro Scientist of Slavery Days," in *The Scientific Monthly* for April, 1946, a century after Rillieux's basic patent, "The great scientific contribution which Rillieux made was in his recognition of the steam economies which can be effected by repeated use of the latent heat in the steam and vapors." Prior to Rillieux's device, sugar was refined by boiling the sugar-cane juice in a series of steaming open kettles, with slaves shifting the juice from one kettle to the next in a slow, cumbersome process by use of long ladles. Not only was the old process slower, but the sugar did not become as white as it did in Rillieux's speedier, more efficient, enclosed process. So it was a black inventor who put the "white" in sugar!

Rillieux traveled throughout the South installing his apparatus on various plantations, such as Bellechasse, the plantation six miles south of New Orleans that belonged to Judah P. Benjamin, who was later Secretary of State of the Confederacy. Planters eagerly listened as Rillieux explained the device that was to enrich them. The basic process (evaporation in multiple effect) devised by Rillieux "is now universally used," George P. Meade points out, "throughout the sugar industry as well as in the manufacture of condensed milk, soap, gelatine, and glue, in the recovery of waste liquors in distilling and paper factories, and in many other processes."

James P. Beckwourth (1798–1867) was a western pioneer. Born in Virginia, apparently a slave, he grew up in St. Louis where he lived as a free man. In 1823 he joined the famous Ashley-Henry expedition organized by General William Ashley and Andrew Henry, co-founders of the Rocky Mountain Fur Company. As blacksmith and wrangler, he participated with them in explorations from 1823 to 1826 that opened up vast areas of the unchartered

West, especially along the Yellowstone, Big Horn, Platte, Green, and Bear rivers in Montana, Wyoming, and Utah. Then, Beckwourth (spelled Beckwith in most of the Western literature) spent a dozen years living with the Crow Indians in Montana and Wyoming, becoming a chief and taking a wife. Subsequently he was an army scout, a hunter, and a fur company agent. He discovered the pass across the Sierra Nevadas to the Sacramento Valley that bears his name today and was used by the goldseekers in the 1850s.

An outstanding Shakespearean actor in the nineteenth century was a black man, Ira Aldridge (1806–1867), who never had a chance to show his talents in his native land. Born in Maryland and reared in New York, he aspired to be an actor, but American stages were barred to black thespians. While studying in Europe, he met the great English actor, Edmund Keane, who encouraged him. Aldridge toured throughout Europe, performing in many roles, often appearing with Keane. Aldridge played Othello, King Lear, Shylock, Macbeth, and Richard III, among other parts.

Robert Duncanson (1817–1872) was a noted landscape artist who was a Midwestern representative of the Hudson River School of painting. Born in New York and educated in Canada and Scotland, he made his home in Cincinnati and Detroit, where he became prominent as a portrait and landscape painter. His works hang in many museums, such as the Cleveland Museum of Art, the Detroit Institute of Art, the Taft Museum, the Cincinnati Art Museum, and the Howard University Gallery. He is best known for the romantic realism of his landscape painting *Flood Waters, Blue Hole, Little Miami River* (1851), which belongs to the Cincinnati Art Museum.

John Chavis (1763–1838), a free-born North Carolinian, attended both Princeton University as a private student of the president, John Witherspoon, and also Washington Academy in Lexington, Virginia, that is now Washington and Lee University. He worked as a Presbyterian minister with white and black congregations in Virginia and North Carolina. He is most noted, however, for the preparatory schools he ran in North Carolina from 1808 to the 1830s, preparing scions of leading families in that slave state for college. He taught them Greek, Latin, English, and math, and was reputed to have the best preparatory schools in the state. The Chief

Justice of North Carolina, Archibald Henderson, sent his sons to Chavis's school. His white pupils went on to such roles as United States Senator, Congressman, Governor, diplomat, lawyer, and physician.

Among other noteworthy blacks were: physician-scientist Dr. James McCune Smith, a graduate of the University of Glasgow, who was also active in the abolitionist movement; slave poet George Moses Horton who taught himself to read by picking out words of familiar church songs in a hymnal and who toiled as a slave janitor at the University of North Carolina while composing poems for students and faculty on request, publishing in 1829 a volume entitled *The Hope of Liberty*; and Tom Molineaux who became the American heavyweight boxing champion but lost to the British champion Tom Cribb in a fight for the world title.

Encountering white hostility and prejudice, blacks developed separate institutions, including: the African Methodist Episcopal Zion (A.M.E.Z.) denomination in 1821; the first black newspaper, *Freedom's Journal* in 1827; Lincoln University in Pennsylvania in 1854; and Wilberforce University in Ohio in 1855.

Blacks were active in the antislavery movement. In a mass meeting in Bethel A.M.E. Church in Philadelphia in January, 1817, blacks, led by James Forten, rejected colonization plans to ship freedmen to Africa, resolving that "Whereas our ancestors" successfully cultivated America, we "feel ourselves entitled to participate in the blessings of her luxuriant soil. . . ." Bishop Richard Allen insisted that "This land . . . is now our *mother country*, and we are well satisfied to stay. . . ." In their opening editorial, on March 16, 1827, the editors of *Freedom's Journal*, Samuel Cornish and John Russwurm, explained: "We wish to plead our own cause. Too long have others spoken for us."

Historians generally date militant abolitionism as beginning with the first issue, on January 1, 1831, of *The Liberator*, the newspaper published in Boston by the white abolitionist William Lloyd Garrison. It is not generally known that his largest support came from blacks, who composed three-fourths of his subscribers by 1834.

Moreover, two years before Garrison's newspaper began, David Walker (1785–1830) issued a militant and widely circulated *Appeal* (1829), published in three editions before he passed away.

Born a free man in Wilmington, North Carolina, Walker had settled in Boston where he had established a clothing business on Brattle Street in 1827. In his *Appeal*, Walker asked his fellow blacks: "Are we Men!! . . . Did our Creator make us to be slaves to dust and ashes like ourselves?" He warned white Americans "that we must and shall be free. . . . And wo, wo, will be to you if we have to obtain our freedom by fighting. . . . Treat us like men, and . . . we will all live in peace and happiness together . . . and we will be your friends." Walker exhorted slaves to throw off their chains, saying: "twelve black men . . . well armed . . . will kill and put to flight fifty whites. . . . If you commence . . . do not trifle . . . kill or be killed . . . had you not rather be killed than to be a slave to a tyrant. . . ."

Inspired by such sentiments, blacks were active as abolitionist lecturers, none more effective than such former slaves as Frederick Douglass and Sojourner Truth. They played a major role in the Underground Railroad, used to help slaves escape to freedom in the North by providing "stations" in which they could hide and be fed during the day and routes over which they could travel during the night. William Still of Philadelphia was a leading black organizer on the railroad. Harriet Tubman was one of the most courageous "conductors." After escaping from slavery in Maryland, she risked her life by returning nineteen times to lead some three hundred slaves to freedom, never losing a passenger and never letting any turn back.

Having struggled for freedom in the abolitionist movement, blacks were ready to fight for freedom on the battlefield during the Civil War.

8

Slavery Issue and the Civil War

1850–1865

One Sunday morning in March, 1864, the men of the First South Carolina Volunteer Regiment assembled for worship. As was their custom, one of their number served as chaplain, delivering an inspirational talk to his comrades. On this particular Sunday, the talk was given by Corporal Thomas Long, an illiterate former slave. Only a short time before, he and his comrades had been somebody's possessions, pieces of chattel, but they had deserted their masters and were now wearing the blue of the Union Army.

Corporal Long was an obscure and lowly soldier, one of 180,-000 black troops in the Federal army. What he said that morning had little significance except as a rare and revealing insight into the thinking of black fighting men. Fortunately, his remarks were taken down by the regiment's white commander (blacks served in segregated units under white officers during the Civil War). His regimental commander was Colonel Thomas Wentworth Higginson, who was an abolitionist, a man of letters, and a scion of a prominent New England family. Higginson recorded Corporal Long's words in the journal he kept of his Civil War experiences. Professor James M. McPherson of Princeton University quoted from Higginson's manuscript journal in his book, *The Negro's Civil War*.

As recorded by Higginson and quoted by McPherson, Long explained to his fellow soldiers in this regiment of blacks: "If we hadn't become sojers, all might have gone back as it was before; our freedom might have slipped through de two houses of Congress & President Linkum's four years might have passed by & notin been done for we. But now tings can never go back, because we have showed our energy & our courage & our naturally manhood."

Corporal Long then went on to tell his comrades in the regiment that had been through some hard and dangerous campaigning:

> Anoder ting is, suppose you had kept your freedom widout enlisting in dis army; your chillen might have grown up free, & been well cultivated so as to be equal to any business; but it would have been always flung in dere faces—"Your fader never fought for he own freedom"—and what could dey answer? Neber can say dat any more, because we first showed dem we could fight by dere side.

Since he was a literary man, Colonel Higginson recorded Long's talk in dialect, with the slurred speech and mispronunciations so common to blacks of the rural South.

Obviously, Corporal Long lacked education, but he was not deficient in wisdom. He saw clearly the symbolic importance of black men fighting to free themselves. He realized that the image of a race in a nation that put such a premium on manhood, courage, and fighting was important. He understood that the Civil War was important to the black man and was a chance for him to show that he deserved freedom and citizenship. Black men fought valiantly in the Civil War, a struggle that to them meant a chance to set their people free. Of the 180,000 black soldiers, 38,000 lost their lives, an extremely high mortality rate, a rate nearly 40 percent higher than that for white soldiers. What is more, since blacks were not allowed in the war at first and since many of them were relegated to garrison duty and noncombat roles, an extraordinarily high percentage of those blacks who served on the front line became casualties.

Nevertheless, despite their sacrifices, most Americans know very little about the role of black soldiers in the Civil War. By omitting them from discussion in textbooks and from exhibits at Civil War battlefield memorials, Americans make a mockery of the courageous efforts of these men to prove themselves and to emancipate their people. Worse still, most Americans, in their ignorance of black troops, would probably agree with the assessment made by a popular writer, W. E. Woodward. In a widely circulated biography, *Meet General Grant* (1928), Woodward asserted that:

> The American negroes are the only people in the history of the world, so far as I know, that ever became free without any effort of

their own. . . . The war that freed them was a war against their masters; their freedom came as an incident of that conflict. . . . It was not their business. They had not started the war nor ended it. They twanged banjos around the railroad stations, sang melodious spirituals, and believed that some Yankee would soon come along and give each of them forty acres of land and a mule.

Woodward knew that there were black soldiers because he discusses them at another place in his biography of Grant. But he minimized their numbers and belittled them, saying, "Before the end of the war there were about one hundred thousand negroes in the Union army. Most of the officers of high rank were not favorably impressed by the negro troops. Sherman considered them a joke, and Grant usually kept them in the rear, guarding his wagon trains."

Contrary to what Woodward says, black soldiers played an active role in General Ulysses S. Grant's prolonged Petersburg Campaign against General Robert E. Lee, a campaign lasting ten months, from June, 1864, to April, 1865. Despite the active participation of blacks in the fighting at Petersburg, a visitor to the Petersburg National Battlefield, operated by the United States government, would come away completely unaware of their presence. Black troops are omitted in the exhibits and narrations, despite the pictures and accounts of them found in unbiased histories and in the official records of the War of the Rebellion. Such neglect is typical of the pattern of omission that leads most Americans to share the ignorant judgment of Woodward (who should have known better from his examination of the records) that the Civil War was not the black man's business.

Blacks were involved both in the war and in the causes leading up to the conflict. The existence of slavery in the states and the burning issue of slavery in the territories were more important in bringing on the war than any other single issue or set of factors. Yet, most adult Americans today received their education at a time when the dominant theory of historical interpretation played down the role of the slavery issue. Accordingly, most of today's adult Americans would not only believe that blacks were not involved in the war, but also that the slavery question, which revolved around black people, was unimportant as a factor leading to the conflict.

Persons who wrote about the Civil War during the first generation after its end were generally too much caught up in the bitterness of the conflict to give the sort of objective appraisals that would gain respectability. From the 1880s to 1920s professional historians, scientifically trained, arrived at the Nationalist Tradition of interpretation of the war's causes and results, stressing slavery as the major divisive factor leading to an inevitable conflict. Slavery, combined with other factors, had created what was essentially two nations with different ways of looking at matters, but the major factor was indeed the existence of slavery in the Southern half of the nation. Historians of this Nationalist Tradition—including Edward Channing, Frederick Jackson Turner, John Bach McMaster, Woodrow Wilson, William E. Dodd, and Arthur C. Cole—judged the Civil War to be beneficial in that it ended slavery and fostered national unity while discrediting secession.

During the 1930s and 1940s, Revisionist historians, led by James G. Randall, Avery Craven, and Charles Ramsdell, rejected this nationalist interpretation. Revisionists were disillusioned by the apparent futility of World War I, which did not fulfill President Wilson's goals of a war to end all wars and making the world safe for democracy. They also were suspicious of our national leadership after witnessing its failures that contributed to the stock market crash of 1929 and the Depression that followed. Doubting the leadership of their time and harboring pacifist tendencies, the Revisionists questioned the concept that the Civil War was inevitable or that it had beneficial results. Instead the Revisionists asserted that the issue of slavery in the territories was a spurious issue invented by extremist agitators. They asserted that the territories in dispute were too dry and not suitable for growing cotton. Ramsdell claimed that conditions of climate and soil would have limited the cotton kingdom (and slavery) from spreading beyond eastern Texas. Hence the debate over slavery in the territories was meaningless.

Revisionists also claimed that a generation of blundering politicians let emotions get out of hand, thus dragging the nation into a needless war. Randall denied that wars have fundamental causes; instead he spoke of nations stumbling into war, of people being dragged into war without reason. He said of wars, "Omit the element of abnormality, of bogus leadership, or inordinate ambition for conquest, and diagnosis fails." As for the Civil War, "If one word or phrase were selected to account for the war, that word would not be slavery, or economic grievance, or state rights, or diverse civilizations. It would have to be such a word as fanaticism." He also suggested that the wars "that have not happened are perhaps best to study" because "There has been as much 'cause' for wars that did not happen as for wars that did." He labeled it an "unhistorical misconception" to say "that you must have war when you have cultural variation, or economic competition, or sectional difference. . . ."

Not only did the Revisionists label the Civil War a war that could have been avoided by sounder and saner leadership, they also contended that it was a pointless war. The Revisionists claimed that slavery was dying out anyway, making all the bloodshed to end it unnecessary. They claimed that slavery was uneconomical, that it needed to expand in order to continue being profitable, that it had reached the limits of its expansion, that cotton prices were falling, making slavery burdensome to the planters, and that the combined effect of all these factors would have been to put an end to slavery. In fact, Revisionists held, the Southern people would have ended slavery on their own if the attacks of the meddling, fanatical abolitionists had not stiffened their resistance to the reform movement. The Revisionist interpretation dominated the teaching of history in the public schools from the 1930s to the early 1960s, thus influencing most of today's adults, even though professional historians had begun to move away from this interpretation during the 1950s.

In the 1950s and 1960s, historians labeled Neo-Nationalists began to return to the earlier interpretation, rejecting the Revisionist arguments. These historians again stressed slavery as the fundamental divisive force, but also emphasized the moral dimension neglected by the Revisionists. Among these Neo-Nationalist historians were Bernard DeVoto, Arthur Schlesinger, Jr., and Pieter Geyl. Schlesinger pointed out that "Because the revisionists felt no moral urgency themselves, they deplored as fanatics those who did feel it, or brushed aside their feelings as the artificial product of emotion and propaganda." Thus, the Revisionists failed to understand the intensity of feeling in the 1850s on the issue of slavery. The Neo-Nationlists were writing after the events of the 1940s, when the world found it necessary to go to war to stop the spread of totalitarian, fascist regimes. They saw in World War II a useful war with sound leadership. Having experienced that war, Schlesinger could write in rebuttal to Randall's premise that all wars are unnecessary. "The unhappy fact is that man occasionally works himself into a log-jam; and that the log-jam must be burst by violence." The Neo-Nationalists rebutted the Revisionist argument that the issue could have been avoided or delayed in order to forestall a clash of arms. As for Ramsdell's contention that with the end of the westward expansion of cotton growing slavery had reached the natural limits, today finds California and Arizona among the leading cotton-growing states.

Ramsdell died in the 1940s and Randall died in the 1950s, but Craven was still living in the late 1960s. In that decade, Craven virtually abandoned the Revisionist position. Although the Revisionist concepts on the causes of the Civil War have little acceptance among historians today, the inevitable lag between up-to-date scholarship and popular belief results in this discredited interpretation retaining considerable public acceptance.

The slavery issue first rocked the nation in the controversy from 1819 to 1821 over the admission of Missouri to the Union as a slave state. Missouri was the first state from the Louisiana Purchase area to apply for admission other than Louisiana, which had had slaves under the French and the Spanish. The controversy developed when Northern Congressmen tried to bar slavery in this new state. The issue, suddenly intruded, provoked such heated debate that Thomas Jefferson commented, "This momentous question, like a fire bell in the night, awakened and filled me with terror." At that time there were eleven free and eleven slave states. Southerners felt a need to retain a parity between slave and free states so that they could have an equal vote in the Senate to block measures adverse to the interests of the South. The growth of population in the North had cast the South into a permanent minority position in the House of Representatives. This first controversy over slavery was decided by the Missouri Compromise of 1820 by which Maine and Missouri were admitted as the twelfth free and slave states, respectively. To avoid future clashes, the Compromise provided that slavery would be prohibited in the rest of the Louisiana Purchase above the

36°30′ line of latitude, which was the southern boundary of Missouri.

The slavery question arose again, however, over the new lands beyond the southwestern section of the Louisiana Purchase. These new lands—primarily the present-day states of New Mexico, Colorado, Arizona, Utah, Nevada, and California—were acquired from Mexico in the course of the Mexican War of 1846–1848. During the war, there were heated debates over the Wilmot Proviso, by which Northern Congressmen sought to bar slavery in any areas acquired as a result of the war. When the gold rush filled California with people and the territory applied for admission as a free state in 1849, the bitter debate continued. The South now faced the prospect of becoming a permanent minority in the Senate as well. California would be the sixteenth free state and additional slave states did not seem in prospect. The South's leading theoretician, Senator John Calhoun of South Carolina, had earlier advocated nullification by Southern states of Federal laws detrimental to their interests, but the determined stance of President Andrew Jackson in the 1832–1833 Nullification Crisis dimmed the luster of that solution. Now, Calhoun opposed the admission of California.

In order for the South to stay within the Union and protect its interests, especially slavery, Calhoun felt that it must be granted protection. He urged a concurrent majority scheme, by which laws affecting the South would have to be approved by a majority of Southern Congressmen as well as by an absolute majority of the entire House or the entire Senate. He also suggested dual presidents, Southern and Northern, each with a veto over bills affecting the interests of his section. Failing some such guarantee that it could protect its institutions from Northern domination, the South would be justified in seceding from the Union and going its own way. The Compromise of 1850 seemed to be a final solution of the issue of slavery in territories. California was admitted as the sixteenth free state under its terms and the rest of the Mexican Cession was to be organized into territories by Congress without any stipulation on slavery, leaving the question to "squatter sovereignty," that is, to the wishes of the residents.

To appease the South, the Compromise of 1850 included a Federal Fugitive Slave Law weighted on the side of the slave-owner.

Federal marshals were to assist in the apprehension and return of fugitive slaves and could deputize bystanders, regardless of their personal beliefs on slavery, to help out. The Federal commissioners, who were to judge cases when slave-owners claimed Northern blacks as runaway slaves, were to receive twice as large a fee for agreeing with the slave-owner and sending the black to enslavement as the amount to be given them if they ruled the slave-owner in error. This discriminatory act aroused great resentment in the North, giving the South a pyrrhic victory at best. Northern states passed personal liberty laws to thwart enforcement of this unpopular Federal law. Attempts were made to block the return of slaves by force, as in the Wellington-Oberlin rescue in Ohio. Bayonet-wielding soldiers, Marines, cavalry, and artillery assembled in Boston to escort Anthony Burns past rescue-minded mobs to the government vessel returning him to slavery in Virginia. Charlotte Forten, who was then a schoolgirl in Salem, Massachusetts, and was also the granddaughter of the black abolitionist and sailmaker of Philadelphia, James Forten, observed the return of Burns. She commented in her journal on June 2, 1854: "With what scorn must that government be regarded, which cowardly assembles thousands of soldiers to satisfy the demands of slaveholders; to deprive of his freedom a man, created in God's own image, whose sole offence is the color of his skin!"

The slavery issue was reopened in the Louisiana Purchase area when Democratic Senator Stephen Douglas of Illinois pushed the Kansas-Nebraska Act of 1854 through Congress. This act repealed the 36°30' line of the Missouri Compromise of 1820. The Nebraska territory was divided into the territory of Kansas (37° to 40°), opposite the slave state of Missouri, and the territory of Nebraska (40° to 49°), which lay to the west of the free state of Iowa and the Minnesota Territory. Slavery would have been banned in both Kansas and Nebraska under the 1820 line. Under Douglas's act, the issue was to be decided by popular sovereignty, letting the residents vote on slavery. This act precipitated the train of events leading on to the Civil War. The Whig Party, which had strength in the North and South, broke up, and the Republican Party came into being. Dedicated to stopping the spread of slavery in the territories, the Republican Party became all-Northern, with almost no open support in the South. Fighting broke out in Kansas as pro- and anti-slavery forces clashed over the issue there. One incident of bloody strife in Kansas was the Pottawatomie Massacre, a murderous assault on slave-owners by John Brown and his followers to avenge an attack on a "free" town by "pro-slavery" forces. And in the Congress, strife reached the point of the cowardly assault by Congressman Preston Brooks of South Carolina on Senator Charles Sumner of Massachusetts. Backed by pistol-wielding fellow Southern Representatives, Brooks beat Sumner unmercifully with a cane on the Senate floor in retribution for Sumner's vituperative attack on Brooks's uncle, Senator Andrew Butler of South Carolina, in a Senate speech on the Kansas question.

By giving slave-owners an opportunity to settle in Kansas and possibly bring it into the Union as the sixteenth slave state, Douglas's Kansas-Nebraska Act of 1854 made him very popular with Southerners. This support seemed to assure him a good chance of securing the Democratic Party's nomination for President in 1860. But the decision by the Supreme Court in a case involving a slave, Dred Scott, eroded Senator Douglas's strength in the South, undermining his prospects of being elected President.

This Dred Scott case began as litigation in courts in Missouri in 1846, but was not finally settled until 1857 when the Supreme Court handed down its epochal decision. Scott had been purchased in 1832 by an army surgeon, Dr. John Emerson. Emerson later was stationed at several posts in Illinois and in what became the Territory of Minnesota. He took his slave, Dred Scott, with him, so that during the period 1834 to 1838 Scott lived in a free state and also in that part of the Louisiana Purchase area that was above the 36°30′ line of the Missouri Compromise. In the Compromise, Congress had prohibited slavery above that line in the Louisiana Purchase. After living in this free state and "free" territory for several years, Scott returned with his master to St. Louis. Emerson passed away in 1843. Three years later, Scott sued in Missouri courts for his freedom, claiming that his period of residence in Minnesota, far north of the Missouri Compromise line, entitled him to freedom. The case went through various courts and finally reached the Supreme Court on appeal as the case of Dred Scott v.

Sandford (1857), one of the most famous cases in the history of the Supreme Court.

Chief Justice Roger B. Taney of Maryland ruled that "Dred Scott was not a citizen of Missouri within the meaning of the Constitution of the United States, and not entitled as such to sue in its courts; . . ." Taney also stripped all American blacks of any legal standing as citizens of the United States holding "that neither the . . . slaves, nor their descendants, whether they had become free or not, were . . . intended to be included" in the terms of the Declaration of Independence and of the Constitution. Furthermore, he commented, blacks were regarded as "so far inferior, that they had no rights which the white man was bound to respect" at the time these documents were drawn up. Not only did the Court rule that Scott was not entitled to sue, it also said that if he were entitled to sue, he should have sued while he was still in the free state or the free territory. By voluntarily returning to Missouri with his master, Dred Scott had reenslaved himself and therefore had no case on that score as well. But, the Court went on, even if entitled to sue and even if suing while in Minnesota (it became a territory in 1849 and a state in 1858), Scott still would not have gained his freedom. The reason being that the 36°30′ Missouri Compromise line was unconstitutional anyway. Taney ruled that the Federal territories belonged to all of the people of the United States, whether from North or South or East or West. All were free to reside in these territories and carry their property along with them. Thus, he ruled, Congress had no right to impede the slave-owning class from settling in any territory by barring slave-owners from bringing their slave property.

The Dred Scott decision of 1857 was a much greater victory for the South than Douglas's Kansas–Nebraska Act of 1854. Douglas, however, stuck by his popular sovereignty views, both in the Senate fight late in 1857 over admission of Kansas under the pro-slave Lecompton constitution opposed by the majority of Kansans, and in the debates with Abraham Lincoln in the 1858 campaign for reelection to the Senate. Douglas's stand cost him his Southern support and led to a split in the Democratic Party. At the nominating convention in 1860, Douglas opposed the proposed Yancey platform plank calling for positive Federal protection and support of slavery in all Federal territories. As a consequence, Southern Democrats bolted from the Party, nominating Senator John Breckenridge of Kentucky for President. The regular Democrats nominated Douglas. This split among the Democrats paved the way for a Republican victory.

Meanwhile, sectional tension increased when John Brown and some twenty followers raided the Harpers Ferry arsenal in October, 1859. Of the five blacks with Brown, only Osborn Anderson escaped. Lewis Leary and Dangerfield Newby were killed in the fighting, and John Copeland and Shields Green were hanged in December, along with Brown.

Lincoln won the election of 1860, bringing to power Republicans determined to prevent the spread of slavery to the territories and to reverse the Dred Scott decision on the territories. Explaining that Lincoln's "opinions and purposes are hostile to Slavery," South Carolina seceded from the Union in December, 1860. It was followed by six other Deep South States in January and February, 1861, which formed the Confederate States of America. In a speech in Savannah, Georgia, in March, 1861, the Confederate Vice President, Alexander Stephens, asserted that "African slavery . . . the proper status of the negro . . . was the immediate cause of the late rupture [secession]. . . ." Stephens then went on to assert that the Confederacy's

> foundations are laid, its cornerstone rests, upon the great truth that the negro is not equal to the white man; that slavery, subordination to the superior race, is his natural and moral condition. . . . our new Government, is the first, in the history of the world, based upon this great physical, philosophical, and moral truth.

When the Confederates attacked Fort Sumter, on April 12, 1861, bringing on the Civil War, blacks rallied to the Union cause. A mass meeting of Negroes in Boston resolved: "we pledge ourselves to raise an army in the country of fifty thousand colored men . . . ready to go at a moment's warning." This and similar offers from blacks in New York, Philadelphia, Cleveland, and elsewhere, were firmly rejected. The Union had four border slave states and the western counties of Virginia on its side along with nineteen free states. Four other Upper South slave states seceded after Appomattox, making eleven states in the Confederacy. Fearing loss of the loyal slave states, Lincoln identified the conflict as a war to save the Union, not to abolish slavery. Hence the War Department refused to enlist Afro-Americans as soldiers, a move that would give the war an abolitionist image. When blacks in Cincinnati tried to form a home guard defense unit, they were abused by the police and told: "We want you . . . to keep out of this; this is a white man's war."

Abolitionists, black and white, pressured Lincoln for black troops and emancipation. Insisting that "all efforts to save the country are vain, unless guided by the principles which the Abolitionists know how to teach," Frederick Douglass maintained that "You must abolish slavery or abandon the Union." But, Archbishop John Hughes of New York, primate of American Roman Catholics, more accurately reflected the sentiments of most Northerners in the first year of the War. Archbishop Hughes said of Catholic fighting men: "a vast majority of our brave troops in the field, have not the slightest idea of carrying on a war that costs so much blood and treasure just to gratify a clique of Abolitionists in the North." Northerners were overwhelmingly opposed at that time (1861) to making the war an abolitionist war.

The Confederates meanwhile used black labor in factories and fields, transporting military supplies, erecting military roads and bridges, tending Confederate soldiers, and building fortifications. The three million Confederate slaves freed many of the six million Confederate whites for military duty, partially offsetting the Union's superiority in numbers.

Gradually, Northern sentiment shifted. As the war dragged on and casualties mounted, the Union side realized that it was neglecting to make use of a large force that could provide a fresh supply of troops to replenish the war-weary ranks. As Lincoln explained:

"Things had gone on from bad to worse, until I felt that we must change our tactics, or lose the game! I now determined upon the adoption of the emancipation policy. . . ."

In July, 1862, he indicated to his Cabinet that he was ready to emancipate the slaves and call upon them to flee their masters and join the Union forces. In so doing, as he explained later, he would be subtracting strength from the Confederates, who made such effective use of blacks, and adding strength to the Union side. But the Secretary of State William H. Seward cautioned against proclaiming emancipation at that time because recent Union reverses on the battlefield would make the Emancipation Proclamation appear to be a "last measure of an exhausted government, a cry for help; the government stretching forth its hands to Ethiopia, instead of Ethiopia stretching forth her hands to the government." Accordingly, Lincoln put off announcing his emancipation policy until September 22, five days after the victory at Antietam, so that emancipation would not seem to be a "last *shriek*, on the retreat."

This effectively disguised, both then and since, the fact that the Federal government was not simply doing the black man a favor, but was desperately calling on blacks to come to the aid of the Union when emancipation was proclaimed. In the preliminary Proclamation of September 22, Lincoln declared that slaves in areas still in rebellion on January 1, 1863, "shall be then, thenceforward, and forever free." In the final Emancipation Proclamation, on January 1, 1863, he promised that the freedmen "will be received into the armed service of the United States."

Thus, in late 1862, the war began to take on a different character. It began to be an abolitionist crusade in which blacks were welcome to serve. Emancipation was also an important diplomatic weapon in that it won the Union the support of many Europeans who favored an end to slavery. Now they would pressure their governments not to aid the Confederacy since it was plain that the Civil War had become a war not only to save the Union but also to end slavery.

Black soldiers began enrolling in late 1862. From September to November, three regiments of Louisiana Native Guards, initially formed to defend their State against the Union's invading forces, switched to the Union side and were enrolled as the first three black regiments officially mustered in. Regiments of former slaves were enrolled in Kansas and South Carolina in January, 1863. The first regiment of Northern free blacks, the 54th Massachusetts, enrolled in April, 1863; Frederick Douglass was a recruiter for this regiment, and his sons, Charles and Lewis, were among the first enlisted. About 140,000 slaves and 40,000 free blacks served in the Union Army and another 30,000 blacks in the Navy.

Combat began even before some units were officially mustered in. In October, 1862, five companies of the developing First Kansas Colored Volunteers fought rebel guerillas near Butler, Missouri. In November, 1862, Company A of the First South Carolina Volunteers, in a raid along the coasts of Georgia and Florida, killed nine Confederates, took three prisoners, and liberated 155 slaves, while suffering only four wounded. The commander, Colonel Beard, reported to General Saxton: "The colored men fought with astonishing coolness and bravery."

Black soldiers labored under handicaps. Pay was unequal: Whites received $10 a month, plus $3 subsistence; blacks $10 from which $3 subsistence was deducted in advance. Blacks generally did not get the bonuses and aid for dependents that local communities supplied to white soldiers. Confederates threatened that they would give no quarter to blacks bearing arms, as in the massacre at Fort Pillow, Tennessee, in April, 1864.

Twenty blacks received the Congressional Medal of Honor or the Navy Medal of Honor. One recipient was Sergeant William Carney of the 54th Massachusetts. Badly wounded in the regiment's gallant charge at Fort Wagner, South Carolina, in July, 1863, he planted the colors on the enemy parapet and kept them flying there until retreat was sounded. Thereupon he crawled back "almost lifeless . . . exhausted by the loss of blood . . . creeping on one knee and one hand . . . but still bearing aloft the colors."

General Nathaniel Banks praised the black Louisiana regiments assaulting Port Hudson, Louisiana, on May 26, 1863. A white officer who saw them in action there declared that "The brigade of negroes behaved magnificently and fought splendidly." Two all-black divisions (a total of seventeen regiments between them) and other black units served under Grant in the Petersburg campaign from June, 1864, to April, 1865. Secretary of War Edwin M. Stanton commented that summer that "the hardest fighting was done by the black troops." He cited General William F. Smith, commander of one of the six corps serving under Grant at Petersburg, as saying the blacks "cannot be exceeded as soldiers. . . ."

Lincoln's enthusiasm showed in a letter he wrote in September, 1864, replying to Isaac Schermerhorn, who had inquired about his use of black troops. Lincoln asserted that the 150,000 blacks then serving were a crucial "physical force. . . . Keep it, and you can save the Union. Throw it away, and the Union goes with it."

The Confederacy saw this also. In November, 1864, President Jefferson Davis began urging the arming of the slaves. In March, 1865, the Confederate Congress passed a law to enlist black troops. But the war ended before this could be accomplished.

Thus blacks fought for freedom and dignity, a struggle they would continue through Reconstruction.

9

Freedmen and Carpetbag Regimes

1865–1877

"I do not think that the colored people would be safe," Dr. Daniel Norton responded when Senator Jacob Howard asked what would happen if the Federal troops and Freedmen's Bureau were removed. "They would be in danger of being hunted and killed," continued the physician who had been practicing in Yorktown, Virginia, for two years.

Dr. Norton was one of seven black men from the tidewater area of Virginia who testified on February 3, 1866, in the nation's capital, before a subcommittee of Senator Howard of Michigan and Representatives Roscoe Conkling of New York and Henry Blow of Missouri. This subcommittee of the Joint Committee on Reconstruction took testimony in regard to Virginia and the Carolinas. The other three subcommittees conducted hearings on the rest of the former Confederate States.

The Joint Committee on Reconstruction had been appointed on December 13, 1865. Its chairman was Senator William Pitt Fessenden of Maine, one of the six Senators on the Committee, but the dominant figure on the committee was Representative Thaddeus Stevens of Pennsylvania, one of nine Representatives on the committee. When Congress convened on December 4, 1865, it refused to seat the Congressmen who showed up to represent the states that had formed the Confederacy and waged war against the Union for four years. Instead, Congress passed, on December 4, a resolution to set up a committee "to inquire into the condition of the states which formed the so-called Confederate States of America, and report whether they, or any of them, are entitled to be represented in either house of Congress." One of the things that Congress was most concerned about was how the former Confederate states would accept the verdict of the war, particularly in regard to freedom for the persons once held in bondage. The war had not begun as an abolitionist crusade, but before it was over the Union was fighting not only to end secession but to end slavery. Much blood had been shed to give the nation a new birth of freedom. Many Northerners, although not strongly antislavery at the start of the war, felt by war's end that lives would have been lost in vain and sacrifices of the wounded would have been made a mockery if the slaves were not given full freedom. Hence, the committee's real concern over the plight of the black man in the South after the Civil War.

Dr. Norton, who testified to Senator Howard's subcommittee on February 3, was a native Virginian, having been born in Williamsburg. He received his education, especially his medical training, in the State of New York. He then returned to help his people. Dr. Norton told the subcommittee that "The spirit of the whites against the blacks is much worse than it was before the war. . . ." A white gentleman had told him that he was well disposed toward the Negro people previously, but that since blacks took up arms against the Confederacy, "he never wanted to have anything to do with them, or to show any spirit of kindness toward them."

The remaining black witnesses that day gave similar testimony about conditions in Virginia. The Reverend William Thornton, a former slave living in Hampton, told of a black woodcutter working on a Negro's land who unwittingly chopped down a tree belonging to a white neighbor. The latter, Thornton testified, "went into the woods and deliberately shot him as he would shoot a bird."

Madison Newby of Surry County was asked by a member of the subcommittee, "Do they whip them just as much as they did before the war?" Newby's answer was "Just the same; I do not see any alteration in that." He further revealed that "They patrol our houses just as formerly. . . . A party of twelve or fifteen men go around at night searching the houses of colored people, turning them out and beating them." When asked if blacks wanted schooling, Newby replied: "Generally . . . but down in my neighborhood they are afraid to be caught with a book." He explained that "There are no colored schools in Surry county; they would kill any one who would go down there and establish colored schools." Newby also told the Congressmen: "I was sent here as a delegate to find out whether the people down there cannot have protection. They are willing to work for a living; all they want is some protection and to know what their rights are; . . . they do not know whether they are free or not, there are so many different stories told them."

Richard Hill of Hampton told the investigators that the whites did not offer fair wages, saying "they are not willing to pay the freemen more than from five to eight dollars a month." Not only was their labor worth more than that, he said, "I do not see how people can live and support their families on those wages." Alexander Dunlop of Williamsburg testified that "We feel in danger of our lives, of our property, and of everything else." Thomas Bain of Norfolk said "The only hope the colored people have is in Uncle Sam's bayonets. . . ." Edmund Parsons of Williamsburg, a former slave like Bain and Hill, testified that blacks feared the whites and that the freedmen "are very anxious to get education. . . ."

This sampling of one day's testimony from residents of one section of a single state indicates both the problems of the freedmen and what Congress was learning about those problems. Many other witnesses, especially Southern whites, painted a much rosier picture of postwar conditions and of white-black relations. The seven Virginia blacks who testified on February 3rd may have been unduly fearful and pessimistic, but their testimony reveals their frame of mind and their outlook on conditions in postwar Virginia. It is difficult to determine how much validity to give to their grim and gloomy testimony when item by item it can be matched by much more cheerful and optimistic testimony from travelers, newspaper correspondents, and other witnesses.

Similarly, conflicting reports on Southern conditions were made to President Andrew Johnson by various observers. Major General Carl Schurz, later a Senator and a Cabinet member, reported that the former Confederate states were still rebellious and not ready for readmission. But journalist Benjamin Truman, Johnson's close friend and aide, reported that these states were loyal and fully ready to return to the Union. Schurz reported to Johnson in September, 1865, Truman reported to the President in April, 1866.

Both men reported that blacks had wandered initially, but had settled down in their old locales. Schurz pointed to a "belief, conviction, or prejudice . . . deeply rooted" among Southern whites that blacks "will not work without physical compulsion. . . ." This influenced leading Southerners to introduce such compulsion into the new system. "Efforts were, indeed, made to hold the negro," said Schurz, "in his old state of subjection. . . ." Truman, by contrast, claimed that "It is the former slave-owners who are the best friends the negro has in the south . . . while it is the 'poor whites' that are his enemies." The poor whites, Truman explained, hated the black man when he was a slave "and now that he is free, there is no striking abatement of this sentiment and the former master no longer feels called by the instinct of interest to extend the protection that he once did."

The controversy over reconstruction policies, symbolized by the conflicting reports of Schurz and Truman, continued in history books. A pro-Southern interpretation emerged at the turn of the century and dominated historical writing until the 1960s. Chiefly responsible was Professor William A. Dunning of Columbia University, whose students wrote the basic histories of Southern states in Reconstruction. Among these writers of Dunning school histories of Reconstruction were Walter L. Fleming, author of *Civil War and Reconstruction in Alabama* (1905), James W. Garner, *Reconstruction in Mississippi* (1901), and J. G. de Roulhac Hamilton, *Reconstruction in North Carolina* (1914). Others writing along these lines included William W. Davis on Florida, C. Mildred Thompson on Georgia, Charles W. Ramsdell on Texas, Hamilton J. Eckenrode on Virginia, John R. Ficklen on Louisiana's reconstruction experiences up to 1868 and Ella Lonn after 1868. A similar approach was followed by Thomas Staples writing on Arkansas and E. Merton Coulter on Kentucky.

These studies varied as to their degree of objectivity and partisanship, but generally they were anti-Negro, anti-radical Republican, anti-Carpetbagger, and ardent sympathizers with, and champions of, the Southern whites in their fight against Republican "meddling" in Southern affairs. The Dunning school interpretation usually included the following:

1. The South was repentant and ready to treat freedmen decently at the end of the Civil War.

2. President Johnson was an unselfish champion of constitutional principles, who faithfully pursued the only sound program, Lincoln's reconstruction plan.

3. Vindictive, power-mad radical Republicans, seeking selfishly to hold office and to exploit the South economically, sent in troops and pushed through a Congressional program of doubtful constitutinal validity giving uneducated freedmen political power.

4. Backed by Federal bayonets, ignorant blacks teamed with fortune-seeking Carpetbaggers and disreputable Southern Scalawags to subject the South to a long orgy of misgovernment, corruption, and crushing debt.

5. Goaded beyond endurance by this misrule, suffering Southern whites formed terroristic groups like the Klan to overthrow these Carpetbag regimes.

The beliefs expressed in this summation of the Dunning school studies have become virtually articles of faith among most Southern whites and were long used, explicitly and implicitly, to justify measures taken to keep blacks out of politics in the South. Many Southern whites still fear that the return of blacks to active participation in politics will bring a return of the "orgy" of misrule that supposedly occurred during Reconstruction. Thomas Dixon's racist novel, *The Clansman*, later made into the motion picture *Birth of a Nation*, tells this story of Reconstruction in extreme form, but is in the general vein of the strongly anti-black, pro-Southern white approach of the most rabid of the Dunning school interpreters.

Only a few historians challenged this interpretation before the 1960s. One of the earliest was John R. Lynch, a Negro who had served as Speaker of the House in the Mississippi legislature and who also represented the state in the United States Congress. Lynch wrote a work entitled *Some Historical Errors of James Ford Rhodes*, correcting the popular and highly regarded historian for his misconceptions of what went on in Reconstruction. During the 1920s, Alrutheus A. Taylor began writing a series of books relating the role of blacks in Reconstruction, including *The Negro in South Carolina During Reconstruction* (1924); his other studies covered Virginia (1926) and Tennessee (1938). In 1935 W. E. B. Du Bois published *Black Reconstruction*, which, despite its Marxist slant, proved an important corrective to the misconceptions concerning the accomplishments of the Carpetbag governments. Horace Mann Bond's book, *Negro Education in Alabama: A Study in Cotton and Steel* (1939), was a much broader study of Reconstruction politics than the title indicates. Also important in correcting the distortions of the Dunning studies was Vernon Lane Wharton's book, *The Negro in Mississippi, 1865–1880* (1947). As a whole, these were lonely voices crying in the wilderness.

In the 1960s, however, many historians have contributed to a substantial rewriting of the history of Reconstruction. They have thus corrected the biased Dunning school accounts. Among the many important new studies of Reconstruction are Eric McKitrick's *Andrew Johnson and Reconstruction* (1960), John Hope Franklin's *Reconstruction after the Civil War* (1961), LaWanda and John Cox's *Politics, Principle, and Prejudice, 1865–1866: Dilemma of Reconstruction in America* (1963), Joel Williamson's *After Slavery: The Negro in South Carolina during Reconstruction, 1861–1877* (1965), Kenneth Stampp's *The Era of Reconstruction, 1865–1877* (1965), and Rembert Patrick's *The Reconstruction of the Nation* (1967). These new books put more emphasis on a period of Reconstruction generally slighted by the Dunning school studies, the two years of Southern home rule at the end of the Civil War, before radical reconstruction began. Although the new interpretations of these revisionist historians of the 1960s have gained widespread acceptance among professional historians, it will take decades to filter down to schoolbooks and laymen.

Early in 1862, President Lincoln began his efforts at reconstruction. Characteristically pragmatic, flexible, and tentative, he experimented in Louisiana, where Federal forces had seized New Orleans in April, 1862. Not until December, 1863, did he announce his plan, extending "full pardon" to all who took an oath "to henceforth faithfully support" the Constitution and the Congressional laws and Presidential proclamations on slavery. Whenever ten percent of the 1860 voters took such an oath, they could form a government that he would recognize.

Lincoln's plan envisaged white governments because only whites were voting in Southern states in 1860. But some blacks felt that they should be given the chance to vote. Early in 1864, representatives of the 18,000 free blacks of New Orleans petitioned President

Lincoln. They pointed out that General Andrew Jackson had called them "fellow-citizens" during the War of 1812 when he urged them "to take up arms to repel the enemies of the country." They also asserted that they were "peaceable citizens, paying their taxes on an assessment of more than fifteen millions of dollars." Therefore, they requested that the blacks of Louisiana, both those born free and those who were lately freed from slavery, be "directed to be inscribed on the registers, and admitted to the rights and privileges of electors." Thereupon, Lincoln did suggest to officials in Louisiana that the educated, propertied blacks be allowed to vote, a suggestion that went unheeded.

Lincoln's stand on Negro suffrage showed his flexibility and his willingness to grow and to adapt to changed conditions. Before the Civil War he had gone on record as being opposed to political and social equality for blacks. He believed then that physical differences between the races would make it impossible for them to live on "the footing of perfect equality" and thus if there had to be a difference between them, he said, "I am in favor of the race to which I belong having the superior position." But that was in 1858. Writing to Brigadier General James S. Wadsworth in January, 1864, Lincoln stated that black troops "have demonstrated in blood their right to the ballot," and that "The restoration of the Rebel States to the Union must rest upon the principle of civil and political equality of both races." Lincoln returned to the subject again in his final public address, made from the balcony of the White House to a crowd celebrating the end of the war. In that address on April 11, 1865, three days before he was shot, Lincoln commented on the reconstructed government in Louisiana, pointing out that some people object to it because "the elective franchise is not given to the colored man." He then went on to comment, "I would myself prefer that it were now conferred on the very intelligent, and on those who serve our cause as soldiers."

Lincoln's ten-percent plan was a wartime measure designed to provide a loyal government to which the wavering, the noncommitted, and the dissident rebels could rally. He believed that the states had not left the Union and that he, as commander-in-chief, could end the "insurrection" and restore them to the Union.

Congress disagreed, insisting that the states had left the Union and that they must apply to Congress for readmission. Congress passed the Wade-Davis Bill in July, 1864. This measure required that fifty percent of the voters must take an oath of loyalty before the state could be considered loyal. The oath that would be administered under the Wade-Davis Bill was the "ironclad oath" that a person had not "voluntarily borne arms against the United States." Until half the state's voters took this oath, the state would not be deemed eligible for readmission. Lincoln blocked this plan with a pocket veto. He explained that he did not want "to be inflexibly committed to any single plan of restoration" although he considered the Congressional program "as one very proper plan for the loyal people of any state choosing to adopt it. . . ." Congress retaliated by barring from their seats in the Senate and the House the Congressional delegations from the states restored by Lincoln: Tennessee, Louisiana, and Arkansas.

Contrary to the viewpoint of many of the Dunning school theorists, the argument of Congress that the Confederate states were no longer in their rightful place in the Union was just as sound constitutionally as the President's contention that the states had never left the Union. Various leaders of Congress offered constitutional arguments to buttress the stand taken by Congress. Senator Charles Sumner of Massachusetts argued that the Confederate states had committed suicide as states by their act of secession and thus would have to apply for statehood all over again. Representative Thaddeus Stevens argued that the area of the Confederacy constituted "conquered provinces" that would have to be admitted to statehood as any new territory acquired by the United States by purchase or war. Congressman Samuel Shellabarger of Ohio offered the "forfeited rights" theory, contending that the Confederate states remained in the Union, but had lost their rights and privileges as states by their secession, with the consequence that they would have to apply to Congress for the restoration of those rights, as would any new state seeking admission. Basically, the entire discussion was a political matter, relating to the exercise of power. During the Civil War the pendulum swung far to the side of executive power, as it always does for the United States in a wartime emergency. After the war, Congress was struggling to redress the balance of power between legislature and President. Lincoln kept the issue on political grounds by always carefully refraining from asserting that his viewpoint was the only sound and constitutional program. His successor, Andrew Johnson, dogmatically and stubbornly converted the political struggle into a constitutional issue by insisting that the Presidential theory had all the constitutional validity while the Congressional theories had none. Too many of the Dunning school interpreters accepted Johnson's view on this.

The assassination of Lincoln by a Southern sympathizer in April, 1865, removed the one man who had the tact, wisdom, charity, and flexibility to resolve the impasse between President and Congress over the issue of restoration of the states to the Union. The radical Republicans, led by Stevens and Sumner, imagined that President Johnson would cooperate with them because of his denunciations of the Southern planter class. But Johnson was a Southerner, a native of North Carolina who moved to Tennessee as a young man. He was also a slave-owner, having owned eight slaves before the Civil War. And he was a Democrat, having run for such offices as Congressman and Senator as a member of the Democratic Party. In 1864, the Republicans had nominated him for Vice President in order to strengthen national unity by having a Southerner who was a Democrat on the ticket. The Republicans had dropped their party label during the war and operated as the Union Party in cooperation with those Northern Democrats and Southern Unionists who opposed secession and the division of the nation. When the war came, Johnson was the only Senator who refused to secede when his state went out of the Union.

Unlike Lincoln, Johnson was doctrinaire, rigid, and determined to have his own way. He ignored the pleas of Congressional leaders not to do anything about restoration until Congress was in session and could cooperate with him in working out an acceptable program. Instead, he rushed ahead with restoration during the late spring and summer of 1865. His plan did not stipulate that even as much as ten percent must take the oath of loyalty before the state would be restored by him. He did require them to ratify the Thirteenth Amendment of December, 1865, which proclaimed that "Neither slavery nor involuntary servitude . . . shall exist within the United States. . . ."

Encouraged by Johnson to disregard Northern sentiment, the

former Confederate states chose leading rebels, many unpardoned, for state offices. They elected to the Congress convening in December, 1865, the Confederate vice president, six Confederate cabinet members, fifty-eight Confederate congressmen, and four Confederate generals. These restored states passed black codes in 1865 that permitted blacks to make contracts, sue and testify, own property, and marry legally, rights not granted under the slave codes in existence before the Civil War. These black codes did not grant blacks the right to vote in any of the Southern states, not even the educated blacks, whom both Presidents Lincoln and Johnson had suggested the states might consider permitting to vote. Although the blacks in Mississippi were basically farmers, that state's black code did not permit "any freedman, free negro, or mulatto to rent or lease any lands or tenements except in incorporated cities or towns. . . ." This was interpreted to mean sale as well as renting thus forcing them to be sharecroppers rather than independent farmers.

The apprenticeship and vagrancy provisions of the black codes especially aroused Northern sentiment against the South. To Southerners, these laws were merely a means of assuring that blacks would work. To Northerners, these measures appeared to be an attempt to restore slavery in a less obvious form. The apprentice laws provided that blacks under eighteen years of age who were orphans or whose parents could not support them were to be apprenticed "to some competent or suitable person" by probate court, "Provided, that the former owner of said minors shall have the preference. . . ." The codes also provided that idle blacks over eighteen could be arrested and charged with vagrancy. If convicted, they could be fined and imprisoned, and then hired out to any person who would pay the fine. When they had worked off the fine, however, the "employer" could notify the sheriff as the "free man" walked away. He could then be arrested, charged, convicted, fined, and jailed again, with his "employer" paying the fine and obtaining his services for free (paying only the fine and the man's upkeep) for another year. Some Southern whites no doubt shared the conviction of Governor William Sharkey of Mississippi, who believed that blacks "were destined to extinction beyond all doubt." Many Northerners were incensed over these violations of the rights of blacks. The Chicago *Tribune*, in an editorial of December 1, 1865, asserted that

> We tell the white men of Mississippi that the men of the North will convert the State of Mississippi into a frog pond before they will allow such laws to disgrace one foot of soil in which the bones of our soldiers sleep and over which the flag of freedom waves.

It was the mistreatment of blacks by these defiant governments restored under Johnson that helped bring on a more severe reconstruction policy under Congressional auspices. The former Confederate states had two years of home rule, from 1865 to 1867, to prove themselves willing to accord decent treatment to the freedmen. Part of their failure to do so was a result of President Johnson's clouding the issue so that they did not comprehend fully what terms they would have to meet to satisfy Northern opinion. Northerners discriminated against blacks in many ways, but they demanded that the South not flagrantly abuse the blacks as the black codes seemed to indicate. Thus, after two years of home rule, the governments in the states restored by Johnson were supplanted, in 1867, and new Carpetbag regimes came into being, bolstered by the votes of blacks.

Some blacks had demanded the right to vote as an essential tool for self-protection and furtherance of their interests. Well aware that only six Northern states permitted Negroes to vote, the great black leader, Frederick Douglass, had demanded in 1865 the unconditional "enfranchisement of the black man, in every State in the Union" because without the ballot "liberty is a mockery" and the freedman the "slave of society. . . ." Meetings of Southern blacks had demanded the right to vote: In Norfolk, Virginia, in June, 1865, they resolved "give us the suffrage, and you may rely upon us to secure justice for ourselves"; and in Alexandria, Virginia, that August, they resolved that "the only salvation for us besides the power of the Government is in the possession of the ballot."

Southern blacks were not enfranchised until 1867. They received the right to vote only after the clash between the radical Republicans and President Johnson had been settled by a Congressional victory that gave Congress the upper hand in controlling reconstruction. When Congress convened in December, 1865, it refused to seat the Congressional delegations from the states restored by Johnson and it also set up the Joint Committee to investigate. In 1866, Congress passed a Civil Rights Act and renewed the Freedmen's Bureau, both measures passed over Johnson's vetoes.

Having found that "the feeling . . . toward emancipated slaves . . . is one of vindictive and malicious hatred," the Joint Committee proposed the Fourteenth Amendment, which was approved by Congress in June, 1866. This amendment restored to blacks the citizenship stripped away by the Dred Scott decision of 1857. It also ensured the civil rights of blacks. Section 1, in which citizenship is granted and rights accorded, has remained a great bulwark of human rights ever since, even though court decisions in the late nineteenth century vitiated the amendment's potency. This section declared that

> All persons born or naturalized in the United States, and subject to the jurisdiction thereof, are citizens of the United States and of the State wherein they reside. No State shall make or enforce any law which shall abridge the privileges or immunities of citizens of the United States; nor shall any State deprive any person of life, liberty, or property, without due process of law; nor deny to any person within its jurisdiction the equal protection of the laws.

Tennessee ratified this amendment in July, 1866, and its Congressional delegation was seated. The other former Confederate states, at Johnson's urging, rejected the amendment. During the Congressional election campaign of 1866, both Johnson and the radical Republicans sought to get more men elected who would support their point of view. Johnson's cause was hurt when white police and mobs rioted, killing 46 blacks in Memphis in May and 34 in New Orleans in July. These riots helped sway Northern opinion to the radicals' view that blacks needed protection from the governments restored by Johnson. Many more blacks, incidentally, had been killed by white mobs in New York during draft riots in July, 1863, but New York was not awaiting a chance to be restored to the Union.

Victorious in the 1866 Congressional elections, the radicals enacted laws in March and July, 1867, and March, 1868. Troops were sent in to enforce this Congressional reconstruction program that revolutionized the South politically. Under these military reconstruction measures, blacks were enrolled by the occupying generals and permitted to help elect delegates to state conventions to draft new constitutions. These constitutions were required to provide for blacks to vote. Furthermore, the states would have to ratify the Fourteenth Amendment as well in order to be permitted to be represented in Congress again. Beginning with Arkansas in June, 1868, and ending with Georgia, in July, 1870, the ten states were readmitted to the Union. The Fourteenth Amendment was finally ratified in July, 1868. The last four states were also required to ratify the Fifteenth Amendment which provided that "The right of citizens of the United States to vote shall not be denied or abridged by the United States or by any State on account of race, color, or previous condition of servitude." This amendment was ratified in March, 1870, thus permitting black men to vote in all states of the Union, including the many Northern states that had barred blacks from voting heretofore.

Most Southern blacks were illiterate because it was a crime to teach them before the war. Generally, they elected to office those Southern blacks with education or else the educated Northern blacks who came South to help out. Twenty-two black men served in Congress, from 1869 to 1901, including two Senators, Hiram Revels (1870–1871) and Blanche Kelso Bruce (1875–1881), both representing Mississippi. Six were elected lieutenant governor, one in Mississippi, two in South Carolina, and three in Louisiana, including P. B. S. Pinchback who was also acting governor of Louisiana for forty-three days. Some idea of the training of the blacks who held such high offices can be seen from the fact that Francis Cardozo, who served as State Treasurer of South Carolina, was a graduate of the University of Glasgow; Jonathan Gibbs, who was Superintendent of Education for the State of Florida, was a graduate of Dartmouth College; and Jonathan J. Wright, who was a Justice of the Supreme Court of South Carolina, was a graduate of the University of Pennsylvania and a highly respected member of the Pennsylvania bar before moving to the South.

There was corruption in Carpetbag governments, but it was part of a general postwar moral breakdown and was influenced by the atmosphere of rampant rising industrialism. The Tweed Ring in New York City stole more than all the Carpetbag governments put together, and there were high scandals in the Grant Administration that touched the Vice Presidency, the Cabinet, and Congress. Also, there was corruption in Southern governments from 1865 to 1867, before blacks began voting, and it continued long after Carpetbag governments ceased. To their credit, Carpetbag governments started public school systems where almost none existed before (with the exception of North Carolina), democratized government, and instituted measures for the public welfare too long neglected in these planter-dominated states. These new responsibilities and the issuance of bonds to bring in railroads and industry account for much of the increased indebtedness.

Carpetbag governments did not take office until 1868. They lasted an average of only four and a half years. Carpetbag rule was overthrown by 1869 in Tennessee and Virginia, by 1870 in North Carolina, 1871 in Georgia, 1873 in Texas, 1874 in Arkansas and Alabama, 1875 in Mississippi, 1876 in South Carolina, and 1877 in Florida and Louisiana. The Ku Klux Klan was founded in Pulaski, Tennessee, in 1866, and had begun beating and murdering blacks and burning their homes, schools, and churches, long before blacks were voting and long before Carpetbag governments started.

The greatest shame of Reconstruction was the failure to provide the freedmen, after centuries of unpaid toil, with land and assistance to make a sound start economically. This failure left a legacy of future troubles.

10

Atlanta Compromise,
Disfranchisement, and Jim Crow
1877–1900

"In all things that are purely social we can be as separate as
the fingers," said the orator, flinging his outstretched hand above
his head, "yet one as the hand [arm still aloft but fingers clenched
in a fist] in all things essential to mutual progress." With that,
according to the dispatch filed from Atlanta, Georgia, on September 18, 1895, by the correspondent of the New York *World*, James
Creelman, "the whole audience was on its feet in a delirium of
applause. . . ."

This was the keynote of a speech that was to have, for several
decades, a decisive impact on the relations of blacks and whites in
America. The speaker was Booker T. Washington, and this was,
Creelman noted, "the first time that a Negro has made a speech in
the South on any important occasion before an audience composed
of white men and women."

Some forty thousand visitors had jammed Atlanta for the opening of the important Cotton States and International Exposition.
The only black speaker at the opening ceremonies in the great
Exposition Building was Washington, who was founder and head of
Tuskegee Institute in Alabama. Creelman described him as being
"tall, bony, straight as a Sioux chief" with "high forehead, straight
nose, heavy jaws . . . piercing eyes, and a commanding manner."

When Washington first took the platform, the blacks sitting in
the balcony cheered, but little applause came from the whites on
the main floor of the hall. But, before he was halfway through his
twenty-minute speech, Creelman reported, "the multitude was in an
uproar of enthusiasm—handkerchiefs were waved, canes were
flourished, hats were tossed in the air. The fairest women of Geor-

gia stood up and cheered. It was as if the orator had bewitched them." Yet, while the whites burst into wild cheering over Washington's statement about being as separate as the fingers, "Most of the Negroes in the audience," Creelman commented, "were crying, perhaps without knowing just why."

In his autobiography, *Up from Slavery* (1901), Washington recalled: "The first thing that I remember, after I had finished speaking, was that [former] Governor [Rufus] Bullock rushed across the platform and took me by the hand. . . ." Creelman stated that "Another shout greeted this demonstration, and for a few minutes the two men stood facing each other, hand in hand." The next day, as Washington tried to walk through the streets of Atlanta, crowds of whites surrounded him and "wished to shake hands," so embarrassing him that he returned to Tuskegee.

The ripples from his speech spread. The editor-publisher of the Atlanta *Constitution*, Clark Howell, telegraphed his impressions to a New York newspaper. Howell described Washington's talk as "one of the most notable speeches, both as to character and as to the warmth of its reception, ever delivered to a Southern audience." Newspapers all over the nation published the speech in full and ran editorials commending it. The Boston *Transcript* editorialized that Washington's speech "seems to have dwarfed all the other proceedings and the Exposition itself. The sensation that it has caused in the press has never been equalled." President Grover Cleveland wrote to Washington on October 6, 1895, thanking him for the copy of the speech that Washington had sent to him. In his letter, President Cleveland stated that "I have read it with intense interest, and I think the Exposition would be fully justified if it did not do more than furnish the opportunity for its delivery."

After his Atlanta Compromise speech, Booker T. Washington was catapulted by white Americans into the position of spokesman of his race for the next two decades. Frederick Douglass, who had been the unchallenged leader of black Americans for almost half a century, died on February 20, 1895, seven months before the Atlanta speech.

Douglass (1817?–1895) and Washington (1856–1915) approached America's racial problems differently. Douglass had been born in Talbot County, Maryland, Washington in Franklin County,

Virginia. Both were brought forth in slavery, conceived by white fathers of slave women. The white fathers of these two baby boys took no responsibility of providing for, caring about, or sustaining their sons. Legally, a white man assaulting a slave woman was not regarded as a criminal rapist; the white man forcing his attention on a slave woman was merely liable to a civil damage suit by the owner if the woman was not his property.

The similarities between Douglass and Washington ended with their being rural-born mulatto slaves who never knew their fathers. Douglass hated slavery, stressing its cruelties, fighting back (commenting "He was whipped oftener who was whipped easiest"), and chafing despite any improvement in condition until he ran away at the age of twenty-one. Washington lived under slavery only nine years, being liberated by the Civil War, but he stressed its kindly aspects, noting that blacks had "no feelings of bitterness against the whites before and during the war. . . ."

Escaping to the North when abolitionist moral fervor was at its peak, Douglass became an abolitionist lecturer and editor, thundering philippics at slaveholding Southerners and apathetic, prejudiced Northerners. Although beaten often by white mobs that invaded abolitionist meetings, and by white hooligans resisting his courageous fights against Jim Crow, this crusader resided in the relative safety of Northern or border cities such as New Bedford, Rochester, and Washington, D.C. He never lived in the rural Deep South where a militant black was likely to be lynched or murdered with little likelihood of his killers ever being apprehended, much less punished.

For five decades, Douglass consistently urged blacks to agitate and to demand full equality. He urged them to seek the ballot box, jury box, and cartridge box. The ballot box would provide political power by which they could advance their interests by exerting pressure on officeholders, as did all groups in America, to obtain better schools, jobs, and services in their neighborhoods. The jury box would give blacks a hand in the administration of justice, breaking the pattern of white police, prosecutors, juries, and judges that punished blacks out of all proportion to the amount of crime for which they were responsible. The cartridge box would enable blacks to defend themselves, thus discouraging white bullies, rapists, lynchers, rioters, and other hostile elements that preyed upon the helpless. He believed that anything worth obtaining had to be fought for, and contended: "If there is no struggle there is no progress. . . . Power concedes nothing without a demand." Those who sought progress without agitation, Douglass asserted, wanted "crops without plowing . . . rain without thunder and lightning . . . the ocean without the awful roar of its many waters." In 1895, as Douglass neared the end of his life, a young black student asked him what advice he would give a young Negro starting out in life. Douglass's answer was: "Agitate! Agitate! Agitate!"

The same student put the identical question to Booker T. Washington in 1899. He got quite a different answer from the man who succeeded to Douglass's mantle of leadership. Washington replied: "Work! Work! Work! Be patient and win by superior service."

The advice to be patient epitomized the difference between the two men, for Washington's patience was matched by Douglass's impatience. Until Booker T. Washington, the dominant theme in black leadership had been militancy. There were always a few who counseled submission, caution, and accommodation, but not until his era was this approach clearly in the ascendancy.

Washington had worked his way through Hampton Institute in Virginia where the emphasis was on practical, industrial training and learning to work with one's hands. During a year of graduate training at Wayland Seminary in Washington, D.C., he became suspicious of formal education divorced from life. Washington was a practical, down-to-earth man, who had learned the trade of brick masonry at Hampton along with his college subjects. He was a man of great sense and a masterful orator, but he tended to feel uncomfortable in the presence of intellectuals. In his Atlanta Compromise speech, as on many occasions, he indicated his aversion for bookish pursuits that lacked practical application to the task of making a living. In Atlanta, he said that the Negro race would "prosper in proportion as we learn to draw the line between the superficial and the substantial, the ornamental gewgaws of life and the useful. No race can prosper till it learns that there is as much dignity in tilling a field as in writing a poem." In 1904, he wrote:

> In a certain way every slave plantation in the south was an industrial school. On these plantations young colored men and women were constantly being trained not only as farmers but as

carpenters, blacksmiths, wheelwrights, brick masons, engineers, cooks, laundresses, sewing women and housekeepers . . . slavery . . . was a curse to both races, but . . . industrial training on the plantations, left the Negro at the close of the war in possession of nearly all the common and skilled labor in the South. . . . For nearly twenty years after the war, except in a few instances, the value of the industrial training given by the plantations was over-looked. Negro men and women were educated in literature, in mathematics and in the sciences. . . . How often have I been discouraged as I have gone through the South, and into the homes of the people of my race, and have found women who could con-verse intelligently upon abstruse subjects, and yet could not tell how to improve the condition of the poorly cooked and still more poorly served bread and meat which they and their families were eating three times a day.

After teaching a few years at Hampton, Washington accepted a call in 1881 to head a new school in Tuskegee, Alabama. This school was the result of a pledge made by a white candidate for the legislature when seeking support among black voters. In return for their support, he promised to secure state aid for a school. Elected with the aid of black voters, he got the legislature to pass a bill authorizing $2,000 yearly for the school and for faculty salaries. The new principal had to secure buildings, teachers, and pupils. Starting from scratch in a Deep South rural community where whites were suspicious that education unfitted blacks for labor, Washington built a great institution with an endowment of $2,000,-000 by 1915 (higher than the endowment of any black and most Southern white colleges then). He gained the support and financial aid of blacks, Southern whites, and Northern philanthropists. Doug-lass's tirades could not have accomplished this. As Washington pointed out in his Atlanta Compromise speech, "It is at the bottom of life we must begin, and not at the top. Nor should we permit our grievances to overshadow our opportunities." Washington was able to build his school and secure support, North and South, by empha-sizing industrial training and the useful skills that his graduates would carry forth, making them assets to their communities. He and his students made the bricks, built the buildings, constructed the furniture, grew the crops, and raised the livestock for his school.

On graduating, his students spread throughout the South creating many "little Tuskegees."

Washington took ignorant, backward blacks living in abysmal poverty as cotton sharecroppers and taught them how to improve their lives by cleanliness, industry, thrift, diversified farming, painting and mending, family budgeting, and better planning. Tuskegee was practicing community involvement, uplifting agricultural extension work and home demonstration techniques long before the terms were invented or the Smith-Lever Act of 1914 was passed. Tuskegee Institute pioneered the "moveable school." To help poor farmers improve their methods, increase their income, and advance their lives, Tuskegee sent out demonstration wagons that carried the school's newest techniques in agriculture and home economics directly to the farmers and farm families, many of whom could not get to the periodic farm conferences held on campus. Tuskegee gained an international reputation for its work and visitors from all over the world, particularly from developing nations, came to learn ways to educate their people. Hired by Booker T. Washington, the great agricultural scientist George Washington Carver served on the Tuskegee faculty from 1896 to 1943, enriching the South and benefitting white and black Southerners by his discoveries. Carver developed countless synthetic products out of peanuts, sweet potatoes, and soybeans, and he pioneered the process of dehydrating foods for longer preservation and less bulky shipping. From 1881 to 1915, Washington headed, and lived at, Tuskegee Institute, learning how to get along with and gain the support of whites in the Deep South. Understandably, his approach to race relations would differ from Douglass's approach.

The downturn in the fortune of the black man in the last quarter of the nineteenth century also affected Washington's outlook. He became convinced that agitation and militancy were useless in the face of a determined drive by Northern and Southern whites to reduce blacks to a degraded, second-class status. He believed that a withdrawal from politics would ease tensions and give blacks a chance to strengthen black communities by economic success as black craftsmen, businessmen, and professionals for a subsequent rise to first-class citizenship. The increasing racism and the drift toward disfranchisement convinced him that submission and accommodation were the best tactics for the times.

Ideas of racial superiority had always existed in America, but they intensified in the late nineteenth century. Social Darwinists seemed to give them scientific sanction when they applied the theory of biological evolution expounded in Charles Darwin's *The Origin of Species* (1859) to the races of men. Social Darwinists insisted that some races had evolved higher than other races. Professor William Graham Sumner of Yale University pointed out that evolution "instead of supporting the natural equality of man, would give a demonstration of their inequality." Sumner attacked the Congressional reconstruction laws that tried to legislate political equality between blacks and whites. He insisted that the government can not "do away with the struggle for existence" and should "not undertake to aid some and handicap others at the outset in order to offset hereditary advantages and disadvantages, or to make them start equally."

Arthur de Gobineau's book, *Essay on the Inequality of Human Races* (1855), was translated from the French late in the century and influenced American thinking. He theorized that there was a gradation of races from Nordic whites at the top down through Alpine and Mediterranean whites and on to nonwhite races, with blacks at the bottom. Houston Stewart Chamberlain, an Englishman and son-in-law of the German composer, Richard Wagner, similarly stressed ideas of superiority of the Teutonic race. These racist ideas of Gobineau and Chamberlain ultimately influenced Adolf Hitler, Nazi Fuehrer of Germany, who tried by conquest to establish the supremacy of the "master Aryan (Nordic) race" over all the world.

The racist concepts of European writers influenced Americans as well. A popular novelist of the early twentieth century, Thomas Nelson Page of Virginia, asserted that blacks for 4,000 years had "exhibited the absence of the essential qualities of a progressive race. . . . In art, in mechanical development, in literature, in mental and moral science, in all the range of mental action, no notable work has up to this time come from the Negro." E. H. Randle of Virginia pronounced education for blacks a failure because their minds seldom developed "beyond that of the twelve-year-old white child. . . ."

Late nineteenth-century imperialism and the Rudyard Kipling notion of taking up the white man's burden to lift backward races from "savagery" fortified American racism. Senator Albert Beveridge of Indiana maintained that "God has . . . been preparing the English-speaking and Teutonic peoples for a thousand years. . . . He has made us master organizers of the world . . . that we may administer government among savage and senile peoples." As the United States acquired overseas colonies, an aberration developed in our policies toward the relationship of older states and newer territories. Up to the late 1890s, operating under terms of the Northwest Ordinance of 1787, we were generally prepared to grant full citizenship and statehood to the areas that were annexed as territories to the original thirteen states. The Northwest Ordinance provided for a regular progression through stages of territorial government to statehood. Each new state was the full equal of the older states. This was unique in the history of the world. We were not to have a mother country and dependent colonies. Instead, all areas added to the United States could look forward to statehood. The one possible exception was Alaska, purchased in 1867, which lacked enough residents for statehood. We could make equal states of the areas acquired up to 1898 because they were contiguous, they were only sparsely settled by the aboriginal Indians, and they were soon filled up by Americans moving out from the older states.

In 1898, there came a break in this pattern when we acquired the Hawaiian Islands and the next year when we acquired American Samoa. Also in 1898, as a result of the Spanish-American War, we gained possession of, or control over, Puerto Rico, Guam, Wake, the Philippines, and Cuba. In 1917, the United States purchased the Danish West Indian possessions, the Virgin Islands. These new possessions or protectorates, acquired in 1898, 1899, and 1917, made the United States a colonial power. We had no intention, at that time, of conferring full-fledged citizenship on the residents of these acquisitions nor of setting these places on the path to progression from territorial government to statehood. The reason was that these places were overseas, were thickly populated by people who were of different race, language, and religion, and were not likely to be filled up by Americans from the older states who would have become a majority. Thus, the United States became a colonial power; the mainland states were the mother country, these island possessions were the colonies. However, Cuba became semi-independent in 1906 and completely free in 1934, and the Philippines gained full freedom in 1946. The other possessions remained dependencies, with the exception of Alaska and Hawaii, which were admitted to the union as the forty-ninth and fiftieth states in 1959. Puerto Rico has, since 1953, enjoyed a special status as a free commonwealth voluntarily associated with the United States.

The fact that we became a colonial power at the turn of the century, with acquisitions all over the world, changed the outlook of many people in America toward the black man. Northerners who had long championed the cause of the Southern blacks could now see the problem of the Southern white more clearly. Northern whites in 1900 were not inclined to grant equal citizenship and statehood to places like Puerto Rico, the Philippines, and Guam, and either as a result of this or coincidentally, their support of the fight of the black man for full equality in the South began to wane. As the editor of the *Atlantic Monthly* noted: "If the stronger and cleverer race . . . is free to impose its will upon 'new-caught, sullen peoples' on the other side of the globe, why not in South Carolina and Mississippi?"

Frederick Douglass had always maintained that the Republican Party, the party of Lincoln and the abolitionists, was the ship (the ark on which blacks might ride out the flood of oppression and be made truly free) while all other parties were the ocean (in which blacks would drown). Yet it was the Republican Party that led the jingoistic drive for taking up the white man's burden and acquiring colonies. Also, as the importance of Midwestern farmers as a voting bloc increased and as growing industrialism made the South's new leaders more sympathetic to Northern capitalism, the Republicans no longer needed black votes to stay in power or to ensure an industrialist-minded Federal government. Now Republicans could begin to abandon the interests of Southern blacks, their former allies, leaving them to the tender mercies of Southern whites who had always maintained that they knew what was best for blacks.

Stereotypes from the leading popular entertainment of that time contributed to American racism. The minstrel shows, Uncle Tom plays, after-dinner jokes, and newspaper cartoons depicted blacks as lazy, stupid, thieving, chicken-stealing, razor-toting, melon-eating comical folk. The only impressions many Americans had of blacks was what they saw on minstrel stages, hardly calculated to improve the black man's image.

Adverse Supreme Court decisions contributed to the deteriorating status of black Americans. One crucial decision was in the civil rights cases of 1883. These cases tested the constitutionality of the Civil Rights Act of 1875 passed by Congress. The first section of that act stated:

> Sec. 1. That all persons within the jurisdiction of the United States shall be entitled to the full and equal enjoyment of the accommodations, advantages, facilities, and privileges of inns, public conveyances on land or water, theatres, and other places of public amusement; subject only to the conditions and limitations established by law, and applicable alike to citizens of every race and color, regardless of any previous condition of servitude. . . .

The Supreme Court, however, denied that Congress had the constitutional power to pass such a law. The Court could not find any warrant in the Thirteenth or Fourteenth Amendments for such legislation. The Court pointed out in the opinion delivered by Justice Joseph P. Bradley of New Jersey, that while "positive rights and privileges are undoubtedly secured by Fourteenth Amendment . . . they are secured by way of prohibition against State laws and State proceedings affecting those rights and privileges. . . ."

The Civil Rights Act of 1875, pointed out Justice Bradley, declares "'certain acts committed by individuals shall be deemed offences" which shall be prosecuted and punished in Federal courts. Thus, the law "imposes a penalty upon any individual who shall deny to any citizen . . . equal accommodations and privileges" in the use of inns, places of amusement, and public conveyances. Such was clearly not intended by the Fourteenth Amendment, which was directed not against discrimination by private entrepreneurs choosing their customers in their places of business, but against state action. Hence, the Court ruled:

> until some State law has been passed, or some State action through its officers or agents has been taken, adverse to the rights of citizens sought to be protected by the Fourteenth Amendment, no

legislation of the United States under said amendment, nor any proceeding under such legislation, can be called into activity; for the prohibitions of the amendment are against State laws and acts done under State authority.

That decision effectively prevented any Congressional action to protect the civil rights of blacks. This was the last civil rights measure passed by Congress until the minor Civil Rights Act of 1957 and it was the last public accommodations measure until the major Civil Rights Act of 1964.

Blacks were still voting in the 1880s, but election frauds, intimidation, and lynching reduced their power. In the 1880s, lynchings of blacks averaged 67 a year, and in the 1890s, lynchings occurred on an average of 116 a year. The peak years were 1892, with 162 blacks lynched, and 1894, when 134 Afro-Americans died at the hands of lynch mobs. In 1892, a black person was murdered by a lynch mob almost every other day throughout the year.

As long as Southern whites voted solidly for the Democratic Party, white supremacy was secure and the black vote (almost all Republican) was ineffectual. In the Populist Party movement of the early 1890s, however, whites split over economic interests. Both sides courted blacks. Economically, blacks should have allied themselves with Populists, a new third party that represented the lower-class elements, small farmers, tenant farmers, farm laborers, factory workers, and laboring people generally. But blacks had usually distrusted lower-class whites. There was hostility between the two elements as a result of friction growing out of competition for jobs, housing, and recreation. The white employer class, unwilling to see lower-class blacks and lower-class whites combine to fight against the capitalist class for their economic interests, had traditionally encouraged hostility between lower-class whites and blacks, playing off both elements against each other while exploiting both. Anyway, many blacks, accustomed to working as maids, cooks, gardeners, valets, and chauffeurs in the homes of middle- and upper-class whites, felt more comfortable with upper-class Democrats, the old master class. Hence, the black vote split between the Populist and Democratic parties, with election frauds ensuing as both parties sought to capture black votes. As long as blacks voted, it was dangerous for whites to split. Blacks made too many gains in the form of political patronage and better schools, roads, and municipal services when they served as the balance of power between Populists and Democrats with both parties courting them ardently.

Accordingly, Southern states began disfranchising blacks by poll taxes, criminal record disqualifications, and discriminatory literacy tests. To protect whites who might lose their right to vote, some states, beginning with Louisiana, passed "grandfather clauses," stating: "No male person who was on January 1st, 1867, or . . . prior thereto, entitled to vote . . . and no son or grandson of any such person . . . shall be denied the right to register and vote . . . by reason of his failure to possess the educational or property qualifications. . . ." Blacks were not voting before the Reconstruction Acts of March, 1867; hence they could not have their right to vote protected under this clause. Mississippi disfranchised blacks in 1890, South Carolina in 1895, Louisiana in 1898, and the rest of the South between 1900 and 1910. The dramatic impact that these measures had on Negro voting can be seen in Louisiana, where in 1896, 130,344 blacks were registered to vote, but in 1900, only 5,320 blacks were registered, a drop of 96 percent.

Confronted by these setbacks, Booker T. Washington's 1895 Atlanta Compromise speech pleaded for economic opportunity. His speech advised blacks to stay in the rural South, becoming useful to, and making friends with, Southern whites. He urged Southern whites to look to the loyal, devoted, non-union, non-striking blacks as their basic labor force. He asserted that blacks erred in beginning at the political top as freedmen rather than at the bottom of life and working up by proving to be substantial citizens. Washington accepted the idea of temporary segregation while blacks proved they were worthy of equality:

> The wisest among my race understand that the agitation of questions of social equality is the extremest folly, and that progress in the enjoyment of all the privileges that will come to us must be the result of severe and constant struggle rather than of artificial forcing. No race that has anything to contribute to the markets of the world is long in any degree ostracized. It is important and right that all privileges of the law be ours, but it is vastly more important that we be prepared for the exercise of these privileges. The

opportunity to earn a dollar in a factory just now is worth infinitely more than the opportunity to spend a dollar in an opera-house.

In 1896, the Supreme Court seemed to agree with him. In the Plessy v. Ferguson case, it approved a law passed by the State of Louisiana that required railroads (whether they wanted to discriminate or not) to provide Jim Crow (separate) facilities for blacks, thus sanctioning "separate but equal." The decision seemed incongruous in relation to what the Court had said in the 1883 civil rights cases. Then, it had ruled that Congress could not prohibit businessmen from discriminating, but it had said that the Fourteenth Amendment would clearly be violated by state law or action. Yet, thirteen years later, in the Plessy case, it upheld the right of the state to pass segregation laws, viewing that as a proper exercise of police power. The opinion, delivered by Justice Henry P. Brown of Michigan, denied that "the enforced separation of the two races stamps the colored race with a badge of inferiority." If so, Brown ruled, it would be "solely because the colored race chooses to put that construction upon it." Brown also said of the argument presented by lawyers for Homer Plessy, a light-skinned Negro, thrown off a train in Louisiana under the state law:

> The argument also assumes that social prejudices may be overcome by legislation, and that equal rights cannot be secured to the negro except by an enforced commingling of the two races. We cannot accept this proposition. If the two races are to meet upon terms of social equality, it must be the result of natural affinities, a mutual appreciation of each other's merits and a voluntary consent of individuals.

How individuals could voluntarily come together when state laws required them to be separated was a question the Court did not answer. The working of the opinion was remarkably akin to the sentiments expressed by Booker T. Washington the year before in his Atlanta speech of 1895.

Both in 1883 and 1896, when the Supreme Court made decisions in the civil rights and Plessy cases destructive of Negro rights, the Court was composed overwhelmingly of Northern Republicans. Both in 1883 and 1896, there were only two Southerners on the Court; the rest came from Northern and Western states. And either seven or eight of the justices were Republicans on the two occasions. Each time, the ruling was by a majority 8 to 1. The lone dissenting voice each time was that of a Southern Republican, Justice John Marshall Harlan of Kentucky. In his dissent in the 1896 Plessy case, Harlan stated that "in view of the Constitution, in the eyes of the law, there is in this country, no superior, dominant, ruling class of citizens. There is no caste here. Our Constitution is color-blind and neither knows nor tolerates classes among citizens." Insofar as segregation laws were concerned, Harlan said unequivocally: "The arbitrary separation of citizens, on the basis of race, while they are on a public highway, is a badge of servitude wholly inconsistent with the civil freedom and the equality before the law established by the Constitution. It cannot be justified upon any legal grounds." And, Harlan commented, "The thin disguise of 'equal' accommodations for passengers in railroad coaches will not mislead any one, nor atone for the wrong this day done."

With Supreme Court sanction, segregation now became the way of life in the South. Where before separation had been by custom or by laws primarily on schools and marriages, now Southern states passed a mass of laws requiring Jim Crow facilities in every sphere imaginable.

Racism, lynching, disfranchisement, and Jim Crow pushed Southern blacks to a low point. Northern blacks also had troubles at the turn of the century.

11

Northward Migration and
Turn-of-the-Century Achievers

1880–1910

The mob surged through the streets of Springfield, Illinois, in August, 1908, shouting "Lincoln freed you, we'll show you where you belong." Several thousand whites had assembled to lynch two blacks who were being held in jail, one suspected of murdering a white man, the other accused of raping a white woman. Their guilt was far from certain, but the mob was ready to execute them without a trial.

The authorities moved the captives away. A white man named Loper who owned a restaurant in Springfield came to the aid of the police in this move to thwart the lynch mob. In his automobile, Loper drove the guards with their prisoners to a nearby town where they boarded a train to a safer jail. The frustrated mob burned Loper's car when they found how their victims had been spirited away. Then the mob invaded Loper's restaurant, drank his whiskey, looted other stores for goods and more whiskey, and set off on a rampage through black neighborhoods, vowing to put blacks in their place and shouting, "We'll show you!"

A journalist, William English Walling, visited Springfield on the second day of rioting, August 16. He wrote an account for *The Independent Magazine*, September 3, 1908, entitled "The Race War in the North." Mob members that he interviewed offered justification for their rampage. They pointed to the two recent crimes, along with other criminality among blacks and politicians' pandering to black voters, "as sufficient explanation why six thousand peaceful and innocent negroes should be driven by the fear of their lives from a town where some of them have lived honorably for half a hundred years."

Moreover, Walling went on, "other thousands" of Springfield whites, including children, women, "and even prosperous business men in automobiles, calmly looked on" while the rioters proceeded to assault blacks, "to sack and plunder their houses and stores, and to burn and murder. . . ." Some whites nailed white handkerchiefs on the fronts of their homes, said news accounts, in order to alert the rioters to the race of the occupants, so that the mob would pass over their houses while beating up, and burning down the homes of, their black neighbors.

Walling concluded that most whites in Springfield supported the riots and the driving out of the blacks, whether they joined the mob themselves or not. "I talked to many of them the day after the massacre and found no difference of opinion on the question. 'Why, the niggers came to think they were as good as we are!' was the final justification offered, not once, but a dozen times." Alarmingly, Northern opinion, he felt, apparently agreed with them and thus did not question Springfield's move to chase away its longtime black residents. Northerners seemed to agree with the whites of Springfield that it was perfectly proper "to hold a whole race responsible for a handful of criminals, and to force it to an inferior place on the social scale."

White mobs had often rioted against blacks in Northern cities. What made this riot so shocking to Walling and other liberals was its occurrence in the city where Abraham Lincoln lay buried and where stood the only house he ever owned.

This riot was a symbol of the friction generated as blacks moved to Northern cities in the early twentieth century. This northward migration betokened the great shift in the black population that was to take place during the century from basically Southern and rural folk to urban ghetto dwellers divided evenly between North and South. This migration was only on a very small scale prior to World War I, but Northerners, unlike Southerners, unaccustomed to living amidst large numbers of blacks, felt suddenly inundated by even a small influx of additional blacks.

Booker T. Washington had counseled his people to stay in the South. He told them in the Atlanta Compromise speech of 1895 to " 'Cast down your bucket where you are'—cast it down in making friends in every manly way of the people of all races by whom we are surrounded. Cast it down in agriculture, mechanics, in commerce, in domestic service, and in the professions. And in this connection it is well to bear in mind that whatever other sins the South may be called to bear, when it comes to business, pure and simple, it is in the South that the Negro is given a man's chance in the commercial world. . . ."

Frederick Douglass likewise advised against a mass exodus from the South. In an article written in 1880 Douglass commented that "we cannot but regard the present agitation of an African exodus from the South as ill-timed, and in some respects hurtful." Blacks should not migrate, he felt, because an exodus "is a surrender" to the forces of oppression in the South. Responding to those who said it was not safe for blacks to remain in a hostile Southland, Douglass asserted that "the business of this nation is to protect its citizens where they are, not to transport them where they will not need protection." He also felt it important to keep the black vote concentrated, saying "In the South the Negro has at least the possibility of power; in the North he has no such possibility," because his votes will be scattered and diluted among too large a populace. Likewise, economic and climatic conditions did not favor an exodus, because too few blacks would have a chance to work in the North or be comfortable in its climate, or be prepared for the competitive life in an energetic, bustling region so different from the easygoing, indolent South in which they had grown up. He contended, therefore, that "the South is the best place for the Negro. Nowhere else is there for him a promise of a happier future." Pointing out that the black man had a monopoly on labor in the South and that the South was utterly dependent on Afro-Americans for both skilled and unskilled labor, Douglass suggested, somewhat unrealistically, that blacks could use the need for labor as a bargaining lever to coerce Southerners into better treatment of them. Douglass reasoned that "a little wisdom and firmness, will enable him to sell his labor there on terms more favorable to himself than he can elsewhere. . . . he can demand living prices with the certainty that the demand will be complied with. Exodus would deprive him of this advantage."

Many blacks ignored this advice from Booker T. Washington and Frederick Douglass. The rural South was conservative and backward, with poor facilities for education and organized recreation. Urban communities, both North and South, were more responsive to reform and progress and provided better schooling, better economic opportunity, and better public amusements. The glamour and excitement of city life and the chance for advancement there compensated for the friction with whites over jobs, housing, and public accommodations that occasionally erupted into race riots. Hence, there was a steady move toward the North and toward cities.

From the first census in 1790 through the eleventh census in 1890, nine-tenths of black Americans lived in the South. In 1790, the percentage of blacks in the South was 91.1, in 1860, 92.2, and in 1890, 90.3. Thereafter, there was a steady migration out of the South. In 1900, 89.7 percent of American blacks lived there, 85 percent in 1920, 75 percent in 1940, and 55 percent in 1960. Sharp increases in migration came during the world wars when availability of factory jobs proved a lure.

Various factors contributed to the outflow. Some of the earlier migration was partly motivated by political setbacks resulting from the overthrow of Carpetbag governments, the withdrawal of Federal troops, and, later, the disfranchisement movement. Black promoters also helped to push migration. Henry Adams of Shreveport, Louisiana, organized a Council on Migration in 1878 and claimed that 100,000 blacks were interested in migrating. Benjamin "Pap" Singleton, a native of Tennessee, organized an exodus to Kansas in 1879.

The basic motive for migration, however, was not persecution, but economic opportunity, a search for better land and a chance to rise from tenancy to ownership. So, much of the migration of the late nineteenth century was southwestward, toward richer, virgin soils. A number of all-black towns, such as Langston and Boley, were founded in Oklahoma at the turn of the century. In the twentieth century, some of the migration was encouraged by employers seeking cheap labor for use in factories, mines, railroads, and other enterprises. More of it was impelled by a quest for job opportunities in cities, especially Northern cities in wartime.

The shift from the country to the city was even more pronounced than the move from the South. In 1890, 80.2 percent of blacks lived in rural areas and only 19.8 percent resided in urban areas. In 1900, the respective figures were 77.3 percent rural and 22.7 percent urban. In 1910, however, 72.6 percent of blacks were rural residents, while 27.4 percent were urban dwellers. This trend continued throughout the century so that by the mid-1960s, 70 percent of blacks lived in cities.

In 1910, Washington, D.C., had more black residents than any other city, with the 94,446 blacks living there constituting 28.5 percent of the population. Four other cities also had more than 80,000 black residents: in New York, the 91,709 blacks were 1.9 percent of that city's vast population; New Orleans had 89,262 blacks (26.3 percent); Baltimore, 84,749 (15.2 percent); and Philadelphia, 84,459 (5.5 percent). Significantly, two of these five cities were Northern, two were along the border between North and South, and only one was in the Deep South.

Among the 43 cities that had 10,000 or more black residents in 1910, five had black majorities: Vicksburg, Mississippi, 57.9 percent; Charleston, South Carolina, 52.8 percent; Savannah, Georgia, 51.1 percent; Jacksonville, Florida, 50.8 percent; and Montgomery, Alabama, 50.7 percent. Of these five, Savannah had the largest number of blacks, 33,246.

Eight of the 43 cities having 10,000 or more black residents were Northern: New York; Philadelphia; Chicago (44,103); Pittsburgh (25,623); Indianapolis (21,816); Cincinnati (19,639); Boston (13,564); and Columbus, Ohio (12,739). Only in four of these Northern cities were blacks as much as five percent of the population: Indianapolis, 9.3 percent; Columbus, 7.0 percent; Philadelphia, 5.5 percent; and Cincinnati, 5.4 percent. When Northern whites rioted against blacks who were crowding them for jobs, housing, and recreation facilities, they did so less from the crush of numbers than from the novelty of suddenly being confronted with larger numbers of competitors from a single ethnic group than at any time since the waves of European immigration began filling up American cities in the 1820s.

Competing for employment in the North and South, black Americans found themselves generally relegated to the lowest paying occupations. Of the 3,073,164 blacks gainfully employed in 1890, 56.2 percent (1,728,325) were engaged in agricultural pursuits, with most of these (1,106,728) being poorly paid agricultural laborers. Another 31.1 percent (956,754) were engaged in domestic and personal service, working as servants, waiters, cooks, porters, launderers, and barbers. Thus, 87.3 percent of American Negroes were in the generally lower-paid agricultural and domestic service categories. Only 57 percent of white Americans were in these categories.

The census statistics listed three other categories of employment that were usually better paying. Only 12.7 percent of blacks were in these categories in 1890, contrasted to 43 percent of whites. Afro-Americans were distributed in these categories as follows: 208,374 (6.8 percent) were in manufacturing and mechanical pursuits; 145,717 (4.8 percent) were in trade and transportation; and only 33,994 (1.1 percent) were in the professions (medicine, law, teaching, etc.). Five percent of white Americans were engaged in the professions.

In the years from 1890 to 1910, more Negroes entered the higher paying categories, but still were far below the proportion of the white population in these categories. In 1910, the proportion of blacks in the two lower paying categories dropped to 81.5 percent, increasing in the three higher paying categories to 18.5 percent. The distribution of Negro workers in 1910 was: agricultural pursuits, 55.4 percent; domestic and personal service, 26.1 percent; manufacturing and mechanical, 10.6 percent; trade and transportation, 6.4 percent; and professions, 1.5 percent.

Since blacks were consigned to lower paying jobs, more black women and children had to go to work to help eke out a decent income for the family. In 1890, only 46.6 percent of all white Americans ten years of age or over were gainfully employed, but 57.6 percent of black Americans ten and over. At that time, 36 percent of the black women had jobs, but only 15 percent of white women. The fact that so many black women had to leave their homes and take jobs to help support their families had a deleterious impact on the Negro family, particularly in depriving black youngsters of the presence of the mother at home in their growing years.

Prejudice and discrimination contributed to the black man's low economic status. Gross inequalities in distribution of educational funds to his schools left him poorly prepared. In 1900, 30 percent of the school-age children in the South were black, yet they received only 13 percent ($4,675,504) of the school funds, while 87 percent of the funds ($31,755,320) went to the white schools, whose pupils constituted 70 percent of the South's school-age children. Yet, somehow blacks were expected to compete on equal terms with whites. Then they were derided for not keeping up, even though their education was so inadequately funded.

Discrimination in licensing craftsmen forced blacks to work as low-paid helpers even when they were as skilled as licensed white craftsmen. No matter how ably blacks performed, many employers gave preference to whites for promotion, thus discouraging black workers and depriving them of incentive to improve. Ignoring the antidiscrimination clause of the American Federation of Labor (A.F.L.) constitution, many craft unions excluded blacks. Since the local A.F.L. unions were virtually autonomous, the A.F.L. president, Samuel Gompers, was unable to bring about compliance with the national body's stand against discrimination in membership. Barred by labor unions, many blacks worked as strikebreakers, being brought in by employers when unions went out on strike. Since unions had done little to aid them, many blacks accepted the role of "scab" or strikebreaker, but this did not cause any friendlier feelings between black and white workers. Friction growing out of black workers taking jobs of white unionists out on strike contributed to some of the race riots of the day.

In spite of all the handicaps and difficulties, some blacks became outstanding. Some people viewed the success of such blacks as proof that the race did not labor under such severe handicaps as the protesters and agitators seemed to indicate. Instead, such persons felt, and Booker T. Washington said, blacks should stress their opportunities rather than their grievances. Viewed conversely, however, the fact that so few talented blacks could make names for themselves might be seen as an indication of the terrible toll taken by a system that crushed down so many more blacks who might likewise have forged ahead if not for the inequities present in American life. For every one who succeeded, there were countless others held back, not by any lack of talent or ability, but because motivation and aspiration were crushed. Also, their chances for training, education, and advancement were crippled from the outset in the separate but unequal institutions that developed in America. Those who did overcome were remarkable indeed, for they ran the race of life with almost insuperable handicaps while confronted with nearly insurmountable obstacles.

Paul Laurence Dunbar emerged in the late nineteenth century as the finest black writer since the time of Phillis Wheatley. Dunbar grew up in Dayton, Ohio, where his outstanding record in the integrated high school should have entitled him to the office job traditionally given the top graduate. Dunbar, being black, was offered a post running an elevator instead. Many black youngsters were crushed by this type of discrimination that told them no matter how well they did in competition with whites, they would be assigned to menial positions. The best was reserved for whites regardless of comparative abilities. Dunbar retained his ambition to be a writer, however, and he continued to write poetry. Finally, in 1896, while in his mid-twenties, he achieved fame with the publication of a volume of his verse, *Lyrics of Lowly Life*. He was especially noted for his dialect poetry, but also wrote fine works in standard English. His use of dialect in some of his poems showed a reaching back toward the roots of Negro experience in the poverty pockets of the rural South and Northern ghettoes. This was a new departure in black awareness. Dunbar also wrote short stories and novels and several other volumes of verse before he passed away in 1906 while in his mid-thirties.

Another notable writer of this time was Charles Waddell Chesnutt, the first black writer to receive serious critical attention and acclaim for his fiction. Chesnutt, like Dunbar, was a native of Ohio. But Chesnutt's parents returned to their native North Carolina after the youngster's early years were spent in Cleveland. In North Carolina, Chesnutt taught school and served as principal of what later became Fayetteville State College. Moving North, he became a court stenographer, studied law, and was later one of the top lawyers in Cleveland. At the same time, he continued to write stories, which began appearing in newspapers and magazines in the 1880s. In 1899, he published two collections of his short stories, *The Conjure Woman*, a collection of tales told in dialect, and *The Wife of His Youth and Other Stories*, a collection written in standard English. From 1900 to 1905, he published three novels: *The House Behind the Cedars, The Marrow of Tradition,* and *The Colonel's Dream.* Thereafter, he abandoned his literary career and returned to the law practice that he had given up to concentrate on his writing. Chesnutt's success as a writer paved the way for the stories and novels of the many twentieth-century black fiction writers. He was a much better short-story writer than novelist, however.

Henry O. Tanner became a famed painter, the first black artist to make a living solely from his art. Tanner's father was a notable religious leader, Bishop Benjamin Tucker Tanner, who wanted his son to follow in his footsteps, but did not discourage him when the youngster displayed an interest in art instead of religion. The family moved from Pittsburgh, where Tanner was born, to Philadelphia, where he studied with the well-known artist Thomas Eakins. Unable to gain sufficient support in this country, as was the case with most artists in a materialistically inclined America then, Tanner moved to Paris. Here he changed from the genre type of painting that produced such early masterpieces as *The Banjo Lesson.* Now, he concentrated especially on religious paintings, such as *The Annunciation, Flight to Egypt, Christ and Nicodemus, Daniel in the Lion's Den,* and *The Resurrection of Lazarus.* Tanner became a big success in Europe, receiving many awards, including the French Legion of Honor. Many museums in Europe and America bought his paintings. Tanner was an inspiration to many black artists who went to Europe to study with him in his studio in Paris where he lived until he passed away in 1937.

One aspect of American life to which blacks contributed in much larger numbers and much more meaningfully than most Americans realize was the cattle frontier in the American West. Of the 40,000 cowboys who rode the range in the heyday of the cowboy, 5,000 were black. Since one out of every eight cowboys was black, but only one man in ten in the population as a whole, they were more heavily represented in the saddle than their proportion in the population. Yet this story has been so generally neglected that most Americans are astounded to learn that there was such a thing as a black cowboy. There was at least one black in most outfits that rode the range. Often blacks were hostlers, wranglers, and cooks. But they also rode the range with the best.

Bronco Sam was a notable black bronco buster who was seldom excelled in the difficult task of breaking wild mustangs. Bob Lemmons was never matched in his ability to capture whole herds of mustangs single-handed. Lemmons would go out alone, follow the herd until it became accustomed to him, move in with the horses, become their leader, and lead them into a corral. Thornt Biggs rose to the position of top hand (foreman over all the cowboys) on a major ranch, an eminence that only a few black cowboys were permitted to attain.

Some of the black cowboys were quite colorful. Nat Love wrote a romanticized autobiography of his days riding the range. His writing was as well read as the most popular dime novels of the day. "Cherokee Bill" Goldsby was a bad man who was part Indian and part Negro. He was feared both for his fast draw with a gun and for his romantic escapades that attracted many women. So feared was he as a gunman that one town passed an ordinance making it a crime for anyone to molest him. They feared not only for the life of the unwary citizen who provoked him, but also for the sheriff who would have to go after him and risk an untimely end. Finally, as with all bad men, Cherokee Bill met his end long before his thirtieth birthday, but not before he had killed more than twenty men.

The most famous of the black cowboys was a spectacular rodeo performer named Bill Pickett. He popularized the sport of bulldogging, leaping on a racing steer from horseback and wrestling it to the ground. He introduced refinements into the art, making him the greatest rodeo performer of his day. After leaping from the horse and seizing the steer's horns with his hands, he would reach up and clamp his strong teeth on the steer's upper lip. Then he would release his hands and let them fly loose so that all spectators in the arena could see that he was holding on only with his teeth. Digging in his feet and twisting down sharply with his teeth, he would then throw the steer. He performed this astounding feat before thousands of fans in Madison Square Garden and before crowned heads of Europe. He overshadowed two other cowboys in the performing group for which he rode, trick roper Will Rogers, who went on to great fame as a humorist, and trick rider Tom Mix, who went on to fame as a movie cowboy.

Blacks were also notable in medical science. Dr. Daniel Hale

Williams was a native of Pennsylvania and a graduate of Northwestern University Medical School. In 1891 he founded Provident Hospital in Chicago, the first hospital in America built, financed, and run by blacks. His hospital was interracial, with 35 whites among its first 189 patients. There, in July, 1893, he performed the unheard-of feat of "sewing up a man's heart." A black laborer, James Cornish, was brought to the hospital on July 9 with a wound suffered in a fight. He went into shock, indicating that the stab in the chest had penetrated to his heart. Medical authorities and textbooks of that day counseled merely rest, cold, and opium, leaving the body to heal itself. A physician was not supposed to attempt to repair the damage directly, but Dr. Dan Williams dared to do so. Without the special instruments, established techniques, and precedents of today's heart surgery, Dr. Williams proceeded to open the man's chest where he found an artery damaged, an inch-long cut in the pericardium, the sac surrounding the heart, and a tenth of an inch penetration into the heart itself. Dr. Williams repaired the damage, sewing up the pericardium. The patient recovered and was soon back at his activities as if he had never been stabbed. Newspapers in Chicago played up the operation and Dr. Williams became widely hailed as the first heart surgeon in the world. It later developed that a similar, but less complex, operation had been performed a little earlier, but was not written up then, so that neither Dr. Williams nor the public knew about it. The success of today's heart surgery and heart transplants can be traced back to the beginning steps taken by this black surgeon.

Another notable black scientist was Ernest E. Just, who earned a Ph.D. degree from the University of Chicago and who taught at Howard University in Washington, D.C. Just spent his summers doing research at the Woods Hole Marine Biological Laboratories. He published two books and sixty scientific papers and was elected vice president of the American Zoological Society.

Several blacks made important discoveries. Jan Matzeliger invented the shoe lasting machine that mechanized that industry. Granville Woods was a successful inventor with many patents. Among other things, he developed the induction telegraph system that made it possible to communicate with moving trains efficiently. Matthew Henson was an explorer who was a friend and companion of Robert Peary, exploring with him for several decades. In 1909 Henson shared the discovery of the North Pole with Peary.

From the last century on, a numbers of blacks have made names for themselves in sports. Nine of the first thirteen Kentucky Derby races were won by black jockeys. Isaac Murphy, a black rider who was one of the greatest jockeys of all time, was the first ever to win the Kentucky Derby twice in a row and the first to ever be the winning jockey three times. He won the race in 1884, 1890, and 1891. When Walter Camp began picking All-American football teams late in the nineteenth century, he included a black football player among his early selections. This was William Henry Lewis, who came from Portsmouth, Virginia, and graduated from Virginia State College. He played football there and then went on to play for Amherst College where he was captain of the team while earning another bachelor's degree. He subsequently played center on the Harvard University football team while going to law school. In those days, there was no limit to the years of player eligibility, and any student, including graduate students, could play. He made All-American in 1892 and 1893 while playing for Harvard. George "Little Chocolate" Dixon became world bantamweight and featherweight champion, and Joe Gans became lightweight boxing champion. But the most famed Negro athlete early in the century was Jack Johnson. Johnson came out of Texas and proved to be one of the greatest prizefighters of all time. He combined the speed and grace of a lightweight with the devastating punch of a heavyweight. He became world heavyweight boxing champion in 1908 and held the title until 1915. Distressed by his arrogance, his high living, and his white wives, America launched a search for a "white hope" who would supplant Johnson. In a sport that has now declined considerably in spectator interest, a black man once reigned supreme. He was Marshall W. "Major" Taylor, who for ten years was the American and world bicycle sprint champion.

There were many black capitalists at this time. Charles Clinton Spaulding went to work in the late 1890s for the North Carolina Mutual Life Insurance Company, a black concern in Durham of which his uncle was a co-founder. Beginning as the sole employee, Spaulding built the business into the largest enterprise owned and run by American blacks. When he passed away in the early 1950s, the company had $33,000,000 in assets and $165,000,000 in policies in force. Madame C. J. Walker had little formal schooling, but she proved adept at business. She developed hair grooming and cosmetic preparations, becoming a millionaire. Her large cosmetics factory in Indianapolis made her one of the very few American women, white or black, who made a fortune of a million dollars on her own. Robert Abbott, Carl Murphy, and Robert Vann were successful newspaper publishers, founding in the late nineteenth and early twentieth century three of the most important and prosperous Negro newspapers, the Chicago *Defender*, the *Afro-American* (of Baltimore), and the Pittsburgh *Courier*, respectively. These newspapers had a wide circulation beyond their original cities, with the *Afro* and *Courier* publishing editions in many different cities. Maggie Lena Walker was a pioneering black banker in Richmond, Virginia.

James Bland was a great minstrel performer who composed some of America's favorite songs, including "Oh, Dem Golden Slippers," "Carry Me Back to Old Virginny," and "In the Evening by the Moonlight." His pseudo-spirituals caused him to be termed the "Black Stephen Foster." The true spirituals, composed by black folk in slavery times, were performed widely by the Fisk University Jubilee Singers in concert tours that both helped to save the school financially and also helped to rescue the spirituals from being lost forever. The outstanding singer-composer Harry T. Burleigh arranged many spirituals. He studied with the great Czech composer, Antonín Dvořák, and assisted Dvořák with the well-known Symphony No. 5 ("From the New World"), that incorporates a spiritual-like melody that became a popular song, "Going Home."

Minstrelsy had been America's most popular entertainment for the last two-thirds of the nineteenth century. Near the century's end, talented black musicians and performers took the lead in helping to transform minstrelsy into a new form. The minstrel show generally had become static with its set patterns. Beginning in the early 1890s, such all-Negro shows as *Creole Show, Octoroons, Oriental America,* and *A Trip to Coontown* broke from the traditional mold by introducing such innovations as an attractive line of black women dancers, a talented singing chorus, concert singers, closing operatic medley, plot, continuity, and characterization. Among the talented black composers, directors, and lyricists were Bob Cole, Will Marion Cook, and J. Rosamond Johnson. Such shows as *Clorindy: The Origin of the Cakewalk* introduced ragtime rhythms on stage and dances developed by black youngsters. The great comedian, Bert Williams, starred in such shows as *In Dahomey* and *Abyssinia* before going on to become the only black star of Ziegfeld's *Follies*. The black shows were the beginnings of the path toward America's present-day gift to the world of entertainment, the musical comedy.

Having proved their talents, many blacks questioned Booker T. Washington's emphasis on industrial education and his retreat from demands for full equality. Increasing opposition to his Atlanta Compromise developed.

12

The Niagara Movement, NAACP, and World War I
1905–1921

Before daybreak on a summer day in 1906, the delegates at the Niagara Movement's second annual conference assembled on the heights above Harpers Ferry. In reverent silence, and shoeless, a hundred dedicated fighters for justice wended their way to an open field. The solemn procession stopped before a small brick building, the old fire engine house that had been reerected in the field.

The delegates stood before this "fort" in which John Brown had made his final stand in his raid on Harpers Ferry, Virginia (now in West Virginia), in October, 1859. There they burst into the strains of the "Battle Hymn of the Republic" while the sun's dawning rays streamed majestically upon their open-air cathedral. The date was August 18, 1906, the closing session of their four-day meeting at Storer College, a black school in Harpers Ferry, West Virginia. They designated this day as John Brown's Day.

Their leader, William Edward Burghardt Du Bois, in his book, *Dusk of Dawn* (1940), wrote years later about the events of that early morning: "we met . . . at Harper's [sic] Ferry, the scene of John Brown's raid, and had in significance if not numbers one of the greatest meetings that American Negroes have ever held. We made pilgrimage at dawn bare-footed to the scene of Brown's martyrdom and we talked some of the plainest English that has been given voice to by black men in America."

This plain English was in the form of a manifesto that a less radical Negro leader, Kelly Miller, derisively labeled "a wild and frantic shriek." In the preamble of the Harpers Ferry resolutions, Du Bois complained that "the work of the Negro hater has flourished. . . the defenders of the rights of American citizens have retreated. The work of stealing the black man's ballot has progressed. Discrimination in travel and public accommodations has . . . spread." Rather than silently acquiescing to such conditions in the hope of making advances along economic lines, which was the tack taken by Booker T. Washington, Du Bois spoke out boldly against these injustices. The preamble continued, in words written by Du Bois:

> Against this the Niagara Movement eternally protests. We will not be satisfied to take one jot or tittle less than our full manhood rights. We claim for ourselves every single right that belongs to a freeborn American, political, civil, and social; and until we get these rights we will never cease to protest and assail the ears of America.

Thus spoke one group of black Americans in 1906.

This Niagara Movement adopted a much more militant tone than had Booker T. Washington, who continued to dominate the scene until 1915. This movement, composed primarily of black Northern intellectuals, assembled at places hallowed by the militant antislavery crusade of the antebellum era. They first met in 1905 at Niagara where fugitive slaves, fleeing slavecatchers who hunted them under the Federal fugitive act of 1850, used to cross the United States' border into safety in Canada. The second meeting was at Harpers Ferry, made sacred to the abolitionist-minded by the courageous stand and heroic sacrifice of John Brown. In 1907, the Niagara Movement assembled in Faneuil Hall in Boston, Massachusetts, the scene of numerous abolitionist rallies. And in 1908 they met at Oberlin, Ohio, where the Reverend Theodore Weld had led the Midwestern branch of the abolitionist movement, making Oberlin College a center of antislavery agitation and activity.

The Niagara Movement represented the beginnings of organized opposition to the Atlanta Compromise. Rejecting Booker T. Washington's moderate stand, this new movement resumed the militant protest tactics of Frederick Douglass. But as a separate movement of black radicals, it was shortlived, for it soon merged into a new civil rights organization of liberal whites and blacks, the National Association for the Advancement of Colored People (NAACP).

On September 18, 1895, seven months after the death of Douglass, who had led blacks militantly since the 1840s, Washington made his Atlanta Compromise speech. In this speech, he indicated willingness to cease the struggle for civil rights for the time being. He hoped that blacks would thereby gain better opportunity to make such progress economically that whites would eventually restore their rights. In his speech, he proclaimed optimistically that "No race that has anything to contribute to the markets of the world is long in any degree ostracized." Six years after the Atlanta Speech, Booker T. Washington expanded on these ideas in his autobiography, *Up from Slavery* (1901). He wrote:

> My own belief is . . . that the time will come when the Negro in the South will be accorded all the political rights which his ability, character, and material possessions entitle him to. . . . there is something in human nature which we cannot blot out, which makes one man, in the end, recognize and reward merit in another, regardless of colour or race. I believe it is the duty of the Negro . . . to deport himself modestly in regard to political claims, depending upon the slow but sure influences that proceed from the possession of property, intelligence, and high character for the full recognition of his political rights. I think that the according of the full exercise of political rights is going to be a matter of natural, slow growth, not an over-night, gourd-vine affair.

Booker T. Washington's references to future equality were so muted, however, that white Americans, especially Southerners, accepted his tactical accommodation as the final solution of the problem. As far as whites were concerned, this new leader had accepted for blacks permanent second-class citizenship, including disfranchisement and segregation. Whites also regarded this black spokesman as assenting to blacks being relegated eternally to menial roles as laborers and servants for white America. Whites, in short, heard what they wanted to hear and distorted the full meaning of his compromise.

Thus, blacks would become invisible people, a servile class that did the dirty work, but did not compete for the better jobs, did not exercise political power, and did not share equally in the use of public accommodations. The endless strife over slavery from the 1830s to 1860s and over civil rights for blacks from the 1860s to

1890s would cease. White Americans, North and South, could now reunite without the black man as a bone of contention between them. National unity would be built on black subjugation. Little wonder then that white America accepted Booker T. Washington as the only black spokesman that whites would heed from 1895 until he passed away in 1915.

Some blacks opposed Washington's Atlanta Compromise from the outset. Professor John Hope (1868–1936) of Roger Williams University, a small black institution at Nashville, Tennessee, was in the audience when Washington spoke. Addressing the black debating society in Nashville on February 22, 1896, he repudiated the Compromise. Hope said:

> If we are not striving for equality, in heaven's name for what are we living? I regard it as cowardly and dishonest for any of our colored men to tell white people or colored people that we are not struggling for equality. I want equality. Nothing less. . . . Now, catch your breath, for I am going to use an adjective: I am going to say we demand social equality. In this republic we shall be less than freemen, if we have a whit less than that which thrift, education, and honor afford other freemen. . . . Why build a wall to keep me out? I am no wild beast, nor am I an unclean thing.

Hope was only an obscure young professor then, a recent graduate (1894) of Brown University. His father was a Scotsman who emigrated to New York, prospered in business, and then settled in Augusta, Georgia, where he fell in love with a beautiful mulatto, Fanny Butts. They had to go North to marry because Georgia forbade miscegenation, but they lived unmolested in Augusta thereafter because of James Hope's eminence. Growing up in this interracial household, devoted to both parents, and fair enough to easily pass for white, John Hope nonetheless proudly proclaimed himself a member of his mother's race.

In 1898, Hope joined the faculty of Atlanta Baptist College, becoming its president in June, 1906. He was the first black man to head one of the black colleges run by such great missionary boards as the American Baptist Home Mission Society and the American Missionary Association (Congregational). Yet, he was the only black college president bold enough to join the Niagara Movement, having been one of those walking barefooted with Du Bois to Brown's shrine at Harpers Ferry.

Hope continued as president of Morehouse College (as the school was renamed in 1913) until it affiliated with Atlanta University and Spelman College in 1929. He was instrumental in forming this great Atlanta System of black colleges (Clark University and Morris Brown College joined later). From 1929 to 1936, Hope served as the first president of the new, larger Atlanta University. One of the greatest of the black educators, Hope stressed liberal arts training while Booker T. Washington, also a great educator, emphasized manual training.

Few black educators dared defy Washington's leadership as Hope did. In *Dusk of Dawn*, Du Bois analyzed Washington's power, citing "the rise at Tuskegee Institute, and centering around Booker T. Washington, of what I may call the Tuskegee Machine." Du Bois pointed out that under Presidents Roosevelt and Taft, from 1901 to 1913, Washington was "the political referee in all Federal appointments or action taken with reference to the Negro. . . ."

Not only Presidents, but governors, Congressmen, and philanthropists consulted Washington before making any appointments of blacks or donations to black institutions. He served on the boards of the major foundations concerned with black education, the Slater Fund, Phelps Stokes Fund, and Anna T. Jeanes Fund. "After a time," Du Bois explained, "almost no Negro institution could collect funds without the recommendation or acquiescence of Mr. Washington." To displease him could dry up the funds vital to a black college's survival.

Du Bois further charged that Northern capitalists, often descendants of abolitionists, hoped to develop a large force of trained blacks as a counterweight to labor union demands and the thrust of white workers for wage increases. Such plans might be disrupted by black colleges offering a liberal-arts-oriented higher education. Washington's philosophy of industrial education fitted so well with the plans of these capitalists that they "proposed by building up his prestige and power to control the Negro group," charged Du Bois. "The Negro intelligentsia was to be suppressed and hammered into conformity."

Washington's Tuskegee Machine influenced black newspapers

and magazines. The Tuskegee News Bureau, directed by Emmett J. Scott, sent out a flood of news releases and canned editorials. By placing or withholding ads, the well-endowed Tuskegee clique persuaded many black editors, most of whose publications were in financial straits, to carry these materials favorable to Washington's viewpoint. Most black newspapers and magazines had a precarious financial existence because they did not get very much of the advertising dollar. Even firms that derived much of their income from black ghettoes seldom bothered advertising in black newspapers and magazines, placing their ads instead in the publications put out by their fellow whites. Thus, Tuskegee ads could make a difference between life and death for some black publications. These subsidies sometimes took the form of Tuskegee buying up a large number of copies of a particular issue of a publication for distribution, bringing in extra funds that were sorely needed by the editor-publisher to keep going. Moreover, the Tuskegee cabal secretly purchased several black periodicals, controlling them unbeknownst to the public.

W. E. B. Du Bois, the leading foe of this Tuskegee Machine, was born in 1868 in Great Barrington, Massachusetts, a town of 5,000 with only 50 black residents. He was the top student in the town's high school. Normally, the top graduate was sent to such leading New England institutions as Amherst College or Williams College. Du Bois, however, was shipped off to a black liberal arts college in Nashville, Tennessee, Fisk University, one of the schools founded after the Civil War by the American Missionary Association. In 1888, Du Bois graduated from Fisk. Subsequently studying at Harvard University and in Germany, he received the Ph.D. degree from Harvard in 1895. Published in 1896, his dissertation, *The Suppression of the African Slave-Trade to the United States of America, 1638–1870,* became the first volume in the Harvard Historical Studies.

Sensitive to the racial rebuffs he experienced despite his brilliant record, Du Bois became aloof, arrogant, and antagonistic. He taught at Wilberforce University for two years. Then he spent fifteen months on the faculty of the University of Pennsylvania while making a pioneering sociological study, published in 1899 as *The Philadelphia Negro: A Social Study.* From 1897 to 1910, he taught sociology at Atlanta University, where he also published an annual series of works on the black man in America. Known as the Atlanta University Publications, these lengthy pamphlets studied Negro education, family life, crime, employment, health, etc. Du Bois's eventual opposition to Booker T. Washington imperiled the school's source of funds, but the white president of Atlanta University, Horace Bumstead, stood by him.

Until 1903, Du Bois did not challenge Washington's Atlanta Compromise of 1895. An admirer of Frederick Douglass, he viewed Washington as sharing Douglass's long-range goals even though employing moderate tactics. But Du Bois became increasingly irritated at the Tuskegee Machine, recalling that "above all I resented the practical buying up of the Negro press and choking off of even mild and reasonable opposition to Mr. Washington in both the Negro press and the white."

The early leadership of the opposition to Washington was taken by such newspaper editors as Harry Smith of the Cleveland *Gazette* and William Monroe Trotter of Boston. The vindictive attack of the Tuskegee Machine on Trotter over the "Boston Riot" of 1903 helped to crystallize Du Bois's opposition to Booker T. Washington.

William Monroe Trotter (1872–1934) was a brilliant Northern intellectual who became the first black Phi Beta Kappa at Harvard University, where he graduated in 1895, while Du Bois was a graduate student there. In 1901 Trotter founded the Boston *Guardian,* soon making it the leading forum of opposition to the accommodationist stand taken by Booker T. Washington. Trotter hammered away at Washington, saying of him "what man is a worse enemy to a race than a leader who looks with equanimity on the disfranchisement of his race in a country where other races have universal suffrage by constitutions that make one rule for his race and another for the dominant race. . . ." Trotter denounced the black politicians who through fear of losing their posts failed to speak out against Washington's "traitorous" surrender of the rights of black men. In an editorial in December, 1902, Trotter said: "silence is tantamount to being virtually an accomplice in the treasonable act of this Benedict Arnold of the Negro race. O, for a black Patrick Henry to save his people from this stigma of cowardice. . . ."

On July 30, 1903, when Washington tried to address a rally at the A.M.E. church in Boston, Trotter and his followers created a disturbance. Trotter interrupted Washington by standing on a chair and hurling such accusatory questions at him as: "Is the rope and torch all the race is to get under your leadership?" Forewarned of the impending disturbance by the spies he infiltrated into the camps of his opposition, Washington and his supporters were prepared. They had police on hand in advance so that Trotter was arrested and order restored. Then, they vindictively instituted a libel suit against Trotter and tried to get Trotter's co-editor, George W. Forbes, fired from his job in the Boston public library system.

The handling of Trotter in this Boston "riot" drove Du Bois firmly into the camp of the opposition to Washington. Earlier that year, he had made his first public criticism of Washington's leadership. In his essay, "Of Mr. Booker T. Washington and Others," published in his book, *The Souls of Black Folk* (1903), Du Bois pointed out that "the hushing of the criticism of honest opponents is a dangerous thing. It leads some of the best of the critics to unfortunate silence and paralysis of effort, and others to burst into speech so passionately and intemperately as to lose listeners. Honest and earnest criticism . . . is the soul of democracy and the safeguard of modern society."

Pointing to the setbacks resulting from Washington's temporary abandonment of black political power, civil rights, and higher education, Du Bois's essay rhetorically asked, "Is it possible, and probable, that nine millions of [black] men can make effective progress in economic lines if they are deprived of political rights, made a servile caste, and allowed only the most meagre chance for developing their exceptional men? If history and reason give any distinct answer to these questions, it is an emphatic No."

Du Bois pointed out in his essay that Washington was striving to develop artisans and property owners among blacks, "but it is utterly impossible, under modern competitive methods, for workingmen and property-owners to defend their rights and exist without the right of suffrage." He contended that Washington expected and advised black men to develop thrift and self-respect, "but at the same time counsels a silent submission to civic inferiority such as is bound to sap the manhood of any race in the long run."

Du Bois resented Washington's emphasis on training blacks in craft skills, some already obsolete, to the neglect of liberally educating the most talented persons of the race. In an article he wrote in 1903 entitled "The Talented Tenth," Du Bois outlined his ideas of education in contrast to the thoughts of Booker T. Washington on what schooling was best for the black man. Du Bois said:

> The Negro race, like all races, is going to be saved by its exceptional men. The problem of education, then, among Negroes must first of all deal with the Talented Tenth; it is the problem of developing the Best of this race that they may guide the Mass. . . . If we make money the object of man-training, we shall develop money-makers but not necessarily men; if we make technical skill the object of education, we may possess artisans but not, in nature, men. Men we shall have only as we make manhood the object of the work of the schools—intelligence, broad sympathy, knowledge of the world that was and is, and of the relation of men to it—this is the curriculum of that Higher Education which must underlie true life.

Du Bois considered himself "an earnest advocate of manual training and trade teaching for black boys, and for white boys, too." Next to the development of black colleges, he considered the development of industrial education for blacks the most important addition to education of blacks since the Civil War. Although he acknowledged the need for manual and craft training for the masses, he insisted on the need of enough men trained in liberal arts college "to leaven the lump, to inspire the masses, to raise the Talented Tenth to leadership. . . ."

Rejecting the counsels of Booker T. Washington concerning voting rights, segregation, and education of blacks, Du Bois issued a call in his book, *The Souls of Black Folk,* for blacks to start fighting again for the things Washington seemed all too willing to surrender tactically. Thus, Du Bois made three demands: (1) "The right to vote"; (2) "Civic equality"; and (3) "The education of youth according to ability."

These basic demands were espoused by the new organization that Du Bois and Trotter formed, the Niagara Movement. A Declaration of Principles incorporating these demands was adopted by the thirty black men who met, at the call of Du Bois and Trotter, in the first Niagara Conference in July, 1905. Encountering hotel discrimination, they met on the Canadian side of the border, at Niagara in Canada, rather than Niagara, New York, where they had planned to meet. The Declaration of Principles adopted there stressed "We believe in manhood suffrage" and also expressed a belief that "all American citizens have the right to equal treatment in places of public accommodation. . . ." The Declaration protested "the denial of equal opportunities to us in economic life" pointing out that "everywhere American prejudice, helped often by iniquitous laws, is making it more difficult for Negro Americans to earn a decent living." The Declaration put the Niagara Movement firmly on record in favor of protest rather than Booker T. Washington's accommodationist stance:

> We refuse to allow the impression to remain that the Negro-American assents to inferiority, is submissive under oppression and apologetic before insults. Through helplessness we may submit, but the voice of protest of ten million Americans must never cease to assail the ears of their fellows, so long as America is unjust.

Du Bois's Niagara Declaration, unlike Washington's Atlanta Compromise, struck boldly at segregation, labeling racial discrimination "barbarous" and a relic of "unreasoning human savagery. . . ." Without naming him, they castigated Washington's leadership, saying the black man in America "needs leadership and is given cowardice and apology. . . ." The sentiment of the black intellectuals was summed up in the statement in the Declaration that "Persistent manly agitation is the way to liberty, and toward this goal the Niagara Movement has started and asks the co-operation of all men of all races."

Although Du Bois and Trotter had called the meeting and drafted this declaration, they finally quarreled and split in 1907, more over personality differences than over policy. The Niagara Movement was the first national organization of militant blacks, but its membership remained small and its financial status was precarious. The Tuskegee Machine infiltrated spies, blocked news coverage, and inspired editorials assailing these radicals. Help was needed.

The race riot of 1908 in Springfield, Illinois, shocked liberal Americans and brought the needed help. William English Walling's article on the riot asked "what large and powerful body of citizens is ready to come to their aid?" A small group of whites, including journalist Walling, social worker Mary White Ovington, and New York *Evening Post* editor Oswald Garrison Villard (grandson of the abolitionist) drafted a call for a meeting to form an organization to help blacks to secure their rights. The call was signed by prominent whites and blacks, including Du Bois. It was issued on February 12, 1909, the centennial of Abraham Lincoln's birth. The call stated that "If Mr. Lincoln could revisit this country in the flesh, he would be disheartened and discouraged" to see blacks segregated, disfranchised, and brutally assaulted.

At the meeting held in New York late in May, 1909, in response to this call, a National Negro Committee was set up. At the second annual conference in May, 1910, it changed its name to the National Association for the Advancement of Colored People (NAACP). The NAACP was dedicated to securing justice, equality of treatment, and integration of blacks into the mainstream of American life. One of its primary goals was "To promote equality of rights and eradicate caste or race prejudice among the citizens of the United States. . . ." The organization also was determined to aid blacks in "securing justice in the courts, education for their children, employment according to their ability, and complete equality before the law."

Du Bois left Atlanta University in 1910 to serve for nearly a quarter of a century, until 1934, as the Director of Publicity and Research for the NAACP. He founded the organization's major publication, *The Crisis,* and rapidly built up this monthly periodical until it had a circulation of more than 100,000. Other than Du Bois, all the officers of the new organization were white. James Weldon Johnson, a notable black poet, became an officer in 1917, when he was made Field Secretary of the NAACP, soon moving up to the position of Executive Secretary. Johnson served as Executive Secretary until 1931 and was followed by Walter White (1931–1955) and Roy Wilkins, since 1955, keeping that key administrative leadership position in the hands of black persons for almost all of the organization's history. Most of the members of the Niagara

Movement came into the NAACP with Du Bois. Some militants, like Trotter, refused to join because they distrusted whites.

The NAACP tactics included publicity, protest, and law suits. Compared to the Atlanta Compromise approach, it was considered a radical, militant group. Its first victory came in Guinn v. United States, in June, 1915, when the Supreme Court ruled the grandfather clause unconstitutional. The legal redress committee of the NAACP was headed by a prominent white lawyer, Arthur Spingarn, who was aided by teams of able black and white lawyers, including the outstanding white attorney, Moorfield Storey of Boston, who was the first President of the NAACP. In addition to the law suits, the NAACP sought Federal laws against lynching, led picketing and protest against the inflammatory, racist film *Birth of a Nation*, and organized a massive protest parade in New York City in 1917 as a protest against assaults on blacks in the East St. Louis race riot that year. Other white officers at the start included Walling as chairman of the Executive Committee and Villard as disbursing treasurer.

Booker T. Washington opposed and fought against the NAACP. He considered its approach too much centered on protest and agitation rather than finding ways to get along with Southern whites. Privately, Washington had battled against disfranchisement and had secretly financed law suits against segregation, but publicly he maintained his submissive stance. As long as he lived, he dominated the racial question, having much readier access to the ears of white America than did the "dangerously radical" NAACP. He passed away in November, 1915, clearing the way for the NAACP to become the dominant voice. With Washington gone and the Tuskegee Machine's stifling grip loosened, blacks were more free to resume militancy.

World War I proved to be an opportunity and a disappointment for blacks in America. When President Woodrow Wilson proclaimed the war a crusade to make the world safe for democracy, the hopes of blacks were raised. In an editorial in *The Crisis* in 1918, Du Bois urged his people: "Let us, while this war lasts, forget our special grievances and close ranks shoulder to shoulder with our own fellow citizens. . . ."

Four hundred thousand blacks served in the army and navy in

World War I. The government refused to provide training for black officers, however. Determined protest and pressure by the NAACP resulted in the army agreeing to set up officer training camps, but on a separate, segregated basis. The highest ranking black man in the regular army, Colonel Charles Young, the first full colonel among black Americans, was put out of the service on grounds of "health" on the eve of America's entrance into the war. He protested, riding horseback from Wilberforce, Ohio, to Washington, D.C., and back, to prove his physical fitness. Nonetheless, this West Pointer who had served with distinction with the black regular army units formed after the Civil War (9th and 10th Cavalry, and 24th and 25th Infantry) was not allowed to continue serving. Many blacks suspected this was to keep him from advancing to general. Henry Johnson and Needham Roberts were heroes who by themselves fought off a large German raiding party trying to capture them in fierce hand-to-hand combat. They received the highest award given by France for exceptional bravery in combat, the Croix de Guerre. Their own government failed to award them the Congressional Medal of Honor. A black regiment, the 369th Infantry from New York City, was on the front line for a longer span of time in this war than any other American outfit.

During the war, half a million blacks emigrated northward to better paying wartime factory jobs. But the democracy they had fought for in the war eluded them. They were dismayed at race riots in wartime at such places as East St. Louis, in 1917, and in the postwar period at such places as Chicago in 1919. The Wilson Administration introduced segregation into Federal facilities in Washington, D.C., that had long been integrated. President Wilson was Southern born and reared and he had married a Southern woman. He brought many Southern Democrats to office with him. Under this leadership a much more Southern climate was introduced into the nation's capital.

The dejected blacks were ripe for the militant program of Marcus Garvey, a program that would stress race pride.

13

UNIA, Harlem Renaissance, and the New Deal

1920–1940

The historic hall in New York City was jammed with one of the largest crowds in its history. Marcus Garvey, leader of the Universal Negro Improvement Association (UNIA), proclaimed to the gathering that there were "Twenty-five thousand Negro delegates assembled in Madison Square Garden in mass meeting, representing 400,000,000 Negroes of the world. . . ." On this night of August 2, 1920, the enthusiastic crowd waved the black, green, and crimson banners of the UNIA, stood to sing their anthem, "Ethiopia, Thou Land of Our Fathers," to the accompaniment of three massed bands, and applauded various entertainers for two hours while waiting to hear their leader.

"When Garvey finally stepped forward to speak, clad in a richly colored academic cap and gown of purple, green, and gold," wrote historian E. David Cronon in his book, *Black Moses: The Story of Marcus Garvey and the Universal Negro Improvement Association,* "he received a tumultuous ovation that lasted for fully five minutes." This rally at the original Madison Square Garden on East 26th Street and Madison Avenue was the highlight of an impressive, month-long convention that made America aware that the Garvey movement was a powerful force among black people.

The convention began on Sunday, August 1, with religious services and a silent march through Harlem. On Monday afternoon, as a prelude to the mass meeting at the Garden, the UNIA paraded down Lenox Avenue in splendor, including its African Legion marching in precision in dark blue uniforms with red trouser stripes, its Black Cross nurses clad in white, its juvenile auxiliary, the convention delegates, and bands and choristers.

Now the 25,000 blacks, gathered in Madison Square Garden in response to the call Garvey had issued for an international convention of dark people, listened intently as the short, stocky, very dark, dynamic, and magnetic orator spoke. "We are the descendants of a suffering people," he said, "determined to suffer no longer." The leader of the first great mass movement among American blacks went on: "We shall now organize to plant the banner of freedom on the great continent of Africa." This Black Moses then told his cheering audience: "We do not desire what has belonged to others. . . . If Europe is for the Europeans, then Africa shall be for the black people of the world. . . . The other races have countries of their own and it is time for the 400,000,000 Negroes to claim Africa for themselves."

Garvey was a black nationalist. He called for a separate homeland in which blacks could take pride. He preached a chauvinistic glorification of blackness. Black Zionism was not new in America, but never before had it attracted such a mass following.

In 1815, Paul Cuffe, a black man of Massachusetts who owned a fleet of sailing vessels, carried thirty-eight black Americans back to Africa. This was the first batch of blacks repatriated from the United States by an American. Earlier, the British had carried away blacks who had fought on their side in the American Revolution. Cuffe landed his blacks at the British colony of Sierra Leone. He hoped to send over Afro-Americans with skills and knowledge who could teach Western technology to their brothers in Africa. In this way, he would be able to develop a thriving commerce between the United States and an increasingly skillful and productive Africa.

The American Colonization Society established Liberia in 1822, naming its capital, Monrovia, after President James Monroe. This organization repatriated 12,000 blacks to that African colony, which became an independent nation in 1847. Most blacks, however, remained suspicious of the Colonization Society, which was dominated by whites and included many Southerners. They sensed that many of its members were more interested in siphoning off free blacks and troublemakers so as to make slavery more secure in the United States than they were in ending slavery.

The first of the Negro Convention Movement meetings, in 1830 at Philadelphia with Bishop Richard Allen presiding, recommended the purchase of a colony in the western part of Canada to which blacks could migrate, so as to get away from the oppressive conditions encountered in the United States. In the 1850s, Dr. Martin R. Delany and other black emigrationists pushed plans for emigration to the Niger River valley in Africa or to Haiti or to Central America.

In subsequent years, other prophets of exodus arose, including Benjamin "Pap" Singleton who urged a migration from the South to the West in the 1870s and Chief Alfred Sam who advocated a return to West Africa at the turn of the century. Nonetheless, most blacks in America, including Garvey's followers, rejected ideas of migrating from their established home, the United States.

Encountering prejudice and discrimination in America, meanwhile, black Americans created a culture within a culture. Black churches, masonic lodges, schools, newspapers, and colleges were the most obvious manifestations of this subculture. Many black leaders, including Frederick Douglass, Booker T. Washington, and W. E. B. Du Bois, counseled creation of a separate black economy and urged blacks to patronize black businesses. Washington founded the National Negro Business League in 1900. After emancipation, burial societies grew into insurance companies and banks, and a black middle class of professional and business men increasingly evolved to serve the needs of black communities. These developments increased awareness of a separate black subculture among blacks. Many wanted to be fully integrated into American life, but on being rejected by white Americans, they developed separate black institutions.

Black leaders voiced the confusion of blacks in America. Du Bois wrote in 1897: "Here, then, is the dilemma. . . . Am I an American or am I a Negro? Can I be both?" Six years later, he wrote in *The Souls of Black Folk:* "One ever feels his twoness,—an American, a Negro; . . . two warring ideals in one dark body. . . ." A black man, he concluded, "would not bleach his Negro soul in a flood of white Americanism, for he knows that Negro blood has a message for the world. He simply wishes to make it possible for a man to be both a Negro and an American, without being cursed and spit upon by his fellows, without having the doors of Opportunity closed roughly in his face."

Conscious of the world-wide linkage of dark men, Du Bois called a Pan-African Congress. The world's first such gathering, it met in Paris in February, 1919, with 57 delegates from Africa, the West Indies, and the United States. Far ahead of his time, Du Bois inspired African nationalists and is generally regarded by the leaders of the new black nations as the spiritual godfather of African independence. While Du Bois was reaching the intellectuals, Garvey was inspiring the black masses in America to take interest, and pride, in Africa.

Many nineteenth-century leaders, such as David Walker, Henry Highland Garnet, and Frederick Douglass, were race conscious and proud to be black men. But many black Americans, from the American Revolution through World War I, apparently did not share this pride. They were constantly reminded of the supremacy of whites in business, in politics, and in almost every sphere. This was reflected in customs (white for weddings, black for funerals), religion (pure white angels versus Satan as the prince of darkness), and language (it's mighty white or noble of you, he's in a black or evil mood). These examples could be multiplied many times over. Mistreated, scorned, and barred from opportunity because of their color, many blacks in America despised their own race. Many of these Negroes became zealously middle-class minded, imitating whites, and accepting the values of whites as the standard in all things. Self-hate became a pervasive characteristic.

Many middle-class blacks were descendants of the favored mulatto house servants. Many could trace their origin back to the white slave-owners who sometimes took pride in these persons conceived in midnight forays to the slave quarters. Some slave-owners made provisions for their mulatto offspring, providing them education at schools and colleges in the North and in Europe and leaving them property in their wills. Often, middle-class blacks, because of their white connections, had an advantageous start over the lower-class blacks, many of whom were descendants of the downtrodden field hands. While many middle-class Afro-Americans dedicated themselves at great sacrifice to helping uplift their black brothers mired in rural and urban poverty, others shunned the black masses, despising the way of life of working-class blacks. Often, they regarded the black masses as uncouth, ignorant, vulgar persons who brought disgrace on all blacks and made more difficult the acceptance of the educated, cultivated blacks by white America.

At times of defeat, despair, and disappointment, however, blacks of all classes tended to become more race conscious and to withdraw from the quest for integration with a society that rejected them. Withdrawal was along the lines of political separation or economic separation or social separation or any combination of these. Political separation looked to emigration from America to a homeland in Africa or some other place free from the oppression of whites or it looked to the creation of a separate, black-run sphere within the United States, either a state or region to be turned over to blacks. Economic separation encouraged the founding of black businesses that could provide employ for blacks and keep profits in the black community to strengthen and build it up. This would free blacks from the exploitation they suffered at the hands of white employers, retailers, and landlords. Social separation involved a heightened awareness of, and pride in, the black heritage and in black institutions free of white involvement or domination.

The crushing of hopes raised during World War I put blacks in a chauvinistic mood. The Great Migration northward during the war filled the ghettoes with two elements: a small group of race conscious intellectuals and a mass of discouraged Southern and West Indian peasants finding it difficult to adjust to urban life. This combination of factors produced both the cultural outpouring known as the Harlem Renaissance and the mass movement led by Garvey.

The year 1919 was one of great discouragement. After fighting for democracy abroad, black fighting men returned in a more assertive mood, determined to stand up for their rights at home as well. Inevitably, there were clashes with whites who were determined to keep blacks "in their place." In the one year 1919 alone, 70 blacks were lynched, including 10 soldiers in uniform. Eleven of the victims were burned alive, reviving a barbarous medieval practice. From June to December in 1919, 26 race riots took place; 23 blacks perished in Chicago alone. During the war the Ku Klux Klan had been revived in the hate-filled atmosphere created in Georgia by the prosecution and eventual lynching of a Jewish manufacturer in Atlanta named Leo Franks for the rape and murder of one of his young white female employees. It was obvious to all the nation and world, outside of Georgia, that Franks did not receive a fair trial and was apparently innocent. The Klan re-emerged in 1915 during the excitement over this Leo Franks case, and spread rapidly in the postwar period of intolerance. Klan membership rose to five million during the 1920s, both in the North and South. Most Southern states, and even a Northern one like Indiana, came to be dominated by the Klan. Klansmen paraded openly in many communities, North and South, including the nation's capital. Also, blacks suffered severe economic setback when the job gains made during the war were wiped out in the postwar letdown. As the white veterans returned, European immigration revived, and Federal contracts for war goods dwindled, more and more blacks found themselves out of work. Blacks were fired and preference in hiring was given to whites, sometimes because the whites were better or more experienced workers, but all too often solely because of racial prejudice and discrimination.

The black masses found little solace in middle-class oriented groups like the NAACP or the newer National Urban League, which had been founded in 1911 to help blacks adjust to city living. New hope was brought them by Marcus Garvey. Garvey had been born in Jamaica in the British West Indies in 1887. His father was a master mason who earned enough from his work in brick and stone to support the family comfortably. Garvey could boast of being a full-blooded black with no trace or taint of white ancestry in his lineage. Leaving school in his teens when the family suffered financial reverses, Garvey became a printer's apprentice, then a printer, later a leader of the printers' union, and a very effective orator. Blacklisted because of his leadership during a strike, he began editing a periodical, *Garvey's Watchman*, and helped found a political organization. Even before he was in his mid-twenties, Garvey was gaining valuable experience as a leader, organizer, orator, and editor, preparing him for his life work in leading the black masses.

While living in London from 1912 to 1914, Garvey came under the influence of a black Egyptian author and editor, Duse Mohammed Ali, who stimulated Garvey's interest in the problems of nonwhite peoples in Africa, Asia, and Latin America. He also met blacks from many places studying in London, and learned of their problems at home. Garvey became fired with the vision of creating a place where blacks would be free from oppression. He envisioned "a new world of black men, not peons, serfs, dogs and slaves, but a nation of sturdy men. . . ." He also dreamed of "uniting all the Negro peoples of the world into one great body to establish a country and Government absolutely their own."

Garvey returned to Jamaica. There, on August 1, 1914, he formed an organization called the Universal Negro Improvement and Conservation Association and African Communities League, later modified to UNIA. The objectives of the new organization, as listed by Garvey, were:

> To establish a Universal Confraternity among the race; to promote the spirit of race pride and love; to reclaim the fallen of the race; to administer to and assist the needy; to assist in civilizing the backward tribes of Africa; to strengthen the imperialism of independent African States; to establish Commissionaries or Agencies in the principal countries of the world for the protection of all Negroes . . . to establish Universities, Colleges and Secondary Schools for the further education and culture of the boys and girls of the race; to conduct a world-wide commercial and industrial intercourse.

Subsequently, a new goal listed was "to establish a central nation for the race." The UNIA motto was "One God! One Aim! One Destiny!" Garvey was President of the organization, headquartered in Kingston, Jamaica.

Garvey became very much interested in the work of Booker T. Washington at Tuskegee. He was greatly influenced by reading Washington's *Up from Slavery*. Garvey wanted to start a trade school in Jamaica, along the lines of Tuskegee, in order to help the black masses. But he found the blacks indifferent, and the mulattoes, who enjoyed their favored status, openly hostile to a program that would train and elevate the black masses. Garvey planned a trip to the United States to confer with and seek the aid of Booker T. Washington, but the latter's passing in November, 1915, occurred before Garvey's trip.

Garvey came to America, anyway, in March, 1916, settling in Harlem. The following year, he founded a branch of the UNIA in New York City. In January, 1918, he established a newspaper, *Negro World*, to push the ideas of the UNIA. Growth at first was slow, but as blacks despaired in the postwar world, the UNIA attracted a large following among the black masses. A great upsurge of membership took place in 1919 and 1920. Garvey claimed that his organization had millions of members, as many as eleven million throughout the world. The exact figures are unknown, because of UNIA secrecy and poor record keeping, but it seems likely that the organization had at least half a million and perhaps as much as two million members, far more than any of the other Negro organizations. By appealing to the black masses while other black groups focused on the middle-class Afro-American, Garvey had a much wider base of support. His newspaper, *Negro World*, had a circulation of several hundred thousand at its peak.

Garvey had a message that fired the dispirited, downtrodden black masses. He said, "I am the equal of any white man," and, he told his followers, "I want you to feel the same way." He urged his people to look to self-reliance asserting "no man will do as much for you as you will do for yourself." He urged black unity saying:

> If we must have justice, we must be strong; if we must be strong, we must come together; if we must come together, we can only do so through the system of organization. . . . Let us not waste time in breathless appeals to the strong while we are weak, but lend our time, energy, and effort to the accumulation of strength among ourselves by which we will voluntarily attract the attention of others.

Garvey instilled pride of race by extolling the glories of blackness and of the African heritage. "When Europe was inhabited by

... a race of savages, naked men, heathens and pagans, Africa was peopled with a race of cultured black men, who were masters in art, science and literature," Garvey asserted. Thus, he stressed, "Black men, you were once great; you shall be great again. Lose not courage, lose not faith, go forward. The thing to do is to get organized." His poem, "The Black Woman," rejected white standards:

> Black queen of beauty, thou hast given color to the world!
> Among other women thou art royal and the fairest!
> Like the brightest jewels in the regal diadem,
> Shin'st thou, Goddess of Africa, Nature's purest emblem!

Garvey opposed integration, receiving open support from such segregationist, white supremacist groups as the Ku Klux Klan and the Anglo-Saxon Clubs. They welcomed such typical pronouncements by Garvey as "I believe in racial purity. . . . I am proud I am a Negro." He also said "To be a Negro is no disgrace, but an honor," and he contended that "we of the U.N.I.A. do not want to become white." He was opposed to "miscegenation and race suicide" believing instead "in the purity of the Negro race and the purity of the white race." He denounced the NAACP, claiming that that group "wants us all to become white by amalgamation, but they are not honest enough to come out with the truth." He warned against the amalgamationist attempts of the "miscegenationists of the white race, and their associates, the hybrids of the Negro race." Garvey approved of the Jim Crow laws that kept the races apart. His UNIA members, he proudly proclaimed, were not among those blacks "who are spending their time imitating the rich whites . . . studying Spanish so as to be able to pass for anything but a Negro, thereby getting a chance to associate with you." UNIA members were black and proud of it. Garvey emphasized that "We are not ashamed of the Race to which we belong and we feel sure that God made black skin and kinky hair because he desired to express Himself in that type." Thus, "we are not seeking social equality," Garvey said, turning his back on the integrationist philosophy of the NAACP. After his first wife died, Frederick Douglass had married a white woman, losing some of his influence among blacks and whites. Garvey would not have approved Douglass's second marriage, saying: "We do not seek intermarriage, nor do we hanker after the impossible."

Garvey had no faith that blacks would ever secure their rights in America. He advocated a return to Africa instead:

> If you cannot live alongside the white man in peace, if you cannot get the same chance and opportunity alongside the white man, even though you are his fellow citizen; if he claims that you are not entitled to this chance or opportunity because the country is his by force of numbers, then find a country of your own and rise to the highest position within that country."

Garvey believed that "Political, social and industrial America will never become so converted as to be willing to share up equitably between black and white." This being the case, he felt, "We want the right to have a country of our own, and there foster and re-establish a culture and civilization exclusively ours." Lynchings and race riots proved that the black man "must build a civilization of his own or forever remain the white man's victim." Garvey did not intend for all American blacks to go back to Africa, however. His black Zionism envisioned setting up a mighty black nation in Africa in which blacks everywhere could take pride and which would give them added prestige in whatever countries they lived. The black motherland could also defend and uphold the rights of blacks throughout the world. "We do not want all the Negroes in Africa," Garvey pointed out, "Some are no good here, and naturally will be no good there." Those with skills, who could help build a great nation in Africa to revive the past glories of the continent, were those who should emigrate primarily, and, of course, any others who wanted to help build the nation.

Garvey was alienated from black intellectuals because of his opposition to integration and because of the intense dislike of mulattoes that he developed after rebuffs in color-conscious Jamaica. Betrayed by incompetent, unscrupulous sycophants in his retinue, Garvey squandered large sums (raised by selling stock in his Black Star Line steamship company) on worthless ships poorly operated. Convicted of mail fraud in 1923, he spent several years in jail and was deported in 1927. The UNIA declined after his jailing. He never returned to America, and passed away in London in 1940.

Garvey's exile was not the end of black nationalism. The Moorish-American Science Temple movement had been begun in Newark in 1913 by Noble Drew Ali, the former Timothy Drew of North Carolina. Drew Ali stressed that blacks were Asiatic Moors and emphasized Islamic beliefs. After he passed away mysteriously in Chicago in 1929, a new prophet suddenly appeared in Detroit in 1930 claiming to be Drew Ali reincarnated. This new prophet was W. D. Fard, sometimes called Master Wallace Fard Muhammad. He founded a Temple of Islam in Detroit and another in Chicago, attracting former followers of Drew and Garvey. Fard's leading lieutenant was Elijah Muhammad, the former Elijah Poole of Georgia. He took over the leadership after Fard disappeared in 1934 as mysteriously as he had appeared. Elijah Muhammad still leads the Black Muslims.

The upsurge of creativity among black intellectuals that developed in the 1920s is known as the Harlem Renaissance. It was stimulated by the cosmopolitan atmosphere of the cities, freeing blacks from the stifling conservatism and conformity of the rural South. The presence of many lower- and middle-class blacks in the Northern ghettoes who could buy books and magazines and go to theaters and clubs provided the financial backing to support the creative blacks who contributed to this Harlem Renaissance. There was a new determination to resist oppression. Claude McKay was a black intellectual from Jamaica who opposed the Garvey movement, siding instead with the black talented tenth, Du Bois, and the NAACP in favoring civil rights and integration. McKay's volume of verse, *Harlem Shadows* (1922), is generally considered to mark the beginning of the Harlem Renaissance. Some lines from his poem, "If We Must Die," indicate the new militant spirit:

> If we must die, let it not be like hogs . . .
> If we must die, O let us nobly die . . .
> Like men we'll face the murderous, cowardly pack,
> Pressed to the wall, dying, but fighting back!

Other outstanding writers of this Renaissance included the poet Countee Cullen and the novelist Richard Wright, who came along in the 1930s with the assistance of the New Deal Federal Writer's Project. Best known of all writers of the Renaissance was Langston Hughes, whose book *Weary Blues* contained poems written in the rhythm of the jazz age.

There were outstanding artists like Hale Woodruff and Richmond Barthé and composers like William Dawson and William Grant Still, but the Harlem Renaissance achieved its greatest notice on stage. Black composers and lyricists created musical revues featuring black performers and often produced and directed by blacks. Such shows as *Shuffle Along, Runnin' Wild, Dinah, Chocolate Dandies, Dixie to Broadway, Blackbirds,* and *Hot Chocolates* were smash hits on Broadway. They introduced such dances invented by Afro-Americans as the "Charleston" and the "Black Bottom." They gave the world such songs as "I'm Just Wild About Harry," and "I Can't Give You Anything but Love." Among the greatest stars were Josephine Baker, who went on to even greater fame in Paris, Florence Mills, and Bill "Bojangles" Robinson. Outstanding black actors of the day included Charles Gilpin, Frank McLendon, Ethel Waters, and Paul Robeson, who appeared on Broadway in plays by such white dramatists as Eugene O'Neill, DuBose and Dorothy Heyward, and Paul Green. Black casts in *Porgy and Bess* and in *Green Pastures* delighted audiences in America and all over the world.

During the 1920s tenor Roland Hayes became the first black vocal artist to become a great star of the concert stage, ranking among the greatest voices in the world. His example inspired others such as Marian Anderson, Paul Robeson, and Dorothy Maynor, all of whom ranked among the highest-paid concert artists in the world. They had world-wide fame, but few Americans were better known than two great black athletes, Jesse Owens and Joe Louis. In the 1936 Olympics at Berlin, Owens set four world or Olympic records in the dashes, broad jump and relays. Louis was the world heavyweight champion from 1937 to 1949, longer than any other man and defended his crown more often, defeating twenty-five challengers. This period was also the Jazz Age, featuring such great performers as blues singer Bessie Smith, hot trumpeter Louis Armstrong, and composer and swing orchestra leader Edward "Duke" Ellington.

Blacks lived in low economic conditions through much of the 1920s. When the stock market crash of 1929 led to the severest economic depression in American history, Afro-Americans were hit even harder. By 1932, 30 percent of whites, but 56 percent of blacks were unemployed. Local relief resources were overwhelmed in this Great Depression, and black Americans desperately needed aid. President Franklin D. Roosevelt's New Deal relief measures aided them. Their needs were communicated to the administration through Mrs. Roosevelt and through such black advisers to Federal departments and agencies as Mary McLeod Bethune, Robert C. Weaver, William H. Hastie, and Ralph J. Bunche. Prodded by John L. Lewis, CIO Industrial unions organized the mass production industries and helped blacks to obtain jobs and upgrading much more effectively than had the restrictive AFL craft unions.

In 1928, Oscar DePriest became the first black sent to Congress from the North. A Republican, like the 22 blacks who represented Southern states in Congress from 1869 to 1901, DePriest represented southside Chicago for three terms. In 1934, he was defeated by Arthur Mitchell, the first black elected to Congress as a Democrat. Mitchell served four terms as a New Deal Congressman before William Dawson succeeded him in 1934. In the 1932 Presidential election, a majority of blacks, as was their tradition, had voted for the Republican candidate, Herbert Hoover. But when Roosevelt ran for reelection in 1936, he became the first Democratic Presidential nominee to secure a majority of the black vote.

Fearful of alienating the powerful Southern Democrats in Congress, Roosevelt did not vigorously push a civil rights program. But blacks had progressed and were on the verge of important new breakthroughs during and after World War II.

14

Era of Progress: World War II Through Desegregation Decision
1941–1955

On April 18, 1946, the stands were packed as the Jersey City Giants opened the International League season at home against the Montreal Royals. This was no ordinary game. The Royals second baseman, Jackie Robinson, later recalled that "everyone present felt some of the same mounting tension I did. This was more than the mere excitement of an opening day. We all sensed that history was in the making. . . . I believe everyone in Roosevelt Stadium that day realized that he was witnessing a significant collapse in the ancient wall of prejudice."

Since the formation of the National League in 1876 and the American League in 1900, major-league baseball had been a game for whites only. An Afro-American named Moses F. Walker had been a star catcher from 1884 to 1888 for the Toledo team in the American Association, which later became a minor league but was then trying to rival the National League as a major league. But from 1888 until 1946, blacks were completely excluded from organized baseball. For those six decades America's national pastime was lily-white on the major-league and minor-league level. When World War II ended, there were no black Americans on the rosters of any of the sixteen teams then in the two major leagues or on any of their affiliated minor-league teams.

All that changed on October 23, 1945, when Branch Rickey, president of the Brooklyn Dodgers, of the National League, announced that he had signed Robinson to a contract to play for the Dodgers' farm (minor-league) club at Montreal. This was the highest minor-league level, only a step below the major leagues.

Reaction to the signing of this black athlete was mixed. Many applauded this democratic step taken five months after V-E Day (May 8, 1945) when Nazi Germany surrendered, thus bringing to an end Adolf Hitler's dreams of a "master race" of Nazi Aryan supermen dominating the rest of the world. Having fought against that racist ideology in World War II, many Americans felt uncomfortable with the racism, segregation, discrimination, and prejudice at home and welcomed a breach in the wall of prejudice that kept baseball and many other organized sports an exclusive preserve for whites. Favorable reaction to "Robbie's" signing came from the South as well as the North. One Southern sportswriter commented in the Norfolk *Virginian Pilot*: "I guarantee that if Jackie Robinson hits homers and plays a whale of a game for Montreal, the fans will soon lose sight of his color."

But there was also considerable opposition. Many persons felt that blacks would not fit into organized baseball. Others feared that the presence of blacks would destroy the game and kill spectator interest. A sportswriter on the Durham, North Carolina, *Morning Herald* predicted that "the Negro player will be so uncomfortable, embarrassed, and out of place in organized baseball, that he will soon get out of his own accord." Unhappy about Rickey's move to integrate the nation's leading sport, the commissioner of minor-league baseball classified the Dodgers' president with "the carpet-bagger stripe of the white race" who by "using the Negro for their own selfish ends . . . retard the race." One of baseball's greatest players of all time, Rogers Hornsby, declared: "it will be tough for a Negro player to become part of a close-knit group such as an organized baseball club. I think Branch Rickey did wrong in signing Robinson to play with Montreal, and it won't work out."

Ignoring his critics, Rickey pushed ahead. Now, in Jersey City on April 18, 1946, Jackie was about to play his first game, ending segregation in professional team sports. Batting second in the top half of the first inning, Robinson recalled that "the Jersey City fans gave me a fine ovation," but he grounded out. He came up again the next inning and "This time I got my first hit in organized baseball." Two of his Montreal teammates were on base, and the Royals were leading 1–0. The count rose to three (balls) and two (strikes). On the three and two pitch, "I swung," said Jackie, "with everything I had. There was a crack like a rifle shot. . . . The ball sailed some 340 feet and disappeared over the left-field fence." His first hit in baseball was a home run. Although their team was now behind 4–0 the "Jersey City fans cheered and applauded. . . ." But Robbie wasn't through. Next time up he displayed his blinding speed by beating out a bunt single, stealing second, racing to third on a ground out, and then worrying the pitcher by quick spurts down the third base line toward home plate until the pitcher made a balk and the umpire waved Jackie home with another run. Before the game ended, he singled twice more for his third and fourth hits, stole another base, and forced another pitcher into a balk. He scored four runs and batted in four that day and also played a good game defensively at second base, even though he had been more accustomed to playing shortstop on the Negro semi-pro team for which he was playing when Rickey signed him.

How did the Jersey City fans react to Robinson leading Montreal to a 14-to-1 victory over their team? Jackie remembered that "the crowd just about mobbed me. Kids were chasing me . . . to get my autograph and grown people were patting me on the back. . . . I was convinced that American sports fans are truly democratic . . . that they would accept me—that they didn't care what color a player was."

Opera patrons likewise welcomed the lowering of the color bar. A step was taken on May 15, 1946, when Camilla Williams appeared as Cio-cio-san in the title role of the New York City Center Opera Company's production of Puccini's *Madame Butterfly*. She was the first soprano of her race to sing with a major opera company in the United States. Another black singer, baritone Todd Duncan (the original Porgy in Gershwin's folk opera, *Porgy and Bess*) had appeared at the City Center the year before in *I Pagliacci* and *Carmen*.

Miss Williams was a native of Danville, Virginia, and a graduate, in 1941, of Virginia State College. She was widely acclaimed for her pioneering performance at the City Center. The great prima donna Geraldine Farrar, who created the role of Cio-cio-san while at the Metropolitan Opera Company from 1906 to 1922, attended the debut and commented that "already she is one of the great Butterflys of our day." Miss Williams added other roles, Nedda in *Pagliacci* in the fall of 1946, Mimi in *La Boheme* in

1947, and the title role in *Aida* in 1948. But the nation's foremost opera company, the Metropolitan, was still closed to black singers, even to a proven artist of the stature of Camilla Williams. *Time Magazine* of September 30, 1946, reported that "As for ambitions to sing at the Met, chronically deaf to Negro voices, Camilla Williams says simply: 'All opera singers aspire to it.'"

The color bar at the Metropolitan Opera Company was not lowered until January 7, 1955, when Marian Anderson appeared as Ulrica in Verdi's *Un Ballo in Maschera*. Miss Anderson had long been famed as the world's greatest contralto. Arturo Toscanini heard her in 1935 and declared: "a voice like yours is heard only once in a hundred years." But it took twenty more years before the Met acknowledged this by permitting her to sing on its stage in the twilight of her long and distinguished career. Although Miss Anderson was the first black singer at the Metropolitan Opera, a black ballerina, Janet Collins, had joined the Metropolitan Opera in 1951, becoming subsequently the prima ballerina.

Of Miss Anderson's debut in 1955, the critic for *Musical America*, Ronald Eyer, wrote: "It was a momentous occasion . . . and it attracted a distinguished, excited audience, rivaling that of opening night." When Ulrica made her one appearance in the second scene of the first act, "the pent-up emotions of the audience broke forth in a tidal wave of cheers and applause as the scene disclosed the impressive figure of Miss Anderson."

In her autobiography, Miss Anderson recalled that "when the audience applauded and applauded before I could sing a note I felt myself tightening into a knot . . . at that moment I was as nervous as a kitten. . . . I should have been firm and secure, but my emotions were too strong. . . . I was not pleased with the first performance." Eyer noted her initial nervousness, but pointed out that she soon settled down "to singing with all her accustomed security, richness and warmth of tone. . . ." Like Jackie Robinson in his "debut," Marion Anderson was grateful at her reception, saying "I will never forget the wholehearted responsiveness of the public."

Jackie Robinson and Marian Anderson symbolize the new status of black Americans in the postwar world. Their breakthroughs in sports and opera were highlights of an era of progress that began during World War II, a war that lasted from 1939 to 1945.

An even greater migration from the South took place during this war than during the First World War. This outward flow was the culmination of a steady move of blacks to the North and West. Half a million blacks migrated northward during World War I, which lasted from 1914 to 1918. Then, during the 1920s, another 1,300,000 Afro-Americans left the South. In the 1930s, 1,500,000 more departed. Opportunities for factory jobs in the Second World War lured another 2,500,000 blacks out of the South in the 1940s. Thus, by 1960, only 55 percent of the Negro population remained in the South, where 90 percent had lived in 1890.

Two signs of progress for blacks occurred before the attack at Pearl Harbor on December 7, 1941, brought the United States into the war. These signs were the appointing of the first black general and the establishment of the Fair Employment Practices Committee (FEPC). Although many black soldiers had served in the nation's wars from the American Revolution onward, most were led by white officers. Only three blacks were graduated from West Point in the entire nineteenth century. Henry Flipper became, in 1877, the first Afro-American ever to graduate from one of the service academies in the United States. John Alexander in 1887 and Charles Young in 1889 were the second and third blacks to graduate from the United States Military Academy at West Point, New York. In World War I, blacks had hoped that Young (1864–1922), their first regular army colonel, would be given an active command and promoted to general, but he was shunted aside by being put out of the army on what seemed to black Americans flimsy grounds of physical unfitness.

The fourth black to be graduated from West Point was Benjamin O. Davis, Jr. He was graduated in 1936. It was his father who, in October 1940, was promoted to the rank of brigadier general. Born in 1877, Benjamin O. Davis, Sr., had served as a lieutenant with a volunteer regiment in the Spanish-American War of 1898 after being graduated from Howard University. Mustered out of the volunteers after the short war, he reenlisted in the regular army in 1899, but subsequently rose from the ranks to become a second lieutenant in the cavalry in 1901. He rose from captain to major during World War I, and became a full colonel in 1930. Then, in the fall of 1940, during President Roosevelt's campaign for a third term as President, Davis was promoted to general. Roosevelt was concerned about the complaints of Afro-Americans over segregation in the drafting and training of men and in the preparation of Negro officers. In promoting Davis, Roosevelt also announced the appointment of two other blacks to positions where they could help to combat the discrimination all too prevalent in the conduct of the selective service system and the armed forces. Campbell Johnson, later to be a colonel, was made executive assistant to the Director of Selective Service, General Lewis Hershey. William H. Hastie was appointed civilian aide to the Secretary of War, Henry Stimson. General Davis served as a brigadier (one-star) general for eight years before retiring in 1948.

When war came in 1939, millions were still unemployed as a result of the lingering effects of the Depression. As defense contracts brought job openings, prejudiced employers and labor unionists discriminated against blacks. Federal officials mildly protested this preferential hiring and upgrading of whites, but blacks demanded firmer action.

The foremost black labor unionist, A. Philip Randolph, president of the Brotherhood of Sleeping Car Porters, called for 100,000 blacks to converge on the nation's capital on July 1, 1941, to protest exclusion of blacks by defense industries. Whites had marched on Washington several times. In 1894, an army of the unemployed, led by Jacob Coxey, came to Washington to demand that Congress provide relief for people suffering from the depression brought on by the Panic of 1893. In 1932, veterans of World War I came to Washington to pressure Congress for assistance in the Depression. This Bonus Expeditionary Force (BEF) of 1932 wanted Congress to pass the bill that would permit immediate cash payment of their adjusted compensation certificates that would not be due for another ten years. President Herbert Hoover panicked and called out the army, under the chief of staff, General Douglas MacArthur, to drive the Bonus marchers out of Washington. Some blacks had participated in both marches, that of Coxey's army and of the BEF.

The march that Randolph called for in 1941 would reveal and dramatize to all the world the racial discrimination prevalent in America. Such a march therefore would weaken the nation's posture as the champion of freedom and democracy against the despicable racist ideology of Adolf Hitler's Nazi Germany. President Roosevelt, both to prevent America's embarrassment and to meet the just demands of Afro-Americans for decent treatment in employment, agreed to issue an executive order on fair hiring. With this agreement, Randolph called off the march. Executive Order 8802, issued on June 25, 1941, proclaimed: "there shall be no discrimination in the employment of workers in defense industries or Government because of race, creed, color, or national origin."

To carry out Roosevelt's order, an anti-discrimination clause was inserted in all defense contracts. The Fair Employment Practices Committee (FEPC) was established to enforce the order and the antidiscrimination clauses. The governor of Alabama vowed opposition because giving blacks equal opportunity at employment would disrupt racial peace. Despite his opposition, the FEPC was an important gain. It opened up many defense jobs and caused a great migration of blacks northward to take advantage of the new opportunities.

Nearly 900,000 black soldiers, sailors, and Marines served in World War II. Half a million went overseas, many in service outfits (quartermaster, engineering, ordnance), but some as combat forces. Among the best known heroes was Messman Dorie Miller of the Battleship *Arizona*. On December 7, 1941, at Pearl Harbor, Miller, who had no gunnery training, manned a machine gun and shot down four Japanese airplanes.

Although 21 black soldiers and sailors won the Congressional Medal of Honor in the Civil War, 15 in the Indian wars, and 7 in the Spanish-American War, none won it in the two world wars. Subsequently, William Thompson and Cornelius Charlton won it in Korea and Milton Olive and Lawrence Joel in Vietnam.

During World War II, Benjamin O. Davis, Jr., rose to colonel in the Air Force, first leading the 99th Fighter Squadron and then the 332nd Fighter Group. Subsequent promotions raised him to the rank of Air Force lieutenant general (three-star) during the Vietnam War, two ranks higher than his father. From 1941 to 1949, nine more blacks were graduated from West Point, making a total of thirteen Negro graduates in the institution's history to that point.

But not until Wesley Brown in 1949 was any black man graduated from the United States Naval Academy at Annapolis, Maryland.

Among the many persons who made important contributions to the war effort, few were more significant than a black medical scientist, Dr. Charles R. Drew. He was a Washingtonian, had been a track star at Amherst College, and was a graduate of the medical school at McGill University in Canada. Drew became a surgeon, head of the department of surgery at the Howard University Medical School in Washington, D.C., and chief surgeon at Freedman's Hospital there. While doing advanced training at Columbia University, Dr. Drew began research into the properties of blood plasma. He became famed for devising techniques for preserving and banking blood. He organized the British Blood Bank that saved so many lives in World War II. His work with blood and with improved surgical techniques was a contribution, like that of an earlier black physician, Dr. Daniel Hale Williams, toward modern heart-transplant work.

Germany surrendered on May 8, 1945, Japan on August 15, 1945. Having defeated race-supremacist fascist dictatorships, Americans were less inclined to be tolerant of bigotry at home. Furthermore, prejudice here proved costly when the nation was seeking friends among Africans and Asians in the Cold War. Blacks stepped up their drive for justice. President Harry Truman's Fair Deal Administration integrated the armed forces during the Korean War.

This new climate aided Jackie Robinson. Born in Cairo, Georgia, in 1919, he grew up in Pasadena, California, where his mother moved the family when her husband left while Jackie was a baby. Jackie was an All-American halfback at the University of California at Los Angeles (UCLA), the top scorer on the basketball team, and a record-breaking track star; he also won letters in baseball. He followed in the athletic footsteps of his older brother, Mack Robinson, who finished second to Jesse Owens in the 1936 Olympics. Jackie left UCLA in 1941, worked a year, served in the Army three years, and played with a black baseball team, the Kansas City Monarchs, before Rickey signed him.

Although Jackie was a fiery competitor, Rickey made him

endure taunts silently so as not to jeopardize the experiment. During spring training in Florida, enforcement of segregation ordinances kept the Montreal Royals from playing in several places and forced Jackie to leave the team in others. During the regular season, Jackie's cold fury at such abuse as the Syracuse players yelling "here's a relative" while releasing a black cat on the field while he was batting made him excel. He led the league in batting and stolen bases. Moving up to the Dodgers, he won the National League Rookie-of-the-Year award in 1947 and the Most Valuable Player award in 1949. He led the Dodgers to six pennants in ten seasons, had a lifetime batting average of .311, and was voted into baseball's Hall of Fame.

Jackie's pioneering ushered in a golden age for black athletes. In 1945, there were no Negroes in major-league professional football, even though All-American Fritz Pollard, Duke Slater, and Joe Lillard were black players in the early history of professional football, from 1919 to 1933. For the next thirteen years, the game was lily-white. In 1946 black players integrated the new All-American Conference and the old National Football League. They soon came to be among the most exciting players in the game, particularly the Cleveland Brown fullback, Jim Brown.

Not until 1950 did major-league professional basketball become integrated. Until the 1958–1959 season, none of the black players were named to the All-Star team of the professional loop, the National Basketball Association (N.B.A.). That year Elgin Baylor and Bill Russell were two of the five All-Star selections. Since then, black players have dominated the League. Bill Russell became the greatest defensive player in the history of the game, and Wilt Chamberlain the greatest offensive player in basketball history. Besides these two great centers, Elgin Baylor at forward and Oscar Robertson at guard became perennial All-Star choices. With a reputed $250,000 a year contract, Chamberlain became the highest salaried player in all professional sports in America.

Many great stars followed Jackie's lead in baseball. His Dodger teammate, catcher Roy Campanella, became the Most Valuable Player three times and was the second black player voted into the Hall of Fame. Don Newcombe of the Dodgers and Juan Marichal of the Giants were among the great pitchers in baseball. But two outfielders, Willie Mays of the Giants and Henry "Hank" Aaron of the Braves, rank among the greatest players in the history of base-ball. At the end of the 1970 season, they had hit more home runs than any players in the history of the game other than Babe Ruth. As of the end of 1970, Aaron with 592 and Mays with 628 were the only active players close to Babe Ruth's career total record of 714 homers.

Afro-Americans did not do as well in other formerly lily-white sports as they did in baseball, football, and basketball. In tennis, only two blacks became stars in the twenty years since the sport was first integrated in 1949. Althea Gibson became the top wom-en's tennis player in the late 1950s and Arthur Ashe, Jr., became the world's top male amateur tennis player in the late 1960s. In professional golf, Ted Rhodes, Charlie Sifford, Pete Brown, and Lee Elder were black pioneers, but none ranked among the top players in the game.

Despite the gains they had made in many sports, black athletes were still restricted. Once their playing days were over, they were dropped while white teammates were assured coaching, mana-gerial, or front-office positions. Many, both in college and profes-sional sports, felt that they were exploited and discarded while long-range benefits went to whites. Not until Bill Russell became player-coach of the Boston Celtics basketball team in 1966 did a black ever direct a professional major-league team. After he retired from the game in 1969, the only other black head coaches in any major-league sports were three men in basketball, Len Wilkins, player-coach of the N.B.A. Seattle Supersonics, Al Attles, player-coach of the N.B.A. San Francisco Warriors, and Johnny McLendon, who coached the Denver Rockets in the rival American Basketball Association (A.B.A.) briefly in 1969.

The failure of baseball and football to appoint a black man as manager or head coach could be attributed only to prejudice. At the start of the 1969 baseball season, Jim "Junior" Gilliam, one of the only four blacks serving as coaches (aides to the manager) for major-league baseball teams, said of the failure to make any blacks manager: "It has to be the color of the skin. . . . There definitely have been qualified men, but the owners aren't ready." Another outstanding black baseball player, Bill White, first baseman for the

Cards and the Phillies in his playing days, explained how his dream
of becoming a manager faded: "They aren't using black people in
the front office and I don't think they're going to in the near future.
. . . I don't feel I have a future in baseball. There aren't enough
progressive-thinking administrative people in baseball who are willing to take a chance on capable black people." The strong resentment of black athletes against the way college and professional
sports exploited their playing talents while discriminating against
them in social affairs and executive positions exploded in a threatened boycott of the 1968 Olympics. Almost completely insensitive
to the plight of the black athlete, many Americans, especially
sports fans, wondered why blacks should rebel against the one area
in which they were given a fair shake and a man's chance, sports.
Too few comprehended the problem and the underlying resentment.

Marian Anderson likewise overcame discrimination and paved
the way for others. Born in Philadelphia in 1902, as a youngster
she began singing professionally in churches. Encouraged and
aided by the great Negro tenor Roland Hayes, she managed to get
professional training for her magnificent voice. Like most American recital artists, she had to make a reputation in Europe before
she gained acceptance in America. Despite her great stature, a
much publicized incident in 1939 aroused suspicions of prejudice.
It was widely reported in the newspapers that she had been denied
an opportunity to sing at Constitution Hall, which was owned by
the Daughters of the American Revolution (DAR). The DAR
officials later denied the charges of discrimination, pointing out
that Miss Anderson sang at their hall subsequently, that blacks
were admitted in the audience there at a time when segregation was
the rule in Washington theaters, and that her manager's request for
a booking date was turned down because the dates he wanted were
already taken. Despite their explanations, the incident was widely
denounced as a case of prejudice. Mrs. Roosevelt resigned from the
DAR. Secretary of the Interior Harold Ickes invited Miss Anderson to sing at the Lincoln Memorial where she gave a concert on
Easter Sunday, 1939, before 75,000 spectators. Her pioneering at
the Metropolitan Opera in 1955 paved the way for other singers
including George Shirley and Grace Bumbry. But the greatest of

the black singers at the Met was the superlative soprano, Leontyne Price, who after making her debut at the Metropolitan in Verdi's *Il Trovatore* in 1961 went on to become reigning prima donna of the Met, and one of its greatest stars.

Many blacks have reached the foremost rank in other entertainment and artistic fields. Bill Cosby and Diahann Carroll pioneered in television, becoming outstanding stars, respectively, on the "I Spy" and "Julia" shows. Sidney Poitier became the first black to achieve the status of a star in the movies. James Baldwin became a widely read essayist and novelist, while Ralph Ellison's novel, *The Invisible Man*, published in 1952, was cited in a poll of American writers taken by the New York *Herald-Tribune* book section in 1965 as the most significant novel written in America in the twenty years since the end of World War II. Poet Gwendolyn Brooks won the Pulitzer Prize in 1949 for her collection of verse, *Annie Allen*, making her the first black ever so honored. Lorraine Hansberry's drama, *Raisin in the Sun*, brought her the greatest acclaim ever bestowed on a black playwright in America. Few popular entertainers of any race have surpassed the appeal of Lena Horne, Harry Belafonte, and Sammy Davis, Jr., in singing, acting, and dancing. Charlie Parker, Dizzy Gillespie, and Miles Davis were among the greatest of the many black innovators in developing modern, progressive jazz. Ray Charles became one of the greatest of blues singers and Mahalia Jackson became the reigning gospel singer. The few persons mentioned typified a great many blacks who made tremendous successes of themselves despite the difficulties they faced and the obstacles they had to overcome.

Progress came too late and too slow for some. Despairing of improvement in the American racial climate, a few blacks became Communist sympathizers in the late 1940s, the most prominent being Paul Robeson and W. E. B. Du Bois. While an NAACP leader from 1910 to 1934, Du Bois was a bitter foe of the Communists, and was still opposed to Communism while teaching at Atlanta University from 1934 to 1944. As a minor NAACP official from 1944 to 1948, he was wooed by the Communists. He finally accepted their cause, with reservations, after leaving the NAACP national office again. Not until 1961, when he was 93 years old, did he join the Communist Party and become a citizen of Ghana, where he died in 1963.

Under the leadership of Walter White as executive secretary, 1931 to 1955, and Thurgood Marshall as chief counsel, 1938 to 1961, the NAACP fought legal battles for voting, fair trials, and other civil rights.

The greatest assault was against the 1896 Plessy ruling under which Southern states spent in 1930 $44.31 per white pupil, but only $12.57 per black pupil, while the national average expenditure for education was $87.22 per pupil. The NAACP first fought for equalization of the separate schools. Then, it launched an attack in the 1930s against segregation in graduate schools, winning victories between 1938 and 1950 in the Gaines, Sipuel, Sweatt, and McLaurin cases, admitting Negroes to white graduate schools in the state universities in Missouri, Oklahoma, and Texas.

The NAACP drive achieved its greatest victory in the unanimous decision rendered by the Supreme Court under Chief Justice Earl Warren on May 17, 1954, in the case of Brown v. Board of Education of Topeka. The Court's ruling said in part:

> Our decision . . . must look . . . to the effect of segregation itself on public education. In approaching this problem, we cannot turn the clock back . . . to 1896 when *Plessy* v. *Ferguson* was written. . . . In these days, it is doubtful that any child may reasonably be expected to succeed in life if he is denied the opportunity of an education. Such an opportunity . . . must be made available to all on equal terms.
>
> We come then to the question presented: Does segregation of children in public schools solely on the basis of race, even though the physical facilities and other "tangible" factors may be equal, deprive the children of the minority group of equal educational opportunities? We believe that it does. . . . To separate them from others of similar age and qualifications solely because of their race generates a feeling of inferiority as to their status in the community that may affect their hearts and minds in a way unlikely ever to be undone. . . .
>
> We conclude that in the field of public education the doctrine of "separate but equal" has no place. Separate educational facilities are inherently unequal. Therefore, we hold that the plaintiffs . . . are, by reason of the segregation complained of, deprived of the

equal protection of the laws guaranteed by the Fourteenth Amendment.

Though hailed by most blacks as a great victory then, more militant blacks in later years would take great objection to the Court's reasoning that separate institutions are necessarily inferior. Following up its initial ruling, the Court ruled on May 31, 1955, that school desegregation must be carried out with "all deliberate speed." Some Court members came to regret the invitation to delay that many Southern communities made out of the word "deliberate."

The Court rulings of 1954–1955 ushered in a civil rights revolution that would begin with a bus boycott late in 1955.

15

Civil Rights Revolution
and New Militancy

1955–1971

"Let us not wallow in the valley of despair," pleaded Martin Luther King, Jr. "I say to you today, my friends, that in spite of the difficulties and frustrations of the moment I still have a dream. . . . I have a dream that one day this nation will rise up and live out the true meaning of its creed: 'We hold these truths to be self-evident; that all men are created equal.' "

The vast throng at the Lincoln Memorial on August 28, 1963, a century after Emancipation, punctuated King's phrases with roars of approval. Two hundred thousand marchers had come to Washington that day in what correspondent E. W. Kenworthy described in *The New York Times* as "the greatest assembly for a redress of grievances that this capital has ever seen." This rally marked the high point of the civil rights movement that began with the bus boycott in Montgomery, Alabama, in 1955. Not only those at the Lincoln Memorial, but millions of Americans at home before their television sets heard King deliver the most eloquent appeal ever made to the nation's conscience for justice long overdue.

"I have a dream that one day on the red hills of Georgia the sons of former slaves and the sons of former slaveowners will be able to sit down together at the table of brotherhood.

"I have a dream that one day even the state of Mississippi . . . will be transformed into an oasis of freedom and justice.

"I have a dream that my four little children will one day live in a nation where they will not be judged by the color of their skin but by the content of their character.

"I have a dream today.

"I have a dream that one day the state of Alabama . . . will be transformed into a situation where little black boys and black girls will be able to join hands with little white boys and white girls and walk together as sisters and brothers."

Standing before Lincoln's statue, King concluded his address to the March-on-Washington with these words:

"This is our hope . . . with this faith we will be able to transform the jangling discords of our nation into a beautiful symphony of brotherhood. . . . And if America is to be a great nation, this must become true. So let freedom ring . . . from every village and every hamlet, from every state and every city . . . to speed up that day when all of God's children, black men and white men, Jews and Gentiles, Protestants and Catholics, will be able to join hands and sing in the words of the old Negro spiritual, 'Free at last! Free at last! Thank God Almighty, we are free at last!' "

In one way or another, blacks had been pleading for fair dealing for two centuries. Tragically, no matter how often this plea was sowed, it seldom brought forth fruit for it generally fell among the thorns of the national dedication to white supremacy and soon was choked by them.

Never had the cause of racial justice been pleaded more cogently than by King at the Lincoln Memorial, but though the nation listened and marked, it did not inwardly digest his words sufficiently. What was needed was a national commitment to stamp out every vestige of racism, to rectify past oppression, to overcome the disadvantages fostered by centuries of deprivation, and to transform his dream of brotherhood into reality. The failure of the American people to undertake such an effort left the nation tragically divided as the 1960s ended, bringing to the fore voices far more strident and tactics far less peaceful than King's. The nation shuddered at the spectre of racial guerilla warfare, but still found it more comfortable to continue along the old lines of white advantage and black disadvantage.

If Martin Luther King was not heeded, it is no wonder that earlier pleadings were ignored. In a petition to the Massachusetts legislature in 1774, a group of slaves in that colony contended that "we have in common with all other men a natural right to our freedoms. . . ." The black scientist, Benjamin Banneker, wrote to Thomas Jefferson in 1791 arguing that "one universal Father hath

. . . endowed us with the same faculties" and urging "you and all others, to wean yourselves from those narrow prejudices" that Jefferson and most whites had toward blacks. In 1829 David Walker threatened "we must and shall be free. . . . And wo, wo, will be to you if we have to obtain our freedom by fighting." Frederick Douglass thundered in 1857: "Power concedes nothing without a demand. . . . If we ever get free from the oppressions and wrongs heaped upon us, we must pay . . . by suffering, by sacrifice, and if needs be, by our lives and the lives of others." Booker T. Washington optimistically concluded in 1895 that "No race that has anything to contribute to the markets of the world is long in any degree ostracized." W. E. B. Du Bois proclaimed in 1905 that "Persistent manly agitation is the way to liberty. . . ." In 1920 Marcus Garvey warned America that blacks were "determined to suffer no longer." Walter White of the NAACP insisted in 1934 that blacks "must, without yielding, continue the grim struggle for integration and against segregation. . . ."

In the perspective of two centuries of vain pleading for justice, the willingness of blacks to take to the streets in 1955 is more understandable. The decade and a half of strife over human rights from 1955 to 1971 alarmed many Americans, but was an outgrowth of centuries of persistent oppression coupled with refusal to rectify wrongs. It all began with an arrest on December 1, 1955, of a black woman who was tired of being pushed around.

Mrs. Rosa Parks, a forty-three-year-old seamstress in a department store in Montgomery, Alabama, was arrested while riding a bus home from a hard day's work. Her crime? She refused to stand so a white man could sit. She was sitting in the first row behind the front section reserved for whites, but the driver ordered her to stand after the white section filled up. Chivalry, Montgomery-style, did not permit a black woman to sit while a white man stood. This sparked a boycott by blacks, furious over accumulated humiliations.

The man who was chosen by the blacks to be their leader in the bus boycott was the twenty-six-year-old pastor of Dexter Avenue Baptist Church in Montgomery, Dr. Martin Luther King, Jr. This young minister was unknown outside of that city, but he had made a good impression since moving to Montgomery the year before.

He was able to unify the civil rights struggle in the city by uniting all factions and appealing to both the masses and the intellectuals.

King had been born in Atlanta, Georgia, on January 15, 1929. His father, the well-respected minister of Ebenezer Baptist Church there, was a persistent fighter for equal treatment who taught his children to stand up for their rights. King graduated from Morehouse College in Atlanta and from Crozer Theological Seminary in Chester, Pennsylvania. He went on to study for a Ph.D. degree at Boston University where he met Coretta Scott, a native of Alabama who was studying at the New England Conservatory of Music. They were married in 1953 and King received his Ph.D. degree in June, 1955.

Guided by King, blacks stood shoulder to shoulder and stayed off the buses. They persisted despite the efforts of whites to harass them and to sow dissension in their ranks. A race riot could have occurred when King's home was bombed, narrowly missing injury to Coretta and their first child, Yolande, but King calmed the mob of angry blacks who had gathered with arms, ready to retaliate.

King became as revered a leader as Frederick Douglass, inspiring millions with his Gandhi-like philosophy of nonviolence. In his book, *Stride Toward Freedom: The Montgomery Story* (1958), King explained his philosophy, pointing out six basic facts about it. "First," he stressed, "nonviolent resistance is not a method for cowards; it does resist." The second basic fact of this nonviolent technique "is that it does not seek to defeat or humiliate the opponent, but to win his friendship and understanding." Tactics such as boycotts, therefore, "are merely means to awaken a sense of moral shame in the opponent" leading to "redemption and reconciliation." As a result, "The aftermath of nonviolence is the creation of the beloved community, while the aftermath of violence is tragic bitterness." The third aspect of nonviolence "is that the attack is directed against forces of evil rather than against persons who happen to be doing the evil."

An important facet of King's philosophy that seemed to escape many of his critics and many of the shoddy imitators was that King did not seek to duck the consequences of his resistance. As he explained:

A fourth point that characterizes nonviolent resistance is a willingness to accept suffering without retaliation, to accept blows . . . without striking back. . . . The nonviolent resister is willing to accept violence if necessary, but never to inflict it. He does not seek to dodge jail. . . . What is the justification for this . . . turning the other cheek? . . . the realization that unearned suffering is redemptive. Suffering . . . has tremendous educational and transforming possibilities.

Fifth, King pointed out, the nonviolent resister "avoids not only external physical violence but also internal violence of spirit." He "refuses to hate" the opponent. The principle of love stands at the center of nonviolence, King explained. Not romantic love or *eros*, not brotherly love or *philia*, but another kind of love, *agape*. He explained that the Greek word "*Agape* means understanding, redeeming good will for all men. It is an overwhelming love which is purely spontaneous, unmotivated, groundless, and creative. . . . It is the love of God operating in the human heart. *Agape* is disinterested love . . . in which the individual seeks not his own good, but the good of his neighbor. . . . It begins by loving others *for their sakes* . . . *agape* makes no distinction between friend and enemy; it is directed toward both." This kind of love springs from the needs of the other person:

> Since the white man's personality is greatly distorted by segregation, and his soul is greatly scarred, he needs the love of the Negro. The Negro must love the white man, because the white man needs his love to remove his tensions, insecurities, and fears. *Agape* is not a weak, passive love. It is love in action. *Agape* is love seeking to preserve and create community.

Agape recognizes that "All humanity is involved in a single process, and all men are brothers." Therefore, King explained, "To the degree that I harm my brother, no matter what he is doing to me, to that extent I am harming myself."

Finally, King pointed out: "A sixth basic fact about nonviolent resistance is that it is based on the conviction that the universe is on the side of justice. Consequently, the believer in nonviolence has deep faith in the future." It was out of the wellsprings of this faith that King uttered his moving "I have a dream" message at the

Lincoln Memorial. It was this faith that held the blacks of Montgomery together and kept them walking until the buses were desegregated.

Inspired by King, Montgomery Negroes boycotted the bus service for twelve long months, despite all the inconvenience and hardship entailed. As one old woman remarked, "my feets are tired, but my soul's refreshed." When the bus segregation ended, however, it was as a result of a Supreme Court ruling in November, 1956, in a law suit brought by the NAACP. The ruling took effect in Montgomery on December 20, 1956, ending the boycott and integrating riders.

Meanwhile, school desegregation encountered opposition. The South's initial stunned acceptance turned into defiance. On March 12, 1956, 99 Southern Congressmen (almost all the Senators and Representatives from the South) signed what has come to be known as the Southern Manifesto opposing and denouncing the ruling and encouraging resistance. It said in part:

> We regard the decision of the Supreme Court in the school cases as a clear abuse of judicial power. . . . undertaking . . . to encroach upon the reserved rights of the states and the people. . . .
>
> This unwarranted exercise of power by the court, contrary to the Constitution is creating chaos and confusion. . . . destroying the amicable relations between the white and Negro races that have been created through ninety years of patient effort by the good people of both races. It has planted hatred and suspicion where there has been heretofore friendship and understanding. . .
>
> We commend . . . those states which have declared the intention to resist forced integration by any lawful means. . . .
>
> We pledge ourselves to use all lawful means to bring about a reversal of this decision which is contrary to the Constitution and to prevent the use of force in its implementation.
>
> In this trying period, as we all seek to right this wrong, we appeal to our people not to be provoked by the agitators and troublemakers invading our states and to scrupulously refrain from disorder and lawless acts.

Despite the Manifesto's closing plea to avoid lawlessness, the example of defiance set by the South's political leadership encouraged the elements that were all too ready to take the law into their own hands by violent means, the kind of violence that had been visited on blacks throughout Southern history.

White Citizens' Councils formed over all the South to fight desegregation. To many persons, the more respectable aura of business and political leadership associated with these councils was merely a screen for activities that caused some observers to term these organizations the "uptown Ku Klux Klan." Despite peaceful compliance with the court orders in many places, violence flared in some, especially in Clinton, Tennessee, in 1956. When Governor Orval Faubus used National Guardsmen to block desegregation of Central High School in Little Rock, Arkansas, in 1957, President Dwight Eisenhower federalized the Guard to protect the small band of black pupils that first Faubus's Guardsmen and then riotous mobs had kept from entering the school. Meanwhile, in Virginia, the General Assembly adopted in September, 1956, the Massive Resistance policy, advocated by the state's political leader, the late Senator Harry F. Byrd, Sr. Under this program there was to be no desegregation of any school, a feat to be accomplished by cutting off state aid to schools that tried to desegregate and, as a last resort, by closing the schools. In 1959, officials in Prince Edward County, Virginia, one of the five counties involved in the original cases decided by the Supeme Court in 1954, closed the county schools under the Massive Resistance program. The white pupils then entered private schools, receiving tuition grants from public monies to pay their expenses of attendance. The black children went without schools. The County did not reopen its schools until ordered by the Supreme Court in 1964. The public schools reopened with almost an all-black enrollment. Only a handful of whites enrolled, the rest remaining in the private schools. More entered after the tuition grants were ruled illegal.

Inspired by the rise of new black nations in Africa, beginning with Ghana in 1957, black Americans became more insistent on achieving their rights. King formed the Southern Christian Leadership Conference (SCLC) in 1957 to continue on a national scale the civil rights work he began in Montgomery. Led by James Farmer, the Congress of Racial Equality (CORE), originally founded in 1942, conducted Freedom Rides to test desegregation on buses in the South in 1957 and 1961. Brutal assaults on the

Freedom Riders shocked America and resulted in the Kennedy Administration's securing Interstate Commerce Commission rulings barring segregated travel.

On February 1, 1960, four black freshmen at North Carolina A. and T. College in Greensboro began a sit-in after being refused service at a Woolworth's lunch counter. The movement spread among black college students as they conducted nonviolent sit-ins, wade-ins, and kneel-ins, courageously enduring beatings and arrests without retaliation. Aided by King's SCLC, they formed the Student Nonviolent Coordinating Committee (SNCC) in 1960.

Massive street demonstrations against segregation led by King in Birmingham in April and May, 1963, aroused national sympathy as fire hoses and police dogs were unleashed on protestors. President John F. Kennedy acted. He had used Federal forces to enroll James Meredith in the University of Mississippi in 1962. He had to resort to force again in June, 1963, when Governor George Wallace tried to stand in the door to block integration at the University of Alabama summer session. But President Kennedy and his chief adviser, his brother Attorney General Robert F. Kennedy, believed, prior to the Birmingham demonstrations and Wallace's stand, that new civil rights legislation would not be needed. In 1957 and 1960, the Senate Majority Leader, Lyndon Johnson of Texas, had piloted through Congress the first civil rights measure passed since 1875. In order to get Southern Democratic Senators not to filibuster the bills to death, they had been watered down considerably, providing primarily for a Civil Rights Commission that would investigate and make recommendations.

Now, because of the events in Birmingham and Wallace's stand in the doorway, President Kennedy spoke over nationwide television on June 11, 1963. He explained why he was demanding much stronger measures, saying in part:

> . . . when Americans are sent to Vietnam . . . we do not ask for whites only. It ought to be possible, therefore, for American students of any color to attend any public institution they select without having to be backed up by troops.
>
> It ought to be possible for American consumers of any color to receive equal service in places of public accommodation . . . without being forced to resort to demonstrations in the street; and it

ought to be possible for American citizens of any color to register
and to vote . . . without interference or fear of reprisal. . . . But
this is not the case.

The Negro baby born in American today . . . has about one-half
as much chance of completing high school as a white baby . . . one-
third as much chance of becoming a professional man, twice as
much chance of becoming unemployed . . . and the prospects of
earning only half as much. . . .

If an American, because his skin is dark . . . cannot enjoy the
full and free life which all of us want, then who among us would
be content to have the color of his skin changed and stand in his
place? Who among us would then be content with the counsels of
patience and delay?

One hundred years of delay have passed since President Lincoln
freed the slaves, yet their heirs. . . . are not yet freed from the
bonds of injustice. . . . from social and economic oppression, and
this nation . . . will not be fully free until all its citizens are free. . . .

We face, therefore, a moral crisis as a country and as a people.
. . . It is time to act in the Congress, in your state and local legislative body and, above all, in all of our daily lives. . . . A great
change is at hand, and our task, our obligation, is to make that
revolution, that change, peaceful and constructive for all. Those
who do nothing are inviting shame as well as violence. . . .

I am therefore asking the Congress to enact legislation giving all
Americans the right to be served in facilities which are open to the
public. . . .

Kennedy was the first American President ever to proclaim publicly that segregation was a moral wrong.

When the new civil rights measure bogged down in Congress,
civil rights groups called for a march on Washington to demonstrate support for the legislation. Some 200,000 black and white
demonstrators came to the nation's capital on August 28, 1963.
Martin Luther King gave his "I Have a Dream" talk, but there was
a much more strident and impatient voice, that of John Lewis, the
young chairman of SNCC. Lewis told the crowd at the Lincoln
Memorial, "They're talking about slow down and stop. . . . We will
not stop. . . . We will march through the South. . . . We shall
fragment the South into 1,000 pieces and put them back together
in the image of democracy." Some of the more militant blacks,

such as Malcolm X of the Black Muslim movement, were disgusted that the moderate forces controlling the demonstration cooperated with the administration in toning down the entire demonstration and in forcing Lewis to cut out many of his more inflammatory passages. Divisions were developing in the movement between those who favored the cautious, legalistic approach of the NAACP, those who backed the dramatic but nonviolent street campaigns led by the moderately inclined King, and those who favored revolutionary action, including retaliatory violence.

Despite the massive demonstration in Washington, the civil rights bill was still not making much progress toward passage when President Kennedy was assassinated on November 22, 1963. His successor, Lyndon Johnson, prodded Congress to act. Cloture was invoked to shut off debate in the Senate. This was the first time that cloture had ever been used successfully in behalf of a civil rights measure. Accordingly, with the Southern filibuster broken, the Civil Rights Act was passed in July, 1964, providing equal access to public accommodations.

Attention turned to voting rights. Led by SNCC, civil rights groups helped blacks register in Mississippi in the summer of 1964. But violence struck again. Prior to that summer, Medgar Evers, NAACP leader in Mississippi, had been cowardly murdered from ambush in June, 1963, and in September, 1963, one month after the March-on-Washington, a bomb exploded in a church in Birmingham, killing four little black girls attending Sunday School. Three of the young civil rights workers, one black and two white, participating in the summer voting registration program were arrested, murdered, and buried under a dam by police and Klansmen in rural Mississippi in June, 1964.

On March 7, 1965, King's followers attempted a march from Selma, Alabama, to the state capital at Montgomery to protest to Governor Wallace over the harassing tactics of the local sheriff during voter registration efforts in Selma. The marchers were brutally assaulted by a sheriff's posse, wielding whips. Thousands of whites and blacks from all over America poured into Selma to join the blacks there in a renewed attempt to make the march. Federal forces had to be sent to Alabama to protect the marchers. Violence continued. In separate incidents in and near Selma, a Southern black and three Northern whites (a minister, housewife, and seminary student) were murdered.

During the struggle for voting rights in Selma, President Johnson addressed a joint session of Congress in a nationally televised speech on March 15, 1965, asking for a law to protect the right to vote. He asserted that "Every American citizen must have an equal right to vote. . . . Yet the harsh fact is that in many places in this country men and women are kept from voting simply because they are Negroes." The President said of this denial: "It is wrong, morally wrong, to deny any of your fellow Americans the right to vote in this country." He indicated that the black man's fight for freedom "must be our cause too . . . it's not just Negroes, but really it's all of us who must overcome the crippling legacy of bigotry and injustice. And we shall overcome." This was not just a sectional problem, not merely a case of Southern injustice, said President Johnson, because "There is no part of America where the promise of equality has been fully kept." Cloture was invoked again and the Voting Rights Act was passed in August, 1965.

Under the Voting Rights Act, the percentage of blacks registered in the states covered increased from 30 percent to 46 percent in just one year, and the number of Afro-Americans serving in the legislatures of Southern states increased from 6 in 1962 to 37 in 1966.

Meanwhile, King won the Nobel Peace Prize for 1964 for his nonviolent crusades. He was the second American black to receive the Nobel Peace Prize, Ralph Bunche having won it in 1950 for his mediation of the Arab-Israeli dispute over Palestine. A third black winner was Chief Albert Luthuli of South Africa who led his people in a nonviolent struggle against the apartheid segregation laws and racial oppression in the Union of South Africa.

The civil rights acts of 1964, ending segregation, and 1965, protecting voting rights, removed obvious injustices, but still left many problems. The nation did not yet fully recognize the exploitation and racism so prevalent in American life. Improved conditions still left far too many blacks impoverished and excluded from an affluent society. Increasingly the Negro problem was becoming a problem of poverty in Northern ghettoes. Public accommodation and voting rights did not make much difference in their lives.

In the 1920 census, for the first time, the United States became urbanized, with 51.4 percent of its people living in cities. At that time, however, only 34 percent of blacks, but 53.4 percent of whites lived in cities. Forty years later, blacks were more concentrated in cities than whites. In 1960, 69.5 percent of whites, but 72.4 percent of nonwhites were urban residents. America's central cities were becoming increasingly black. Almost one-fifth of the black population lived in just six cities in 1960: New York with 1,087,931 blacks; Chicago with 812,637; Philadelphia 529,240; Detroit 482,223; Washington 411,737; and Los Angeles 334,916. Except for Washington (a border city), these were Northern and Western cities. More blacks lived in New York City alone in 1960 than in any states other than the state of New York (which led the nation with 1,417,511 blacks), Texas, Georgia, and North Carolina. Although blacks were only 11 percent of the national population in 1965, seven of America's ten largest cities were one-fourth black, ranging from 25 percent in Houston to 63 percent in Washington. Although Washington was the only one of the nation's sixty largest cities to have a population more than 45 percent black in 1960, census projections showed that Detroit, Baltimore, St. Louis, New Orleans, Newark, Richmond, and Jacksonville would all be more than 45 percent black by 1970. More and more whites were moving to the suburbs causing the central cities to become increasingly black. From 1960 to 1968, the populations of all the metropolitan areas in the United States rose 14 percent to a total of 128,000,000. But the population of the central city portion of the metropolitan areas only increased by one percent in that span while the suburbs increased by 28 percent. The number of whites living in the central cities declined by 5 percent from 1960 to 1968 while the number of black residents in the central cities increased by 25 percent. Meanwhile, the black population in the suburbs remained stable, being 5 percent in both 1960 and 1968. The pattern was clear. A few blacks were able to move to the suburbs, enough to maintain a constant percentage there, but whites were increasingly becoming suburbanites abandoning the central cities to blacks, more and more of whom were flocking there from the rural South.

Cramped into urban ghettoes, hampered by inadequate schools

in those ghettoes, and discriminated against in hiring and upgrading, the economic condition of black Americans remained far below that of whites. Consistently, twice as many blacks were without jobs. In 1950, 4.9 percent of whites, but 9.0 percent of blacks were unemployed; in 1960, it was 4.9 percent of whites and 10.2 percent of nonwhites, and the respective figures, as of February, 1969, stood at 2.9 percent for whites, but 5.7 percent for blacks. When employed, a majority of blacks were concentrated in the lower-paying blue-collar jobs because preference generally was given to whites, regardless of qualification, for the higher-paying white-collar positions. Although the picture was improving, blacks were still left far behind. In 1940, 44.8 percent of white men and 52.4 percent of white women held professional, managerial, sales, clerical, skilled, and technical positions, while only 10 percent of black men and 6.9 percent of black women held such positions. More than 90 percent of the employed blacks held such jobs as laborer, service worker, domestic servant, farmer and farm laborer, and factory operative. By 1962, the percentage of blacks in the upper categories had increased to 25 percent for the men and 22.2 percent for the women, but whites had not stood still meanwhile so that 61.1 percent of white men and 62.1 percent of white women were then in those higher-paying and white-collar positions. The discrimination in hiring, assignment, and upgrading of workers was reflected in the differences in family income. In 1950, the median family income for whites was $3,445, for blacks $1,869; in 1960, the respective figures were $5,835 for whites and $3,233 for blacks. In 1968, the median earnings for central city blacks amounted to $5,623, but $8,294 for whites. Clear evidence of discrimination could be seen in the fact that in 1964, the median income for whites with only an eighth-grade education, $5,386, was higher than the median income for nonwhites who were high school graduates, $5,039. Similarly, whites who had completed only 1-3 years of high school (ninth to eleventh grades) had a higher median income, $6,512, than blacks who had completed 1-3 years of college (equivalent to thirteenth to fifteenth grades), $5,907. Thus, even a college-trained black was generally relegated to a lower-paying job than a white who had not even finished high school.

There was a concentration of blacks among the nation's poor. In the late 1960s, only 28 percent of nonwhites had a family income of more than $7,000, while 55 percent of white families were in that category. Blacks were much more concentrated at the other end of the income scale. Of the nearly thirty million people with incomes below $3,000, two-thirds (20,300,000) were white and only one-third (9,400,000) were nonwhite. But the twenty million whites living in poverty constituted only 12 percent (one of eight) of the white population, while the nine and a half million blacks living in poverty constituted 41 percent (or two out of five) of the nonwhite population. Likewise, because they had less choice in the housing market, were poorer, and were at the mercy of slumlords, many more blacks lived in dilapidated, rat-infested housing than whites. In fact, in the late 1960s, nearly one out of three blacks lived in substandard housing, but only one out of twelve whites. Moreover, poor blacks living in ghettoes were often victimized by slum merchants who sold them poor quality goods at usurious interest rates.

Frustrated, angered, and embittered at their plight and at being exploited, the ghettoes were ready to explode. Clashes with the police—who were both symbols of the oppressive white power structure and often prejudiced toward, and unnecessarily rough and discourteous in their dealings with, ghetto blacks—touched off explosions. The nation was awakened to the dangerous situation by the riots in such ghettoes as the Watts section of Los Angeles in 1965 and in Newark and Detroit in 1967.

Many blacks were rejecting King's nonviolent tactics and his goal of an integrated society. Speaking out in March, 1964, Elijah Muhammad, leader of the Black Muslims, advocated separatism:

> We want . . . to be allowed to establish a separate state or territory . . . either on this continent or elsewhere. . . . We believe that our former slave-masters are obligated to maintain and supply our needs in this separate territory for the next twenty to twenty-five years—until we are able to produce and supply our own needs.
>
> Since we cannot get along with them in peace and equality . . . we . . . demand . . . complete separation. . . .

Elijah Muhammad warned that "Integration is a clever trick of the devils [whites]. We should not be deceived . . . in thinking that this offer of integration . . . is leading us into a better life." The Black Muslims believed in retaliatory violence, in fighting back when attacked.

Robert F. Williams of Monroe, North Carolina, was another advocate of self-defense. As leader of the local NAACP, Williams led a campaign in June, 1961, to integrate recreational facilities. When Klansmen attacked the civil rights pickets, he pointed out, authorities stood by while helpless blacks were beaten. But, under his leadership, the blacks armed themselves. Now the local authorities stepped in to prevent the Klan from provoking a general bloodletting. Accused of kidnapping a white couple in the course of a demonstration, Williams fled the nation and did not return until 1969. In his book, *Negroes with Guns* (1962), he pointed out that it had always been "an accepted right of Americans" where the law would not or could not keep order to "act in self-defense against lawless violence." He approved nonviolence where feasible, but called for fighting back when attacked. He asked, "Why do the white liberals ask us to be non-violent? We are not the aggressors . . . they . . . come to the downtrodden Negroes, who are already oppressed and too submissive as a group, and they ask them not to fight back." He wondered why the black leaders opposed black violence but not America's warmongering abroad. From exile in Cuba, Williams attacked American policies on racial and foreign matters and, according to some reports, he organized undercover groups of militant blacks in America who plotted revolutionary means to achieve their goals.

The man who became a leading spokesman for the new militancy was Malcolm X, the dynamic leader of the Black Muslims in New York. Born Malcolm Little in Omaha, Nebraska, in 1925, he had encountered American racism and violence early in life. His father was a follower of Garvey and a part-time Baptist preacher who was brutally attacked, because of his beliefs, in Omaha and in Lansing, Michigan, where the family moved. Finally, his father was killed in 1931 in an "accident" that struck most people as murder. Malcolm's mother had to be committed to a mental institution and the family was scattered. Malcolm went to live with relatives in Boston where he did well in school and aspired to be a lawyer until a white teacher told him that law school was an unrealistic goal for a black, even one like Malcolm who was first student in his class, suggesting that he take up carpentry instead. Disgusted with school, Malcolm turned to a life of crime in New York and received, he said, an unduly harsh sentence when apprehended—because he had a white girl friend. In jail, he was converted to the Black Muslim philosophy which gave him new hope. After his release from jail, he became active in the movement and soon became its most effective speaker and dynamic publicist, heading the Muslim Mosque in New York City. The charismatic appeal of Malcolm X made him a great hero to militant young blacks.

In March, 1964, Malcolm X broke with the Black Muslim leader Elijah Muhammad. He discarded the Black Muslim notion that all whites were devils. He cooperated in civil rights efforts, but urged blacks to respond to violence in kind. He set up his own group, the Organization for Afro-American Unity (OAAU). Free from Elijah Muhammad's domination, Malcolm asserted that all blacks had suffered "political oppression . . . economic exploitation . . . and social degradation at the hands of the white man." To assert this, he said "doesn't mean that we're anti-white, but it does mean we're anti-exploitation, we're anti-degradation, we're anti-oppression. And if the white man doesn't want us to be anti-him, let him stop oppressing and exploiting and degrading us." He proclaimed that he was not an American, but was "One of the 22 million black people who are the victims of democracy. . . . And I see America through the eyes of the victim. I don't see any American dream; I see an American nightmare."

Speaking at a public meeting sponsored by the Cleveland chapter of CORE in April, 1964, Malcolm X explained why blacks must control their own communities:

> A segregated school system produces children who . . . graduate with crippled minds. But this does not mean that a school is segregated because it's all black. A segregated school means a school that is controlled by people who have no real interest in it whatsoever.
>
> Let me explain. . . . They never refer to the white section as a

segregated community. . . . The white man controls his own school, his own bank, his own economy, his own politics, his own everything, his own community—but he also controls yours. When you're under someone else's control, you're segregated. They'll always give you the lowest or the worst there is to offer, but it doesn't mean you're segregated just because you have your own. You've got to *control* your own. Just like the white man has control of his, you need to control yours.

. . . it's time now for our people to become conscious of the importance of controlling the economy of our own community. If we own the stores, if we operate the businesses . . . we are creating employment for our own kind. Once you gain control of the economy of your own community, then you don't have to picket and boycott and beg . . . downtown for a job. . . .

Thus, Malcolm expressed the essence of Black Power two years before the term was popularized by Stokely Carmichael.

Malcolm X continued to grow, becoming broader in his outlook when freed from the fetters of Black Muslim doctrine. But he was assassinated in New York on February 21, 1965, while addressing a rally of the OAAU in a public meeting hall. Three days before his death, in his last formal speech, he told an overflow audience at Columbia University that "It is incorrect to classify the revolt of the Negro as simply a racial conflict of black against white, or as a purely American problem. Rather, we are today seeing a global revolution of the oppressed against the oppressor, the exploited against the exploiter."

Inspired by Malcolm X and recalling the teachings of Marcus Garvey, thousands of blacks became more militant, advocating black pride, black awareness, and black power. New militant leaders such as Floyd McKissick and Roy Innis of CORE and Stokely Carmichael and Rap Brown of SNCC emerged. Black Power first came to national attention when Carmichael espoused it during the Meredith March Against Fear through Mississippi in June, 1966, a march designed to encourage blacks to register and vote.

Black Power stressed: pride in blackness; black political control where blacks were a majority and proportionate influence in other areas; black officeholders and leaders chosen by and responsive to the black masses; policy-making by blacks in civil rights organizations, with whites working to change their own communities; black control of economic institutions in areas with black majorities; strong black political blocs that could negotiate with the larger community from positions of real strength; deemphasis of integration and instead stress on tactical separation so as to build strong black communities; concentration on improving the lot of the downtrodden black masses; and meeting violence with violence.

The writings of the black Algerian psychiatrist and revolutionist, Frantz Fanon, in such books as *The Wretched of the Earth* (1961), provided a rationale for the use of violence. He claimed that "violence is a cleansing force. It frees the native from his inferiority complex and from his despair and inaction." In October, 1966, the Black Panther Party was founded in Oakland, California, by Huey Newton and Bobby Seale. The Party became involved in fatal shoot-outs with police in various cities as it undertook the mission of protecting black communities from brutality by police, termed "pigs" in Panther literature. The Panthers became allied with white revolutionists in their struggle against what they termed the aggression of capitalist America visited on the nonwhite peasants of Vietnam and the exploited nonwhite (Third World) minorities in the United States. Eldridge Cleaver, a leading Panther and author of a bestseller, *Soul on Ice*, worked with a leading magazine of the radical New Left, *Ramparts*. Cleaver fled into exile in Cuba and Algeria to avoid jailing for his involvement in a shoot-out.

The traditional middle-class black leadership—Roy Wilkins of the NAACP, Whitney Young of the Urban League, and Martin Luther King of SCLC—initially rejected Black Power, but eventually accepted many of its tenets. They still stressed integration and nonviolence, however, opposing the violent confrontations favored by the Black Panthers.

As was the case with Garvey, most black Americans accepted Black Power's stress on black pride while rejecting its separatist tendencies. Political advances through the normal democratic process lessened the appeal of separation. Afro-Americans were elected mayors of major cities, including Carl Stokes in Cleveland, Ohio, Richard Hatcher in Gary, Indiana, and Kenneth Gibson in Newark, New Jersey, and of Southern cities, including Charles Evers (brother of Medgar) in Fayette, Mississippi. Maynard Jackson was elected Vice Mayor of Atlanta, and Thomas Bradley and Richard Austin came close in 1969 to being elected mayors of Los Angeles and Detroit, respectively, attracting many white votes. Edward Brooke of Massachusetts was elected to the United States Senate in 1966, the first black popularly elected to a Senate seat (the two black United States Senators of the Reconstruction era had been chosen by the state legislature, as were all Senators until the Seventeenth Amendment of 1913 provided for direct election). In 1966, Robert C. Weaver was appointed Secretary of the new Department of Housing and Urban Development, making him the first black to serve in the Cabinet. The next year President Johnson also named the first black to serve on the Supreme Court, Thurgood Marshall. When the 92nd Congress convened in January, 1971, it had more black members than at any pervious time, including Representative Shirley Chisholm of Brooklyn, the first black woman in Congress. But the most powerful of the black congressmen, Adam Clayton Powell, Jr., of New York, had lost his committee chairmanship and seniority in 1967 and 1969, a major setback for black political power. His defeat in the 1970 primary ended his 26 years of service in Congress.

Nonviolence, however, lost much of its appeal when Martin Luther King, Jr., the leading apostle of this approach, was assassinated on April 4, 1968, by a white sniper, James Earl Ray, in Memphis, Tennessee, where King had come to support striking sanitation workers. The slain leader was only thirty-nine years old. Some 100,000 persons assembled in Atlanta five days later for the funeral at his father's church. The mourners included the humble and the mighty, among them Robert Kennedy, Richard Nixon, Hubert Humphrey, Nelson Rockefeller, Ronald Reagan, Edward Brooke, George Romney, and Jacqueline Kennedy. At the funeral, they played the tape of the last sermon King had delivered at the church, two months before when he said:

> When I have to meet my day, I don't want a long funeral. . . . I'd like for somebody to say that day that Martin Luther King, Jr., tried to love somebody. . . . that I tried to love and serve humanity. Yes, if you want to, say that I was a drum major. Say that I was a drum major for peace . . . for righteousness. . . .

King's passing raised the spectre of racial guerilla warfare. Floyd McKissick pronounced King "the last prince of nonviolence" and maintained that now "Nonviolence is a dead philosophy," killed by white racists. Stokely Carmichael gave voice to the thoughts of many black Americans in his declaration that "When white America killed Dr. King last night she declared war on us. . . . He was the one man in our race who was trying to teach our people to have love, compassion and mercy for white people."

After King's death, Congress rushed to passage a fair housing bill that had been languishing. But Americans found it hard to face up to the grim realities inherent in the determination of a long-suffering, exploited people to suffer no more. This was demonstrated by the general derision and anger with which whites greeted a manifesto demanding reparations for injustices done blacks. Led by a former head of SNCC, James Forman, the National Black Economic Development Conference adopted a manifesto demanding $500,000,000 from American churches as atonement for centuries of exploitation in April, 1969, a year after King's slaying. The figure was subsequently increased to three billion dollars. Church leaders were initially shocked, but increasing numbers of them recognized the responsibility of white America to assist blacks to overcome the handicaps imposed on them by white America. But most white churchgoers denounced their leaders for such "appeasement."

Most white Americans were simply too comfortable with the economic and social advantages of being white to make the needed commitment to a total national effort to end racism and exploitation and to overcome the ill effects of centuries of black deprivation. Only time will tell if the apathy will end while there is still time to turn the jangling discords into harmonious brotherhood.

Suggestions for Additional Reading

This brief listing indicates some of the abundance of materials available for further reading on the history of blacks in America. The works are listed by chapters, with a select group of general works included at the end. Works known to be already available in paperback are marked with an asterisk; many others may be appearing soon in paperback editions.

Chapter 1 African Background (Prehistory to 1591)

*ARDREY, ROBERT. African Genesis. New York: Atheneum, 1965.

BALANDIER, GEORGES. Daily Life in the Kingdom of the Kongo, from the Sixteenth to the Eighteenth Century. New York: Random House, 1968.

*BOHANNAN, PAUL. Africa and Africans. Garden City, N.Y.: Natural History Press, 1964.

*COLLINS, ROBERT O., ED. Problems in African History. Englewood Cliffs, N.J.: Prentice-Hall, 1968.

*CHU, DANIEL, and SKINNER, ELLIOTT. A Glorious Age in Africa: The Story of Three Great African Empires. Garden City, N.Y.: Doubleday, 1965.

DAVIDSON, BASIL. Africa: History of a Continent. New York: Macmillan, 1966.

*DAVIDSON, BASIL. The Lost Cities of Africa. Boston: Little, Brown, 1959.

*DELAFOSSE, MAURICE. The Negroes of Africa: History and Culture. Washington, D.C.: The Associated Publishers, 1931.

*FAGE, J. D. An Introduction to the History of West Africa. Cambridge: Cambridge University Press, 1961.

*FAGE, WILLIAM, and PLASS, MARGARET. African Sculpture: An Anthology. New York: E. P. Dutton, 1964.

*HERSKOVITS, MELVILLE J. The Myth of the Negro Past. Boston: Beacon Press, 1958.

LEAKEY, L. S. B. The Progress and Evolution of Man in Africa. London: Oxford, 1961.

*OLIVER, ROLAND, ED. The Dawn of African History. London: Oxford, 1961.

*OLIVER, ROLAND, and FAGE, J. D. *A Short History of Africa.* Baltimore: Penguin, 1962.

PANIKKAR, K. MADHU. *The Serpent and the Cresent: A History of the Negro Empires of Western Africa.* Bombay: Asia Publishing House, 1963.

ROBBINS, WARREN M. *African Art in American Collections.* New York: Praeger, 1966.

TROWELL, MARGARET. *Classical African Sculpture.* New York: Praeger, 1964.

*VANSINA, JAN. *Kingdoms of the Savanna.* Madison: University of Wisconsin Press, 1966.

*WIEDNER, DONALD L. *A History of Africa South of the Sahara.* New York: Vintage, 1962.

WOODSON, CARTER G. *The African Background Outlined.* Washington, D.C.: The Association for the Study of Negro Life and History, 1936.

Chapter 2 *The Slave Trade and Latin American Slavery (1441–1565)*

BROWNING, JAMES B. "Negro Companions of the Spanish Pioneers in the New World," *Howard University Studies in History.* Washington, D.C.: Howard University, 1930.

*CURTIN, PHILIP D., ED. *Africa Remembered: Narratives by West Africans from the Era of the Slave Trade.* Madison: University of Wisconsin Press, 1967.

*DAVIDSON, BASIL. *Black Mother: The Years of the African Slave Trade.* Boston: Little, Brown, 1961.

DONNAN, ELIZABETH, ED. *Documents Illustrative of the History of the Slave Trade to America.* 4 vols. Washington, D.C.: Carnegie Institution, 1930–1935.

DU BOIS, WILLIAM EDGAR BURGHARDT. *The Suppression of the African Slave-Trade to the United States, 1638–1870.* New York: Longmans, Green, 1896.

*HARRIS, MARVIN. *Patterns of Race in the Americas.* New York: Walker & Company, 1963.

*HORGAN, PAUL. *Conquistadores in North American History.* New York: Farrar, Strauss, 1963.

KLEIN, HERBERT S. *Slavery in the Americas: A Comparative Study of Virginia and Cuba.* Chicago: University of Chicago Press, 1967.

*MANNIX, DANIEL P., and COWLEY, MALCOLM. *Black Cargoes: A History of the Atlantic Slave Trade, 1518–1865.* New York: Viking Press, 1965.

*TANNENBAUM, FRANK. *Slave and Citizen: The Negro in the Americas.* New York: Vintage, 1963.

*WILLIAMS, ERIC. *Capitalism and Slavery.* Chapel Hill: University of North Carolina Press, 1944. (Paperback edition published by G. P. Putnam's Sons, New York.)

Chapter 3 Slavery in the British Colonies (1619–1763)

DAVIS, DAVID BRION. *The Problem of Slavery in Western Culture.* Ithaca, N.Y.: Cornell University Press, 1966.

FLANDERS, RALPH BETTS. *Plantation Slavery in Georgia.* Chapel Hill, N.C.: University of North Carolina Press, 1933.

*GREENE, LORENZO J. *The Negro in Colonial New England, 1620–1776.* New York: Columbia University Press, 1942. (Atheneum Paperback, New York.)

JERNEGAN, MARCUS W. *Laboring and Dependent Classes in Colonial America.* Chicago: University of Chicago Press, 1931.

*JORDAN, WINTHROP D. *White Over Black: American Attitudes Toward the Negro, 1550–1812.* Chapel Hill: University of North Carolina Press, 1968. (Paperback edition by Penguin Books, Baltimore, Md.)

KLINGBERG, FRANK J. *An Appraisal of the Negro in Colonial South Carolina.* Washington, D.C.: The Associated Publishers, 1941.

McMANUS, EDGAR J. *A History of Negro Slavery in New York.* Syracuse, N.Y.: Syracuse University Press, 1966.

*PHILLIPS, ULRICH B. *Life and Labor in the Old South.* Boston: Little, Brown, 1963. (Reprint of 1929 book.)

RUSSELL, JOHN H. *The Free Negro in Virginia, 1619–1865.* Baltimore: The Johns Hopkins Press, 1913.

STEINER, BERNARD C. *History of Slavery in Connecticut.* Baltimore: The Johns Hopkins Press, 1893.

*STEPHENSON, WENDELL HOLMES. *A Basic History of the Old South.* Princeton, N.J.: Van Nostrand, 1950.

*TATE, THADDEUS W. *The Negro in Eighteenth-Century Williamsburg.* Charlottesville: The University Press of Virginia, 1965.

TURNER, EDWARD RAYMOND. *The Negro in Pennsylvania: Slavery, Servitude, Freedom, 1639–1861.* Washington, D.C.: The American Historical Association, 1911.

Writer's Program, Work Projects Administration. *The Negro in Virginia.* New York: Hastings House, 1940.

Chapter 4 Afro-Americans in the Revolutionary Era (1763–1800)

*APTHEKER, HERBERT. *Essays in the History of the American Negro.* New York: International Publishers, 1964.

BINDER, FREDERICK M. *The Color Problem in Early National America.* The Hague, The Netherlands: Mouton & Company, 1968.

BRAWLEY, BENJAMIN. *Early Negro American Writers.* Chapel Hill: University of North Carolina Press, 1935.

CRAWFORD, GEORGE W. *Prince Hall and His Followers.* New York: The Crisis, 1914.

*DOBLER, LAVINIA, and TOPPIN, EDGAR. *Pioneers and Patriots: The Lives of Six Negroes of the Revolutionary Era.* Garden City, N.Y.: Doubleday, 1965.

FRAZIER, E. FRANKLIN. *The Negro Church in America.* New York.: Schocken Books, 1964.

JACKSON, LUTHER P. *Virginia Negro Soldiers and Seamen in the Revolutionary War.* Norfolk, Va.: Guide Quality Press, 1944.

*QUARLES, BENJAMIN. *The Negro in the American Revolution.* Chapel Hill: University of North Carolina Press, 1961.

RUCHAMES, LOUIS, ED. *Racial Thought in America*, vol. I, *From the Puritans to Abraham Lincoln: A Documentary History.* Amherst: University of Massachusetts Press, 1969.

*WASHINGTON, JOSEPH R. *Black Religion: The Negro and Christianity in the United States.* Boston: Beacon Press, 1964.

WESLEY, CHARLES H. *Richard Allen, Apostle of Freedom.* Washington, D.C.: The Associated Publishers, 1969. (Revision of 1935 book.)

WOODSON, CARTER G. *The History of the Negro Church.* Washington, D.C.: The Associated Publishers, 1921.

ZILVERSMIT, ARTHUR. *The First Emancipation: The Abolition of Negro Slavery in the North.* Chicago: University of Chicago Press, 1967.

Chapter 5 Cotton Kingdom and Plantation Slavery (1791–1860)

DUIGNAN, PETER, and CLENDENEN, CLARENCE. *The United States and the African Slave Trade, 1619–1862.* Stanford, Calif.: Stanford University, 1963.

EATON, CLEMENT. *A History of the Old South.* New York: Macmillan, 1949.

FRANKLIN, JOHN HOPE. *The Free Negro in North Carolina, 1790–1860.* Chapel Hill: University of North Carolina Press, 1943.

GENOVESE, EUGENE D. *The Political Economy of Slavery; Studies in the Economy and Society of the Slave South.* New York: Pantheon Books, 1965.

HOWARD, WARREN S. *American Slavers and the Federal Law, 1837–1862.* Berkeley: University of California Press, 1963.

JACKSON, LUTHER P. *Free Negro Labor and Property Holding in Virginia, 1830–1860.* New York: Appleton-Century, 1942.

McCONNELL, ROLAND C. *Negro Troops of Antebellum Louisiana: A History of the Battalion of Free Men of Color.* Baton Rouge: Louisiana State University Press, 1968.

MIRSKY, JEANETTE, and NEVINS, ALLAN. *The World of Eli Whitney.* New York: Macmillan, 1952.

*SYDNOR, CHARLES S. *Slavery in Mississippi.* Baton Rouge: Louisiana State University Press, 1966.

TAYLOR, ORVILLE W. *Negro Slavery in Arkansas*. Durham, N.C.: Duke University Press, 1958.

*WADE, RICHARD C. *Slavery in the Cities: The South, 1820–1860*. New York: Oxford University Press, 1964.

Chapter 6 Slave Life and Revolts (1800–1860)

*APTHEKER, HERBERT. *American Negro Slave Revolts*. New York: Columbia University Press, 1943.

APTHEKER, HERBERT. *Nat Turner's Slave Rebellion*. New York: Humanities Press, 1966.

BANCROFT, FREDERIC. *Slave Trading in the Old South*. Baltimore: J. H. Furst, 1931.

BAUER, RAYMOND, and BAUER, ALICE. "Day by Day Resistance to Slavery," *The Journal of Negro History*, XXVII (October, 1942), 388–419.

*BOTKIN, B. A., ED. *Lay My Burden Down: A Folk History of Slavery*. Chicago: University of Chicago Press, 1945.

*BROWN, WILLIAM WELLS. *The Narrative of William W. Brown, a Fugitive Slave*. Reading, Mass.: Addison-Wesley, 1969.

*EATON, CLEMENT. *The Growth of Southern Civilization, 1790–1860*. New York: Harper, 1961.

*ELKINS, STANLEY M. *Slavery: A Problem in American Institutional and Intellectual Life*, New York: Grossett & Dunlap, 1963.

FISHER, MILES MARK. *Negro Slave Songs in the United States*. Ithaca, N.Y.: Cornell University Press, 1953.

*HENSON, JOSIAH. *Father Henson's Story of His Own Life*. New York: Corinth, 1962.

LOCKE, ALAIN. *The Negro and His Music*. Washington, D.C.: The Associates in Negro Folk Education, 1936.

LOFTON, JOHN. *Insurrection in South Carolina: The Turbulent World of Denmark Vesey*. Yellow Springs, Ohio: Antioch Press, 1964.

NORTHRUP, SOLOMON *Twelve Years a Slave*. Edited by SUE EAKIN and JOSEPH LOGSDON. Baton Rouge: Louisiana State University Press, 1968.

*OLMSTED, FREDERICK LAW. *The Slave States (Before the Civil War)*. Edited by HARVEY WISH. New York: G. P. Putnam's Sons, 1959.

*OSOFSKY, GILBERT, ED. *Puttin' On Ole Massa: The Slave Narratives of Henry Bibb, Williams Wells Brown and Solomon Northrup*. New York: Harper, 1969.

*PHILLIPS, ULRICH B. *American Negro Slavery*. Baton Rouge: Louisiana State University Press, 1966. (Reprint of 1918 book.)

*STAMPP, KENNETH M. *The Peculiar Institution: Slavery in the Ante-Bellum South*. New York: Vintage Books, 1956.

WALKER, DAVID. *David Walker's Appeal*. New York: Hill and Wang, 1965.

*WEINSTEIN, ALLEN, and GATELL, FRANK OTTO. *American Negro Slavery: A Modern Reader*. New York: Oxford University Press, 1968.

*WISH, HARVEY, ED. *Slavery in the South: First-Hand Accounts of the Ante-Bellum American Southland from Northern & Southern Whites, Negroes & Foreign Observers.* New York: Farrar, Straus, 1964.

Chapter 7 North of Slavery and Black Abolitionists (1800–1860)

*BENNETT, LERONE, JR. *Pioneers in Protest.* Chicago: Johnson Publishing Company, 1968. (Paperback edition by Penguin Books, Baltimore, Md.)

*BONTEMPS, ARNA, and CONROY, JACK. *Anyplace but Here.* New York: Hill and Wang, 1966.

BONNER, T. D., ED. *The Life and Adventures of James P. Beckwourth.* New York: Knopf, 1931.

BRADFORD, SARAH. *Harriet Tubman, the Moses of Her People.* New York: Corinth, 1961. (Reprint of 1886 book.)

BRAWLEY, BENJAMIN. *The Negro Genius; A New Appraisal of the American Negro in Literature and the Fine Arts.* New York: Dodd, Mead, 1937.

BROWN, STERLING. *Negro Poetry and Drama.* Washington, D.C.: The Associates in Negro Folk Education, 1937.

BUCKMASTER, HENRIETTA. *Let My People Go; The Story of the Underground Railroad.* New York: Harper & Brothers, 1941.

*DOUGLASS, FREDERICK. *Life and Times of Frederick Douglass.* New York: Collier Books, 1962. (Reprint of 1892 book.)

DOVER, CEDRIC. *American Negro Art.* Greenwich, Conn.: New York Graphic Society, 1960.

*DUBERMAN, MARTIN, ED. *The Antislavery Vanguard: New Essays on the Abolitionists.* Princeton, N.J.: Princeton University Press, 1965.

*DUMOND, DWIGHT L. *Antislavery: The Crusade for Freedom in America.* Ann Arbor: University of Michigan Press, 1961. (Paperback edition by Norton, New York.)

FARRISON, WILLIAM EDWARD. *William Wells Brown: Author and Reformer.* Chicago: University of Chicago Press, 1969.

FAUSET, ARTHUR H. *Sojourner Truth: God's Faithful Pilgrim.* Chapel Hill: University of North Carolina Press, 1938.

FONER, PHILLIP S. *Frederick Douglass.* New York: Citadel Press, 1964.

FONER, PHILIP S. *The Life and Writings of Frederick Douglass.* 4 vols. New York: International Publishers, 1950.

FORTEN, CHARLOTTE. *The Journal of Charlotte Forten.* Edited by RAY ALLEN BILLINGTON. New York: The Dryden Press, 1953.

*GARA, LARRY. *The Liberty Line: The Legend of the Underground Railroad.* Lexington: University of Kentucky Press, 1961.

HARE, MAUD CUNEY. *Negro Musicians and Their Music.* Washington: The Associated Publishers, 1936.

*LITWACK, LEON F. *North of Slavery: The Negro in the Free States, 1790–1860.* Chicago: University of Chicago Press, 1961.

MALVIN, JOHN. *North into Freedom: The Autobiography of John Malvin, Free Negro, 1795–1880.* Edited by ALLAN PESKIN. Cleveland: The Press of Western Reserve University, 1966.

MARSHALL, HERBERT, and STOCK, MILDRED. *Ira Aldridge, the Negro Tragedian.* New York: Macmillan, 1958.

*PORTER, JAMES A. *Modern Negro Art.* New York: The Dryden Press, 1943. (Paperback edition by Grosset & Dunlap, New York.)

QUARLES, BENJAMIN. *Black Abolitionists.* New York: Oxford University Press, 1969.

QUARLES, BENJAMIN. *Frederick Douglass.* Washington, D.C.: The Associated Publishers, 1948.

*QUARLES, BENJAMIN, ED. *Frederick Douglass* (Great Lives Observed Series). Englewood Cliffs, N.J.: Prentice-Hall, 1969.

*STERLING, PHILIP, and LOGAN, RAYFORD. *Four Took Freedom: The Lives of Harriet Tubman, Frederick Douglass, Robert Smalls, and Blanche K. Bruce.* Garden City, N.Y.: Doubleday, 1967.

WOODSON, CARTER G. *The Education of the Negro Prior to 1861.* New York: G. P. Putnam's Sons, 1919.

Chapter 8 Slavery Issue and the Civil War (1850–1865)

BREWER, JAMES H. *The Confederate Negro: Virginia's Craftsmen and Military Laborers, 1861–1865.* Durham, N.C.: Duke University Press, 1969.

*CORNISH, DUDLEY TAYLOR. *The Sable Arm: Negro Troops in the Union Army, 1861–1865.* New York: Norton, 1966.

*DUMOND, DWIGHT L. *Antislavery Origins of the Civil War in the United States.* Ann Arbor: University of Michigan Press, 1960.

FRANKLIN, JOHN HOPE. *The Emancipation Proclamation.* Garden City, N.Y.: Doubleday, 1963.

*FRANKLIN, JOHN HOPE. *The Militant South, 1800–1861.* Boston: Beacon Press, 1964.

HUGHES, LANGSTON. *Famous Negro Heroes of America.* New York: Dodd, Mead, 1958.

*KUTLER, STANLEY I., ED. *The Dred Scott Decision: Law or Politics?* Boston: Houghton Mifflin, 1967.

*MCCARTHY, AGNES, and REDDICK, LAWRENCE. *Worth Fighting For: A History of the Negro in the United States during the Civil War and Reconstruction.* Garden City, N.Y.: Doubleday, 1965.

*MCPHERSON, JAMES M. *The Negro's Civil War: How American Negroes Felt and Acted during the War for the Union.* New York: Random House Pantheon Book, 1965.

QUARLES, BENJAMIN. *Lincoln and the Negro.* New York: Oxford University Press, 1962.

QUARLES, BENJAMIN. *The Negro in the Civil War.* Boston: Little, Brown, 1953.

*ROZWENC, EDWIN, ED. *Slavery as a Cause of the Civil War.* Boston: Heath, 1963.

STANTON, WILLIAM R. *The Leopard's Spots; Scientific Attitudes toward Race in America, 1815–1859.* Chicago: University of Chicago Press, 1966.

VOEGELI, V. JACQUE. *Free but Not Equal: The Midwest and the Negro During the Civil War.* Chicago: University of Chicago Press, 1967.

*WILEY, BELL IRVIN. *Southern Negroes, 1861–1865.* New Haven: Yale University Press, 1938.

Chapter 9 Freedmen and Carpetbag Regimes (1865–1877)

*BUCKMASTER, HENRIETTA. *Freedom Bound.* New York: Macmillan, 1967.

COX, LAWANDA, and COX, JOHN. *Politics, Principle, and Prejudice, 1865–1866: Dilemma of Reconstruction America.* New York: Macmillan Free Press, 1963.

*CRAVEN, AVERY. *Reconstruction: The Ending of the Civil War.* New York: Holt, Rinehart, 1969.

*CROWE, CHARLES, ED. *The Age of Civil War and Reconstruction, 1830–1900. A Book of Interpretive Essays.* Homewood, Ill.: Dorsey, 1966.

*CRUDEN, ROBERT. *The Negro in Reconstruction.* Englewood Cliffs, N.J.: Prentice-Hall, 1969.

DONALD, HENDERSON. *The Negro Freedman: Life Conditions of the American Negro in the Early Years after Emancipation.* New York: H. Schuman, 1952.

*DU BOIS, W. E. B. *Black Reconstruction.* New York: Harcourt, Brace, 1935.

*DUNNING, WILLIAM A. *Reconstruction, Political and Economic, 1865–1877.* New York: Harper Torchbook, 1962. (Reprint of 1907 book.)

DURDEN, ROBERT F. *James Shepherd Pike: Republicanism and the American Negro, 1850–1882.* Durham, N.C.: Duke University Press, 1957.

*FLEMING, WALTER L., ED. *Documentary History of Reconstruction . . . 1865 to 1906.* 2 vols. New York: McGraw-Hill, 1966. (Reprint of 1906–1907 book.)

*FRANKLIN, JOHN HOPE. *Reconstruction after the Civil War.* Chicago: University of Chicago Press, 1951.

KORNGOLD, RALPH. *Thaddeus Stevens.* New York: Harcourt, Brace, 1955.

*MCKITRICK, ERIC L. *Andrew Johnson and Reconstruction.* Chicago: University of Chicago Press, 1960.

*MCPHERSON, JAMES. *The Struggle for Equality: Abolitionists and the Negro* *in the Civil War and Reconstruction*. Princeton, N.J.: Princeton University Press, 1964.

*PATRICK, REMBERT W. *The Reconstruction of the Nation*. New York: Oxford University Press, 1967.

*ROSE, WILLIE LEE. *Rehearsal for Reconstruction: The Port Royal Experiment*. Indianapolis: Bobbs, Merrill, 1964.

*SHENTON, JAMES P. *The Reconstruction: A Documentary History, 1865–1877*. New York: Putnam's, 1963.

*SINGLETARY, OTIS A. *Negro Militia and Reconstruction*. New York: McGraw-Hill, 1963.

SMITH, SAMUEL DENNY. *The Negro in Congress, 1870–1901*. Chapel Hill: University of North Carolina Press, 1940.

*STAMPP, KENNETH M. *The Era of Reconstruction, 1865–1877*. New York: Knopf, 1965.

TAYLOR, ALRUTHEUS A. *The Negro in South Carolina During Reconstruction*. Washington, D.C.: Association for the Study of Negro Life and History, 1924.

TAYLOR, ALRUTHEUS A. *The Negro in Tennessee, 1865–1880*. Washington, D.C.: The Associated Publishers, 1941.

TAYLOR, ALRUTHEUS A. *The Negro in the Reconstruction of Virginia*. Washington, D.C.: Association for the Study of Negro Life and History, 1926.

*WHARTON, VERNON LANE. *The Negro in Mississippi, 1865–1890*. New York: Harper Torchbook, 1965. (Reprint of 1947 book.)

WILLIAMSON, JOEL. *After Slavery: The Negro in South Carolina During Reconstruction, 1861–1877*. Chapel Hill: University of North Carolina Press, 1965.

WILSON, THEODORE BRANTNER. *The Black Codes of the South*. University, Ala.: University of Alabama Press, 1965.

Chapter 10 Atlanta Compromise, Disfranchisement, and Jim Crow (1877–1900)

*BAKER, RAY STANNARD. *Following the Color Line: American Negro Citizenship in the Progressive Era*. New York: Harper, 1964. (Reprint of 1908 book.)

*BLAIR, LEWIS H. *A Southern Prophecy: The Prosperity of the South Dependent upon the Elevation of the Negro*. Boston: Little, Brown, 1964. (Reprint of 1889 book.)

BOND, HORACE MANN. *The Education of the Negro in the American Social Order*. New York: Prentice-Hall, 1934.

*CABLE, GEORGE W. *The Negro Question: A Selection of Writings on Civil Rights in the South*. Edited by ARLIN TURNER. New York: Norton, 1968.

EDMONDS, HELEN G. *The Negro and Fusion Politics in North Carolina, 1894–1901*. Chapel Hill: University of North Carolina Press, 1951.

*FURNAS, J. C. *Goodbye to Uncle Tom*. New York: William Sloane Associates, 1956.

*HARLAN, LOUIS R. *Separate and Unequal: Public School Campaigns and Racism in the Southern Seaboard States, 1901–1915*. Chapel Hill: University of North Carolina Press, 1958.

HARRIS, ROBERT J. *The Quest for Equality: The Constitution, Congress and the Supreme Court*. Baton Rouge: Louisiana State University Press, 1960.

*HAWKINS, HUGH, ED. *Booker T. Washington and His Critics: The Problem of Negro Leadership*. Boston: Heath, 1962.

*LEWINSON, PAUL. *Race, Class, and Party: A History of Negro Suffrage and White Politics in the South*. New York: Grosset & Dunlap, 1965. (Reprint of 1932 book.)

LOGAN, FRENISE A. *The Negro in North Carolina, 1876–1894*. Chapel Hill: University of North Carolina Press, 1964.

LOGAN, RAYFORD. *The Negro in American Life and Thought: The Nadir, 1877–1901*. New York: Dial, 1954.

MATHEWS, BASIL. *Booker T. Washington: Educator and Interracial Interpreter*. Cambridge, Mass.: Harvard University Press, 1948.

*MEIER, AUGUST. *Negro Thought in America, 1880–1915: Racial Ideologies in the Age of Booker T. Washington*. Ann Arbor: University of Michigan Press, 1963.

NEWBY, I. A. *Jim Crow's Defense: Anti-Negro Thought in America, 1900–1930*. Baton Rouge: Louisiana State University Press, 1965.

RAPER, ARTHUR. *The Tragedy of Lynching*. Chapel Hill: University of North Carolina Press, 1933.

SEABROOK, ISAAC DUBOSE. *Before and After, or, The Relations of the Races at the South*. Baton Rouge: Louisiana State University Press, 1967.

*SPENCER, SAMUEL R. *Booker T. Washington and the Negro's Place in American Life*. Boston: Little, Brown, 1955.

*THORNBROUGH, EMMA LOU, ED. *Booker T. Washington* (Great Lives Observed Series). Englewood Cliffs, N.J.: Prentice-Hall, 1969.

*TINDALL, GEORGE BROWN. *South Carolina Negroes, 1877–1900*. Louisiana State University Press, 1966. (Reprint of 1952 book.)

WASHINGTON, BOOKER T. *My Larger Education: Being Chapters from my Experience*. Garden City, N.Y.: Doubleday, Page, 1911.

*WASHINGTON, BOOKER T. *Up from Slavery*. New York: Dell, 1965. (Reprint of 1902 book.)

*WISH, HARVEY, ED. *The Negro Since Emancipation*. Englewood Cliffs, N.J.: Prentice-Hall, 1964.

*WOODWARD, C. VANN. *The Strange Career of Jim Crow*. Revised edition. New York: Oxford University Press, 1957.

WYNES, CHARLES E. *Race Relations in Virginia, 1870–1902*. Charlottesville: University of Virginia Press, 1961.

*ZIEGLER, BENJAMIN MUNN, ED. *Desegregation and the Supreme Court*. Boston: Heath, 1958.

Chapter 11 Northward Migration and Turn-of-the-Century Achievers (1880–1910)

BRAWLEY, BENJAMIN. *Paul Laurence Dunbar: Poet of His People*. Chapel Hill: University of North Carolina Press, 1936.

BUCKLER, HELEN. *Dr. Dan: Pioneer in American Surgery*. Boston: Little, Brown, 1954.

CHESNUTT, HELEN M. *Charles Waddell Chesnutt: Pioneer of the Color Line*. Chapel Hill: University of North Carolina Press, 1952.

COURLANDER, HAROLD. *Negro Folk Music, U.S.A.* New York: Columbia University Press, 1963.

*DRISKO, CAROL F., and TOPPIN, EDGAR A. *The Unfinished March: The Negro in the United States, Reconstruction to World War I*. Garden City, N.Y.: Doubleday, 1967.

DURHAM, PHILLIP, and JONES, EVERETT L. *The Negro Cowboys*. New York: Dodd, Mead, 1965.

ELLIOTT, LAWRENCE. *George Washington Carver: The Man Who Overcame*. Englewood Cliffs, N.J.: Prentice-Hall, 1966.

EMANUEL, JAMES A., and GROSS, THEODORE L., EDS. *Dark Symphony: Negro Literature in America*. New York: Macmillan Free Press, 1968.

*FRAZIER, E. FRANKLIN. *The Negro Family in the United States*. Revised and abridged. Chicago: University of Chicago Press, 1966.

GREENE, LORENZO, and WOODSON, CARTER G. *The Negro Wage Earner*. Washington, D.C.: Association for the Study of Negro Life and History, 1930.

HANDY, W. C. *Father of the Blues: An Autobiography*. New York: Macmillan, 1947.

HARRIS, ABRAM L. *The Negro as Capitalist: A Study of Banking and Business Among American Negroes*. Philadelphia: American Academy of Political and Social Science, 1936.

HENDERSON, EDWIN B. *The Negro in Sports*. Revised edition. Washington, D.C.: The Associated Publishers, 1949.

*LOCKE, ALAIN. *Negro Art: Past and Present*. Washington, D.C.: Associates in Negro Folk Education, 1936. (Paperback edition by Grosset & Dunlap, New York).

LOGGINS, VERNON. *The Negro Author, His Development in America to 1900*. Port Washington, N.Y.: Kennikat Press, 1964.

MATHEWS, MARCIA M. *Henry Ossawa Tanner: American Artist*. Chicago: University of Chicago Press, 1969.

OTTLEY, ROI. *The Lonely Warrior: The Life and Times of Robert S. Abbott*. Chicago: Regnery, 1955.

REDDING, J. SAUNDERS. *To Make a Poet Black*. Chapel Hill: University of North Carolina Press, 1939.

REID, IRA DE A. *The Negro Immigrant, His Background, Characteristics, and Social Adjustment, 1899–1937.* New York: Columbia University Press, 1939.

*ROBINSON, BRADLEY. (with MATTHEW HENSON). *Dark Companion: The Story of Matthew Henson.* Revised edition. New York: Fawcett, 1967.

SCHEINER, SETH M. *Negro Mecca; A History of the Negro in New York City, 1865–1920.* New York: New York University Press, 1965.

SPEAR, ALLAN H. *Black Chicago: The Making of a Negro Ghetto, 1890–1920.* Chicago: University of Chicago Press, 1967.

*SPERO, STERLING, and HARRIS, ABRAM L. *The Black Worker: The Negro and the Labor Movement.* New York: Columbia University Press, 1931.

WESLEY, CHARLES H. *Negro Labor in the United States, 1850–1925.* New York: Vanguard, 1927.

WOODSON, CARTER G. *A Century of Negro Migration.* Washington, D.C.: Association for the Study of Negro Life and History, 1918.

Chapter 12 The Niagara Movement, NAACP, and World War I (1905–1921)

*BRODERICK, FRANCIS L. *W. E. B. DuBois: Negro Leader in a Time of Crisis.* Stanford, Calif.: Stanford University Press, 1959.

*BRODERICK, FRANCIS L., and MEIER, AUGUST, EDS. *Negro Protest Thought in the Twentieth Century.* Indianapolis: Bobbs-Merrill, 1965.

*DU BOIS, W. E. B. *The Souls of Black Folk: Essays and Sketches.* Chicago: A. C. McClurg, 1903. (Paperback edition by Fawcett, New York.)

*FULLINWIDER, S. P. *The Mind and Mood of Black America: 20th Century Thought.* Homewood, Ill.: The Dorsey Press, 1969.

*HUGHES, LANGSTON. *Fight for Freedom: The Story of the NAACP.* New York: Berkley, 1962.

JACK, ROBERT L. *History of the National Association for the Advancement of Colored People.* Boston: Meador, 1943.

*JOHNSON, JAMES WELDON. *Along This Way . . . Autobiography.* New York: Viking, 1933.

KELLOGG, CHARLES FLINT. *A History of the National Association for the Advancement of Colored People, Volume I, 1909–1920.* Baltimore: Johns Hopkins University Press, 1967.

*LOGAN, RAYFORD W. *The Betrayal of the Negro: From Rutherford B. Hayes to Woodrow Wilson.* New York: Collier, 1965. (Revised and enlarged edition of *The Negro in American Life and Thought: The Nadir*)

MILLER, LOREN. *The Petitioners: The Story of the Supreme Court of the United States and the Negro.* New York: Random House, 1966.

*NEWBY, I. A., ED. *The Development of Segregationist Thought.* Homewood, Ill.: The Dorsey Press, 1968.

OVINGTON, MARY WHITE. *The Walls Came Tumbling Down.* New York: Harcourt, Brace, 1947.

RUDWICK, ELLIOTT M. *Race Riot at East St. Louis, July 2, 1917.* Carbondale: Southern Illinois University Press, 1964.

RUDWICK, ELLIOTT M. *W. E. B. DuBois: A Study in Minority Group Leadership.* Philadelphia: University of Pennsylvania Press, 1960.

SCOTT, EMMETT J. *Scott's Official History of the American Negro in the World War.* Chicago: Homewood Press, 1919 .

*STERLING, DOROTHY, and QUARLES, BENJAMIN. *Lift Every Voice: The Lives of Booker T. Washington, W. E. B. DuBois, Mary Church Terrell, and James Weldon Johnson.* Garden City, N.Y.: Doubleday, 1965.

TERRELL, MARY CHURCH. *A Colored Woman in a White World.* Washington, D.C.: Ransdell, 1940.

TORRENCE, RIDGELY. *The Story of John Hope.* New York: Macmillan, 1948.

WHITE, WALTER. *Rope and Faggot, A Biography of Judge Lynch.* New York: Knopf, 1929.

Chapter 13 UNIA, Harlem Renaissance, and the New Deal (1920–1940)

BOND, FREDERICK W. *The Negro and the Drama.* Washington, D.C.: The Associated Publishers, 1940.

BROWN, STERLING. *The Negro in American Fiction.* Washington, D.C.: Associates in Negro Folk Education, 1937.

BUNI, ANDREW. *The Negro in Virginia Politics, 1902–1965.* Charlottesville: The University Press of Virginia, 1967.

CAYTON, HORACE R., and MITCHELL, GEORGE S. *Black Workers and the New Unions.* Chapel Hill: University of North Carolina Press, 1939.

*CRONON, EDMUND DAVID. *Black Moses: The Story of Marcus Garvey and the Universal Negro Improvement Association.* Madison: University of Wisconsin Press, 1966.

*DRAKE, ST. CLAIR, and CAYTON, HORACE R. *Black Metropolis: A Study of Negro Life in a Northern City.* Revised and enlarged edition. 2 vols. New York: Harper & Row, 1962.

GARVEY, MRS. AMY JACQUES, ED. *Philosophy and Opinions of Marcus Garvey.* 2 vols. New York: Universal, 1923-1925.

GLOSTER, HUGH M. *Negro Voices in American Fiction.* Chapel Hill: University of North Carolina Press, 1948.

*GOSNELL, HAROLD F. *Negro Politicians: The Rise of Negro Politics in Chicago.* Chicago: University of Chicago Press, 1967. (Reprint of 1935 book.)

ISAACS, EDITH J. R. *The Negro in the American Theatre.* New York: Theatre Arts, 1947.

*JACOBSON, JULIUS, ED. *The Negro and the American Labor Movement.* Garden City, N.Y.: Doubleday, 1968.

JOHNSON, JAMES WELDON. *Black Manhattan.* New York: Knopf, 1930.

*JONES, LEROI. *Blues People: Negro Music in White America.* New York: William Morrow & Company, 1963.

*KEIL, CHARLES. *Urban Blues.* Chicago: University of Chicago Press, 1966.

KENNEDY, LOUISE V. *The Negro Peasant Turns Cityward: Effects of Recent Migrations to Northern Centers.* New York: Columbia University Press, 1930.

LOCKE, ALAIN, ED. *The Negro in Art: A Pictorial Record of the Negro Artist and of the Negro Theme in Art.* Washington, D.C.: Associates in Negro Folk Education, 1940.

LOCKE, ALAIN, ED. *The New Negro: An Interpretation.* New York: A. & C. Boni, 1925.

MARSHALL, RAY. *The Negro and Organized Labor.* New York: Wiley, 1965.

*MELTZER, MILTON, and MEIER, AUGUST. *Time of Trial, Time of Hope: The Negro in America, 1919–1941.* Garden City, N.Y.: Doubleday, 1966.

MITCHELL, LOFTON. *Black Drama; The Story of the American Negro in the Theatre.* New York: Hawthorn, 1967.

NORTHRUP, HERBERT R. *Organized Labor and the Negro.* New York: Harper, 1944.

OSOFSKY, GILBERT. *Harlem: The Making of a Ghetto; Negro New York, 1890–1930.* New York: Harper, 1966.

RECORD, WILSON. *The Negro and the Communist Party.* Chapel Hill: University of North Carolina Press, 1951.

WEAVER, ROBERT C. *Negro Labor, A National Problem.* New York: Harcourt, Brace, 1946.

*WRIGHT, RICHARD. *Native Son.* New York: Harper, 1940. (Paperback edition by Signet, New York.)

Chapter 14 Era of Progress: World War II Through Desegregation Decision (1941–1955)

ANDERSON, MARIAN. *My Lord, What a Morning: An Autobiography.* New York: Viking, 1956.

*ASHMORE, HARRY S. *The Negro and the Schools.* Revised edition. Chapel Hill: University of North Carolina Press, 1954.

*BALDWIN, JAMES. *Go Tell It on the Mountain.* New York: Dell, 1953.

*BONE, ROBERT A. *The Negro Novel in America.* New Haven, Conn.: Yale University Press, 1965.

BULLOCK, HENRY ALLEN. *A History of Negro Education in the South: From 1619 to the Present.* Cambridge, Mass.: Harvard University Press, 1967.

CLARK, KENNETH. *Prejudice and Your Child.* Boston: Beacon Press, 1955.

CLIFT, VIRGIL, and others. *Negro Education in America: Its Adequacy, Problems, and Needs.* New York: Harper, 1962.

*ELLISON, RALPH. *Invisible Man.* New York: Signet, 1952.

*ELLISON, RALPH. *Shadow and Act.* New York: Signet, 1964.

*FRANKLIN, JOHN HOPE, and STARR, ISIDORE, EDS. *The Negro in Twentieth Century America: A Reader on the Struggle for Civil Rights.* New York: Vintage Books, 1967.

*GROSS, SEYMOUR L., and HARDY, JOHN EDWARD, EDS. *Images of the Negro in American Literature.* Chicago: University of Chicago Press, 1966.

HILL, HERBERT, ED. *Soon One Morning: New Writing by American Negroes, 1940–1962.* New York: Knopf, 1963.

HUGHES, LANGSTON, and MELTZER, MILTON. *Black Magic: A Pictorial History of the Negro in American Entertainment.* Englewood Cliffs, N.J.: Prentice-Hall, 1967.

*ISAACS, HAROLD R. *The New World of Negro Americans.* New York: John Day, 1963.

LEE, ULYSSES. *The Employment of Negro Troops.* (U.S. Army, History of World War II). Washington, D.C.: Government Printing Office, 1966.

*LEWIS, ANTHONY, and THE NEW YORK TIMES. *Portrait of a Decade: The Second American Revolution (1954–1964).* New York: Random House, 1964.

LOGAN, RAYFORD W. *The Negro and the Post-War World: A Primer.* Washington, D.C.: The Minorities Publishers, 1945.

MANN, ARTHUR. *The Jackie Robinson Story.* New York: Grosset & Dunlap, 1963.

ROBINSON, JACKIE. *Jackie Robinson: My Own Story,* as told to WENDELL SMITH. New York: Greenberg, 1948.

RUCHAMES, LOUIS. *Race, Jobs and Politics: The Story of FEPC.* New York: Columbia University Press, 1953.

*SMITH, BOB. *They Closed Their Schools: Prince Edward County, Virginia, 1951–1964.* Chapel Hill: University of North Carolina Press, 1965.

ST. JAMES, WARREN D. *The National Association for the Advancement of Colored People: A Case Study in Pressure Groups.* New York: Exposition Press, 1958.

*UNITED STATES COMMISSION ON CIVIL RIGHTS. *Freedom to the Free: Century of Emancipation, 1863–1963.* Washington, D.C.: Government Printing Office, 1963.

WHITE, WALTER. *A Man Called White . . . Autobiography.* New York: Viking, 1948.

WHITE, WALTER. *How Far the Promised Land.* New York: Viking, 1955.

WHITE, WALTER. *A Rising Wind.* Garden City, N.Y.: Doubleday, Doran, 1945.

YOUNG, A. S. "DOC." *Negro Firsts in Sports.* Chicago: Johnson Publishing Company, 1963.

Chapter 15 Civil Rights Revolution and New Militancy (1955–1971)

*BARBOUR, FLOYD B., ED. *The Black Power Revolt: A Collection of Essays.* Boston: Porter Sargent, 1968.

*BELL, INGE POWELL. *CORE and the Strategy of Nonviolence.* New York: Random House, 1968.

*BENNETT, LERONE. *Confrontation: Black and White.* Baltimore: Penguin, 1965.

*BENNETT, LERONE. *What Manner of Man: A Biography of Martin Luther King, Jr.* Chicago: Johnson Publishing Company, 1965.

*BRINK, WILLIAM J., and HARRIS, LOUIS. *The Negro Revolution in America.* New York: Simon and Schuster, 1964.

*BROOM, LEONARD, and GLENN, NORVAL. *Transformation of the Negro American.* New York: Harper & Row, 1967.

*BURNS, W. HAYWOOD. *The Voices of Negro Protest in America.* New York: Oxford University Press, 1963.

*CARMICHAEL, STOKELY, and HAMILTON, CHARLES V. *Black Power: The Politics of Liberation in America.* New York: Vintage Books, 1967.

*CLARK, KENNETH B. *Dark Ghetto: Dilemmas of Social Power.* New York: Harper & Row, 1965.

*CLEAVER, ELDRIDGE. *Soul on Ice.* New York: Dell, 1968.

 CRUSE, HAROLD. *The Crisis of the Negro Intellectual.* New York: William Morrow, 1967.

*ESSIEN-UDOM, E. U. *Black Nationalism: A Search for an Identity in America.* New York: Dell, 1962.

*FANON, FRANTZ. *The Wretched of the Earth.* New York: Grove, 1966.

 GINZBERG, ELI. *The Negro Potential.* New York: Columbia University Press, 1956.

*GRIER, WILLIAM H., and COBBS, PRICE M. *Black Rage.* New York: Bantam Books, 1968.

*HARRINGTON, MICHAEL. *The Other America: Poverty in the United States.* Baltimore: Penguin, 1963.

*HENTOFF, NAT. *The New Equality.* New York: Viking, 1965.

*KING, MARTIN LUTHER, JR. *Stride Toward Freedom: The Montgomery Story.* New York: Harper & Row, 1958.

*KING, MARTIN LUTHER, JR. *Why We Can't Wait.* New York: Signet, 1964.

*KONVITZ, MILTON. *A Century of Civil Rights.* New York: Columbia University Press, 1961.

*LESTER, JULIUS. *Look Out, Whitey!* New York: Grove, 1969.

*LINCOLN, C. ERIC. *The Black Muslims in America.* Boston: Beacon Press, 1961.

*LITTLE, MALCOLM. *The Autobiography of Malcolm X.* Boston: Beacon Press, 1961.

*LITTLE, MALCOLM. *Malcolm X Speaks.* New York: Grove, 1965.

*LOMAX, LOUIS E. *The Negro Revolt.* New York: Signet, 1963.

MILLER, WILLIAM ROBERT. *Martin Luther King, Jr.: His Life, Martyrdom and Meaning for the World.* New York: Weybright and Talley, 1968.

PROUDFOOT, MERRILL. *Diary of a Sit-In.* Chapel Hill: University of North Carolina Press, 1962.

REDDICK, LAWRENCE D. *Crusader Without Violence.* (Biography of Martin Luther King, Jr.) New York: Harper, 1959.

*ROCHE, JOHN P. *The Quest for the Dream: The Development of Civil Rights and Human Relations in Modern America.* Chicago: Quadrangle, 1963.

*SILBERMAN, CHARLES E. *Crisis in Black and White.* New York: Vintage Books, 1964.

*U.S. RIOT COMMISSION. *Report of the National Advisory Commission on Civil Disorders.* New York: Bantam, 1968.

*WASKOW, ARTHUR I. *From Race Riot to Sit-In, 1919 and the 1960's: A Study in the Connections between Conflict and Violence.* Garden City, N.Y.: Doubleday, 1966.

WEAVER, ROBERT C. *The Negro Ghetto.* New York: Harcourt, Brace, 1948.

*WRIGHT, NATHAN, JR. *Black Power and Urban Unrest: Creative Possibilities.* New York: Hawthorn, 1967.

*YOUNG, WHITNEY. *To Be Equal.* New York: McGraw-Hill, 1964.

*ZINN, HOWARD. *SNCC: The New Abolitionists.* Boston: Beacon, 1964.

General Bibliography (for all 15 chapters)

ADAMS, RUSSELL L. *Great Negroes: Past and Present.* Chicago: Afro-Am Publishing Company, 1964.

*BARDOLPH, RICHARD. *The Negro Vanguard.* New York: Vintage Books, 1961.

*BENNETT, LERONE, JR. *Before the Mayflower: A History of the Negro in America, 1619–1964.* Baltimore: Penguin, 1966.

*BUTCHER, MARGARET JUST. *The Negro in American Culture; Based on Materials Left by Alain Locke.* New York: Knopf, 1956.

*CUBAN, LARRY. *The Negro in America.* Chicago: Scott, Foresman, 1964.

DRIMMER, MELVIN, ED. *Black History: A Reappraisal.* Garden City, N.Y.: Doubleday, 1968.

*DUBERMAN, MARTIN. *In White America: A Documentary Play.* New York: Signet, 1964.

*FISHEL, LESLIE H., JR., and QUARLES, BENJAMIN, EDS. *The Negro American: A Documentary History.* Glenview, Ill.: Scott, Foresman, 1967.

*FRANKLIN, JOHN HOPE. *From Slavery to Freedom: A History of Negro Americans.* Third edition. New York: Knopf, 1967.

FRAZIER, E. FRANKLIN. *The Negro in the United States.* Revised edition. New York: Macmillan, 1957.

*GOODE, KENNETH G. *From Africa to the United States and Then . . . : A Concise Afro-American History.* Glenview, Ill.: Scott, Foresman, 1969.

HUGHES, LANGSTON, and MELTZER, MILTON. *A Pictorial History of the Negro in America.* New York: Crown, 1963.

*KATZ, WILLIAM LOREN, ED. *Eyewitness: The Negro in American History.* New York: Pitman, 1967.

*KATZ, WILLIAM LOREN. *Teachers' Guide to American Negro History.* Chicago: Quadrangle, 1968.

*LINCOLN, C. ERIC. *The Negro Pilgrimage in America.* New York: Bantam, 1967.

*LOGAN, RAYFORD W. *The Negro in the United States: A Brief History.* Princeton, N.J.: Van Nostrand, 1957.

*LOGAN, RAYFORD, and COHEN, IRVING. *The American Negro: Old World Background and New World Experience.* Boston: Houghton Mifflin, 1967.

*MEIER, AUGUST, and RUDWICK, ELLIOTT M. *From Plantation to Ghetto: An Interpretive History of American Negroes.* New York: Hill and Wang, 1966.

*MELTZER, MILTON, ED. *In Their Own Words: A History of the American Negro.* 3 vols. New York: Thomas Y. Crowell, 1964–1967. I, 1619–1865 (1964); II, 1865–1916 (1965); III, 1916–1966 (1967).

*MILLER, ELIZABETH W. *The Negro in America: A Bibliography.* Cambridge, Mass.: Harvard University Press, 1966.

*MYRDAL, GUNNAR. *An American Dilemma: The Negro Problem and Modern Democracy.* 2 vols. New York: McGrall-Hill, 1964. (Reprint of 1944 book.)

*OSOFSKY, GILBERT, ED. *Burden of Race: A Democracy History of Negro-White Relations in America.* New York: Harper & Row, 1969.

*PENN, JOSEPH E., et. al. *The Negro American in Paperback: A Selected List . . . Annotated for Secondary School Students.* Washington, D.C.: National Education Association, 1967.

*PINKNEY, ALPHONSO. *Black Americans.* Englewood Cliffs, N.J.: Prentice-Hall, 1967.

*QUARLES, BENJAMIN. *The Negro in the Making of America.* New York: Collier, 1964.

REDDING, JAY SAUNDERS. *The Lonesome Road; The Story of the Negro's Part in America.* Garden City, N.Y.: Doubleday, 1958.

SALK, ERWIN. *A Layman's Guide to Negro History.* New York: McGraw-Hill, 1967.

*TOPPIN, EDGAR A. *A Mark Well Made: The Negro Contribution to American Culture.* Chicago: Rand McNally, 1967.

*WADE, RICHARD C., ED. *The Negro in American Life: Selected Readings.* Boston: Houghton Mifflin, 1965.

*WELSCH, ERWIN K. *The Negro in the United States: A Research Guide.*
Bloomington: Indiana University Press, 1965.

WOODSON, CARTER G., and WESLEY, CHARLES H. *The Negro in Our History.*
Tenth edition. Washington, D.C.: The Associated Publishers, 1962.

WOODSON, CARTER G., and WESLEY, CHARLES H. *The Story of the Negro
Retold.* Revised edition. Washington, D.C.: The Associated Publishers,
1959.

*WOODWARD, C. VANN. *The Burden of Southern History.* New York:
Vintage, 1961.

Biographies of Notable Black Americans

The lives of many outstanding men and women demonstrate the range of achievement of black Americans. For each of the 145 representatives selected for this purpose, other equally talented persons come easily to mind, and many of these are mentioned, although only briefly, here and elsewhere in this book. Short biographies of 145 persons appear below. The twenty fields in which these men and women made names for themselves are:

Art (7):
Bannister, Edward
Barthé, Richard
Duncanson, Robert

Lewis, Edmonia
Tanner, Henry
White, Charles

Woodruff, Hale

Athletics (11):
Ashe, Arthur
Brown, Jim
Chamberlain, Wilt
Gibson, Althea

Johnson, Jack
Louis, Joe
Mays, Willie
Murphy, Isaac

Owens, Jesse
Robinson, Jackie
Russell, Bill

Business and Labor (8):
Alexander, Archie
Forten, James
Leidesdorff, William

Randolph, A. Phillip
Russell, Harvey
Spaulding, C. C.

Walker, Madame C. J.
Williams, Paul

Composing (7):
Bland, James
Burleigh, Harry T.
Cole, Bob

Cook, Will Marion
Handy, W. C.
Johnson, Hall

Still, William Grant

Dance (3):
Collins, Janet

Dunham, Katherine

Robinson, Bill

Education (5):
Bethune, Mary McLeod
Chavis, John

Hope, John
Johnson, Charles S.

Wharton, Clifton R., Jr.

241

Exploration (4):

Beckwourth, James	Estevanico
De Sable, Jean	Henson, Matthew

Government Service (14):

Brimmer, Andrew	Chisholm, Shirley	Powell, Adam Clayton
Brooke, Edward	Dawson, William	Rowan, Carl
Bruce, Blanche Kelso	Evers, Charles	Stokes, Carl
Bunche, Ralph	Hastie, William	Weaver, Robert C.
Cardozo, Francis	Marshall, Thurgood	

Invention (3):

Morgan, Garrett	Rillieux, Norbert	Woods, Granville

Leadership (19):

Carmichael, Stokely	Malcolm X	Washington, Booker T.
Douglass, Frederick	Newton, Huey	Wells, Ida B.
DuBois, W. E. B.	Seale, Bobby	White, Walter
Farmer, James	Terrell, Mary Church	Wilkins, Roy
Garvey, Marcus	Truth, Sojourner	Young, Whitney
Hall, Prince	Tubman, Harriet	
King, Martin Luther	Turner, Nat	

Literature (11):

Baldwin, James	Ellison, Ralph	McKay, Claude
Brooks, Gwendolyn	Hughes, Langston	Wheatley, Phillis
Chesnutt, Charles W.	Johnson, James Weldon	Wright, Richard
Dunbar, Paul Laurence	Jones, LeRoi	

Medicine (3):

Derham, James	Drew, Charles R.	Williams, Daniel Hale

Military (4):

Carney, William	Salem, Peter
Davis, B. O., Jr.	Young, Charles

Music (12):

Anderson, Marian	Dixon, Dean	Gillespie, Dizzy
Armstrong, Louis	Ellington, Duke	Hayes, Roland
Charles, Ray	Fitzgerald, Ella	Jackson, Mahalia
Cole, Nat "King"	Garner, Erroll	Price, Leontyne

Publishing and Editing (4):

Abbott, Robert	Russwurm, John
Johnson, John H.	Vann, Robert

Religion (6):

Allen, Richard	Divine, Father	Muhammad, Elijah
Burgess, John	Healy, James A.	Payne, Daniel A.

Science (4):

Banneker, Benjamin	Julian, Percy
Carver, George W.	Just, Ernest

Social Science (5):

Franklin, John Hope	Harris, Abram L.	Woodson, Carter G.
Frazier, E. Franklin	Locke, Alain	

Television, Movies, and Entertainment (9):

Belafonte, Harry	Davis, Sammy	Parks, Gordon
Carroll, Diahann	Horne, Lena	Poitier, Sidney
Cosby, Bill	Mills, Florence	Williams, Bert

Theater (6):

Aldridge, Ira	Gilpin, Charles	Robeson, Paul
Duncan, Todd	Hansberry, Lorraine	Waters, Ethel

Their rise to fame or their most important contribution places these outstanding men and women in the following historical periods:

Earliest Achievers, 1530–1830:

Allen, Richard	De Sable, Jean	Russwurm, John
Banneker, Benjamin	Estevanico	Salem, Peter
Chavis, John	Forten, James	Wheatley, Phillis
Derham, James	Hall, Prince	

Black Abolitionists to Disfranchisement, 1830–1890:

Aldridge, Ira	Douglass, Frederick	Rillieux, Norbert
Bannister, Edward	Duncanson, Robert	Truth, Sojourner
Beckwourth, James	Healy, James A.	Tubman, Harriet
Bland, James	Leidesdorff, William	Turner, Nat
Bruce, Blanche Kalso	Lewis, Edmonia	Woods, Granville
Cardozo, Francis	Murphy, Isaac	
Carney, William	Payne, Daniel A.	

Atlanta Compromise to NAACP, 1890–1920:

Abbott, Robert	Henson, Matthew	Walker, Madame C. J.
Carver, George W.	Hope, John	Washington, Booker T.
Chesnutt, Charles W.	Johnson, Jack	Wells, Ida
Cole, Bob	Johnson, James Weldon	Williams, Bert
Cook, Will Marion	Just, Ernest	Williams, Daniel Hale
Du Bois, W. E. B.	Morgan, Garrett	Woodson, Carter G.
Dunbar, Paul Laurence	Tanner, Henry	Young, Charles
Handy, W. C.	Terrell, Mary Church	

Harlem Renaissance to Second World War, 1920–1945:

Alexander, Archie	Armstrong, Louis	Bethune, Mary McLeod
Anderson, Marian	Barthé, Richmond	Burleigh, Harry T.

Divine, Father
Dixon, Dean
Drew, Charles R.
Duncan, Todd
Dunham, Katherine
Ellington, Duke
Fitzgerald, Ella
Frazier, E. Franklin
Garvey, Marcus
Gilpin, Charles
Harris, Abram L.
Hastie, William

Hayes, Roland
Horne, Lena
Hughes, Langston
Johnson, Charles
Johnson, Hall
Julian, Percy
Locke, Alain
Louis, Joe
McKay, Claude
Mills, Florence
Muhammad, Elijah
Owens, Jesse

Randolph, A. Philip
Robeson, Paul
Robinson, Bill
Spaulding, C. C.
Still, William Grant
Vann, Robert
Waters, Ethel
White, Walter
Williams, Paul
Woodruff, Hale
Wright, Richard

Civil Rights Revolution, 1945–1970:

Ashe, Arthur
Baldwin, James
Belafonte, Harry
Brimmer, Andrew
Brooke, Edward
Brooks, Gwendolyn
Brown, Jim
Bunche, Ralph
Burgess, John
Carmichael, Stokely
Carroll, Diahann
Chamberlain, Wilt
Charles, Ray
Chisholm, Shirley
Cole, Nat "King"
Collins, Janet
Cosby, Bill

Davis, B. O., Jr.
Davis, Sammy
Dawson, William
Ellison, Ralph
Evers, Charles
Farmer, James
Franklin, John Hope
Garner, Erroll
Gibson, Althea
Gillespie, Dizzy
Hansberry, Lorraine
Jackson, Mahalia
Johnson, John H.
Jones, LeRoi
King, Martin Luther
Malcolm X
Marshall, Thurgood

Mays, Willie
Newton, Huey
Parks, Gordon
Poitier, Sydney
Powell, Adam Clayton
Price, Leontyne
Robinson, Jackie
Rowan, Carl
Russell, Bill
Russell, Harvey
Seale, Bobby
Stokes, Carl
Weaver, Robert C.
Wharton, Clifton
White, Charles
Wilkins, Roy
Young, Whitney

Abbott, Robert S. (1870–1940), Founder-Editor, Chicago Defender

Robert Sengstacke Abbott founded the *Chicago Defender* in 1905. This crusading editor-publisher made it one of the largest and most influential of the many black newspapers. Only the multi-edition *Pittsburgh Courier* and the *Afro-American* chain of newspapers surpassed it.

Abbott was born on St. Simon Island off the coast of Georgia. His parents had been slaves—his father a butler, his mother a field hand. After emancipation, they ran a grocery store. Following his father's passing, his mother married John J. Sengstacke, who later edited a little newssheet, the *Woodville Times, Savannah News.*

Helping his stepfather with his paper, Abbott became interested in journalism. After attending Beach Institute in Savannah, Ga., and Claflin College in Orangeburg, S.C. he was graduated from Hampton Institute in Virginia where, following his stepfather's advice, he learned the printing trade.

After moving to Chicago in 1896, Abbott worked at printing and odd jobs while attending Kent Law School. He earned his law degree three years later, and practiced law for a while in Topeka, Kans., and in Gary, Ind.

Later, however, he returned to his first love, journalism, and founded the *Chicago Defender*. Although the first four-page issue, on May 5, 1905, had a circulation of only 300, Abbott's use of sensational yellow-journalism tactics soon attracted Chicago's black masses. The *Defender* engaged in many crusades, particularly urging blacks to migrate from the South. By 1956, when his nephew and heir, John H. Sengstacke, converted the semi-weekly into a daily, the *Defender* had grown to a circulation of more than 200,000. Abbott spotted some talented people early in their careers, recruiting future novelist Willard Motley for his staff and publishing schoolgirl poems of future Pulitzer prizewinner Gwendolyn Brooks (*q.v.*).

Other outstanding black editor-publishers of his day included William Monroe Trotter of the *Boston Guardian,* Carl Murphy of the *Afro-American*, and Robert Vann (*q.v.*) of the *Pittsburgh Courier*.

Aldridge, Ira F. (1807–1867), Shakespearean Actor

Ira Frederick Aldridge was for thirty years one of the world's most distinguished actors. He gave command performances before, and was honored by, monarchs of Sweden, Prussia, Austria, and Russia. Best known for his portrayal of Othello, he also appeared as Shylock, Lear, Macbeth, and Hamlet, as well as in many non-Shakespearean roles.

His birthplace is uncertain. Some accounts say he was born in New York City in 1807 while his parents, who made their home in Maryland, were temporarily residing in the North. Others say he was born in Maryland in 1805. His grandfather is said to have been an African chief. Aldridge attended the African Free School in New York City and is reported to have served an apprenticeship with a carpenter in Maryland.

His interest in drama was aroused early and he joined the African Theater Company which had been formed in New York City by James Hewlett. White rioters disrupted their performances.

Aldridge moved to Europe in 1824, studied briefly in Glasgow, and then embarked on a stage career in London. The great English tragedian

Edmund Keane encouraged him. In 1833, Aldridge appeared at the Theatre Royal, Covent Garden, London, as Othello. He soon was well known as an actor.

His first wife was an Englishwoman; after she passed away, he married a Swedish opera singer. Their children, Luranah, Ira, and Amanda, became singer-actors. The talented tragedian Aldridge was never seen on stage in his native land: he passed away in Poland while arrangements were being made for an American tour. However, his daughter Amanda (1866–1956), who became a famous voice teacher, taught several of America's finest black singers in the twentieth century. Among these who traveled to England to study with her were Marian Anderson (*q.v.*), Roland Hayes (*q.v.*), and Paul Robeson (*q.v.*). Robeson, who was an actor as well as a singer, became a famed Othello, as had Aldridge.

Alexander, Archie A. (1888–1958), Contracting Engineer; Territorial Governor

Archie Alphonso Alexander was a successful businessman, who headed his own civil engineering firm for more than forty years, and also became Governor of the Virgin Islands.

Alexander was born in Ottumwa, Iowa. His father was a janitor who later moved to a farm near Des Moines where Alexander graduated from high school. After working several years, he enrolled in the College of Engineering at the University of Iowa. Officials tried to discourage the black boy from continuing in this field, but Alexander persevered. He worked long hours to support himself, but in spite of this, managed to make good grades, join a fraternity, and play football. An outstanding tackle (1909–1911), he became known as "Alexander the Great."

He graduated in 1912 with a B.S. in civil engineering, then worked as a design engineer for the Marsh bridge engineering firm of Des Moines. In 1914, while only in his mid-20s, he formed his own firm, Alexander and Higbee, in partnership with a white fellow employee. The firm secured contracts to build bridges, sewer systems, viaducts, and also a conduit for the University of Iowa. His partner met with an accident, and the firm continued as A. A. Alexander, Inc., for four years, until 1929 when Alexander joined a white classmate in the engineering firm of Alexander and Repass. They built a million-dollar sewage disposal plant at Grand Rapids, Mich., a civilian airfield at Tuskegee, Ala., the $1,000,000 Tidal Basin Bridge in the District of Columbia, a power plant in Nebraska, the K Street Freeway in Washington, D.C., and railroad bridges in Iowa and Missouri. Like architect Paul Williams (*q.v.*), Alexander's business extended beyond the black ghettoes into national competition with white companies.

In April, 1954, President Dwight D. Eisenhower appointed Alexander Governor of the Virgin Islands. This made Alexander the second Afro-American territorial governor, the first having been William H. Hastie (*q.v.*). Ill health forced Governor Alexander to resign in August, 1955.

Allen, Richard (1760–1831), A.M.E. Founding Bishop and Race Leader

Richard Allen founded the first major black institution in America, the African Methodist Episcopal (A.M.E.) denomination. He was also the earliest leader of his race in the United States.

Allen was born a slave in Philadelphia but grew up on a plantation in Delaware. After becoming a zealous Methodist, Allen preached to and converted many, including his master who let him buy his freedom. In the 1780s, Allen traveled through the Middle Atlantic states preaching while supporting himself with odd jobs. The Methodist leader Francis Asbury encouraged him, but Allen declined to accompany him on missionary journeys through the South.

Allen settled in Philadelphia in 1786, working to bring blacks into St. George's Methodist Church where he preached to his black brethren at odd hours. Friction developed as Allen brought more and more blacks into the church. He proposed a separate church, but whites and blacks objected.

In April, 1787, Allen formed the Free African Society, along with Absalom Jones, a former slave who had moved from Delaware to Philadelphia with his grocer-owner, and bought his freedom. The first organization of black Americans, the Society was dedicated to self-improvement and advancement.

In November, 1787, whites banished blacks to the gallery at St. George's Church and tried to remove some when they knelt too far forward. Allen and Jones led an exodus out of the church. Two black churches resulted. Jones and most of the Free African Society members established St. Thomas Free African Church within the Protestant Episcopal denomination. Allen formed the Bethel African Methodist Episcopal Church. Each church's new building was consecrated in 1794.

Bishop Asbury ordained Allen in 1799. White elders of St. George's Church controlled the new congregation until Allen won a court suit early in 1816 gaining complete independence. In April, 1816, delegates from sixteen A.M.E. churches in various states met in Philadelphia to form a separate denomination. Allen was the first consecrated A.M.E. bishop.

In the yellow fever epidemic of 1793, Allen organized blacks in Philadelphia to care for the afflicted. In 1817, he took a prominent role in the anti-colonization rally held in Philadelphia. And in 1830, he was the chairman and leading force in calling the first of the conventions held periodically to express the black man's position.

Anderson, Marian (1902–   ), Singer

Her great contralto voice and quiet dignity make Marian Anderson one of America's most beloved and admired celebrities. Late in her career, the Metropolitan Opera lowered its racial bars for her.

Miss Anderson was born in Philadelphia. Her father, a laborer, was chief usher at Union Baptist Church. Her mother, a schoolteacher from Virginia, sacrificed her career for her family and then worked as a maid at Wanamaker's after her husband passed away. Miss Anderson began singing in her church's junior choir. She earned money singing at various churches. She experienced racial rebuffs early, being barred from a music school in Philadelphia and consigned to humiliating Jim Crow facilities on Southern tours.

Tenor Roland Hayes (q.v.) encouraged her, helping her church raise money for her voice lessons. Her Town Hall debut, before a disappointingly tiny audience, was a failure. But after she won a major competition that resulted in an appearance with the New York Philharmonic in August, 1925, prospects improved.

Aided by Rosenwald fellowships, she made several trips to Europe to study and to build a reputation. On her European tour of 1933–1935, Sol Hurok took her under his management, and Arturo Toscanini's glowing praise brought her world fame.

She returned to America where she triumphed in recitals at Town Hall and Carnegie Hall. Hurok's backing opened for her doors of halls heretofore closed to blacks. She became a premier attraction. The celebrated affair of Constitution Hall, whose owners, members of the D.A.R., wrote Miss Anderson, "decreed that it could not be used by one of my race," led to her performance in a memorable Easter concert at the Lincoln Memorial before a crowd of 75,000. Later, she did sing at Constitution Hall.

It was not until 1955 that she appeared at the Metropolitan Opera as Ulrica in *The Masked Ball*. Blacks had sung at opera houses in Europe and America, but she was the first at the Met.

Armstrong, Louis (1900–   ), King of Jazz

Throughout the world, Louis "Satchmo" Armstrong and jazz are synonymous. He is the world's greatest trumpet player.

Daniel Louis Armstrong was born on July 4, 1900, in New Orleans, birthplace of jazz. In the famed Storyville "red-light" section, he heard such great Dixieland groups as the Eagle and Superior Bands and such musicians as cornetists Bunk Johnson and Joe "King" Oliver. Louis formed a street-singing quartet of youngsters.

His father, a factory worker, left his mother, who was a domestic servant, and Louis grew up with his grandmother, sister, mother, and a succession of "stepfathers." Sometimes neglected, 12-year-old Louis was arrested for shooting off one of his stepfather's guns celebrating New Year's Eve. Sentenced to a boys' home for eighteen months, he joined the band there and learned the bugle and cornet. Afterwards, he played in various honkytonks in the evenings while working during the day on coal and milk wagons.

When Storyville was shut down in World War I and King Oliver moved to Chicago to play in Lincoln Gardens, Armstrong took his place playing with Kid Ory. He also played summers in Fate Marable's band on Mississippi steamboats, later joining the prestigious Tuxedo Brass Band in New Orleans.

In August, 1922, Armstrong joined King Oliver's band in Chicago, then played a year with a New York orchestra, after which he formed his own band in 1925, playing trumpet. He cut a historic series of records with his group, anticipating almost all the innovations of modern jazz.

Armstrong invented scat singing. In 1930, he began fronting big bands and singing popular tunes. His world tours brought frenzied responses both from ordinary people and from crowned heads. His thousands of recordings have sold millions of copies, especially his "Blueberry Hill" and "Hello, Dolly." He played in many movies. He is a living legend and has acted as a goodwill ambassador for the State Department.

Ashe, Arthur (1943–   ), Tennis Champion

Arthur Ashe, Jr., is one of the world's foremost tennis players. He led America to successive Davis Cup championships. He won the first U.S. Open Championship against the top professionals and amateurs.

Ashe was born in Richmond, Va., son of a city playground caretaker and landscape contractor. Ashe began playing tennis when he was 7, on the nearby segregated Negro playground. His skill brought him to the attention of a Lynchburg physician, Dr. Robert "Whirlwind" Johnson, who coached promising youngsters for the black American Tennis Association. This black coach's best known protégé up to this time had been Althea Gibson (*q.v.*). Ashe spent summers under Dr. Johnson's tutelage, winning the National Junior Indoor Singles championships in 1960 and 1961.

Ashe, who had enrolled at the University of California at Los Angeles, was named to the Davis Cup Team in 1963, rising in the national rankings from eighteenth in 1963 to third in 1965 to first in 1968. In 1965 he won the National Collegiate Athletic Association singles and doubles titles and led U.C.L.A. to the N.C.A.A. team championship. In 1967 he won the national indoor doubles title. In 1968 Ashe won both the United States amateur championship and the first U.S. Open.

In the 1968 world combined amateur and professional tennis rankings, Ashe ranked second, after Australian professional Rod Laver. In 1968 and 1969, Ashe led the United States team to Davis Cup International championships, America's first successive wins since 1948–1949.

Ashe remains the only ranking black male tennis player just as the only black woman ever ranked in American tennis was Althea Gibson in the 1950s. Blacks have little opportunity to compete in a game run through segregated country clubs where only a nationally prominent Ashe or Gibson could enter tournaments.

Baldwin, James A. (1924–   ), Writer

James Arthur Baldwin is an influential writer whose perceptive essays interpret for America the race problem and black anger.

Born in Harlem of Southern migrant parents, Baldwin was reared in a stringently religious atmosphere dominated by his clergyman father. In his early teens, Baldwin became a Pentecostal preacher, but his early love of literature persisted. He edited the literary magazine at his high school. Upon graduation he worked in a defense plant where he experienced painful discrimination and prejudice. After his father's passing in 1943, he moved to Greenwich Village, working at odd jobs and nearly starving, but continuing to write. Magazines published his book reviews and essays. He began a novel, was encouraged by Richard Wright (*q.v.*), and won several fellowships.

Baldwin left America in 1948 for a ten-year stay in stimulating, prejudice-free Paris. There he completed his novel, *Go Tell It on the Mountain* (1953), a brilliant, partly autobiographical account of storefront religion in Harlem. In 1955 he published *Notes of a Native Son,* a collection of essays. His second novel, *Giovanni's Room* (1956), dealt with white homosexuals in France, but like his next two novels, *Another Country* (1963) and *Tell Me How Long the Train's Been Gone* (1968), was not as highly regarded as his first novel.

Meanwhile, Baldwin returned to America, becoming an important interpreter of the race problem, particularly in the polemical essays *Nobody Knows My Name* (1961) and *The Fire Next Time* (1964). His other writings include two plays, *Blues for Mister Charlie* (1964) and *The Amen Corner* (1968), and a collection of short stories, *Going to Meet the Man* (1965).

Baldwin contends incisively that whites create the race problem because in their own insecurity they need someone to dominate. "I'm not a nigger, I am a man," he insists, "but if you think I'm a nigger, it means you need it."

Banneker, Benjamin (1731–1806), Scientist

Benjamin Banneker was a mathematician, astronomer, clock-maker, and surveyor. He helped lay out the nation's capital. He made the first clock constructed wholly in America. From 1791 to 1802, he published yearly almanacs, a high scientific and literary accomplishment. Along with Phillis Wheatley (*q.v.*), he was the most prominent black in early America.

Banneker was born free on a farm about ten miles from Baltimore, Md. His grandmother, an English indentured servant, had married an African chief, Bannaky (later Banneker), who was brought to America in chains. Banneker's grandmother taught him to read and he attended an integrated Quaker school nearby.

He was gifted mathematically, and devised mathematical puzzles in verse that stumped experts. About 1761, without having seen one, he made a clock with wooden parts that became a local tourist attraction.

The Ellicotts, a Quaker milling family that moved to Maryland from Pennsylvania in the 1770s, befriended Banneker and he began studying astronomy in his late 50s, mastering it rapidly and issuing almanacs within five years. His almanac for 1793 contained a remarkable peace plan proposing a Secretary of Peace, free schools, repeal of capital punishment, and a ban on military dress, titles, and displays.

Meanwhile, in 1791, President George Washington appointed him to assist Andrew Ellicott, III (later America's first Surveyor-General), and Major Pierre-Charles L'Enfant of France in surveying Washington, D.C. Banneker was the first black Presidential appointee. Ellicott and Banneker reproduced L'Enfant's plan from memory when the Frenchman quit after a dispute with Federal officials.

Banneker's correspondence with Thomas Jefferson in August, 1791, criticized Jefferson's racist thinking. Liberals throughout the world cited Banneker and Dr. James Derham, the first black physician in America, as proof of what blacks could do when freed from oppression and discrimination.

Bannister, Edward M. (1828–1901), Landscape Painter

Edward Mitchell Bannister was more widely recognized than any other black artist in nineteenth-century America. Specializing in landscapes of poetical quality, he won a first price in the Centennial Exhibition in Philadelphia in 1876 and was a founder of the Providence Art Club.

Bannister was born in Canada, at St. Andrews, New Brunswick, his mother's home; his father came from the West Indies. Bannister, who loved to sketch, attended school in St. Andrews and later shipped out on a coastal vessel.

He moved to Boston at the age of 18, and became a photographer, making solarized prints. In the evenings, he studied art at the Lowell Institute, learning anatomy from Dr. William Rimmer. By 1854, Bannister had his first commission, painting "The Ship Outward Bound." He shared a studio with a white artist, Edwin Lord Weeks, and exhibited with the Boston Art Club. He was inspired to do his best by a racial slur in the New York *Herald* of 1867 which said that blacks seemed to appreciate art even though incapable of producing it.

In 1871, he moved to Providence, R.I., where he could sail on Narragansett Bay while studying scenery. Officials tried to withdraw the prize he won at Philadelphia's Exposition in 1876 when the artist proved to be black, but white artists insisted that the jury's decision stand. Subsequently, he sold this prize painting, "Under the Oaks," in Boston for $1,500. Among his other oil paintings are "Sabin Point, Narragansett Bay," in the collection of Brown University and "After the Storm," belonging to the Museum of the Rhode Island School of Design.

Informal meetings between Bannister and two white artists in his studio led to the formation of the Providence Art Club in 1880. This club was the seedbed of the important Rhode Island School of Design.

Barthé, Richmond (1901–   ), Sculptor

Richmond Barthé's sculpture is included in such collections as the Whitney Museum of American Art, the Philadelphia Museum, and the Metropolitan Museum of Art. Noted for his sensitive portrayal and natural plasticity, he is America's preeminent black sculptor. He was the first black sculptor commissioned to do a public monument dedicated to a white person: the relief medallion portrait for the Fifth Avenue Memorial to *New York Evening Journal* editor-columnist Arthur Brisbane.

Barthé was born in Bay St. Louis, Miss., and grew up in New Orleans. He left school at the age of 14, and worked as a butler for a white family that encouraged him to pursue his interest in art. The art editor of a New Orleans daily newspaper also encouraged him, though unable to run a story about his talents. After Barthé was refused admittance by a New Orleans art school, a Catholic priest raised money to send him to the Chicago Art Institute in 1924. Barthé waited tables to earn a living during his four years at the Art Institute.

Beginning as a painter, he changed to sculpture in 1928. Among his finest pieces are such small bronzes as "Shoe Shine Boy" in the Oberlin College Museum of Art and "The Boxer" at the Metropolitan. He did the marble bust of Booker T. Washington for New York University's Hall of Fame. For Haiti, he made monumental statues of liberators Toussaint L'Ouverture and Jacques Dessalines. He did portrait busts of actress Katherine Cornell and actor John Gielgud and carved a large frieze depicting the theme "The Green Pastures" on a Harlem housing project. Leading museums in Africa, Austria, Canada, England, France, Germany, and the U.S. own his works.

Along with Henry Tanner (*q.v.*) and William E. Scott, Barthé was one of the few black artists successful enough to make a full-time living from his art. Since the 1950s, he has resided in Jamaica in the British West Indies. Other great twentieth-century black sculptors include Augusta Savage, Sargent Johnson, and Elizabeth Prophet.

Beckwourth, James (1798–1867), Western Pioneer

James P. Beckwourth, also spelled Beckwith, was a pioneering mountain man who discovered a western pass. His autobiography recaptures the flavor of the fur-trade era.

He was born in Fredericksburg, Va. Apparently, his mother was a mulatto slave, his father their white owner. They moved to St. Louis where Beckwourth, who had been freed, was apprenticed to a blacksmith, but ran away and worked as a miner.

Returning, he joined the expeditions of General William H. Ashley and Andrew Henry. Beckwourth traveled with their Rocky Mountain Fur Company expeditions from 1823 to 1826 along the Yellowstone, Big Horn, Platte, Green, Bear, and Beaver rivers in Montana, Wyoming, Colorado, and Utah, exploring with such pioneers as Jim Bridger and Tom Fitzpatrick and running a company post in dangerous Blackfoot Indian country.

Beckwourth lived with the Crow Indians, who took him for a long-lost Crow, from 1826 to 1837, marrying a Crow, becoming a chief, and participating in their wars. Afterwards, he worked as a guide, trapper, fur-company agent, Army scout, and hunter.

In the early 1850s, he discovered a pass across the Sierra Nevada Mountains to the Sacramento Valley. Beckwourth Pass, near the head-waters of the Feather River in Plumas County, Calif., was used in the gold rush and is now traversed by the Western Pacific Railway. He set up a combined ranch, post, and inn there. In 1859 he moved to Denver, setting up a ranch and store. In 1864 he was a guide for the Chivington Expedition that massacred Cheyennes. Three years later the government sent Bridger, Hank Williams, and Beckwourth to pacify his Crow brothers. He became ill and passed away on this mission.

Belafonte, Harry (1927–   ), Singer-Actor

Harold George Belafonte, Jr., is one of America's greatest folk ballad singers, and a nightclub entertainer, recording artist, actor, television performer, and matinee idol. His TV specials, such as his show with Julie Andrews in the fall of 1969, provide some of the brightest moments in television history.

Harry Belafonte was born in New York City of West Indian parents, his father from Martinique, his mother from Jamaica. From the ages of 9 to 13, he lived in Jamaica. Later, he attended St. Thomas parochial school in Harlem, but dropped out of George Washington High School before his senior year. He enrolled in the Navy and afterwards worked as a janitor. Late in 1945, a tenant gave him tickets to the first play he had ever seen, which aroused his interest in acting.

He attended a drama workshop for two years under the G.I. Bill, with Marlon Brando, Tony Curtis, and Sidney Poitier as classmates. But acting jobs were scarce. Instead, he became a nightclub singer from January, 1949, to December, 1950. He began as a jazz singer at the Royal Roost in New York and quit while performing as a pop singer at the Five O'Clock Club in Miami. He did not like the popular songs he sang.

Belafonte wanted to sing folk ballads. He spent months researching folk music. In November, 1951, he began at the Village Vanguard, wearing the open-neck shirt and tight black pants that became his trademark. He was a sensation. His singing and recording of such calypso songs as "Matilda," "The Banana Boat Song," "Mary Ann," and "Hold Him Joe" brought him popularity and earnings theretofore unparalleled for a folk singer in America.

He went on to become an actor and producer. He starred in such movies as *Carmen Jones* and *Odds Against Tomorrow* and such Broadway shows as *Almanac* and *Three for Tonight.*

Bethune, Mary McLeod (1875–1955), Educator

Mary McLeod Bethune was an educator, leader of her race, and founder of Bethune-Cookman College. She was an adviser to President Franklin Roosevelt and a close friend to his wife.

Mary Jane McLeod was born in a log cabin near Mayesville, S.C. She was the fifteenth of seventeen children of hardworking, ex-slave cotton farmers. Although their masters had sold most of their older children, her parents managed to reunite the entire family after emancipation.

When she was 11, Presbyterian missionaries founded a Negro school at Mayesville. For four years, she eagerly walked five miles each way to attend. A white Quaker schoolteacher in Denver, Colo., donated money out of her extra earnings as a seamstress to send her to Scotia Seminary for Negro girls in Concord, N.C., for seven years and for one year to Moody Bible Institute in Chicago, where she was the only black student. She then taught at Presbyterian schools in South Carolina, Georgia, and Florida. In the meantime, she married Albertus Bethune.

In 1904, without funds, with only five pupils, but with faith to move mountains, Mary Bethune founded a normal and industrial school for Negro girls in Daytona Beach, Fla. She began in a rented house, then bought a town dump near the Negro section. In 1907, the school moved into Faith Hall erected on the former dump. In 1923, the now 600-student school affiliated with the Board of Education of the Methodist Church and absorbed its Cookman Institute for Boys at Jacksonville to form Bethune-Cookman Institute (later Bethune-Cookman College), with Mrs. Bethune as president until 1947 and president emeritus and trustee thereafter.

As president of the National Association of Colored Women, 1926–1930, and as founder-president of the National Council of Negro Women from 1935 to 1949, she became widely known. Presidents from Coolidge to Truman appointed her to various posts. From 1935 to 1944, she was President Roosevelt's Special Adviser on Minority

Affairs. From 1936 to 1944, she was Director of the Division of Negro Affairs of the National Youth Administration, the first black woman to head a Federal office. She formed an informal "Black Cabinet" of New Deal Negro advisers, including Ralph Bunche, William Hastie, and Robert C. Weaver (*q.q.v.*).

Bland, James (1854–1911), Minstrel Composer

People sing or hum "Oh Dem Golden Slippers" and "In the Evening by the Moonlight" without knowing James A. Bland composed them. This minstrel performer's composition, "Carry Me Back to Old Virginny," became Virginia's official state song.

Bland was born in Flushing on Long Island, N.Y., and grew up in Philadelphia. His Southern-born parents came of families long free in Delaware and South Carolina. His father had attended Oberlin College and graduated from Wilberforce University. In 1867, his father became the first Negro Patent Office examiner and they moved to Washington. When the son finished high school and entered Howard University, the father also enrolled, and earned a law degree at night school. More interested in banjo music than scholarship, the son neglected his studies to perform evenings in hotels. His family's hopes to make him a lawyer or doctor faded.

Bland left college to perform in Haverly's Colored Minstrels who performed his compositions, including "Oh! Lucinda," "In the Morning by the Bright Light," "You Could Have Been True," "Listen to the Silver Trumpets," and "The Old Fashioned Cottage." When the troupe played in London in the early 1880s, the British idolized Bland. He stayed there twenty years, earning and spending grandly. He returned to Washington early in the twentieth century, but ministrelsy was declining and his inspiration had waned. He spent his last years in Philadelphia.

Like Stephen Foster (1826–1864), the Northern white minstrel composer, Bland was penniless at the end of his life. Both enriched America with their music, but passed away neglected. Many songs that they failed to copyright were pirated by others.

Brimmer, Andrew F. (1926–), Federal Reserve Officer

In February, 1966, Andrew Felton Brimmer became the first Negro on the Federal Reserve governing board. He had been born in Newellton, La., son of a sharecropping warehouseman.

On graduating from high school, he went to live with an older sister in Bremerton, Wash. After serving in the Army, he entered the University of Washington on the G.I. Bill. He received a B.A. degree in economics in 1950, and continued his education on a John Hay Whitney Foundation Opportunity Fellowship, earning his M.A. in 1951. Then he studied at the Delhi School of Economics and University of Bombay, on a Fulbright fellowship, later publishing an article and a monograph on India's economy.

He became a research assistant at M.I.T.'s Center for International Studies and a teaching fellow at Harvard. While writing his dissertation, "Some Studies in Monetary Policy, Interest Rates, and the Investment Behavior of Life Insurance Companies," he also worked as an economist for the Federal Reserve Bank of New York City. In 1957, he received his Ph.D. from Harvard.

He became an assistant professor of economics at Michigan State University. While there he wrote *Life Insurance Companies in the Capital Markets*, published in 1962, and many articles. From 1961 to 1963, he taught at the Wharton School of the University of Pennsylvania.

In 1963, he joined the Commerce Department, and in 1965 became Assistant Secretary of Commerce for Economic Affairs. He traveled throughout America, persuading businessmen to curb overseas investments voluntarily in order to reduce America's deficit in international payments. President Lyndon Johnson appointed him to the seven-member Board of Governors of the Federal Reserve System. Governor Brimmer is a fiscal moderate who swings between the Board's liberal and conservative blocs, but supports tight-money policies to fight inflation.

Brooke, Edward W. (1919–   ), Senator

Edward William Brooke is the only Afro-American ever elected to the U.S. Senate by popular vote. This Protestant, Negro Republican has won statewide elections handily in Catholic, Democratic Massachusetts, where blacks are only two percent of the population.

He was born into an upper-middle-class black family in Washington, D.C., son of a Veterans Administration lawyer. His mother's family in Virginia claims descent from Thomas Jefferson and British Admiral Philip Broke, and relation to the English poet Rupert Brooke (1887–1915). Brooke graduated from Howard University in 1941, was an infantry officer in World War II, and graduated from Boston University Law School in 1948.

Brooke first practiced law in Roxbury, outside Boston. In 1950 and 1952, running for the state legislature, he won the Republican nomination but lost to the Democrat. In 1960, Republicans ran him for secretary of state—the first black nominated for statewide office in Massachusetts. He polled 1,195,000 votes, losing to his Democratic opponent by less than 12,000.

In 1962, Brooke won the Republican nomination for attorney general, beating out a millionaire blueblood Boston lawyer. He received 1,143,000 votes that fall, almost 260,000 more than his Democratic opponent, and he was the only Republican to win statewide office in Massachusetts. He was the only Negro in America ever chosen attorney general. He soon had a crimebuster reputation. In 1964, Brooke was reelected, getting 1,543,000 votes and a record margin of 797,000, at a time when Republicans everywhere followed Barry Goldwater to defeat.

In 1966, Brooke was nominated for the U.S. Senate. His opponent, former Governor Endicott Peabody, was backed by Senator Edward Kennedy. But Brooke received 1,213,000 votes, winning by more than 400,000. Although two other blacks, Blanche Bruce (*q.v.*) and Hiram Revels, had served in the Senate, they were elected by the Mississippi legislature during Reconstruction, long before the Seventeenth Amendment (1913) provided for direct, popular election of U.S. Senators.

Brooks, Gwendolyn (1917–　　), Poet

The poetry of Gwendolyn Brooks Blakely brilliantly evokes Northern ghetto life, universalizing human experience in contemporary garb. She is the only Afro-American to win the Pulitzer Prize.

Except for one month in her birthplace, Topeka, Kans., Miss Brooks has always lived in Chicago. She was reared in an artistic atmosphere, her mother a composer, her father a music house employee, and her brother an artist. She began writing poetry at 7, publishing her first poem when she was 13. She lived near the Chicago *Defender*, which published her early poems. After graduating from Wilson Junior College in 1936, she did newspaper, magazine, and office work. Marrying a Chicago businessman, she wrote poetry in spare time from being a housewife and mother.

Recognition came with poetry awards in 1943 and 1944 at summer writer's conferences at Northwestern University. Her poems began to appear in *Poetry, Harper's, Saturday Review of Literature*, and *Yale Review*. In 1945, her first volume, *A Street in Bronzeville*, won wide acclaim. Her second volume of verse, *Annie Allen* (1949)—portraying a woman's feelings as daughter, wife, and mother—won the Pulitzer Prize. She has written a novel, *Maud Martha* (1953), a children's book, *Bronzeville Boys and Girls* (1956), and two more volumes of poetry, *The Bean Eaters* (1956), and *Selected Poems* (1963). The opening lines of the second stanza of "The Children of the Poor" in *Selected Poems* went:

What shall I give my children? who are poor,
Who are adjudged the leastwise of the land,
Who are my sweetest lepers, who demand
No velvet and no velvety velour;

Her poetry has been anthologized in many collections and she has won many awards. In the late 1960s, this shy, unassuming, well-read, and observant poet began teaching creative writing classes at neighboring colleges, then joined the faculty of Chicago Teachers College.

Brown, Jim (1936–   ), Football Star

Jim Brown was the greatest runner, and perhaps the greatest player, in the history of football. From 1957 to 1965 he was the National Football League's top attraction and highest-paid player.

James Nathaniel Brown was born on St. Simon Island, Ga. After his father, who once boxed professionally, left, his grandmother reared him. At age 7, he joined his mother, a domestic servant in Manhasset, Long Island, N.Y. At Manhasset High School, he starred in baseball, basketball, football, and lacrosse, setting scoring records in basketball. Major-league baseball teams wanted him, but he entered Syracuse University, winning ten varsity letters, three each in football and lacrosse, two each in basketball and track. Scoring seven touchdowns in one game, he made the 1956 All-American team.

In nine seasons, 1957–1966, as fullback for the Cleveland Browns of the NFL, Jim Brown led the league in rushing every season except 1962 and rushed for at least 1,000 yards each season but two. He holds the records for most yards gained in a season (1,863), career touchdowns (126), and career rushing yardage (12,312). He was NFL Rookie-of-the-Year in 1957 and NFL Player-of-the-Year in 1958, 1963, and 1965.

Quitting football at his peak, Brown became an actor, starring in such movies as *Rio Conchos* and *The Dirty Dozen*. Other black football stars include All-Americans Paul Robeson (*q.v.*), Brud Holland, and Kenny Washington, Heisman trophy winners Ernie Davis, Mike Garrett, and O. J. Simpson, and pro stars Ollie Matson, Emlen Tunnell, Lenny Moore, Deacon Jones, and Gale Sayers.

Bruce, Blanche K. (1841–1898), Senator

Blanche Kelso Bruce was the first black to serve a full term in the U.S. Senate. He represented Mississippi from 1875 to 1881.

He was born near Farmville in Prince Edward County, Va., son of a wealthy planter and his slave. A body servant to his white half-brother, Bruce was taught by plantation tutors. In the late 1850s, he was carried to Missouri, learning the printer's trade in the town of Brunswick. His young master joined the Confederate Army taking Bruce as his valet, but Bruce ran away. He opened Negro schools in Lawrence, Kans., and Hannibal, Mo., continuing his avid reading. In 1866 he entered Oberlin College for further studies.

In 1868 he moved to Mississippi and became a well-to-do planter, entered politics, and held such posts as sergeant-at-arms in Mississippi's senate, assessor of Bolivar County, levee commissioner, county sheriff and tax collector, and county superintendent of schools.

In 1874, Mississippi's legislature elected him to the U.S. Senate. Subsequently, Presidents Garfield, Harrison, and McKinley appointed him Register of the Treasury (1881–1885 and 1897–1898) and Recorder of Deeds in the District of Columbia (1891–1893). As Register, his signature appeared upon the nation's paper money.

Bruce was not the first black in the Senate. Hiram Revels (1822–1901) served one year, 1870 to 1871, filling out an unexpired Mississippi term in the seat once held by Jefferson Davis. Twenty other Afro-Americans served in the House of Representatives from 1870 to 1901.

Bunche, Ralph J. (1904–   ), Statesman

As Under Secretary for Special Political Affairs, Ralph Johnson Bunche is the highest ranking American in the United Nations, one of seven under secretaries to Secretary General U Thant. He was the first black to win the Nobel Peace Prize.

Bunche was born in Detroit, son of a struggling barber and grandson of a slave. When he was 11, his family moved to New Mexico where his parents passed away. His grandmother moved the family to Los Angeles where Bunche attended Jefferson High School and U.C.L.A., starring in basketball, working as a gymnasium janitor, and graduating *summa cum laude* in 1927. Too poor to use a tuition scholarship to Harvard Graduate School, he was aided by Negro clubwomen who raised a thousand dollars.

He received his master's degree from Harvard in 1928, and established a department of political science at Howard University, heading it, though often on leave, until 1950. Returning to Harvard, on a Rosenwald fellowship for a year of research in African mandates, he received his Ph.D. in 1934, the first American black with a doctorate in political science. Later, he worked closely with Gunnar Myrdal in his study of the race problem, preparing research memoranda for Myrdal's classic, *An American Dilemma* (1944).

In World War II, Bunche worked for the Office of Strategic Services, eventually heading the Africa section. With the State Department, 1944 to 1946, he wrote the trusteeship portions of the U.N. Charter. Secretary General Trygve Lie selected him in 1946 to head the U.N. Trusteeship Division and in 1948 made him secretary of the peace-seeking Palestine Commission. Replacing the assassinated U.N. Mediator Count Folke Bernadotte later in 1948, Bunche brought an end to the Arab-Israeli war in 1949. He received the Nobel Peace Prize in 1950. Bunche continued with the U.N., becoming under secretary to Dag Hammarskjold in 1955 and serving as his special representative in the Congo crisis in 1960.

Two other blacks received the Nobel Peace Prize, both for leading nonviolent crusades against racial injustice: Chief Albert John Luthuli of South Africa in 1960 and Martin Luther King (*q.v.*) in 1964.

Burgess, John M. (1909–   ), Episcopal Bishop

John Melville Burgess is the first black to preside over a diocese of the Protestant Episcopal Church in America. He heads the diocese of Massachusetts. Previously, black bishops headed only the missionary diocese of Liberia, Africa.

Bishop Burgess was born in Grand Rapids, Mich., son of a dining-car waiter. Waiting on tables in fraternity houses, he earned A.B. (1930) and M.A. (1931) degrees in sociology at the University of Michigan. He planned on social work, but decided to go into the ministry.

Graduating from the Episcopal Theological School at Cambridge, Mass., in 1934, he began his ministry as vicar of St. Phillip's in his home town. For a dozen years he served mission churches there and in Cincinnati. From 1946 to 1951, he was the Episcopal chaplain at Howard University in Washington, D.C. For the next five years, he was a canon at the Washington Cathedral under Woodrow Wilson's grandson, Francis Sayre, dean of the cathedral.

In 1956, he became Archdeacon of Boston and supervisor of the Episcopal City Mission. As suffragan (assistant) bishop of the diocese of Massachusetts, he was the first to supervise white and black parishes; Arkansas and North Carolina had each had a black suffragan bishop limited to supervising black congregations. In 1969, he was elected coadjutor (successor) bishop to retiring Bishop Stokes.

Since his election as suffragan bishop, another black, Richard B. Martin, has become suffragan bishop of the diocese of Long Island. Other black bishops of predominantly white dioceses include Robert Jones, first in a Methodist diocese in America (New Orleans), and

Catholic bishops James Healy (*q.v.*) and Harold Perry. Several blacks served terms as heads of such denominations: Bishop Prince Taylor was president of the Methodist Board of Bishops; Hollis Price was moderator of the United Church of Christ; and Joseph H. Jackson, longtime leader of six million blacks in the National Baptist Convention, was president of the World Council of Churches.

Burleigh, Harry T. (1866–1949), Singer-Composer

The most famous black musician in the first decades of the twentieth century was Harry Thacker Burleigh. A noted baritone and church soloist, he composed many art songs. He also arranged and preserved many spirituals. He was a pupil and friend of Antonín Dvořák whose Fifth Symphony, "From the New World," contains melodies of spirituals Burleigh sang to him.

Burleigh was born in Erie, Pa. His parents were employed as domestics by a wealthy family that patronized renowned musicians. Burleigh was so eager to hear one pianist that he stood outside the drawing-room window in the snow. The employer then hired him to hold doors at future musicals so that he might listen in comfort. On graduating from high school, he worked as a stenographer and sang in churches and synagogues in Erie.

In 1892, he came to New York and won a scholarship to the National Conservatory of Music, whose staff included Dvořák and Victor Herbert. After graduating in 1896, he taught voice there several years. In 1894, he applied to be baritone soloist at St. George's Episcopal Church on Stuyvesant Square, where J. P. Morgan worshipped. Black soloists were unheard of, but he won over 59 white applicants. He sang there until he retired in 1946, rendering "Palms" annually for 52 years. He also became solo singer in 1900 at Temple Emanuel, the nation's richest synagogue. He sang in Morgan's home often and at his funeral. He sang before American and European audiences, twice giving command performances for King Edward VII.

Cardozo, Francis L. (1837–1903), State Official

Francis Louis Cardozo held high posts in South Carolina during Reconstruction. Well-educated and able, he refutes charges of incompetence leveled at black officeholders of that period.

He was born in Charleston, S.C. His father was a Jewish economist, his mother was of mixed ancestry. After attending a school for free blacks in Charleston, he was apprenticed to a carpenter and worked at this trade until he had saved a thousand dollars toward his further education. He then attended the University of Glasgow in Scotland for four years, where his education cost much more than he had saved, but he worked during vacations and also won a thousand-dollar competitive scholarship. He next attended Presbyterian seminaries in Edinburgh and London for three years, then returned to America, where he became pastor of Temple Street Congregational Church in New Haven, Conn.

After the Civil War, he moved back to his native city to head for three years Avery Institute, a normal school for freedmen set up by the American Missionary Association in 1865. Elected a delegate to the South Carolina constitutional convention of 1868, he served on key committees. As chairman of the Committee on Education, he helped establish the public school system.

Cardozo was then elected Secretary of State of South Carolina, 1868–1872, taking leave in 1871 to teach Latin at Howard University in Washington, D.C. Returning to South Carolina in 1872, he was elected State Treasurer. Reelected in 1876, he served until the Democrats overthrew the carpetbag government in 1877. Although Cardozo had discharged his duties with great integrity, the Democrats later convicted him in a trial so clearly unfair that Democratic Governor Wade Hampton pardoned him immediately.

Cardozo moved to Washington, serving in the Treasury and Post Office departments. From 1884 to 1896, he was principal of the city's high school for blacks.

Carmichael, Stokely (1941–   ), Black Power Militant

Stokely Carmichael symbolizes revolutionary black leadership.

Born in Port of Spain, Trinidad, West Indies, he knew black police, judges, and merchants. But in Harlem, where he was brought at the age of 11, he found white police, judges, and merchants predominant. An inquiring and somewhat rebellious boy, he became a gang member and tried marijuana before his parents moved to an all-white block in the Bronx. His father, a hardworking carpenter and cab driver, passed away young and his mother held the family together on her wages as a maid. In the new neighborhood, Carmichael joined an auto-stealing gang of middle-class white boys. He later pulled away from them, however, while attending Bronx High School of Science, reserved for gifted students.

During his senior year, televised brutality against sit-inners inspired Carmichael to join CORE's youth group in picketing Woolworth's in New York. He refused scholarships to white universities to enter Howard University. While majoring in philosophy, he found time to devote himself to causes: Freedom Rides in Mississippi; demonstrations in

Cambridge, Md.; and the Mississippi Freedom Project. He was arrested and beaten often.

After graduation in 1964, he worked full-time for the Student Non-violent Coordinating Committee (SNCC), becoming senior field secretary in Alabama. He organized the Lowndes County Freedom Organization as an independent political party using the black panther as a symbol. This third party spread to other counties.

In May, 1966, SNCC chose Carmichael and Ruby Robinson for chairman and executive secretary, replacing, respectively, the less radical John Lewis and James Forman. On the Meredith March that June, Carmichael's speeches publicized Black Power. In May, 1967, he stepped down in favor of H. Rap Brown, who succeeded him as SNCC leader, Carmichael remaining in the organization as a field worker.

Early in 1968, he became Prime Minister of the Black Panther Party (formed in 1966 in California by Bobby Seale and Huey Newton), then allied with SNCC. But SNCC expelled him that July when he kept his Panther post after the alliance disintegrated. He married South African jazz singer Miriam Makeba.

Other militant black leaders include Georgia legislator Julian Bond, Los Angeles's Ron Karenga, and nationalist Robert Williams.

Carney, William (1840– ?), Soldier

Sergeant William Harvey Carney received the Congressional Medal of Honor for heroism at Fort Wagner in 1863. His was the first such award given to a black soldier.

Most sources list New Bedford, Mass., as Carney's birthplace, but Benjamin Quarles (*The Negro in the Civil War*) lists Norfolk, Va. Some state that Carney attended New Bedford schools but Quarles quotes Carney as saying he "attended a private and secret school kept by a minister" when 14, and "in my fifteenth year I embraced the gospel." Probably Carney migrated to New Bedford in his mid-teens. There, Quarles reported, Carney worked at odd jobs, retaining his interest in the ministry. He was also a seaman.

On February 17, 1863, Carney enlisted in Company C of the Fifty-Fourth Massachusetts Infantry, the first Union regiment of Northern free blacks. The first companies—recruited in Boston, Philadelphia, Pennsylvania, and New Bedford—were mustered in on March 30, the last companies on May 13. Two weeks later, the regiment left for the South Carolina front.

On July 18, 1863, the Fifty-Fourth led the Union assault on Fort Wagner at Charleston. Many fell, including the color bearer. Sergeant

Carney seized the flag. Though severely wounded in head, thigh, and shoulder, he kept it flying, later crawling back to the Union line still bearing the colors aloft. Entering the hospital, he said, "Boys, the old flag never touched the ground." He was awarded the Congressional Medal of Honor. Twenty-one black soldiers and sailors received it in the Civil War, another twenty-two in Indian campaigns and the Spanish-American War, and six in Korea and Vietnam.

After the war, Carney lived briefly in California. From 1870 to 1901, he was a postman in New Bedford. He spent his last years in Boston as an employee at the state capitol, living until at least 1904.

Carroll, Diahann (1935–   ), Television Star

Next to Bill Cosby (*q.v.*), Diahann Carroll is the most successful black in television. Millions of viewers know her as "Julia."

She was born Carol Diahann Johnson in the Bronx, daughter of a subway conductor and a nurse. As early as the age of 6, she began acting in school plays and singing with the children's choir in church. At ten, she won a Metropolitan Opera scholarship for singing lessons. At 15, she began modeling for fashion photographers. She attended the High School of Music and Art for talented pupils in New York City. At her parents' insistence, she entered New York University, but soon won a spot on a television talent show. Her parents let her leave college on the condition that she would reenter if she made no progress as an entertainer.

But she was a success from the start, singing in supper clubs from New York to Hollywood. During 1954, while still in her teens, she played Myrt in the movie *Carmen Jones*, appeared on Red Skelton's television show, and made a great impression as Ottilie in the short-lived Broadway musical, *House of Flowers*. Composer Richard Rodgers vowed to write a show for her. Meanwhile, she played Clara in the film *Porgy and Bess* (1959), cut record albums, and appeared in a non-singing role opposite Sidney Poitier (*q.v.*) in the movie *Paris Blues* (1961).

In 1962, Rodgers wrote a Broadway musical, *No Strings*, for her, starring Miss Carroll as a model loved by a white novelist. Subsequently, she continued appearing in clubs, movies, and on television shows: the "Peter Gunn" series, Jack Parr, and others. She starred in the television special produced by Harry Belafonte (*q.v.*) in 1966, "Strolling Twenties."

In 1968, she began her own television comedy series, "Julia." Playing a widowed nurse with a young son, she became an instant, enduring hit.

Carver, George W. (1861–1943), Scientist

Working in his humble laboratory at Tuskegee, George Washington Carver freed the South from dependence on cotton by developing hundreds of uses for peanuts and sweet potatoes.

He was born in slavery near Diamond Grove, Mo. (now a national monument). When George, his older sister, and mother were kidnapped, their owner, Moses Carver, sent a man to track and recover them. The females were never found, but the sickly, "worthless" baby was recovered. Carver "ransomed" George by giving the tracker his racehorse. After emancipation, he remained on the farm with the kindly Carvers.

At 14, he left to attend school in Neosho, Mo. Later, he roamed through Kansas, Colorado, Minnesota, and Iowa, working at innumerable jobs and enduring hardship while continuing his education. He completed high school in his mid-20s. After more wandering, working, homesteading, and saving, he attended two Iowa colleges, Simpson at Indianola and Iowa State at Ames. He graduated in 1894, and became assistant botanist and head of the greenhouse at Iowa State, earning his master's degree in agriculture and bacterial botany two years later. Also an excellent pianist and artist, Carver's paintings took prizes at the Columbian Exposition in Chicago.

He was hired by Booker T. Washington at Tuskegee Institute and taught from 1896 to 1943. He built a demonstration wagon to reach backwoods farmers taking this "movable school" to them. Thus he pioneered agricultural extension. In an attempt to free Southerners from the tyranny of cotton and the boll weevil, he devised numerous uses for peanuts and sweet potatoes. He made over 300 products out of peanuts, including polish, coffee, and facial cream. He pioneered in chemurgy (synthesizing industrial products from plant life chemically) before the science came into being. He developed dehydrated foods; the U.S. Army used his sweet potato flour in World War I. Subsequently neglected, dehydration was rediscovered two decades later as if he had never existed.

Henry Ford and Thomas Edison tried to lure him to their laboratories. But Carver donated his discoveries to humanity, never seeking to patent, or profit from them.

Chamberlain, Wilt (1936–   ), Basketball Star

Wilton Norman Chamberlain is the greatest scorer and gate attraction in basketball history. His yearly salary, $250,000, is the highest ever in any sport.

The seven-foot, one-inch Chamberlain was born in Philadelphia. Like his father, a handyman, and his mother, a part-time maid, he was of normal height until his 14th summer when he sprang up four inches. He began playing basketball and was six feet, eleven inches tall on entering Overbrook High School. A sportswriter dubbed him "Wilt the Stilt," a nickname he hates, preferring "The Big Dipper," as he was called in college.

Wilt scored 2,252 points in three years in high school, becoming the nation's most publicized schoolboy. The National Basketball Association (NBA) passed a special rule to let the Philadelphia Warriors draft him while still in high school. Sought by two hundred colleges, he selected the University of Kansas. In two seasons, he averaged thirty points a game and led Kansas to the finals of the national championship. He quit college and toured a year with the Harlem Globetrotters.

In his first season with the Warriors, 1959–1960, he broke many NBA records. He led the league in scoring his first seven years. He scored an incredible 4,209 points (an average of 50.4 points a game) during the 1961–1962 season. In ten seasons, he scored 27,098 points, far beyond any player past or present.

Twice college All-American, NBA Rookie-of-the-Year, and four times the NBA's Most Valuable Player, nonetheless he played on only one championship team. In his eighth season, 1966–1967, he led the Philadelphia 76ers to a record 68 victories (only 13 losses) and the NBA championship in the playoffs.

He has been traded several times, from the Warriors (who had moved to San Francisco) to the 76ers to the Los Angeles Lakers.

Charles, Ray (1932–   ), "Soul" Musician

Ray Charles Robinson is outstanding as a singer, pianist, bandleader, composer, and saxophonist, and few musicians have approached his commercial success.

Charles was born in Albany, Ga., where his father was a mechanic, his mother a sawmill worker, but soon they moved to Greenville, Fla., where they passed away when he was in his mid-teens.

Starting at age 5, Ray gradually became blind. He attended a state school for the blind in St. Augustine, where he learned Braille, piano, and clarinet. He could memorize great quantities of music. Upon graduation from the school for the blind, Charles began touring with hillbilly and rhythm and blues combinations, settling in Seattle, Wash., about 1950. He dropped his surname to avoid confusion with boxer "Sugar"

Ray Robinson. Charles taught himself to arrange and compose music. He has perfect pitch.

Synthesizing the gospel music of his childhood with blues and jazz absorbed later, he began recording his unique style of soul music for Atlantic Records in 1954. Five years later, he moved to the ABC-Paramount label, recording "Georgia on My Mind" in a hoarse, soulful rendition that became a smash hit. An astute businessman, he receives royalties far beyond most performers. Braving opposition, he proved his versatility in 1962 by recording an album, *Modern Sounds in Country and Western Music*, that sold a million copies. One song from the album, "I Can't Stop Loving You," sold two and a half million records when released alone.

His Ray Charles Enterprises, that includes his band, Raelets quartet, bus, and airplanes, earns handsomely from his concerts ($30,000 weekly average), records, and television work. He has had trouble with the authorities over his drug addiction. For many years, jazz critics polled by *Down Beat* rated him America's top male vocalist.

Chavis, John (c. 1763–1838), Educator

John Chavis was a black teacher who taught white pupils from leading families in antebellum North Carolina. Among his pupils were future governors, congressmen, and diplomats.

Apparently, he was born free, probably near Oxford, N.C. Contemporaries described him as being of pure African appearance and well educated. Where he began his schooling is uncertain. Eventually, he attended Princeton University, probably as a private student of Dr. John Witherspoon, president from 1768 to 1794. In the late 1790s, he enrolled at Washington Academy of Lexington, Va., now Washington and Lee University. His acceptance there may have been due to his service as a soldier in the American Revolution.

Chavis was licensed as a minister by the Lexington Presbytery in Virginia and became a missionary among blacks in Maryland, Virginia, and North Carolina. About 1805 he moved to North Carolina, becoming a supply minister for both white and black churches in the Orange Presbytery.

By 1808, he was running schools. He taught whites daytime and blacks evenings, at the request of white patrons. But he charged blacks less, so that the whites in effect subsidized them. Chavis taught Greek, Latin, English, mathematics, and other subjects to boys and girls, conducting schools in Wake, Granville, Chatham, and Orange counties.

His pupils included Archibald and John Henderson, sons of North

Carolina's Chief Justice. Two pupils, Charles Manly and Abraham Rencher, became governors of North Carolina and New Mexico, respectively. Rencher and Willie P. Mangum became congressmen; Rencher also was a diplomat. Other pupils became physicians, lawyers, ministers, and professors. Chavis reputedly ran the best college preparatory schools in North Carolina.

Restrictions imposed after Nat Turner's Revolt (1831) ended his teaching and ministry. The Orange Presbytery supported Chavis and his widow thereafter.

Chesnutt, Charles Waddell (1858–1932), Writer

In 1898 and 1900, respectively, Paul Laurence Dunbar (*q.v.*) and Charles Waddell Chesnutt published the first noteworthy novels by blacks. Their chief fame, however, comes from Dunbar's poems and Chesnutt's short stories.

In a wagon train of free blacks fleeing Southern oppression in 1856, Chesnutt's father and mother left their homes in Fayetteville, N.C., for Indiana and Ohio, respectively. They fell in love on this journey; were later reunited in 1857, and were married in Cleveland where Charles was born. All three were light enough in complexion to get opportunities denied darker persons. Charles's father was a Cleveland horsecar driver-conductor, who became a Union Army teamster during the Civil War. At war's end, the family returned to Fayetteville where the father became a grocer and later a farmer.

When Charles was 14, his school principal, Robert Harris, made him a salaried pupil-teacher to keep him from dropping out to help support his family. Next year, Chesnutt became full-time assistant principal to Harris's brother, Cicero, in Charlotte. During three years there, he continued his own studies zealously. In 1877, he became English teacher and first assistant to Robert Harris in the new Fayetteville State Normal School, succeeding Harris as its head in 1880.

Chesnutt was unhappy with Southern restrictions and left Fayetteville in 1883. He had trained himself to take dictation at a rate of 200 words a minute, and became a stenographer, first for Dow Jones on Wall Street and then for a railroad in Cleveland. Although he studied law and passed the Ohio bar in 1887, his legal stenography business and work as a court reporter in Cleveland paid too well to drop.

As a schoolboy, he had published stories in a black newspaper. On Wall Street, he wrote a daily gossip column for the *New York Mail and Express*. Starting in 1885, he wrote many stories and poems for newspapers and magazines in his spare time. His first important work, "The

Goophered Grapevine," appeared in *Atlantic Monthly* in 1887. Others followed, without critics and readers realizing that he was black.

In 1899, he published two widely acclaimed collections of short stories, *The Conjure Woman* and *The Wife of His Youth*. From 1899 to 1901, he abandoned business to write, returning when literary income lagged. He published three novels, *The House Behind the Cedars* (1900), *The Marrow of Tradition)* (1901), and *The Colonel's Dream* (1905), which was his last book.

Chisholm, Shirley (1924–   ), Congresswoman

In 1968, Shirley Chisholm attained the highest elective post ever held by a black woman in America, and is the first black woman in Congress. She represents the Bedford-Stuyvesant section of Brooklyn, where she was born Shirley Anita St. Hill. Her father, a factory worker, migrated to New York from British Guiana. Her mother, a seamstress and domestic, came from Barbados. Between the ages of 3 and 11, Shirley lived with her stern, proud, upright grandmother in Barbados. Graduating from a girl's high school in Brooklyn, she received a scholarship to Brooklyn College where she majored in sociology. After being graduated *cum laude*, she taught in a nursery school and earned a master's degree in elementary education at Columbia University. She married Conrad Chisholm who had migrated to Brooklyn from the West Indian island of Jamaica. Mrs. Chisholm became an authority in her field, directing a nursery in Brownsville, heading Manhattan child-care center from 1953 to 1959, and serving from 1959 to 1964 as educational consultant to New York City on day care for welfare children.

Active in such groups as the Brooklyn NAACP and the Bedford-Stuyvesant Political League, she was noted for being outspoken, independent-minded, and trustworthy. Bucking the Democratic machine, she was elected to the state legislature in 1964 and was subsequently reelected. An impressive debater, she secured laws for public day-care centers, unemployment insurance for domestics, and college training for disadvantaged blacks and Puerto Ricans.

Early in 1968, court-ordered reapportionment made her Assembly district part of New York's new Twelfth Congressional District. She won the Democratic primary against two machine-sponsored blacks in a district seventy percent black and Puerto Rican and eighty percent Democratic. Then, she easily defeated her nationally known Liberal Republican opponent, James Farmer (*q.v.*), former head of CORE, who was unfamiliar with the district. She publicly opposed House leaders over her assignment to committees on forests and villages, forcing an unprecedented reassignment to the Veterans Affairs Committee.

Prior to Mrs. Chisholm's election, NAACP lawyer Constance Baker Motley held the highest elective post ever won by a black woman. She was elected Borough President of Manhattan. President Lyndon Johnson later made her a Federal judge.

Cole, Bob (1868–1911) Cook, Will (1869–1944), Pioneer Composers of Musicals

Two black composers led the way in converting minstrelsy to musical comedy: Bob Cole and Will Cook. Cole wrote, composed, directed, danced, sang, joked, and acted in shows. Besides composing, Cook pioneered with jazz orchestras.

Both were well trained. Robert Cole was born in Athens, Ga., and was a graduate of Atlanta University. Will Marion Cook was born on the campus of Howard University where his father was secretary to the University and acting dean of the law school. When Cook's father passed away, his mother, an Oberlin graduate, began teaching at Howard. After attending Oberlin, he was trained in classical violin and harmony by Joachim at the Berlin Conservatory and also studied under Antonín Dvořák. Both Cole and Cook lived in New York City in the late 1890s as musical comedy was developing.

The first break with minstrelsy was a singing-dancing chorus of sixteen beautiful girls in an all-black show that opened in Boston in 1890, *The Creole Show*. It played five years in various cities. From 1891 to 1893 it was a hit at the Chicago World's Fair. Bob Cole was among its performers. Afterwards, he headed a Negro stock company in New York. Two white promoters hired him in 1897 to write words and music for a show built around black operatic singer, Madame Sissieretta Jones, famed as "The Black Patti." The show, *Black Patti's Troubadors*, played successfully many years. Breaking with the promoters in a financial dispute, Cole decided to do his own show.

In 1898, both Cole and Cook wrote pathbreaking shows. Aided by Billy Johnson, Cole wrote, produced, and directed *A Trip to Coontown*, the first show ever to be planned, directed, managed, and promoted entirely by blacks. It was a complete departure from minstrelsy and the beginning of musical comedy since it had a plot and well-developed characters. The show opened in New York in April, 1898, and ran three seasons.

Cook, fresh from his studies, composed *Clorindy: The Origin of the Cakewalk*, with lyrics by poet Paul Laurence Dunbar (*q.v.*). In the summer of 1898, *Clorindy* introduced syncopated Negro ragtime music on stage to New York and featured comedian Ernest Hogan. In Cook's 1899 show, *Jes Lak White Folks,* singer-dancer-actress Abbie Mitchell began her long stage career. Only 14, she married the 30-year-old Cook.

From 1901 to 1909, two black companies were prominent. Bob Cole led one company, teaming with two brothers, composer J. Rosamond Johnson and lyricist James Weldon Johnson (*q.v.*) (not related to his earlier partner, William Johnson). Cakewalking comedians Bert Williams (*q.v.*) and George Walker headed the other company, with Cook composing their *In Dahomey* (1902), *Abyssinia* (1906), and *Bandanna Land* (1907). Cole and Rosamond Johnson became vaudeville headliners and also wrote and appeared in the first black operettas, *The Shoofly Regiment* (1906) and *The Red Moon* (1908). Both shows played on Broadway, a breakthrough for blacks. Among Cole's hit songs were "Under the Bamboo Tree," "The Maiden with the Dreamy Eyes," and "Oh, Didn't He Ramble." For Williams and Walker, Cook wrote such popular songs as "Bon Bon Buddy," "Rain Song," and "I May Be Crazy But I Ain't No Fool." Walker's incapacitating stroke in 1909 and Cole's passing two years later disrupted both companies.

Meanwhile, Cook was also pioneering with jazz orchestras. The Memphis Students Band, composed of professional New York musicians, was trained and directed by Cook, though fronted by dancing conductor Will Dixon. In 1905 it became the first jazz band to play a theater engagement, appearing at Proctor's Theatre in New York before going on a tour of Europe. In 1914, a former member of this band, Jim Europe, gave a Carnegie Hall jazz concert with his 125-piece Clef Club Syncopated Orchestra, aided by Cook. In 1919, Cook formed the American Syncopated Orchestra which played a long engagement at New York's 44th Street Theatre and also gave concerts in Berlin, London, and Paris. Cook was giving classical jazz concerts long before Paul Whiteman's supposedly pioneering concert of 1924.

Mercer Cook, son of Will and Abbie Mitchell Cook, became a noted scholar on black literature and head of the Romance Languages department at Howard University. He was President Lyndon Johnson's ambassador to Senegal and to Niger.

Cole, Nat (1919–1965), Singer and Pianist

Nat King Cole transformed from a jazz pianist into a popular singer. He sold fifty million records, including "Sweet Lorraine," "Nature Boy," and "Mona Lisa."

Son of a minister, he was born Nathaniel Adams Coles in Montgomery, Ala. He changed the spelling of his name on forming his trio. The family moved to Chicago when Nat was five. All the children were good musicians, trained by the mother who was choir director in her husband's Baptist church. By the age of 12, Nat was a pianist and church organist. In high school, he formed a band and also played in his brother's sextet.

In 1936, Nat became pianist for a touring black revue, *Shuffle Along.* In the following year, stranded in Hollywood when the show closed there, he became a pianist in small nightclubs, and then formed a trio, with bass and guitar. This fine "combo" developed a large following of jazz fans in Hollywood's leading clubs and on tour. Cole sang as well as played.

In 1943, the King Cole Trio began recording for Capitol. Their first recording was Nat's own composition, "Straighten Up and Fly Right," which sold half a million copies. Many other hits followed. Increasingly, Cole concentrated on singing. His styling, rather than his voice, was distinctive, and superb on such hits as "It's Only a Paper Moon," "Too Young," "Walking My Baby Back Home," and "The Christmas Song."

In the 1940s, he was the only black performer with his own commercial network radio program. During the 1956–1957 season, he became the first black entertainer with his own national television show. NBC carried it many months, but commercial sponsors, afraid of adverse reaction of Southern whites, refused to back it.

Like other black performers, Cole was abused and humiliated in the South. Three whites assaulted him on stage in Birmingham, Ala., in 1956. An indication of progress is the decline of such abuse and the readiness of business to sponsor black shows on television in the late 1960s.

Cook, Will Marion (1869–1944), Composer
See: Cole, Bob and Cook, Will

Collins, Janet (1923–   ), Ballerina
The first black outstanding in ballet, Janet Collins has been prima ballerina with the Metropolitan Opera since 1951. She joined the Met four seasons before contralto Marian Anderson (*q.v.*).

Daughter of a tailor, Miss Collins was born in New Orleans. When she was 4, her family moved to Los Angeles. She began dance lessons at a neighborhood Catholic center at the age of 10. When still in junior high school, she did professional adagio dancing. She attended Los Angeles City College and the Los Angeles Art Center School—she was also an accomplished painter. She studied with many famous dance teachers, and went on the initial tour of the Katherine Dunham (*q.v.*) troupe. Later, Miss Collins auditioned for Ballet Russe de Monte Carlo. When she was told she could be hired if she used white makeup to disguise her race, she refused.

To secure concert bureau backing for a tour, she had to create her own dances and present a solo concert. Aided by a Rosenwald Fellowship, she prepared for three years, studying classic, dramatic, Hebrew, and Negro dances. Critics praised her solo concert at Las Palmas theater in Los Angeles in 1947, but the concert bureaus were unmoved by a West Coast debut. She had to prove herself in New York City. By dancing and portrait painting, she earned enough to move to New York in 1949. She attracted great notice with her solo concert in the Y.M.H.A. dance series. She became lead dancer for Cole Porter's Broadway hit musical, *Out of This World*, often stopping the show.

After she joined the ballet troupe at the Met, she appeared as prima ballerina in *Aida* on opening night of the 1951 season. She shared the premiere-danseuse roles that year. The next season, she was the star soloist for the three dozen dancers in the corps de ballet. In December, 1952, she starred in her first classic ballet, "Dance of the Hours" in *La Gioconda*.

She is a professor at the School of American Ballet. On tours she displays her own compositions, some based on Negro spirituals.

Cosby, Bill (1938–   ), Comedian and Television Actor

Comedian Bill Cosby smashed color barriers in television, becoming the first black starring in a non-black role. His success in "I Spy" paved the way for Diahann Carroll (*q.v.*) in "Julia."

Cosby was born in Germantown, outside Philadelphia, son of a Navy mess steward. In fifth grade, he did a comedy routine that his teachers and classmates found hilarious. Although very bright, he enjoyed clowning more than studying and dropped out in the tenth grade. During a four-year hitch in the Navy, he received his diploma equivalence by examination. Enrolling at Temple University on a track and football scholarship, he was talented enough as a defensive back to be pro football material.

But Cosby was more interested in becoming a comedian. While at Temple, he began performing at coffee houses in Philadelphia, starting at five dollars a night. He quit Temple after his sophomore year to perform in nightclubs in New York. His salary rose from $175 a week in 1962 to $25,000 a week three years later. His story-telling convulsed audiences. Avoiding racial nuances, he simply related childhood or everyday experiences pushed to absurd lengths, adding funny noises, rubbery face movements, and character acting. Cosby writes all his comedy material.

In 1965, he began a three-year run, co-starring with Robert Culp, in the dramatic series "I Spy." Featuring the two men as C.I.A. agents disguised as tennis stars, it gave Cosby a role unrelated to race or comedy. On this top-rated show, Cosby won the Emmy award in 1966 and 1967 as television's best male actor. In 1969, he began a new series, the *Bill Cosby Show*, playing a high school teacher in comic situations. His success paved the way for the highly successful Flip Wilson show in the 1970–1971 season.

He appears on other shows also. His record albums, such as *I Started Out As a Child*, are best sellers.

Davis, Benjamin O., Jr. (1912–   ), Air Force General

Lieutenant-General Benjamin Oliver Davis, Jr., held the highest military rank reached by an American black. His father was the first black general.

Davis was born in Washington, D.C. At the age of 8, he moved to Tuskegee Institute where his father taught military science. Later they moved to Cleveland where Ben was senior class president at integrated Central High School. He spent a year at Western Reserve University and two years at the University of Chicago before being appointed in 1932 to the U.S. Military Academy at West Point. Although his father had become a colonel in 1930, Davis was hesitant. Prejudice had relegated his father to segregated units and made him take thirty-two years to rise to colonel. Also, no black had graduated from West Point since Charles Young (*q.v.*) in 1889.

Uncertain about a military career, Davis failed the entrance examination, but then zealously studied and passed it on a second attempt. After a few pleasant days at West Point, he was suddenly subjected to a complete boycott and silent treatment from all other cadets. As the only black at the isolated academy, he had no one to talk to during his freshman year. He weathered this cruel treatment and had good relations his other three years. In 1936, he became the fourth black ever to graduate from West Point.

Davis wanted to fly, but the Army Air Corps barred blacks at that time. He became an infantry lieutenant and an R.O.T.C. instructor at Tuskegee, rising to captain in 1940. That year his father was promoted to brigadier general, retiring eight years later. When the Air Corps dropped its color bar, Davis enrolled in the first class of black air cadets, graduating in 1942. Having moved up to lieutenant-colonel, he became commander of the 99th Fighter Squadron, an all-black unit that fought under him in North Africa, Sicily, and Italy. He then trained and commanded a larger all-black unit, the 332nd Fighter Group. In 1944 his group knocked out German radar installations, facilitating the allied invasion of southern France. He won the Silver Star for gallantry and the Distinguished Flying Cross, meanwhile becoming a full colonel, only eight years after leaving West Point.

Later, he commanded the 477th Fighter-Bomber Group at Lock-bourne Air Base. After attending the Air War College, he became a staff planning officer and later chief of the fighter branch at Air Force Headquarters. He commanded the 51st Fighter Interceptor Wing in Korea in 1953, then became director of operations and training for the Far East Air Forces. In 1954, President Eisenhower promoted him to brigadier general. In 1957, he became Deputy Chief of Staff of the 12th Air Force in Germany. He was promoted to major general in 1959 and lieutenant general in 1965. He became Chief of Staff of the U.S. Air Force in East Asia in 1965, and in 1968 became second in command of the U.S. Strike Command at McDill Field in Florida.

On Davis's retirement early in 1970, Mayor Carl Stokes (*q.v.*) appointed him Director of Public Safety for Cleveland. He left that post later that year to become head of the force of Federal Marshals formed to halt airplane hijacking. The third and fourth black generals were appointed in 1968 and 1970, respectively, Brigadier General Frederic Davison in the Army and Brigadier General Daniel "Chappie" James in the Air Force.

Davis, Sammy, Jr. (1925–   ), Entertainer

Sammy Davis, Jr., has been in show business all his life. *Mr. Wonderful* and *Golden Boy* were Broadway musicals built around him.

Sammy's father and mother were top dancers in Holiday in Dixieland, a vaudeville troupe led by Will Mastin, Sammy's adopted uncle. His mother performed until two weeks before Sammy was born in Harlem and soon left him with friends in Brooklyn so that she could return to the show. When his parents broke up, the father took the 3-year-old boy on tour. A born mugger, Sammy was soon on stage, mimicking others and dancing. When only 6, he played in two movies, *Rufus Jones for President*, with Ethel Waters (*q.v.*), and *Season's Greetings*. When he was 8, Mastin formed the Will Mastin Trio, featuring little Sammy. Tapdancer Bill Robinson (*q.v.*) gave Sammy some help with his dancing. Increasingly, Sammy was the star of the act, singing, dancing, and mimicking popular singers and actors, while his father and Mastin stayed in the background. In 1954, Sammy cut an album for Decca, *Starring Sammy Davis, Jr.*, imitating famous personalities, and another album with his own singing voice, *Just for Lovers.*

Late in 1954, he lost his left eye in an auto accident, but was soon back on stage wearing an eye patch. Later he got an artificial eye. He began making television appearances. In 1956, *Mr. Wonderful* featured the Will Mastin Trio, but Sammy's dynamic singing, dancing, and mimicking made it virtually a one-man show. A close friend of Frank Sinatra, Sammy acted in a series of movies with Sinatra, Dean Martin, and Peter Lawford, such as *Ocean's 11* in 1960. Sammy also played the role of Sportin' Life in the MGM movie version of *Porgy and Bess* in 1959. His biggest success came in 1964 in *Golden Boy*, the musical version of Clifford Odets's drama about a boxer. In 1966, the Sammy Davis Variety Hour ran on NBC-TV with commercial backing, but did not last long.

Dawson, William L. (1886–1970), Congressman

William Levi Dawson has been in Congress longer than any other black. He has served fourteen consecutive terms from the First Illinois district.

Dawson was born in Albany, Ga., grandson of slaves and son of a barber. He attended Albany Normal School and Fisk University, graduating *magna cum laude* in 1909. Although 23, he had never voted because of disfranchisement of blacks. In 1912, he moved to Chicago, studying law at Kent College and Northwestern University.

After he was admitted to the bar in 1920, he began practicing law, but devoted much of his time to politics, starting as a precinct worker in the machine of Republican Mayor William Thompson. In 1928, Dawson ran against Congressman Martin Madden in the Republican primary, but lost. Madden soon passed away and the machine selected alderman Oscar DePriest as the Republican nominee. The first northern black in Congress, DePriest served from 1929 to 1935. Meanwhile, Republicans sent Dawson to the state central committee, 1928 to 1930. Elected alderman of the Second Ward, he served on City Council from 1933 to 1939. Shifting to the New Deal, blacks replaced DePriest with the first black Democratic Congressman, Arthur Mitchell. This former Republican served from 1935 to 1943. In 1939, Dawson also switched parties, becoming Democratic National Committeeman and later vice chairman of the Democratic National Committee.

When Mitchell refused to seek a fifth term in 1942, Dawson won the Democratic primary and the election, making him the third Northern black and second black Democrat in Congress. A machine politician, Dawson held tight rein on his district by patronage, careful organization, and accessibility to voters. Quiet and regular, he was not a flamboyant fighter for black rights as was Adam Clayton Powell (*q.v.*), who joined him in Congress in 1945.

Dawson was chairman from 1949 to 1970 of the House Committee on Government Operations. Although twenty-four blacks served in the House or Senate before him, he was the first to head a standing committee in either body. His cousin, William L. Dawson of Anniston, Ala., became a recognized composer.

Derham, James (1762– ?), Pioneer Physician

Dr. James Derham was the first black physician in America. He was born into slavery in Philadelphia, and as a boy, became the property of a physician, Dr. John Kearsley, who trained him to be his assistant in dispensing medicine. He learned to read and write from Dr. Kearsley, and absorbed all the knowledge he could.

During the Revolution, Derham was sold to a British physician, Dr. George West, surgeon of the Sixteenth British Regiment. Working as West's assistant, Derham learned more about medicine, especially treating wounds. When the British departed, Derham was sold to a physician in New Orleans, Dr. Robert Dove. As his assistant, Derham learned about as much as any medical doctor knew at that time.

Dr. Dove allowed Derham to purchase his freedom on generous terms and encouraged him to set up his own practice. By 1789, Dr. Derham had a thriving practice, earning more than $3,000 a year. Speaking French, Spanish, and English, he became very skilled at diagnosing and prescribing. Dr. Benjamin Rush of Philadelphia, who was Surgeon-General of the Continental Army and a signer of the Declaration of Independence, visited Dr. Derham in New Orleans, saying of him:

> I have conversed with him upon most of the acute and epidemic diseases of the country where he lives, and was pleased to find him perfectly acquainted with the modern simple mode of practice in those diseases. I expected to have suggested some new medicines to him; but he suggested many more to me.

Dr. James McCune Smith and Dr. Martin R. Delany were among other skilled black physicians of the early nineteenth century.

De Sable, Jean (c. 1745–1818), Pioneer

Jean Baptiste Pointe De Sable founded America's second largest city, Chicago.

Born in Haiti, he migrated to Louisiana as a young man. He became a friend and business associate of Jacques Clamorgan, a white merchant who engaged in fur trading near St. Louis. De Sable married a woman of the Potawatomi tribe in an Indian ceremony about 1771, but in 1778 a Catholic priest remarried them formally at Cahokia, Ill. They had a son, Jean, and daugher, Suzanne. Land records show that De Sable had a farm in Peoria, Ill., as early as 1773.

About 1775, De Sable set up a trading post at the important portage between the Chicago and Des Plaines rivers, which linked the Great Lakes and the Mississippi River. He moved his family to this post, while still maintaining his farm in Peoria and also managing other trading posts at Michigan City (1779) and near Port Huron, Mich. (1780-1784). After 1784 he concentrated his efforts at his Chicago post.

He built a thriving establishment. White traders and Indians settled around it. His daughter married a man named Pelletier in 1790. Their child, Eulalie, De Sable's granddaughter, was born at Chicago in 1796, the first birth on record there. In 1800, De Sable sold his post to Jean Lalime for six thousand livres. By then, it consisted of ten buildings, more than one hundred livestock, and elaborate furnishings as described on the deed recorded in Detroit.

Concerning Chicago, the Indians said, "the first white man who settled here was a Negro." The city grew up around the site of De Sable's post. After selling out, he moved farther west, and spent his last years in St. Charles, Mo.

Divine, Father (c. 1874–1965), Cult Leader

George "Father Divine" Baker had millions of followers, black and white. They pooled their resources in flourishing enterprises and lived communally, worshipping their leader as God.

Born to sharecroppers on Hutchinsons's Island, near Savannah, Ga., Baker moved to Baltimore by 1899. A gardener and part-time Baptist preacher, he became "The Messenger and Son" of Samuel "Father Jehoviah" Morris, who claimed Godship. In 1912, Baker moved southward, proclaiming his own divinity. Prosecuted for disruptions in Valdosta, Ga., his flock moved in 1915 to New York City, where he learned from the Church of the Living God of John "Bishop St. John The Vine" Hickerson, another disciple of Father Jehoviah.

Settling in Brooklyn, The Messenger had his followers (called angels) renounce attachments to husbands, wives, children, and parents. He forbade sexual relations. His wife, Peninah "Sister Penny" Baker of Valdosta, slept in the women's quarters and he in the men's. Since his devoted followers donated all their earnings to the movement, he could serve free banquets to believers and outsiders.

Renamed Major Morgan J. Devine, he moved to Sayville, Long Island, in 1919, helping his followers, mostly domestics, find employment. Under Reverend Devine's discipline, even dissolute, shiftless, criminal persons became dependable, honest, and hardworking. In 1928, his communal cult had forty disciples. Expanding aggressively thereafter, he brought busloads of Harlem's poor to his free banquets, making converts with his largesse and preachings. Renamed Father Divine in 1930, he attracted whites, many educated and well-to-do, who likewise gave their possessions to the movement, finding bliss and healing in his teachings of peace, happiness, health, abundance, equality, brotherhood, and eternal life. He forbade illness and death; any Divine angel who got sick or passed away was said to have lacked true faith.

Prosecuted as a public nuisance and jailed by a harsh Long Island judge in 1932, Father Divine gained national attention and thousands of followers when the judge died five days later. Converts deemed Divine omnipotent. Now moving to Harlem, he founded communal "heavens," feeding and housing thousands of Depression victims. Peace restaurants, barber shops, laundries, and other businesses sprang up, undercutting competitors by good service at unbelievably low prices. Followers hailed patrons and each other with the movement's universal greeting, "Peace," and response, "It's Truly Wonderful." Soon, even large luxury hotels were being purchased in cash (he called loans sinful) by this Peace Mission Movement. Attracting converts worldwide by his banquets, healings, enterprises, and newspaper (*The New Day*), Father Divine claimed twenty million adherents, but probably had only two million.

Stubbornly fleeing New York in 1941 to avoid paying a small judgment secured by two disillusioned angels seeking to withdraw their funds, he made Philadelphia his headquarters. In 1946, several years after his first wife passed away (her passing, like that of other angels, went unacknowledged by Divine), he married a young, white Canadian follower, Edna "Sweet Angel" Ritchings, setting her up as a spotless, virginal wife in his sexless kingdom.

A passionate believer in racial equality, he ostentatiously exhibited his white and black followers living harmoniously. His movement lost much of its impetus when its God finally succumbed to old age.

Dixon, Dean (1915–   ), Conductor

Charles Dean Dixon is the first black renowned as a symphonic conductor. Although his pioneering paved the way for others, he had to move to Europe for permanent employment.

Dixon was born in New York City. His father passed away early. His mother set out to make her son a music lover, carrying him to Carnegie Hall concerts before he could walk. She limited exposure to popular music by keeping their radio "out of order." She started him on violin lessons when he was 3, forcing him to continue when he rebelled and even when a teacher quit ten years later on grounds that he had no special talent.

But Dixon had absolute pitch and he dreamed of conducting. Black conductors were unheard of and all but his mother tried to dissuade him, but he persisted. In his senior year in high school, he formed the Dean Dixon Symphony Orchestra in the Harlem Y.M.C.A. Beginning with only a violinist and pianist, he had seventy players within five years.

He entered the Juilliard Institute of Musical Art on the basis of a violin audition, but switched to public school music. After graduation in 1936, he won a three-year conducting fellowship to the Juilliard Graduate School. Early in 1941, he led his Dean Dixon Symphony in a concert at the Heckscher Theatre attended by Eleanor Roosevelt and the musical director of the NBC Symphony. He was then invited to direct the NBC Symphony for two concerts that June. In August, 1941, at Lewisohn Stadium, he became the first black guest conductor of the New York Philharmonic. In succeeding years, he made other guest appearances leading the NBC and Philharmonic orchestras. He also led the National Youth Administration Orchestra. In 1944, he organized the American Youth Orchestra, leading it for five years until financial support dwindled.

He had to move to Europe to become a permanent director. From 1949 to 1960, he was one of three resident conductors of the Gothenburg Symphony in Sweden's second largest city. He conducted major orchestras all over Europe in guest appearances. In 1960, he became director of the Hessian Radio Symphony in Frankfurt, Germany.

Meanwhile, younger blacks got conducting posts in America. Henry Lewis was associate conductor of the Los Angeles Philharmonic for three years before becoming musical director of the Los Angeles Opera Company in 1965. Paul Freeman became associate conductor of the Dallas Symphony in 1968.

Douglass, Frederick (c. 1817–1895), Leader

From 1847 to 1895, Frederick Douglass was the leader of his race. His unceasing militancy inspired blacks of his day and of today to fight against slavery, segregation, discrimination, exploitation, and all forms of oppression.

Born to a slave woman, by an unknown white man, at Tuckahoe in Talbot County on Maryland's Eastern Shore, he was originally named Frederick Bailey. He learned early that slaves who resisted were whipped more severely once, but not nearly as often as those who submitted meekly. From the age of 9 to 16 he lived in Baltimore with Hugh Auld, brother of his owner's son-in-law. When Auld angrily told his wife that her helping him learn the alphabet unfitted him for slavery, Frederick became more determined to learn. Unwittingly aided by white playmates, he learned to read, beginning his lifelong zealous studies. When the son-in-law, Tom Auld, took him back to the Eastern Shore, he was so rebellious that he was sent to a professional slavebreaker. The slavebreaker crushed his spirit for six months until he remembered his earlier lessons and fought back, mastering the slavebreaker.

Sent back to Baltimore at the age of 19, he plotted his escape while apprenticed as a calker. In 1838, he borrowed a free black seaman's identification papers and rode public transportation to freedom in the North. He changed his name to Frederick Douglass to avoid recapture.

Settling in Massachusetts, he attended abolitionist meetings, speaking out so ably at a meeting in 1841 that the Antislavery Society hired him as a lecturer. He was a most effective abolitionist, eloquently narrating from personal experience the many evils of slavery. He also protested and resisted discrimination, segregation, and prejudice wherever he found them in the North.

In publishing his *Narrative* (1845) to prove to skeptics that despite his learning and polish he was a fugitive slave, his real identity became known. For safety, he fled to England, lecturing at antislavery rallies there. English abolitionists raised money to buy his freedom and donated the excess funds to let him establish a newspaper, *The North Star*, which he published in Rochester, N.Y., from 1847 to 1863, renaming it *Frederick Douglass's Newspaper* in the early 1850s. His was by far the most successful, long-lasting, and outstanding of pre-Civil War black newspapers. He became the chief spokesman for his people. He was also active in many other causes, especially women's rights.

He became a friend of President Abraham Lincoln, pressuring him to make the Civil War a crusade against slavery. He closed his newspaper to concentrate on recruiting black soldiers. His sons served in the 54th Massachusetts.

Douglass demanded voting rights for blacks during Reconstruction and became a prominent Republican orator. He moved to Washington, D.C., and briefly published a newspaper, *New National Era*. President Rutherford Hayes appointed him U.S. Marshal for the District of Columbia in 1877 and President James Garfield made him Recorder of Deeds for the District of Columbia in 1881, making him the first black man in either post. From 1889 to 1891, he was the U.S. Minister to Haiti, appointed by President Benjamin Harrison. He had declined this post when President Ulysses Grant offered it twenty years earlier, which would have made him America's first black diplomatic representative, but he felt his people needed him at home in 1869.

Drew, Charles R. (1904–1950), Father of Blood Plasma and Blood Banks

Dr. Charles Richard Drew's research made possible the use of blood plasma to save countless lives. He founded and directed the world's first two major blood banks.

Drew was born in Washington, D.C., son of a carpetlayer. His mother was a graduate of Miner Teacher's College. He graduated from the best black high school in the nation, Dunbar, of which Francis Cardozo (*q.v.*) was once principal and from which famous Washington blacks like William Hastie and Robert Weaver (*qq.v.*) graduated. Drew starred in baseball, basketball, football, and track. He won a scholarship to Amherst College, graduating in 1926 after being star quarterback, captain of the track team, and becoming national high-hurdles champion. He then worked for two years at Morgan State College in Baltimore, as athletic director, football coach, and instructor in chemistry and biology.

His grades at Amherst were only average, but he wanted a medical career, and managed to enter the medical school of McGill University in Montreal, Canada. There he became an excellent student, won fellowships, ran track, and joined Dr. John Beattie, a British instructor, in doing research on blood. In 1933, he received his M.D. and Master of Surgery degrees, interning at Montreal General Hospital where he continued his research on blood and also completed a residency in surgery. In 1935, he returned to his hometown, becoming instructor in pathology at Howard University's College of Medicine. The next year, he became assistant in surgery at the College and at adjacent Freedmen's Hospital.

In 1938, Drew received a Rockefeller fellowship for advanced training at the Columbia Medical Center in New York City. There he continued his surgical training, but focused on blood research with Dr. John Scudder. Drew's work in the experimental blood bank set up at the medical center under his direction in 1939 resulted in his discoveries that blood plasma, which kept for months, could replace whole blood, which deteriorated in a few days, in transfusions. In 1940, he received from Columbia University's College of Physicians and Surgeons the Doctor of Medical Science degree (akin to a Ph.D. in medicine), the first black awarded this degree. His thesis, "Banked Blood," was a major contribution in medical history.

Drs. Drew, Scudder, and E. H. L. Corwin prepared plans for the Blood Transfusion Association for using banked blood plasma in France, but the sudden fall of France cancelled the project. Drew returned to Howard, but after a month went on leave in October, 1940, to set up and direct the British Blood Bank, collecting blood in New York, converting it into plasma, and shipping it to Britain, saving persons injured by Nazi bombing during the Battle of Britain. When that project ended in 1941, Drew was appointed the director of the American Red Cross project to collect and bank the blood of 100,000 donors. A controversy subsequently developed when the Red Cross agreed to Army and Navy insistence that blood of black donors be refused. Drew fought such segregation, publicly stating that there was no scientific difference whatever between blood from persons of different races.

Dropped from the program, he returned to Howard University where he rose to the posts of Professor of Surgery and head of the Department of Surgery in the College of Medicine and also Chief Surgeon, Chief of Staff, and then Medical Director of Freedmen's Hospital. In April, 1950, he was killed in an automobile accident in North Carolina.

Du Bois, W. E. B. (1868–1963), Scholar and Spokesman

William Edward Burghardt Du Bois spanned the eras of the main black leaders—Douglass, Washington, Garvey, Malcolm X, and King (qq.v.). Too scholarly and arrogant to have a large personal following, he influenced all twentieth-century black protest thought and helped found the NAACP.

Du Bois was born in Great Barrington, Mass., a town with few blacks. His mother's family, the Burghardts, had farmed in New England ever since her grandfather was emancipated for service in the Revolution. Du Bois's father, a barber and son of a mulatto steward on ships plying the Caribbean, had been born in Haiti, later moving to Connecticut. He soon abandoned the family and Will grew up on his grandfather's farm. When he reached school age, his mother returned to town, doing domestic work so Will could get a good education. He was the only black in his high school graduating class, and its outstanding pupil. The resulting scholarship, normally to a New England college, sent him instead to a black school, Fisk University in Nashville, Tenn., where he first encountered widespread racial prejudice and separation. He taught during summer vacations in rural Tennessee schools.

After graduating from Fisk in 1888, he attended Harvard University two years, receiving an A.B. in philosophy in 1890, spending another two years of graduate study in political economy and history. Experiencing racial rebuffs on campus and in Boston, he became increasingly withdrawn and caustic. With aid from the Slater Fund, he studied abroad for two years, primarily sociology at the University of Berlin. After his return, he taught at Wilberforce University in Ohio, 1894 to 1896, meanwhile completing his dissertation for his Ph.D. from Harvard in 1895. Published in 1896, Du Bois's dissertation, *Suppression of the African Slave Trade*, became the first volume in the Harvard Historical Studies.

In 1896, he became a sociology instructor at the University of Pennsylvania, and carried out a pioneering sociological investigation that became his second book, *The Philadelphia Negro* (1897). From 1897 to 1910, he taught at Atlanta University, supervising the publication of sixteen monographs, the Atlanta University studies of Afro-Americans in regard to such matters as education, business, crime, and health.

Du Bois challenged the accommodationist leadership of Booker T. Washington, seeking to revive the militancy of Douglass. In 1903, he published *Souls of Black Folk* which criticized Washington's tactics. Two years later, Du Bois founded the Niagara Movement and in 1910 became a founder of the NAACP. He left Atlanta University to serve as NAACP Director of Research and Publicity as its only black officer. In 1910 he became founder and editor of the NAACP's monthly magazine, *The Crisis*; he built its circulation from 1,000 then to 104,000 in 1919. He used its pages to attack Marcus Garvey and to foster Pan-Africanism, labor solidarity, racial chauvinism, and a separate black economic-cultural order, ignoring the NAACP's integrationist platform.

At odds with fellow directors, he resigned from the NAACP in 1934, returning to Atlanta University for a decade. There, he founded *Phylon Magazine* and wrote such books as *Black Reconstruction* (1935) and *Dusk of Dawn* (1940). His criticism of the school and his use of *Phylon* for propaganda contributed to his being dropped in 1944. He returned to the NAACP in a minor post for four years. He sponsored a great Pan-

African Conference in London in 1945. His leadership in this field since his first Pan-African Conference in 1919 makes him revered as the "Godfather of African Independence." The NAACP dismissed him in 1948 after his activity in Henry Wallace's Progressive Party and his attacks on NAACP Executive Secretary Walter White (*q.v.*).

More and more, Du Bois became a fellow traveler of the Communist Party line in the early 1950s, despairing of America ever ending racism and exploitation under the capitalist system. Settling in Ghana, he became a Ghanaian citizen, joined the Communist Party at the age of 93, and was compiling an *Encyclopedia Africana* when he passed away. He had also written such novels as *Dark Princess* (1928) and many stories and poems, some collected in *Darkwater* (1921). He passed away the day of Martin Luther King's March on Washington (August 28, 1963), eighteen months before Malcolm X was assassinated.

Dunbar, Paul Laurence (1872–1906), Poet

Paul Laurence Dunbar towers above all black writers prior to the flowering of black talent in the 1920s. Although best known for his poems in dialect, he also wrote beautiful poems in standard English, as well as novels and stories.

Son of former slaves, he was born in Dayton, Ohio. His father, a plasterer, escaped to Canada from Kentucky, served in the 55th Massachusetts, and settled in Dayton after the War. His mother, a laundress, had also been a slave in Kentucky, moving to Dayton after emancipation. Self-taught, she loved books and started Paul early on reading and writing. He was writing poems when six and gave a public recital of his verse at thirteen. Upon his father's death, twelve-year-old Paul and his mother struggled to maintain themselves, with Paul delivering her laundry bundles and working part-time in hotels, even though small and sickly.

Dunbar attended Dayton's sole high school, the only black in his graduating class. A good student and well-liked, he was elected president of the school literary society and editor of the school newspaper. He wrote the class song for the graduating exercises in 1891. Recognizing his talent, his teachers encouraged him. As he lacked money for college, he sought employment in journalism or clerical work, hoping to devote his spare time to a literary career. But newspapers and offices had nothing to offer a black boy. Whether subtle or brusque, the inevitable rejection let him know that such positions were reserved for whites. Eventually, he got a job as an elevator operator at four dollars a week, far less than what white classmates of much less ability could earn. He continued his writing, however, gave dramatic readings, and sent poems to newspapers. James Whitcomb Riley saw one of his poems in a newspaper and wrote him an encouraging letter.

Late in 1892, he asked a local publisher to print a volume of his verse on a regular royalty basis. Told to put up $125 to cover the cost of printing, he turned away discouraged, but an executive advanced the funds out of his own pocket. *Oak and Ivy,* though out before Christmas in 1892, was dated 1893. Several of the poems, like "The Ol' Tunes," were in dialect. Dunbar sold enough copies to people riding his elevator and to friends to repay the $125 guarantee in a few weeks.

More years of poverty and struggle followed. With the aid of patrons, a second privately printed volume of verse, *Majors and Minors,* appeared early in 1896. It contained many of his most famous poems, such as "Ships That Pass in the Night" and "When Malindy Sings." William Dean Howells reviewed it in *Harper's Weekly* that summer, bringing Dunbar overnight fame. Later in 1896, his best known work, *Lyrics of Lowly Life,* reprinting the best works from the two earlier collections along with an introduction by Howells, was published by Dodd, Mead. An instant success, it sold 3,500 copies a year for many years, remarkable for a collection of verse.

Dunbar toured England reading his verse in 1897, returning that fall to a job in the reading room of the Library of Congress. Next year, he married Alice Ruth Moore, a promising black writer from New Orleans who was teaching in Brooklyn. By 1899, his health was failing increasingly, and he nearly died of pneumonia. He continued writing but gave fewer and fewer readings. Dodd, Mead published his other volumes of verse, including *Lyrics of the Hearthside* (1899) and *Lyrics of Love and Laughter* (1903), his four novels, including *The Sport of the Gods* (1902), and his four collections of stories, including *The Heart of Happy Hollow* (1904).

Despite his hardships and tragic illness, his poems expressed a joy in life. But they fail to confront sufficiently the cruel mistreatment of his people.

Duncan, Todd (1903–   ), Concert Baritone and Actor

Robert Todd Duncan was the original Porgy in George Gershwin's *Porgy and Bess.* His warm baritone voice made him a concert favorite as well.

Duncan was born in Danville, Ky., son of a prosperous garage owner and a music teacher. The family soon moved to Indianapolis where young Robert picked out pieces on the piano and began taking lessons from his mother at age 5. He was only an average student in high school, but his great talents began to emerge at Butler University in Indianapolis. While still an undergraduate, he trained choirs, gave piano lessons, and studied voice and theory at an Indianapolis conservatory, the College of Music and Fine Arts. On graduating from Butler in 1925, he taught at a local junior high school for one year and then became instructor in English and music at Louisville Municipal College for Negroes. He directed operettas at this Kentucky college. In 1929, he began taking voice lessons in New York and enrolled at Columbia University, receiving his Master's degree in 1930. He became professor of voice and head of the department of public school music at Howard University in Washington, D. C., a position he held until 1945, with numerous interruptions for theater and concert work.

In 1934, he appeared as Alfio in an all-black production of *Cavalleria Rusticana*. The single performance of this opera at Mecca Temple soon paid off. When Gershwin was interviewing scores of black singers in 1935 without finding one just right for the lead in his opera, someone recalled Todd Duncan's memorable performances as Alfio. Gershwin sent for him, and Duncan won the part. He was magnificent, appearing then and in revivals in 1938 and 1942. In between he taught at Howard and also made concert tours.

Before retiring from stage and concert tours to give private voice lessons in Washington, D.C., Duncan appeared in White House concerts for the Roosevelts in 1935, in the Broadway musicals *Cabin in the Sky* (1940) and *Lost in the Stars* (1950), in the movie *Syncopation* (1940), and as frequent soloist with major symphonies throughout the world. He appeared in New York City Center operas in 1945 as Tonio in *Pagliacci* and Escamillo in *Carmen*, but came along too early to benefit from the subsequent lowering of the color bar at the Metropolitan. In 1950, he won the Critics Award for the best male performance in a Broadway musical.

Duncanson, Robert (1817–1872), Artist

Robert Duncanson was a Midwestern representative of the Hudson River School of painting. Contemporary boosters hailed him as the best American landscape painter west of the Appalachians.

He was born in New York in 1817 of a black mother and a white Canadian father of Scotch descent. They sent him to a school in Canada. The Anti-Slavery League sent him to Edinburgh, Scotland, where he apparently studied such subjects as English literature and classical history. About 1840, Duncanson settled in Cincinnati where he owned a

Daguerreotypy (silver-plate process photography) studio by 1842, and was also a painter.

He joined the flourishing group of Hudson River School artists in Cincinnati, becoming an active member of the Cincinnati Art Union and possibly the Academy of Art. Although some of his early paintings— such as "The Trial of Shakespeare" (1843)—reflected his European training, he was mainly influenced by fellow artists in Cincinnati.

Increasingly, Duncanson received commissions to do portraits for prominent families in Cincinnati and Detroit, opening up a studio in the latter in 1849 while retaining his studio in Cincinnati. In 1848, a wealthy Ohio grapegrower and landowner, Nicholas Longworth, I, whose descendant married Theodore Roosevelt's daughter, selected Duncanson to paint eight landscape murals in his palatial home, Belmont, in Cincinnati. It is now the Taft Museum. Duncanson painted many portraits, including members of the Berthelet family of Detroit and Longworth of Cincinnati.

About 1862 Duncanson toured Europe, exhibiting his highly lauded, but now lost, painting, "The Lotus Eaters" (1861), based on Lord Tennyson's poem. He evidently visited the poet laureate Tennyson. Duncanson's masterpiece was a landscape, "Blue Hole, Flood Waters, Little Miami River" (1851), now in the Cincinnati Art Museum, which also has his "Seascape" (1871). He passed away in Detroit. A number of his paintings, such as "The Drunkard's Plight" (1845) and "Fruit Piece" (c. 1860) are in the Detroit Institute of Arts.

Dunham, Katherine (1910–   ), Dancer, Choreographer

Well trained in anthropology, Katherine Dunham pioneered in studying and choreographing primitive Afro-American dances for the concert stage. One of America's most honored choreographer-dancers, she formed an outstanding modern dance troupe.

Although sources conflict on whether she was born in Chicago or Joliet, Ill., her beautifully written, romanticized autobiographical memoir of growing up, *A Touch of Innocence* (1959), perhaps resolves the matter. She claims she was born and spent her first few years in the Chicago suburb of Glen Ellyn, Ill., then lived with relatives in Chicago for several pre-school years after her mother's passing, and settled in Joliet when her father remarried. She, her older brother, and her stepmother lived behind and worked in her father's cleaning and dyeing establishment in Joliet.

As a youngster, she showed interest in the dance. At the age of 8, she caused a crisis in the Methodist church her family attended in Joliet when she staged a "cabaret party" that raised $32 for the church. While in high school, Miss Dunham taught dance to neighborhood youngsters. At the University of Chicago, she took anthropology, not teacher preparation as her family wanted. She supported herself by giving dancing lessons. With two friends, she founded a Negro school of the dance which gave concerts at the Chicago Civic Opera and other places. She also studied anthropology at Northwestern University and spent a year of field study in the West Indies on a Rosenwald Fellowship, 1936–1937. On returning, she received a Master's degree from Chicago University, writing her thesis on Afro-American dance rituals. She wrote magazine articles on these dances and also a book, *Journey to Accompong* (1946), about her anthropological trip.

Based on her studies of primitive rituals, she choreographed exciting dances for her troupe that brought rave notices in New York concerts in 1940. She acted and danced in the Broadway musical, *Cabin in the Sky* (1940), and in such movies as *Stormy Weather* (1943). She was the choreographer for the movie *Pardon My Sarong* (1942) and the Broadway musical *Windy City* (1946). Among shows she choreographed and produced for the Katherine Dunham Dance Troupe were *Tropical Revue* (1943), *Bal Nègre* (1946), and *Bamboche* (1962).

In 1963, she became the first Negro choreographer at the Metropolitan Opera, designing and directing dances for a new production of *Aida*. Among other great black dancers are opera company soloists Janet Collins (*q.v.*), Carmen de Lavallade, and Arthur Mitchell, choreographers Donald McKayle and Talley Beatty, and dance troupe leaders Pearl Primus and Alvin Ailey. Beatty, Collins, and actress Eartha Kitt were Dunham dancers.

Ellington, Duke (1899–   ), Composer, Orchestra Leader

Since the 1920s, Edward Kennedy Ellington has led the most outstanding and enduring of all jazz orchestras. Successful before the big band era of the 1930s and 1940s, he continues touring in the 1970s, long after the other big bands faded. As a jazz composer, Duke Ellington is beyond compare, pioneering with extended orchestral jazz compositions.

Ellington was born in Washington, D.C., son of a butler who later became a Navy Yard blueprint tracer, and who provided well for the family. The nickname "Duke," first applied by a playmate when Edward was only 8, stuck because of Duke's neat, confident, charming, and regal manner. He began piano lessons at the age of seven but had more interest in art and drawing by the time he was a student at Armstrong

High School. He was talented enough to win a scholarship to the Pratt Institute of Applied Arts in Brooklyn, but turned it down because he was now gravitating toward a musical career.

While still in high school, he became a popular ragtime pianist at local socials, rent parties, and night spots. Several young Washingtonians like saxophonist Otto Hardwick and cornetist Arthur Whetsol played regularly with him. Jerking sodas and playing the piano after school at the Poodle Dog Café, Ellington composed his first piece, "Soda Fountain Rag." After playing in various local bands, he advertised his own society band, securing many bookings.

In 1922, Duke went to New York with four of his boys, including Hardwick, Whetsol, and drummer Sonny Greer of New Jersey who joined Duke in 1919 after an engagement in Washington, remaining in the band until 1950. Running out of bookings and money, they returned to Washington. They tried the big city again in 1923, playing at the Kentucky Club in mid-Manhattan until 1927, with a few side excursions. By 1924, trombonist Charlie Irvis and growl trumpeter Bubber Miley, both New Yorkers, had joined the group, and gave a hotter sound to the sweet music of the Washingtonians, as Ellington's band was called. Harry Carney, who became the world's greatest baritone saxophonist, joined the orchestra in 1926 and was still playing in it in 1970. Growl trombonist Joe "Tricky Sam" Nanton also joined in 1926.

Impresario Irving Mills heard the band in 1926, became its promoter-manager, and arranged recordings for it in 1927 with big companies like Columbia and Victor. Duke had begun recording in 1926 for minor labels. Late in 1927, the band, enlarged from a seven-piece to a ten-piece group, became a fixture at the Cotton Club, also broadcasting on the CBS radio network.

Long before the Benny Goodman band of 1935 launched the big band swing era, Duke Ellington's band had international renown, making movies and playing in theaters, hotels, nightclubs, and concert halls, here and abroad. Many of the greatest jazz musicians became members, including trumpeter Cootie Williams, alto saxophonist Johnny Hodges, trombonist Lawrence Brown, clarinetist Barney Bigard, and bass player Jimmy Blanton.

Duke composed and arranged pieces that best displayed his aggregation of all-stars, brilliantly combining the orchestra's ensemble playing with the mini-concerto improvisations of their prescribed solos. After he joined the band as an arranger in 1939, Billy Strayhorn also composed such pieces as "Take the A Train." Ellington has written at least a thousand compositions including such short pieces as "Mood Indigo,"

"Sophisticated Lady," "Solitude," "I Let a Song Go Out of My Heart," "Don't Get Around Much Any More," and "Black and Tan Fantasy," and such long pieces as *Black, Brown and Beige* (1943), *Liberian Suite* (1948), and *A Concert of Sacred Music* (1965). He has also written the scores for such movies as *Anatomy of a Murder* and *Paris Blues* and such musicals as *Jump for Joy.*

He has won many polls and awards. President Richard Nixon gave him a 70th birthday party at the White House. His only son, Mercer, led his own band as early as 1941, but now plays in and manages for his father's orchestra. Mercer's daughter is one of the June Taylor Dancers on Jackie Gleason's television show.

Ellison, Ralph W. (1914–   ), Writer

Ralph Waldo Ellison's novel, *Invisible Man* (1952), is the finest literary effort by any American black. Already on its way to becoming an American classic, it was voted "the most distinguished single work" published in America during the twenty-year span, 1945–1965, in a poll of two hundred of the nation's leading critics, editors, and writers, taken by the New York *Herald Tribune's Book Week* Magazine in 1965.

Ellison was born in Oklahoma City. His father, who was a construction worker and tradesman, passed away when Ellison was 3. His mother supported herself and her son by domestic work. She encouraged his interest in literature and music by bringing home old records and magazines from the households in which she worked. A jazz fan, Ellison played trumpet in his high school band. Hoping to be a symphonic composer, he majored in music at Tuskegee Institute, 1933 to 1936. He came to New York in 1936 to study sculpture and music. There he worked on the WPA Federal Writers Project and met two great black writers, Langston Hughes and Richard Wright (*qq.v.*). An avid reader, Ellison had long been absorbing Hemingway and Eliot. Wright encouraged him to be a writer and stimulated his interest in Conrad, James, and Dostoevski.

In 1939, Ellison launched his writing career, publishing short stories, essays, and reviews in *New Masses, Antioch Review, New Challenge, The Negro Quarterly,* and other publications. He dabbled briefly in left-wing causes, but was too individualistic to be a joiner. After 1943, he concentrated on his art and ceased activism. During World War II, he served in the merchant marine. Afterwards, he received a Rosenwald Fellowship that enabled him to concentrate on writing his novel, *Invisible Man.* This work received the National Book Award for fiction in 1953—in competition with a Hemingway novel—the first such award for a black writer. Partly autobiographical, this great novel tells of the frustrating and humiliating experiences of a young black idealist at the hands of racists, South and North.

Ellison has been a guest lecturer and visiting professor at many institutions, particularly Bard, Rutgers, and Yale. Although his short stories and essays have been published in many magazines and anthologies, his only book besides his novel is the collection of essays, *Shadow and Act*, published in 1964. Despite his limited output, he is acclaimed one of America's greatest writers.

Estevanico (c. 1500–1539), Explorer

Estevanico (Little Stephen), also called Estevan or Esteban (Stephen), helped inspire the expeditions of De Soto and Coronado. Eighty years before the Pilgrims arrived on the *Mayflower,* Estevanico crossed the continent from Florida to the Gulf of California and became the first non-Indian to enter Arizona and New Mexico.

A black African from Azamor in western Morocco, Estevanico was on the Narvaez expedition that set out from Spain in 1527 to explore the western shores of the Gulf of Mexico. When it was blown off course, the expedition landed at Tampa Bay on Florida's west coast. Narvaez foolishly sent the ships westward while he and several hundred men walked overland to the region of Tallahassee. Here they built makeshift boats, drifted westward in the Gulf sighting the mouth of the Mississippi, and shipwrecked in 1528 on Galveston Island off the coast of Texas. Eventually, only one black (Estevanico) and three whites (Cabeza de Vaca, Castillo, and Dorantes) survived. Estevanico was the slave of Dorantes.

Enslaved by hostile Indians for several years, the four men finally escaped to friendlier tribes that accepted them as healers. Aided by friendly Indians, they gradually made their way westward through Texas and southwestward through Mexico, finally reaching Spanish settlements along the Gulf of California in 1536. The three Spaniards soon left Mexico, but the Viceroy purchased Estevanico to serve as a guide in seeking the seven golden cities of Cibola. The four survivors had learned of Cibola from Indians who talked mainly with Estevanico because the Spaniards held themselves aloof. When Cabeza de Vaca returned to Spain and told of Cibola, De Soto set out on an expedition, 1539–1543, through the southeastern United States searching for Cibola but only finding the Mississippi River.

Meanwhile the Viceroy in Mexico assigned Coronado to search for Cibola. In 1539, Coronado sent out an advance party led by Friar

Marcos but guided by Estevanico. Since Estevanico got along well with Indians, he was sent far ahead and thus was first to enter Arizona and New Mexico. The Indians at Cibola, now Zuni, N.M., imprisoned and killed him. Learning of his death from friendly Indians, Friar Marcos only viewed Cibola from a safe distance, reporting back to Coronado that it gleamed like gold. Coronado's gold-hunting expedition of 1540–1542 through the southwestern United States learned that Cibola was not golden, but only pueblo dwellings that glistened in sunlight.

Evers, Charles (1923–   ), NAACP Official and Southern Mayor

Charles Evers succeeded his slain brother, Medgar Evers (1925–1963), as Mississippi's NAACP director. Subsequently, he organized black voters and became mayor of Fayette.

He was born in Decatur, Miss. His energetic parents and uncle owned several businesses, including a lumber contracting firm. Charles and Medgar trudged two miles down muddy roads to the "separate-but-equal" one-room (for all eight grades), deskless Decatur Consolidated School while whites rode past in shiny yellow buses to their well-equipped school. The brothers went to high school in Newton, Miss., rooming with a kindly white woman in whose restaurant Charles worked after school. Charles dropped out to serve in the Army during World War II, returned to finish high school, and received a B.A. in social science at Mississippi's Alcorn A. & M. College in 1950.

After a year in Korea with Army reserves, Charles settled in Philadelphia, Miss., where he managed a funeral parlor owned by his parents and also opened a restaurant, hotel, gas station, and taxi service. Medgar also moved there, working in insurance. They secretly recruited local blacks into the NAACP, a "dangerously radical" organization to white Mississippians. Medgar moved to Jackson in 1954 as the state's first NAACP field director. Charles became the first black disc jockey in Mississippi on station WHOC in Philadelphia. He daringly launched voter-registration campaigns. Segregationist whites harassed and economically pressured his businesses, employees, and broadcasting job. Consequently, he fled to Chicago in 1957 where he worked three jobs (meat handler, hotel porter, and bartender) simultaneously for two years, saving enough money to open several cocktail lounges. After Medgar was cowardly assassinated from ambush while returning home on June 12, 1963, Charles asked the national NAACP for his brother's post. They agreed at once and he moved to Jackson immediately to continue the work.

He organized effective economic boycotts in such places as Natchez and Port Gibson, securing jobs and desegregating facilities. After the Voting Rights Act of 1965, he moved his office to Fayette in Jefferson County, tirelessly persuading blacks there and in adjacent Claiborne County to join NAACP chapters and register to vote. Soon black voters there outnumbered whites two to one. Splendidly mobilized, 95 percent of the registered blacks voted in 1966 and one was elected to Jefferson County's School Board, the first black elected to any office in Mississippi in this century. With 29 of the state's 82 counties having more blacks than whites, Evers pushed his organizing drive getting enough blacks registered to control the election outcome in nine southwestern counties by 1967. Astutely persuading the black majorities to elect both whites and blacks to office, he kept the white businessmen from fleeing these economically depressed counties.

In a special congressional election in 1968, Evers led six segregationists, but lost the runoff to the runner up, 87,000 to 43,000. In 1969, he was elected mayor of Fayette, a town of 1,626 in which he owns the Medgar Evers Shopping Center that contains grocery and liquor stores, radio repair shop, cocktail lounge, and ballroom.

Farmer, James L. (1920–   ), Civil Rights Leader
James Leonard Farmer helped found the Congress of Racial Equality (CORE). Under his leadership, CORE pioneered in using such nonviolent techniques as sit-ins and Freedom Rides.

Farmer was born in Marshall, Tex., and grew up on the campus of Wiley College there. His father, who had a Ph.D. degree from Boston University, was a member of the faculty. The campus sheltered Farmer from much of the cruelty of Southern segregation, and he first learned of racial discrimination as a youngster when his mother told him that only whites could get a drink of water in a nearby drugstore. Earning a B.S. degree in chemistry at Wiley when he was only 18, Farmer started to study medicine, but switched to religion. Training for the Methodist ministry at the School of Religion of Howard University, he received the Bachelor of Divinity degree in 1941, but refused to be ordained because the Methodist Church was segregated.

While attending Howard, he had been active in religious organizations, serving as vice chairman of the National Council of Methodist Youth. He now turned full time to social action work. From 1941 to 1945, he was race relations secretary of the pacifist group, the Fellowship of Reconciliation. He was an organizer for the Upholsterer's Union for several years and later an international representative for the State, County, and Municipal Employees Union.

In 1942, in Chicago, he helped found CORE, along with a group of students at the University of Chicago. The next year, CORE staged a sit-in that forced a restaurant in Chicago's Loop to serve blacks. CORE also effectively used standing-line protests, whereby its disciplined white and black members stood peacefully but firmly in line before ticket windows to force these facilities to admit blacks. In 1947, CORE led a Journey of Reconciliation through the upper South in which sixteen white and black riders challenged bus segregation.

From 1942 to 1956, CORE worked primarily through autonomous local chapters with its national office manned only by volunteers. Unpaid as national chairman, Farmer earned his living otherwise. From 1959 to 1961, he worked for the national NAACP, serving as its program director under Executive Secretary Roy Wilkins (q.v.). Late in 1960, the NAACP won a Supreme Court suit barring segregation in bus terminals. Unable to get the NAACP to test implementation by sponsoring a Freedom Ride similar to CORE's 1947 ride, Farmer quit the NAACP in February, 1961, to become CORE's first full-time, paid national director. The violence met in the Deep South in May, 1961, by the six white and seven black Freedom Riders, including Farmer, dramatically revealed that segregation persisted despite court orders. The direct mass action work of CORE for the next five years under Farmer's leadership made it a leading civil rights group and put Farmer in the front rank of civil rights leaders.

In 1966, he left CORE (which became increasingly militant under his successors, Floyd McKissick and Roy Innis) to head a national literacy and job training program, but lack of funding crippled the project. Farmer became a professor of social work at Lincoln University in Pennsylvania. In 1968, he ran unsuccessfully against Shirley Chisholm (q.v.) for a seat in Congress. In 1969, President Richard Nixon appointed him assistant secretary of the Department of Health, Education, and Welfare. He resigned from his post in the Nixon administration in December, 1970.

Fitzgerald, Ella (1918–   ), Singer

Widely acclaimed as "The First Lady of Song," Ella Fitzgerald ranks with the all-time favorites among popular singers. Whether doing blues, Dixieland tunes, ballads, swing numbers, calypso, pop songs, or her unique scat singing, she is an incomparable vocalist.

Born in Newport News, Va., she was orphaned early in life. She came to New York as a child, where she received her schooling at an orphanage in Yonkers. At the age of 15, she entered the regular amateur contest at the Apollo Theater in Harlem, listing herself as a singer and dancer. Too nervous to dance that night, she stuck to the singing. Drummer-band leader Chick Webb, who heard her then, hired her as a vocalist for his band. Tutored by him, she developed rapidly.

She became nationally known in 1938 through her singing and recording of a song she wrote in collaboration with Webb, "A-Tisket A-Tasket," based on a nursery rhyme she remembered from childhood. Webb passed away the next year, but turned his band over to Ella when he knew the end was near. She led it for three years before venturing out as a solo singer. She was booked into the leading theaters, clubs, and hotels, becoming one of the biggest drawing cards in America. She began touring in America and abroad with the Norman Granz "Jazz at the Philharmonic" in the late 1940s. She has appeared in many movies, such as *Pete Kelly's Blues*.

Among the many songs that she has recorded (largely for Decca) are "Stone Cold Dead in the Market," "That's My Desire," "Into Each Life Some Rain Must Fall," and "How High the Moon." Her album of Broadway show tunes, *Cole Porter Song Book* (Verve Records, 1956), was an inspired mating of Ella's styling with Porter's compositions. Other songs she has composed include "You Showed Me the Way," and "Oh! But I Do."

Perenially, she has led the *Down Beat* and *Metronome* polls as top female vocalist in America. Other great black vocalists included Billie Holiday and Sarah Vaughan in Ella's earlier days and Nancy Wilson and Dionne Warwick more recently.

Forten, James (1766–1842), Businessman, Abolitionist

Sail manufacturer James Forten was one of the earliest black businessmen. He was also an influential abolitionist, persuading William Lloyd Garrison to advocate racial equality.

Forten was born in Philadelphia. His great-grandfather came from Africa in chains, his grandfather was born a slave but became free, and his father was born free. He attended the school of the famous Quaker abolitionist, Anthony Benezet, but quit to take a job in 1775 when his father passed away. He worked in a grocery store to support his mother, but eventually convinced her to let him enlist.

Thus, at the age of 15, he became powder boy aboard a privateer, *Royal Louis*, commanded by Stephen Decatur, Sr. (whose son proclaimed "our country, right or wrong" in the War of 1812). When the privateer was captured by the British frigate *Amphyon*, the blacks, who formed a tenth of the crew of two hundred, faced enslavement in the

West Indies. Forten was spared because the captain's son had taken a liking to him when they played marbles together and persuaded his father, Sir John Beasly, to keep him aboard. Growing increasingly fond of Forten, the wealthy Captain Beasly offered to educate and rear him in England with his son, but Forten refused to desert his own country. Beasly then sent him to the prison ship *Jersey*, anchored in a bay of Long Island. Thousands died on the disease-swept hulk, but Forten passed up a chance to escape in the chest of an officer who was being exchanged. Instead, he persuaded another young prisoner who was sicker to escape in his place. Released from his seven-month imprisonment, Forten returned home near the Revolution's end. He then spent a year in England where British abolitionists impressed him.

Returning home, he apprenticed himself to a white Philadelphia sailmaker, Robert Bridges. Forten was so able that several years later, in 1786, Bridges made this 20-year-old black youth the foreman of the sail loft. When Bridges retired in 1798, Forten took control of the business. He prospered, employing as many as forty men, white and black, and amassing a fortune of $100,000 by 1832. A major role in Forten's success was his invention of a device to handle sails. He lived elegantly in a spacious house at 92 Lombard Street, supporting his family and assorted relatives. The Humane Society cited him in 1821 for rescuing drowning persons. He recruited 2,500 blacks to work on defensive fortifications in 1814 when Philadelphia feared British invasion.

Despite his prominence, taxpaying, and philanthropy, Forten, like other blacks in Philadelphia, was frequently insulted and humiliated. He became a leading fighter for his people's rights. In 1800 he circulated petitions protesting fugitive slave legislation and published a pamphlet in 1813 denouncing bills to bar free blacks from Pennsylvania. Standing firmly in favor of racial equality, he rejected American Colonization Society arguments that blacks were inferior and should return to Africa. Seeking his support, the Society offered him high posts in their prospective colony, Liberia, but he spurned the offers. With Bishop Richard Allen (*q.v.*), he called and chaired a series of protest meetings in 1817 and thereafter against colonization. Forten was a leader in the Negro Convention movement of 1830 onward. He supported Garrison, enlisted black subscribers for his *Liberator*, served on the Board of Managers of Garrison's American Anti-Slavery Society, and contributed more money to the abolitionist cause than anyone other than the wealthy white merchant brothers, Arthur and Lewis Tappan. Garrison and other prominent abolitionists stayed at Forten's home often. More than any other, he influenced Garrison to believe in racial equality and to favor educational and employment opportunities that would let blacks prove they were not inferior in ability.

Abolitionist poet John Greenleaf Whittier wrote a poem, "To the Daughters of James Forten." Forten's son-in-law, Robert Purvis, was a leading black abolitionist. *The Journal of Charlotte L. Forten* (1953), kept by Forten's granddaughter, Charlotte (1837–1914), gives revealing insights into the life of nineteenth-century blacks.

Franklin, John Hope (1915–   ), Historian

John Hope Franklin is an eminent historian who became chairman of the department of history at the University of Chicago in 1967. He has written many books, including the standard history of black Americans, *From Slavery to Freedom* (third edition, 1967).

He was born in Rentiesville, Okla. The Tulsa office of his father, one of the first black lawyers in Oklahoma and an uncompromising foe of segregation, was burned by rioting whites. Franklin graduated from Booker T. Washington High School in Tulsa, where he was active in debating and singing. At Fisk University in Nashville, Tenn., he was a history major. He was elected to Phi Beta Kappa and graduated *magna cum laude* in 1935. He received his M.A. in history from Harvard University in 1936. After teaching a year at Fisk, 1936–1937, he returned to Harvard, supported by Austin and Rosenwald fellowships, receiving the Ph.D. degree in history in 1941.

Although preeminent in his graduate work, he had to seek employment at small black colleges while white fellow students of lesser ability received appointments at major universities. Joining the faculty of St. Augustine's College in Raleigh, N.C., in 1939, he published his first book, *The Free Negro in North Carolina, 1790–1860* in 1943. Moving to North Carolina College in Durham that year, he published his authoritative work, *From Slavery to Freedom*, four years later. While on the faculty of Howard University in Washington, D.C., 1947–1956, he wrote *The Militant South, 1800–1860* (1956), only the second book by a black to be included in the Harvard Historical Studies in its first six decades; W. E. B. Du Bois (*q.v.*) was author of the first book in the series. From 1956 to 1964, Franklin was chairman of the department of history at Brooklyn College where he published *Reconstruction after the Civil War* (1961) and *The Emancipation Proclamation* (1963). In 1964, he became professor of history at the University of Chicago.

Noted for his balance and objectivity, Franklin is outspoken but courteous, charming, and popular. He serves in many high historical offices including the executive committee of the American Historical

Association and the presidency of the Southern Historical Association. He received Guggenheim and other research grants. He has been a visiting professor at such universities as Cambridge, Wisconsin, Harvard, Australia, and Cornell, and at the Salzburg Seminar. Despite spending considerable time lecturing to scholars and laymen, he has written many articles, contributed chapters to several books, edited several books on the Civil War era, and co-authored a junior high school textbook, *Land of the Free* (1966). He is co-editor of the Crowell American History Series. The leading black historians contemporaneous with Franklin are Benjamin Quarles, Rayford Logan, Charles Wesley, and Merze Tate.

Frazier, E. Franklin (1894–1962), Sociologist

The distinguished sociologist, Edward Franklin Frazier, was the most renowned black in the field. His book, *The Negro Family in the United States*, is a major contribution to the literature of sociology and has become a classic.

Frazier was born in Baltimore, Md. His father was a bank messenger who had never been to school, his mother a former slave. They urged him to get an education. After graduating from Baltimore High School, he attended Howard University in Washington, D.C., graduating *cum laude* in 1916. He spent the next three years teaching mathematics at three schools: Tuskegee Institute in Alabama, St. Paul's Normal School in Virginia, and Baltimore High School.

Entering Clark University in Worcester, Mass., he received an M.A. in sociology in 1920. On research fellowships, he spent one year at the New York School of Social Work and another year at the University of Copenhagen. He taught sociology at Morehouse College in Atlanta, 1922–1924, and was director of the Atlanta School of Social Work the next three years. A white mob forced him out of Atlanta after publication in *Forum* (June, 1927) of his essay, "The Pathology of Race Prejudice," drawing an analogy between the thought processes of prejudiced Southerners and insane persons.

He attended the University of Chicago as a research assistant in the department of sociology from 1927 to 1929, receiving the Ph.D. degree in 1931. Meanwhile, he joined the faculty of Fisk University in Nashville, teaching there five years. In 1934, he became professor and head of the department of sociology at Howard University, continuing to teach there after retiring from the chair in 1960.

His first books, *The Negro Family in Chicago* and *The Free Negro Family*, were both published in 1932. His epochal study, *The Negro*

Family in the United States (1939), altered sociological thinking by presenting an objective analysis of racial problems in terms of historical socio-economic forces. His other books included *Negro Youth at the Crossroads* (1940), *The Negro in the United States* (1949), *Race and Culture Contacts in the Modern World* (1957), the controversial *Black Bourgeoisie* (1957) with its sharp attack on the shortcomings of the black middle class, and *The Negro Church in America*, published posthumously in 1964.

Unlike many black scholars who get pulled from their research into active roles in crusades and causes, Frazier, as Du Bois observed, stuck to his academic knitting. He rarely accepted non-academic assignments, but he did direct for Mayor Fiorello La Guardia a study of the causes of the Harlem riot of 1935 and served as Chief of the Division of Applied Social Sciences of UNESCO from 1951 to 1953. He has written many articles and received many honors, including a Guggenheim research grant. He was visiting professor at Sarah Lawrence College, the University of Southern California, and New York University, among others. In 1948 he was president of the American Sociological Association, making him the first black to head the main scholarly organization in any field. Other outstanding black sociologists of his day include Ira de A. Reid, Hylan Lewis, Mozelle Hill, C. Eric Lincoln, and Daniel Thompson.

Garner, Erroll (1921–   ), Jazz Pianist

The world's greatest jazz pianist, Erroll Louis Garner, does not read music. But he has sold far more records than any other jazz instrumentalist and is the first one to tour under management of concert impresario Sol Hurok.

Born in Pittsburgh, Pa., he was the youngest of six children in a musical family. His father worked in the Westinghouse plant but was an amateur player of guitar and mandolin. Four of Erroll's older brothers and sisters were musicians and the oldest, Linton, became a professional pianist and arranger. Before he was 3 years old, the precocious Erroll began picking out on the piano tunes he heard on the phonograph. At 6 he took lessons, but the teacher soon dropped him because he memorized her examples instead of learning to read music. That brief instruction was his only formal training.

He learned to play so well on his own that he made his professional debut the next year. He became a regular radio performer on KDKA in Pittsburgh with a group called the Candy Kids. As an elementary school pupil, he sometimes played piano on Allegheny River boats. At Pittsburgh's Westinghouse High School, he played tuba in the marching band, having been barred from the piano because he could not read sheet music. After school, he was a pianist in local clubs, restaurants, and taverns. When playing with bands, he memorized the score or simply improvised.

Garner quit high school to play in a local dance orchestra. In 1939, he became accompanist for singer Ann Lewis, going to New York and touring a year with her. For a while he played organ in a theater in upstate New York. Inducted in the Army in 1942, he was discharged within a year because of asthma. He began playing in New York nightclubs, rapidly gaining popularity. He then formed a trio with bass player "Slam" Stewart and guitarist "Tiny" Grimes, touring the East. While the trio played the Strand Theater in New York City in 1946, Garner was asked to make some recordings for Savoy Records. After walking up fifteen floors to their studio because of an elevator strike, he was too tired to play his familiar bouncy numbers. Instead, he recorded ballads, especially "Laura," which became a best seller with sales of half a million, bringing him national recognition.

His reputation grew steadily. In 1950 at Music Hall in Cleveland, he became the first modern jazz instrumentalist to give a solo recital in America. Later that year he gave a Town Hall concert in New York and signed with Columbia Records. To preserve his brilliant improvisations, too often lost, he began composing at the keyboard with an assistant writing down the music in a special notation system devised by Garner. In 1957, he gave a recital of his compositions with the Cleveland Symphony Orchestra. The next year he signed with Sol Hurok.

Garner composes scores for ballet, movies, and Broadway musicals. His most popular tune is "Misty" and his most notable album, *Concert by the Sea. Down Beat*'s poll of international jazz critics judged him the world's best pianist. Other great jazz pianists of his day include the late "Fats" Waller who composed "Ain't Misbehavin" and "Honeysuckle Rose," Oscar Peterson, and Thelonious Monk.

Garvey, Marcus (1887–1940), Black Nationalist

In the 1920s, Marcus Moziah Garvey was preaching black pride, racial separation, and the resurrection of a great black empire in Africa. His doctrines attracted at least a million followers, mainly Northern ghetto blacks, making him the first black leader in America with a mass following.

Garvey was born in the town of St. Ann's Bay in Jamaica, British West Indies, a descendant of Maroons who escaped from slavery and resisted reenslavement. His parents had little formal schooling, but his father was a skilled mason and avid reader. Garvey attended local schools, but had to stop at the age of 14 because of the family's financial setbacks. Apprenticed to a printer who was his godfather, he read extensively in his library.

Though very well read, Garvey was ever sensitive about his lack of extensive higher education and antagonistic toward intellectuals of his race. He also disliked and distrusted light-skinned Negroes because they joined the whites in oppressing and holding down the black masses in Jamaica's rigid color-caste system.

At the age of 17, he moved to the capital city, Kingston, working as a printer. Fascinated by street debates, he tried to join in but was told "Country boy, shut your mouth!" Determined to participate, he zealously worked at the art of public speaking, becoming a magnetic platform orator. He progressed rapidly at work, becoming a master printer and foreman for one of the island's largest printers when only 20 years old. Blacklisted by employers after becoming leader of a strike in 1907, he took a job in the government printing office. In 1910, he founded a periodical, *Garvey's Watchman*, which failed, and then formed a political club.

Moving to a higher-paying job in Costa Rica as a United Fruit Company banana plantation timekeeper, he soon quit over the exploitations of the peasants, many of them black migrants from Jamaica. He found British officials unconcerned. Working and sometimes starting newspapers in Colombia, Venezuela, and various Central American republics, he found the black peasantry everywhere exploited and apathetic with whites and mulattoes unwilling to aid the downtrodden.

In 1912, he went to London to learn about the plight of blacks elsewhere in the British Empire. A black Egyptian editor and author, Duse Mohammed Ali, awakened his interest there in Africa and its exploitation by European colonialists. Garvey became a black nationalist. In London, he also met blacks from many places, learning about his people's problems worldwide. He eagerly read books on Africa and on his race. The autobiography of Booker T. Washington (*q.v.*), *Up from Slavery*, inspired him to become a leader of his race, to unite blacks everywhere to establish a nation and government of their own.

Returning to Jamaica in 1914, he founded the Universal Negro Improvement Association (U.N.I.A.), urging blacks everywhere to unite and advance under the motto, "One God! One Aim! One Destiny!" He planned to establish a Tuskegee Institute in Jamaica to uplift the black masses, but they were indifferent and the mulattoes actively opposed him. In 1915, he planned a trip to America to visit Tuskegee and meet Washington, but the latter's passing that November foiled his plans.

He came to America in March, 1916, anyway, setting up a branch of the U.N.I.A. in Harlem the next year. Harlemites generally ignored him at first. He toured thirty-eight states to learn the conditions of blacks. He became convinced that the race's leaders, mostly mulattoes, were opportunists who helped exploit the masses and relied too much on white philanthropy. In January, 1918, he founded a weekly newspaper the *Negro World*, that reached 50,000 circulation in 1920 and was said to have attained a peak of 200,000. An attempted assassination of Garvey in October, 1919, by an unbalanced former employee brought him sympathy and notoriety. The Harlem branch of U.N.I.A. became world headquarters and membership soared.

In 1919, Garvey began selling stock in his Black Star Line, which acquired ships for commerce with, and transportation to, Africa. The Negro Factories Corporation he founded in 1919 set up cooperative businesses. He called a mammoth international convention of blacks that met in New York in 1920. Under his leadership, it adopted a "Declaration of the Rights of the Negro Peoples of the World" and established an African Republic with Garvey chosen as Provisional President. He established Black Cross Nurses, an African Legion, and an African Orthodox Church, with a black God and Christ.

Although Garvey instilled needed race pride in the despairing black masses, the intellectuals of the race distrusted him as a demagogue and charlatan. They fumed over his opposition to integration, his call to separate and return to Africa, his acceptance of support from segregationists and the Ku Klux Klan, and his harsh denunciations of mulattoes and intellectuals.

In 1922, Garvey was indicted on mail fraud charges concerning sale of Black Star Line stock. Although convicted in 1923, it was evident that he was personally honest but naive in business and victimized by unscrupulous, flattering advisers. He went to jail in February, 1925, but was released and deported in December, 1927. His movement dwindled in America in his absence.

He was triumphantly hailed in Jamaica after being deported and revitalized the U.N.I.A. branch there and opened branches in London and Paris. Jailed by Jamaican judges for intemperate remarks in political campaigns, his prospects of leadership in his native island faded. In 1933, he closed his failing newspaper, *Negro World*, and began a magazine, *Black Man*, which limped along for five years. By 1935 he moved his headquarters to London where he passed away five years later.

Gibson, Althea (1927–   ), Tennis Champion

Althea Gibson broke the color bar in lawn tennis in 1950, and went on to become a star, winning the Wimbledon and Forest Hill championships seven years later. Many people contributed to her success.

Born of cotton sharecroppers in Silver, S.C., she grew up on 143rd Street in Harlem after her father became a handyman in New York. Whippings did not cure her of fighting, stealing, playing hooky, and running away. Tomboyish and athletic, she won the city paddle-tennis championship at the age of 12. Her teachers promoted her to get rid of her, and she finished junior high school in 1941. Disliking trade school, she soon dropped out, securing working papers despite being underage on her pledge (which she promptly ignored) to take night classes. She was often fired because of absenteeism and poor work.

Concerned people helped salvage a wasted life. Observing her playing paddle tennis, a black recreation worker purchased some second-hand rackets for her in 1941 and introduced her to regular tennis. She showed great promise. He and his wife befriended her, taking her to the Harlem River Tennis Courts. A black schoolteacher took her from there to Harlem's exclusive Cosmopolitan Tennis Club where wealthy blacks chipped in to provide her a junior membership and lessons by the club professional. A well-to-do black woman, who had lost her own daughter, outfitted and practically adopted Althea, struggling to impart the polish the ghetto roughneck needed in tennis. In 1942, Althea won the first tournament she ever entered, one sponsored by the predominantly black American Tennis Association (A.T.A.). She won the national A.T.A. girls singles in 1944 and 1945. She met boxer Sugar Ray Robinson through a roommate who knew his wife, Edna. Ray and Edna took her under wing, encouraged her, and bought a saxophone for the music-loving youngster.

Reaching the finals of the A.T.A. women's championship at Wilberforce, Ohio, in 1946, she was observed by two tennis-playing black surgeons who were leaders in the A.T.A., Dr. Hubert Eaton of Wilmington, N.C., and Dr. Robert "Whirlwind" Johnson of Lynchburg, Va. On recommending that she seek a tennis scholarship at a black college, they learned she had never been to high school. Seeing in her a top prospect to crack tennis's color bar, they proposed that she live with Dr. Eaton's family and attend high school, spending her summers with Dr. Johnson's family. Reluctant to leave New York, she assented only after Sugar Ray insisted education would help her in tennis or music.

Living in the luxurious Eaton household, she learned to stop brawling, cheating, lying, and stealing. Knuckling down to her studies and playing in the marching band, she graduated from Williston High School at the age of 21. She played tennis daily on the beautiful regulation court in Dr. Eaton's backyard, the only court for blacks in the city. Intensive summer instruction on a similar court behind the Lynchburg home of Dr. Johnson, who later tutored Arthur Ashe (*q.v.*), readied her for A.T.A. competition. She won the A.T.A. women's championship in 1947 and for the next nine years.

The two physicians worked to open other doors for her. Entering the Eastern and the National Indoor Championships in New York early in 1949, she reached the quarter finals in both. Another black had earlier played in the National Indoor meet, but grass courts still barred blacks. Entering Florida A. & M. College on a tennis scholarship in 1949, she graduated in 1953. Meanwhile, tennis barriers toppled. In her second National Indoor Tournament early in 1950, she reached the finals, but United States Lawn Tennis Association (U.S.L.T.A.) officials ignored her as the big summer grass-court tournaments approached. A great former champion, Alice Marble, wrote a sharp editorial in *American Lawn Tennis* (July, 1950) denouncing their inaction. Soon Althea was invited to the Eastern Grass Courts Championship, losing in the second round. She reached the quarter-finals of the national Clay Courts Championship and then was allowed to enter the national championships at Forest Hills, Long Island, in August, 1950. Although she lost in the second round there, she had become the first black in major lawn tennis competition.

The next six years were discouraging. Although blacks in Detroit, led by former heavyweight champion Joe Louis (*q.v.*), paid her way to become in June, 1951, the first American black to play in the English championship tournament at Wimbledon, she lost in the quarter-finals. Failing through the years to win the National Indoor, National Clay, Forest Hills, or Wimbledon championships, her ratings slipped. She had advanced from ninth ranked in 1952 to seventh in 1953, but fell to thirteenth in 1954.

Discouraged, she was on the verge of joining the Women's Army Corps in 1955 and giving up tennis and teaching—she taught physical education at Lincoln University in Missouri from 1953 to 1955. Fortunately, she was invited to go on a State Department good-will Asian tennis tour that fall with three white stars. Her interest revived. In 1956 she won fourteen consecutive tournaments and rose to second ranked, but lost in the finals at Wimbledon and Forest Hills.

Miss Gibson reached the pinnacle in 1957 and 1958. Both years she won the English and American championships at Wimbledon and Forest

Hills, and led American women to Wightman Cup team victories over the British women's team. She became America's top ranking player and the best in the world.

She retired in 1958 to become a professional golfer.

Gillespie, Dizzy (1917–   ), Modern Jazz Musician

Trumpeter Dizzy Gillespie helped develop bebop. This began modern jazz, pointing to progressive and cool jazz.

John Birks Gillespie was born in Cheraw, S.C., youngest of nine children of a bricklayer. Since his father also led a local band and kept instruments in the house, John experimented with drums, piano, trumpet, and trombone. Two years after his father passed away in 1929 he began music lessons, starting on trombone but switching to trumpet. He formed a band when he was 14, becoming sufficiently recognized to win a scholarship to Laurinburg Institute, an industrial high school in North Carolina. There he studied harmony and theory. Several months before graduation, he withdrew to move to Philadelphia with his family in 1935.

There he began playing in a local band, imitating trumpeter Roy Eldridge after hearing him on radio. Two years later he joined Teddy Hill's band in New York, making his first recorded solo, "King Porter Stomp." His eccentric and undisciplined behavior led to his nickname, "Dizzy." While playing with Cab Calloway's band from 1939 to 1941, he and other innovative jazzmen began working out the fast, intricate, less danceable bebop style in afterhours jam sessions at Minton's and other places. Then he played in various bands, including the Earl Hines orchestra when it included alto saxophonist Charlie "Yardbird" Parker, bass violist Oscar Pettiford, and vocalists Billy Eckstine and Sarah Vaughan. In 1943, Gillespie and Pettiford led a quintet, including drummer Max Roach, that introduced bebop to the public, in arrangements by Gillespie. Audiences disliked the dissonance of the controversial new sounds. Gillespie then joined Billy Eckstine's new band, becoming widely known as it toured nationally. Early in 1945, Gillespie formed a quintet, including "Yardbird" Parker. As played by Gillespie and Parker, and also by such others as pianist Thelonious Monk, bebop gained acceptance among knowledgeable New Yorkers.

Gillespie formed his own big band that summer, but it flopped on tour because people outside New York were unprepared for bebop. He tried again in 1946 and this time succeeded; the new jazz was catching on. From 1946 to 1950, bebop was the rage, with Gillespie's band recording such numbers as "Ool-Ya-Koo," "Cool Breeze," "Cubana Bop," and

"Oo-Pop-a-Da." His band played in Carnegie Hall and toured Europe, but the bebop fad soon faded.

He dissolved his band in 1950. Until 1956, he led smaller groups, usually quintets. Like other progressive jazz groups, his incorporated and went beyond bebop techniques. He also played solo with Norman Granz's Jazz at the Philharmonic. In 1956, Gillespie led a big band in a State-Department-sponsored tour of Europe and Asia, the first time the government sponsored a jazz band.

He has been chosen best trumpeter in *Down Beat* polls. Among his many compositions is "Night in Tunisia." Besides Gillespie, Monk, and Parker, other big names in modern jazz include trumpeter Miles Davis, saxophonists Coleman Hawkins, Lester Young, John Coltrane, and Cannonball Adderly, pianist Bud Powell, and trombonist J. J. Johnson.

Gilpin, Charles S. (1872–1930), Actor

Charles Sidney Gilpin was the first famed black dramatic actor in America. He created the role of Emperor Jones.

Gilpin was born in Richmond, Va., youngest child of a steel-mill laborer and a nurse. He attended St. Francis School for black Catholics until the age of 12 when he became a printer's devil on a black weekly, the *Richmond Planet*. Interested in acting, he became a variety performer, first appearing on stage in Richmond in 1890. Unable to make a living thereby, he supported himself between roles as a printer or job pressman for such concerns as the Philadelphia *Standard* (early 1890s). He performed in song and dance routines at fairs, restaurants, and variety theaters. In the mid 1890s, he toured with Purkis & Davis's Great Southern Minstrels. At the turn of the century he sandwiched acting in between jobs as an elevator operator, porter, printer, switchboard operator, and trainer of prize-fighters.

Joining the Canadian Jubilee Singers of Hamilton, Ontario, in 1903, Gilpin devoted himself to acting thereafter. In 1905, he appeared in the Bert Williams (*q.v.*) and George Walker show, *Abyssinia*, and toured with Gus Hill's Smart Set Company the next year. He was with the Pekin Stock Company in Chicago from 1907 to 1909, getting his first chance at straight dramatic roles. For the next six years Gilpin was on tour: in vaudeville a year; with the Pan-American Octette two years; with the Rogers & Creamers Old Man's Boy Company two years; and then another year in vaudeville.

Moving to New York, Gilpin joined the stock company started by actress Anita Bush at the Lincoln Theater in Harlem during the interlude (1910–1917) when the only black performing downtown was Bert Williams (*q.v.*) in Ziegfield's *Follies*. In 1916, Gilpin helped organize and also managed the Lafayette Players, a dramatic stock company at Harlem's Lafayette Theater.

He first appeared on Broadway in 1919 in the role of a black clergy-man in John Drinkwater's play *Abraham Lincoln*. Next year he was selected for the role of Brutus Jones, an ex-convict and Pullman porter who makes himself emperor of a West Indian island. In this demanding role in the Provinctown Players production of Eugene O'Neill's drama, Gilpin appeared alone in six of the eight scenes, fleeing the rebelling islanders in mounting terror as their tom-toms draw nearer. The play ran in New York from November, 1920, to 1924; it made theater history and established Gilpin, whose performance was a sensation, as one of the nation's great actors.

Earlier, an Afro-American, Ira Aldridge (*q.v.*) became a famed actor, but only in Europe. Gilpin's success paved the way for other blacks in straight dramatic roles, such as Frank Wilson and Rose Mc-Clendon in *In Abraham's Bosom*, Richard Harrison in *Green Pastures*, and Paul Robeson (*q.v.*). Gilpin lost his voice in 1926, retired, ran an elevator, and made a comeback in touring revivals of *Emperor Jones*. Failing health forced his retirement in 1929.

Hall, Prince (1748–1897), Fraternal Leader

Prince Hall, a Revolutionary Era leader, founded Masonry among Afro-Americans. Lodges of black Masons bear his name.

Hall was born at Bridgetown in the British West Indian island of Barbados, probably in 1748, according to muster rolls showing his Army enlistment in 1778 at age 30. The obituary listing his age as 72, making his birthyear 1735, probably erred. His father, an Englishman, was a leather worker, his mother was a free black of French extraction. He learned his father's trade but, seeking wider opportunity, left Barbados. He sailed to Boston in 1765, working for his passage.

In Boston, Hall worked at his trade, acquired real estate, and was voting by the age of 25. Census records list him as a soap manufacturer. He took lessons at night to overcome his lack of schooling. He studied the Bible zealously and became the minister of a Methodist church in Cambridge.

Hall became a leader among Boston blacks. In 1775, he urged the Committee of Safety to let slaves enlist. He sent petitions to the Massachusetts legislature in 1777 urging emancipation because slavery was incompatible with the patriot cause. Hall served in the Revolution himself, enlisting for a nine-month term in 1778 from Medford. He worked for the education of black children, petitioning the legislature in 1787 to open schools, urging his fellow blacks in 1792 to establish a school of their own, and requesting the Selectmen of Boston in 1796 to provide a schoolhouse.

A month before fighting broke out at Lexington, Hall and fourteen other free blacks were initiated into Masonry in Boston on March 6, 1775, by British Army Lodge No. 441 of the 38th Regiment of Irish infantry. Later, other blacks were inducted by this regimental lodge after Hall and his fourteen friends became the first Afro-American Masons. Before the British evacuated Boston in March, 1776, the Army lodge granted a license to permit Hall and his fellow black Masons to continue meeting and functioning, but not to confer degrees. Under this license, African Lodge No. 1, the first organized body of black Masons in America, was established on July 3, 1776.

Subsequently, Prince Hall applied for a charter from white Provincial Masonic authorities in America, without success. He then wrote to the British Grand Lodge in 1784 and a charter was granted on September 29, 1784. Because of a mixup, the charter was not delivered for three years. Under this charter, African Lodge No. 459 was formally organized on May 6, 1787, with Prince Hall as Master. Four years later, following accepted Masonic usage of that time, the African Grand Lodge was formed by an assembly of the craft in June, 1791, with Hall as Grand Master. In 1797, Hall granted warrants to establish a lodge in Philadelphia and another in Providence.

While on a charitable mission in November, 1807, Prince Hall caught a cold that developed into pneumonia, and passed away a month later. The next year, at a delegate convention of the three lodges of black Masons, the African Grand Lodge was renamed the Prince Hall Grand Lodge and Nero Prince was elected Grand Master in succession to Hall. Next to Prince Hall, the best known black fraternal leader was J. Finley Wilson, the Grand Exalted Ruler of the black Elks from 1921 to 1952.

Handy, W. C. (1873–1958), Blues Composer

William Christopher Handy is rightfully called "Father of the Blues." His "St. Louis Blues" is one of the world's most popular songs and has sold more copies than any song ever written.

Born in Florence, Ala., son and grandson of former slaves and A.M.E. ministers, he received no encouragement. His parents considered popular music sinful, but Handy loved it, inspired by a country fiddler and a church cornetist. He painstakingly saved to buy a guitar, which his outraged parents termed "a devil's plaything" and exchanged for a dictionary. When schoolmates listed more dignified professions, but Handy chose musician as a future career, his teacher berated him and his father whipped him, saying he'd rather see him dead.

But Handy persisted, secretly buying a cornet and playing in a band. Over his parents' objections, he attended dances and sang in a minstrel quartet. Graduating from high school, he passed the teacher examination in Birmingham, but took a higher-paying ironworking job in Bessemer, organizing a brass band. Left jobless by the 1893 depression, he formed a quartet in Birmingham that hoboed and worked its way to the Chicago World's Fair. En route, Handy lived in such poverty and degradation in St. Louis that he contemplated returning to a "respectable" profession in Florence, but couldn't concede his parents were right and he wrong.

Things improved when he joined the Hampton Cornet Band in Evansville, Ind. In 1896, he joined Mahara's Minstrels in Chicago and soon gained a reputation as a cornet soloist, touring America and Cuba with them. His now proud father congratulated him after a performance in Huntsville. Handy taught music at Alabama A. & M. College in Huntsville, 1900–1902, then returned to Mahara's Minstrels for another year.

In 1903, turning down an offer to lead a white municipal band in Michigan, he became director of a black fraternal band in Clarksdale, Miss., hearing again blues strains he had heard as a youngster. On playing a dance at a nearby town, his orchestra was upstaged by a three-piece country band of black youngsters who, in spelling Handy's men, played and sang primitive folk blues. Handy decided to forget conventional music and to arrange and compose music rooted in the black folk experience. His band's popularity and income soared.

He moved to Memphis, Tenn., forming a band that became the city's best, playing for Beale Street saloons, picnics, funerals, and political campaigns. He composed for candidate Ed Crump in the 1909 Memphis mayoral campaign a song, "Mr. Crump" (later retitled "Memphis Blues"), that in 1912 became the first published blues composition.

Handy went on to compose such songs as "St. Louis Blues" (1914), "Joe Turner Blues" (1915), and "Beale Street Blues" (1917). Many were published by Pace & Handy Music Company, a firm he formed with Harry Pace, a black banker and insurance man of Memphis and Atlanta who was also a lyricist. Handy also arranged many spirituals. He lived to see his beloved blues venerated as one of America's greatest contributions to world music.

Hansberry, Lorraine (1930–1965), Playwright

Lorraine Hansberry wrote the most successful and highly acclaimed play by any American black, *A Raisin in the Sun*. It won the New York Drama Critics Circle Award for 1959 over such dramas as Archibald MacLeish's *J.B.* and Tennessee Williams's *Sweet Bird of Youth*.

Miss Hansberry was born into an upper-class black family in Chicago. Her father was a wealthy realtor and former U.S. Marshal who spent considerable money and energy fighting a restricted covenant case to the Supreme Court. Victorious but embittered, he passed away in Mexico in 1945 while preparing to move his family into exile. Her family could have sent her to private schools, but preferred that she share the deprived ghetto schools of Chicago's South Side. While attending Englewood High School, she fell in love with drama, hanging around theaters and acting groups thenceforward. After graduating in 1948, she spent two years at the University of Wisconsin studying stage design and drama. She also studied painting at the Chicago Art Institute and other places.

Considering herself untalented, she moved to New York City, studied briefly at the New School for Social Research and worked as a store clerk and theatrical producer's aide. She began several plays, finishing none, and wrote some short stories, without publishing them. Working as a waitress, hostess, and cashier in a Greenwich Village restaurant owned by the family of music publisher and song writer Robert Nemiroff, she fell in love with and married him in 1953.

One evening, while working at home, she became so disgusted with the play she was working on that she threw the manuscript in the air. Nemiroff patiently picked up the scattered pages, reassured her, and she then finished *A Raisin in the Sun*, which some friends undertook to publish after hearing a reading at their apartment. After trial runs in New Haven and Philadelphia, it opened at the Ethel Barrymore Theater on Broadway on March 11, 1959. This long-run drama—starring Claudia McNeil, Ruby Dee, and Sidney Poitier (*q.v.*) with a black director, Lloyd Richards—was a big moneymaker, netting Miss Hansberry royalties of $80,000 in its first four months alone, with the movie rights selling for $300,000. Her second play, *The Sign in Sidney Brustein's Window*, opened on Broadway on October 15, 1964, but the young playwright passed away three months later as its run ended.

Only a handful of plays by blacks reached Broadway, the first not until 1925, but none ran as long as *Raisin*. Among the best were plays by James Baldwin (*q.v.*) in the 1960s, Langston Hughes (*q.v.*), 1930s to 1960s, Hall Johnson (*q.v.*) in 1933, Richard Wright (*q.v.*) in 1941, and Louis Peterson's *Take a Giant Step* (1953). In 1970 the Pulitzer

Prize for drama was awarded to Charles Gordone for *No Place to Be Somebody*, the first time any black dramatist or any off-Broadway play won the award.

Harris, Abram L. (1899–1963), Economist

The most outstanding academic economist among American blacks was Abram Lincoln Harris. Author of several major studies, he divided his teaching career between a black school, Howard University (1927–1945), and a white school, the University of Chicago (1946–1963).

Harris was born into comfortable circumstances in Richmond, Va. His father was the only black butcher in a large market, his mother a normal school graduate. Their home was well stocked with books, and the youngster received a good education at one of the most outstanding black secondary schools in the nation, Armstrong High in Richmond.

Harris then attended Virginia Union University in Richmond, graduating in 1922. Another two years of study earned him a M.A. degree at the University of Pittsburgh. He became Instructor of Economics at West Virginia State College in 1924, executive secretary of the Minneapolis Urban League in 1925, and a researcher for Columbia University's Department of Banking in a study of money markets in 1926.

The next year, he became assistant professor at Howard University in Washington, D.C., rising to head of the Department of Economics in 1930 and full professor in 1936. Meanwhile, on a Social Science Research Council fellowship (1928–1930), he resumed his work at Columbia University, earning the Ph.D. degree in economics in 1931. Subsequently he held Simon Nelson Patten (1932–33) and Guggenheim Foundation (1935–36, 1943–44, 1953–54) research fellowships.

He co-authored with Sterling Spero *The Black Worker* (1931). His best known work was *The Negro as Capitalist* (1936), a definitive study of the black man in banking, insurance, and other enterprises. He has published many articles, including "The Social Philosophy of Karl Marx," and is author of *Economics and Social Reform* (1958).

Harris went to the University of Chicago as a visiting professor of economics in 1946, and stayed on there. He was also a visiting professor during summers at such places as City College of New York (1942) and University of Puerto Rico (1957). Reserve Board Governor Andrew Brimmer (*q.v.*) is a black economist who attained greater visibility than Harris by serving in government.

Hastie, William H. (1904–   ), Judge and Governor

William Henry Hastie was the first Afro-American to become a Federal district judge, a territorial governor, and a Federal appellate judge.

As civilian aide to the Secretary of War, he denounced discrimination in World War II.

Hastie was born in Knoxville, Tenn., but his family moved to Washington, D.C., where his father, a trained pharmacist, became a Federal clerk. His mother was a schoolteacher. Like Washington's other elite black families, the Hasties would send their son to Dunbar High School and to New England colleges. Hastie's cousin, Charles H. Houston (1895–1950), son of a prominent Howard University professor and lawyer, attended Amherst College and Harvard Law school, joined his father's law firm, and became legal counsel for the NAACP, plotting the desegregation strategy and grooming Thurgood Marshall (*q.v.*) as his successor.

Hastie graduated from Dunbar High School, a class ahead of the future surgeon, Charles Drew (*q.v.*). Winning a scholarship to Amherst, he became Phi Beta Kappa as had his cousin a decade earlier. Hastie graduated at the head of his Amherst class in 1925. After teaching two years at the Bordentown Manual Training School in New Jersey, Hastie entered the Harvard University Law School. A top student, he was elected to the staff of the *Harvard Law Review*, receiving his L.L.B. in 1930. Ralph Bunche and Robert Weaver (*qq.v.*) were among his friends at Harvard.

In 1930, Hastie joined the faculty of the School of Law at Howard University in Washington, D.C., where his cousin, Charles Houston, was vice dean. Admitted to the District of Columbia bar the next year, Hastie joined the firm of Houston and Houston. Continuing his studies, he received the degree of Doctor of Juridical Science from Harvard University in 1932. That year was also a turning point in the career of Attorney Benjamin J. Davis, Jr., who came from a wealthy Atlanta family and attended Amherst College and Harvard Law School with Hastie. As defense lawyer in 1932 for Angelo Herndon on trial in Atlanta for circulating Marxist leaflets to local unemployed, Davis found the judge turning his back and reading newspapers whenever Davis spoke while the prosecutor was permitted to call Davis "nigger" and "darky lawyer" in court. Herndon was sentenced to twenty years on the chain gang. The embittered Davis joined the Communist Party, moved to New York City, and was elected to City Council in 1943.

Meanwhile, Hastie became one of the corps of bright young blacks brought into Federal service in Franklin Roosevelt's New Deal administration. Hastie became Assistant Solicitor in the Department of Interior despite Southern objections to his "leftist" leanings and NAACP connections. With Bunche, Weaver, and other black New Deal appointees,

Hastie served in Roosevelt's "Black Cabinet" under the leadership of Mary McLeod Bethune (*q.v.*).

In 1937, President Roosevelt appointed Hastie judge of the Federal district court for the Virgin Islands. After a two-year term there, he returned to Howard University in 1939 as professor of law and dean of the Law School. From November, 1940, to January, 1943, he was on leave serving as civilian aide to Secretary of War Henry L. Stimson. He quit in protest over continued segregation practices by the Army and the Air Corps. Returning to his professorship and deanship at Howard, he remained for three years until President Harry Truman appointed him Governor of the Virgin Islands. After three years as governor, 1946 to 1949, Truman appointed him a judge of the Third Circuit United States Court of Appeals. That same year, his classmate Ben Davis was convicted and jailed as one of the top eleven leaders of the Communist Party.

Long after Hastie, other blacks, such as Wade McCree, James Parsons, and Constance Baker Motley became judges of Federal district courts in the continental United States. Not until Thurgood Marshall in 1961 did another black become a Federal appellate judge. Marshall moved up to the Supreme Court in 1967, leaving Hastie as the only black appellate judge.

Hayes, Roland (1887–   ), Singer

Few singers approach the artistry and appeal of Roland Hayes in singing lieder, spirituals, and arias. His pioneering broke down barriers for black singers as serious concert artists.

Hayes was born in a cabin in Little Row, now Curryville, Ga. Former slaves who met after the war, his parents worked a ten-acre tenant farm near the plantation on which his mother, Fanny or "Angel Mo," grew up. A skilled carpenter but indifferent farmer who loved hunting, his father taught him the beauty of Nature's songs. He passed away when Roland was 11. Determined to get a better education for the three sons left at home, Mrs. Hayes worked zealously with her boys for several years to pay off all debts and move the family to Chattanooga, Tenn. Roland and his older brother were to attend school and work alternately while the youngest attended steadily. Carrying molten iron in ladles to the molds in a sash-weight factory for eighty cents a day, Roland often burned his feet and legs.

At 16, when he was just a third-grader, his singing in church choirs attracted his first music teacher, Arthur Calhoun, an Oberlin-trained black. Associating professional singing with loose-living minstrels, the strongly religious Angel Mo consented only reluctantly to her son's lessons. One evening, Calhoun took him to the home of the editor of a white daily in Chattanooga who played recordings for Hayes, introducing him to classical music by great voices, including Caruso. Aroused at first hearing such music, Hayes determined to become a classical singer.

In 1905 he set out with his portion from the family savings, fifty dollars, hoping to get formal musical instruction at Oberlin. Stopping in Nashville, Tenn., he was accepted at Fisk University as a sixth grader in the preparatory department, but received a solid grounding in classical music from the college faculty. Professor Jennie Robinson, head of music at Fisk, secretly raised money for his tuition and fees, while his work as a houseboy provided other expenses. Annoyed by the time he spent with the Fisk Jubilee Singers, who sang popular music, the austere Miss Robinson had him expelled from Fisk after four years.

Moving to Louisville, Ky., he became a singing waiter in a men's club. After a visiting Boston businessman, Henry Putnam, encouraged him to resume his training in New England, Hayes accepted an offer to sing lead tenor with the Fisk Jubilee Singers at a summer conference in Boston in 1911. Putnam arranged separate auditions with five famous Boston voice teachers. These five whites agreed lessons would be a waste of time because white concert audiences would not accept a black classical singer. Heretofore, black vocal artists were restricted to a circuit of black colleges, churches, and halls. Nevertheless, two of the five agreed to take him on; he chose Arthur Hubbard.

There followed a long and arduous struggle for recognition. Working as a bellhop, insurance company messenger, and church singer, he paid for his lessons with Hubbard and moved his mother to Boston; Angel Mo insisted on taking in washing, even after he became famous, to pay her way. In 1914, he was hired to sing duets with Harry T. Burleigh (*q.v.*) on lecture tours accompanying Booker T. Washington (*q.v.*). The next summer he toured with a trio of his own, singing classical numbers. Since professional managers would not sponsor his concert debut at Boston's Jordan Hall late in 1915, he did so himself, losing $200 but getting good notices. After touring black churches and schools for two years, he had enough capital late in 1917 to rent Boston's august Symphony Hall, $400 in advance, for a concert, the first there for a black artist. Friends feared he couldn't fill it, but by his own exertions Hayes sold enough tickets to have an overflow crowd and clear $2,000. Promoters still would not back him so he toured as his own promoter-manager. He had been so anxious to gain acceptance by whites that he had neglected his black heritage of suffering that imparted a special tonal quality to his classically trained voice, but he finally realized this and fused the two into a supreme artistry.

Still unaccepted in America, he went to England in 1920 to study and to build his reputation. He became a great success there and on the Continent, singing in command performance at Buckingham Palace for King George V and Queen Mary in 1921. Returning briefly in 1922 to see his ailing mother for the last time (she passed away the next year), he remained overseas until he returned in triumph near the end of 1923 to begin prolonged transcontinental tours of America under professional management.

Roland Hayes paved the way for Marian Anderson, Paul Robeson (*qq.v.*) and other great black concert artists by earning several hundreds of thousands annually in concert tours. His prominence brought him no respite, however, from the humiliations and hardships of American prejudice, including his being hauled to jail and beaten by police in Rome, Ga., in 1942, after his wife and daughter unknowingly sat in a section of a shoe store reserved for white customers.

Healy, James A. (1830–1900), Catholic Bishop

From 1875 to 1900, a black man, James Augustine Healy, was Bishop of Portland, Me., heading the 45,000 square-mile Roman Catholic Diocese comprising Maine and New Hampshire. Spiritual leader for 80,000 Catholics, only 300 of whom were black, he began with 57 parish churches and 33 mission stations in both states, but finished with 86 parishes and 79 missions in Maine alone, after New Hampshire became a separate diocese in 1884 with its bishop at Manchester. His brother became president of Georgetown University in Washington, D.C.

Healy was the eldest child of a Georgia planter. His father, Michael Healy (1796–1850), was an Irish soldier who came to Canada with a British regiment near the end of the War of 1812. Settling in Georgia penniless, he worked his way up to ownership of sixty slaves and a 1,600-acre cotton plantation near Macon. Ignoring Georgia laws forbidding interracial marriage, in 1829 he married a slave, Eliza Crawford (1813–1850), mulatto daughter of a prosperous cotton gin owner. Ten children were born on their plantation, beginning with four sons, James, Hugh, Patrick, and Sherwood. To shield his son from insults in Georgia, Michael Healy placed James in a Quaker elementary school in Flushing, Long Island, after which he attended a Quaker secondary school, Franklin Park, in Burlington, N.J. As they reached school age, his brothers followed him northward.

John Fitzpatrick, coadjutor (assistant) bishop of Boston, met Michael Healy in 1844 and persuaded him to place the boys at the new Jesuit college in the diocese. Unhappy at racial slurs in New Jersey and Long Island, the three Healy brothers, now joined by Sherwood, were delighted to enroll in grammar, secondary, and collegiate schools on the campus of Holy Cross College in Worcester, Mass. Here they found full acceptance. The four brothers were baptized as Roman Catholics along with the two sons of the famed New England reformer, Orestes Brownson, becoming lifelong friends. The Healys were excellent students. When Holy Cross College held its first graduation exercises in 1849, James Healy was valedictorian, John Brownson second, and Hugh Healy fourth.

James wanted to become a Jesuit, but their novitiate (training house) was in the slave state of Maryland, which posed difficulties. Patrick, who was lighter skinned, entered the novitiate after graduating from Holy Cross in 1850. James entered the Sulpician Seminary in Montreal, Canada, in September, 1849, to train for the priesthood. The death of his father in August, 1850, four months after his mother died, made James head of the family, threatening an end to his studies. Fortunately, his brother Hugh, a clerk in a New York City store, took charge, bringing the three youngest children (Josephine, Eliza, and Eugene) from the plantation; Martha and Michael, Jr., were already studying in the North and the seventh child had died in infancy. Also, their father's will, leaving his $40,000 estate in trust to his nine surviving children, was honored. Since Georgia law forbade freeing the slaves, the bondsmen the Healys inherited were hired out for $1,500 annually.

In 1852, James Healy transferred to the Sulpician Seminary in Paris, France. He planned to go on for a doctorate and become a seminary professor. But after Hugh's passing in 1853, he decided to return to America to become a priest and take care of the family. Completing seminary, he was ordained at Notre Dame Cathedral in Paris in 1854. He returned to Boston that August and became assistant priest in a parish. Under his father's will, the slaves were not to be sold until the youngest of the Healy children was 21, but feeling it incongruous for a priest (James), Jesuit (Patrick,) nun (Martha), and seminarian (Sherwood) to continue as slave-owners, Father James Healy arranged for the slaves to be sold in 1855, netting $33,000.

Bishop Fitzpatrick, head of the diocese of Boston from 1846 until his death in 1866, had become a second father to the Healy brothers after persuading their father to send them to Holy Cross. Late in 1854, he made James his personal secretary. Next year he named him chancellor of the diocese to handle administrative details. Healy bought a home in West Newton (a suburb of Boston) for the family, especially the younger children. After eleven years as the bishop's secretary and the diocesan chancellor, Father James Healy became in 1866 pastor of St. James Church in South Boston. This was one of the largest churches in the diocese and seated two thousand people per mass. Its congregation, mostly Irish, readily accepted their black priest. Healy replaced John Williams as pastor when Williams succeeded Fitzpatrick as bishop. Sherwood Healy (1836–1875), who showed his African ancestry even more than James, became the favorite of Bishop Williams. Ordained in Rome in 1858 and earning a doctorate in canon law two years later, Sherwood had come to Boston as a priest in 1860 and gone on to become professor, vice president, and director of the new provincial Catholic seminary at Troy, N.Y. Sherwood became theologian and companion to Bishop Williams and in 1870 was appointed by him rector of the new Holy Cross Cathedral being constructed in Boston. The two brothers were friendly rivals.

When the bishops of Portland and Hartford both passed away late in 1874, James and Sherwood were among favorites to succeed them. In February, 1875, Pope Pius IX named James Healy bishop of Portland. Williams, now an archbishop, appointed Sherwood Healy to succeed his brother as pastor of St. James Church. Sherwood, often ill, passed away that October. Bishop Healy's flock, mostly poor Irish immigrants, became devoted to a bishop who showed such great concern for the poor. Many named sons James or Augustine and daughters Augusta after their beloved black bishop. In June, 1900, at the celebration of Bishop Healy's twenty-fifth anniversary as head of the diocese, Pope Leo XIII sent word that he had appointed him an Assistant to the Papal Throne, one of the highest honors in Roman Catholicism, just below cardinal. Bishop Healy passed away two months later. His successor as Bishop of Portland, William O'Connell, succeeded Archbishop Williams in Boston in 1906 and later became Cardinal O'Connell.

Besides James and Sherwood, two other Healy children rose high in Catholicism. Patrick Healy, S.J. (1834–1910), taught at St. Joseph's College in Philadelphia and was President of Georgetown University from 1874 to 1883. Josephine and Eliza Healy became nuns, with Eliza (1847–c. 1917) becoming mother superior of the Congregation of Notre Dame at convents in Montreal, Canada; St. Albans, Vt.; and Staten Island, N.Y.

Henson, Matthew A. (1866–1955), Arctic Explorer

On April 6, 1909, six men reached the North Pole, climaxing one of the greatest epics of heroism, discovery, and adventure in human history. One was white, the commander, Robert E. Peary (1856–1920). One was black, Matthew Alexander Henson, Peary's companion since 1887, including six previous arctic trips, 1891 to 1906. The other four were Eskimos, Ootah and Seeglo, who had been with Peary and Henson in 1906, and Egingwah and Ooqueah, recruited for the last successful dash.

Recognition and honors came to Peary after an interlude in which an imposter's claims to have reached the Pole first confused the public. But Henson generally went unheeded by a nation too prejudiced to accept the fact that a black man could be a hero of polar exploration. Most historians and writers, from ignorance or prejudice, dismiss Henson as merely Peary's servant, but Henson was far more than that. He was the indispensable partner essential to the success of Peary's expedition because of his ability, knowledge, rapport with the Eskimos, endurance, courage, resourcefulness, and steadfastness.

Henson was born on a farm in Charles County, Md. In his autobiographical account, *A Negro Explorer at the North Pole* (1912), he states briefly that his parents soon moved to Washington, D.C., that his mother passed away when he was 7, that an uncle sent him to school in Washington for six years, that he went to sea from Baltimore at 12, and that he sailed the world a half dozen years before meeting Peary in Washington and being hired by him. Henson's biographers—Bradley Robinson, with whom Henson collaborated, in *Dark Companion* (1947), and Floyd Miller in *Ahdoolo!* (1963)—gave a different version. Robinson states that Henson's mother passed away on the farm when he was 2, that his father remarried but passed away when he was 8, and that his stepmother cruelly abused and whipped him, refusing to let him attend school. Running away from the farm when he was 11, he walked to Washington where a black restaurateur gave him room and board for his dishwashing but left him no time for schooling. He then walked to Baltimore and went to sea as a cabin boy. Robinson and Miller identify the ship as the merchant vessel *Katie Hines*, commanded by a Captain Childs who took along books to give the lad daily lessons. Becoming an able-bodied seaman, Henson sailed with the kindly captain until the latter passed away when Henson was 18.

Later, Henson worked as a Boston stevedore, Providence bellhop, Buffalo laborer, and New York coachman, before returning to Washington at 19. He was working as a stock clerk in the Steinmetz hat store when Lieutenant Robert Peary entered in 1887 seeking a sun helmet. Steinmetz recommended Henson as the valet Peary needed for his trip to survey a canal route through Nicaragua. Hiring Henson, Peary found him a great aid in the dangerous work of hacking and charting a path through the swamps and jungles. Henson's experiences at sea made him so resourceful that Peary gave him responsibilities greater than those of a servant.

After this initial venture, Henson accompanied Peary on all his re- maining explorations. Peary had made one trip to the arctic in 1886 before meeting Henson. On the next seven journeys to the hazardous, 50° below zero, northern wastelands (1891–92, 1893–95, 1896, 1897, 1898–1902, 1905–06, and 1908–09), Henson was at Peary's side. Be- tween expeditions, he worked at various jobs, such as a messenger for the Navy and an aide in mounting arctic exhibits for New York's Mu- seum of Natural History. He and Peary became the most experienced and seasoned arctic explorers, breaking in almost a complete new crew for each trip. Henson was the only man with Peary on more than two ventures into the arctic. Gradually, Peary realized Henson's value. From the second trip onward, his journal entries list Henson as his assistant rather than his servant.

Like an earlier black explorer, Estevanico (*q.v.*), Henson became the key to cooperation from the natives who regarded him as a brother because his skin was, like theirs, not white. The meaningless word, "Ahdoolo," that Henson coined to rouse the Eskimos every morning, was incorporated into their language. Decades later, Eskimos still spoke of him with affection and veneration. Henson saved Peary's life several times: rescuing him from a crevasse; coolly killing a musk-ox which charged him; and nursing him back to health when his feet froze. Ever courageous, Henson braved dangers and hardships sharing Peary's in- domitable spirit of going forward when others trembled and wavered.

When the final successful dash across 450 miles of dangerous, shift- ing, splitting Arctic Ocean ice was made in 1909, the whites on the expedition—Dr. J. W. Goodsell, Donald MacMillan, Ross Marvin, George Borup, and Captain Bob Bartlett—were sent back one by one with the teams of Eskimos and dog sledges they led. Each had per- formed his function as a support team. Only Henson was selected to go all the way with the team he led. In his book, *How Peary Reached the Pole* (1934), Commander MacMillan explained why:

> He was the most popular man aboard the ship with the Eskimos. He could talk their language like a native. He made all

the sledges which went to the Pole. He made all the stoves. Henson, the colored man, went to the Pole with Peary because he was a better man than any of his white assistants.

Peary, who felt compelled to explain to color-conscious Americans why a black man was given preference over a white man, stated:

> Matthew Henson, my Negro assistant, has been with me since 1887. I have taken him on each and all of my expeditions, except the first, and also without exception on each of my farthest sledge trips. This position I have given him primarily because of his adaptability and fitness for the work, and secondly on account of his loyalty. He is a better dog driver and can handle a sledge better than any man living except some of the best Eskimo hunters. I couldn't get along without him.

The controversy caused by Dr. Frederick Cook's claims to have reached the pole on April 21, 1908, a year before Peary, delayed Peary's well-merited rewards. Once Cook's claims were exposed as a complete hoax, honors were showered upon Peary, including promotion to Rear Admiral, an $8,000 pension, medals and scrolls from societies, and a Congressional resolution of thanks. Ignored and forgotten, Henson asked for nothing. He was parking cars in a Brooklyn garage when a black politician, acting independently, in 1913 secured for the 47-year-old hero a government job in the custom house, as a messenger boy at $900 a year. Working his way up to clerk at $2,000 a year, Henson retired at the age of 70. Four times (1926, 1936, 1938, 1949), bills to grant him a Federal pension as a reward for his arctic explorations were bottled up in committee by an ungrateful Congress.

Fortunately, Henson lived long enough to receive some belated honors from neglectful Americans: In 1937 the Explorers Club made him a member; Congress issued in 1944 a medal jointly honoring the five whites and one black with Peary in 1909; President Truman saluted him in ceremonies at the Pentagon in 1950; President Eisenhower honored him at the White House in 1954; and in 1961 Maryland posthumously passed a bill providing for a bronze plaque in the State House hailing Henson as co-discoverer of the North Pole.

Hope, John (1868–1936), Educator

When John Hope became president in 1906 of what is now Morehouse College, he was the first of his race to head one of the black colleges established after the Civil War by such major denominational boards as the American Missionary Association and the American Baptist Home Mission Society. He went on to found and serve as first president of the Atlanta University system, the leading educational complex for blacks in America.

Hope was born in Augusta, Ga. His mother, Mary Frances (Fanny) Butts, was born there of an open interracial union between a former Virginia planter and a free black woman. Fanny herself became the mate of a prominent Augusta physician-professor, and after his passing lived with his close friend James Hope. A native of Scotland and a descendant of Sir Thomas Hope, James had prospered in merchandising in New York with his brothers before moving to Augusta, where he eventually became a cotton mill owner. Since interracial marriage was illegal in Georgia, James and Fanny finally moved to New York in 1866 to marry and settle. Fanny was homesick, and they returned to Augusta the next year. Although he had married across the racial line, James Hope remained a prominent, respected, prosperous businessman in Augusta, often entertaining business associates, but not their wives, in his home. After he passed away in 1876, however, callous executors, with the sanction of prejudiced Georgians, robbed the family of their inheritance.

Consequently, John Hope had a hard struggle to get through school. Aided by scholarships, he worked his way through Worcester Academy in Massachusetts and through Brown University in Rhode Island, graduating from the latter in 1894. His teaching career began at Roger Williams University, a black school in Nashville, Tenn., run by the American Baptist Home Mission Society, where he taught science and classical languages for four years. In 1898, he became professor of classics at Atlanta Baptist College, another of the Society's schools. Founded as Augusta Institute in 1867, it had moved to Atlanta in 1879 as Atlanta Baptist Seminary and had been renamed Atlanta Baptist College in 1897 before becoming Morehouse College in 1913. Hope became the school's president in June, 1906.

The blond, blue-eyed Hope could easily be taken for white, but he chose to ally with his mother's race. He denounced the Atlanta Compromise of Booker T. Washington (*q.v.*) and was the only black college president to join the militant Niagara Movement, led by his close friend Professor W. E. B. Du Bois (*q.v.*) of Atlanta University. Hope was the only college president, white or black, present at the founding meeting of the NAACP in 1909. In 1919, he was asked by a leading Southern white reformer, Will W. Alexander, to join an unprecedented Southern biracial reform group, the Commission on Interracial Cooperation. Disillusioned by his failure as a Y.M.C.A. secretary to get better treatment for black soldiers overseas, Hope hesitated, but joined in 1920. In 1932, he became president of the Commission, an unusual honor for a black man in the South. In 1944, this Commission became the Southern Regional Council.

Hope capped his career in 1929 when he put together the Atlanta University system, designed to coordinate the six competing denominational colleges for blacks in Atlanta. Under Hope's plan, Atlanta University, founded as an undergraduate school in 1867 by the Congregational denomination's American Missionary Association, was converted into a graduate institution, the first black university devoted solely to graduate work. Morehouse and Spelman colleges were affiliated with it as the independent, undergraduate colleges for men and women, respectively.

Hope served as the first president of the new Atlanta University from 1929 to 1936. He planned for all six schools to become affiliates with it, but many years elapsed before Gammon Theological Seminary and Clark and Morris Brown colleges cooperated.

Horne, Lena (1917–   ), Singer, Actress

For three decades, Lena Horne has been one of America's favorite entertainers. Extraordinarily pretty and glamorous, she combines poise and sex appeal in her popular rendition of blues and ballads. She aided in the long struggle to have blacks treated with dignity in movies.

She was born in Brooklyn, the only child of parents whose lives were unstable. Refusing to work for whites, her handsome father became a professional gambler. Her mother wanted to be an actress. They were divorced when the child was 3. On both the maternal and paternal sides, Miss Horne was descended from well-educated, prospering, middle-class, light-skinned families. Her father's mother, Cora Calhoun Horne, claimed descent from John C. Calhoun and was active in the NAACP, Urban League, and Ethical Culture Society. Living with her father's parents in what was then the integrated Bedford section of Brooklyn, Lena was introduced to books, concerts, plays, and museums, and attended the Ethical Culture School.

But Miss Horne's beautiful mother took her away on tour with theatrical troupes, and Lena loved the backstage life. When the road shows folded, her mother would leave her with friends or relatives while seeking a new role in other cities. Thus she lived and attended schools in various places including Atlanta, Miami, Jacksonville, Macon, and Birmingham, returning to stay with her grandparents in Brooklyn from time to time. For a while, she stayed with her uncle, Frank Horne, a poet who was Dean of Students at Fort Valley State College in Georgia; later, Dr. Horne became a New Deal housing expert.

Miss Horne's interest in dramatics was encouraged by a friend of the family with whom she stayed after her grandparents died. She went to dancing school, and won an award with a dance group, launching her stage career with a week of ballet at the Harlem Opera House. She went to live with her mother and stepfather, a white of Spanish descent who was unable to get work in the Depression. To help out, she quit Girls' High School in Brooklyn at 16 and secured a job as a chorus girl at the famous Cotton Club in Harlem, which had featured the bands of Duke Ellington (*q.v.*) and Cab Calloway and the "Stormy Weather" revue with Ethel Waters (*q.v.*). She danced and sang at the Cotton Club for two years and also appeared in a short-lived Broadway play, *Dance with Your Gods*, in 1934.

Subsequently, Miss Horne became the vocalist for Noble Sissle's band for three years, and appeared briefly in the 1939 *Blackbirds* revue. In 1940, she became vocalist for Charlie Barnet's orchestra, the first time a black woman was feature singer for a white band. On her own, she became a sensational soloist at Cafe Society Downtown in 1941. Singing songs like "The Man I Love" and "Embraceable You," she was a great hit there and at clubs in Hollywood in 1942.

She was signed to an M-G-M contract in 1942, and was featured in the all-black *Cabin in the Sky* and *Stormy Weather* in 1943, and *Broadway Rhythm* the next year, among others. During the early 1950s, however, she was blacklisted because of her long friendship with Paul Robeson (*q.v.*) who brought her into the Council for African Affairs, an organization that became listed as a front for Communist causes. She was completely innocent of any involvement in subversive causes, but the atmosphere of hysteria and guilt by association kept her out of jobs until 1957.

After her name was cleared, she was signed to be the star of the integrated cast of Harold Arlen's Broadway musical, *Jamaica*, with Ricardo Montalban as her leading man. A huge success, *Jamaica* ran from the end of 1957 to the spring of 1959. Lena Horne also became a frequent guest on television shows and co-starred in a memorable special with Harry Belafonte in 1970.

She has fought for racial dignity throughout her career. She quit an Army entertainment tour during World War II because prejudiced officials arranged segregated seating in Arkansas that placed white German prisoners of war in choice front rows ahead of black American soldiers. She cancelled an engagement in Miami Beach in 1955 when the hotel in whose show she was to star refused to rent her a room.

Hughes, Langston (1902–1967), Poet Laureate and Author

One of America's finest and most versatile writers, James Langston Hughes was a major literary figure for forty years. Generally considered the "Poet Laureate" of his people, he wrote not only great poetry, but also outstanding works in almost every literary form.

Langston Hughes was by far the most prolific of all black writers. He published ten volumes of poetry: sixty-six short stories; more than a hundred essays; five volumes of "Simple" stories about his famous creation, Jesse B. Semple; three other volumes of short stories; more than twenty theatrical works, including dramas, musicals, gospel song-plays, and operas; seven anthologies; eleven books of Negro life and history for young and old; two novels; and two autobiographies.

Hughes was born in Joplin, Mo., but spent most of his youth in Lawrence, Kans., with his grandmother, and upon her passing, her friend, Auntie Reed. His parents had separated in his infancy. His father went to Mexico to make money and live among whites. Langston Hughes sometimes lived in Topeka, Buffalo, and other places with his mother, a stenographer who moved about seeking better jobs. His grandmother's first husband, Sheridan Leary, had fought and died beside John Brown at Harpers Ferry. She had then married Charles Langston, whose brother, John Mercer Langston, later became the only black Congressman from Virginia. The lonely boy was an avid reader during his years with Mrs. Langston and Auntie Reed in Lawrence. At 14 he went to live with his mother and stepfather in Lincoln, Ill., where he completed grade school. Elected class poet in the overwhelmingly white school because his classmates assumed any black had rhythm enough to be a poet, he proceeded to write his first poem, and read it at the graduation exercises. His family moved to Cleveland, Ohio, where he attended Central High School and wrote poems and stories.

In his late teens, he spent some months with his father in Mexico, but found him, though well off, thoroughly unlikable. In 1921, he published his first work, the famous poem "The Negro Speaks of Rivers," in *The Crisis* magazine edited by W. E. B. Du Bois (*q.v.*). That year, financed by his father, he entered Columbia University, but lost interest and dropped out. He worked at odd jobs in New York, then went to sea as a mess boy, visiting Africa and then spending ten months in Europe learning a lot about life while working in night clubs in Paris and beachcombing in Italy and Spain.

He returned to America, and he joined his mother in Washington, D.C. While working as a busboy in the Wardman Park Hotel there, he was discovered by poet-critic Vachel Lindsay, who brought him to the attention of the literary world. Hughes became one of the most heralded writers of the Harlem Renaissance. His first book, *The Weary Blues* (1926), vividly portrayed Negro urban folk life in poems that blended syncopated blues and jazz rhythms with black street dialogue. A second volume of poetry, *Fine Clothes to the Jew*, followed in 1927. Meanwhile, he returned to college attending a black school, Lincoln University in Pennsylvania, from which he graduated in 1930. During his senior year, he completed his first novel, *Not Without Laughter* (1930).

Hughes went on to display mastery of many literary forms. His poems were published in such collections as *Scottsboro Limited* (1932), and his short stories in *The Ways of White Folks* (1934). He wrote many plays, including *Mulatto* (1930), which became a hit on Broadway five years later. He founded community theater groups in the black ghettoes of Harlem in 1938, Los Angeles the next year, and Chicago in 1941. Later, he developed and popularized a new art form, the "gospel song-play," beginning with the huge success of his *Black Nativity* on Broadway in 1961. He produced various others in this genre, including *Tambourines to Glory* in 1963, based on his 1958 novel of the same name.

In 1942, he created an enduring fictional character, Jesse B. Semple, known as "Simple." Simple's humorous observations of American life through the eyes of a man who spends his evenings in a Harlem bar after laboring all day make him loom as large in American humor as Finley Peter Dunne's famous Mr. Dooley. Appearing originally as a weekly column in the Chicago *Defender*, these hilarious tales about Jesse Semple were collected in such volumes as *Simple Speaks His Mind* (1950), *Simple Stakes a Claim* (1957), and *Simple's Uncle Sam* (1965). Hughes's musical folk comedy, *Simply Heavenly* (1957), ran on Broadway.

Among his accounts of Afro-American history and life are *Fight for Freedom: The Story of the NAACP* (1962) and *Black Magic: A Pictorial History of the Negro in American Entertainment* (1967), addressed to adults, and *The First Book of Jazz* (1955), *Famous Negro Heroes of America* (1958), and *The First Book of Africa* (1964) for young readers. He edited such anthologies as *The Poetry of the Negro, 1746–1949* (1949), with Arna Bontemps as co-editor, *An African Treasury* (1961), and *New Negro Poets, U.S.A.* (1964). Among his later books of poetry are *Shakespeare in Harlem* (1942); *Montage of a Dream Deferred* (1951), which contains the lines "What happens to a dream deferred? / Does it dry up / like a raisin in the sun?", which inspired the great play by Lorraine Hansberry (*q.v.*); *Ask Your Mamma* (1961); and the posthumously published *The Panther and the Lash* (1967), dealing with Black Panthers and the white backlash.

Except for having a white patroness with whom he broke in 1930, Hughes lived solely from his earnings as a professional writer and a reader of poetry, for four decades. He was the only black poet to live from his professional earnings throughout his career. His two autobiographies, *The Big Sea* (1940), covering the years to 1930, and *I Wonder as I Wander* (1956), bringing the story to 1937, tell of his early life and career. Unfortunately, he did not live to fulfill his plans to issue a third volume on his later years.

Jackson, Mahalia (1911–   ), Gospel Singer

Mahalia Jackson is America's greatest gospel singer. Her moving renditions of gospel songs in her powerful contralto voice attract millions of fans to whom her work has great appeal less for its religious content and meaning than for its artistry and its resemblance to jazz and blues.

She was born in New Orleans, La., the third of six children. Her father was a stevedore and barber and also preached for a small church. Although he had several sisters in theatrical and vaudeville work, he permitted only sacred music in his home and discouraged his children from thoughts of the entertainment world. Living in New Orleans, the cradle of jazz, Mahalia could not be isolated from worldly music, hearing in friends' homes recordings of blues singer Bessie Smith and operatic tenor Enrico Caruso. Although she enjoyed blues and opera, Mahalia was interested in singing only church music, and joined her father's choir as a child. She dropped out of school after the eighth grade and worked as a laundress and maid.

At the age of 16, Miss Jackson moved to Chicago where she worked in a factory and as a hotel maid. She hoped to save enough money to study nursing or beauty culture. Joining the Greater Salem Baptist Church during her first week in Chicago, she sang in the church choir and soon became soloist. The choir director formed a quintet featuring her that traveled from church to church singing for silver offerings from the congregation. With her earnings, she enrolled in beautician's school and opened a beauty shop.

As early as 1934, seven years after moving to the North, she made her first recording, "God Gonna Separate the Wheat from the Tares." This Decca record enjoyed great popularity in the South among lovers of gospel music. Unlike spirituals, which are antebellum spontaneous folk creations, gospels are modern songs composed by black writers and singers in Negro churches. Unlike blues, which are sad laments, gospels are joyous songs raised to the Lord. Miss Jackson's fame spread in gospel circles. In 1945, her recording for Apollo Records of "Move on Up a Little Higher" brought nationwide attention because fans of jazz, blues, and popular music began buying this record also. It sold over a million copies, the first gospel record to do so. Through her, the gospel songs, heretofore largely church music, began reaching the general public.

Her first concert in New York's Carnegie Hall in 1950 was a sellout, and was followed by annual appearances there. She toured Europe singing in concert halls in leading cities. From 1954 to 1955 she had a weekly network show called "Mahalia" on CBS Radio. She began recording for Columbia Records, cutting such albums as *Sweet Little Jesus Boy*. She refused to sing in nightclubs and theaters or to sing songs she considered sacrilegious or just too worldly. Her performance at the Newport (R.I.) Jazz Festival in 1957 was electrifying.

Mahalia Jackson has made guest appearances on many television shows. Her largest television audience, however, undoubtedly was in 1968 when, with tears streaming, she sang a solo at the memorial service for Martin Luther King, Jr. (*q.v.*), on the Morehouse College campus in Atlanta just before his burial. Many stories of warm and compassionate acts are told of this woman of deep faith. An example is the time she trudged through the snowy streets of Chicago after midnight to sing and pray beside the bed of a dying woman who was unknown to her but whose daughter, also a stranger, asked her to do so at the end of a concert performance in a little Southside church.

Johnson, Charles S. (1893–1956), Sociologist and Educator

Charles Spurgeon Johnson was a pioneer black sociologist and a widely consulted expert on race relations. He wrote numerous books on Negro life, some of which became classics and bestsellers. He was the first black to become president of Fisk University, serving from 1947 until he passed away in 1956.

Johnson was born in Bristol, Va., the eldest of five children of a former slave. His father's former master had tutored his ex-slave in the classics along with his own son. This foundation enabled Johnson's father to go to Richmond Institute, later part of Virginia Union University, where he earned the Bachelor of Divinity degree. Reverend Johnson worked to bring religion to the rough, immoral railway workers living in the black section of Bristol.

Even as a youngster, Charlie Johnson learned to study both books and people. He avidly read the books in his father's library. He analyzed the behavior of the white customers and black barbers in the barber shop in which he worked during his boyhood. He developed habits of seeking to understand rather than condemn. He learned fearlessness from his diminutive father who tried singlehandedly and armed only with his Bible to halt a lynch mob. Though failing to stop the lynchers, he so shamed them by courageously denouncing their sinful misconduct to their faces that lynchings ceased in Bristol.

Bristol did not have a high school for blacks. Johnson left home to attend Wayland Academy in Richmond. Finishing the Academy, which was the high school part of Virginia Union University, he then enrolled in the college, completing the four-year course in only three years and graduating with honors in 1917. While working his way through high school and college, he was also active as a debater, editor, member of the college quartet, football manager, and student council president. He did considerable reading in summers while working as a watchman on a steamer running between New York and Providence.

In 1917, he entered the University of Chicago, waiting tables in a hotel and holding other jobs as well to pay his way. He studied under preeminent sociologists like Robert E. Park, called the "father of American Sociology." During his first year in Chicago, Johnson set up the research department for the new Urban League branch in Chicago. He enlisted early in 1918 and fought in France. Returning in 1919 from World War I, he saw the postwar racial rioting in Norfolk and Washington. He reached the University of Chicago a week before the biggest riot broke out, leaving 15 dead and 538 wounded in Chicago. He was in the thick of it and was shot at. Called to testify before the governor's commission, he was so impressive with his knowledge of the sociological conditions underlying the 1919 riot that he was appointed to the commission's staff. The 600-page report he co-authored, *The Negro in Chicago* (1922), was called a landmark in social research. It is generally acknowledged the best analysis of the background of a race riot. Meanwhile, he graduated from the University of Chicago with the Ph.B. degree.

From 1921 to 1928, Johnson served as director of research for the national Urban League at its headquarters in New York. In 1923, he founded for the League a magazine called *Opportunity*, which not only published social reports, but also featured the works of such young black writers, artists, and musicians as Langston Hughes, Richmond Barthé, and William Grant Still (*qq.v.*). Edited by Charles Johnson from 1923 to 1928, *Opportunity* was an important force in the Harlem Renaissance.

In 1928, Johnson became professor of sociology and director of the Institute of Social Science at Fisk University in Nashville, Tenn., a leading black college founded by the American Missionary Association in 1867. Immersed in his first loves—social research and interpreting the races to one another—he wrote many books, including *The Negro in American Civilization* (1930), the bestselling *Shadow of the Plantation* (1934), a textbook entitled *Race Relations* (1935), *Growing Up in the Black Belt* (1941), and *Patterns of Negro Segregation* (1943).

Despite the burdens of the presidency of Fisk, which he assumed in 1947, he continued writing, publishing *Education and the Cultural Crisis* in 1951. Fellow scholars recognized him by electing him president of the Southern Sociological Society (1945–1946). He served on many commissions, including the three-man League of Nations Commission of 1930 to investigate peonage in Liberia and the 26-member State Department Mission of 1946 that helped General Douglas MacArthur restructure Japan's educational system. President Harry Truman appointed him to the United States delegation to UNESCO. The leading expert on race relations in his day, he became in 1943 director of the racial relations programs of both the Rosenwald Foundation and the American Missionary Association.

Johnson, Hall (1888–1970), Choral Director and Composer-Arranger

In 1925, Hall Johnson formed a singing group that made him the nation's best known black choral director. His efforts helped bring to a wide audience Negro folk music sung in the original manner rather than in the polished concert versions to which audiences had been accustomed. He is also famed as a composer for his arrangements of spirituals and other folk music of his people. He wrote a Broadway show and was a Hollywood composer-arranger.

Johnson was born in Athens, Ga., the son of an African Methodist Episcopal minister. His mother and grandmother were former slaves. He learned many old spirituals from his grandmother, Mary Hall Jones, who was his only source for some of the songs he introduced through his choir.

As a child, he started to study piano with an older sister, but did not take up music seriously until his sophomore year in college. After finishing Knox Institute in Athens, Ga., at 15, he attended Atlanta University for a year. He then transferred to Allen University in Columbia, S.C., where his father, the Reverend William Decker Johnson, had become president. There Johnson taught himself to play the violin his mother had given him, and learned enough to play in the orchestra at a nearby summer resort.

He thus earned enough money in college to be able to go to Philadelphia to study music after his graduation from Allen in 1908. In Philadelphia, he studied violin at the Hahn School of Music and also enrolled in the School of Music at the University of Pennsylvania. In graduating from the latter in 1910, he took the prize for best composition for orchestra and chorus.

Johnson moved to New York in 1914, and found work with various bands. He played in the orchestra of the renowned white dance team, Vernon and Irene Castle, in theater orchestras and, during the war, with Jim Europe's famed regimental band. He was in the orchestra for the famed all-black musical revue, *Shuffle Along*, that opened in 1921. Throughout, he continued studying music at such places as the Institute of Musical Art.

Seeking to form a black choir comparable to the Russian Don Cossack chorus, he founded the Hall Johnson Negro Choir in Harlem in December, 1925. He began with eight voices, and had expanded to twenty by the time his choir gave its first concert in a regular New York auditorium, the Pythian Temple, in February, 1928. The next month, the group sang at Town Hall. That August, it began the first of six consecutive seasons of appearances with the Philharmonic Symphony in its summer series at CCNY's Lewisohn Stadium. The Hall Johnson Choir received great critical acclaim for its authentic singing of spirituals, work songs, folk ballads, and other Afro-American folk music in pristine versions. Even before forming his choir, Johnson had published his transcriptions of several spirituals and continued to introduce many through his ensemble.

Johnson's choir sang in, and he arranged and helped direct the music of, the famed Broadway musical written by whites for a black cast, *Green Pastures*, that opened in 1930. In 1933, his own show, *Run Little Chillun*, for which he wrote the book and music, opened on Broadway. It featured the conflict between two black religious groups—a Baptist church and a nature cult. It was generally panned as a play and drama, but Johnson's choral portions were applauded as superb entertainment.

Johnson moved his choir to Hollywood in 1935 to work on the film version of *Green Pastures,* released the next year. Thereafter they made the film capital their home, making appearances in movies while Johnson did arranging and composing for films. Johnson and the choir had a hand in such pictures as *Lost Horizons* (1937), *Way Down South* (1939), *Swanee River* (1941), and *Cabin in the Sky* (1943). Upon retiring from active choral direction, he continued working as an arranger.

Other famed black choirs and directors rivaled his work. Among them can be counted the Fisk Jubilee Singers, the Hampton Institute Choir under Nathaniel Dett, the Wings Over Jordan radio choir, Leonard DePaur's Infantry Chorus, and Warner Lawson's Howard University Choir.

Johnson, Jack (1878–1946), Champion Boxer

Many historians of boxing consider Jack Johnson the greatest fighter ever to climb into a ring. He had a heavyweight's power but a lightweight's grace, displaying the strength of a bull, the speed of a panther, and a punch like the kick of a mule. He was the first black to become world heavyweight boxing champion. Racial prejudice and Johnson's deportment combined to cloud recognition of his great talent.

Johnson was born in Galveston, Tex., son of a devout black school janitor. Quitting school after the fifth grade, Jack Johnson became a milkwagon helper at $1.25 a week. He later worked in a livery stable and as a baker's apprentice. While working on the docks he thrashed the local bully, but was reproached by his pious parents, who disliked fighting. He hung around a gym and showed great promise as a boxer. Restless, he left home to roam the nation, hopping freight trains and living by odd jobs, begging, and gambling.

Returning to the Galveston docks, he gained local fame by knocking out a professional boxer traveling with a circus, who promised $5 to anyone who could last four rounds. This gave him a start fighting as a semiprofessional in Galveston. Roaming again, he worked on a Florida fishing boat, then rode the rails northward, becoming a professional boxer by 1897. In Chicago he became a sparring mate for a West Indian fighter, Joe Walcott of Barbados, who polished Johnson's style. Walcott later became welterweight champ, 1901–1904, the first black titleholder in that division. Overmatched against an experienced black heavyweight known as Klondike, Johnson was knocked out for the first time. After joining a troupe of touring boxers, he knocked out Klondike several times. Johnson also learned a lot from a top-ranking heavyweight, Joe Choyinski (a Polish Jew), who knocked him out in a Galveston bout that landed both in jail for three weeks, since professional boxing was illegal in Texas. Sparring daily with Choyinski to entertain their jailers, he received valuable lessons in dodging blows.

Thereafter, Johnson crisscrossed the nation, fighting dozens of bouts in many places. His first wife deserted him and the next woman he took up with broke his heart by running off with another man, stealing his belongings. Thenceforward, Johnson shunned black women and concentrated on blondes, angering the public and causing him trouble.

In 1902, he beat George Gardner, who claimed the lightheavyweight championship. But Gardner was not recognized as champion until the following year, when that division was officially established. From 1902 through 1907, Johnson won 57 bouts, many against the leading black heavyweights such as Sam Langford and Joe Jeannette. Among his victims was Bob Fitzsimmons, who was world heavyweight champ from 1897 to 1899 but was in his mid-40s when Johnson kayoed him in 1906. After Fitzsimmons's successor, James J. Jeffries, retired in 1905 after six years as undefeated world heavyweight champion, the title was held by mediocre fighters Marvin Hart and Tommy Burns.

Burns, a Canadian, ducked Johnson for two years but finally agreed to a title bout in Australia on Christmas Day, 1908. Burns was no match. Johnson toyed with and taunted him, and as was his custom, carried on a running conversation with ringsiders while humiliating his hapless foe. Johnson was so superb and outclassed his opponents so far in his prime that only Langford gave him any trouble. But many spectators, failing to see that Johnson's great ability made it hard for him to take his foes seriously, detested Johnson for what they considered his arrogance, lack of sportsmanship, and clowning in the ring. When the fight with Burns was stopped by police in the fourteenth round to save the helpless Burns from severe injury, Johnson became world champion.

Thus a black man became heavyweight titleholder at a time when racist concepts of white superiority enjoyed wide circulation and popularity. There were earlier black boxing champions, like featherweight George Dixon (1892–1900) and lightweight Joe Gans (1901–1908), but the heavyweight crown had far greater prestige and publicity. Immediately a search began for a "great white hope" to restore the title to the superior race. At once claims went up that the retired champion, Jim Jeffries was still the champ. Unless Johnson beat him, his claim to the title was suspect in the eyes of prejudiced whites. Great pressure was mounted on Jeffries to make him come out of retirement. Meanwhile, in

1909, Johnson knocked out middleweight champion Stanley Ketchel, 35 pounds lighter than him. He also fought exhibitions with several out-classed foes including Victor McLaglen (who later turned actor and won Hollywood's Academy Award in 1935). On July 4, 1910, Johnson easily knocked out The Great White Hope, Jeffries, at Reno, Nev. This bout was Johnson's biggest payday, earning him more than $100,000 in pre-income tax, noninflated dollars. Fatal racial rioting occurred in many places in America after the Burns and Jeffries fights.

Johnson successfully defended his title four more times, once in 1912, twice in 1913, and again in 1914, also winning a nontitle bout late in 1914 and an exhibition early in 1915. He held the heavyweight crown until April 5, 1915, when, past his prime and badly out of condition, he was knocked out in a controversial, 26-round bout in Havana, Cuba, by the much younger, bigger, and stronger Jess Willard. Johnson later claimed that he threw the fight, but ring experts agree that he did not take Willard seriously and was not in shape to handle a man who was in excellent condition.

Meanwhile, Johnson's personal misfortunes and fast living con-tributed to his decline. He drank heavily and partied into the late hours, often with the blondes who hung around his nightclub and his training quarters. He married three white women; the first committed suicide in 1912 after 20 months of marriage, the second divorced him in 1924 after 12 years of marriage, and the third, whom he took in 1925, re-mained by him to the end. He was convicted in 1913 on trumped-up Mann Act charges pressed relentlessly by white reformers and prose-cutors through a blonde hanger-on who chased after him and lived and traveled with him before he ditched her. Johnson fled the country to avoid imprisonment. With wife and handlers, he lived abroad for seven years. Returning from exile, he served in Leavenworth Prison for ten months. Subsequently, he resumed his ring career, but mostly lived by appearances in theaters, vaudeville, traveling shows, and boxing ex-hibitions, fighting as late as 1945. A reckless driver with many speed-ing tickets, Johnson lost his life in a crash in North Carolina.

All the unfavorable publicity and the bitterness of many whites to-ward this flamboyant noncomformist could not obscure his merits in the eyes of unprejudiced experts. Boxing's greatest authority, Nat Fleischer —longtime editor of boxing's bible, *Ring Magazine*—ranked him the greatest heavyweight fighter of all time, listing Jack Dempsey fourth and Joe Louis (*q.v.*) sixth. Johnson was elected in the first group chosen for Boxing's Hall of Fame when it opened in 1954.

Johnson, James Weldon (1871–1938), Poet and Reformer

Best known for his poetry, James Weldon Johnson was a Renaissance man in his versatility. He was a poet, novelist, lyricist, essayist, librettist, critic, translator, anthologist, and historian. But he was also a school principal, editor, lawyer, vaudevillian, college professor, and diplomat. Moreover, he was a leader in the national NAACP for fourteen years, including a decade as its first black Executive Secretary.

Johnson was born in Jacksonville, Fla., son of a headwaiter in a leading hotel. His self-taught father was a Virginian who had been a headwaiter in New York where he met his wife. A native of Nassau in the Bahamas, his mother had been raised in New York City. Both of his parents loved literature and music, but his mother also was a choir singer and an amateur poet and artist. A white neighbor became Johnson's white mammy and lifelong friend when his mother was unable to nurse him. After finishing grade school, Johnson was sent to the high school department of Atlanta University because Jacksonville made no provision for secondary education for blacks. On finishing high school, he entered the college where he was a top-ranking student, athlete, campus leader, and singer in the fund-raising, touring college quartet. Teaching school in Georgia's cotton belt one summer introduced him to downtrodden rural blacks.

After graduating from Atlanta University in 1894, Johnson became principal of the Stanton School in Jacksonville. Tactfully, he expanded it by simply having his eighth-graders repeat for enough additional years of advanced work to carry them through high school. When confronted with his *fait accompli*, school officials assented to this quiet revolution so that Jacksonville now formally began high school training for blacks. Meanwhile, Johnson founded and edited a short-lived newspaper, the *Daily American*, and also studied law by reading for the bar in a white lawyer's office. In 1897 he became the first black ever admitted to the Florida bar through open examination in court. He practiced law in time he spared after performing his duties as principal.

But his first loves, poetry and songwriting, came to the fore when his brother, John Rosamond Johnson, two years his junior, returned from studying at the Conservatory of Music in Boston. They collaborated on songs, James doing the words, John the music. For a Lincoln's birthday observance in 1900, they wrote a song, "Lift Every Voice and Sing," first sung at the celebration by a children's chorus from Jacksonville's black schools. This widely-used, majestic song has come to be known as the Negro National Anthem.

In 1901, the brothers gave up their posts as principal and music teacher, respectively, in the Jacksonville school system. They moved to New York City to try their hand in writing songs for Tin Pan Alley and for the black musical comedies of the day. They soon were friends of the leading composers, lyricists, and performers of the day, including Bob Cole, Will Cook, Paul L. Dunbar, Harry Burleigh, and Bert Williams (*qq.v.*). The Johnson brothers teamed with Cole to form a highly successful vaudeville troupe. The hit songs written by this team were sung not only by black performers but by the leading white popular singers of the day, including Lillian Russell and May Irwin. Among their hits were "Under the Bamboo Tree," "The Congo Love Song," "Since You Went Away," and "The Maiden with the Dreamy Eyes." James helped his brother and Cole with their hit operetta, *The Shoofly Regiment* (1906).

Meanwhile, Johnson had been studying literature at Columbia University. In 1904, he worked in President Theodore Roosevelt's successful election campaign. His reward came with diplomatic posts as the American Consul at Puerto Cabello, Venezuela, from 1906–1909 and at Corinto, Nicaragua, from 1909–1913. Charming, urbane, and tactful, Johnson proved an able diplomat. While consul, he published anonymously *The Autobiography of an Ex-Colored Man* (1912), a novel about a mulatto who passed for white.

Returning to America after the Democrats came to power under Woodrow Wilson, he became editor of the New York *Age*, and wrote editorials and columns for this Negro weekly for ten years. After he translated the libretto of the opera *Goyescas* it was performed at the Metropolitan Opera in the 1915–1916 season. In 1917, he published a collection of his verse, *Fifty Years and Other Poems*. His critical anthology, *The Book of American Negro Poetry*, appeared in 1922. With his brother, he edited *The Book of American Negro Spirituals* (1925), followed by a second volume in 1926. His best work was *God's Trombones: Seven Negro Sermons in Verse* (1927). One poem in this book, "The Creation," remains an extremely popular declamation piece. Johnson was the elder statesman of the Harlem Renaissance, and an inspiration to younger talents.

Meanwhile, Johnson had gone to work for the NAACP. Serving as field secretary from 1916 to 1920, he traveled about building up branches. He helped organize the huge, silent parade in New York City in 1917 to protest the East St. Louis riots. He led a delegation to President Wilson to plead for clemency for black soldiers condemned for their part in the Houston riot of 1917. In 1920, he investigated and presented facts on the brutal occupation of Haiti by American Marines. Later that year, he moved up to the post of Executive Secretary of the

NAACP, the first black in the position. He led the fight for the Dyer Anti-Lynching Bill and raised funds for the successful defense of the Sweet family of Detroit, who were tried for firing fatal shots into a mob besieging their home in a previously all-white neighborhood. He served ably until 1930 when he went on leave to be succeeded by Walter White (*q.v.*) in 1931 and by Roy Wilkins (*q.v.*) in 1955, both of whom, like Johnson, came from writing backgrounds.

In 1931, Johnson joined the faculty of Fisk University in Nashville, Tenn., teaching creative writing. His *Black Manhattan* (1930) is a revealing insider's history of blacks in New York, especially in the theatrical world. Among his other books in the 1930s was his autobiography, *Along This Way* (1933). Beginning in 1934, he served as a visiting professor each fall quarter in New York University. His career ended in an automobile accident near his summer home in Maine.

Johnson, John H. (1918–   ), Publisher

John Harold Johnson is one of America's leading publishers. The Johnson Publishing Company grosses about $12 million a year from its four magazines and its book publishing. His leading magazines, the monthly *Ebony* and weekly *Jet*, have circulations of 1,138,412 and 453,095, respectively. By far the leading publisher in the history of black America, he is also one of the wealthiest and most successful businessmen his race has ever had.

An only child, Johnson was born in Arkansas City, Ark., son of a sawmill worker. When he was only 6, he lost his father in a mill accident. His mother, a domestic servant, later married another millworker. When Johnson was 15, his mother took him on a week's visit to the Chicago World's Fair. They decided to stay and his stepfather joined them. They lived on relief for eighteen months until the stepfather received a WPA job and Johnson became a part-time worker under the National Youth Administration's work-relief program. The fact that Chicago playmates laughed at his home-made clothes gave Johnson added impetus to become a success. He was an honor student at DuSable High School as well as class president, a debater, managing editor of the school newspaper and yearbook, and student council president.

In 1936, he was asked to speak at the annual Chicago Urban League banquet in honor of high school seniors. Harry Pace, president of the largest black business in the North, Supreme Liberty Life Insurance Company of Chicago, gave the main address. Impressed by Johnson, he hired him as his office boy and aided his part-time study for two years at the University of Chicago. In 1938, Johnson became Pace's assistant, continuing his studies at the School of Commerce on Northwestern University's Chicago campus for two more years at night. Having majored in journalism and business in college, Johnson then devoted himself full-time to Supreme Liberty.

One of his duties was preparing a summary of news about blacks for use by Pace in the company's house organ. Finding great interest among acquaintances in such a condensation, Johnson borrowed $500 in 1942, using his mother's furniture as collateral. He mailed letters to 20,000 Supreme Liberty customers offering charter subscriptions at $2.00 to a new magazine, *Negro Digest*. Three thousand responded. His monthly *Negro Digest* began in November, 1942, with a press run of 5,000 copies, which sold out in a week. By October, 1943, circulation was 50,000. When he conceived a series, "If I Were a Negro," with Mrs. Eleanor Roosevelt leading off, circulation jumped to more than 100,000.

In November, 1945, Johnson launched a picture magazine, *Ebony*, which quickly sold out its first press run of 25,000. Patterned after *Life*, his slick picture magazine soon attracted major advertisers, making it the first black magazine with substantial ads from firms selling to the general public. Through aggressive salesmanship, neglected by other black publishers, Johnson's publications are still the only black magazines with significant general advertising. In 1967, *Ebony* reached the million mark in circulation (putting it among the nation's top fifty magazines) and had yearly advertising revenues of $7 million.

In 1950, Johnson launched a sensationalist monthly, *Tan Confessions*, which has now been converted into a more sedate woman's magazine under the title *Tan*. Its circulation is 125,000. In 1951, he brought out *Jet* as a pocket-sized weekly news magazine. A feature magazine called *Hue* was dropped soon after its start in 1951. *Negro Digest* was suspended in 1951, but revived ten years later as a monthly literary magazine emphasizing black militancy. Without ads and with a circulation of only 50,000, *Negro Digest* loses money, but Johnson carries it to give a voice to a different perspective than his other, slick, success-story oriented magazines. Since 1962, his company has also published books.

Johnson began buying Supreme Life stock in 1955, becoming chief stockholder in 1964. He is now board chairman of the company for which he began as an office boy. He also owns a cosmetics company. In 1951 Johnson became the first black ever to be named one of the ten outstanding young men of the year by the Junior Chamber of Commerce.

Jones, LeRoi (1934–   ), Militant Poet-Playwriter and Separatist

Everett LeRoi Jones began his career as an avant-garde poet living a bohemian life among whites in Greenwich Village. Giving up on racist America, he became an ardent black nationalist and separatist, immersing himself in cultural and political activities in the black ghetto.

Jones was born into comfortable, middle-class circumstances in Newark, N.J., his father a postal supervisor and his mother a social worker. He had one sister. In seventh grade at Central Avenue School, he created a comic strip, "The Crime Wave," and wrote science fiction for the school magazine at Barringer High. A bright pupil, he graduated from high school two years ahead of his age group. He first attended the Newark extension of Rutgers University and then entered Howard University in Washington, D.C., graduating in 1953. Originally interested in becoming a minister, he majored in English. He did graduate work at the New School for Social Research in New York and then served a hitch in the Air Force, where he continued writing poetry.

Upon his discharge, he settled in New York, and did graduate work at Columbia University. He soon became a notable figure in the Beat Generation literary movement in Greenwich Village. He married a white girl, publishing one of the better underground poetry magazines, *Yugen*, with her. He also co-edited an underground literary newsletter. In the late 1950s and early 1960s, he was lecturing on poetry, writing, and theater arts at the New School and Columbia. He was a co-founder of the American Theatre for Poets, an avant-garde dramatic troupe started in 1961 in the Village. He read his poetry in Village coffee houses. A visit to Cuba in 1960 made him a political activist and convinced him that America was decadent and doomed with only Afro-Americans having rightful claims to survive in the coming new world.

Considering himself primarily a poet, Jones has published several volumes of his verse, notably *Preface to a Twenty Volume Suicide Note* (1961) and *The Dead Lecturer* (1964). But he is best known for his controversial plays. In March, 1964, *The Dutchman* opened at the Cherry Lane Theater off Broadway and ran until the following February. A shocking confrontation in searing language between a taunting white prostitute and a middle-class minded black intellectual, it won the Obie Award as Off Broadway's best play in 1964. During the 1964–1965 season, the St. Mark's Playhouse off Broadway ran a twin bill of his even more shocking short plays, *The Toilet* and *The Slave*.

Thereafter, Jones gave up trying to address whites and focused on his own people. He left his wife and children in 1965, and settled in Harlem. He published an autobiographical novel, *The System of Dante's*

Hell (1965), and founded a cultural workshop, the Black Arts Repertory Theatre. In 1966, he moved his cultural center to the Newark ghetto, setting up in a slum building called Spirit House. Arrested in 1967 for illegally possessing a gun during the Newark riot, he was given a two-to-three-year sentence in 1968 by a judge who disliked Jones's published ideas. He remains out on appeal bond. In 1968, he formed a black nationalist group, patterned after Ron Karenga's Los Angeles group, US. Jones's Black Community Development and Defense Organization adopted African dress, Swahili as a second language, and the Kawaida branch of the Muslim religion. Jones became the group's minister or Imamu. Meanwhile, he married a black divorcée. He, his wife, their son, and her three daughters have African names and wear African garb. Jones is active in Newark politics and racial confrontations.

Besides his plays and activism, LeRoi Jones is perhaps best known for his critiques of Afro-American music, *Blues People* (1963) and *Black Music* (1967). He has written many essays and articles, published a collection of essays, *Home* (1966), and has edited several anthologies of poetry such as *The Moderns* (1963). Among plays he wrote for his black workshops is *Slave Ship*. Eldridge Cleaver of the Black Panthers is another militant writer, but differs from Jones in that he favors allying with white radicals.

Julian, Percy (1899–   ), Research Chemist

Next to George Washington Carver and Charles Drew (*qq.v.*), who passed away in 1943 and 1950, respectively, Percy Lavon Julian is America's best known black scientist. The research of this distinguished industrial chemist for the Glidden Company and for his own Julian Laboratories resulted in the discovery of vital new uses for soybeans.

Julian was the eldest of six children born in Montgomery, Ala., to a railway mail clerk and his schoolteacher wife. Julian's grandfather was a slave whose right hand was mutilated as punishment for his trying to learn to read. Julian's parents assigned their children topics to research and books to review to be presented before the whole family. Public schools for blacks in Montgomery were limited to the eighth grade. Passing the white high school on his way home from school one day, Percy climbed a fence to watch students working in the chemistry laboratory. A white policeman pulled him down and told him to run along because that was not for him. But his parents encouraged his ambition to be a chemist. He attended the State Normal School in Montgomery where he received some high school grounding while taking teacher training.

Upon graduating from Alabama State in 1916, he entered De Pauw University in Greencastle, Ind., but his early training was so inadequate that he was classified as a sub-freshman for two years. He carried a double load of high school deficiency subjects and regular college courses. To help pay his way, he slept in the attic of the white fraternity house where he waited tables, played in a jazz band, and tended furnaces. Yet, he became a Phi Beta Kappa and graduated in 1920 as the class valedictorian. Dean William Blanchard, who was also professor of chemistry, had tried to discourage him from majoring in chemistry, fearing that there was no future for blacks in it. But he persisted in his choice of major and was later elected to the Sigma Xi science research honor society. His family was so delighted at his success at De Pauw that his mother and the other children moved to Greencastle so that they could attend college. Remaining at his job in Alabama, his father sent the bulk of his wages to them. All six children graduated from De Pauw, and Julian's three sisters went on to get master's degrees, two becoming Y.W.C.A. workers and one a teacher, while his two brothers went on to secure doctorates and become practicing physicians.

Despite his being the top graduate, Julian's teachers did not award him a fellowship for graduate study in chemistry, because they considered his color a bar to success in the field. Instead, he went to Fisk University in Nashville, Tenn., where he taught chemistry for two years. He was a very able teacher and when he sent Dean Blanchard a copy of his lectures, his former professor was so impressed that he encouraged him to study further. Julian applied at Harvard, and received the Austin Fellowship in chemistry, 1922–1923. Making all A's, he earned his Master's degree in 1923. Had he been white, he would have been made a teaching assistant while he went on to study toward a doctorate, but Harvard officials feared that their white students from the South would not accept him. Instead, he was granted research assistantships of a lesser status, enabling him to study biophysics and chemistry at Harvard from 1923 to 1926.

Julian taught chemistry at West Virginia State College for Negroes in 1926 and 1927, then became associate professor and acting head of the chemistry department at Howard University in Washington, D.C., 1927 to 1929. Meanwhile, he had been doing research along the lines mapped out by the famed Dr. Ernst Späth, who had synthesized nicotine. In 1929, with a General Education Board fellowship, Julian went to study at the University of Vienna under Dr. Späth, receiving his Ph.D. in organic chemistry in 1931. He returned to Howard as full professor and department head, 1931–1932, and then joined the faculty of his alma mater, De Pauw, as research fellow and teacher of organic chemistry, for four years. At De Pauw, he synthesized a drug, physostigmine, used in treating glaucoma. He boldly challenged the recently published findings of that drug's chemical structure made by the world-renowned head of Oxford University's chemistry department, Sir Robert Robinson, and was proved right. Dean Blanchard wanted to make him head of the department but his colleagues balked at the idea of a black leader.

Meanwhile, the Glidden Company of Chicago, manufacturers of paint, varnish, food products, and chemical goods, asked Julian to do soybean research as director of Glidden's soya products division. He accepted and held that post from 1936 until 1953, and also took over as manager of Glidden's fine chemicals development division in 1945. More than fifty chemists served on the staff under him. He perfected a soya protein, cheaper than milk casein, for use in coating paper. National Foam Company engineers used Julian's soya protein to make the Aero-Foam extinguisher widely used by the Navy in World War II to put out oil and gasoline fires. The research of Julian and his associates led to Glidden's being able to manufacture in quantity soya sterols (crystals), testosterone and progesterone (male and female hormones). From soybean sterols, he also devised "Compound S," an inexpensive substitute for the costly hormone cortisone used in treating arthritis.

His work with "Compound S" led him to set up his own Julian Laboratories, Inc., in Franklin Park, Ill., in 1954, with a companion laboratory in Mexico City in 1955. He now made "Compound S" from a Mexican plant at lower cost than from soybeans. His laboratory manufactured other drugs also. In 1961, his companies were merged with a large Philadelphia drug firm.

Dr. Julian published more than a hundred scientific papers and held more than fifty patents. He became a millionaire. Yet, when he purchased a home in the Oak Park suburb of Chicago in 1951, he was threatened, his son and daughter were harassed, and attempts were made to bomb and burn him out. He stood firm, hiring armed guards to protect his home for two years. Finally, he gained acceptance and one of his children was elected student council president.

Among the other notable black scientists of Julian's day were dermatologist Theodore Lawless, statistician David Blackwell, syphilologist William Hinton, chemists Lloyd Hall, Robert Barnes, and Lloyd Ferguson, physicists Elmer Imes and Herman Branson, and pathologist Julian Lewis.

Just, Ernest E. (1883–1941), Biologist

The first recipient of the highly coveted Spingarn award was an unassuming young biologist, Ernest Everett Just. This gold medal is presented annually by the NAACP "to the man or woman of African descent and American citizenship, who shall have made the highest achievement during the preceding year or years in any honorable field of endeavor." When Just received it in 1915, he was only in his early 30s and had not completed his studies for the doctorate. But he had already achieved distinction in his field by publishing half a dozen important scientific papers based on his research on egg fertilization and the functioning of cells.

Just was born in Charleston, S.C., the eldest of three children of a wharf builder. His father and grandfather had together erected some of the largest docks in Charleston. But Just's father passed away when the lad was only 4 years old. Just's mother was a Charleston schoolteacher who, when widowed, worked in, and aided residents of, the phosphate fields community three miles outside Charleston. Opening a school and church there, she persuaded the phosphate laborers to form the town of Maryville, and she sold her own property to found an industrial school there.

After going to his mother's school, Just spent six years, until he was 17, in secondary training at the State College for blacks in Orangeburg. Wishing to continue his studies at Kimball Academy, a Northern institution he had read about in a religious newspaper, he left South Carolina in 1900, working his way to New York City on a Clyde Line ship. He worked in the city a month to earn train fare to Meriden, N.H., site of Kimball Academy. To his disappointment, despite his earlier training, he was placed in the lowest class, meaning four more years of study to finish high school. But he worked hard and completed all the work in only three years, becoming president of the debating society and editor of the school newspaper. He then attended Dartmouth College at Hanover, N.H., on scholarships and loans. Dedicated to intellectual pursuits, he was demoralized to find the students wrapped up in football instead. He became indifferent to his own studies and was ready to quit during his second year. Then, during his first course in biology, he became absorbed in science through reading a paper on the development of the egg. He switched his major from the classics to biology, making cytology (the study of cells) his lifelong work. He took all of Dartmouth's biology offerings and began research in his senior year. He was the sole *magna cum laude* graduate in his class, received a Phi Beta Kappa key, and was the only student to take special honors in two subjects.

Upon graduating from Dartmouth in 1907, Just joined the faculty of Howard University in Washington, D.C., where he taught, except for short leaves, for the remainder of his career. At the beginning he taught English as well as science, and he helped found Howard's drama group. In the summer of 1909, Just went to Woods Hole, Mass., to do research and study at the Marine Biological Laboratory with Dr. Frank Lillie. Just reveled in pure scientific research and returned there every summer but two from 1909 to 1930. He became a leading authority, doing experiments that contributed to later cancer research. Eventually he became a colleague of Lillie's and a member of the Corporation (ruling board) of the laboratory.

Just took leave from Howard during the 1915–1916 school year to study at the University of Chicago, where he received the Ph.D. in zoology and physiology in 1916. He published sixty papers in the leading journals and wrote two books, both published in 1939, *Basic Methods for Experiments of Marine Animals* and *The Biology of the Cell Surface.* He was elected vice-president of the American Society of Zoologists and served on the editorial boards of such scholarly journals as *Biological Bulletin* and the *Journal of Morphology.* He became the only black to have a star (designating distinction) beside his name in the authoritative compilation, *American Men of Science.* During the 1930s, aided by Rosenwald, General Education Board, and Carnegie grants, he left Woods Hole, doing his research at biological institutes and marine laboratories in Berlin, Paris, and Naples.

Part of the reason for his immersion in his research was his frustration, bitterness, and sensitivity over rebuffs arising from color. He suffered in the restrictive, segregated atmosphere of Washington, D.C., but was not invited, despite his stature, to the staff of any major Northern institution. The Rockefeller Institute closed its doors to him. He deserved to be president, not just vice president, of the national zoological society.

Another early black biologist, Charles Henry Turner (1867–1923) also had a Ph.D. from the University of Chicago and published 49 papers on invertebrates in major journals. Although he was an authority on insect behavior, Turner's career was spent teaching at Sumner High School in St. Louis. Just's daughter, Margaret Butcher, long a professor of English at Howard University, wrote a widely-used account of black cultural contributions, based on materials assembled by her father's friend, Professor Alain Locke (*q.v.*).

King, Martin Luther, Jr. (1929–1968), Apostle of Nonviolence

Martin Luther King, Jr., attracted broader support than any other black leader in American history. He had a strong appeal to diverse blacks, from humble Southern peasants to sophisticated Northern intellectuals, from devout, elderly, rural churchgoers to skeptical young radicals on college campuses. He also attracted more ardent and active support from whites, especially liberals and college students, than any other black leader.

During a decade of nonviolent demonstrations, from the Montgomery bus boycott of 1955–1956 through the Selma March of 1965, he helped to revolutionize the status of the Southern black. He thus ended the segregation and disfranchisement that Booker T. Washington tacitly accepted in the Atlanta Compromise of 1895.

King was born in Atlanta. Originally he was named Michael Luther King, Jr., but during his childhood, his father changed the first name of his son and himself to Martin. King's mother had been a schoolteacher before her marriage. Her father, the Reverend Alfred Daniel Williams, had founded Ebenezer Baptist Church in Atlanta in 1895. King's father succeeded his father-in-law as pastor of Ebenezer in 1932. The senior King built the church into one of Atlanta's more important black churches.

King came from a militant heritage. His grandfather, Reverend Williams, was a founding member of the Atlanta chapter of the NAACP. Reverend Williams was a leader in the drive by Atlanta blacks in the 1920s to defeat bond issues until a high school was promised to blacks; there had been white public high schools in Atlanta for half a century before then. The grandfather also led a boycott that put out of business a newspaper that ridiculed the blacks for their fight for equal schooling. As a boy, King learned militancy from his father's example. When a traffic cop, in the customary insulting manner of Southern whites, called Reverend King "Boy," he angrily pointed to his son, retorting, "That's a boy. I'm a man." When the clerk in a downtown store told King and his father to move to the rear of the store, Reverend King refused, saying "We'll either buy shoes sitting here or we won't buy any shoes at all." He then stalked out of the store with his son.

King attended the public schools of Atlanta, including Booker T. Washington High School that had opened in 1924 as a result of the fight his grandfather and other NAACP leaders had waged. Having been skipped at the ninth- and twelfth-grade levels, King was only 15 when he entered his father's alma mater, Morehouse College in Atlanta. He planned to be a doctor, but soon found that he wasn't cut out for science courses and switched his major from premedical to sociology. Before the end of his junior year, however, he was so influenced by the college president, Benjamin Mays, and by such professors as George Kelsey that he decided to go into the ministry. Accordingly, he was ordained in his father's church in 1947.

Upon graduating from Morehouse in 1948, King entered Crozer Theological Seminary in Chester, Pa. One of only six blacks among the 100 students, he became president of the senior class, won the Plafker Award as the most outstanding student, and was awarded the Crozer Fellowship for graduate study at any university he chose. He started at the School of Theology at Boston University in 1951, also taking two years of philosophy courses at Harvard. In Boston, he met and married an Antioch College graduate, Coretta Scott from Marion, Ala., who was studying voice at the New England Conservatory of Music.

After completing his coursework and starting the research on his doctoral dissertation, King accepted a call in 1954 to become pastor of the Dexter Avenue Baptist Church in Montgomery, Ala., near the state capitol building. King had had several offers of Northern pastorates, but decided to return to the South and make this church the beginning of his full-time ministry. During his first year at Dexter Avenue, he completed his dissertation and received the Ph.D. degree from Boston University in 1955.

The arrest of Rosa Parks on December 1, 1955, for refusing to surrender her seat on a bus to a white man triggered a boycott of the buses by Montgomery's blacks. They turned to Dr. King to lead the boycott. Using Gandhi's principles of passive resistance, he held them together united and nonviolent for 381 days, despite harassment, provocation, and violence by whites, including the bombing of King's home. The boycott was called off in December, 1956, after a court ruling ended segregated seating.

Black America had found a new leader. In 1957, he brought together Southern black ministers to begin organizing what would become the Southern Christian Leadership Conference (SCLC) to carry on nonviolent crusades against the evils of second-class citizenship throughout the South. Late in 1959, he gave up his pastorate in Montgomery and moved to Atlanta to serve as co-pastor with his father at Ebenezer, a post he held until the end. The sit-in movement by black college students, inspired partly by King, led to formation of the Student Nonviolent Coordinating Committee (SNCC) in 1960 under King's auspices. His crusades failed to dent white intransigence in some places, especially St. Augustine, Fla., but he was notably successful in the results of the

Birmingham demonstrations of 1963 and the Selma March of 1965 that led, respectively, to the Civil Rights Acts of 1964 and 1965.

King reached the peak of his influence on America when he concluded his "I have a dream" oration at Lincoln Memorial during the August 28, 1963, March on Washington. He was awarded the Nobel Peace Prize in 1964, a prize won by only two other blacks, America's Ralph Bunche (*q.v.*) and South Africa's Albert Luthuli. King wrote half a dozen books including *Stride Toward Freedom: The Montgomery Story* (1958), *Strength to Love* (1963), *Why We Can't Wait* (1964), and *Where Do We Go from Here: Chaos or Community?* (1967).

King had greater success against the obvious injustices of Southern segregation and disfranchisement than against the hard-core problems of joblessness, underemployment, inadequate training, poorly-funded schools, ill housing, and poverty that ground down many blacks nationwide. When he conducted open housing marches in white neighborhoods in Chicago in 1966, he encountered rock-throwing mobs and greater race hatred than he had ever seen in the South. Out of sympathy at first with the Black Power ideas of young militants in SNCC, he came to see its merits increasingly. He still insisted on nonviolence, however, as the only approach that would heal and unite rather than divide and increase mutual hatred. In 1967, he came out against the Vietnam War as a drain on American energies and funds needed to improve conditions at home.

In March, 1968, King called for a Poor People's March on Washington to demonstrate the need for greater Federal action. But on April 4, 1968, while helping sanitation workers on strike in Memphis, Tenn., he was killed by a hired assassin, James Earl Ray. More than 150,000 persons, including Robert Kennedy, Hubert Humphrey, Nelson Rockefeller, and Richard Nixon, came to Atlanta to attend his funeral at Ebenezer Baptist Church and to walk behind the mule cart bearing his body to the memorial service on the Morehouse campus. The shock of his death led to the passage of the Civil Rights Act of 1968 to provide for open housing and for protection to civil rights workers. The SCLC, under his successor, Ralph Abernathy, supported by his widow, Coretta Scott King, held the Poor People's March in June, 1968. The brutal slaying of the leading apostle of nonviolence strengthened the hands of militants who had been saying for many months that nonviolence was futile and that Americans don't respect or heed a defenseless man. In 1969, SNCC dropped the word Nonviolent from its title, substituting National.

America may never again see a black leader with as broad an appeal as King. The increasingly disparate conditions of the 25,000,000 blacks make it unlikely that so many will enlist again under one banner or behind one leader as they did for King's nonviolent crusades. His day was a dream world when it seemed that merely walking through streets protesting peacefully and suffering brutality in silence would awaken the American conscience enough to usher in the millennium. The extent to which this dream became a nightmare instead is an index of the degree to which the racism King optimistically hoped to erase permeates America.

Leidesdorff, William (1810–1848), Pioneer Merchant and Diplomat

William Alexander Leidesdorff was a pioneer merchant, landowner, and civil leader in pre-gold rush California. As vice consul to American Consul Thomas Larkin, he was active in the intrigues leading to California's gaining freedom from Mexico.

Leidesdorff was born on the island of St. Croix in the Danish West Indies (now the Virgin Islands). His father was a Danish sugar planter named William Leidesdorff, his mother a mulatto islander named Anna Marie Spark. They were not legally married and their son was born out of wedlock, but in 1837, under Denmark's flexible laws, the father legalized his son in court, making him his heir. The son spoke many languages fluently in later life and gave evidence of being well educated and highly refined.

He came to the United States, settling in New Orleans and taking out naturalization papers in 1834 in the Federal Eastern District of Louisiana. He became a ship captain sailing on vessels between New Orleans and New York, later moving to New York. On one trip, Captain Leidesdorff sailed from New York to the Hawaiian Islands.

In 1841, he served as the pilot for the 106-ton schooner *Julia Ann*, which sailed from New York around South America to California. The vessel was owned by J. D. Jones of New York, the American Consul in Hawaii. Leidesdorff sailed in California coastal waters, then settled down in the village of Yerba Buena (now San Francisco) after Jones sold the vessel late in 1841.

Leidesdorff went into business as a merchant in Yerba Buena, importing goods for sale in California and selling supplies to ships that visited San Francisco Bay. The village, founded in 1836, had only thirty families when he moved there. He became prosperous, and travelers' accounts indicate that he was one of the most prominent men of Yerba Buena. In 1844 he built a warehouse on the beach. That year he also built the City Hotel, the first in San Francisco, on land he had bought at the corner of what is now Clay and Kearney Streets.

Since California was ruled by Mexico, many American settlers, including Leidesdorff, took out Mexican citizenship to gain such advantages as grants of land. Leidesdorff gained his Mexican citizenship in 1844 and received from the Mexican government a grant of 35,000 acres of land in the Sacramento Valley. Located along the left bank of the American River, the grant was called Rio del Rancho Americano. It adjoined the land of John Sutter.

Becoming a friend of Thomas Larkin, the only American Consul in California, Leidesdorff entered diplomatic work. Larkin was stationed at Monterey, then capital of California. He asked Leidesdorff to help him, appointing him American vice consul (also called sub-consul) for the Port of San Francisco, a post Leidesdorff held from 1845 until July, 1846. Many letters were exchanged between Larkin and Leidesdorff as American settlers plotted for California's revolt from Mexico. Leidesdorff met with Captain John Fremont. He helped Commander John Montgomery free San Francisco from Mexican rule. He translated into Spanish for all to read Commodore John Sloat's July 9, 1846, proclamation that California was part of the United States. When Sloat's successor, Commodore Robert Stockton, visited San Francisco in September, 1846, he was honored at a ball in Leidesdorff's house. A bachelor, Leidesdorff had the most imposing house in the city and gave many lavish parties with hundreds of guests.

Leidesdorff was active in civic affairs in San Francisco, the name Yerba Buena took in 1847. He was elected to the first city council, becoming the treasurer. He chaired the investigating committee that cleared the first American mayor, Washington Bartlett, of charges of misuse of funds. Leidesdorff was also a member of the four-man committee that set up San Francisco's first public schools. Late in 1847, Leidesdorff introduced the first steamboat to California. Hoping to speed transportation from San Francisco to Sacramento, he bought a steamer built by an American at Sitka, Alaska, for Russians. It proved unsuitable, taking six days for a trip a man could walk in less time, and the venture failed. He also staged California's first horse race, in 1847.

When he passed away suddenly from brain fever in 1848, there was an imposing funeral procession with gun salutes and flags at half-mast. He was buried in San Francisco's oldest building, Mission Dolores. His land so increased in value with the gold discoveries that his estate was worth $1,500,000. Army quartermaster Captain Joseph Libby Folsom bought it from Leidesdorff's mother, who was still living in St. Croix, for only $75,000. Folsom City now occupies part of the tract. Leidesdorff

Street is a small street in San Francisco named in honor of this black pioneer.

Lewis, Edmonia (1845–1890), Sculptor

Mary Edmonia Lewis was the first black woman in America to be a sculptor. For a while, in the 1870s, her neo-classical works were much in demand.

She was born in Albany, N.Y. Her father was black, her mother a Chippewa Indian. Orphaned early, she evidently grew up mostly with her mother's tribe, also living for a while in an orphanage. Little is known of her early training, but she apparently attended grade school sporadically.

She attended Oberlin College where she was involved in a scandal. Earlier doubts about her attendance and about the scandal were dispelled by a recent article of Professor Geoffrey Blodgett, based on his search of college records and local newspapers. She entered Oberlin's Preparatory Department in 1859, boarding with a dozen white girls at the home of a member of the college board. Considered wild earlier, she now applied herself satisfactorily. In January, 1862, however, during the mid-term recess, she apparently tried to play a prank on two fellow boarders who were going on a sleigh ride. Fixing them a drink of hot spiced wine, she slipped in a passion-stimulating drug. The lark backfired when they became ill on the ride.

They recovered and authorities tried to hush up the case, fearing scandal and damage to Oberlin's liberal reputation. But vigilantes seized and brutally beat Edmonia. Now charges were brought. Her lawyer was John Mercer Langston (1829–1897), a former slave and Oberlin graduate who became Ohio's first black lawyer and an Oberlin councilman. In the two-day preliminary hearing late in February, he got the charges dropped on grounds that the supposed poison had not been recovered from the victims nor been preserved or analyzed. Edmonia was free, but she left Oberlin later that year. Langston went on to become the first president of Virginia State College and Virginia's only black congressman. His brother's grandson was Langston Hughes (*q.v.*).

Edmonia went from Oberlin to Boston. Encouraged by friends to study art, she visited the Boston studio of sculptor Edmund Brackett. Getting materials, tools, and a model of a foot, she returned in two weeks with the good copy she made. With his instruction and encouragement, and the backing of a benefactor, she opened a studio. She took well to sculpture. Her first piece was a medallion head of John Brown. Her next work, a bust of the late Civil War hero Colonel Robert Gould

Shaw, was purchased by his family and exhibited at the Boston Soldier's Aid Fair of 1864. It was so well liked that she sold a hundred copies of it, earning enough to move to Europe, with aid from the famous Story family of Boston.

Settling in Rome in 1865, she continued studying and sculpting. Her creativity was shown in the next few years in rough but imaginative works such as "Hiawatha," "Hagar in the Wilderness," and "Forever Free."

She then turned to a more disciplined, neo-classical style that was smoother, but also too sentimental and derivative, lacking her original refreshing spontaneity. Among these works of the 1870s were two groups of babies in marble, "Awake" and "Asleep," and also busts of such persons as Charles Sumner, Abraham Lincoln, and Jesse Peck Thomas. With the Greek Revival at its height, there was great demand for her work. She received many commissions to do pieces for patrons in America and Europe, including aristocracy. She was a striking success at the Philadelphia Centennial Exhibition of 1876, in which another black, Edward Bannister (q.v.) took a top prize for painting. At this Centennial, she displayed the marble babies, busts of Henry Wadsworth Longfellow and John Brown, and her notable, almost clinical, "The Death of Cleopatra." As the neo-classical vogue faded in the 1880s, the formerly celebrated Edmonia Lewis sank into such obscurity that historians are not sure when she passed away. The year usually given, 1890, is not verified.

Eugene Warbourg (1825–1861) was a black sculptor who preceded her. Her main successors among black women sculptors were Meta Warrick Fuller and May Howard Jackson, both born in 1876, and Augusta Savage, born in 1900. Though they are generally considered to have excelled her in artistry, they did not attain the popularity she reached at her peak. Her pioneering showed the way.

Locke, Alain (1886–1954), Scholar

Alain LeRoy Locke was the first black to be a Rhodes Scholar. This professor of philosophy also became the leading spokesman of the Harlem Renaissance and the foremost critic and historian of Afro-American culture.

Locke was born in Philadelphia, the son of Pliny I. Locke who had received a law degree in 1874 in the fourth class ever graduated from the law school at Howard University in Washington, D.C. He attended Central High School, the Philadelphia School of Pedagogy, and Harvard University, where he was elected to Phi Beta Kappa and received his

B.A. in 1907. Meanwhile, he won the highly coveted Rhodes Scholarship, an award for two years of study at Oxford University in England. Instituted in 1902 with funds left by empire-builder Cecil Rhodes, the scholarship is granted to 32 recipients selected each year after rigorous examinations and interviews throughout the United States. Locke was the only black selected in the first six decades of the program; not until 1962 was there another black Rhodes Scholar. Receiving an extension on his grant, Locke studied at Oxford from 1907 to 1910. Then he spent another two years in graduate study in philosophy at the University of Berlin.

Returning to America in 1912, Locke became assistant professor of philosophy and English at Howard University. Except for leaves, he remained at Howard until he retired in 1953. After further study at Harvard, 1916–1917, he received the Ph.D. degree in 1918. He was promoted to full professor upon his return from Harvard and soon became head of the department of philosophy. He was an exchange professor at Fisk University, 1927–1928, and was Inter-American Exchange Professor to Haiti in 1943. He was a visiting professor at the University of Wisconsin, 1945–1946, and at the New School for Social Research in 1947.

Locke published his first book, *Race Contacts and Inter Racial Relations*, in 1916. His next work was his doctoral dissertation, *The Problem of Classification in the Theory of Value* (1918).

He is best known for his writings about the cultural contributions of his people. His critiques and encouragement stimulated black artists, writers, and musicians. His book, *The New Negro: An Interpretation* (1925), explained the Harlem Renaissance to America and presented representative writings of the movement. In March, 1925, he served as editor for the issue of *Survey Graphic* that was devoted to Harlem, publishing poems, fiction, essays, and illustrations by promising young blacks. He co-edited *Plays of Negro Life* and edited *Four Negro Poets*, both anthologies appearing in 1927.

In 1934, he founded the Associates in Negro Folk Education, serving as editor for its series of eight Bronze Booklets. He wrote three of the booklets, *Negro Art: Past and Present* (1936), *The Negro and His Music* (1936), and *The Negro in Art: A Pictorial Record of the Negro Artist and of the Negro Theme in Art* (1940). These books are invaluable contributions that no student of Afro-American culture can afford to overlook. Among his other writings were *The Negro in America* (1933) and *When Peoples Meet: A Study in Race and Culture Contacts*, which he edited in 1942.

Locke became ill while hard at work on his *magnum opus*, which was to be a comprehensive study of black cultural contributions, bringing together in definitive form the things he had been saying in his various small books and his many articles. He had collected the materials and prepared tentative outlines when the end came. A colleague and friend, English professor Margaret Just Butcher, daughter of biologist Ernest Just (*q.v.*), completed the work, publishing it in 1956 under the title, *The Negro in American Culture: Based on Materials left by Alain Locke.*

Louis, Joe (1914–   ), Heavyweight Boxing Champion

Joe Louis held the world heavyweight boxing championship longer (12 years), and defended it more often (25 times), than anyone else. But more than his boxing skill and powerful punch, it was his deportment that endeared him to hundreds of millions of people all over the world. He was a clean fighter, sportsmanlike, kind and considerate to all opponents, and a person of integrity, honesty, and modesty. Joe was a champion in the ring or out. He rescued boxing from the odium of scandal, made it easier for blacks to break into major league sports, and did much to improve relations between the races. At his peak, polls showed that he was better known throughout the world than any American other than President Franklin Roosevelt.

He was born Joseph Louis Barrow to poverty-stricken cotton sharecroppers deep in the Buckalew Mountain region of Alabama, near Lafayette in Chambers County. His mother recalled that he loved to eat and sleep but did not speak until he was six. The strain of struggling to provide for his large family on the rocky land proved too much for Joe's father, who was broken physically and mentally, and was institutionalized when Joe was only 4. His wife and children worked harder to scratch out a living in his absence. Mrs. Barrow expected to hear the sad news that belatedly reached their remote cabin, that her husband had passed away and been buried in the mental institution in Mobile. A strong, God-fearing woman, she brought her children up to be honest, decent, clean, reliable, churchgoing people. When Joe was 7, she married a widower named Patrick Brooks. Sixteen years later, in 1937, Joe's father was discovered alive in the institution, his death report an error of mistaken identity. But, out of touch with reality and unable to realize his son was famous, he passed away the next year.

Meanwhile, Joe's stepfather moved to Detroit, secured a job in an auto plant, and sent for the family when Joe was 10. Placed in a grade with much younger children because of his poor early schooling and unable to overcome his weak background, Joe struggled manfully but hopelessly. He next tried vocational school, hoping to become a cabinetmaker. His mother also had him take violin lessons. When his stepfather lost his job, 12-year-old Joe got work carrying ice after school for $1.00 a week, but building his muscles also. His mother reluctantly accepted $269 of welfare money over seven months to ward off starvation for her family in the Depression. But, unhappy about having to accept charity, she did not rest until Joe repaid the full sum in 1935 out of his early earnings as a boxer.

Joe joined his gang of pals in the usual mischief of ghetto youngsters, but true to the stern upbringing his mother gave him, avoided any serious infraction. A former friend who had become a good amateur boxer persuaded 16-year-old Joe to go to Brewster's East Side Gymnasium to spar with him. Finding he was too tough for his friend to handle, Joe Louis decided to become a boxer himself. He joined the boxing club and began training for amateur bouts. Meanwhile, he secured a job in an auto plant as a lathe operator at $1.00 a day. His mother hoped he would abandon the foolish idea of boxing and concentrate on steady factory work.

In his first amateur bout, late in 1932, Louis was badly overmatched with a veteran boxer. He took a bad pounding and was knocked down seven times in the first two rounds, but showed his courage by rising each time to finish the three-round bout on his feet. More determined than ever, he resumed training, working harder and learning rapidly. He knocked out his opponents in his next three fights. He became Detroit's light heavyweight Golden Gloves champion in 1932. In 1933, he secured a better-paying job in the Ford Factory, at $25 a week. From his amateur fights, he received only merchandise checks worth about $7.50 apiece. In his two years as an amateur, Joe Louis won 54 fights, 43 by knockouts and 7 by decision. He lost four times, including his first fight, but two losses were by highly questionable decisions. In 1933, he reached the finals of the national amateur boxing championship and in April, 1934, he won, becoming at the age of 19 America's amateur light heavyweight boxing champion.

He decided to turn professional, and was taken over by three blacks in Detroit who molded him into a champion. They were businessmen John Roxborough and Julian Black, who became his co-managers, and trainer Jack "Chappie" Blackburn who found him an apt pupil. Since the reign from 1908 to 1915 of Jack Johnson (*q.v.*) as world heavyweight champion, not a single black had had a shot at the title. Jack Dempsey refused to fight the outstanding black fighter, Harry Wills.

Johnson's image—his taunting of opponents, his loose living, and his white women—had soured America on a black heavyweight king. To correct this image, Louis was instructed to keep a deadpan expression and never show emotion in the ring, never to smile or gloat over a fallen foe, to say not a word in the ring and as few as possible before and after bouts, to speak respectfully of his opponents, never to fight a crooked (fixed) bout, never to boast or brag, to live a clean life, and to take a black wife. Louis needed little instructing in such matters, however, because modesty, sportsmanship, honesty, and integrity were ingrained in him. Aware of his poor schooling, background, and diction, he was also naturally taciturn around all but his closest friends. When he did speak, as when he said we would win World War II because we were on God's side, the wisdom he expressed so simply showed him to possess far more sense than many people who considered their education and eloquence as placing them far above him.

In his first professional fight, on July 4, 1934, in Chicago, Louis knocked out Jack Kracken in the first round, earning $59. In his twelve fights in 1934, all in Detroit or Chicago, he knocked out ten foes and beat the other two by decision. By mid-1935, Mike Jacobs became the promoter for Louis's fights, bringing him to New York in June, 1935, where he knocked out the former champion Primo Carnera in the sixth round at Yankee Stadium. That September, Louis fought Max Baer, who had just lost the world championship to Jimmy Braddock in June, and kayoed him in the fourth round. In beating Baer before 90,000 people in Yankee Stadium, Louis restored boxing to its heyday of the million-dollar-gate Jack Dempsey–Gene Tunney fights of the mid-1920s. Louis, who got married just before the fight, earned $240,000 in beating Baer.

Blacks were elated over Louis's success. After broadcasts of his fights, they poured from their ghetto homes in wild, good-natured celebrations. Many whites also increasingly admired this modest, clean youth. Few were prepared for the setback that came against Max Schmeling. The former world heavyweight champion from Germany had spotted a flaw—Louis could be hit by a quick right cross after he threw a left jab because he momentarily dropped his left hand. When they met in Yankee Stadium in June, 1936, in Louis's 28th professional fight, Schmeling almost knocked him out in the fourth round, caught him with a right after the bell ended the next round, and then pounded unmercifully on the dazed Louis, who fought on only on instinct and courage until knocked out in the twelfth.

The Nazi propaganda machine, with Schmeling chiming in, made such great capital over a German knocking out a man of an inferior race when America's white hopes were unable to do so, that Jimmy Braddock, pressured by anti-Nazi groups, ignored his promise to fight Schmeling. Meanwhile, Louis made a comeback in August, 1936, knocking out in three rounds former champion Jack Sharkey who had dethroned Schmeling. After Jess Willard beat Jack Johnson, the title was held successively by Dempsey, Tunney, Schmeling, Sharkey, Carnera, Baer, and Braddock. Before the end of 1936, Louis kayoed three more foes, including a one-punch, 26-second fight.

On June 22, 1937, Louis met Jimmy Braddock for the world championship and knocked him out in the eighth round, making Louis, who was just 23, the youngest heavyweight champion till then. True to his promise to be a fighting champion, Louis took on all who dared, fighting one a month at one stretch from December, 1940, to June, 1941. His most satisfying triumph came in his rematch with Schmeling in June, 1938, in Yankee Stadium. He demolished Hitler's symbol of Aryan supremacy with an unbelievable barrage of blows delivered in cold fury, knocking him out in only 2 minutes and 4 seconds of the first round. Louis far outclassed his opponents. He won 22 of 25 title defenses by knockouts, five in the first round. Only Tommy Farr, Arturo Godoy, and Jersey Joe Walcott lasted a full 15 rounds. He knocked out the latter two in their second bouts with him.

Louis's first defense was against Farr in August, 1937; his 25th and last was the return bout with Walcott in June, 1948. He had a close call in his first bout with Billy Conn, knocking him out in the 13th round when Conn was far ahead on points. This bout typified Louis's sportsmanship. When Conn slipped in the 10th round, losing his balance and leaving himself wide open, Louis stepped back rather than take advantage, even though to hit his foe in such a situation was perfectly within the rules of boxing. Some of Louis's toughest fights were with Conn, Walcott, Tony Galento, and Buddy Baer.

Louis retired as undefeated champion in March, 1949. His only professional defeat until then was to Schmeling before becoming champ. After coming out of retirement he lost two more fights: his successor as world champion, Ezzard Charles, decisioned him in 15 rounds in a title fight in 1950, and a future champion, Rocky Marciano, knocked him out in 1951. Louis's biggest purse was $625,916 for his second fight with Conn. His total earnings in his 76 professional fights (he won 73, including 61 knockouts, and lost only 3) came to $4,626,721. In 1942, he risked his title in two fights in which he did not earn a penny because he donated his entire purse to charity, fighting Buddy Baer for Navy

Relief and Abe Simon for Army Relief. He served without complaint in the Army during World War II.

Generous to a fault with old friends and hangers-on and not careful to work out the most advantageous financial program in light of taxes, Louis found himself in later life owing huge amounts of Federal income tax; a settlement was made. Most of his financial ventures in retirement were unsuccessful. His marriages did not work out too well. In 1970, he had to be committed for treatments for delusions of persecution. Millions prayed for his recovery.

Boxing's greatest authority, Nat Fleischer, placed Jack Johnson first, Jim Jeffries second, Bob Fitzsimmons third, Jack Dempsey fourth, Jim Corbett fifth, Joe Louis sixth, and Sam Langford seventh when he ranked the greatest heavyweights of all time. Not all experts would agree with placing Louis only sixth, but even if all were unanimous on that as his standing in terms of fighting prowess, none can deny that Louis is the most popular fighter of all time. He is also the most beloved of all black athletes of all time in any sport. Moreover, Louis did more for boxing than any other man and he outranks all other fighters of any weight as a champion gentleman, an idol to youngsters, and a model worthy of great admiration and emulation.

Malcolm X (1925–1965), Revolutionary

Malcolm X was a charismatic leader who became the foremost spokesman for the downtrodden ghetto black and the greatest hero of black revolutionaries. By far the most effective salesman of the Black Muslim movement, he broke with its leader, Elijah Muhammad (q.v.) in the last year of his life and moderated his anti-white views.

He was born Malcolm Little in Omaha, Neb., the fourth of eight children. His father was a Baptist preacher and Garveyite from Georgia, his mother a mulatto from Grenada, British West Indies. Whites objected to his father teaching the doctrines of Marcus Garvey (q.v.), stressing black pride and unity. Having seen one of his brothers lynched and two others also slain by whites, Reverend Little fearlessly organized blacks for Garvey's return-to-Africa crusade. Klansmen threatened them in Omaha and broke their windows. The family moved briefly to Milwaukee and then settled in Lansing, Mich., where whites burned down their first home and constantly harassed them. The father took Malcolm to his Garvey movement rallies. When Malcolm was 6, his father was bludgeoned and laid across a Lansing streetcar track to be crushed. The police labeled it accidental and did not seek his killers; one insurance company labeled it suicide and refused to pay. Breaking under the strain of caring for eight children while being hounded by overbearing welfare officials, Malcolm's mother was committed to a mental institution when he was 12.

In trouble for stealing, Malcolm had been placed in a foster home several months before the family broke up. He also stayed in trouble in school and was expelled when 13. He was sent to the detention home in Mason, a town with only one black family, a dozen miles from Lansing. Having taken a liking to him, the white couple in charge kept him there when the time came for him to go to the reform school. Instead, he was sent to Mason Junior High, where he played on the basketball team, made very high grades, and was elected class president in the seventh grade.

On going to Boston in the summer of 1940 to visit his father's three children by a previous marriage, he fell in love with the exciting big city ghetto. He became restless with smalltown Midwestern life where the few blacks scattered among whites were never truly accepted or allowed to rise. Midway through eighth grade, his English teacher discouraged his ambition to be a lawyer, telling him that that was impractical for blacks and urging him instead to learn a trade like carpentry. This same white teacher, Malcolm learned, encouraged white youngsters whose grades were much lower than his to try for any profession their hearts desired. That was a turning point in Malcolm's life, making him realize whites would never accept him, no matter how well he did. To them, he would always be just another black, somehow lower than they. He now lost interest in school, became sullen and uncooperative, and dropped out after eighth grade, taking the bus to Boston in June, 1941, to live with his half-sister.

In Boston, Malcolm worked as a ballroom shoeshine boy and a drugstore soda jerk. Zoot-suited, conk-haired, and a lindy-hopper, 16-year-old Malcolm gained status among ghetto hustlers when a glamorous girl from Beacon Hill's white society set fell in love with him. While working on a railroad dining car running between Boston and New York, he became fond of Harlem and after being fired from the railroad in 1942 for cursing at demanding white passengers, he was hired as a waiter at Small's Paradise there. Early in 1943, he was fired from Small's for procuring business for a house of ill-fame from a "soldier" who was a military spy. Since Malcolm's record was clean theretofore, the police did not book him. Out of work, "Detroit Red," as Malcolm was nicknamed, drifted into crime, beginning as a peddler of "reefers" (marijuana cigarettes). Most of his customers were musicians. At 17, he was clearing sixty dollars a day, but narcotics officers ran him out of Harlem. He began traveling on his old railroad pass, selling to his musician friends in towns they were playing. He continued seeing his Beacon Hill girl friend. When his draft call came, he put on a crazy act at the induction center, was rejected as psychologically unfit for service, and received a 4-F card.

His traveling reefer-peddling business ended when railroads black-balled him for pulling a gun on a fellow black employee during a card game argument. He now turned to small robberies and stickups, becoming a cocaine addict also. After his partner was wounded, Malcolm shifted to other things, delivering numbers bets, steering masochistic wealthy whites to prearranged appointments with sadistic black prostitutes, and delivering bootleg whiskey. He moved back to Boston late in 1945 when several hustlers were gunning for him after various run-ins. Needing large sums for his drug habit, he formed a burglary ring in Boston. He recruited two black pals and two white women—his well-to-do girl friend and her kid sister who was in love with one of his two friends. Inevitably, they were caught. Normally, they would have gotten two years as first offenders, but the police, caseworkers, prosecutor, and judge were enraged that well-bred white girls would love and work for low-class black criminals. Malcolm and his pal (the third man escaped) received ten-year sentences in February, 1946, three months before Malcolm's 21st birthday.

In prison, Malcolm was nicknamed "Satan" because of his pronounced anti-religious attitude. Writing to him in 1948, one of his brothers told him of his new faith, the Nation of Islam of Elijah Muhammad. Another brother wrote him to abandon pork and cigarettes and he would show him a way out. Malcolm obeyed. His relatives had become Black Muslims. They indoctrinated him, saying all whites were doomed devils and only blacks, through Muhammad, would be saved by Allah. Remembering the white oppressors and racists he had known all his life, Malcolm could readily agree whites caused his downfall.

His relatives urged him to write Elijah Muhammad, who sometimes visited his brother's home in Detroit. He corresponded with the Muslim leader, learning to pray and to abstain from narcotics, liquor, immorality, and all harmful things. Conscious that reliance on ghetto slang and profanity had greatly limited his vocabulary, he began studying and copying a dictionary page by page. As his word base broadened, he began reading extensively, especially history, philosophy, and the black man's past. Reading of the horrors of imperialism, colonialism, slavery, and the other oppression and exploitation by whites, reinforced Elijah

Muhammad's teachings that whites were devils. He began recruiting other convicts and also became an outstanding prison debater.

Malcolm was released in August, 1952, in custody of a brother who managed a furniture store owned by whites in Detroit's ghetto. As a salesman there, Malcolm saw how slum merchants preyed on blacks, selling inferior goods at inflated prices on seemingly attractive terms (little down, low payments), but at usurious interest rates that netted the merchant many times the item's worth. Malcolm became active in the Detroit temple, recruiting ghetto blacks whose language he could speak from his years as a hustler. Membership tripled. Elijah Muhammad, whom he met on visits to Muslim headquarters in Chicago, was well pleased with him. Malcolm Little now became Malcolm X. In the summer of 1953, he became Assistant Minister of the Detroit temple, meanwhile working in a truck factory, then in a Ford plant.

Deciding to become a fulltime Muslim minister, Malcolm quit his job and spent months in intensive training under Elijah Muhammad in Chicago. Sent to Boston near the end of 1953, he converted enough persons to start a temple in only three months. By March, 1954, this temple, the eleventh in America, was well organized and Malcolm moved on to Philadelphia, establishing Temple Twelve there by May. Because of his successes, Elijah Muhammad made him minister of Temple Seven in New York City in June, 1954. The temple then had less than one hundred members, not one in a thousand Harlemites had heard of the Muslims, and less than 500 whites all over America knew they existed. His temple grew slowly but steadily. He traveled around the nation, founding and speaking at other temples also. In 1957, Malcolm founded the Muslim newspaper, *Muhammad Speaks*. In 1958, Harlem became aware of the Muslims when Malcolm and his temple brothers forced authorities to transfer a Muslim clubbed by police from a jail cell to a hospital. A nationally televised documentary in 1959 alerted whites to the Muslim presence. They reacted in startled fear on learning that such an antiwhite group preaching separatism existed. Malcolm was kept busy furiously rebutting the white foes and also the black leaders who attacked the Muslim movement. The resulting publicity led to Muslim mass rallies in the early 1960s with many thousands present and with representatives from temples all over America, most of which Malcolm had started.

Malcolm became in greater demand as a speaker on college campuses than any person other than Senator Barry Goldwater. Elijah Muhammad, who felt ill-equipped to address college audiences, was growing resentful. Other Muslim leaders shared his jealousy of Malcolm's prominence. Malcolm began realizing this envy was at work when the Muslim newspaper stopped mentioning him. Meanwhile his faith in Elijah Muhammad was being shaken by persistent rumors out of Chicago that he could no longer ignore, rumors of adulterous conduct by his saintly leader who had members suspended or expelled for the slightest moral infractions. Confronting Muhammad, he tried to help his leader devise a counter strategy to protect the movement's integrity if the scandal leaked too far. Muhammad was pleasant to him, but afterwards Malcolm learned of a hate campaign against himself that apparently emanated from the movement's leader. He soon learned that Muhammad was labeling him ambitious and dangerous, using him as a scapegoat to screen his own misconduct. In November, 1963, Malcolm X made an intemperate remark about President Kennedy's assassination, referring to chickens coming home to roost, meaning that unchecked white violence against blacks had spread until it engulfed the nation's leader. Muhammad used that as a pretext to suspend him from all duties and speaking for 90 days. Malcolm obeyed, but soon learned, from Muslims sent to do the job, that orders to slay him had come down from Muslim headquarters. Malcolm was crushed. He had come into the movement when it had only 400 members, had been instrumental in building it to a membership of 40,000, and had remained completely devoted to Muhammad. Yet the leader had turned on him.

On March 12, 1964, Malcolm X announced his withdrawal from the Nation of Islam, founding instead the Muslim Mosque, Inc. Only a few defected with him. Even his own brothers remained loyal to Muhammad, continuing as ministers of the Muslim mosques in Detroit and Lansing. From April 13 to May 21, Malcolm traveled to Mecca, visiting many Arab lands en route. He learned the true Islamic religion and realized how much Elijah Muhammad had distorted its teachings. Malcolm became El Hajj Malik El Shabazz there. To his amazement, he found white Moslems having true brotherhood with black Moslems. He found greater peace, acceptance, and friendship than he ever knew in America. His views changed. He realized that all whites were not devils, that the exploitative system in America encouraged most whites to be racists and oppressors, but also that some whites could become genuine brothers. On June 28, 1964, Malcolm founded a new secular group, the Organization for Afro-American Unity (OAAU), to work for black unity and freedom and to cooperate with other civil rights groups. Although he dropped the white hatred and separatist ideas he had voiced as a Black Muslim, the news media continued to twist his words into the old mold, refusing to give credit to the new Malcolm. From July 9 to November 24, he was abroad again, visiting Africa and the Middle East, attending as an observer the summit meeting of African heads of states held in Cairo. Ignoring threats on his life, he plunged on his return into the task of building the OAAU and spreading his new ideas. But little time remained.

He was fighting in court to remain in the house in East Elmhurst, Long Island, that the Black Muslims were trying to evict him from when it was firebombed on February 14, 1965, while he, his pregnant wife, and four daughters were asleep. They barely escaped. A week later, on February 21, Malcolm was assassinated as he addressed a rally in New York's Audubon Ballroom. He was 39 years old, the same age at which Martin Luther King (*q.v.*) would be gunned down three years later. Two of the three gunmen who slew Malcolm were Black Muslim enforcers; the three received life imprisonment.

The voice of Malcolm X was stilled, but his ideas lived on. He taught blacks to be fearless and to see that "progress" in civil rights left the black masses still the helpless victims of racist exploitation and oppression. He exposed the selfish black leaders and exploiters who cooperated with whites while lower class blacks were ground under. More than any other, he was the inspiration for the nationwide fight against white racism and for black dignity that took off from where the civil rights movement, focused on Southern segregation and disfranchisement, left off. Malcolm's monument is the thousands of dedicated, young, black militants determined to unite their people and bring real freedom for all blacks of all classes.

Marshall, Thurgood (1908–   ), Civil Rights Lawyer; Supreme Court Justice

Serving as NAACP counsel from 1938 to 1961, Thurgood Marshall became the nation's foremost civil rights lawyer. In 1967, he became the first black on the U.S. Supreme Court.

Marshall was born in Baltimore, Md., great-grandson of an African slave who by defiance gained his freedom in Maryland. Marshall's father was a country club steward, his mother a teacher. After graduating with honors from Douglass High School, he attended Lincoln University, Pa. He worked his way through college as a grocery clerk, dining car waiter, and bellhop, but was also on the debating team. Although loud, good-naturedly rough, uncouth, and funloving, he graduated *cum laude* in 1930. He then enrolled in the law school at Howard University in Washington, D.C. Completely absorbed by law, he now became studious, being noted for his meticulous research, prodigious memory, and brilliant mind. He led his class, graduating *magna cum laude* in 1933.

Admitted to the Maryland bar that year, Marshall practiced in Baltimore. Most of his cases involved civil rights, gaining him satisfaction and respect, but hardly enough income to pay office expenses. While practicing law in Baltimore from 1933 to 1938, he also served as counsel for the Baltimore branch of the National Association for the Advancement of Colored People (NAACP). He participated in fights to have Maryland's board of education equalize salaries (white teachers received double the pay of blacks) and he won a case in Maryland's Court of Appeals gaining a black, Donald Murray, admittance to the Law School of the University of Maryland.

In 1936, he became a part-time assistant to Charles H. Houston, the special counsel to the NAACP who had taught him at Howard. Houston and he plotted the NAACP strategy in attacking segregation. Marshall prepared the brief in the 1938 Supreme Court case granting Lloyd Gaines the right to enter the University of Missouri Law School. In 1938, Houston retired to private practice and Marshall moved to New York to succeed him as special counsel at NAACP headquarters.

Representing the NAACP, Marshall made numerous trips to Southern communities, often at the risk of his life, being threatened and run out of town several times. He was admitted to practice before the U.S. Supreme Court. His success resulted from extremely meticulous preparation of, and a sharp mind in arguments on, his cases. His knowledge of constitutional doctrine was overpowering. He won such key cases as Smith v. Allwright (1944) ending white primaries; Morgan v. Virginia (1946) invalidating state laws segregating interstate passengers; Shelley v. Kraemer (1948) barring state courts from enforcing restrictive covenants; and Sweatt v. Painter (1950) blocking efforts to make blacks attend a hastily-created law school designed to keep them out of the University of Texas. Marshall's greatest victory was the 1954 school desegregation decision. He then led NAACP legal efforts in the considerable litigation growing out of the civil rights movement of the 1950s.

In September, 1961, President John F. Kennedy nominated Marshall to serve on the Second Circuit U.S. Court of Appeals, covering Connecticut, Vermont, and New York, and sitting in New York City. He was the second black to become a Federal appeals judge. Charles Houston's cousin, William Hastie (*q.v.*), has been serving on the Third Circuit Court of Appeals, sitting in Philadelphia, since 1949. In August, 1965, President Lyndon Johnson appointed Marshall to the post of Solicitor-General, in which he represented the Federal government in arguing cases before the Supreme Court. He was the first black in that position. In June, 1967, President Johnson nominated Marshall to the Supreme Court. Confirmed by the Senate in late August by 69 to 11, he took the oath of office in October, becoming the first black justice.

Mays, Willie (1931–), Baseball Star

One of baseball's greatest stars, Willie Howard Mays is the only player in the history of the game to reach both 600 home runs and 3,000 hits during his career. His amazing feats as a centerfielder, his bubbling enthusiasm, his batting and baserunning, all combine to make him the most exciting all-around player in the history of baseball. A top attraction, he was for many years the highest paid player.

Born in Westfield, Ala., a steeltown suburb a dozen miles from Birmingham, Mays came from an athletic family. His grandfather, Walter Mays, was a noted pitcher for Negro amateur teams at Tuscaloosa, Ala. His father, William Howard Mays, was a semi-pro outfielder who worked as a plumber's assistant in a steel mill in Fairfield, a larger suburb on Birmingham's outskirts. Willie's mother had been a high school track star. His parents were divorced before he was 3. When his mother remarried (eventually giving him two half-brothers and eight half-sisters), Willie was brought up by his father's sister, Aunt Sarah, who lived in Fairfield. Since his father remained single and continued to eat his lunch there, he and Willie saw a lot of each other. Known as "Kitty Cat" because of his grace on the playing field, the father taught Willie how to throw, catch, and hit long before he started to school and later took him to games of the company team on which he played.

Willie, who idolized the Yankees's Joe Dimaggio, was all wrapped up in baseball. Still, he was an all-around athlete at Fairfield Industrial High School. In basketball, he was the leading scorer in Jefferson County, averaging 20 to 25 points per game. In football, he was a quarterback, an outstanding passer (five touchdown passes in one game), and a good punter. The school lacked a baseball team, but he had started playing sandlot ball at 10, being so good that he played with boys four to five years older than he. By the time he was 14, he was playing for a semi-pro steel mill baseball team, but his father would not let him work in the mills for fear that he would get trapped there and never realize his full athletic potential. Willie had been a pitcher in sandlot and semi-pro ball, but his father made the 14-year-old switch to the outfield because Willie, who was the industrial team's leading batter, baserunner, and powerhitter, was exhausting himself trying to do everything.

In the spring of 1948, soon after Mays turned 17, his father arranged a tryout for him with the Birmingham Black Barons of the Negro National League. He was hired at $300 a season. With two more years of high school ahead, Mays played on weekends when his team was in town, joining them full time only during summer vacations. When the regular centerfielder was injured, Mays got a chance at his post. Although his hitting lagged, his fielding and throwing were so impressive that he won the centerfield spot. Now his 35-year-old father stopped playing himself, satisfied that his son would make the grade. In his next two seasons Mays's hitting improved greatly, making him a promising prospect for the major leagues. The Boston Braves and Chicago White Sox were interested, but major league rules forbade signing a high school youngster. Two scouts from the New York Giants who came to look at the Barons' first baseman in May, 1950, were so much more impressed with Mays that they urged the club to sign him. Mays agreed. The Giants paid the Barons $10,000 and gave Mays a bonus of $6,000 when he graduated from high school in June and could sign the contract.

Mays hit .353 the rest of the season with the Giants' farm team at Trenton in the Class B Inter-State League. In 1951, he was promoted to the Triple A Minneapolis Millers of the American Association, where he batted .477 and hit eight home runs in the team's first 35 games. Meanwhile, the Giants had lost eleven in a row early that season. Manager Leo Durocher sent for Mays. Mays played his first major league game on May 25, 1951, in Shibe Park in Philadelphia against the Phillies. He went hitless in five trips to the plate and also went hitless six more times up in the next two games, although the Giants won all three games. But in his twelfth time at bat, the first time in the Giants's Polo Grounds ballpark, he hit a homer off Warren Spahn of the Braves. Then he began another hitless streak, leaving him with 1 hit in his first 26 at bats. He then went on a batting spree that raised his average well over .300, but a late season slump caused him to wind up at .274, with 20 homers. His sensational fielding—his trademark "breadbasket catches," his phenomenal range, his tremendous throws—electrified the fans. Catching fire from him, the Giants overtook the Brooklyn Dodgers, tying them for the pennant and beating them in a best of three playoff, where Mays made a fantastic throw to the plate to cut off a Dodger run. The Giants lost the World Series to the New York Yankees, but Mays was named the National League rookie of the year for 1951.

He played in 34 games in 1952 (batting .236) before he was drafted into the Army. In uniform for 22 months, mostly at Fort Eustis, Va., he played service ball with his customary infectious enjoyment. The Giants were in first place when he was called up, but fell to second in ten days, winding up that season in second and the next in fifth. Mays returned in March, 1954. In his first full season, he hit .345 with 41 homers and 110 runs batted in. The Giants won the pennant and beat the Cleveland Indians in four straight games in the World Series. Mays, whose average was highest in either league, was named the Most Valuable Player in the National League for 1954. His sensational World Series over-the-shoulder catch of Vic Wertz's long drive and his whirling bullet throw to second to hold the runner on first had fans talking for years. Willie's salary jumped from $13,000 for 1954 to $40,000 for 1955.

The "Say-hey Kid" (as Mays came to be known) never again led the league in batting, although hitting .333 in 1957, the Giants's last year in New York and .347 in 1958, their first year in San Francisco. He compiled a lifetime batting average of .306 as of the start of his 19th season (1970). He led the National League in home runs four times, with 51 in 1955, 49 in 1962, 47 in 1964, and 52 in 1965. In 1965, he was named the Most Valuable Player for the second time. By the early 1960s Mays was earning more than $100,000 a year, more than any other player, and in 1966 he was drawing $125,000, a higher salary than any baseball player had ever before received.

In 1969, he hit his 600th homer and added 28 more by the end of 1970. The only player in baseball history to hit as many as 600 home runs was Babe Ruth, who retired with 714. During the 1970 season, Mays became the tenth player in baseball history to reach 3,000 hits (Ruth had 2,873). Henry Aaron was the ninth player to reach the 3,000 hit mark, earlier in 1970. Since he is three years younger than Mays, did not lose any seasons to military service, has a .313 lifetime average, and had 592 home runs by the end of 1970, Aaron seems likely to eclipse Mays's lifetime marks.

Mays and Aaron are the black superstars of baseball. Next to them, the greatest black ballplayers would include infielders Jackie Robinson (*q.v.*), Maury Wills, and Ernie Banks, pitchers Don Newcombe, Juan Marichal, and Bob Gibson, catcher Roy Campanella, and outfielders Roberto Clemente and Frank Robinson.

McKay, Claude (1890–1948), Poet and Novelist

Claude McKay was a leading poet of the Harlem Renaissance of the 1920s. The militant spirit expressed in his collection of verse, *Harlem Shadows*, typified the movement.

McKay was born in the village of Sunny Ville on the island of Jamaica in the British West Indies. He was the youngest of eleven children of prospering peasant landowners who grew coffee, cocoa, bananas, and sugar cane. At the age of 6, he moved to the home of his older brother who was a schoolteacher and an Anglican lay preacher. This freethinking brother influenced McKay to read widely and think for himself. When he was 16, an English squire, Walter Jekyll, broadened his reading by introducing him to major English and American poets. A specialist in Jamaican folklore, Jekyll helped him incorporate native dialect into his poems.

McKay's interest was writing poetry, but he had to earn a living also. At 17, he became an apprentice cabinetmaker on a Government Trade Scholarship; at 19, he became a constable. He continued writing poems in Jamaican dialect, publishing *Constab Ballads* in 1912, and a collection of verse, *Songs From Jamaica* (1912). In 1912, he came to the United States and entered Tuskegee Institute. Unhappy with the regimentation there, he transferred to the department of agriculture at Kansas State University. He had little interest in a career of agriculture, however, and was glad two years later when he inherited several thousand dollars, enabling him to quit.

He moved to Harlem to become a freelance writer. Initially, he worked as a bartender, waiter, porter, longshoreman—anything to sustain himself until he built a name. His poetry appeared increasingly in magazines. In 1919, he went to England where his next volume of verse, *Spring in New Hampshire and Other Poems*, was published in 1920. Returning to New York that year, McKay became associate editor of *The Liberator* and *The Masses*.

In 1922, his most important work, *Harlem Shadows*, appeared. This volume contains an exceptionally good collection of sonnets and lyrics, including such poems as "If We Must Die," "The White House," and "The Lynching." McKay was attracted to Communism and visited Russia in 1922, speaking at the Third Internationale as a representative of the American Workers Party. He became ill from unsanitary conditions in Russia and he traveled in Europe and Africa, living several years in Spain. He remained abroad during most of the 1920s.

After returning to America, McKay published a trilogy of novels, *Home to Harlem* (1928), set in New York, *Banjo* (1929), set in Marseilles, and *Banana Bottom* (1930), set in Jamaica. A central thread in these novels is the conflict between the pure and primitive instincts of the natural man and the inhibitions of the decadent, overly civilized intellectual. He also brought out a collection of short stories, *Gingertown* (1932).

McKay's final works were his autobiography, *A Long Way From Home* (1937), and a sociological study, *Harlem: Negro Metropolis* (1940). During his last decade, he came increasingly under the influence of Roman Catholicism and converted to that faith in 1944. He devoted his last years to working with the Catholic Youth Organization in Chicago. *Selected Poems of Claude McKay* was published posthumously in 1953. Other great poets of the Harlem Renaissance included Langston Hughes (*q.v.*), Countee Cullen, and Jean Toomer.

Mills, Florence (1895–1927), Broadway Musical Star

Although little remembered now, Florence Mills was a leading Broadway star in the 1920s. Few entertainers were ever better loved by audiences, fellow performers, directors, and management than this elfin, birdlike pixie who sang, danced, and acted her way into the hearts of Americans and Europeans before the final curtain closed too soon.

Born in Washington, D.C., Miss Mills performed almost her entire life. At 5, she was a singing-dancing amateur in salons of Washington society. "Baby Florence" performed so delightfully at the residence of Baron Julian Pauncefote, British ambassador from 1889 to 1902, that Lady Pauncefote gave her a gold bracelet. Flo also won medals for her skill as a cakewalker and buck-dancer.

This child performer made her professional debut at the Empire Theater in Washington with the second company of the Bert Williams (*q.v.*) and George Walker show, *Sons of Ham*. She appeared as an extra attraction, making a hit singing "Hannah from Savannah" and drawing encores by her dancing. Afterwards, the 6-year-old trouper traveled for a while with the company.

The young performer's family moved to Harlem in 1903. She continued to appear in various road companies and in such vaudeville acts as the Mills Sisters, formed in 1910 by Florence and her two sisters, Maude and Olivia. Another of her acts was the Panama Trio with Cora Green and Ada "Bricktop" Smith. Relatively unknown then, all three of these young performers became famous. Ada's Montmartre Club, Chez Bricktop, was the most fashionable nightspot in Paris from the late 1920s through the 1930s. The three young performers—Ada, Cora, and Flo—also toured as part of the Tennessee Ten. It was a hard life for the frail Flo Mills, traveling from coast to coast performing and throwing herself so energetically into her shows, but the years of experience were paying off in mastery of her craft. Financial rewards were slow in coming, but showed improvement. She had begun at $9 a week in the early 1900s and had worked her way up to about $50 a week by 1920.

Her big chance for stardom came in the summer of 1921 while she was appearing in a Harlem cabaret. That year *Shuffle Along*, written, composed, directed, and performed by blacks, exploded onto the New York scene, making entertainment history and launching the Harlem Renaissance. Although composers Noble Sissle and Eubie Blake and the writing-comedian team of Flournoy Miller and Aubrey Lyles opened their show in May, 1921, with Gertrude Saunders as singer-dancer, Florence Mills was called in to replace her when she became ill that summer. With such hit songs as "I'm Just Wild About Harry," the show was a huge success, running a year at New York's 63rd Street Theater and touring for two more years. Although the show was built around the team of Miller and Lyles, it provided Flo Mills a chance to display her skills before a wider audience and brought her stardom. Josephine Baker rose from the chorus of this show to become, for decades, one of the greatest entertainers in Paris.

In 1922, Miss Mills left *Shuffle Along* to star in Lew Leslie's *Plantation Revue*, beginning at his 50th Street Club and moving to Broadway's 48th Street Theater that July. This revue was enlarged into *From Dover to Dixie* and carried, in 1923, to London, where the British raved over her. In modified form, it was brought to Broadway's Broadhurst Theater in October, 1924, as *Dixie to Broadway*, playing well into 1925. Flo Mills was a smash hit in what was essentially the first Negro revue, i.e., the first show built around a female singing-dancing star rather than around the traditional blackface male comedy team. As the toast of Broadway, Florence Mills was also in great demand in nightclubs, appearing in a trio with her husband, U. S. Thompson, and another man, Fredi Johnson.

In the spring of 1926, Leslie developed another revue, *Blackbirds*, built around Miss Mills. It played at the Alhambra Theater in Harlem a month and a half and then went abroad, playing in Paris for five months and in London for six months. Singing her theme song, "I'm a Little Blackbird Looking for a Bluebird," Miss Mills captivated audiences. The Prince of Wales (later Edward VIII and now Duke of Windsor) saw the show sixteen times and described Miss Mills as "ripping." But success never spoiled her. She remained so sweet, kind, unselfish, modest, and generous that many persons, high and low, described her as the most lovable person they had ever met.

She was such a sensation abroad that American audiences eagerly awaited her return to prepare for opening her new revue *Blackbirds of 1928*. But the hardworking Miss Mills had delayed too long caring for an inflamed appendix. Two operations in New York in October failed to save her. Sixty thousand people viewed her body, five thousand packed the church for her funeral on November 6, 1927, while more than one hundred thousand jammed the streets outside to pay their last respects to the beloved performer.

Blackbirds of 1928 went on without her but centered around dancer Bill "Bojangles" Robinson (*q.v.*) and such hit parade songs as "I Can't Give You Anything But Love." Florence Mills gave her all before taking her final bow.

Morgan, Garrett A. (1875–1963), Inventor

Garrett A. Morgan contributed a smoke inhalator and an automatic stoplight to American life.

Born in Paris, Tenn., Morgan moved to Ohio as a penniless youth in 1895. In Cleveland in 1901, the mechanically minded young man developed his first invention, a belt fastener for sewing machines. He sold this for $150.

His next major invention was a breathing helmet and smoke protector. For this device, he won the First Grand Prize gold medal in 1914 at the Second International Exposition of Sanitation and Safety. *Crisis* magazine reported early in 1914 that Morgan's device was being used by fire departments in several large cities in Ohio, Pennsylvania, and New York, and was also being considered by New York City.

In 1916, Morgan had a chance to demonstrate the utility of his safety device when an explosion in a tunnel at the Cleveland Waterways trapped several dozen men 228 feet below Lake Erie, five miles from shore. Smoke and debris prevented rescuers from reaching the trapped men or even finding out if they were still alive. Someone recalled that Morgan had been displaying a gas inhalator to prospective manufacturers, and in response to the urgent plea for help, Garrett Morgan and his brother Frank rushed to the disaster scene. The two brothers, and two volunteers, went into the tunnel wearing Morgan's invention, and returned to the surface with unconscious men. They made the trip over and over, saving more than twenty of the seemingly doomed workers. The City of Cleveland awarded Morgan a solid gold medal for his heroic rescue.

The resulting publicity aroused interest among manufacturers and fire departments nationwide. Morgan was asked to demonstrate the device in many cities and towns. In the South, Morgan had to hire a white man to make the demonstrations. Many cities placed orders but business began to slacken later, perhaps because the inventor's racial identity became better known. In World War I, Morgan's inhalator was transformed into a gas mask to protect soldiers.

Morgan continued his work. In 1923, he developed an automatic stoplight to aid rapid, orderly movement of traffic in cities. He sold the rights to his stop signal to General Electric for $40,000. With development by that company, there was no problem concerning the race of the inventor.

Useful inventions came from other blacks. Among them were the sugar refining process of Norbert Rillieux (*q.v.*), the lubricating devices of Elijah McCoy, the shoe lasting machine of Jan Matzeliger, and the induction telegraph system of Granville Woods (*q.v.*).

Muhammad, Elijah (1897–   ), Cult Leader

Elijah Muhammad is the leader of a militant, disciplined, anti-Christian cult, the Lost-Found Nation of Islam. His doctrines stress black superiority and oppose integration with whites, whom he labels a doomed race of devils. He calls for a separate area of America to be turned over to blacks to rule.

He was born Elijah Poole in Sandersville, Ga., seventh of thirteen children of Wali and Marie Poole. His father was a Baptist preacher, sawmill worker, and tenant farmer. Though frail throughout his life, Elijah displayed leadership ability early, serving as peacemaker in disputes among his brothers and sisters. Helping the family by his earnings as a field boy and sawmill worker slowed his progress through school. When he quit to work full-time at 16, he had completed only the fourth grade. An older sister continued to teach him at night. From boyhood on, he spent hours poring over the Bible, trying to fathom its mysteries.

He showed a strong race consciousness, objecting to the manner in which white employers frequently cursed and abused their black workers. He told them politely but firmly to fire him if his work was poor, but never to curse him. He was such a good and trustworthy worker, however, that he sometimes became foreman. Conscious of the shortcomings of his people, he tried to find reasons to explain their condition rather than simply to condemn their faults, such as tardiness, laziness, and shoddy work. He worked in Sandersville and in Macon, Ga., where he was a laborer for the Southern Railroad and a foreman at the Cherokee Brick Company. When an employer did curse him early in 1923, he decided to move northward to avoid trouble.

Detroit, supposedly a paradise for blacks, lured him. At the age of 25, he moved there, taking the wife he had married in 1919 and their two children. Five more were born in Detroit and one in Chicago, giving them six sons and two daughters. From 1923 to 1929, he worked in the Chevrolet factory in Detroit, but he found the North far from the expected haven. Though prejudice and exploitation there were more subtle, the black man was oppressed just as in the South. When the Depression came and blacks were fired so whites could work, Elijah Poole became more embittered. He was on relief from 1929 to 1931, suffering like other blacks from overbearing welfare workers who kept blacks waiting while they took care of white clients first.

In the Depression summer of 1930, a mysterious silk peddler and prophet appeared among Detroit's deprived blacks. Variously called Master W. D. Fard or Wali Farrad or Wallace Fard Muhammad, he taught blacks that they were members of the original superior race, descendants of Muslims of Afro-Asia. He told them he was sent by Allah (God) to reclaim his lost people, to rescue them from the offshoot race of white devils who had made a hell on earth for them. He claimed Christianity was a false religion used by whites to keep blacks in subjection. Detroit's ghetto blacks, including Elijah Poole, were ripe for such teachings. Believers soon hired a hall so that many could hear this prophet. Thus the Black Muslim movement was born. It now became more tightly organized, with stiff requirements for membership and strict rules of conduct. Fard attracted followers of two earlier black nationlist groups, the religiously oriented Moorish Science Temple Movement founded in Newark, N.J., in 1913 by North Carolina born Timothy Drew or Noble Drew Ali and the more secular African Nationalist (UNIA) movement founded in 1914 in his native Jamaica, British West Indies, by Marcus Garvey (*q.v.*) and brought to America two years later. Both movements floundered after Garvey was deported in 1927 and Drew Ali passed away suddenly in 1929.

Elijah Poole became Fard's closest aide. Fard gave hs followers their "true" Muslim family names to replace the names gotten from "white devil" slave masters. Poole became Elijah Karriem. Fard established a University of Islam in Detroit to give elementary and secondary level instruction to blacks. He selected certain male followers to train as ministers in the movements's Temple Number One in Detroit. As Fard retired more into the background, he designated Elijah to be the Supreme Minister and renamed him Elijah Muhammad. Some of the other ministers were jealous because they had more formal education, but Elijah Muhammad was more dedicated to Fard. He believed Fard to be the Mahdi, sent by Allah to establish a reign of righteousness.

In 1932, Elijah Muhammad went to Chicago where he set up Temple Number Two and where he apparently worked as a dairy deliveryman. He and Fard made a start on Temple Number Three in Milwaukee. Muhammad soon returned to Detroit to aid Fard, who was sent to jail in 1932 because of a follower's sacrificial killing of a brother. Released and ordered out of Detroit in 1933, Fard sought a haven with Muhammad in Chicago but was jailed there also. Elijah aided him and risked jail trying to conceal Fard from persecution by police who felt he stirred up blacks dangerously by his anti-white, black supremacist teachings. Once freed in Chicago, Fard increasingly stayed out of sight and Muhammad ran the Detroit temple. Threatening factional disputes within the movement, as well as police persecution from without, impelled Fard's retirement. He formed a protective, militaristic group, the Fruit of Islam. In 1934, Fard disappeared as mysteriously as he had suddenly appeared.

Elijah Muhammad now became leader of the movement. He deified Fard, proclaiming that he had really been Allah in disguise. He claimed that Allah (Fard) had been instructing him for three years, giving him secrets imparted to no one else. Muhammad now declared himself to be "The Messenger of Allah to the Lost-Found Nation of Islam in the Wilderness of North America."

Membership had climbed to about 8,000 under Fard, but now declined as Muhammad encountered difficulties. In 1934, he was arrested because he and his followers sent their children to the unaccredited University of Islam rather than to Detroit's public schools. Muhammad was convicted and put on six months' probation. Even greater trouble loomed from rivals seeking to wrest control of the movement from him. He fled from Detroit later in 1934 and designated the Chicago Temple as the new headquarters. Threats to his life caused him to leave Chicago. From 1935 to 1942, he lived a fugitive's existence, mostly in Washington, D.C., where he founded Temple Number Four and where he read books at the Library of Congress that bolstered Fard's teachings. For safety, he had to change residences and cities frequently. In May, 1942, tipped off by his enemies, police arrested him in Washington, D.C., on draft resistance and sedition charges. As a result of his teachings, he and his followers refused to bear arms for America in World War II. Muslims objected to military service unless called by Allah to fight in his holy cause. Convicted of encouraging resistance to the draft, Elijah Muhammad was sentenced to five years in jail, actually serving three and a half years in a Federal prison in Michigan before his release in 1946.

By 1945, Muslim membership had fallen to only 1,000. On his return from jail, Muhammad began building it again. His weekly column in the Pittsburgh *Courier* and other black newspapers attracted notice. By early 1959, aided by such dynamic ministers as Malcolm X (*q.v.*), the movement had thirty temples and about 12,000 members. Because of secretiveness, membership can only be estimated. After Mike Wallace's television documentary on the Muslims, "The Hate That Hate Produced," In July, 1959, the mass media discovered, publicized, and inadvertently promoted the movement. By the end of 1960, membership had probably reached 100,000.

The most famous Black Muslim, Malcolm X, broke with Elijah Muhammad in 1964 and tried to found his own movement, but was assassinated the next year. Failing health causes Muhammad to spend much of each year in the house the Muslims bought for him in Phoenix, Ariz., in 1961. One of Muhammad's sons, Wallace D. Muhammad, minister of the Philadelphia temple, is generally acknowledged to be his likely successor. Another son, Herbert, is Muslim public relations director and Elijah, Jr., is second in command of the Fruit of Islam order, which is commanded by Muhammad's son-in-law Raymond Sharrief.

Membership in the movement has fallen off in recent years and may be less than 20,000. Members are taught to abstain from tobacco, pork, alcohol, gambling, dancing, cardplaying, drugs, cosmetics, immorality, and adultery. They are dedicated, enterprising workers on their jobs and in numerous Muslim businesses, including restaurants, supermarkets, cleaning and laundry establishments, pharmacies, and apartment buildings. Many members who were once degraded or criminal become honest, clean-living, hardworking people as Muslims. Those who slip in their devotion to Muslim teachings and codes of conduct are suspended or expelled. Like Father Divine (*q.v.*), Elijah Muhammad is able to rescue and remold people untouched by Christianity or civil rights organizations.

Murphy, Isaac (1856–1896), Jockey

Though a rarity today, black jockeys and trainers once dominated horseracing. In the 1953 edition of his authoritative *Encyclopedia of Sports* Frank Menke states that many veteran horsemen consider a black rider, Isaac Murphy, the greatest jockey of all time. In his peak years, 1884 to 1892, Murphy compiled probably the highest winning average of any jockey in racing history. He was the first jockey to win the Kentucky Derby three times.

Murphy was born in Kentucky's famous horse-breeding Blue Grass

Country, at Pleasant Green Hill in Fayette County, and rode his first race while a teenager. Christened Isaac Murphy Burns, he dropped his surname when he went racing.

Before he left his teens, a black jockey had won the Kentucky Derby. When the first Kentucky Derby was run, at Churchill Downs in Louisville in 1875, fourteen of the fifteen jockeys were blacks. A black named Oliver Lewis rode Aristide to victory. From 1875 to 1902, thirteen Kentucky Derby races were won by nine black jockeys. Black trainers, such as James Williams in 1876, Alex Perry in 1885, and Dud Allen in 1891, trained many winning Derby horses.

Isaac Murphy first won the Kentucky Derby on Buchanan in 1884. Then, on Riley in 1890 and Kingman in 1891, he became the first jockey to win two consecutive Kentucky Derbys. Another black jockey, Jimmy Winkfield, won it in consecutive years, 1901 and 1902. But not until Earle Sande won his third Kentucky Derby in 1930 did another jockey win the race three times. Eddie Arcaro later won it five times.

Murphy was an outstanding rider at many tracks. At Chicago's Washington Park, he won four of the first five runnings of the American Derby in 1884, 1885, 1886, and 1888. A black trainer, Albert Cooper, trained the winning horse in this race in 1885, 1886, and 1888. Murphy won the Suburban Handicap at Belmont Park in New York with Salvatore in 1889, and on Salvatore again, beat the great jockey Ed "Snapper" Garrison at Sheepshead Bay, N.Y., in 1890. In the 1892 Saratoga season, Murphy won 49 of the 51 races he entered.

Murphy owned a race horse, Playfellow, whom he rode to a third-place finish at Lexington in 1886. When Murphy succumbed to an attack of pneumonia at the age of 40, he left an estate worth $50,000.

Winkfield was the last black to win the Kentucky Derby, in 1902, but the last black jockey in the race was Jess Conley, who finished third in 1911. Another notable black jockey, Willie Simms, won the Belmont Stakes in 1893 and 1894, the Kentucky Derby in 1896, and the Preakness in 1898. A black jockey named Monk Overton rode six winners out of six mounts at Washington Park on July 10, 1891.

Newton, Huey, and Seale, Bobby: Black Panther Leaders

The Black Panther Party was founded in Oakland, California, in 1966 by Huey Newton (1942–   ) and Bobby Seale (1937–   ). By courageously confronting and defying police brutality toward, and capitalistic exploitation of, the black masses in the ghettoes, Panthers have won wide admiration among black Americans, especially the young.

Both Panther founders were born in the South of poor families that migrated to California near the end of World War II. Newton was born in Grove, La., youngest of seven children of a laborer who was a part-time Baptist preacher. When Huey was 2, the family moved to California, living in several places before settling in Oakland. Seale was born in Dallas, Tex. When he was 7, his family moved to Oakland.

Newton and Seale learned to fight in Oakland's ghetto. Bobby's first remembrances of Oakland involved aiding his brother and sister fight neighborhood youngsters who refused to share their swings. From the age of 5 onward, Huey was a fearless fighter, usually winning but showing "guts" even when losing.

Both encountered white racism. Huey remembered police brutality. Whenever disturbances occurred at the movies, police would kick out ghetto youngsters, calling them "niggers." Bobby attributed his being barred from playing on his high school basketball and football teams to prejudice. Losing interest in school, he dropped out, joining the Air Force where, like most black servicemen, he often encountered racism at the hands of prejudiced whites even though he was risking his life to help defend the nation and them. Huey became an avid reader of Shakespearean poetry and ancient Chinese philosophy during his second year at Oakland's Technical High School. Seeking a better academic training, he moved in with a married sister in order to attend high school in Berkeley. After some boys jumped him and beat him badly there, he took a hammer to school the next day, striking one of them when they renewed the assault. Jailed and released, he was not permitted to enter Berkeley High School when officials learned that his parents lived in Oakland. He returned to, and graduated from, Tech High where counselors advised him against college, suggesting a trade school or job instead. He was furious that prejudiced counselors would seek to thwart his ambitions for higher education.

Although both grew up in Oakland, the five-year gap in their ages kept Newton and Seale from ever meeting until they were both students at a two-year institution, Merritt College in Oakland, in the early 1960s. Newton enrolled there determined to go to college despite the adverse advice of his high school counselors. After leaving the Air Force, Seale earned his high school diploma in night school while working as a journeyman sheet metal worker in an aircraft electronics plant, then entered Merritt. Both were active in the Afro-American Association at the college, but they came to feel that the organization's emphasis on the African heritage and the black man's past achievements was a retreat into cultural nationalism and away from meeting head on the problems of the current political oppression and economic exploitation of blacks. They withdrew from the assocation and began considering forming their own group. Meanwhile, Newton ran afoul of the law several times, being arrested for theft and burglary and sentenced for assault with a deadly weapon. He also attended a law school in San Francisco, across the bay from Oakland, but dropped out.

Inspired by the teachings of the late Malcolm X (*q.v.*), Newton and Seale founded the Black Panther Party in October, 1966. The party was based on a ten-point program, drafted by Newton, including: black power; full employment; restitution for past exploitation; decent housing; education geared to black needs; exemption from military service for blacks; an end to police brutality; release of all black prisoners; and trial of blacks only before juries drawn from the black community. Other rules and principles established discipline regarding such matters as regular reports to party headquarters, handling of finances, party work assignments, drunkenness and drug addiction, and courtesy to and respect for the black masses. Panthers demanded "power to the people" while raising clenched fists in salute. They wore black berets and jackets and carried guns openly. They called for replacing capitalism with a people-controlled socialistic economy. They provided free breakfasts, along with indoctrination, to hungry ghetto schoolchildren. They raised funds at rallies and by sale of the Panther newspaper.

Soon came clashes with the police. Panthers patrolled the ghettoes to protect the black masses who had long been brutalized, trampled upon, and abused by the police, white businessmen, and other authorities in disregard of constitutional rights. Panther literature termed the police fascist pigs who were tools of greedy slum merchants and landlords. Unaccustomed to being challenged in their freedom to push around blacks, police instituted a vendetta. Panthers were harassed on sidewalks, in traffic, and at their offices and homes by police who seemed anxious to provoke a showdown with these young black militants. Panther Defense Minister Huey Newton was wounded and charged with murder of an Oakland policeman in a shootout in 1967, but was convicted only of manslaughter. In 1970, he was released on bail when an appeals court ordered a new trial. Seale led armed Panthers in a demonstration in the gallery of the California legislature in 1967. In April 1968, police killed an unarmed Panther, Bobby Hutton, and wounded the Panther Minister of Information, Eldridge Cleaver, former convict and famed author of *Soul on Ice*. Cleaver fled to Algeria to avoid being jailed on parole violation charges that he felt were designed not to serve justice but to muzzle his trenchant criticism of American racism.

The Black Panthers have always been an all-black party, but they welcomed active cooperation with white revolutionaries. From exile, Cleaver ran as the 1968 Presidential candidate of the Peace and Freedom Party, an alliance of Panthers and white radicals. Late in 1969, Panther party chairman Bobby Seale went on trial in Chicago along with seven white radicals for conspiracy to foment disruptive demonstrations during the 1968 Democratic nominating convention in Chicago. Seale was given a four-year contempt sentence and set aside for a separate trial because of his courtroom outbursts.

Such vindictiveness as the 1969 slaying in bed of Illinois Panthers by police who raided a Chicago apartment with guns blazing before dawn, aroused sympathy for Panthers. Prominent whites raised money to defend Panthers persecuted by excessive bail and other harassment. Rallies supported Panthers on trial in 1970: thirteen in Connecticut, including Seale, charged with murder of an informer; and twenty-one in New York, charged in a bomb plot.

Twenty-eight Panthers have been killed by police and many more have been jailed, threatening the party's existence. Nonetheless, next to the inspirational Malcolm X, Newton and Seale are the most revered heroes of the Black Revolution because of their fearlessness in the face of oppressive forces that have long intimidated most blacks.

Owens, Jesse (1913–   ), Track Star

During the dozen years from 1933 to 1945, two black athletes reigned as America's greatest and best known sports heroes. By their prowess and their conduct in the only two sports in which blacks then competed freely, boxer Joe Louis (*q.v.*) and track star Jesse Owens paved the way for subsequent breakthroughs, by blacks in major league baseball, football, and basketball. A one-man track team in high school, college, and the 1936 Olympics, Owens was an amazing performer, setting many records in the sprints, hurdles, and running broad jump.

He was born James Cleveland Owens at Danville in northern Alabama, fifteen miles southwest of Decatur. He was the seventh of eleven children of cotton tenant farmers. His family was so poor that sometimes only potato peelings stood between them and starvation. He was called "J.C." by his family, but a teacher misunderstood the mumbled response of the shy lad when he was asked his name the first day of school. After the teacher wrote it down as Jesse, he was too bashful to correct the error, becoming Jesse Owens.

In 1924, when Jesse was 11, his family moved to Cleveland, Ohio. He worked hard to overcome the deficiencies of his rural Alabama education, and had caught up with his class by the time he was 14. When he entered sidewalk track tryouts for students of Fairmount Junior High School on East 107th Street, he astounded the teacher in charge, Charles Riley, by beating older boys and winning the 100-yard dash in ten seconds flat, a junior high school record. He and Riley became close friends as Riley worked intensively to develop Jesse's talents. When Jesse went on to Cleveland's East Technical High School, Coach Riley moved up also, to become track coach there. Meanwhile, the Owens family faced financial troubles as Mr. Owens lost his foundry job in the depressed economy. Jesse worked afternoons and weekends at the shine stand in a shoe repair shop throughout secondary school. His classmates at the integrated high school elected him Student Council president.

He was a one-man track team at East Tech. At the National Inter-scholastic Championship meet in Chicago, on June 17, 1933, Jesse won the 100-yard dash in 9.4 seconds, equaling the world record. He also won the 200-yard dash in 20.7 seconds, close to a world record, and he set a high school broad jump record of 24 feet, 9⅝ inches. Jesse won 75 of the 79 events he entered in high school competition. He lost three other races in his junior year at high school, including one in the 1932 Olympic Games tryouts in Los Angeles where he was beaten by the great black sprinter, Ralph Metcalfe of Marquette University, an Olympic winner. In 1971 Metcalfe entered Congress as successor to William Dawson (q.v.).

Owens entered Ohio State University in Columbus in the fall of 1933, working his way through as a gas station attendant at first, but later being appointed a legislative page through the intercession of a black legislator. In one track meet, he collected 40 of the 45 points Ohio State received. Another time, representing Ohio State in the Big Ten championship meet at Ann Arbor, Michigan, on May 25, 1933, the "Buckeye Bullet" (as he was called) had a fantastic day. In just 75 minutes, he set three world records and tied another, equaling the 100-yard record of 9.4 seconds, and setting a 220-yard mark of 20.3 seconds, a 220-yard low hurdles record of 22.6 seconds, and broad jumping 26 feet, 8¼ inches. Many experts regard this as the greatest single day in track history. His broad jump record stood for a quarter of a century, longest lasting of any track and field record. Another black broad jumper, Ralph Boston of Tennessee A. & I. State University, broke it in 1961 by jumping more than 27 feet.

In the 1936 Olympics at Berlin, Jesse Owens single-handedly demolished Aryan supremacy myths of Adolf Hitler's Nazi movement. Owens was awarded four gold medals for winning the 100 meters in 10.3 seconds, the 200 meters in 20.7 seconds, and the broad jump in 26 feet, 5/16 inches, and for leading America's winning 400-meter relay team that won in 39.8 seconds. Each of these marks set or equaled a world or Olympic record. Owens was the first athlete to win four gold medals (for first-place finishes) in one Olympics. Not until American swimmer Don Schollander in 1964 was this feat duplicated.

After the 1936 Olympic Games, Jesse Owens turned professional and earned enough money in appearances and exhibitions to buy his parents a new eleven-room house in Cleveland by the end of the year. In later years, he tried his hand at various business, some unsuccessful, but did best as a worldwide goodwill ambassador for America and as a molder of youngsters in his position on the Illinois Youth Commission after moving to Chicago.

Besides Owens, Metcalfe, and Boston, some of America's great black track stars include sprinter-jumper De Hart Hubbard, sprinters Howard Drew, Eddie Tolan, Bob Hayes, and Jim Hines; hurdlers Harrison Dillard and Lee Calhoun; middle distance runners John Taylor, John Woodruff, Mal Whitfield, and Lee Evans; broad jumper Bob Beamon; high jumpers Charlie Dumas and John Thomas; pentathlon champion John Borican; decathlon champion Rafer Johnson; and women sprinters Wilma Rudolph and Wyomia Tyus.

Like Joe Louis (*q.v.*), Owens was a good sport who neither took unfair advantage nor made excuses for his defeats nor complained about racial slights and insults. Instead, he simply went out and always did his best, winning, like Louis, many friends for his people by his sincerity and modesty.

Parks, Gordon (1912–   ), Photographer, Writer, and Movie Director

An award-winning creative photographer, Gordon Parks is also a writer and composer. He is the first black to direct full-length movies for a major Hollywood studio.

Parks was the youngest of fifteen children born to a poor farm family in Fort Scott, Kan. Sixteen-year-old George Washington Carver (*q.v.*) had come to this same town from Missouri in 1877 to seek a high school education, but fled westward after a brutal lynching there. Whites were cruel, abusive, and violent toward blacks in this small Kansas town, but Parks rose above hatred. His mother had passed away when he was 16, but she had filled him with ambition and determination to overcome poverty and bigotry with the weapons of love, dignity, and hard work. She taught Gordon never to hate whites and never to give up trying to be somebody simply because blacks faced so many obstacles.

After his mother's funeral, Gordon moved to St. Paul, Minn., where he lived a few weeks with a married sister. Thrown out by his brother-in-law after a quarrel, the 16-year-old lad was on his own, sometimes without a place to lay his head. When several sisters and his father came to St. Paul in the spring of 1929, he roomed with them, while attending Mechanical Arts High School and then the Central High School. He earned his keep during high school by such jobs as waiting tables, being janitor in a flophouse, and playing the piano in a brothel. Between jobs, hunger and bitterness almost drove him to the point of robbery, but he remembered his mother's teachings and turned away in shame.

Forced by poverty to drop out of high school to work full-time, he refused to wallow in despair. Instead, he read voraciously in public libraries in his spare time. Although he could not read music, he wrote many songs, mostly melancholic. He also tried painting, sculpturing, and writing, as well as playing semi-pro basketball. He drove himself so hard that he collapsed in October, 1931, and was dangerously ill for six months. During his convalescence, he decided to keep pushing but not to try to do it all overnight, girding instead for a long climb. On recovering, he worked as a busboy at hotels in St. Paul. Larry Duncan, band leader at one hotel, orchestrated and performed Parks's song, "No Love," after hearing him playing it on the piano. Parks became the only black member of the band, and toured with it until it broke up in New York in 1933, leaving him stranded and penniless in Harlem. He became a Civilian Conservation Corps worker for fifteen months and then went to Minneapolis in July, 1934, to live with the family of the woman he had married the year before.

In the late 1930s, he found the calling for which he searched. While working as a railroad porter and bar car waiter, he was greatly moved by a photographic spread in a magazine left by a passenger. The photos of migrant workers were taken by such great camera artists as Carl Mydans and Ben Shahn, working under Roy Stryker at the Farm Security Administration (FSA). Then, visiting a movie house during a stop-over in Chicago in December, 1937, Parks was overwhelmed by the superb photography of Norman Alley's newsreel footage of the Japanese sinking of the U.S. gunboat *Panay*. He decided to become a photographer. Famed cameramen, such as Robert Capa, whom he met as train passengers, encouraged him.

Buying a Voightlander Brilliant camera in a pawnshop for $12.50, Parks began taking pictures. Within two months, he had his initial exhibit, in an Eastman Kodak store window in downtown Minneapolis. His photographs of attractive young black women began appearing, without fee, in local weekly newspapers. Marva Louis, wife of the heavyweight boxing champion, saw some of his fashion photos in an exclusive St. Paul dress shop and arranged for him to move to Chicago where he was given a darkroom in David Ross's South Side Community Art Center in return for photographing center activities. Mrs. Louis helped him secure a lucrative clientele of society women, white and black, who wanted their portraits done.

His leisure time was spent in more challenging work, photographing poverty in Chicago's South Side. An exhibit of his ghetto photographs at the South Side Center in September, 1941, won him a Rosenwald Fellowship, the first ever granted for studying photography. He spent the last part of his fellowship year studying with Roy Stryker at FSA, and went to work for him afterwards. In 1943, Parks became an Office of War Information (OWI) correspondent. In 1944, he quit in disgust and moved to Harlem when an assignment for him to photograph black combat troops was cancelled because of pressure from bigoted Congressmen who resented publicizing black fighting men.

From 1944 to 1948, he worked under Stryker on a seven-man team doing documentaries for Standard Oil. In 1948, *Life* magazine bought and ran his free-lance photographic article on a young Harlem gang leader. Shortly, Parks was hired by *Life*. He served as a staff photographer from 1948 to 1968, doing photographic essays on segregation, crime, fashions, Black Muslims, Stokely Carmichael (*q.v.*), heavyweight champion Mohammed Ali, a Brazilian slum boy named Flavio, and also a superb spread illustrating his favorite lines from great poetry.

Meanwhile, the versatile Parks was doing writing, television, and movie and musical work. He wrote a novel, *The Learning Tree* (1963), based on his Fort Scott childhood, and an autobiography of his years from his migration northward through his work with OWI, *A Choice of Weapons* (1966). He filmed three documentaries on life in the black ghetto for National Educational Television. Also, in the 1960s he filmed and narrated a television adaptation of his autobiography.

In June, 1968, he signed a contract with Warner Brothers-Seven Arts to direct four motion pictures. The first movie he directed was *The Learning Tree*, an adaptation of his novel. He also wrote the musical

score for this movie. Among his other musical compositions are a piano
concerto, performed first in Vienna in 1953, and three piano sonatas,
initially performed in Philadelphia in 1955.

Payne, Daniel A. (1811–1893), Bishop and Educator

Next to Richard Allen (*q.v.*), Daniel Alexander Payne was the greatest figure in African Methodist Episcopal (A.M.E.) history. He worked
to educate A.M.E. ministers, purchasing Wilberforce University for the
denomination and serving as its president.

Payne was born of free parents in Charleston, S.C. When they passed
away before he was 10, a great-aunt reared him. At the age of 8, he
began attending a Minor's Moralist Society School run by Charleston
free blacks. He later mastered Greek, Latin, French, English, and
mathematics under a private tutor. Meanwhile, he learned trades, being
apprenticed to a shoemaker and a tailor and working four years, 1824–
1828, in a carpentry shop. He was converted and joined the Methodist
Episcopal Church when he was 15.

In 1829, he began instructing three children in their home, but soon
had so many pupils that he set up a school. He had the most successful
school for blacks in Charleston. But, as an aftermath of the uprising led
by Nat Turner (*q.v.*) in 1831, increasingly restrictive measures were
enacted. Finally, the state legislature passed a law in December, 1834,
making it a crime, punishable by fines and whippings, for free blacks to
teach either slaves or other free blacks to read or write. The law took
effect in April, 1835. Payne closed his school, leaving South Carolina in
May.

He entered the Lutheran Theological Seminary at Gettysburg, Pa.,
supporting himself by such jobs as waiting tables and bootblacking.
While there, he held Sunday school for local black children and also
assisted at an A.M.E. church in Carlisle. Although licensed to preach in
1837 and ordained a Lutheran minister in 1839, his first pastorate was
in a Presbyterian church in East Troy, N.Y. He worked so hard that he
injured his throat and was speechless for a year. Near the end of 1840,
as his voice was returning, he moved to Philadelphia and opened a
school, which had sixty pupils by 1843.

In 1841, Payne joined Philadelphia's Bethel A.M.E. Church, the
mother church of the A.M.E. denomination. He became a local A.M.E.
preacher within two years and a full-fledged A.M.E. minister in 1844.
One of his reforms while helping at Bethel in Philadelphia was the
introduction of a trained choir despite opposition of longtime worship-

pers who could not read music. His first pastorate was at Israel A.M.E. church in Washington, D.C., in 1844 where he used his knowledge of carpentry to construct pews for his poor congregation. From 1845 to 1850, as pastor of Bethel A.M.E. Church in Baltimore, reform-minded Payne made it the first A.M.E. church with instrumental music. He also conducted a school for Baltimore children.

As early as 1842, Payne began pushing for an educated ministry, offering resolutions at A.M.E. conferences to require regular courses of study for prospective ministers. He published somewhat tactless epistles in A.M.E. periodicals ridiculing the shortcomings of the ministry and stressing the urgency of having an educated ministry. Generally haughty and dogmatic in pushing reforms, the zealous Payne antagonized many A.M.E. clergy and laity. Attacks on him were so bitter that he tried to withdraw as a delegate to the 1844 General Conference but went at his bishop's insistence. His resolution for a committee to draft a course of study was overwhelmingly rejected, but was subsequently repassed when a tactful and respected elder statesman eloquently pleaded for this needed reform.

In 1850, a church to which Payne was appointed refused to accept him because of his well known insistence on such reforms as dignified worship services. In the impasse, his bishop assigned him to prepare a history of the denomination. Traveling widely to gather material, he made many friends. In 1852, he was elected a bishop despite his tearful insistence that he was unworthy. He worked zealously to raise the level of the denomination's worshippers by promoting literary societies and lyceums. During the Civil War, he visited the White House often, urging President Lincoln to free the slaves.

In 1863, without any money, he boldly contracted for the A.M.E. denomination to purchase Wilberforce University. The school had been founded near Xenia, Ohio, in 1855 for the education of blacks, making it the second oldest black college in America (Lincoln University in Pennsylvania was first in 1854). Wilberforce was founded by a white denomination, the Methodist Episcopal Church, and was run by whites for seven years even though its student body was black. Having purchased it, Bishop Payne became its first black president, serving thirteen years, 1863 to 1876.

In 1881, he served impressively as an A.M.E. delegate to the Methodist Ecumenical Conference held in London. Among the books he published was *The History of the A.M.E. Church from 1816 to 1856* (1891).

Poitier, Sidney (1924–   ), Hollywood Star

Sidney Poitier is the first black actor to become a top-ranking Hollywood star. He was the first Afro-American to be featured in movies as a straight, dramatic actor rather than as an entertainer (singer, dancer, comedian) turned actor. He helped break Hollywood's senseless and tasteless stereotypes depicting blacks primarily as menials who were shiftless, stupid, and terrified of ghosts. He is the only black to win the top Academy Award as best actor of the year.

Born in Miami, Fla., the youngest of eight children, Poitier was carried in infancy to the Bahama Islands where he was reared on his parents' tomato farm on Cat Island. After early private tutoring, he attended Western Senior High School and Governor's High School, both in Nassau. He had to drop out of school to go to work because of slackening demand for tomatoes in the Depression and because arthritic rheumatism incapacitated his father.

At the age of 15, Sidney returned to Miami and lived with a married brother. His West Indian accent was so pronounced that it was nearly impossible for an American to understand him. Nonetheless, he secured a job as a messenger in a drugstore. In Miami he become acutely conscious of segregation and prejudice, which caused him, he recalled, to be confused and frustrated. Wishing to go North, but lacking money, he "rode the rails," and arrived in Harlem with only $1.50. He secured a job as a dishwasher and slept on a roof across from the Capitol Theatre. He enlisted after Pearl Harbor, was trained as a physiotherapist by the Army, and served until 1945.

He returned to New York, where he worked in unsatisfying menial jobs. When he learned that the American Negro Theatre—a Harlem community theater in a library basement—was looking for actors, he applied. Poitier's accent was still so thick and he knew so little of acting that he failed the audition miserably and was rejected by director Frederick O'Neal, who later became the first black to be elected president of the acting union, Actors Equity. Determined to become an actor, Poitier bought a cheap radio and spent six months listening to, and imitating the cultivated voices of, radio announcers and actors. Returning to the American Negro Theatre, he received acting lessons from O'Neal in exchange for serving as a janitor and stagehand. Soon he was appearing in their productions, alternating with Harry Belafonte (*q.v.*) in the lead role in *Days of Our Youth*, and also appearing in such other plays as *On Striver's Row*, *You Can't Take It With You*, and *Riders to the Sea*. In 1946, he was hired at $75 a week for an all-black production of *Lysistrata* that closed after four performances. In 1948, he played in various roles in *Anna Lucasta* on Broadway and played the male lead when it went on tour.

He then shifted to movies, and did not return to Broadway for a decade. His first film was a 1949 Army Signal Corps documentary, *From Whom Cometh My Help.* His first Hollywood role was as a doctor in *No Way Out* in 1950. From that movie onward, he played parts depicting blacks with dignity and respect. Among the films in which he had major roles during the 1950s were *Cry the Beloved Country* (1952), *Blackboard Jungle* (1955), *Something of Value* (1957), and *Edge of the City* (1957). For *The Defiant Ones* (1958), he received the Silver Bear Award at the Berlin film festival of 1958 and also a New York Film Critics' citation. In that film, he played an escaped convict chained to a white convict; the two hated each other but had to cooperate for mutual survival. He also played Porgy in the 1959 Samuel Goldwyn production of *Porgy and Bess*, with the Metropolitan Opera's black baritone, Robert McFerrin, dubbing in Porgy's singing parts. Returning to Broadway in 1959, Poitier gave an electrifying performance as Claudia McNeil's son in the great play by Lorraine Hansberry (*q.v.*), *A Raisin in the Sun.* He also starred in the 1960 film version of that play.

Subsequently, Poitier starred in a long succession of memorable motion pictures, such as *Paris Blues* (1960), *Lilies of the Field* (1963), *A Patch of Blue* (1966), *The Bedford Incident* (1966), *In the Heat of the Night* (1967), *To Sir with Love* (1967), *Guess Who's Coming to Dinner* (1967), *For Love of Ivy* (1968), and *They Call Me Master Tibbs* (1970). He won the Oscar for best actor for his role in *Lilies of the Field* as an itinerant carpenter who helps a group of nuns in the Southwest to overcome local prejudices and construct a church. Previously, Hattie McDaniel had won an academy award in 1939 for her role as a mammy in *Gone with the Wind*, but it was for best supporting actress, not best actress. Poitier had a banner year in 1967: his movie *In the Heat of the Night,* won the Academy Award for best picture of the year, his co-star in that film, Rod Steiger, won the Oscar for best actor, and his co-star in *Guess Who's Coming to Dinner*, Katherine Hepburn, was chosen best actress. Miss Hepburn played the mother of Poitier's fiancée in a movie based on the formerly taboo subject of interracial marriage.

Among the many other notable black movie actors and actresses can be counted Louise Beavers, Harry Belafonte (*q.v.*), Diahann Carroll (*q.v.*), Dorothy Dandridge, Sammy Davis, Jr. (*q.v.*), Ossie Davis and his wife Ruby Dee, Ivan Dixon, Lena Horne (*q.v.*), Rex Ingram,

Canada Lee, Abbey Lincoln, Hattie McDaniel, William Marshall, Clarence Muse, Brock Peters, Frank Silvera, Ethel Waters (*q.v.*), and Leigh Whipper. In 1971 James Earl Jones was nominated for the Oscar for his lead role in *The Great White Hope*.

Powell, Adam Clayton, Jr. (1908–   ), Congressman

As chairman of the important House Committee on Education and Labor during the 1960s, Harlem's representative, Congressman Adam Clayton Powell, Jr., exercised more power than any other black who ever served in the United States Congress. Although possessed of enormous ability and although at times a brilliant legislator, he had shortcomings that led to his fall from power.

Powell had a good start in life through his famous father, Adam Clayton Powell, Sr. (1865–1953). Adam Clayton Powell, Jr., was born in New Haven, Conn., where his father was serving as pastor of Immanuel Baptist Church and taking courses at Yale University Divinity School. The family moved to New York soon after his birth when his father became pastor of 100-year-old Abyssinia Baptist Church, a black church on 40th Street in lower Manhattan with 1,600 members and a heavy debt. Reverend Powell was a great success, building, and moving the church into, a $335,000 Gothic edifice on 138th Street in Harlem in 1923. By the mid-1930's he had 14,000 members, making Abyssinia the largest Protestant church in America. He was also a vigorous crusader against vice and prostitution and a reformer who fed the Depression poor while fighting for better jobs for blacks and better city services for Harlem.

Having known great hardship in his younger life, Reverend Powell tried to shield his son from privation but perhaps overindulged him. Moreover, the younger Powell was so handsome and personable from childhood onward that parishioners pampered him. Spoiled and petted, and smart enough to get by on minimum effort, young Powell concentrated more on good times than on his classes, with the result that he was expelled from City College. His father then sent him to a men's school, Colgate University, in tiny Hamilton, N.Y. Away from wine, women, and high life, he buckled down to his studies and received his bachelor's degree in 1930. He was awarded his master's degree from Columbia University in 1932.

Powell's first job was as manager of his father's church in 1930. He soon became assistant pastor and after his father retired in 1937 became the pastor of Abyssinia. Some parishioners had been upset by young Powell's life style even before he succeeded his father. He drove sporty foreign cars, drank, smoked, dressed like a fashion plate, went night-clubbing, and dated gorgeous showgirls. When parishioners objected to his plans to marry a divorced actress in 1933, he threatened to quit the church and they backed down. Some members, however, both then and subsequently, took vicarious pleasure in their pastor's high living. Powell's first three marriages, to the actress, to an outstanding nightclub pianist, and to a pretty congressional secretary from Puerto Rico, ended in divorce. His fourth wife was a young black beauty queen.

His playboy image was only one side of him. Young Powell joined his father as a powerful crusader on behalf of Harlem's black masses. Light-skinned and blue-eyed, and easily mistaken for white, he nonetheless identified with and became a powerful spokesman for the black man on the street corner. He spoke the language of the people and appealed greatly to them with his demagogic harangues. While Martin Luther King (*q.v.*) was still an infant, the Reverend Adam Clayton Powell, Jr., was leading Harlem's masses in picketing, boycotts, and street demon-strations. A flaming, fiery orator, and a vociferous radical, he led suc-cessful campaigns, from 1931 to 1941, for better hospital care, for black administration of Harlem relief, for lower rent, and for jobs in Harlem. When Powell began his campaigns, almost all of the clerks in retail stores in Harlem were whites who lived outside the ghetto. Nearly all the customers were black but blacks were hired only in such menial roles as janitors and delivery boys. All the buses and subway trains passing through Harlem were driven by whites and the subway change booths were manned by whites. Powell led a bus boycott in 1940 that resulted in the hiring of blacks in all capacities, including as drivers. He led a picket line that resulted in the 1939 World's Fair increasing its black employees from 200 to 732. He also campaigned to have black pharmacists employed in Harlem drugstores, almost all of which, like most Harlem businesses, were owned by whites who lived outside the ghetto and took the profits home. His drive was so successful that by the fall of 1941 all of Harlem's black pharmacists had jobs. He opened up white-collar employment for blacks at the telephone company. In the early 1940s, he pressured the Board of Education to hire blacks on the faculties of its institutions of higher learning, City, Hunter, Queens, and Brooklyn colleges. America had many qualified black scholars but there were none among the 2,000 faculty members of New York City's col-leges because of the incredible prejudice and insensitivity of those re-sponsible for hiring.

Powell's fiery crusading and spellbinding oratory so endeared him to residents of Harlem that they long overlooked his playboy activities and irresponsible behavior. With his pastorate at Abyssinia Baptist Church as his power base in the community and with his proved record of fighting for the black masses, Powell was able to launch a highly successful political career. In 1941, he was elected to the City Council in New York, making him the first black ever to serve on the Council. In 1944, he was elected to the U.S. Congress and reelected continuously thereafter. From 1945 to 1955, he and William L. Dawson (*q.v.*) of Chicago were the only blacks in Congress.

His strong fights for civil rights and other measures on behalf of blacks offset his poor record of attendance to his duties in Congress. He missed many committee meetings, floor debates, and crucial votes. Nonetheless, he became a great hero to many blacks because he defied and took the measure of racist Congressmen, especially Southern Democrats. Haughty and arrogant, and refusing to play the role of the humble, modest, grateful black, he alienated powerful Democrats. The party tried to purge him in 1958 by denying him its support in his bid for reelection at a time when he also faced indictment on tax irregularities. But Harlem's voters rallied to his cause, renominating and reelecting him overwhelmingly over the man endorsed by the party bosses.

In 1960, he became chairman of the vital Education and Labor Committee. A brilliant parliamentary tactician, he piloted through Congress the major antipoverty and aid to education bills of the Kennedy and Johnson Administrations. But his continued absenteeism, his high-handedness toward his congressional colleagues and committee members, and his cavalier disregard of accepted conventions gave his foes a means of removing him from positions where he could aid his people so powerfully. To avoid paying a court-ordered slander judgment won by a black woman he accused of being in racketeering, he fled from Harlem to a haven in the Bahamas, returning only infrequently. He was also accused of taking kickbacks from the salary checks paid his third wife as his office secretary at a time when she was actually living in Puerto Rico. While still married to her he was accused of taking European tours on committee funds with the beauty queen who served on his staff and later became his fourth wife. All Powell's irregularities were the sort of things that some white Congressmen had long been doing with impunity. But for a black man to play the game as they did, and to do so with such style and verve, upset the powers that be in Congress.

In 1967, the House excluded him from his seat on grounds of his misuse of funds. But he was reelected in a special election in 1967 and in the regular election in 1968. He was finally seated in January, 1969, but was fined and stripped of his seniority. The Supreme Court ruled in

June, 1969, that he had been excluded unconstitutionally and gave him the right to recover back pay. But the powerful chairmanship he held from 1960 to 1967 was gone forever.

Blacks had lost out because his irresponsible behavior gave their enemies a chance to strike at them by emasculating him. Congressmen Dawson also headed a standing committee but he was too unimaginative and too much of a party regular ever to be an independent-minded maverick like Powell. In the June, 1970, Democratic primary, Harlem blacks finally turned against Powell, giving the nomination to another black, State Assemblyman Charles B. Rangel, who was later elected congressman.

Price, Leontyne (1927–   ), Opera Star

During the 1960s, Leontyne Price became the reigning prima donna of the Metropolitan Opera Company and was widely acknowledged to be one of the great sopranos of opera history. Her career was aided by white Mississippians who remain close friends.

She was born Mary Leontyne Price in Laurel, Miss. Her father was a sawmill carpenter, her mother a midwife. Both of her grandfathers were Methodist ministers. She and her brother were given a strict, religious upbringing, worshipping regularly in St. Paul's Methodist Church where she sang in the choir. Upon graduating from Oak Park High School in 1944, she entered Wilberforce University in Ohio to study to become a public school music teacher. While she was there, a cleavage led to the division of the campus into state-supported Central State College under President Charles Wesley (who formerly headed the total institution) and A.M.E.-affiliated Wilberforce University under newly appointed President Leander Hill. Her music education curriculum put her with Central State. Dr. Wesley—a music-minded historian whose daughter, Charlotte Wesley Holloman, later became a leading opera singer in Europe—encouraged Miss Price to become a professional singer, which, by the time she graduated in 1948, she decided to do.

Lacking money, she faced the dismal prospect of doing popular singing to accumulate funds for serious vocal training, a detour that often proved a dead end. Her aunt, who worked for the white Chisholm family in Laurel, apprised them of Leontyne's plight. Mrs. Elizabeth Chisholm, who had long watched Leontyne's progress and who had faith in her ability, paid Miss Price's living expenses during four years of study at the Juilliard School of Music in New York on a scholarship. Without this aid, she could not have accepted the scholarship. The Chisholms, whom Miss Price regards as her second family, have followed her career closely ever since, attending her important debuts. Both whites and blacks in Laurel take great pride in the success of this home town girl and welcome her warmly on her visits there, which she makes as often as possible because of the warmth she finds.

A former concert singer, Florence Page Kimball, was her vocal coach at Juilliard, 1948–1952, and continued her teacher, friend, and adviser thereafter. At Juilliard, Miss Price's performance as Mistress Ford in the student production of Verdi's *Falstaff* led composer Virgil Thomson to choose her to sing the role of Saint Cecilia in the April, 1952, Broadway revival of his *Four Saints in Three Acts*, originally presented on Broadway in 1934, with an all-black cast. Her fine work at Juilliard also brought invitations to sing at the Tanglewood Festival.

Attracted by her performance in *Four Saints*, lyricist Ira Gershwin had her audition for a revival of his brother's opera, *Porgy and Bess*, first presented in 1935, two years before composer George Gershwin passed away. With Miss Price as Bess and with Arkansas-born concert baritone William Warfield as Porgy, the revival played to packed houses from June, 1952, to June, 1954, including a nationwide tour, eight months on Broadway, and a State Department tour of Europe, including Russia. Having better success than Porgy had with Bess, Mr. Warfield married Miss Price in 1952.

After her triumph as Bess, Miss Price climbed steadily to the top of the opera world. She made her Town Hall concert debut in November, 1954. She sang the role of Floria Tosca in the NBC-TV production of Puccini's *Tosca* in 1955, and later sang leading roles in such other operas on television as Mozart's *Magic Flute* in 1956 and his *Don Giovanni* in 1960.

Her first appearance in an opera house was as Madame Lidoine in Francis Poulenc's *Dialogues of the Carmelites* for the San Francisco Opera Company in 1957. In later seasons, she sang the lead roles for them in such operas as Verdi's *Aida* and *Il Trovatore*. With the Lyric Opera of Chicago, she sang the lead roles in such operas as Massenet's *Thaïs* in 1959 and Puccini's *Madame Butterfly* in 1960. Rapidly establishing herself as the greatest Aida of all time, she sang the role at the Vienna State Opera in 1959 and at the great Teatro alla Scala in Milan in 1960.

Her Metropolitan Opera debut came on January 27, 1961, as the Countess Leonora in Verdi's *Il Trovatore*, in which she scored a great operatic triumph. That season, she sang such lead roles as Cio-cio-san in *Madame Butterfly* and Lui in Puccini's *Turandot*. She had the honor of opening the Met's 1961–1962 season, singing the lead role of Minnie in

Puccini's *La Fanciulla del West* (The Girl of the Golden West). The reigning soprano at the Metropolitan, its prima donna absoluta, she sang the lead role in the historic opening opera, Samuel Barber's specially commissioned *Antony and Cleopatra*, when the Metropolitan Opera Company moved into its new home at the Lincoln Center for the Performing Arts on September 16, 1966.

Among the other blacks who have sung leading roles at the Metropolitan Opera since contralto Marian Anderson (*q.v.*) debuted there in 1955 are baritone Robert McFerrin, tenor George Shirley, sopranos Mattiwilda Dobbs, Gloria Davey, Martina Arroyo, and Reri Grist, and mezzo-soprano Grace Bumbry.

Randolph, A. Philip (1889–), Labor Leader

As founding president of the first black union chartered by a major labor federation, Asa Philip Randolph is America's leading black unionist. He is also one of the most revered leaders in the civil rights movement.

Randolph was born in Crescent City, Fla., where his father was a struggling African Methodist minister. To help out, Philip worked at many jobs that stretched out his schooling, including newsboy, grocery clerk, and railroad section hand. He completed high school at Methodist-run Cookman Institute in Jacksonville, later merged with Mary McLeod Bethune's (*q.v.*) school at Daytona Beach.

On finishing Cookman, Randolph migrated to New York City, where he held such jobs as waiter on Fall River Line Boats, Consolidated Edison porter, and elevator operator. Meanwhile, he took evening courses, especially government, economics, literature, and philosophy, at City College (CCNY).

Appalled at working conditions, he was not content to push ahead himself, but worked to organize his fellow workers to better conditions through unity. He was fired from the Fall River job when the manager overheard him planning a mass protest against deplorable work conditions. In 1917, he organized a small union of elevator operators in New York City. He also aided in organizing campaigns among such other groups as the garment workers.

Randolph moved increasingly to the left. He spoke on street-corner soapboxes about Afro-American problems, capitalism's shortcomings, and Socialist prospects. In 1917, he and a brilliant, witty law student, Chandler Owen, founded a monthly magazine, *The Messenger,* subtitled "The Only Radical Negro Magazine in America." As Socialists and pacifists, they opposed, in editorials and speeches, American participation in World War I. Randolph refused to serve. He was arrested in Cleveland, Ohio, in June, 1918, and jailed, but only for a few days, because of his antiwar stance. Becoming well-known as *The Messenger*'s co-editor, Randolph also wrote articles for such other magazines as *Opportunity* and *Survey Graphic*. He became an instructor at the Rand School of Social Science in New York. During and after the war, he ran unsuccessfully on the Socialist ticket for such posts as state legislator and congressman. Although a radical and Socialist, Randolph steadfastly opposed Communism.

Despite his early union activities, he considered himself primarily a writer and editor, until 1925. That year, Randolph set out to organize workers on railroad sleeping cars. He had long been concerned about the exploitation of Pullman car porters and maids who worked on trains about 350 hours a month for only $70 monthly, including tips. When they tried to organize, the Pullman Company fired activists and set up a worthless company union. Meeting in Harlem with half a dozen porter representatives in August, 1925, Randolph agreed to organize a real union. The group elected him president. He gave *The Messenger* a new subtitle, "The Official Organ of the Brotherhood of Sleeping Car Porters."

The company attacked Randolph as a radical, red, and outsider (he had never worked as a Pullman porter). Some moderate black leaders, editors, and preachers likewise denounced him as an "atheistic agitator." Ignoring attacks, Randolph pushed ahead. By 1928, he signed up over half the workers and prepared to strike for recognition and better hours and conditions. But the American Federation of Labor (AFL) withheld aid and Randolph had to call it off. Discouraged, many dropped out. Randolph was offered a large sum of money by company supporters to abandon the effort, but, though needing it, he turned it down. He kept on and workers again signed up. Railway labor law changes in 1934 gave him another chance. In 1935, workers voted 5,931 to 1,422 for the Brotherhood to represent them in collective bargaining. In 1937, the Pullman Company signed a contract recognizing Randolph's union. The Brotherhood immediately got hours reduced to 240 a month with $2,000,000 in wage increases, and much better job conditions. By 1950, the Pullman car workers received a minimum of $240 a month for 205 hours of work and had 18,000 members. The union belonged to the AFL. In 1957, Randolph became a vice president of the merged AFL-CIO.

Throughout, Randolph also fought for civil rights. He was advocating nonviolent protest demonstrations in 1940, a decade and a half before they caught on. During World War II—which he supported as a war of survival for democracy against totalitarian facism—he threatened a March on Washington to protest job discrimination. This led to President Franklin Roosevelt's Executive Order 8802 establishing the Fair Employment Practices Committee (FEPC). Randolph was a prime mover behind the 1963 March on Washington. Respected as the elder statesman of the civil rights movement, he helped unify moderate and radical forces in the movement.

After forty-three years as president of the Sleeping Car Porters, he retired in 1968 to devote his energies to the A. Philip Randolph Institute, directed by civil rights strategist Bayard Rustin. Other leading black labor unionists include: Isaac Myers, who served as president of the National Labor Union in 1870; Willard Townsend, who organized the redcaps into the United Transport Service Employees, served as a CIO vice president, and joined Randolph on the Executive Board of the merged AFL-CIO; and George L. P. Weaver, an executive of the Electrical, Radio, & Machine Workers Union, who was appointed Assistant Secretary of Labor by President John Kennedy.

Rillieux, Norbert (1806–1894), Inventor

Norbert Rillieux invented the revolutionary multiple-effect vacuum evaporation process, refining sugar whiter and grainier. His technique became the basic manufacturing process in many industries.

Rillieux was born free in New Orleans, La. His father, Vincent Rillieux, was a white engineer; his mother, Constance Vivant, was apparently a free mulatto. The father had invented such things as a steam-operated cotton-baling press. Since Norbert was so bright, his father sent him to school in Paris.

Rillieux showed such ability in engineering that he became an instructor of applied mechanics at L'École Centrale in Paris in 1830. That year, he published outstanding scientific papers on steam engines and efficient use of steam. He probably developed the theory for his invention at this time.

Heretofore, sugar was refined by the "Jamaica train" process, which involved boiling sugar cane juice in a series of open vats, with slaves using long ladles to transfer the boiling juice from one to another. Much was lost by evaporation in this slow, cumbersome process that left the sugar brownish and lumpy. A "single-effect" vacuum pan to boil sugar solution to grain was developed in 1812. Other inventors sought to devise a multiple-effect process to reuse the latent heat from the boiling process.

Rillieux's genius found the solution. He enclosed condensing coils in a vacuum chamber, using the vapor from the first chamber to evaporate the juice in a second vacuum chamber, and so on. Unable to interest French machinery manufacturers, he agreed to be chief engineer of a new refinery Edmund Forstall was building in New Orleans, but quit shortly because of a dispute between his father and Forstall. Rillieux tried to get a wealthy free black planter named Durnford in Plaquemines Parish (county) to try out his process, but he refused. The first test of the system was made with a triple-effect evaporator Rillieux built and installed in 1834 on the Louisiana plantation of Zenon Ramon. For some reason, it failed, as did another attempt in 1841.

But in 1845 he succeeded with machinery built to his specifications by Merrick & Towne of Philadelphia and installed by him on Theodore Packwood's Myrtle Grove Plantation below New Orleans. Rillieux's two American patents were Numbers 3,237 (August, 1843) and 4,879 (December, 1846). For the next decade, he traveled from plantation to plantation installing his system. Judah P. Benjamin, later Confederate Secretary of State, had him install it on his Louisiana plantation, Bellechasse. Since social custom forbade entertaining this black engineer at home, most planters apparently provided him a special house with a staff of slave servants so that they and neighboring planters could confer and dine with him while the installation proceeded.

Rillieux also worked out a brilliant plan for draining the lowlands of New Orleans. But the influential Forstall, now his enemy, persuaded state legislators and city aldermen not to award the project to Rillieux. Instead, a company headed by Forstall, with an engineer he chose, received the contract. With restrictions on free blacks increasing, Rillieux returned to France about 1861.

He found that a German worker at Merrick & Towne had copied his drawings and sold them to a factory in Magdeburg. Thus, Europe's first multiple-effect vacuum evaporator was installed in a sugar beet factory in France's Nord region in 1852. But, lacking proper understanding of Rillieux's designs, it and subsequent attempts failed. For nearly two decades, Rillieux abandoned engineering for Egyptology, and worked on deciphering hieroglyphics.

In 1881, he resumed his work in engineering, devising the system now universally used in cane and sugar beet refineries. But he lost out in bitter patent fights in France that apparently broke his heart and put him in his grave in Paris. Today, his basic technique is used in manufacturing sugar, condensed milk, soap, gelatin, and glue and in many other manufacturing processes, such as recovering waste liquids in distilleries and paper factories. Although he is little known, Rillieux made one of the world's great inventions.

Robeson, Paul (1898–   ), Athlete, Actor, Singer

Many critics and playgoers regard Paul Bustill Robeson as the finest Othello ever to act the part since Shakespeare wrote it. Similarly, he put more meaning into Negro spirituals with his rich baritone voice than any other concert singer. Moreover, he was a brilliant student and All-American athlete. Despite such success, he found racial insults so unbearable that he blighted his career during the Cold War by courageously speaking out against American intolerance while openly praising Soviet Russia as free of racial prejudice.

Robeson was born in Princeton, N. J., youngest by far of eight children. His father was a Methodist minister who had been a slave on the Robeson plantation in North Carolina before he escaped to freedom in 1860 and worked his way through Lincoln University. His part-Indian mother came from a distinguished Philadelphia family of free blacks. She had a fatal cookstove accident when Paul was 6, leaving him alone with his 59-year-old father, since the other children had grown up and moved away. Reverend Robeson and his son grew very close, moving to Westfield and then settling in Somerville, N. J., when Paul was 13. Reverend Robeson set high standards, demanding perfection always. When Paul had a 97 average in high school, his father was disappointed that he had fallen short of a perfect 100. When Paul made seven A's and one B in his first year of college, his father asked why he fell to a B in one course.

Paul enjoyed high school and college. The top student and athlete at Somerville's integrated high school, he was welcomed at the homes and parties of white schoolmates. Meanwhile, he sang in the choir of his father's church. In statewide competition, he won a scholarship to Rutgers University at New Brunswick, making him the third black ever enrolled in New Jersey's state university. At Rutgers, he was a brilliant Phi Beta Kappa student and also a 12-letter athlete, winning varsity letters three seasons in each of four sports. As a football end, he was chosen All-American in 1917 and 1918, and also starred at center for the basketball team. He did not sing in the glee club, but won honors in oratory, extemporaneous speaking, and debating, was student commencement speaker, and was one of the four seniors selected for the Cap and Skull Society.

His father, who passed away just before his senior year, wanted him to be a minister, but when Paul balked, they agreed he should study law. Upon graduating from Rutgers in 1919, Robeson moved to Harlem and entered Columbia University Law School. But he was unenthusiastic about law. While a law student, he played a few games of professional football in 1921 for the Akron Indians, a mostly white major league team coached by halfback Fritz Pollard, the second black All-American (Brown University, 1916). The pathologist Robeson married that year, Eslanda Goode, noted his lack of interest in law or pro football and pushed him into a stage career. His father had detested acting as sinful, but after repeated efforts Eslanda persuaded Paul to play the cross-bearer in the Harlem Y.W.C.A. production of Ridgely Torrence's *Simon the Cyrenian*. She persuaded members of the famed Provincetown Players to come from their Greenwich Village playhouse to see and meet the athlete turned actor. Robeson took a liking to these theatrical professionals. Through his wife's efforts, he secured a part in *Taboo* that played briefly on Broadway in 1922.

On graduating from Columbia in 1922 and passing the state bar, Robeson was taken into the firm of a Rutgers man who was a prominent New York lawyer. But Robeson soon found the work little to his liking and noted that the white law clerks and a senior partner resented having a black, even a famed athlete, in the firm. He left to open a small law office in Harlem.

Meanwhile, his acting friends were incorporating the reluctant Robeson into the company at their Provincetown Playhouse on Mac-dougal Street in the village. He was well received in the title role of their revival of Eugene O'Neill's *Emperor Jones*, a role first made famous by Charles Gilpin (*q.v.*). He gave up law forever. He became a friend and admirer of O'Neill who worked closely with, and whose plays brought fame to, the Provincetown group. In 1924, Robeson played the male lead in O'Neill's daring drama about interracial marriage, *All God's Chillun Got Wings*.

In 1925, his friends discovered that Robeson could also sing. One day early in April, Eslanda heard him relaxing by singing spirituals played by his composer-pianist friend, Lawrence Brown. Paul was always singing, but she now realized he had enormous talent. She alerted the Provincetown players. They listened, agreed he had great ability, and hired Greenwich Village Theatre for an April concert. Ticket sales lagged until columnist Heywood Broun plugged it after hearing a preview at a party. Although the April 19 concert was Robeson's first public appearance as a singer, it was a sellout and a huge success. America acclaimed a new talent. He sang only Negro spirituals and folk songs, the first time a concert artist had not included some of the standard repertoire of classical arias and art songs. A promoter signed Robeson and Brown, who formerly accompanied tenor Roland Hayes (*q.v.*), to a concert tour.

In the fall of 1925, Robeson was an artistic hit in a London revival of *Emperor Jones*. Returning, he resumed his concert tours before sellout audiences. To save his voice from overstrain, he had to take training from such teachers as Amanda "Montague Ring" Aldridge of England, daughter of the great black Shakespearean actor, Ira Aldridge (*q.v.*). But he insisted on retaining his natural style of singing spirituals as he had heard them in rural black churches pastored by his father. He appeared in other plays, such as *Black Boy* in 1926. In the 1930 revival of the Jerome Kern-Oscar Hammerstein II hit, *Show Boat,* he movingly sang "Old Man River," sung in the original production four years earlier by the outstanding black dramatic baritone Jules Bledsoe.

During the 1930s, Robeson lived mostly in Europe, partly in protest of American racism. There he starred in such plays as *Stevedore* and O'Neill's *The Hairy Ape*, also making such movies as *Sanders of the River*. His most satisfying role was when he finally played Othello for the first time, in 1930, in London, to tremendous critical acclaim. Subsequently, he made such Hollywood films as *Emperor Jones, Show Boat*, and *King Solomon's Mines*. In movies he had to play parts he disliked, parts in line with Hollywood's offensive stereotyping of blacks that reflected white prejudices. Robeson was sensitive also to such insults as being relegated to a hotel freight elevator right after a Carnegie Hall ovation, being denied service in a San Francisco restaurant, and even being refused a glass of water to wash down an aspirin in a Times Square drugstore. He sent his only child to school in Switzerland and Russia to shield him from American prejudice. He began including little lectures against racial bias in the middle of his concerts, to the great annoyance of many who came to hear him sing, not complain about America's way of life.

Despite his growing estrangement with American ways, his greatest triumph came in October, 1943, when *Othello* opened on Broadway, starring him along with José Ferrer as Iago and Ferrer's wife, Uta Hagen, as Desdemona. It ran well into 1944, for a record-breaking 296 performances, longer than any Shakespearean drama theretofore. Robeson was selected actor of the year. He was at his peak in the 1940s, earning more than $100,000 a year as a Broadway and Hollywood actor, as a concert artist, and a recording star.

But his popularity began to slip in 1947 as he spoke out increasingly against Jim Crow. In 1948, he campaigned for Progressive Party nominee Henry Wallace and associated with Marxist groups. When he publicly doubted whether black Americans would fight for racist America against what he saw as nondiscriminatory Soviet Russia, his career was ruined. By 1950, his recital income dwindled to less than $2,000. Moreover, the State Department cancelled his passport, cutting him off from lucrative European appearances.

A comeback in the late 1950s failed when he continued his outspoken indictment of the ills of American society. Many black actors, musicians, athletes, singers, and other entertainers of Robeson's day simply bit their lips and endured insults silently, hoping that their performances would win friends and gradually break down prejudice. Robeson could not take that passive path, even at the cost of his career. It is to America's shame and loss that his great talents were stifled because he refused to suffer abuse in silence.

Robinson, Bill (1878–1949), Tap Dancer

Bill "Bojangles" Robinson was one of America's greatest tap dancers. He delighted millions of people, and made millions of dollars, with the rhythmic patter of his feet in Broadway musicals and in Hollywood movies, especially with Shirley Temple.

He was born Luther Robinson in Richmond, Va., but changed his name to Bill. His father worked in a machine shop and his mother was a choir singer, but he was orphaned as a baby and raised by a grandmother who had once been a slave. When only six, he was dancing for nickels and dimes at Richmond beer gardens. Since Bill was always fighting, his teachers were relieved when he quit school at the age of 8 and hitched rides to Washington, D.C., to work in a stable. Wanting to be a jockey, he eagerly carried water for racehorse grooms. Other stable boys taught him the buck-and-wing and other dancing steps they performed on street corners for extra money.

He began dancing professionally with minstrel Eddie Leonard for $5 a week and board, touring in a show, *The South Before the War,* which Bill joined when it came through town. Subsequently, he traveled with other shows and also worked for a long stretch as a waiter in a Richmond restaurant.

In 1906, he abandoned all else for nightclub and vaudeville dancing. He began at $75 a week and rose steadily to earnings of more than $1,000 a week at America's greatest vaudeville house, the Palace Theater in New York, just off Times Square and Broadway. Bojangles, as he was nicknamed, had been a vaudeville headliner for many years before he came to the attention of drama and music critics by dancing onto the legitimate stage in *Blackbirds of 1928.*

That show, produced by white promoter Lew Leslie, was to have starred Florence Mills (*q.v.*), but she succumbed late in 1927. Leslie had a good show, with singers Adelaide Hall and Ada Ward, comic pantomimist Johnnie Hudgins, and such songs as "Diga Diga Do," "I Must Have That Man," and "I Can't Give You Anything but Love." But he needed a strong performer to hold it together as Flo Mills had done in *Blackbirds of 1926*. Since Bill Robinson was unknown to Broadway musical fans, except the few who also went to vaudeville shows, building the show around him was a gamble. But it paid off— Robinson was a great success and a national star. The show ran at the Liberty Theatre on Broadway more than a year, for 518 performances.

After starring in another Broadway show, *Brown Buddies*, that closed in 1930, the 52-year-old tap dancer went to Hollywood. From 1930 to 1939, Bojangles made fourteen motion pictures for major studios. The biggest box-office hits among these movies co-starred child actress Shirley Temple with him in such films as *The Little Colonel, Littlest Rebel,* and *Rebecca of Sunnybrook Farm.*

He returned to the stage in 1939 in *The Hot Mikado*, a parody of the Gilbert and Sullivan operetta. Co-starring black comic Eddie Green (later on radio's "Duffy's Tavern" program), *Hot Mikado* was a smash hit at the New York World's Fair. Robinson's Broadway musical, *Memphis Bound,* folded quickly, however. In 1943, he starred in the movie *Stormy Weather* with Lena Horne (*q.v.*). A carefree, simple person, Robinson made about $3,000,000 in his career, but he spent it generously if not always wisely and was penniless at the end.

Bojangles invented the stair tap dance, dancing up and down steps in an unbelieveably rhythmic pattern. His feet could make and coordinate more distinct rhythms simultaneously than any other tap dancer. Robinson inspired many white and black dancers, but none matched the master. Among the many other great black popular dancers are cakewalker Ida Forsyne; Buck and Bubbles (John Bubbles was the original Sportin' Life in *Porgy and Bess*); a later Sportin' Life, Avon Long; the Nicholas Brothers (Harold and Fayard); and Bunny Briggs.

Robinson, Jackie (1919–   ), Baseball Star

A great and exciting player, Jackie Robinson was elected to baseball's exclusive Hall of Fame. His successful pioneering smashed the color bar in baseball and in all major-league team sports.

He was born John Roosevelt Robinson in Cairo, Ga., youngest of five children of poor cotton sharecroppers. His father abandoned them when Jackie was a baby. Left with five children under 10, Mrs. Robinson migrated to Pasadena, Calif., where her brother lived. A devout, hard-working woman, Mrs. Robinson did laundering, ironing, and day's work, and saved her pennies to buy a house large enough to take in roomers. Like the other children, Jackie helped out by working at odd jobs—newsboy, shine boy, gardener, caddie, and Rose Bowl vendor.

Jackie idolized his brother Matthew, called Mack, who was a track star at Pasadena Junior College and the University of Oregon. Six years Jackie's senior, Mack set a junior college broad jump record, a 20.7 second world 220-yard record soon broken by Jesse Owens (*q.v.*), and finished second to Owens in the 200 meters at the 1936 Olympics in Berlin.

Jackie became a football, basketball, track, and baseball star at John Muir Technical High School in Pasadena, from which he graduated in 1937. At Pasadena Junior College, 1937 to 1939, he batted .417 and .466 in two seasons, stealing 25 bases in 24 games one season. Chicago White Sox manager Jimmy Dykes labeled him major-league caliber then. But Jackie enjoyed football, basketball, and track much more, setting a junior college broad jump record of 25 feet, 6½ inches (breaking his brother's record), and scoring 28 points in one basketball game. In his second season as halfback, he led Pasadena to eleven straight victories and the national junior college championship, scoring 131 points and gaining more than 1,000 yards.

He entered the University of California at Los Angeles in 1939, teaming with power-running Kenny Washington to become the UCLA Touchdown Twins. In 1939, the Twins, along with end Woody Strode (now a movie actor), led UCLA to an undefeated season. Jackie, who averaged a fantastic twelve yards per carry, drew some All-American nominations, but Kenny was the consensus All-American. Playing forward in basketball, Jackie led the Pacific Coast Conference in scoring two successive years. In his first UCLA baseball game, he stole five bases, including home. In track, he was the 1940 National Collegiate Athletic Association (NCAA) broad jump champion.

Robinson dropped out of college to take a job in the spring of 1941, only a few months short of graduation. The family needed his earnings and he wanted to save to get married. His job as a camp athletic director petered out shortly. But he performed so sensationally in the August, 1941, All-Star Game—scoring one of the two touchdowns the college seniors managed against the powerful professional Chicago Bears—that the Los Angeles Bulldogs hired him. This was a professional football team in the Pacific Coast league, a top minor league that was integrated. Robinson was always less interested in baseball than in football and basketball because some topflight football and basketball minor leagues had black players, whereas organized baseball was lily-white from the major leagues down to the smallest minor league. Robinson was also selected to play on the College All-Star basketball team.

Drafted in April, 1942, Robinson went to Officers Candidate School, after his protests exposed the deliberate rejections of all black applicants at his camp. Upon his discharge as a first lieutenant late in 1944, he became basketball coach at Sam Houston College for blacks in Austin, Tex. Since the pay was low and he needed more money to help his mother and to prepare for marriage, he quit to join a black baseball team, the Kansas City Monarchs, in spring training at Houston, for $400 a month. A few days later, in April, 1945, he and two other black ballplayers were given a tryout by Boston Red Sox officials at Fenway Park. It was a farce—the Red Sox were merely trying to ease mounting pressures to end baseball segregation and had no intention of signing them. During the 1945 season as Monarchs shortstop, Robinson batted .345.

Meanwhile, Branch Rickey, president of the Brooklyn Dodgers, was carefully laying plans to really integrate baseball. From careful scouting reports, he chose Jackie Robinson as the player most likely to succeed on ability and character. Signing Robinson for a $3,500 bonus and $600 monthly salary, Ricky gave the outspoken scrapper strict instructions to accept abuse silently his first years so as not to jeopardize the experiment.

In October, 1945, the world learned that Robinson was the first black in the modern major leagues, having been signed to play with the Dodgers' top farm team, the Montreal Royals of the Triple-A International League. Playing for Montreal during 1946 at second base, Robbie topped the league in batting with .349, stole 40 bases, and led the Royals to the league and Little World Series championships. Moving up to the Dodgers as a first baseman in 1947, he played spectacularly and was named National League Rookie of the Year. His finest season was 1949, when, playing second base, he led the league in batting with .342, hit 16 home runs, 12 triples, and 38 doubles, drove in 124 runs, and led the Dodgers to the National League pennant. In his ten seasons on the Brooklyn Dodgers, 1947–1956, the team won the pennant six times and won its only World Series, in 1955. (It later took three World Series as the Los Angeles Dodgers in 1959, 1963, and 1965). Robbie retired before the 1957 season began, having played every position except catcher and pitcher and having a .311 lifetime major-league average.

His pathbreaking efforts caused other sports to integrate. The first black players in the National Football League were his UCLA teammates, Washington and Strode, hired by the Los Angeles Rams in the spring of 1946. In 1962, Robinson received the great honor of being named to baseball's Hall of Fame at the first election at which he was eligible. His teammate, catcher Roy Campanella, became in 1969 the second black among baseball's 115 greats thus far elected to the Hall. After retiring, Robinson went into business and politics, serving in such posts as the vice presidency of the Chock Full O' Nuts restaurant chain and as a political aide to Republican Governor Nelson A. Rockefeller of New York.

Rowan, Carl (1925–), Journalist; Federal Executive

Carl Thomas Rowan is a prize-winning journalist. As head of the United States Information Agency (USIA), he was the first black to serve on the National Security Council.

Rowan was one of five children born in Ravenscroft, Tenn., to a poor family that later moved to McMinnville. There he hoed bulb grass for ten cents an hour. On Saturdays and in summers, he waited on the corner with other black laborers to be hired at 25 cents an hour.

But he desired to rise above casual manual labor. His first writing, a poem composed when he was 13, was good enough to be read on the high school stage. An ambitious student, he was class president and valedictorian at Bernard High School in 1942. His earnings in a tuberculosis hospital that summer enabled him to enroll at Tennessee Agricultural and Industrial State College in Nashville. There he passed stiff nationally competitive Navy examinations to enter the V-12 Naval officer training program. Heretofore the Navy lacked black officers. His acceptance by classmates and instructors, 1943–44, in the naval training program on a Kansas campus where he was the only black in a company of 334 trainees, strengthened his resolve to be somebody. Becoming in 1944 one of the first fifteen blacks to earn a commission in the Navy, he served as communications officer on two Atlantic ships.

After his discharge, Rowan returned to Oberlin College in Ohio where he had taken part of his naval training, and graduated in 1947 with a major in mathematics. He then entered the University of Minnesota, earning a master's degree in journalism and simultaneously writing for two black weeklies, the Minneapolis *Spokesman* and the St. Paul *Recorder*. He did public opinion surveys for another black newspaper, the Baltimore *Afro-American*, during the 1948 Presidential campaign.

In November, 1948, the 23-year-old Rowan was hired as a copyreader by the leading newspaper in Minnesota, the Minneapolis *Tribune*. In 1950, he became a general assignment reporter, one of the few black reporters on a white daily. Other pioneering black journalists included Ted Poston of the New York *Post* and Roi Ottley of the Chicago *Tribune.*

In December, 1950, Rowan set out to tour the South to write a series on life under segregation. More letters arrived on this "How Far from Slavery?" series, than on any other that ever ran in the *Tribune. Look* reprinted excerpts. The articles were expanded into Rowan's first book, *South of Freedom* (1952). *The Pitful and the Proud* (1956) was based on his observations in India during 1954 as a State Department international exchange lecturer. Parts of this book first appeared as articles in the *Tribune* and thirty other newspapers. Rowan became the only newspaperman to win three successive Sigma Delta Chi awards for reporting: 1954, for the nation's best general reporting for his 1953 articles on school segregation cases; in 1955 for best foreign correspondence for his articles on India; and in 1956 for political coverage in reporting the turmoil in Southeast Asia and the Bandung Conference. His third book, *Go South to Sorrow* (1957) was based on a return tour of the South. He also wrote *Wait Till Next Year* (1960), a biography in collaboration with Jackie Robinson (*q.v.*).

From 1961 to 1963, Rowan was the deputy assistant secretary of state for public affairs. He was the American ambassador to Finland from 1963 to 1964. On January 21, 1964, President Lyndon Johnson appointed Rowan to succeed Edward R. Murrow as head of the USIA, making the 38-year-old Rowan the highest ranking black in the Federal Government then and one of the few ever to head a Government agency. Under his jurisdiction was the Voice of America, the radio arm of USIA, with 100 transmitters in 18 locations in the U.S. and overseas. As head of the Government's propaganda agency, Rowan served on the National Security Council.

Leaving Government service in 1965, Rowan returned to much more lucrative work, journalism, as a Chicago *Daily News* columnist. His column is syndicated in many newspapers and he lectures widely.

Russell, Bill (1934–   ), Basketball Ace and Coach

Bill Russell, greatest defensive player ever, revolutionized basketball style while leading the Boston Celtics to eight straight world championships. He was the first black to direct any modern major-league team.

He was born William Felton Russell, younger of two sons of a paper-bag factory worker in Monroe, La. A Monroe policeman threatened to jail Bill's mother for dressing as fashionably as whites. A clerk pulled a gun on Bill and his father when they started to leave after he ignored them to wait on whites who entered behind them. Tired of such racism and limited opportunities for blacks, the Russells moved when Bill was 9, settling in Oakland, Calif. But Oakland police arrested his brother for shining shoes, giving the 12-year-old a police record, whereas white shineboys were merely chased away.

Bill began playing on a housing project playground while his mother and father worked separate Oakland shipyard shifts. Bill's father also drove trucks, but quit that and the shipyard after his wife passed away, taking a foundry job to have more time for his young sons. Being a good athlete in junior high school, Bill's brother was able to go to prestigious, predominantly white Oakland Technical High School. Bill could not follow in his shoes. Unable to make any sports team at Hoover Junior High, Bill went to predominantly black McClymonds High. A gangly, 6'5", 158-pounder, Bill tried for defensive end on McClymonds' football team, but failed. He was rejected for varsity basketball also. But the junior varsity coach, his former home room teacher at Hoover, encouraged Bill. This white coach's faith in him was the turning point of Bill's life, rescuing him from despair and possible delinquency. Although he had only 15 uniforms, he carried Bill as his 16th player, letting him alternate with the 15th in suiting up for games. Next year, Bill made the varsity as the last substitute when his jayvee coach moved up to varsity coach. In his senior year, everything fell into place and McClymonds won the city championship. Although Bill scored little, his coach valued his defensive play, encouraging him to concentrate on it.

Fortunately, a scout, who came to watch an Oakland High All-Star player, saw McClymonds win easily with Bill playing his customary outstanding defensive game and also scoring the most points he ever got in a high school game, 14. Thus, Bill received a scholarship to the University of San Francisco (USF), a small Jesuit school without a gymnasium. But, led by 6' 9" Russell at center and his little roommate, guard K. C. Jones, the USF Dons became a basketball powerhouse, winning 14 and losing 7 when they were sophomores playing their first varsity season. Early in their junior year, they lost to UCLA, but then the Dons won a recordbreaking 56 consecutive games for the rest of their junior and senior years, including the NCAA championship in 1955 and 1956. Russell's tremendous shotblocking dismayed opponents, forcing them to hurry shots and to shoot from farther out. He changed the concept of defense in basketball. Further, his great rebounding gave his team ball control. Since Russell was so slender, many people wondered if he could do well in the rugged professional game against heavier foes.

After playing on the 1956 U.S. Olympics team, Russell joined the Boston Celtics, a high-scoring team that had never won a National Basketball Association (NBA) championship because of weakness in defense and rebounding. Since the St. Louis Hawks had draft rights to Russell, Celtics coach Arnold "Red" Auerbach gave the Hawks an established star, center Easy Ed McCauley, and an outstanding rookie, forward Cliff Hagan, in order to get Russell. Auerbach told Russell not to worry about scoring, but simply to block shots, get the rebounds, and start the fastbreak for such hotshooting Celtics guards and forwards as Bob Cousy, Bill Sharman, and Tom Heinsohn in the initial season and Sam Jones, Tom Sanders, K. C. Jones, and John Havlicek in later seasons. In Russell's rookie season, 1956–57, the Celtics finished on top in the NBA Eastern Division for the first time in their history. They then beat Western Division leader St. Louis in the playoff finals for their first NBA championship. The next season, they led the Eastern Division but lost to St. Louis in the playoff finals after Russell hurt his knee. Then starting with the 1959 playoffs climaxing Russell's third season, 1958–1959, Boston reeled off an incredible eight straight NBA championships (1959–1966). Closest to the Celtics' feat are the New York Yankees' five straight World Series baseball championships, 1949–1953, and the Montreal Canadiens' five straight Stanley Cup hockey championships, 1956–1960.

In the 1958–59 season, Russell and Los Angeles Laker Elgin Baylor became the first blacks ever named to the NBA All-Star team. Since then, Baylor at forward, Cicinnati Royal Oscar Robertson at guard, and either Russell or Wilt Chamberlain (*q.v.*) at center, have been perennial All-Star selections, making them the four black superstars of basketball. During his first nine seasons, 1956–57 to 1964–65, Bill Russell was voted the NBA's Most Valuable Player (MVP) five times (1958, 1961, 1962, 1963, 1965); the other winners were Cousy in 1957, Bob Pettit of St. Louis in 1959, Chamberlain in 1960, and Robertson in 1964. Chamberlain was the MVP the next three seasons (1966–1968), Wes Unseld of Baltimore won in 1969, and Willis Reed of New York in 1970. Blacks thus won 12 of the 15 MVP awards since Pettit won in the first year it was awarded (1956), with only Pettit (twice) and Cousy breaking their string.

When Cousy retired in 1964, Russell became the Celtics' captain. In April, 1966, after winning the eighth championship in a row, Auerbach retired and Russell was named to succeed him as coach of the Celtics. Russell was the first black to become manager or head coach of a major-league team in any professional sport in modern times. His only predecessors were Fritz Pollard, who was player-coach of the Akron Indians football team for four seasons (1919–1921 and 1925) in professional football's infancy, and Johnny McLendon, who was coach of the Cleveland Pipers most of the team's 1961–62 season in the American Basketball League, a short-lived rival of the NBA that never established itself as a real major league. In Russell's first season as player-coach, 1966–67, the Celtics lost to Philadelphia in the Eastern Division playoff. But in the next two seasons, 1967–68 and 1968–69, they won two more NBA championships. Russell retired at the end of his third season as player-coach. In his 13 seasons with the Celtics, the team won the championship 11 times. In the first season after his retirement (he no longer coached or played), 1969–70, the Celtics finished last in the Eastern Division and didn't even get into the divisional playoffs, an indication of how much Russell was missed. With Russell's retirement, the only black major-league head coaches or managers in any sports are two NBA player-coaches, Lenny Wilkins of the Seattle Supersonics and Al Attles of the San Francisco Warriors; Wilkins was appointed before, and Attles during, the 1969–70 season. McLendon coached the Denver Rockets of the well-established rival American Basketball Association at the beginning of that season before being replaced.

From the beginning much more outspoken than most black athletes, Russell evidently helped to change some distasteful practices such as the tacit quota system that once limited each NBA team to only two or three black players, and the callous subjecting of black players to embarrassing discrimination and segregation on Southern tours. Militantly proud of his Afro-American heritage, Russell focused on his rubber plantations in Liberia on his ancestral continent when he left basketball.

Ranging from 12.5 points per game in the 1967–68 season to 18.9 in 1961–62, Russell never approached Chamberlain in scoring, but his value is seen in the Celtics' eleven championships whereas Chamberlain's teams won the NBA championship only once. The newest black superstar, Lew Alcindor, who played his first NBA season in 1969–70 after Russell retired, may well surpass both to become basketball's greatest all-time player. The 7' 2" Alcindor led UCLA to an unprecedented three straight NCAA championships with one 47-game winning streak and only two defeats in three seasons. Alcindor can score as well as Chamberlain but is also, like Russell, a team player and great shot blocker. In just one season, Alcindor lifted the last-place Milwaukee Bucks expansion team into a strong championship contender, finishing second in the Eastern Division and pushing the eventual NBA championship New York Knicks to the limit in the Eastern playoff finals.

Russell, Harvey (1918–   ), Corporate Executive

On January 25, 1962, Harvey Clarence Russell, Jr., became a vice president of the Pepsi-Cola Corporation. He was the first black at that executive level in a leading American corporation.

Russell was one of five children born of educators in Louisville, Ky. His grandparents were college graduates, his father became a college president, and his mother was a high school teacher. He enrolled at Kentucky State College for blacks, in Frankfort, where he played football and majored in sociology. Upon graduating in 1939, he pursued graduate studies at Indiana University for two years, waiting tables to help pay his way, and at the University of Michigan for another year. During World War II, he served for four years in the U. S. Coast Guard, becoming a lieutenant junior grade. He was the first black to be a deck officer in the Coast Guard.

Upon leaving the Coast Guard in 1946, Russell embarked upon a career in business. To learn about sales promotion, he worked for six months without pay for William P. Graham Associates, a New York advertising firm. When Graham promoted a punch named for heavyweight champion Joe Louis (*q.v.*), Russell was hired formally. Continuing with Graham Associates until 1948, he learned about the soft-drink business from ingredients through bottling, advertising, and sales. Then, from 1948 to 1950, he was sales manager for the Rosa-Meta Cosmetics Company of New York.

In 1950, Russell went to work for Pepsi-Cola, beginning as supervisor of a dozen black salesmen. By 1957, he worked his way up to director of the special markets department. In a company reorganization in 1962, Russell and several other departments heads were made vice presidents. He was one of the 28 vice presidents in the corporation. After three years as vice president in charge of special markets, he was promoted, in 1965, to vice president in charge of planning. In 1969, he became vice president for community affairs.

Five years before Russell became a Pepsi vice president, retired baseball player Jackie Robinson (*q.v.*) had become the first black vice president of a large white company. But Robinson worked for an essentially regional firm, the Chock Full O' Nuts restaurant chain, whereas Russell became vice president of a much larger company, Pepsi, which is internationally known and is one of the 300 largest corporations in America.

A pioneering black corporate executive, Ramon Scruggs, became public relations manager for American Telephone and Telegraph in 1963 after serving eight years as manager of customer relations for Michigan Bell Telephone. Among the other black corporate executives is Charles F. Harris who manages a major division of the Random House Publishing Company.

Russwurm, John (1799–1851), Pioneer Journalist and Colonizationist

John Brown Russwurm was a founding editor of the first black newspaper in America, *Freedom's Journal*. Switching to colonization, he held posts in colonies set up by private American groups in Africa.

Russwurm was born in Jamaica in the British West Indies. His father was a white American, his mother a black Jamaican. Upon leaving Jamaica, the father put his son in school in Canada under the name John Brown to avoid embarrassment. His father then married a white woman in Maine. When she learned about his mulatto son, she insisted that John should be brought into the family and be given his father's name, Russwurm. After John's father died and she remarried, this kind white stepmother still took care of John, sending him to schools and college in Maine.

John B. Russwurm graduated from Bowdoin College in Brunswick, Me., in the summer of 1826. A white classmate was John P. Hale (Bowdoin, 1827), a native of New Hampshire who became a leading opponent of slavery while serving in the U.S. Senate between 1847 and 1865 and who was the Free Soil Party's nominee for President in 1852. Russwurm has generally been regarded as the first American black to graduate from college, but it has been learned recently that another black, Edward Jones, graduated from Amherst College in Massachusetts in August, 1826, two weeks before Russwurm.

After college, Russwurm settled in New York City. There he became co-founder and co-editor of *Freedom's Journal*, along with the Reverend Samuel Cornish. A free black from Delaware, Cornish had been a Presbyterian minister in Philadelphia before coming to New York City to found the first black Presbyterian church there, in 1822. The first issue of their newspaper appeared March 16, 1827, beginning black journalism in America. The paper initially took a strong antislavery stand and opposed the recolonization of Afro-Americans in Africa. When Russwurm began to moderate his stand against colonization, a rift developed between the co-editors. Cornish resigned from the paper in September, 1827.

Russwurm continued as sole editor and proprietor. In February, 1829, he announced his conversion to the colonizationist point of view. Contending that blacks would never get their rights and that their ambitions would wane in restrictive America, he urged them to go to Africa where limitless opportunities would stimulate their ambitions. Former friends, supporters, and subscribers bitterly denounced him as an apostate. He was burned in effigy and accused of selling out to the American Colonization Society. He was forced to resign the editorship of the newspaper he founded. Cornish took over in March, 1829, renamed it *The Rights of All,* and continued publishing it until 1830.

Meanwhile, Russwurm left for Africa in the summer of 1829. He became the first superintendent of public schools in Liberia, the colony founded by the American Colonization Society in 1822 for repatriating American blacks in Africa. From 1830 to 1834, he also served as colonial secretary and edited a newspaper he founded, the *Liberia Herald.* In 1836, Russwurm was appointed governor of the Maryland Colony, founded in 1833 at Cape Palmas on the southeastern edge of Liberia by the Maryland State Colonization Society.

Russwurm served as governor for the remaining sixteen years of his life. He cooperated closely with Joseph Jenkins Roberts, a native of Virginia, who in 1841 became the first black governor of Liberia and then was elected Liberia's first President when it became an independent republic in 1847. Through the groundwork laid by Roberts and Russwurm, the Maryland Colony was annexed by Liberia in 1857.

Salem, Peter (c. 1750–1816), Revolutionary War Hero

Peter Salem was a hero at the Battle of Bunker Hill, June 17, 1775. He served in Massachusetts regiments throughout the American Revolution.

He was born a slave in Framingham, Mass. His master, Captain Jeremiah Belknap, came from Salem, Mass.; hence Peter's name. Belknap sold him to Major Lawson Buckminster, a leading citizen of Framingham. Buckminster let Salem enlist in the colonial forces. By serving, Salem gained his freedom.

When the American Revolution began on April 19, 1775, Peter Salem was a member of a 75-man Framingham Minute Men Company commanded by Captain Simon Edgell. Hearing of the attack at Lexington, this company marched to Concord, where Salem and his comrades fought on the opening day of the War for American Independence.

On April 23, Massachusetts called for 13,500 eight-month volunteers. Next day, Thomas Drury, a lieutenant in Edgell's company, resigned to form an eight-month company that joined the 5th Regiment, Mass., commanded by Colonel John Nixon of nearby Sudbury and his brother, Lieutenant-Colonel Thomas Nixon of Framingham. Peter Salem enlisted on April 24 as a private in Captain Drury's company in Colonel Nixon's regiment.

On June 17, 1775, British forces under General William Howe landed on Charlestown Peninsula on Boston's north side, to dislodge the colonial forces under Colonel William Prescott that had fortified Breed's Hill there, with Bunker Hill as a secondary line. General Artemas Ward sent in additional regiments, including Colonel Nixon's, to help defend the site. The main American position was a redoubt (earthwork enclosure) on the side of Breed's Hill facing Boston. Drury's Company, including Salem, fought from within the redoubt. On the third and successful British assault that day, Major John Pitcairn, who led the British who fired on the Minute Men at Lexington, mounted the redoubt and ordered the colonists to surrender. The patriots hesitated and were about to be overwhelmed when Peter Salem stepped forward and fired the shot that mortally wounded Pitcairn. The British assault wavered momentarily, giving the colonists time for an orderly retreat.

Some writers question Peter Salem's role as a hero in this battle. So many of the early accounts give credit to Salem that the tradition that he fired the shot that felled Pitcairn seems well founded. John Trumbull's famous painting of the battle prominently depicts black soldiers, probably including Salem.

After vacillating on whether to have blacks in his army, the new colonial commander, General George Washington, decided to let black soldiers reenlist. The printed muster rolls for Massachusetts servicemen indicate that Peter Salem reenlisted in January, 1776, this time in Captain Simon Edgell's company of Colonel John Nixon's regiment. In September, 1776, he began serving with Captain Micajah Gleason's company in the same regiment, but under Colonel Thomas Nixon after John Nixon became a general. On January 1, 1777, Salem signed up as a three-year volunteer in Colonel Thomas Nixon's regiment, serving two years in Captain Thomas Barnes's company and one in Captain John Holden's company

On January 1, 1780, he reenlisted for a final three-year term. In addition to fighting at Concord and Bunker Hill, he served at Saratoga, which proved the turning point of the war when General John Burgoyne surrendered his entire army to colonial forces in October, 1777. Throughout the war, Salem was usually the only black in his company.

After the war, Peter Salem married and settled in Framingham. In 1793, he moved to Leicester, Mass., where he stayed until he returned to Framingham in 1815 to spend his last year. In the 1880s, the Sons of the American Revolution erected a memorial over his grave in Framingham. In 1910, the Daughters of the American Revolution placed an inscription on the site where he lived in Leicester.

Seale, Bobby (1937–   ), Black Panther Leader
See: Newton, Huey, and Seale, Bobby

Spaulding, C. C. (1874–1952), Insurance Executive

Charles Clinton Spaulding built the North Carolina Mutual Life Insurance Company into the largest business owned and operated by Afro-
Americans. He began as its manager and sole full-time employee in
1899 and became its third president in 1923, succeeding the co-
founders, John Merrick and Spaulding's uncle Aaron McDuffie Moore.
After three decades of his presidency, the company had $165,000,000
of policies in force.

Spaulding was born on a farm at Clarkton, N. C. One of fourteen
children of hardworking parents who owned the land they worked, he
began tilling the soil as soon as he was old enough to handle a plow.
Work on the farm interrupted his schooling after only the first few
grades. Anxious to better himself, he begged to be allowed to go to
Durham, N. C., to join his uncle, Dr. Moore, a physician who set up
practice there after graduating from Leonard Medical College of Shaw
University in nearby Raleigh.

In Durham, young Spaulding began work as a dishwasher in a hotel at
$10 a month. He soon became head bellboy and then a waiter. Finding
he could not continue his schooling while working in the hotel, he became a cook for a white judge, serving him for two years while completing his elementary education at the Whitted Grade School in Durham.
Determined to be educated, Spaulding sat in that school awkwardly with
children only half his age. He was nearly 24 years old when he finished
Whitted in 1898. Upon graduating, he took a job as manager of a
grocery company in which twenty-five of Durham's leading black citizens invested $10 apiece. When the company ran into financial troubles
and the others withdrew, Spaulding was left in 1899 with a $300 indebt-
edness from the insolvent business. He did not let that burden crush him
and did not try to shirk it. Although it took five years and much sacrifice, he paid off every penny of the debt.

Meanwhile, led by Merrick as president and Moore as treasurer and
medical director, seven black men had gotten together in October, 1898,
to form an industrial assessment insurance association, the North Carolina Mutual and Provident Association. Merrick (1859–1919) was
born in Clinton and grew up in Raleigh, where he learned the trades of
brickmasonry and barbering. He moved to Durham in 1880, where he
eventually owned five barber shops, two for black and three for white
patrons, becoming personal barber to tobacco tycoon Washington Duke.
At the same time, the enterprising Merrick invested in real estate and

also became a contractor, building many homes for Durham blacks. Each of the seven founders put up $50 and the company began operating April 1, 1899. Business was so slow that the other five founders became discouraged. Merrick and Moore bought them out and started all over again later in 1899.

Now, they hired Moore's nephew, C. C. Spaulding, fresh from his failure in the grocery business. When Spaulding became general manager in 1899, the company's weekly collection was $29.40 and he was not only manager, but agent, clerk, promoter, bookkeeper, office boy, and janitor. As sole employee and working on a commission basis, he sold the policies, collected the premiums, and kept the records. Merrick, who handled the finances, and Dr. Moore, who examined and passed upon applicants for policies, served in their spare time as unsalaried president-treasurer and medical director respectively, continuing their respective barbering-real estate business and medical practice. With a desk and two chairs as its main possessions initially, the company operated in a corner of Dr. Moore's office, rented for two dollars a month. When the first claim was filed for $40 upon the passing of a policyholder, the company did not have enough money on hand to pay it and would have failed had not Merrick and Moore dug into their own pockets. Spaulding rushed the $40 check to the widow and used the signed receipt as an effective persuasion to others to sign up with a company that paid promptly. In its first year of operation, 1899, North Carolina Mutual had $395 income, assets of $350, and only $247 of insurance in force.

Spaulding worked indefatigably, traveling all over the state to build up the business. A firm believer in saturation advertising, he saw to it that calendars, pens and pencils, matchbooks, fans, thermometers, brushes, and paperweights extolling the company were distributed through black stores, churches, offices, lodges, and funeral parlors, reaching many homes in the black community. He also ran ads in the black press. To instill confidence, he dressed impeccably in a high collar and hired schoolteachers as agents. In 1909, the company was reorganized into an old line mutual legal reserve life insurance company without capital or stock, and its name was changed to North Carolina Mutual Life Insurance Company. The Mechanics and Farmers Bank was formed in Durham in 1907 with the company's aid.

In 1919, Merrick passed away and Moore became president. Spaulding succeeded Moore in 1923. In 1921, while Spaulding was still general manager, a new six-story, plus basement, office building was erected for the company in Durham at a cost of $250,000. By 1926, the company's yearly income had reached the $2,000,000 mark. In 1928, Spaulding's fifth year as president, it had $35,000,000 of insurance in force. In 1935, North Carolina Mutual employed 1,153 persons, including 93 in the Durham home office, and paid out nearly $800,000 in claims. When Spaulding passed on in 1952, the company had $33,000,-000 in assets as well as $165,000,000 in policies.

Despite his success, Spaulding encountered racism. He could not eat in restaurants in buildings owned by his company. When he ordered a soft drink at a soda stand adjoining a building his company owned, the clerk roughly pushed him out for unwittingly challenging the South's cherished way of life.

Among the many other blacks in insurance and banking were A. F. Herndon, who built the Atlanta Life Insurance Company; Jesse Binga, founder of the Binga State Bank in Chicago; Truman Gibson and Harry Pace, co-founders of Supreme Liberty Life Insurance Company of Chicago; Jesse Mitchell, founder of the Industrial Bank of Washington, D.C.; and Spaulding's nephew, Asa T. Spaulding, the first trained black actuary in America, who was president of North Carolina Mutual from 1959 to 1968. During his tenure, North Carolina Mutual opened its new fourteen-story office building in Durham late in 1966. Vice President Hubert Humphrey spoke at the 1967 dedication ceremonies for the building, which cost more than $5,000,000. In 1968, North Carolina Mutual had $26,000,000 income, assets of $98,000,000, and $480,-000,000 of insurance in force. Before 1970, it had gone over the one hundred million mark in assets and had half a billion dollars of insurance in force, far surpassing any other black business in magnitude.

Still, William Grant (1895–   ), Composer

William Grant Still is America's greatest black composer and one of the top twentieth-century American composers. His symphonies, suites, ballets, and other works based on Afro-American themes have won him many honors and competitive commissions and are played by major American and European symphonies.

Born in Woodville, Miss., Still was of Scotch-Irish, Spanish, Cherokee, and African descent. His parents taught at Alabama A. & M. College in Huntsville before moving to Mississippi. Besides mathematics, his father taught music, played a cornet, led a Woodville band, and tried composing.

His father passed away when Billy was a baby, and his mother moved to Little Rock, Ark., to live with her sister and mother. She taught literature in the local high school while her mother tended Billy. Since his grandmother constantly sang hymns and spirituals, Billy was introduced to the rich heritage of black folk music. When he was 8, his mother married a railway postal clerk, Charles Shepperson, who was a music lover. He brought a phonograph, Red Seal records, and opera librettos home. Enraptured while listening for hours, Billy decided to become a composer. Skilled at making things, he whittled a fiddle on which he made such screechy noises that the family secured a violin and music teacher for him. As soon as Billy learned to read music, he began writing it on scratch pads on which he ruled out staff lines. He organized schoolmates into little bands to play his melodies.

Still was determined to be a composer but his mother and stepfather considered that an impossible dream. Insisting that he train for a secure profession, they sent him to Wilberforce University in Ohio in 1911 to major in science. But music absorbed him. Playing in the band, he learned all the reed instruments. Eventually, he arranged, orchestrated, led, and composed for the band. A concert was given solely of his pieces. He yearned to transfer to Oberlin College to study music, but his mother, wanting him to be a physician, insisted that he remain at Wilberforce. Uninterested in his courses, he mischievously broke rules, stayed in trouble, and finally was expelled four months before graduation.

Still now began a long hard struggle to achieve his ambition. Lacking a degree, he worked at odd jobs until he came into a small inheritance from his father at age 21. He enrolled at Oberlin College's Conservatory of Music in 1916, working as a waiter and janitor to stretch his meager funds. Impressed by his talents, his teachers created a special scholarship to help him along. He joined the Navy in 1918, he served during World War I as a messboy. Afterward, he joined famed blues composer W. C. Handy (q.v.), working daytime in Handy's music publishing firm in Memphis and playing nights in Handy's band. Hating the sordid night life of Memphis and other towns Handy's band played, Still tasted the dregs his mother had warned him awaited black musicians.

Still's prospects improved when he moved to New York City in the early 1920s. He not only worked in Handy's new music publishing firm there, but also arranged for and played in jazz and theater orchestras at greater pay than in Memphis. In 1921, he played oboe in Eubie Blake's orchestra for the great black musical *Shuffle Along*, featuring Florence Mills (q.v.). He played in and became leader of the band at the Plantation Club, wrote arrangements for such performers as Sophie Tucker, Paul Whiteman, and Handy, and orchestrated for the "Deep River" radio program on Station WOR. He had now earned enough to enroll at the New England Conservatory of Music in Boston where he studied composing under George Chadwick, who was so impressed with Still that he refused to accept payment. Returning to New York subsequently, Still studied under the modernist composer, Edgard Varèse. Influenced by Varèse, he composed music that critics found too dissonant and intellectual.

He then began drawing themes from Afro-American folk and jazz idioms. His early works included a symphonic poem, *Darker America* (1924), the lively *From the Black Belt* (1926), and a ballet with a West Indian setting, *La Guiablesse* (1927). Howard Hanson, director of the Eastman School of Music and Rochester Symphony, encouraged Still and performed his works. One of Still's best known works is his symphonic poem, *Africa* (1930), but his *Afro-American Symphony* (1931) is generally regarded as the greatest work. Premiered in Rochester, it was soon played by the New York Philharmonic, by the Philadelphia Orchestra under Leopold Stokowski, and by the Berlin, Leipzig, and Stuttgart symphonies. His *New Symphony in G. Minor* (1937) was premiered by Stokowski's orchestra. The Rochester Symphony and Philadelphia Orchestra, under Hanson and Stokowski, are among orchestras that have made recordings of Still's works. Still settled permanently in Los Angeles before World War II. He composed for several Hollywood movies, but overthrew his most lucrative contract in 1943 when a director insisted on converting a film on blacks into the traditional degrading Hollywood "darky" stereotype.

He has won many honors, including Guggenheim Fellowships (1934 and 1935) and Rosenwald Fellowships (1939 and 1940). He was the first Afro-American to conduct a major symphony, leading the Los Angeles Philharmonic in a performance of his works at the Hollywood Bowl in 1936. Millions attending the World's Fair in New York in 1939 heard Still's musical accompaniment for the continuous six-minute showings of "Democracity" at the Perisphere, performed 120 times a day, without realizing a black composed it. The jury that selected the composer for this World's Fair theme played many recordings without knowing their composers. Of all the works heard, the two they liked best were a suite, *From a Deserted Plantation* (1933), and a ballet, *Lenox Avenue* (1937), both by Still. The latter had been commissioned by CBS Radio in its first American Composers Series. Still's *Plain-Chant for America* (1941) was commissioned for the 100th anniversary of the New York Philharmonic. In 1944, competing against 37 other composers, Still's *Festive Overture* was selected unanimously for the commemoration of the Cincinnati Orchestra's 50th anniversary, and was awarded a $1,000 War Bond. His opera, *Troubled Island* (1937), set in Haiti with a libretto by Langston Hughes (*q.v.*), was presented by the New York City Center Opera Company in 1949, celebrating its fifth anniversary. This was the first time an opera composed by a black was performed by a major American opera company.

Still's other operas include *Blue Steel* (1935), *A Bayou Legend* (1940), *Costaso* (1949), and *Highway No. 1, U.S.A.* (1963). Among his other ballets are *Sahdji* (1930), with an African setting, and *Miss Sally's Party* (1940). Two of his frequently performed works for chorus and orchestra are *And They Lynched Him on a Tree* (1940) and *Those Who Wait* (1943). Such concertos as *Kaintuck* (1935) and *Pastorela* (1946) are performed often as are such short orchestral works as *Ebon Chronicle* (1936), *Caribbean Melodies* (1941), *Poem for Orchestra* (1944), and *To You, America* (1952). His third and fourth symphonies were composed in 1945 and 1949. Among his best known songs are "Levee Land," written for Flo Mills; "Winter's Approach," setting a poem of Paul Laurence Dunbar (*q.v.*); and "Breath of a Rose."

Besides Still, the greatest black composers are William Dawson, Ulysses Kay, and Howard Swanson. The promising career of Edmund Jenkins, composer of *Charlestonia: A Negro Rhapsody,* was cut short by his untimely passing in 1924.

Stokes, Carl (1927–   ), Mayor of Cleveland

In 1967, Carl Burton Stokes was elected mayor of Cleveland, Ohio, one of the nation's ten largest cities. He was the first black ever elected mayor of so large a city.

Stokes was born in a poor black neighborhood in Cleveland, younger of two sons of a laundry worker and cleaning woman. After his father passed away when Carl was 2, his mother struggled to support the family, sometimes needing welfare aid to do so. Carl and his brother Louis sold newspapers and worked in neighborhood stores to help out. Mrs. Stokes preached the importance of education to her sons, but Carl dropped out of East Technical High School in 1944, holding a foundry job until he joined the Army a year later. Serving in occupied Germany, he decided to finish school.

After his discharge as a corporal in 1946, Carl returned to Cleveland and earned his high school diploma in 1947. He began his college training at West Virginia State College and continued at Cleveland College of Western Reserve University, majoring in psychology. But he left college to become a state liquor agent, sometimes getting into gun battles. After three years in Ohio liquor enforcement, he enrolled at the

University of Minnesota and worked weekends as a dining car waiter. He received the B.S. degree in law in 1954. Stokes was a probation officer for the Cleveland Municipal Court, 1954–1958. He took evening courses at the Cleveland-Marshall Law School, and received his law degree (L.L.B) in 1956. In 1957, he passed the Ohio bar and began practicing law.

In 1958, Mayor Anthony Celebreeze appointed Stokes assistant city prosecutor under the city law director, Ralph Locher. Active in the community, Stokes served on the executive committee of the Cleveland NAACP, on the Community Council of his middle-class residential section, Mount Pleasant, and on the executive committee of the Democratic Party in Cuyahoga County, where Cleveland is located. In 1962, Stokes quit his city post to form a law partnership with his brother Louis, who had attended Western Reserve University and had graduated from Cleveland-Marhsall Law School in 1953.

Carl Stokes was elected to the Ohio House of Representatives in 1962. The first black Democrat ever elected to the state legislature, he served three terms, taking a moderate stance on issues. In 1965, he decided to run for mayor when blacks became aroused over Mayor Ralph Locher's refusal to meet with civil rights groups to discuss the racist outlook of Cleveland's police chief. Stokes ran as an independent Democrat without entering the primary. He surprised observers by polling 85,375 votes to Mayor Locher's 87,833 in a three-way race, closing the gap still more in a recount.

In 1967, Stokes entered the Democratic primary against Mayor Locher and a third candidate, Frank Celeste. Stokes's mere presence seemed to have a calming effect on blacks incensed over high unemployment and police brutality, thus preventing recurrence, of the rioting that rocked Cleveland in 1966. He won the primary election on October 3, 1967, soundly defeating the incumbent mayor. Grandson of a slave, Stokes ran in the final election against Republican Seth C. Taft, nephew of Senator Robert A. Taft and grandson of President William H. Taft. As in the primary, Stokes skillfully won white support by his moderate outlook without alienating black militants. Handsome, witty, charming, and a good television debater, Stokes defeated Taft by a margin of 2,500, with 43,000 whites voting for him.

On November 3, 1967, he was sworn in as mayor of America's eighth largest city (Cleveland had 876,000 residents in the 1960 census). This prominent black mayor attracted considerable Federal aid to ease Cleveland's squeeze in housing and employment, reformed law enforcement administration to improve relations between the police and the black ghetto, kept tempers cool, and generally ran a clean, forward-looking administration. In September, 1969, he defeated "law and order" candidate Robert Kelly in the Democratic primary, getting 60 percent of the vote, and then defeated Republican nominee Ralph Perk by nearly 4,000 votes out of 240,000 cast in the November election, giving him a second two-year term as Cleveland's mayor.

Of the many other black mayors, the most prominent next to Stokes are Walter E. Washington, appointed mayor of the nation's ninth largest city, Washington, D.C., by President Lyndon Johnson in 1967; Richard Hatcher, elected mayor in 1967 of the 70th largest city, Gary Ind.; and Kenneth Gibson, elected mayor of America's 30th largest city, Newark, N. J., in 1970. Louis Stokes (1925–   ), the mayor's brother, was elected to Congress from Cleveland in 1968.

Tanner, Henry O. (1859–1937), Painter

Henry Ossawa Tanner was an outstanding American artist. He switched from his early scenes of everyday life among his fellow blacks to the Biblical paintings for which he is best known.

Tanner was born in Pittsburgh, Pa., eldest of seven children of an A.M.E. minister, Benjamin Tucker Tanner (1835–1923). Sometime after Reverend Tanner became in 1868 the chief A.M.E. secretary and editor of the A.M.E. *Christian Recorder*, the family settled in Philadelphia, where the denomination had its headquarters. Strolling with his father in that city's Fairmount Park, 13-year-old Henry watched a landscape artist working and became interested in an artistic career. Next day, using housepaint brushes and the back of an old book, he tried to paint like that artist. His family wanted him to train for the ministry; his increasingly eminent father became a notable bishop, 1888 to 1908. When Henry persisted in his objective, the family continued trying to persuade him to follow in his father's footsteps, but supported him in his pursuit of a career in art.

Young Henry spent his afterschool hours and weekends painting and visiting galleries and museums. He made clay models of zoo animals. His family financed his study at the Pennsylvania Academy of the Fine Arts, 1884–1888, where the famed artist Thomas Eakins was his main teacher. Meanwhile, having seen an exhibit of seascapes, Tanner saved his money for a trip to Atlantic City to paint marine scenes. An exhibit of these early works was arranged by a friend and one of them, "A Windy Day on the Meadows," sold for $100 and hangs in the Pennsylvania Academy. Influenced and encouraged by Eakins, Tanner produced warm and penetrating works in this first phrase of his career, including oil portraits of his father and mother. Eakins did a portrait of Tanner.

On completing his studies as one of the top students at the Pennsylvania Academy, Tanner was disappointed and embittered at not receiving the scholarship aid for study abroad that usually went to the better students. Financial returns from his art work were meager as he only sold a picture occasionally. He moved in 1888 to Atlanta, Ga., where one of his brothers was pastor of a leading church. Tanner opened a photographic studio there to eke out a living while teaching a few classes in drawing at one of Atlanta's black schools, Clark College. A.M.E. Bishop Daniel A. Payne (*q.v.*) was one of his patrons, buying several paintings for Wilberforce University. Tanner's most famous painting during this first phase was a genre (everyday life) scene, showing the influence of Eakins, "The Banjo Lesson" (1890, oil), that hangs in Hampton Institute.

Another early patron was a white Methodist bishop, Joseph C. Hartzell, who arranged for an exhibition in Cincinnati in 1890, to help Tanner raise money to study abroad. Many of the works exhibited were landscape paintings Tanner had done in the mountains of North Carolina. Although the works did not sell, Bishop Hartzell bought the collection for $300 and raised additional funds among his friends to help Tanner go abroad. In 1891, Tanner left for Europe, planning to study in Rome.

He settled in Paris, however, where he studied at the Académie Julian, 1891–1896, under such leading artists as Benjamin Constant and Jean Paul Laurens. Like other struggling, unknown artists, he lived a poverty-stricken existence. At first, he continued painting genre scenes of peasant life in Brittany and Normandy in such works as "The Young Sabot Maker," "The Bagpipe Lesson," and "Return of the Fishing Boats." In 1895, one of his pictures was accepted by the Paris Salon. The next year, his oil painting of "Daniel in the Lion's Den" was so well received, gaining an honorable mention in the Paris Salon, that he devoted himself to painting religious scenes, launching his second phase.

In 1897, he painted his best known work, "The Resurrection of Lazarus," which received the third place medal at the Paris Salon and was purchased by the French Government to hang in the Luxembourg Gallery Collection, a high mark of distinction for contemporary artists. With this honor, Tanner's reputation was made and commissions flowed in. A wealthy art patron who was on a visit to Paris, Lewis Rodman Wanamaker of the Philadelphia department store family, was attracted to Tanner by this painting. Wanamaker became Tanner's patron, and financed several trips to the Holy Land, beginning with a visit in 1897. Now an established artist, Tanner set up his studio in an artist's colony at Trépied, outside Paris.

Leading museums acquired many of his oils, such as "Christ and Nicodemus on the Housetop" (1899) and "The Wailing Wall" (1915), both purchased by the Pennsylvania Academy of the Fine Arts; "Judas" (1899), purchased by the Carnegie Institute; and "The Three Marys" (1912), in the collection of the Art Institute of Chicago. Tanner reached the peak of his art in two paintings: "The Annunciation" (1898), in the Wilstach Collection of the Philadelphia Museum of Art; and "Two Disciples at the Tomb" (1906), in the Chicago Art Institute. He won many prizes, including silver medals at such places as the Paris Exposition in 1900 and Louisiana Purchase Exposition at St. Louis in 1904; a gold medal at the San Francisco Exposition in 1915; and the French Legion of Honor.

Tanner made occasional trips to the United States. Sensitive, shy, and wishing to be judged only on his art, he was appalled at the adulation he attracted in America because of his race. For a while in World War I, he supervised a Red Cross canteen near Paris and painted a few military camp scenes. Entering his third phase during the war, Tanner continued depicting Biblical scenes, but increasingly turned out landscapes, still lifes, and some genre scenes, eventually settling into semi-retirement at his country home in Étaples, Normandy, where he lived until the end. Among the best of his works in this last phase are a genre scene, "The Wailing Wall," and a Biblical scene, "Christ at Emmaus."

Sustaining himself and even becoming prosperous from his art alone, Tanner was an inspiration to younger black artists. Some of them, particularly William A. Harper and William Edouard Scott, came to Paris to study with Tanner.

Terrell, Mary Church (1863–1954), Civic Leader

As a victim of race and sex discrimination, Mary Church Terrell fought prejudice all her life. She sought to liberate blacks and women from their unequal status.

She was born Mary Eliza Church in Memphis, Tenn., younger of two children of prosperous former slaves. Her father, Robert Reed Church, worked his way up from dishwasher to cook to chief steward on the Memphis riverboats of his slaveowner-father, Captain C. B. Church. Gaining freedom, he became a successful businessman, eventually amassing almost a million dollars from real estate operations. Her mother, Louisa Ayres Church, had a store in downtown Memphis, selling hairpieces to, and dressing hair for, aristocratic white women of Memphis. Her parents separated when she was young and Mollie (as Mary was callled) and her brother Thomas were reared by their mother.

Her father remained close to the children, taking Mollie on trips. She first encountered racism when her father, who looked white, had to pull his pistol to stop a conductor from dragging bewildered, 5-year-old Mollie from the first-class coach in which they rode. Mollie started in the inadequately financed schools Memphis provided for blacks. Her mother soon sent her to the Model School conducted by Antioch College at Yellow Springs in southwestern Ohio. Living with townspeople, she attended that school two years and public schools there another two years before transferring to the eighth grade of the high school at Oberlin in northern Ohio. Having excelled in high school, Mollie enrolled in Oberlin's four-year, classical curriculum rather than the two-year certificate program most women took. Her father cheerfully financed the longer course. At Oberlin, she was freshman class poet, an editor of the college newspaper, and a leader in the literary society. But she was rejected for summer positions in New York as private secretary to well-to-do women as soon as they detected her race. She graduated from Oberlin in 1884, one of the first black women with a college degree.

She wanted to teach but her father, emulating Southern aristocrats, considered teaching beneath her. Her mother had moved to New York City and opened a thriving Sixth Avenue shop. Her father married a friend of his wife's. After a year of pampered ease at her father's new mansion in Memphis, Miss Church spent a summer with her mother and then put her training to use by joining the faculty of Wilberforce University in Ohio in 1885. For two years, she taught five courses, including French, at this black college. Furious at first, her father relented and assented.

In 1887, she began teaching Latin in the black high school (now Dunbar High) in Washington, D.C. She was courted by her department head, Robert H. Terrell, an alumnus of the school and a top graduate and commencement orator at Harvard University in 1884. Going on a summer tour of Europe with her father, she remained abroad at his expense, for two years, 1888–1890, living in rooming houses in Lausanne, Berlin, and Florence, and studying at private schools so that she became fluent in French, German, and Italian. Some malicious American whites abroad went out of their way to try to persuade Europeans to segregate Miss Church as was done in America. Nonetheless, four whites, including a German baron, an American student, and a prosperous American businessman, all aware of her race, proposed marriage to her.

Upon her return to the teaching job in Washington in 1890, Terrell renewed his courtship. When Oberlin College appointed her registrar and faculty member in 1891, she declined, preferring to marry Terrell and settle in Washington with him. Seeking decent housing, they met the bitter humiliations and frustrations blacks experience buying in a restricted housing market.

Mrs. Terrell became a busy civic worker and fighter for rights. In 1895, she was appointed to the Board of Education of Washington, D.C., the first black woman on an American school board. She served until 1900, resigning upon her husband's appointment as principal of the black high school. In 1901, President Theodore Roosevelt appointed her husband, who had studied law while teaching in District schools, to a four-year term as a judge of the Municipal Court of the District of Columbia. Judge Terrell was reappointed by Presidents Roosevelt in 1905, Taft in 1909, Wilson in 1913 and 1917, and Harding in 1921, despite strenuous objection by the Senate's Southern demagogues. From 1906 to 1911, Mrs. Terrell served on the reorganized School Board of Washington.

She was active in many movements. Fighting for women's suffrage she spoke in 1898 and 1900 at biennial sessions of the Woman Suffrage Association. Invited to speak at the International Congress of Women in Berlin in 1904, a trip made on funds supplied by her father, she made a spectacular impression by giving her thirty-minute address in fluent German, then repeating it in French and English, the only speaker able to do so. She was a founder of the leading organization of black women, the National Association of Colored Women, and served as its first president, 1896 to 1901. Despite the fact that her husband owed his judgeship to the powerful race leader Booker T. Washington (q.v.), Mrs. Terrell was a charter and active member of the NAACP which bitterly opposed Washington's stands. Increasingly, she was called upon to express her views on racial matters, both on lecture tours all over America and in such magazine and newspaper articles as "Lynching from a Negro's Point of View" in *North American Review* in 1904.

Working as a Federal clerk during the World War I manpower shortage, she was disgusted at the vicious segregation practices under the Southern-oriented Wilson Administration. After the war, she was a delegate to the International Congress of Women held in Zurich in 1919 in conjunction with the Paris Peace Conference. She also worked in political campaigns at Republican eastern headquarters for the 1920 Presidential race and as chairman for black women in Ruth Hanna McCormick's quest for a U.S. Senate seat from Illinois in 1929. Her half-brother from her father's second marriage, R. R. Church, Jr., became a power in both Tennessee and national Republican politics during the 1920s and 1930s.

Her autobiography, *A Colored Woman in a White World* (1940), eloquently pleaded for racial justice by its recital of indignities suffered continually even by so distinguished and talented a black woman. She battled to the end. Fed up with the hardships of life in segregated Washington, Mrs. Terrell, in her late 80s, led the drive and brought the Thompson restaurant suit that resulted in the 1953 Supreme Court ruling ending segregation in public accommodations in the nation's capital. She lived to see the Supreme Court declare school segregation unconstitutional everywhere, passing away two months after the May, 1954, desegregation decision.

Truth, Sojourner (c. 1797–1883), Antislavery Prophet

Believing herself God's chosen instrument, Sojourner Truth toured America denouncing slavery, sinfulness, and injustice. Illiterate, but possessing great faith and surprising wisdom, she became an impressive lecturer for abolitionism and other causes.

She was born Isabella, slave of the prominent Hardenbergh patroonship family of Ulster County, N. Y. Although she fostered impressions that she was several decades older, she was born only a few years before the eighteenth century ended. Next to youngest of twelve children of James and Elizabeth (called Baumfree and Mau-Mau-Bett), Isabella hardly knew her older siblings before they were sold away. The unhealthy slave quarters—the Hardenbergh inn-house's dank, planked cellar—aged and crippled her parents. Upon the master's death, their last two children were auctioned off, but the useless old couple were set free, destitute and helpless, to provide for themselves.

Knowing only low Dutch but sold to an English-speaking couple, uncomprehending Isabella was beaten severely and repeatedly. Recalling her mother's teachings about an omnipotent God, perplexed Isabella prayed for deliverance. Miraculously, she soon acquired an easygoing, tavernkeeping master who never whipped her hard. Attracted to the homely but striking tavern slave, a prosperous New Paltz landowner next bought her. He had five children by the mystic-minded girl captivated by his godly visage, giving her an elderly slave husband for appearances.

Under New York's gradual emancipation law, Isabella was to become free in 1827, but her master promised to free her a year earlier for hard, devoted service. When he reneged, she walked away with her youngest baby, confident that God would protect her. Sure enough, the kindly Van Wagener family took her in, paid her irate master for her last year, freed her as Isabella Van Wagener, and hired her. After a year with this pious but dull family, she prepared to return to the arms of her former master. But she experienced the overwhelming presence of God revealing to her that it would be an awful sin to submit when free to the abuse of her body she had to tolerate in slavery. Cleansed of sinful yearning and thenceforth chaste, she searched for God's purpose for her.

New York laws forbade sales of slave children beyond the state, but despite the fact that her former owner sold their 5-year-old son, Peter, within the state he wound up, through subsequent transactions, on an Alabama plantation. Blacks dared not challenge lawbreaking whites, but Isabella, certain of divine backing, raised a fuss, pestering citizens, lawyers, and courts until, incredibly, Peter was returned to her.

In 1829, she moved to New York City, still seeking God and Jesus and her quest. She soon became a follower of a wealthy cultist who stressed fasting, reincarnation, and self-healing. She remained a believer when the "kingdom" was taken over in 1832 by a bearded "Messiah" who converted it into a feasting, free-loving sect. The only black member, she devotedly poured her savings, earnings, and labor into it, but remained aloof from the puzzling debauchery. Her reputation for integrity preserved her when, in 1834, the commune collapsed in scandal, involving false accusations of murder of the original leader, and true charges of alienation of affections, fraud, and theft. She even sued and won a $125 slander judgement against a socially prominent, disillusioned cultist who, deliberately falsifying, labeled her a murderous co-conspirator.

After several years of toil for various employers, Isabella learned her mission from a second revelation. On June 1, 1843, she left New York City to carry God's message to America. Adopting the name Sojourner Truth, she became a familiar figure at religious revivals, women's suffrage meetings, abolitionist rallies, and other gatherings in the mid-Atlantic, New England, and Midwestern states. She took care of her expenses by working at odd jobs at first and later by peddling her narrative, dictated and published in 1850. As a former Northern slave, she was a unique attraction on abolition platforms. Her deep faith, keen insights, and ready quips overcame hostile scoffers. Derided because she couldn't read Scripture, she said educated people read His word but God addressed her directly. When male-supremacy ministers were over-whelming feminists at an Akron, Ohio, meeting, she routed them with such retorts as that Christ came from God and a woman—man had nothing to do with it. After she gave a strong antislavery speech, a man said he cared no more for her talk than a fleabite, but she vowed, God willing, to keep him scratching. When a physician at an Indiana rally called her a man masquerading as a woman, she crushed him by baring her breasts on stage, saying white babies had suckled and asking if he wished to do so, too. When Frederick Douglass (*q.v.*) concluded a speech pessimistically assessing the black man's prospects, Sojourner's famous question, "Frederick, is God dead?" changed the audience's gloomy mood.

William Lloyd Garrison, Harriet Beecher Stowe, and Abraham Lincoln were among the many, high and low, impressed by this woman. Visiting Lincoln at the White House in 1864, she stayed to help runaway blacks piling up in misery in Washington. She preached doctrines of cleanliness and hard work. She fought and helped end Jim Crow streetcars in Washington, taking her crusade and lawsuit threats to the transit company president. When two white women objected to her riding on the same car with white ladies, she replied that streetcars were for poor whites and blacks and that if they were ladies they would have the money to hire a carriage.

Her last decades of traveling lectures were devoted to futile efforts to arouse white America to support her solution to the race problem, which was to train the freedmen and recolonize them in the undeveloped West. The end came in the house she had bought in 1857 near Battle Creek, Mich., her final resting place.

Tubman, Harriet (c. 1821–1913), Heroic Liberator

Escaping from slavery to freedom in the North, Harriet Tubman courageously returned South nineteen times, leading some 300 slaves out of bondage. Illiterate but shrewd, this "Black Moses" daringly carried out her risky operations, outwitting slave patrols and pursuing slaveowners. She never lost one of her passengers on this dangerous "underground railroad." She was one of the world's bravest women.

She was born Araminta Ross, slave of Edward Broadus, at Bucktown, near Cambridge, in Dorchester County on Maryland's Eastern Shore. Her parents, Benjamin Ross and Harriet Greene, were devoted to each other and their eleven sons and daughters but could not, under the laws of slavery, be legally married. Early in life, Araminta began to be called Harriet or Rit after her mother. Rit's father was a valuable slave who supervised timber cutting and hauling, but Rit's defiant spirit reduced her value.

Like all slave children, little Harriet was put to work early. At 6, she was placed with James Cook to learn weaving under his wife, but Cook also made her wade through water to tend his muskrat traps. Sent out once when ill with measles, she contracted pneumonia and barely survived, causing Cook to return the "worthless" child. When her mother had nursed her back to health and she had been hired to the Cooks again, Rit stubbornly resisted learning weaving, preferring outdoor work to being a house servant close to slaveowners. Hired out to other families, proud, "uppity" Rit received many brutal whippings. One cruel woman, seeking her money's worth, made her do housework all day long and then expected her to sit up all night rocking her sick baby's cradle; she whipped her severely whenever she dozed off and let the baby cry. Accordingly, Rit's neck and shoulders forever showed a mass of whip scars. Too troublesome to be a house servant, Harriet had her way, and finally became a field hand.

Working as a hired hand in her early teens, she observed an overseer trailing a slave who was sneaking from work toward the store one evening. She tried to head him off to prevent a whipping, but arrived too late. The overseer seized him and told Harriet and other slaves to help tie the man up so he could be whipped mercilessly. She refused, and when the slave twisted loose and darted from the store, stood in the doorway to block pursuit. Seizing a two-pound iron weight, the furious overseer hurled it at the fleeing slave. It stuck Harriet in the head, causing a deep, nearly fatal, skull indentation. To everyone's surprise, she recovered, but thenceforward was subject to cataleptic seizures. In the midst of the work or conversation she would suddenly fall into deep slumber, waking from her stupor after some time and resuming where she had left off as if there had been no interruption.

She regained her strength in strenuous field work and lumbering. She could lift loads and do heavy work that would tax strong men. About the age of 24, her master, seeking to increase his stock of slaves, married her to a free black, John Tubman, but they were childless. Chafing under slavery, Harriet Tubman yearned to run away, but John was content to have her remain a slave and to benefit from her labors. In 1849, she decided to escape. The passing away of her latest owner posed the danger of a slave auction that might send a sullen, headstrong slave like her to the Deep South. She fled with two of her brothers, hiding in caves and graveyards by day and traveling at night, guided by the North Star when visible or by feeling the moss on trees on cloudy nights. She thwarted slavecatchers' dogs by walking upstream for hours in the Choptank River. Her brothers turned back. In the adjacent slave state, Delaware, Quaker sympathizers aided her to cross the Delaware River into southern New Jersey. She did not breathe easily until she was safely in Philadelphia with its large black population.

Free, she vowed to help her parents, brothers, and sisters to escape from slavery. She found work in Philadelphia and saved money to carry out her project. Aided by William Still, a free black who directed eastern seaboard underground railroad operations from Philadelphia, she engineered the escape of her sister, Mary Ann Bowley, married to a free black, and their two children, late in 1850. She had Still write John Bowley instructions to secure a boat to carry his family up Chesapeake Bay from Cambridge to Baltimore where Harriet met them and smuggled all four the rest of the way. Early in 1851, she went home and led one brother and two other men to freedom. In the fall of 1851, she came back to guide her husband northward but found that he had abandoned her and taken another wife. Harriet Tubman then led a party of ten northward, including another brother and his wife. Returning at Christmas time, 1851, she brought out two more brothers, a sister-in-law, and eight other people, this time taking them all the way to Canada because the Fugitive Slave Law was making it difficult for runaways in the free states. She remained there with them that winter, laboring mightily to help them survive.

Thus, Harriet Tubman became the most famous conductor on the underground railroad. Prominent abolitionists contributed money to add to the pennies she saved from jobs as cook or maid between rescues to finance operations. Her life was filled with peril. She carried a pistol which she would point at any wavering souls who wanted to turn back, vowing they would go on or be buried on the spot. She never let any "passenger" turn back, fearing betrayal, whether voluntarily or after torture. She carried paregoric to drug babies to keep them from crying and giving away the hiding slaves. Quakers like Thomas Garrett of Wilmington, Del., hid them in the daytime, fed them, and assisted their nighttime travel. Harriet had a deep faith that God would guide and protect her and an uncanny sense of danger. Once, she instinctively turned her party from its path and thus escaped capture by a large band of slavecatchers staked out ahead. Rewards totaling $40,000 were posted for her. Once when pursuers were on her trail, she boldly bought a train ticket and rode southward, guessing rightly that they would not look for her to head toward them. Another time, walking through Bucktown carrying two chickens, she saw a slaveowner approaching for whom she had worked on hire for six years. She quickly let the chickens loose and bent over chasing after them, thus hiding her face. Walking through slave quarters, she sang songs to convey messages and instructions to slaves. When slavecatchers were guarding the Delaware River bridge, she and Garrett smuggled her party across under a wagonload of bricks and masonry equipment. Another time, she had to hide runaways under a wagonload of manure with straws for breathing.

Her most perilous rescue was bringing out her aging parents in 1857. They had refused to escape until her father was in danger of prosecution for aiding runaways. Too feeble to walk, they were carried in a makeshift wagon Harriet rigged up to drive them to the passenger train, giving them forged passes to Wilmington. There, Garrett took them to his home where Harriet came to smuggle them the rest of the way to freedom. She settled them in a home in Auburn, N. Y., on land that an underground railroad sympathizer, Senator William Henry Seward (later Secretary of State), sold to her on generous terms. Her final Southern rescue mission came in December, 1860. She rescued all her family and many others, more than 300 in all, on her nineteen trips. She also aided in the spectacular rescue in Troy, N. Y., in April, 1859, of a runaway, Charles Nalle, who had been arrested and was about to be returned to Virginia under the Fugitive Slave Law. Despite taking a severe clubbing, she led a mob of antislavery citizens and blacks that took Nalle from the police and marshals as he was being carried away from the jail in irons under heavy guard. Meeting John Brown and learning of his intended raid on Harpers Ferry in the fall of 1859, she planned to join him but missed the rendezvous because of a cataleptic seizure.

During the Civil War, she aided the Union Army as a spy, nurse, and liaison with contraband slaves. Governor John Andrew of Massachusetts arranged her passage to Union-occupied Port Royal, S. C. There, early in June, 1863, she guided and directed a detachment of 150 black troops under Colonel James Montgomery's nominal command in a raid she planned up the nearby Combahee River, destroying Confederate mines, storehouses, crops, and plantations, and liberating nearly 800 slaves. Despite Seward's strenuous postwar efforts, Congress refused to vote a pension to this courageous woman for her unpaid wartime services. In 1869, she married Nelson Davis, a young Civil War veteran. On his passing in 1890, Harriet Tubman Davis received a widow's pension of $8 a month, increased to $20 monthly in 1898. In Auburn, she raised money to set up a home for elderly, indigent blacks, pouring all her substance into it the rest of her life, leaving her penniless at the end.

Another rebellious slave, Frederick Douglass (*q.v.*), 1817–1895, had been born less than twenty miles from her, in adjacent Talbot County, Md. Her home still stands in Auburn and a courthouse plaque there commemorates the deeds of this heroine.

Turner, Nat (1800–1831), Slave Revolt Leader

Nat Turner spread terror among slaveholders everywhere by the revolt he led in the Tidewater region of Virginia in 1831. Nearly sixty whites were slain in this desperate bid for freedom.

He was born in Southampton County in southeastern Virginia, slave of Benjamin Turner. In August, 1800, two months before his birth, Gabriel Prosser led several thousand fellow slaves in an aborted revolt outside Richmond, sixty miles north of Nat's home county. That same year, Denmark Vesey—who led the 1822 conspiracy at Charleston, S. C., involving 10,000 slaves, free blacks, and whites allies—purchased his freedom. Nat's mother, Nancy, who had been kidnapped in Africa and brought to America, was never reconciled to enslavement, and instilled defiance in him. His father, mother, and grandmother encouraged the bright lad, aiding him to learn to read at an early age. When Nat was a youngster, his rebellious father escaped.

In childhood, Nat gave signs of being unusual. At about the age of 4, while playing with other youngsters, he began to tell of things that his mother, overhearing him, said occurred before his birth. He was able to relate other such incidents, causing adults to tell him he must be a prophet. People also told him he had too much sense to remain a slave. His grandmother and master, both devout, exposed him to Scriptures and a religious atmosphere that molded his inquisitive mind. He avidly read the Bible. Neither drinking, stealing, nor mixing with carousers, he stayed aloof, awaiting a sign of his special purpose. Other blacks, impressed by his intelligence and bearing, respected his superior judgment. After his original master, he successively was owned by Samuel Turner, Thomas Moore, and Putnam Moore.

Praying while ploughing one day in early adulthood, he heard a voice, he related in his *Confessions*, like the Spirit that spoke to prophets of old. Astonished, he prayed continually for two years, when he had another revelation, confirming his belief that "I was ordained for some great purpose in the hands of the Almighty." Never ordained or licensed as a preacher, he became a slave exhorter, often addressing and influencing his fellow blacks at Sabbath meetings. He ran away from a harsh overseer but, after hiding in the woods for thirty days, returned, to the astonishment of fellow slaves who had expected him to flee forever like his father. But he had heeded the voice of the Spirit telling him to return for chastening as preparation for his mission.

Turner began having visions. He saw white and black spirits battling, the sun darkened, and blood flowing, and heard a voice saying, "Such is your luck . . . let it come rough or smooth, you must surely bear it." He withdrew from close association with fellow blacks. Additional revelations came in 1825 and subsequently. Then he began seeing signs; drops of blood on corn like dew from heaven, and hieroglyphics in blood on leaves. Now, he confessed, the Holy Ghost appeared to him, telling him that Christ was about to lay down his yoke. Shortly afterward, he was able to convert and purify a white man, Ethelred Brantley, turning him from wickedness. In May, 1828, Nat Turner heard a loud noise in the heavens and the Spirit told him he must take on Christ's yoke, but to wait for a sign before slaying the enemies with their own weapons.

In January, 1830, he was hired out to an owner he liked, kindly Joseph Travis, who had married the widow of a previous owner, Thomas Moore. In February, 1831, he received the sign, an eclipse of the sun. He then took four slaves, Henry, Hark, Nelson, and Sam, into his confidence. They began devising plans, selecting July 4 as the day to begin the revolt, but Nat became ill, forcing a postponement. Another sign came with a reddening of the sun, August 13. On Sunday, August 21, 1831, accordingly, Turner's four confederates, along with Turner and two new recruits, Will and Jack, met at a secret rendezvous in the woods and agreed to begin that night, starting at the Travis home, and sparing none to sound the alarm, there or elsewhere, until they had sufficient strength to ward off counterattack.

Murdering the five members of the Travis family, including an infant, they secured guns and ammunition to supplement the axe and hatchet they started out with. Then, they proceeded from house to house in rural Southampton County, slaying occupants, liberating slaves, some of whom joined them, and procuring weapons, horses, money, and drink. Working all that night and into the next day, they killed fifty-five to sixty-five whites. The band grew from seven to from fifty to seventy. Nat moved them toward the county seat, Jerusalem (now named Courtland), hoping to get a large supply of guns and ammunition there. He planned to control the county as a base of operations for liberating slaves or else to set up a guerrilla camp in nearby Dismal Swamp for the same purpose.

But a pitched battle in a field near James Parker's house on Monday, August 22, disrupted his plans. By now, the countryside was aroused and armed. Detachments of soldiers were rushing to the scene from Fort Monroe. Rallying some of his men and recruiting others, Turner and about twenty followers rested Monday night and resumed the attack at dawn on Tuesday, but were routed in attacking a house. He sent word for a rendezvous at the original meeting place, to rally to begin anew. He waited there until Wednesday evening, but all his comrades were fallen or captured. He went into hiding in a dugout two miles from the Travis place. He was captured six weeks later on October 30, jailed in Jerusalem, tried on November 5, and hanged there on November 11, 1831. The other rebels had all been slain or tried and executed by then. In jail, Thomas Gray took down Turner's *Confessions* and published them immediately.

Many hundreds of innocent blacks were slain in Southampton County and surrounding areas by panicky and vengeful whites during those harrowing August days. Even more repressive measures than were enacted in the late 1820s were now passed, stifling free blacks especially.

Turner's resistance, like that of other blacks who fought desperately for freedom, explodes the myth of the docile, devoted slave. To many blacks, he is a hero for trying to overthrow cruel and inhuman bondage. History, looking at his color and at the color of the enemies he slew, refuses to enshrine him among the patriots and heroes who fought tyranny.

Vann, Robert L. (1887–1940), Newspaper Publisher

After founding the *Pittsburgh Courier* in 1910, Robert Lee Vann built it into the largest and most widely read of the many weekly newspapers published by American blacks. Switching temporarily from the Republicans, this astute editor-publisher served in the New Deal administration.

Vann was born in Ahoskie in northeastern North Carolina. His parents, former slaves, eked out a living as tobacco tenant farmers in rural Hertford County, of which Ahoskie (4,500 people in 1960) was the metropolis. They were so poor and traveled so little from their backwoods area that Robert was 10 before he saw a railroad train.

Ambitious to make something of himself, he struggled through school. He attended Waters Normal Institute at the county seat, Winton, and continued his schooling until 1903 in the academic department of Virginia Union University in Richmond. He then went on to the University of Pittsburgh, paying his way by working as a bellhop in summer resort hotels at Bar Harbor, Me. He earned his law degree, LL.B., in 1909, from the law school at the University of Pittsburgh, passed the Pennsylvania bar examination, and opened a law office.

Like any young lawyer, especially one serving the impoverished black ghetto, Vann was finding it hard to make a living. He became interested in a little, two-page news sheet that was issued in his spare time by a black factory hand in a Pittsburgh pickle plant. Used largely as a vehicle for his poetry, it was surprisingly popular. Vann saw that it might be a success as a newspaper. The poet-editor, delighted at a chance to convert his personal journal into a real newspaper, agreed. Several others joined in the project. Vann, as lawyer, drew up the charter. They had little capital and, serving a black market, very little advertising revenue. As did all black newspapers, theirs depended heavily on subscribers, necessitating selling copies at a relatively high price.

The first edition of this newspaper, the *Pittsburgh Courier*, appeared on March 10, 1910. By 1912, Vann had sole control and became editor. Circulation climbed steadily, reaching 50,000 by 1920. By 1930, editions of the influential *Courier* were published from coast to coast. It outstripped its rivals. In 1936, the *Pittsburgh Courier*'s circulation of 174,000, for all its editions, dwarfed the other leading black newspapers, the *Afro-American* chain with a combined circulation of 70,000 and the *Chicago Defender* with 50,000.

Meanwhile, Vann became active in politics, beginning as a Republican. From 1917 to 1921, he was Assistant City Solicitor for Pittsburgh. He served as national director of Negro publicity in the Republican Presidential campaigns of Warren Harding in 1920, Calvin Coolidge in 1924, and Herbert Hoover in 1928. He began switching to the Democrats in 1930 and came out for Franklin Roosevelt against President Hoover in 1932. Although most blacks remained Republicans, supporting Hoover, Vann's backing swung many votes to Roosevelt. Blacks of Allegheny County, of which Pittsburgh is county seat, voted for Roosevelt and carried the county for him. Vann's reward was appointment in 1933 to the post of Special Assistant to the Attorney General of the United States. The first black in such a post under the Democrats, he was part of the New Deal Administration "Black Cabinet" or "Black Brain Trust" of advisers. He resigned this post in 1936 to be freer in his campaign stance because Vann opposed blind allegiance to either party. He urged blacks to stay loose and use their votes as a swing factor, keeping the parties from taking them for granted. Thus they could exert maximum pressure to secure their rights. He did support Roosevelt again in 1936 and 80 percent of blacks voted for the Democratic ticket.

In 1936, Vann gave up his law practice to concentrate on running his newspaper. By 1938, sensing that blacks were putting too much trust in the Democrats, he began urging them to judge men and issues and not get tied to one party. He also began in 1938 a crusade for equality in the armed forces, pressuring the Democrats to prove their good faith. Unhappy with their performance, he switched parties and backed the Republican nominee, Wendell Willkie, against President Roosevelt in 1940. But Vann's health was failing, and he passed away two weeks before the election in which Roosevelt handily defeated Willkie. By then, Vann's *Pittsburgh Courier* had reached 200,000 in circulation. His widow, Jessie Matthews Vann, whom he had married in 1910, succeeded him as publisher, continuing at the helm another two decades.

Walker, Madame C. J. (1867–1919), Cosmetics Manufacturer

Beginning as a humble washerwoman, Sarah Breedlove Walker became rich by inventing and manufacturing cosmetics products, particularly hair preparations. One of the first American women to be a self-made millionaire, Madame C. J. Walker was also the biggest success in manufacturing among blacks in America.

Sarah Breedlove was born in Delta, La., to poor black farmers. She knew poverty and deprivation in childhood. Orphaned when only 6, Sarah was reared by an older sister. In 1882, at 14, she married C. J. Walker. Settling in Vicksburg, Miss., the couple had one child. Walker's passing six years later left his 20-year-old wife and young daughter in poverty. Moving to St. Louis, Mo., his widow worked as a washerwoman. Her daughter attended public schools by day while she attended evenings.

Madame C. J. Walker noted the difficulties black women had in styling their naturally curly hair. To straighten out kinks, they had to press an iron against batches of their hair placed against a flat surface. She sought an easier way. Investing two dollars and using trial and error methods, she finally came up with a formula for a preparation that would stiffen strands of hair, making it easier to press and style. She then designed a metal comb that could be heated and used in pressing and styling hair much better than any previous device.

She invented the hair conditioner in 1905. Trying it out on herself and relatives until she had a commercially acceptable product, she then began making it in tubs, packing it in jars, and peddling it door-to-door in St. Louis. Deciding to expand, she spent a year in preliminary work in

Denver, Colo., and then toured for two years, promoting her products. She built up a large mail-order clientele by advertising in black newspapers and magazines and traveling around demonstrating and pushing her products. She set up a branch office in Pittsburgh, Pa., in 1908, to handle mail orders, with her daughter, now in her early 20's, in charge.

Madame Walker continued traveling, promoting the business. By 1910, she decided to build a factory in Indianapolis, Ind., to manufacture her hair preparations, facial creams, and other products. Along with her research and production laboratories there, she set up a school, both to train her salesmen and to teach the "Walker System" of styling hair to beauticians from all over America. At the peak of her career, she had 2,000 salesmen selling the ever-lengthening line of Walker products, an annual payroll of $200,000, and business amounting to $500,000 annually. A superb businesswoman, she had many original ideas, copied subsequently by other businesses. For example, she organized her agents into clubs to promote mutual business, social, philanthropic, and civic ends; arranged periodic three-day conventions attended by delegates from these clubs; and gave cash prizes to the clubs that did most to aid their communities.

Until the end, she remained modest, generous, kindly, and genuinely interested in promoting projects beneficial to her people and nation. Still, she lived in a style befitting her fortune. She built a $250,000 mansion, Villa Lewaro, at exclusive Irvington-on-the-Hudson, N. Y., which she furnished lavishly. Her will provided for dividing her estate of nearly two million dollars between her daughter (one-third) and schools and charities (two-thirds).

Another outstanding black businesswoman sometimes confused with Madame C. J. Walker was Maggie L. Walker (1867–1934). Born Maggie Lena Mitchell in Richmond, Va., she grew up in poverty but went to school and became a teacher. Taking business training, in 1889 she became executive secretary, at $8.00 a month, of the Order of St. Luke, a Richmond burial society with 3,400 members but no reserve or property. Meanwhile, she married Armstead Walker. She expanded the Order, becoming secretary-treasurer in 1899. Mrs. Walker made it into a solid insurance enterprise, adding a bank and a newspaper. By 1924, the Order had more than 100,000 members, a $70,000 emergency fund, a $100,000 office building in Richmond, 55 home office employees, 145 field workers, and a newspaper, the *St. Luke Herald*. In 1902, she founded in Richmond the Order's independent bank, the St. Luke Penny Savings Bank which, under her leadership as president, grew into a leading black bank, the St. Luke Bank and Trust Company. A high school in Richmond was named for this successful insurance and banking leader.

Washington, Booker T. (1856–1915), Educator and Spokesman

From 1895 to 1915, Booker Taliaferro Washington was the leading spokesman of black Americans. His advice was heeded by Presidents, governors, Congressmen, and philanthropists, giving him great power over the destinies of his fellow blacks. He stressed reconciliation with Southern whites and cessation of agitation for rights, urging blacks instead to develop skills that would make them so useful to their communities that whites would eventually grant them full citizenship. The great educational institution he founded at Tuskegee in 1881 emphasized manual training to lift blacks out of backwardness and poverty and start them toward becoming useful, prospering persons, deserving of all rights.

He was born a slave on the plantation of James Burroughs at Hale's Ford in Franklin County, in the western part of Virginia, sixteen miles south of Roanoke. His mother, Jane Burroughs, a slave, was a cook on the small, ten-slave plantation. His father was a white man from a nearby plantation. Booker's elder brother, John, was also a mulatto. Called only by his first name, Booker did not know that his mother had initially named him Booker Taliaferro, giving him his father's surname. Looking back later on his nine years as a slave, Booker T. Washington recalled that there were hardships and deprivations because of the inadequate food, clothing, and shelter that was the lot of the slave everywhere, but he also remembered mutual affection and kindly relations between the master and the slaves.

Early in the Civil War, Booker's mother married Washington Ferguson, a slave on a neighboring plantation whose master allowed him only infrequently to make the trip to see his wife and their daughter, Amanda. Ferguson ran away during the Civil War and settled in Malden, W. Va., taking a job in the salt works. When the slaves were emancipated in 1865, by Union armies enforcing Lincoln's proclamation of two years before, Ferguson sent for his wife, stepsons, and daughter. He secured jobs for the boys packing salt in barrels. His kindly wife adopted a homeless lad, James, who toiled in the salt works, giving John and Booker a younger foster brother.

None of Malden's blacks were literate, but Booker, securing a discarded copy of Webster's blue-back speller, mastered the alphabet. When a black school opened, he was anxious to attend, but his stepfather wanted him to keep working and earning. Booker received sporadic lessons at night in the teacher's spare time. Eventually, Ferguson relented and let him attend school daytimes, but he had to work in the salt "mines" from 4:00 a.m. to 9:00 a.m. daily, and after school. On the 10-year-old lad's initial day in school, he discovered that other pupils had two names. Knowing only Booker, he assumed a name famous in American history, telling the teacher his name was Booker Washington. Learning later of his original surname, he made that his middle name. Booker T. Washington's brothers, John and James, and sister, Amanda, accepted Washington as their last name also.

Upon overhearing miners talking about a black college at Hampton, Va., Booker yearned to go. Meanwhile, he became houseboy for General Lew Ruffner, owner of the Malden coal mines and salt works. Mrs. Ruffner was a rigorous Vermont Yankee who drilled Booker on spotless housecleaning. She also encouraged him to continue his studies. In 1872, Booker set out to attend Hampton Institute, but his money gave out when he had gotten to Richmond, where he slept under wooden sidewalks while seeking to earn money to resume his trip. Working at odd jobs, begging rides, and walking, he soon traveled the remaining eighty miles. When the disheveled 16-year-old lad asked for admission and scholarship aid, Hampton officials tested him by asking him to clean a room. Well trained by Mrs. Ruffner, he swept three times and dusted four times, easily passing the "white glove" inspection. He was admitted and given a job as janitor to pay for his room and board. His tuition was paid by a Northern friend of the school's white president, Samuel C. Armstrong, who had founded Hampton Institute in 1868 after serving as a Union Army general.

Born in Hawaii of Yankee missionaries who taught work habits to the natives, Armstrong stressed manual training in his school. All students worked on campus and learned useful trades as well as academic subjects. President Armstrong took a liking to Washington, who learned brickmasonry along with his collegiate courses. After graduating in 1876, Washington taught school in Malden for two years and then attended Wayland Seminary in Washington, D.C., 1878–1879. He found big city life unpleasant and he disliked the classical curriculum at Wayland, a Baptist seminary founded in 1865. (Wayland merged in 1899 with Richmond Theological Institute, founded in 1867, to form Virginia Union University in Richmond.) Washington felt that Wayland's students desired education in order to rise above, and live off, the black masses. He preferred Hampton's practical training, which he felt would elevate his race, much more than the higher learning divorced from reality given at Wayland and other classically oriented black colleges. From 1879 to 1881 he served on Hampton's faculty, particularly supervising 100 American Indians admitted experimentally.

In 1881, President Armstrong recommended Booker T. Washington to a committee seeking a principal for a new black school in Tuskegee, Ala. As a political payoff to Macon County blacks who helped elect him, a white state legislator secured passage of a bill appropriating $2,000 annually to pay faculty salaries for a black college at the county seat, Tuskegee. As principal, Washington had to recruit teachers and also secure land, buildings, and pupils for the school. He faced hostility from whites in that rural county who feared education would unfit blacks to do the laboring tasks for which they were needed.

He began his school with forty pupils in a dilapidated shanty near a black church. He soon contracted to buy an abandoned plantation, using the plantation structures for temporary classroom buildings and dormitories. He had to raise funds to pay for this campus purchased only on faith. Patterning his school after Hampton, he won the support of Southern whites and Northern philanthropists. He demonstrated that his students were learning practical trades that would make them useful persons, adding to the prosperity and stability of their communities. By encouraging blacks to remain among and make friends of Southern whites, he helped to ease tension and increase his school's friends. He and his students built a kiln and made bricks with which they erected campus buildings. They also grew food, raised livestock, and built furniture for the school.

Under Washington's thirty-four years of leadership, Tuskegee Institute became an important, innovative educational institution. He took rural blacks mired in cotton tenancy and taught them to improve their lives by diversified farming, careful budgeting, better sanitation, more balanced diets, and personal hygiene. Community involvement and outreach were Tuskegee bywords. Periodic farmers' conferences on campus introduced improved agricultural techniques to local farmers. For those who could not attend, Tuskegee pioneered the "movable school," sending out demonstration wagons to carry the classrooms to outlying farms. Years later, the Federal Government began agricultural extension and home demonstration work, using some of Tuskegee's techniques. Washington brought George Washington Carver (*q.v.*) to the Tuskegee faculty in 1896. Carver's researches for nearly half a century in his Tuskegee laboratory immensely enriched the South. By 1915, Tuskegee had 2,000 acres of land, an annual budget of $290,000, 1,500 students, almost 200 faculty members, and an endowment of nearly $2,000,000, larger by far than any other black college or university and larger than many Southern white colleges. Washington wrote half a dozen books about blacks, his work, and Tuskegee. His classic autobiography, *Up from Slavery* (1901), was translated into many languages. In 1901, he became the first black to have dinner at the White House when he dined with President Theodore Roosevelt, an occurrence that angered the race-conscious South.

Meanwhile, Washington's work spread far beyond Tuskegee. Encouraging black capitalism, he founded the National Negro Business League in 1900. He also fostered such other useful institutions as National Negro Health Week, begun in 1914. Increasingly in the 1880s and early 1890s, the successful founder of thriving Tuskegee was called upon to speak at educational meetings and other gatherings on such matters as black education and race relations. In September, 1895, seven months after the passing of the militant leader Frederick Douglass (*q.v.*), Washington made his important speech at the Cotton States Exposition in Atlanta. Washington said what he had often said before, but now his remarks received national attention. In essence, his Atlanta Compromise suggested that blacks should stop agitating for political and social rights in return for whites' granting them better economic opportunity to earn these rights by building a solid base of skilled and prospering black laborers, farmers, craftsmen, professionals, and homeowners. Whites were overjoyed at this solution to the racial problem, misreading it to mean blacks would remain permanently a laboring, servant caste, without political or social rights.

Dismayed at what they considered his "surrender" of their rights, black intellectuals, mostly Northerners, opposed him. The control he had over Federal appointments for blacks and over foundation grants to black institutions greatly curtailed his opposition. The Tuskegee Institute News Bureau flooded newspapers with releases supporting Washington's side of the controversy. He and his supporters secretly subsidized, or bought control of, several influential black newspapers and magazines, in which they promoted Washington's viewpoint without the public being aware that these periodicals were controlled by him.

For two decades, Booker T. Washington's views prevailed. In those twenty years, disfranchisement, segregation, and numerous lynchings occurred. The economic status of the black man did not improve as much as Washington had hoped in the optimistic belief that whites really wanted blacks to rise. He did secretly finance and encourage lawsuits and other efforts to prevent disfranchisement and segregation of blacks, but these covert attempts failed. After he passed from the scene in 1915, the opposition, led by W. E. B. Du Bois (*q.v.*), restored militant protest

—as focused in the NAACP that Du Bois helped found in 1910—to center stage, reuniting blacks in a renewal of the fight for full equality, a fight that Frederick Douglass made for half a century before Washington rose to leadership in 1895.

Waters, Ethel (1900–   ), Singer and Actress

Singing or acting, Ethel Waters has given many memorable performances. Sustained by faith, she rose from squalor to stardom.

She was born out of wedlock in Chester, Pa., to a 12-year-old raped in her family's Philadelphia hovel by a youth named Waters. Ethel was unwanted and unloved. Her mother's affection centered on the legitimate daughter born of a subsequent marriage. Raised mostly by her grandmother, whom she called Mom, Ethel seldom stayed in one place more than a few weeks, except for one fifteen-month period when the entire family shared a three-room shanty in a red-light district of Philadelphia. Constantly in the streets of Philadelphia or nearby Chester, she learned to swear like a sailor and serve as lookout for gamblers and prostitutes. She saw life at its seamiest. Neglected by her carousing aunts, she was so hungry she was driven to steal. Nuns in a parochial school she attended briefly invented errands for her in order to have excuses to feed their hungry, but proud and sensitive, pupil.

Surrounded by depravity, but also seeing the miserable consequences of whiskey, narcotics, and sensuality, Ethel Waters determined to do better. Her grandmother, despairing of elevating the sights of her own children, focused on her. Ethel pretended to be regular among her peers, but carefully refrained from indulging in harmful vices. Finding solace in God, whether through Catholic services, storefront churches, or evangelistic revivals, all of which she enjoyed, helped her to rise above her miserable environs. She dreamed of becoming traveling companion to a rich lady. Having sung and recited in a church program at age 5, she also fancied herself as a performer, imitating vaudevillians. She possessed an exceptional memory, and absorbed blues songs plaintively sung by her aunts and other ghetto flotsam to relieve their misery and release their pent-up emotions. Her hopes of bettering herself received a jolt when she wed at age 13 while still in sixth grade. Saddled with her during the grandmother's terminal illness, her mother pushed her into marriage with a man nearly twice her age. Ethel left her unfaithful husband within a year. On her own and large for her age, the 14-year-old got a job making $4.75 weekly as a menial in a Philadelphia apartment hotel.

On her seventeenth birthday, she attended a Halloween party at a

Philadelphia nightclub where friends prevailed upon her to sing a tune. Hearing her, two vaudevillians persuaded her to join their troupe in a two-week engagement at Baltimore's Lincoln Theater for $10.00 a week. Billed as Sweet Mamma Stringbean, she stopped the show with her low-keyed rendition of the "St. Louis Blues" of W. C. Handy (*q.v.*), so unlike the shouting style of blues queens Bessie Smith and Ma Rainey. Discovering that the vaudevillians received $25 for her act but paid her only $10, she quit, joining up with the Hill Sisters who also left the troupe. She toured sleazy theaters in the South with them for almost a year, steadily building up a following. She nearly lost a leg in Anniston, Ala., because of malpractice by a white hospital physician. He was trying to punish her for having injured it in an accident that wrecked the fancy car of a prominent white whose chauffeur gave joy rides to showpeople.

Soloing later, she sang in a Philadelphia saloon, Harlem's Lincoln Theater, and the Edmond's Cellar nightspot in Harlem. Edmond's pianist persuaded her to expand by adding popular ballads to her blues repertoire. Her act attracted increasing attention, drawing customers away from fancier clubs. But she was rejected for a part in tryouts for the great black musical *Shuffle Along* because she was identified with low-class clubs. Anxious to prove herself, she signed with a traveling show, *Hello 1919,* whose showgirls had to stay in bawdy houses on tour. She cut records for several companies. On Pace and Handy's Black Swan label, she sang such songs as "Oh Daddy" and "There'll Be Some Changes Made." She also toured with Fletcher Henderson's Black Swan Jazz Masters band. Singing "Georgia Blues," she starred in a shortlived road show, *Oh! Joy!* at $125 weekly, her first appearance as a name performer. She then toured black theaters all over America with her own troupe. She had to flee Atlanta without her belongings in order to escape being severely beaten by the white owner of the black theater there who was furious at her impertinence in insisting that a piano be properly tuned. Safely up North, she cut records for Columbia at $250 each and continued stage and club appearances.

Up to now she had played only in black theaters and nightspots. Fearful that white audiences would not accept her blues singing, Miss Waters had steadfastly refused offers from big, downtown clubs and theaters. Pestered by a black performer, Earl Dancer, she finally made a trial three-day run at the Kedzie Theatre in Chicago. Accustomed to frenzied ovations by black audiences, she interpreted the decorous applause by whites to mean she was a flop, and was not convinced until the theater enthusiastically signed her for a week at $350 and the critics wrote glowing reviews. Forming an act with Dancer, she began touring the bigtime, white vaudeville circuit.

In 1924, she made her first big splash in New York, introducing a new song, "Dinah," as the summer replacement for Florence Mills (*q.v.*) in the hit revue at the Plantation Club downtown. Doing such numbers as "Shake That Thing," Miss Waters appeared in 1927 in her first Broadway musical, *Africana,* a revue produced by her erstwhile partner, Earl Dancer. Subsequently, she drew down $1,250 a week at the Palace Theater in Chicago.

Making her first film, she sang "Am I Blue" in Darryl Zanuck's *On With the Show.* Meanwhile, after a succession of unhappy love affairs, she married again. She starred in Lew Leslie's show, *Blackbirds of 1930*, and appeared in *Rhapsody in Black* in 1931 and a new edition of that show in 1932. Later, playing at Harlem's classiest nightspot, the Cotton Club, she introduced Harold Arlen's new song, "Stormy Weather." Pouring into it the anguish of her unhappy childhood, miserable romances, and disintegrating second marriage, she made it her best-known number, virtually a theme song of her life. Irving Berlin heard her and arranged for her to sing four songs in his new Broadway show, *As Thousands Cheer* (1933), starring Clifton Webb and Marilyn Miller. Two of the four tunes were the hit-parade number "Having a Heat Wave," and the haunting "Supper Time," sung by a woman who learns while preparing their meal that her husband has just been lynched. That season, she was Broadway's highest-paid performer, drawing $5,000 a week, combined, from the show, a nightclub act, and a permanent guest spot on a radio network program. On Broadway and on tour, she spent two years in *As Thousands Cheer.* In the 1935–1936 season, she co-starred with Beatrice Lillie in another musical, *At Home Abroad.*

Meeting DuBose and Dorothy Heyward, collaborators on such plays as *Porgy* and *Mamba's Daughters,* Miss Waters agreed to create on stage the role of Hagar, daughter of Mamba, because Hagar reminded her of her own mother. Barnstorming to promote her new love affair's band-leading venture, she patiently waited two years for the Heywards to get financial backing to produce the play. It finally opened in January, 1939, at the great Empire Theater. In her first non-singing role, Ethel Waters not only was the first black woman ever starred in a Broadway drama but also was a stunning success as an actress. *Mamba's Daughters* had a long run on Broadway, an extended tour, and a lengthy Broadway re-run. Critics acclaimed Miss Waters for making the difficult transition from a singing idol to a superb dramatic actress.

Subsequently, she returned to musicals, singing "Taking a Chance on

Love," "Happiness Is Just a Thing Called Joe," and the title song in the all-black Broadway show *Cabin in the Sky,* 1940–1941. She appeared in more Hollywood movies, with Paul Robeson (*q.v.*) in an episode in *Tales of Manhattan* (1941), in *Cairo* (1942), and the screen version of *Cabin in the Sky* (1943). In 1942, she bought her first house, in Los Angeles. Then came a puzzling hiatus in her career. From 1943 to 1949, her bookings dwindled to almost nothing, and people termed her "washed up." By late 1948, she was almost broke and was reduced to singing in cheap saloons. But then she bounced back, with featured roles in the movie *Pinky* (1949), the long-run, prizewinning Broadway drama *The Member of the Wedding* (1950), and the movie version of that drama in 1953.

By the late 1950s, her career had skidded once more. Broke, down and out, she bounced back again, not in show business, but as a member of evangelist Billy Graham's revival team during the 1960s. Working for God, she found at last the peace, happiness, and love for which she groped so long. Her autobiography, *His Eye Is on the Sparrow* (1951), took its title from the spiritual she sang so beautifully in *The Member of Wedding.*

Weaver, Robert C. (1907–   ), Cabinet Member

On January 13, 1966, President Lyndon B. Johnson appointed Robert Clifton Weaver to head a newly created Federal department combining various agencies dealing with cities and with housing. Five days later, the Senate confirmed him. As Secretary of Housing and Urban Development, Weaver was the first black to serve in the Cabinet of an American President.

Great-grandson of a slave, he was born in Washington, D.C., of that city's middle-class black elite. The famous singer-composer Harry T. Burleigh (*q.v.*) was his uncle, and his maternal grandfather, Dr. Robert Tanner Freeman, was the first Afro-American with a dental degree, having graduated in the initial class at Harvard University's Dental School in 1869. His father was a postal clerk. Robert grew up in a suburb of Washington where only seven black families lived among 3,000 whites. Robert and his brother were not permitted to attend the neighborhood school around the corner. Instead, they had to travel nearly an hour crosstown to reach a black school. Like such other outstanding black Washingtonians as Charles Drew and William Hastie (*qq.v*), Robert attended Dunbar High School. Skilled and enterprising, he earned money as an electrician during his junior year there and ran his own electrical business as a senior.

An outstanding student in high school, Weaver won the scholarship to Harvard University awarded top Dunbar graduates. There he majored in economics, graduating with honors in 1929, and received a master's degree in economics in 1931. He taught for one year at Agricultural and Technical College in Greensboro, the land-grant school for North Carolina blacks. Returning to Harvard as an Austin Scholar (1932–1933), he earned the Ph.D. in economics in 1934. Showing exceptional ability in his doctoral work, he disproved the contention of one professor, an eminent economist, who claimed that blacks lacked aptitude for graduate work in economics.

Along with other bright young blacks like Hastie and Ralph Bunche (*q.v.*), Weaver was brought into Government service by President Franklin Roosevelt's New Deal Administration. Most began as race relations advisers to Federal departments. Led by Weaver and Mary McLeod Bethune (*q.v.*), they formed a "Black Cabinet." Proving their ability, some advanced to increasingly important administrative posts transcending minority matters. Weaver served as adviser on Negro Affairs to Secretary of the Interior Harold Ickes from 1933 to 1937. For the next three years, he was special assistant to the administrator of the United States Housing Authority. From 1940 to 1944, during World War II, he held administrative positions dealing with employment and training of minorities, serving successively with the National Defense Advisory Commission, Office of Production Management, War Production Board, and War Manpower Commission. His wartime experience led to his first book, *Negro Labor: A National Problem* (1946).

Leaving Federal service, Weaver served as executive director of the Mayor's Committee on Race Relations in Chicago, 1945–1946. He also held housing posts with the Metropolitan Housing Council of Chicago and the National Council on Housing. His work in housing led to his second book, *The Negro Ghetto* (1948). Meanwhile he also served with the United Nations Relief and Rehabilitation Administration (UN RRA) mission in Russia's Ukraine, where he rose from supply officer to reports officer to acting deputy chief of mission. Returning to teaching, Weaver served as lecturer or visiting professor or professor of economics between 1947 and 1951 at Northwestern University, Columbia University Teachers College, New York University School of Education, and the New School for Social Research. He also served from 1949 to 1954 as director of the John Hay Whitney Foundation's Opportunity Fellowships Program.

Weaver was active in Democratic politics and in the NAACP, eventually becoming chairman of the board of the latter. He resumed Government work when the Democrats, under Averell Harriman, returned to power in New York in 1955. Governor Harriman appointed Weaver to be Deputy Commissioner of the Division of Housing. That December, Weaver, acknowledged to be one of the nation's foremost housing experts, became State Rent Administrator. He thus became the first black in New York's Cabinet. He served until January, 1959, when the Republicans came to power under Governor Nelson Rockefeller. From 1959 to 1960, Weaver was a Ford Foundation consultant. He then served under Democratic Mayor Robert Wagner as vice chairman of New York City's Housing and Redevelopment Board, 1960–1961. On December 31, 1960, President-elect John F. Kennedy appointed Weaver to a higher post than any black had ever before held in the executive branch of the national government: Administrator of the Housing and Home Finance Agency. The Senate confirmed him in February, 1961. He was still heading that large ($340,000,000 budget in 1961) and important Federal agency when it became in 1966 the core of the new Department of Housing and Urban Development (HUD), which President Johnson appointed him to head.

Weaver's other two books are *The Urban Complex* (1964) and *Dilemmas of Urban America* (1965), the latter being the Godkin Lectures given at Harvard University. Leaving HUD on January 1, 1969, on the eve of the return of the Republicans to power under President Richard M. Nixon, Weaver took office as president of Bernard M. Baruch College of the City University of New York.

The President's Cabinet has not always been very representative of the nation's makeup. Not until Henry Morgenthau and Frances Perkins, both in 1933, did a Jew or woman, respectively, ever serve. Not until Anthony Celebreeze and John Gronouski, both in 1963, did an Italian-American or Polish-American, respectively, sit in the Cabinet.

Wells, Ida B. (1869–1931), Anti-lynching Crusader

Mrs. Ida Baker Wells Barnett was a crusading journalist who tried to arouse public opinion to end the horror of lynching. She dared to publish the truth about lynching while living in the South.

Ida B. Wells was born in Holly Springs, Miss. While growing up there, she observed Ku Klux Klan terrorists depriving blacks of their rights. She determined to secure an education to help her people. Her plans seemed stymied at the age of 14 when her parents, stricken by yellow fever, passed away. Left with four younger children, plucky Ida managed to support them and still continue her education. She took the Normal course at Rust College in Holly Springs, and studied one summer at Fisk University in Nashville, Tenn., where she wrote for the campus magazine.

In her late teens, she became a teacher in a country school, and later taught in Memphis, Tenn. She wrote for a local black weekly, *Living Word*. Using the pseudonym "Iola," she published articles in other black magazines and newspapers throughout America.

Having been a schoolteacher six years and having saved some money, Miss Wells resigned to become editor and co-owner of the weekly Memphis *Free Speech*. Her crusading for racial justice rapidly gained her wide readership among blacks in the lower Mississippi Valley. Prosperity beckoned, provided her newspaper could remain in existence. She was threatened often, but, carrying two pistols for protection, she fearlessly continued her campaigns. In 1892 she revealed the background of, and official culpability in, the lynching of three Memphis blacks. Their only crime had been competing successfully as grocers, taking away business from white grocers who, monopolizing trade in a black neighborhood, overcharged and abused customers. The white grocers and their friends provoked a disturbance to get the three black businessmen thrown in jail. The mob took them from their cells with little effort by authorities to avert their murder or apprehend the lynchers. The night after her exposé appeared on newsstands, a mob of whites descended upon her newspaper and demolished the printing press and editorial office. They went looking for Miss Wells but friends smuggled her out of the city. Whites openly threatened to lynch her if she ever came back.

She fled to New York. She tried to get Northern dailies to print the black man's side of the lynching issue, but was turned down. She was hired by a black weekly, the New York *Age*, whose editor-publisher, T. Thomas Fortune, had often published dispatches she sent from Memphis. Miss Wells began issuing publications documenting the facts about lynching, including *Southern Horrors* (1892) and *A Red Record* (1894). The first to compile and publish statistics on lynching, she showed that black lynch victims were accused of rape in less than one-fourth of the lynchings and that some were lynched for such trivial causes as insulting whites or failing to move aside. Yet many prominent men, including some Southern governors and congressmen, justified lynching as necessary to protect white women from rape. Miss Wells denounced the North for acquiescing in the crime of lynching by failing to take positive action against it.

She became greatly in demand as an anti-lynching lecturer. She went to England late in 1892 where she greatly stirred the English by her accounts of the bestial and inhuman practice. Her trip was financed by the Women's Loyal Union, formed among New York blacks to support her crusade. Going to Chicago during the 1893 World's Columbian Exposition, she collaborated with other blacks in a booklet citing achievements of Afro-Americans, to counteract the derogatory impression given in the daily press. In Chicago, she investigated and reported on a lynching for the Chicago *Inter-Ocean* newspaper. Settling in Chicago, she founded and headed thenceforward the Ida B. Wells Club, the first organization of black women there. She traveled widely to help found other clubs of black women. Eventually there came a federation of such clubs.

In 1895, in Chicago, she married Ferdinand L. Barnett, a journalist who helped write the World's Fair booklet. A native of Alabama, he had attended Fisk and Northwestern universities, became an attorney in Chicago, and in 1878 founded the *Conservator*, the first black newspaper in Illinois. The Barnetts became leading opponents of Booker T. Washington's (*q.v.*) Atlanta Compromise policies. Ida B. Wells-Barnett continued writing for black newspapers, especially the Chicago *Defender* of Robert Abbott (*q.v.*). Her anti-lynching articles also appeared in leading magazines, including pieces in *The Arena* in January, 1900, *The Independent* (May 16, 1901), and *Survey* (February 1, 1913). She led a delegation to see President William McKinley in 1898 to protest lynchings. She headed the Anti-lynching Speakers Bureau of the Afro-American Council and she founded the Negro Fellowship League in 1908, becoming its first president. She was among the prominent blacks who signed the 1909 call for the meeting that led to formation of the NAACP, where her fiery militancy and distrust of whites stirred up controversy in the new organization.

In 1913, Mrs. Barnett was appointed adult probation officer in Chicago, the first of her race in such a post. Two years later, she was elected vice president of Chicago's Equal Rights League. In 1940, the Ida B. Wells housing project in Chicago was dedicated to commemorate this courageous battler for justice.

Wharton, Clifton R., Jr. (1927–   ), University President

On January 2, 1970, Clifton Reginald Wharton, Jr., assumed office as the fourteenth president in the 114-year history of Michigan State University. Enrolling 44,400 students on its campus at East Lansing, Michigan State is one of the seven largest institutions of higher learning in America. Wharton was the first black to become president of a major university.

He was born in Boston, Mass., eldest of four children of a distinguished career diplomat, Clifton R. Wharton, Sr. (1899–   ). A native of Baltimore, Md., the elder Wharton attended Boston English High School and received bachelor's and master's degrees in law from Boston University. He practiced law in Boston three years and worked almost two years for Federal agencies in Washington, D.C. Passing the career examination in 1925 he entered the Foreign Service, a professional, nonpolitical corps of American diplomats begun in 1924. During its first two decades, Wharton was the only black career diplomat in the Foreign Service. Beginning at the lowest level as third secretary and vice consul in Monrovia, Liberia, in 1925, he advanced through successively higher posts in the Canary Islands, Madagascar, and the Azores, becoming eventually Consul General in Lisbon, Portugal, in 1950 and in Marseilles, France, in 1953. In 1958, President Eisenhower appointed him to be the U. S. Minister to Romania, the first black career diplomat to become America's top representative in a foreign nation. In 1961, President Kennedy appointed him American Ambassador to Norway, the post in which he served until his retirement in 1964. He was the first black to be America's ambassador to a white nation.

Clifton Wharton, Jr., attended prestigious Boston Latin High School. Founded in 1635, this private school is the oldest secondary school in the United States. His father's high school, Boston English, founded in 1821, is the oldest public high school in the nation. Young Wharton enrolled in the nation's oldest college, Harvard University, founded in 1636. He was a student leader there, helping to found the National Student Association and serving as its national secretary, 1946–1947. He graduated with highest honors at the top of his class in 1947, receiving a B.A. in history. He then became the first black ever admitted to the School for Advanced International Studies at Johns Hopkins University in Baltimore, where he earned an M.A. in international studies in 1948.

Dedicated to helping underdeveloped areas progress, Wharton became an expert on growth problems of Latin America and Southeast Asia. He also became a specialist in American foreign policy and international education. Specializing first in Latin America, he served five years with the American International Association for Economic and Social Development, learning to speak Spanish fluently. He resumed his studies at the University of Chicago and in 1956 received another master's degree, in economics. In 1958 he became the first black to receive a Ph.D. in economics from that institution.

Turning to problems of Asian development, he went to work for a private, nonprofit organization founded by John D. Rockefeller III as the Council on Economic and Cultural Affairs, subsequently renamed the Agricultural Development Council. Headquartered in New York, the council finances research and teaching connected with economic and human problems of agricultural development, mainly in Asia. From 1958 to 1963, he was stationed in Malaysia, directing the council's program in Cambodia, Malaysia, Thailand, and Vietnam. When President Lyndon Johnson sent a ten-man task force to Vietnam, Wharton was the only member with extensive first-hand knowledge of that land. While in Malaysia, he was a visiting professor at the University of Malaya and wrote numerous articles on development problems of Southeast Asia.

From 1963 to 1968, Dr. Wharton directed the Agricultural Development Council's American Universities Research Program (AURP). Aided by a $1,500,000 Ford Foundation grant, AURP encouraged American professors to conduct research on agricultural development problems in foreign lands. Some 140 professors from sixty colleges and universities in Canada and the United States received grants under this program. On leave in 1964, Wharton was a visiting professor at Stanford University, in the Research Center in Economic Growth. In 1968, he became vice president of the Agricultural Development Council. He wrote a book, *Subsistence Agriculture and Economic Development*, scheduled for publication in 1970. He became, in 1969, a director of the Equitable Life Assurance Society, making him the first black to serve on the board of one of America's ten largest corporations.

Since Michigan State University has long been a leader in conducting international technical and advisory assistance programs in Africa, Asia, and Latin America, Wharton's background made him an ideal choice for president. The student-faculty-administration steering committee— set up to help select a successor to Dr. John A. Hannah, who became head of the Federal Agency for International Development in April, 1969—strongly recommended Wharton. The other three nominees, including former Michigan governor G. Mennen Williams, were white, but Wharton was selected by the board of trustees in October, 1969.

He was not the first black to head a predominantly white institution. Dr. James A. Colston (1909–   ), a native of Quincy, Fla., and graduate of Morehouse College, Atlanta University, and New York University, became president in 1966 of Bronx Community College (1969 enrollment: 6,800), a two-year school in the City University of New York system, after previous service as president of Bethune-Cookman College and Knoxville College. Dr. Robert C. Weaver (*q.v.*) became president of Baruch College (1969 enrollment: 9,500) in that same system in 1969.

Wheatley, Phillis (c. 1753–1784), Poetess

Phillis Wheatley was the most notable black writer in America from the Colonial-Revolutionary era in which she wrote until the advent about 1900 of poet Paul Laurence Dunbar and novelist Charles Waddell Chesnutt (*qq.v.*). She was the first Afro-American, and second American woman, to write a book.

She was born about 1753 somewhere in West Africa, possibly Senegal. At about the age of 8, she was kidnapped and brought to America on a slave ship that sold her in Boston, Mass., in August, 1761. The purchaser was a prosperous merchant-tailor, John Wheatley, who had an imposing residence on fashionable King Street (now State Street) in Boston. The household consisted of him, his wife Susannah, their 18-year-old twins, Nathaniel and Mary, and a few elderly slaves. He bought Phillis to train her to help Mrs. Wheatley in her advancing years. She was sold cheaply because the captain feared the frail child might not survive.

Noting that Phillis was bright, alert, and eager to learn, the Wheatleys, especially Mary, helped her learn her letters. She progressed so rapidly that although she spoke only her native tongue when she arrived in Boston, she learned to read English in only sixteen months. She also learned to write and was corresponding with prominent people by 1765. She also began composing poems. Her earliest surviving poem, "To the University of Cambridge, In New England, 1767," was written when she was only 13. Among her other early poetry was a poem in 1768 hailing King George's repeal of the Stamp Act and elegies on Reverend Joseph Sewall in 1769 and on evangelist George Whitefield in 1770. The latter was printed as a broadside (large, single, printed sheet), making it her first published poem. Another early black poet, Jupiter Hammon (c. 1720-c. 1800), a slave on Long Island, N. Y., had published a poem in broadside in 1761. The novelty of a young slave from Africa writing poetry superior to that of most well-educated persons attracted considerable notice for Phillis in Boston. The Wheatleys gave her only light household duties, treating her almost as a member of the family. She flowered under their kind treatment. She had privileges seldom given a slave, such as light and heat in her room so that she could arise and write whenever inspiration came.

Delicate and sickly, Phillis became so ill in the early 1770s that the Wheatley family physician advised a trip abroad to improve her health. Since Nathaniel Wheatley had to go to England on business, Phillis went with him, in May, 1773. Mary might have accompanied them, but she had married in 1771 and had her own household to attend. Some persons in England eagerly awaited Phillis, especially Selina Shirley, Countess of Huntingdon, mentioned in her elegy on Whitefield because she was his patron and an executor of his estate: "Great *Countess*, we Americans revere / Thy Name, and mingle in thy grief sincere." The Countess lionized Phillis and introduced her to British society. A charming conversationalist, Phillis made many friends. The highlight of her trip was the publication of her book, *Poems on Various Subjects, Religious and Moral* (1773). Dedicated to the Countess of Huntingdon, it was printed by a London firm and sold by a Boston firm. Many subsequent editions appeared. This book, which contained thirty-eight of her poems, including those mentioned above, was the first ever written by an American black and only the second by an American woman.

The Countess arranged to present Phillis to King George III at court, but Phillis had to rush back to America without meeting the monarch, because Mrs. Wheatley was gravely ill. When Mrs. Wheatley passed away in March, 1774, Phillis wrote her closest friend, Obour, slave of the Tanner family of Newport, R.I., that she felt the loss as if it were her own mother.

When George Washington became commander of the colonial forces in the Revolution, Phillis wrote a poem on him, entitled "His Excellency Gen. Washington." On October 26, 1775, while she was staying temporarily in Providence, R.I., she wrote a letter to him, enclosing the poem. Four times in this poem, she referred to this nation as Columbia, believed to be the earliest such usage. She also termed Washington "first in peace and honours" in this poem, fourteen years before Henry Lee's famous eulogy, "first in war, first in peace, first in the hearts of his countrymen!" On February 28, 1776, General Washington responded belatedly to Phillis, praising her poetic ability and inviting her to visit him at his headquarters in Cambridge, which she did in March, 1776.

She was still a slave then—she did not become free until her master, John Wheatley, passed on in March, 1778, whereupon the daughter, Mary, emancipated her informally. Next month Phillis married a talented free black whose failure in various business and professional undertakings in Boston left them in financial straits. Her husband's proud manner cut her off from white friends who might have helped, and the Wheatley twins passed away, Mary late in 1778 and Nathaniel, long a resident of England, in 1783. Needing money, Phillis tried to publish a second collection of poems in 1779 but lack of subscribers cancelled the project. Phillis's husband went to debtors' prison and Phillis worked in a cheap lodging house, but the arduous labor brought the sickly young poet to an end in her early 30s.

Her poetry was too artificial, too imitative of Alexander Pope, and too confined by classical restraint to be great poetry. Her true sentiments are veiled and she avoided subjects on which she might have written with great feeling. Nonetheless, it is remarkable that she wrote such elegant, if stilted, poetry considering her handicaps of status and training.

White, Charles (1918–), Artist

Charles White is the most admired and inspirational of all contemporary black artists. The social realism of his heroic drawings in charcoal or ink or crayon fit well the current mood of black awareness but his art antedates the present temper by several decades. For thirty years, White has turned out greatly admired portraits and murals of blacks, both ordinary persons and great historical figures. While his subject matter is the Afro-Americans from whom he sprang, the bold lines, massive figures, stolid dignity, and worn but noble faces he portrays transcend ethnic lines. He achieves universality by affirming mankind's triumph over adversity, an eloquent testament to White's belief in the ultimate goodness and perfectibility of man.

White was born in Chicago, only child of Southern migrants. His mother was a domestic worker, his father a Creek Indian who did construction and railroad work. His passing when Charles was 8 left mother and son struggling to exist. On his seventh birthday, his mother had bought Charles a set of oil paints to occupy him while he waited for her at her maid's job. When he painted the window shades, she spanked him, hid the paints, bought him a violin, and started him on lessons. But he preferred painting. On his way home from elementary school one day, he came upon an outdoor art class whose students taught him how to mix paints, rekindling his interest. In spare time from work as a delivery boy and shoeshine boy, Charles wandered through the main library, admiring the paintings, especially those of Winslow Homer. He attended Saturday art lectures for promising public school youngsters, and won prizes for ably executing weekly assignments.

Charles had done well in elementary school and began well in high school. But his interest in black heroes had been fired up by his avid reading of library books, especially *The New Negro* by Alain Locke (*q.v.*). On finding that these figures were left out of his schoolbooks, he began to lose interest. He would play hookey to read in the public library or wander through the galleries of the Chicago Art Institute, admiring paintings and dreaming of becoming an artist. At the age of 14, he began painting signs for beauty and barber ships, theaters, and other local businesses. He became the youngest member of an Arts and Crafts Guild formed by young black signpainters who aspired to careers in art. By pooling their earnings and raising money by putting on parties, they paid one member's way each week to a lesson at the Chicago Art Institute, with the chosen one then teaching the others what he learned.

Charles's art teachers in high school encouraged him to enter art competitions. He won scholarships to the Chicago Academy of Fine Arts and to the Mizen Academy of Art but was rejected when the recipient turned out to be black. These cruel rebuffs made the sensitive youngster more withdrawn. Taking refuge in his drawing, he won first prize in a nationwide high school pencil sketching contest. His prize work was sold for five dollars and reproduced in a magazine, which boosted his confidence. Determined to make a career in art, he redoubled his efforts, made up his failing grades, and completed high school in June, 1937.

That May, he had won a tuition scholarship to the Art Institute of Chicago for a year of full-time study in art. To pay for his art supplies, carfare, and other expenses, he worked as a cook and valet for a man and also taught a class in drawing at a Catholic high school. Employed by the Federal Arts Project of the Works Progress Administration (WPA), 1938–1941, White had his first chance to work professionally with mature artists.

Increasingly, recognition came his way. As early as November, 1936, while still in high school, he had been included in a group exhibition along with two artists who were university graduates. That December, one of his drawings was reproduced in a magazine article on promising Chicago artists. His drawing titled "There Were No Crops This Year" won a first award at the American Negro Exposition in Chicago in 1940. While teaching at the Chicago Community Art Center in 1941, he became a close friend of photographer Gordon Parks (q.v.) whose photographs of ghetto life matched White's sketches.

In 1941, White married a talented black sculptress, Alice Elizabeth Catlett. Shortly afterward, he received a Rosenwald Fellowship. The young couple used it for travel in the South where White made sketches for a mural he had agreed to do for Hampton Institute. Unaccustomed to segregation, he was severely beaten in New Orleans for entering a forbidden restaurant and was forced at gunpoint to the back of a streetcar in Hampton, Va. During the fall semester, 1942, with his fellowship renewed, he studied tempera and fresco painting under Harry Sternberg at the Art Students' League in New York City, where he made his home for a decade and a half. Then, the Whites spent nine months at Hampton Institute in 1943 where he did his great 18- by 60-foot mural in tempera, "The Contribution of the Negro to American Democracy," featuring such persons as Frederick Douglass, Harriet Tubman, and George Washington Carver (*qq.v.*). The resulting publicity led to other commissions, such as the mural on the history of the black press commissioned by the Associated Negro Press.

Drafted into the Army in 1944, he developed serious lung infections while on duty combatting Mississippi and Ohio river floods. Given a medical discharge, he spent three years in a Veteran's Administration Hospital. After his release in 1947, he had his first one-man show, to great critical acclaim. White spent a year as artist-in-residence at Howard University and then was hospitalized for another year following a lung operation. His first marriage foundered meanwhile and he married a social worker in 1950. On their honeymoon trip to Europe, he found many Europeans were familiar with, and fond of, his work. The kind treatment received abroad gave him a new appreciation for his fellow man.

More and more honors came his way as increasing compassion, power, dignity, and universality emerged in his work. In 1952, the Whitney Museum purchased his "Preacher" and the Metropolitan Museum of Art exhibited his work. In 1955, he received a John Hay Whitney Foundation Opportunity Fellowship. He had one-man shows at many institutions, including New York University. Failing health forced him to move west to the Los Angeles suburb of Altadena, Calif., where he settled in 1956, and still lives with his wife and two adopted children in a house nestled at the foot of the San Gabriel Mountains. In 1959 he won a first prize in an invitational show in Germany in which Pablo Picasso and other notables exhibited. The Berlin Museum purchased his "Micah" print.

An insight into his appeal may be gained by viewing the eighty-eight works reproduced in *Images of Dignity: The Drawings of Charles White* (1967). Other outstanding contemporary black artists include Eldzier Cortor, Romare Bearden, and Jacob Lawrence.

White, Walter (1893–1955), Civil Rights Leader

As assistant secretary of the National Association for the Advancement of Colored People (NAACP) from 1918 to 1931, blue-eyed blonde-haired Walter Francis White daringly investigated lynchings in communities where they had just occurred. For nearly a quarter of a century, 1931–1955, he was the NAACP's Executive Secretary. He was an uncompromising fighter and writer for equality.

He was born in Atlanta, Ga., younger of two sons among seven children born to a former schoolteacher and a postman. The thrifty, hardworking, puritanical family owned a well-kept eight-room house on the edge of a ghetto. All nine were light enough to pass for white but took pride in and identified with the black race. To avoid humiliation on Jim Crow streetcars, they walked everywhere or rode the surrey Walter's father scrimped to buy.

At the onset of the Atlanta race riot of 1906—stirred up by race-baiting politicians and newspapers—13-year-old Walter was making the rounds with his father in his horse-drawn mail cart. Mistaking them for white, mobs of whites bypassed them while hunting down and murdering helpless blacks. When a mob of whites invaded their section of town the next night, father and son stood guard. Shouting that such a residence was too good for blacks, the mob prepared to burn the "uppity" mail-man's house. Walter and his father cocked their guns to shoot the first rioters to enter their yard, but, before they could fire, shots from blacks in a neighboring building sent the cowardly mob scampering in search of unarmed black victims.

Walter worked summers as an errand boy and an office boy. One summer he applied for a bellboy job at Atlanta's most luxurious hotel. Hired as a page-boy instead, he only learned a week later that it was a post reserved for whites. Friends advised him to keep the job since it was an honest mistake. At summer's end when the manager wanted to promote the highly capable youth to key clerk, Walter informed him that he was black and of course did not get the job. The following summer he sold policies for a black Atlanta insurance company, Standard Life.

He attended Atlanta's public schools in the ill-equipped, cast-off buildings alloted to blacks, staffed by lower-salaried black teachers, and scheduled for double sessions (he attended 8:00 to 2:00). Although his father's taxes helped support public high schools for whites, he had to pay tuition to send his son to the high school department of private black colleges in Atlanta, since there were no public high schools for blacks anywhere in Georgia. The dedicated efforts of New England whites who toiled on the faculties of these black colleges overcame the bitterness that Walter might have had toward whites from his experiences with Southern mobs and injustice.

Upon graduating from the high school department of Atlanta University, White entered the college, and received his B.A. degree in 1916. He was offered the principalship of a small rural school, but went to work as a clerk for Standard Life Insurance Company instead. Able and efficient, he was soon promoted to cashier. In December, 1916, he was a leader in efforts to form an Atlanta branch of the NAACP. Until then, only three of the organization's seventy-one branches were in Southern cities. White became secretary of the Atlanta branch. Standard Life's founder-president, Heman Perry, was a founding member of the branch and the company's secretary-treasurer, Harry Pace, became branch president. Later, Pace helped composer W. C. Handy and publisher John H. Johnson (*qq.v.*). James Weldon Johnson (*q.v.*), the writer who became NAACP field secretary and branch organizer in December, 1916, was greatly impressed with White on his visits to the Atlanta branch in February and March, 1917. White was a leader in the branch's drive to force Atlanta to improve the black schools.

Later in 1917, when the expanding national NAACP needed an assistant to its chief administrative officer, secretary Roy Nash, a white man, Johnson recommended White. He went to work on January 31, 1918, serving under John Shillady, another white who replaced Army-bound Nash. Twelve days later, White volunteered to go to Tennessee to investigate a Lincoln's birthday lynching in which a black sharecropper had been slowly burned by a mob for defending himself from a beating by his employer. Staying at the main hotel and posing as a white man interested in buying farm land, White learned from whites that the sharecropper's employer was a mean, thoroughly disliked person who had no justification for beating the sharecropper. But the whites took the black's life anyway, explaining that blacks might get out of hand if even one was allowed to get away with hitting a white man, even if justifiably. Returning to New York, White reported their barbarous outlook to newspapers and Congressional committees. NAACP studies showed that only 19 percent of the 5,000 blacks lynched from 1889 to 1918 were accused of rape, the crime that supposedly justified lynchings.

In 1919 John Shillady went to Austin, Tex., to confer with Governor William Hobby about Texas's demand that the New York-chartered NAACP cease operations in Texas until it got a state charter. On his way from the hotel to keep his appointment with the governor, Shillady was badly mauled by a mob led by a judge and a sheriff. Governor Hobby—who later married the woman who became Secretary of Health, Education, and Welfare (HEW) in 1953—rejected NAACP appeals to prosecute Shillady's attackers, contending that he got what he deserved and what any white would get who interfered with Texas's handling of blacks. Shillady never recovered from the beating; he resigned his post several months later, and passed away soon afterward. Johnson replaced him, becoming the first black to be the NAACP secretary.

Despite the hazards, White continued his forays, investigating a dozen race riots and twoscore lynchings. He usually posed as a white reporter from a Northern daily anxious to get and print the South's version. When he interviewed Governor Charles Brough of Arkansas, the governor praised him for his willingness to correct the "lies" the NAACP was telling. He had some narrow escapes. One sheriff pinned a deputy's badge on him, telling him he was free to slay blacks with the power of the law behind him. He was given a gun and sent out in a car with other gun-toting deputy sheriffs to get some blacks, but fortunately all were in hiding from rioting whites. In Helena, Ark., on his way to the jail to interview some blacks who were being railroaded to a legal lynching because of their activity in a sharecropper union, a black man whispered to him that the whites were planning to ambush him. White immediately ducked out of sight and boarded the next train North. The conductor told this stranger that he was leaving too soon, that the townspeople were planning a surprise lynching for a "high yellow Negro" snooping around passing for white. White said he was sorry to have to miss the fun. He sweated out the train's slow journey to safety. On another occasion, he was invited to join the Ku Klux Klan in Georgia, but backed out. Out of his experience came several books: a remarkable, highly praised novel, *Fire in the Flint* (1924); a second novel, *Flight* (1926); and a sociological study written while on leave with a 1927 Guggenheim Fellowship for creative writing, *Rope and Faggot: A Biography of Judge Lynch* (1929).

Walter White became acting secretary of the NAACP in 1929 when Johnson took leave with a Rosenwald Fellowship for creative writing. In this post, White directed the NAACP's fight in 1930 to block confirmation of Judge John J. Parker of North Carolina to the Supreme Court. In a successful lobby coordinated by White, labor unions, and civil rights groups applied so much pressure over Parker's antiunion and anti-Negro rights views that the Senate, by a 41 to 39 vote, refused to confirm him despite strong backing by President Herbert Hoover. Parker later proved to be a fair-minded jurist in civil rights cases before the fourth circuit appellate court. When Johnson's leave ended, his physicians advised against resuming the heavy burden of NAACP secretary. He became a Fisk University professor and White replaced him in 1931 as NAACP secretary. When W. E. B. Du Bois (*q.v.*) who had been NAACP research director and *Crisis* editor from the beginning resigned in 1934,

White became the sole guiding force of the NAACP. He directed its campaigns for antilynching legislation, pressuring the House into passing the Costigan-Wagner bill in 1934 and the Gavigan bill in 1937, but a Senate filibuster stymied the former in 1935 and the latter in 1938. The constant publicity and campaigning, however, helped to change public opinion, removing the sanction that permitted lynchings. Owing largely to White's efforts, lynchings virtually ceased.

As executive secretary, White led NAACP campaigns for voting rights and against the poll tax. He also worked to end job discrimination, joining A. Philip Randolph (*q.v.*) in the 1941 March-on-Washington movement. White's investigations of discrimination in the armed forces laid the groundwork for President Harry Truman's order desegregating the military in 1948. White directed the NAACP fight for equalization of schools and then for integration. He lived ten months past the great triumph of the May, 1954, school desegregation decision.

White also wrote *A Rising Wind* (1945), an autobiography, *A Man Called White* (1948), and the posthumously published *How Far the Promised Land?* (1955). In addition to his civil rights work, he served as an adviser to the Federal Government concerning the United Nations and also the Virgin Islands.

Wilkins, Roy (1901–   ), NAACP Leader

For four decades, Roy Wilkins has been a leading figure in the National Association for the Advancement of Colored People (NAACP). He served under Walter White (*q.v.*) from 1931 to 1955, succeeding him as executive secretary on April 11, 1955.

Wilkins was born in St. Louis, Mo., grandson of a Mississippi slave. His parents left Mississippi after their marriage in 1900, settling in St. Louis. His father was a college graduate and minister, but could only find employment tending a brick kiln in St. Louis. His mother succumbed to illness when he was 3. His father then sent Roy and the two younger children to live with an aunt and uncle in St. Paul, Minn. Growing up in a low-income mixed neighborhood, Roy attended St. Paul's integrated schools. He was editor of the high school magazine.

Upon graduating from high school in 1919, he entered the University of Minnesota, majoring in sociology, but also taking journalism courses. He worked his way through college as a redcap, dining car waiter, and stockyard laborer. He also was night editor of the university newspaper, the Minnesota *Daily*, which had a circulation of 10,000. In addition, he was editor of a black weekly, the St. Paul *Appeal*, while still an undergraduate. Active in the community, Wilkins served as secretary of the

St. Paul chapter of the NAACP. While he was in college, a brutal mass lynching in Duluth, Minn., prompted him to enter the university's oratorical contest where he won first prize with a strong anti-lynching speech.

On receiving his A.B. degree in 1923, he joined the staff of a leading black newspaper, the weekly Kansas City *Call*. He soon moved up to managing editor. Living in Missouri's second largest city, Wilkins for the first time encountered wholesale segregation. Appalled at Jim Crow, the sensitive young man fought back through his newspaper writings and NAACP activity. He was elected secretary of the Kansas City chapter. In 1930, he attracted attention of the organization's national leaders by the vigorous fight he mounted statewide against the reelection of a Kansas segregationist to the U.S. Senate.

In 1931, when Walter White moved up to executive secretary, the national NAACP hired Wilkins as assistant secretary under him. In 1932, Wilkins and journalist George Schuyler, posing as black day laborers, secured jobs on an Army Engineer Mississippi River flood control project to investigate charges of maltreatment of black workers. They found that blacks were paid much less than white workers in constructing flood-prevention levees, averaging only ten cents an hour. Moreover, these underpaid black workers were forced by the contractors to buy all their supplies from commissaries at exorbitant prices. Any who protested were brutally beaten and the bodies of those who did not survive such beatings were concealed by burial in the levees. Becoming suspicious, police arrested Schuyler at a rooming house in Vicksburg, Miss., took his money, pen, and notebooks, and told him to leave the state if he hoped to stay alive. Wilkins, who was staying at another rooming house, escaped arrest. The two bravely continued their investigations in northwestern Mississippi, garnering data that the NAACP used to secure a Congressional investigation and corrective legislation. In 1934, Wilkins was arrested in Washington, D.C., while participating in a demonstration, picketing the Attorney General for failure to include lynching on the agenda of a national conference on crime.

When W. E. B. Du Bois (*q.v.*) left the NAACP in 1934, Wilkins replaced him as editor of *The Crisis*, the NAACP's official organ. Continuing as assistant secretary also, Wilkins was *Crisis* editor until 1949. He also traveled widely speaking for the NAACP and wrote many articles on racial issues for magazines and books. In 1943, he went to Philadelphia for the NAACP to represent blacks when transit workers went on strike because eight blacks were promoted to motormen, a relatively high-paying job previously reserved for whites. After six days, the strike ended and the blacks kept their jobs. Along with White and

Du Bois (who rejoined the NAACP's national staff from 1944 to 1948), Wilkins was a consultant to the American delegation at the founding conference of the United Nations in San Francisco in 1945. During the 1940s, Wilkins appeared as a panelist on a weekly radio program, "Pride and Prejudice," broadcast from New York.

While White was on a one-year leave of absence, beginning in June, 1949, Wilkins served as acting executive secretary. He also chaired the National Emergency Civil Rights Mobilization convened in Washington in January, 1950, to lobby for fair employment and other civil rights measures. When White returned in June, 1950, the NAACP was reorganized, with Wilkins appointed to the post of internal administrator, giving him complete management of the national office, while the executive secretary concentrated on the organization's outward affairs. A month after White passed away, NAACP directors unanimously appointed Wilkins executive secretary.

For a decade and a half, Wilkins has directed NAACP campaigns seeking to implement school desegregation, to abolish the poll tax and secure Federal protection for voting rights, and to end discrimination in public accommodations, housing, and jobs. Under his leadership, the NAACP has adopted a more militant and activist stance, joining in demonstrations such as the 1963 March on Washington as well as continuing its traditional tactics of law suits, publicity, and lobbying. Wilkins marched at many hotspots, such as Selma in 1965 and the renewed Meredith March Against Fear in 1966. Along with Martin Luther King, A. Philip Randolph, James Farmer, and Whitney Young (*qq.v.*), Wilkins was one of the Big Five civil rights leaders consulted by American Presidents. NAACP lawyers and funds rescued and defended the militant protestors of more activist organizations when they were arrested by stalwarts of segregation and the status quo. Nonetheless, the rush of events has caused the NAACP, once feared and condemned for being a radical, revolutionary, "communist" group, to be labeled by militants of the 1960s and 1970s a conservative, white-run, "Uncle Tom" organization.

Wilkins was the third black to become the NAACP's executive secretary. The first secretaries, 1910 to 1919, were white. Three blacks have served since then: James Weldon Johnson (*q.v.*), 1920 to 1931; Walter White (*q.v.*), 1931 to 1955; and Roy Wilkins, since 1955.

Williams, Bert (c. 1874–1922), Comedian

Many knowledgeable persons consider Bert Williams the greatest comedian in the history of American entertainment. W. C. Fields said he was the funniest man he ever saw.

He was born Egbert Austin Williams in Antigua, British West Indies. His paternal grandfather, a white man and Danish consul on the island, married a native Antiguan, one-fourth African and three-fourths Spanish. Their son also married a quadroon. Bert's early childhood was spent on the lovely family plantation, but when he was 7 a serious illness cost his father his fortune. On a physician's advice, Bert's father moved his family to America, settling in California. Bert went to school in San Francisco and yearned to study engineering at Stanford University in nearby Palo Alto, but lacked the money. Like his father, he loved books and remained an avid reader of Goethe, Schopenhauer, Voltaire, and others all his life.

Bert loved music and learned to play many instruments, especially the banjo. As a youngster, he sang and danced in the streets for coins when school was out. A gifted mimic and natural singer, he could imitate the speech and manner of anyone he met. Playing his banjo, singing, and doing mimicry, he became an entertainer in cafés and honkytonks along San Francisco's Barbary Coast. In 1895, he met George Nash Walker, an entertainer from Lawrence, Kan. They formed a vaudeville team. Initially, the short, dark-skinned Walker played the comic stooge and dancer while the tall, light-skinned Williams was the straight man and serious singer. Realizing soon that Williams attracted more laughs, they switched roles with Walker as the well-dressed, fast-talking, sharp-dancing, dapper straight man and Williams as the dim-witted, drawling buffoon and singer. Since Williams looked too much like a white man to be accepted by American audiences in this role, he reluctantly donned burnt-cork makeup.

A smash hit in San Francisco, the team of Williams and Walker went on tour and reached New York City in 1896. Appearing in a show at the Casino Theatre, they were a hit with New Yorkers even though the show flopped. They played a record-breaking 28 consecutive weeks at Koster and Bial's Theatre, raising the cakewalk dance to new heights of popularity. They then tried London music halls, but without much success. Back in New York, they flopped with such shows of their own as *A Senegambian Carnival*. But the show they brought out in 1900, *The Sons of Ham*, was a big success, playing more than two years. In this show, Williams sang "I'm a Jonah Man," creating the character of a sad, luckless, ever-failing, dull Southern black. The Jonah Man was such a hit with audiences that Williams could not escape being that character thenceforward.

In 1902, Williams and Walker made theatrical history for blacks by opening their new show, *In Dahomey*, on Broadway at the prestigious

New York Theatre in Times Square. Their wives, Lottie Thompson Williams and Ada Overton Walker, had important parts in the cast. The composer and lyricist were Will Marion Cook and Paul Laurence Dunbar (*qq.v.*), respectively. In the spring of 1903, they took the show to London, playing at the Shaftesbury Theatre with only moderate success at first. But then they were invited to give a command performance at Buckingham Palace on June 23, 1903, for the ninth birthday of the king's grandson, Edward, (now the Duke of Windsor). Now the show became a big attraction, staying in London six more months and touring the Continent, making cakewalking the rage of Britain and France.

Other hits followed. *In Abyssinia* opened at the Majestic Theatre in Columbus Circle in New York in 1906. Their last hit, *Bandana Land*, opened in 1907. After its successful New York run, the show went on the road, but Walker became ill, collapsed, and retired to his home in Kansas, passing on in 1911. Williams continued to divide his income with Walker until then.

On his own, Williams did a show in 1909, *Mr. Lode of Kole*, that was only a modest success. In 1910, Abraham Erlanger, the nation's leading theatrical magnate, signed him to appear in the *Follies*, produced by Florenz Ziegfeld. Signed initially for three years, he remained for ten. From 1910 to 1917, he was the only black performing on Broadway. Black musical shows that had run downtown theretofore did not return until the 1920s. Not until Charles Gilpin (*q.v.*) in 1917 did another black actor appear downtown. Although Williams was the comic star of the *Follies*, he often had to use freight elevators and rear entrances when the show toured. He wanted to try serious roles but out of gratitude to Erlanger and Ziegfeld for giving him a break turned down a tempting offer to act in a David Belasco production.

After leaving the Follies, he starred in 1920 in *Broadway Brevities* at the Winter Garden. Then the Shuberts signed him as the lead in Sigmund Romberg's *Underneath the Bamboo Tree*, in which he was playing when he suffered a fatal seizure of pneumonia.

Few comedians approached the inventive, comic genius of Bert Williams. A cultivated, intelligent man, he played drawling dim-witted roles so convincingly that many onlookers were sure he was being himself. Before emerging on stage he would stick out his white-gloved hands and evoke gales of laughter simply by the droll movement of his fingers. No one matched him at telling tales, such as the story about "Waiting for Martin," or in such pantomimes as his poker game act. Applause thundered after his wry singing of such songs as "I May Be Crazy but I Ain't No Fool," "Bon, Bon Buddy, the Chocolate Drop," "I'm in the Right

Church but the Wrong Pew," and "Nobody." Eddie Cantor, Al Jolson, W. C. Fields, Jack Benny, and Red Skelton became better known, but critics rank Bert Williams ahead of any of them.

Ernest Hogan was a contemporary black comedian who rivaled Williams. Since their day, outstanding black comedians have included Rochester Anderson, Dusty Fletcher, Moms Mabley, Dick Gregory, and Flip Wilson.

Williams, Daniel Hale (1856–1931), Pioneer Heart Surgeon

In 1893, Dr. Daniel Hale Williams performed an operation publicized as the world's first successful heart surgery. This eminent surgeon founded the Provident Hospital in Chicago, the first hospital operated by Afro-Americans.

He was born in Hollidaysburg, Pa., fifth of seven children and younger of two sons. His father was a descendant of German settlers in Pennsylvania who had intermarried extensively with Indian, Irish, Scotch, and Welsh, and occasionally with blacks. His mother came from a respected, light-skinned free black family of Annapolis, Md. Dan's father, who was a businessman, abolitionist, and equal rights spokesman, passed away when the boy was 11. His widow apprenticed Dan to a Baltimore shoemaker and moved to Rockford, Ill., with her two eldest daughters, leaving the others in Maryland. After some months, forlorn, 12-year-old Dan followed them westward. When his restless mother moved back East leaving him in Rockford with a sister and cousins, he worked in barber shops and on lake boats. Moving to Wisconsin, he operated a barber shop in the village of Edgerton when he was 17, but soon moved to nearby Janesville.

There he was befriended by Charles Anderson, a black barber who owned the largest, most exclusive shop in town. Working part-time at Anderson's, Dan, who had attended black schools in Hollidaysburg and Annapolis, resumed his studies at Janesville's high school. He dropped out when the burden of working and caring for himself became too great. Anxious to go to college, he later attended classes at a classical academy in town, from which he graduated in 1877. Only one family withdrew a child because this private academy admitted the young black barber. He studied in a law office briefly, but his real interest was medicine. The town's leading physician, Dr. Henry Palmer, Wisconsin's surgeon-general and a customer of the barber shop, accepted Dan and two whites as apprentices in 1878. Two years later, the physician felt all three were ready for medical school. When the other two chose Chicago Medical College, an affiliate of Northwestern University, Dan went with them in the fall of 1880. Boarding with the widow of the wealthy black realtor, John Jones, and subsisting on a succession of loans from Anderson, Dan Williams completed his course in 1883. He had served an internship in adjacent Mercy Hospital the previous spring and summer.

He opened an office at 31st and Michigan in a well-to-do mixed neighborhood with white doctors in adjoining suites. Dr. Williams always proudly identified with his race but he was so fair-skinned that people usually mistook him for white. He got along well with his white fellow students and professors, and kept up his professional associations. When a former professor retired, he had Williams appointed to replace him as staff physician of the Protestant Orphan Asylum, an unpaid job valuable for experience and prestige. A dedicated physicain and skillful surgeon, Dr. Dan's reputation grew rapidly and his clientele, both white and black, swelled. He was appointed to the surgical staff of the South Side Dispensary and became a part-time anatomy and surgical instructor at his alma mater, Chicago Medical College of Northwestern University. He also became a surgeon of the City Railway Company and in 1889 was appointed to the Illinois State Board of Health. Nonetheless, bars were drawn, preventing him, for example, from joining the South Side Medico-Social Society. He was admitted to the Chicago Medical Society.

Feeling keenly the need for a hospital where black interns, nurses, and physicians—usually rejected by prejudiced, white-controlled hospitals—could train and enjoy staff privileges, Williams launched a drive in 1890 to found a hospital. Incorporated early in 1891 and opened as a twelve-bed institution that May, Provident Hospital at 27th and Dearborn was the first hospital in America founded or fully controlled by blacks. Funds were raised from blacks in the community and wealthy white donors. Under his exacting leadership, Provident set high standards, had an integrated staff and patients, built a good reputation, and soon became a mecca for black interns, nurses, and patients from all over America. Many were relieved to find a hospital where they were not abused, neglected, or used for guinea pigs simply because of their color.

It was here that Williams performed his famous operation on July 9, 1893, boldly opening the chest and sewing the pericardial sac of James Cornish, a laborer stabbed in a brawl. Medical thinking of the day demanded that heart punctures be left, either to heal themselves or prove fatal. Dr. Dan dared to do the unthinkable operation, risking his reputation and that of his fledgling hospital to save Cornish, who was sinking fast. The operation succeeded. Cornish walked out in 51 days and lived another twenty years. Extensive nationwide newspaper publicity was given to the unprecedented operation. Four years later, medical journals learned that a similar operation, unknown to Williams, had been performed successfully by Dr. H. C. Dalton in St. Louis in 1891, but his patient remained hospitalized 103 days and it was not known how long he lived thereafter. Standard texts continued to list Williams's case as the first fully successful heart operation. Operating without any of today's modern devices, techniques, and experience, Daniel Hale Williams took the first step down the path to today's spectacular heart transplants.

In later years, he succeeded in many other daring operations far ahead of his time, including two heart stab cases, several Caesarean deliveries, removal of difficult uterine tumors, brain surgery, and suturing of spleens. Leading white physicians and surgeons, as well as blacks, traveled long distances and crowded into amphitheaters to watch this skillful surgeon in his breathtaking lecture-demonstration-operations. In 1894, he was appointed by President Grover Cleveland surgeon-in-chief of 200-bed Freedmen's Hospital in Washington, D.C., where he served for four years, elevating the run-down institution, associated with Howard University, to respectable status. Returning to Provident and his Chicago practice in 1898, he served on the surgical staff of Cook County Hospital, 1900–1906, and became associate attending surgeon at St. Luke's Hospital, 1907–1931. Appointed visiting professor of clinical surgery at Meharry Medical College in Nashville, Tenn., in 1899, he made periodic visits, instituting surgical clinics and building up that black school. Under his forceful persuasion and guidance, blacks in Nashville and some thirty other cities throughout America founded hospitals. He was a founder and first vice president of the National Medical Association, an organization of black physicians. When the American College of Surgeons was founded in 1913, he was the only black invited to become a charter member. He wrote many important articles for major medical journals and spoke brilliantly before medical societies.

An inspiration to countless young doctors, he was so wrapped up in his work and so little attuned to medical politics that he failed to pander to powerful people and to protect himself from envious, ruthless, backbiting, ambitious men. Undercut and outmaneuvered, he was forced to resign in 1912 from the staff of Provident, which had expanded to a sixty-five-bed hospital in a new building at 36th and Dearborn. He never fully recovered from that display of ingratitude.

Williams, Paul R. (1894–   ), Architect

For four decades, Paul Revere Williams has been one of the West Coast's top architects. He is the most successful Afro-American in this field.

Born in Los Angeles, he was orphaned at 3. He sold newspapers and ran errands while going to grade school. The fair-skinned youngster was not conscious of racial differences while growing up in a mixed neighborhood and attending integrated schools. But when he applied for jobs after school hours, he suffered rebuffs on account of his color. Bewildered and resentful at first, he resolved to prove himself and to show that he could succeed at anything. While attending Polytechnic High School in Los Angeles, he decided he wanted to be an architect. Paul's instructors tried to dissuade him, asking who had ever heard of a black architect and pointing out that blacks were too poor to pay architects' fees. They urged him to become a physician since even the poor got sick and could find money for medical fees. Their arguments simply made Paul more determined. He had faith that he would be judged as an individual on his ability rather than lumped with the mass of his people who had little chance to develop their talents because of prejudice.

He worked his way through the University of Southern California making watch-fobs out of brass and gold-plating them. Becoming an art instructor in Los Angeles, he continued his studies of drafting and design in evening art schools. He later attended the Beaux Arts Institute of Design and was awarded their Beaux Arts medal for superior work. Looking up the addresses of architects in the Los Angeles Telephone directory, he trudged from office to office on the list until he found an architect willing to employ a black draftsman. He started at the bottom as a $15 a week general utility man, and slowly worked his way up to chief draftsman. As he had confidently expected, the Society of Los Angeles Architects accepted him on merit and he became a certified architect in 1915. He served under residential architect Reginald Johnson for half a dozen years and under commercial architect John Austin for three years, and learned many facets of the profession.

In 1923, Williams opened his own office. When prospective home-builders, suspecting his race, tried to leave his office, he devised tricks to get their attention. Asking what price home they planned to build, he indicated that the sum (whatever it was) was below the level at which he took work. But he offered to pause from his supposedly heavy load of commissions to give them some suggestions free of charge if they had a moment. Sometimes they would stay and he often wound up getting a client once they had a chance to hear him out. Another trick was his learning to draw rapidly upside down so that as a prospective client sat across from him describing his ideas, Williams would make a quick, rough sketch of the plans upside down from his side but right side up for the amazed client. When he had a chance at a big order, to build a house of more than $100,000, he would tell the client the blueprints would be ready next day, whereas most architects took several weeks. What the surprised client did not know on seeing the completed blueprints next day was that Williams had dropped everything else and worked through the night to get the job done. He soon saw big oaks growing out of his little acorns. Automaker Errett L. Cord was so impressed upon seeing one of the small homes Williams designed that he looked up the architect and commissioned him to do his thirty-two-room, $300,000 mansion.

Gradually, he built up a thriving practice. So many requests for his services came from all over America that he had to turn down many. By the late 1940s, he had a staff of twenty, including two blacks, working under him in his plush Wilshire Boulevard office and had a net income in excess of $50,000. At one time he was planning thirty-three buildings simultaneously, including homes, office buildings, and apartment houses. He has offices in Washington and Los Angeles and serves on the Los Angeles Municipal Housing Commission.

Paul Williams has designed more than 3,000 houses, ranging in value from $10,000 to $600,000, including homes for such Hollywood stars as Lon Chaney, Cary Grant, Bert Lahr, Julie London, Bojangles Robinson (q.v.), Frank Sinatra, and Danny Thomas. He designed the Beverly Hills mansion of CBS board chairman William Paley, the Sunset Plaza Apartments in Hollywood, the Saks Fifth Avenue store in Beverly Hills, the high-rise Wilson High School in Los Angeles, the Music Corporation of America office buildings in New York and Beverly Hills, the Palm Springs Tennis Club, the Beverly Wilshire Hotel, three buildings on UCLA's campus, and ten branches of the Bank of America. Williams served as associate architect for the $27,000,000 Federal Customs and Office Building in Los Angeles and the $50,000,000 Los Angeles International Airport. He has written two books, *Small Homes of Tomorrow* and *New Homes for Today*.

Woodruff, Hale (1900–   ), Artist

During the Harlem Renaissance movement of the 1920s, Hale Aspacio Woodruff emerged as one of the most promising of Afro-American artists. His use of color and his quality of design have kept him in the front rank of American artists even though some recent critics consider him lacking in militancy and social awareness.

Woodruff was born in Cairo, Ill. His ancestors lived in slavery in Alabama. His semi-literate father was a farmer and part-time musician, his mother was a domestic worker all her life. Their burdens multiplied when his father passed away during Hale's third year. After attending public schools in Nashville, Tenn., Hale made his way through the John Herron Art Institute in Indianapolis, Ind., on the hard-won earnings of his mother and himself. He then served four years on the staff of the Indianapolis Y.M.C.A., meanwhile doing such paintings as his oil portrait in 1926 of Countee Cullen, a leading poet of the Harlem Renaissance.

Woodruff was encouraged to study further by his winning of a bronze Harmon award in 1926, the first year the Harmon Foundation gave competitive prizes to stimulate Afro-American artists. When the foundation sponsored the nation's first all-black art exhibit in 1928, beginning an annual event, Woodruff was one of the artists represented. At that time he was studying in Paris. He had gone there in 1926 to study at the Académie Moderne and Académie Scandinave, and with Henry Tanner (*q.v.*). Art lovers of Indianapolis helped to finance his study abroad. Financier and art patron Otto Kahn also aided him after Walter White (*q.v.*) of the NAACP brought Woodruff to Kahn's attention. Working in Paris, Woodruff was influenced by French modernists, especially the cubism of Pablo Picasso as seen in such Woodruff works as "The Card Players" (oil, 1930) and "Abstract Composition" (oil, 1931).

Returning to America, Woodruff moved South to seek materials in the life of the black masses. He joined the faculty of Atlanta University as an art instructor, and drew on his observations of Southern life to do paintings and several series of etchings and woodcuts of Georgia town scenes. For a W.P.A. project series, he did panels of black neighborhoods entitled "Shantytown" and "Mudhill Row." As social commentary, his art showed bleak poverty so starkly that city fathers were shamed into corrective steps. Among the block prints he turned out in this period were "Giddap" (1938), showing the start of a lynching, "By Parties Unknown" (1938), showing a lynching's aftermath, and "Sunday Promenade," "Returning Home," and "Three Musicians," all in 1939. The versatile Woodruff also did many landscapes such as his 1934 water color, "The Teamster's Place," and his 1936 oil, "Atlanta Landscape," and many portraits such as his 1939 oils, "Suzetta" and "Little Boy." An Atlanta school developed around him, with such pupils as printmaker Wilmer Jennings and painter Frederick Flemister becoming eminent artists. Woodruff instituted the important annual Atlanta University art shows in 1941.

Woodruff is best known for the superb set of murals in oil tempera on canvas done during 1938 at Savery Library of Talladega College in Talladega, Ala. Unveiled and dedicated on April 15, 1939, "The Amistad Murals" were commissioned by the college in commemoration of the centennial of a famous slave uprising. Led by their tribal chieftain, Cinque, African slaves rebelled in June, 1839, aboard a Spanish slave schooner, *Amistad*. After killing or imprisoning officers and crew, they ordered the helmsmen to return to Africa but he steered them to Connecticut where the mutinous slaves were jailed and tried in 1840. With prominent New Englanders and abolitionists rallying to their cause, the verdict went for them. They were freed and—led by educated, re-christened Joseph Cinque—returned to Africa, landing in Sierra Leone in January, 1842. A masterpiece of color and design, the murals tell the dramatic story in three panels: "The Mutiny Aboard the Amistad," "The Amistad Slaves on Trial at New Haven, Connecticut," and "The Return to Africa."

In 1946, Woodruff became Professor of Art Education at New York University, where he served until his retirement. He put increasing stress on design and abstraction as seen, respectively, in his "Girls Skipping" (oil, 1949) and "American Land of Many Moons" (oil, 1954). He has won many prizes, had many exhibits, and is represented in important collections. Other leading artists of his generation include Aaron Douglass, Archibald Motley, Laura Wheeler Waring, and James Wells.

Woods, Granville T. (1856–1910), Inventor

Granville T. Woods was an electro-mechanical genius thought by some contemporary boosters to be on a par with Thomas Edison. Devices patented by Woods, especially his induction telegraph system, greatly increased safety of rail travel.

Born in Columbus, Ohio, Granville attended school there until the age of 10. He then served an apprenticeship in a machine shop, where he mastered the trades of machinist and blacksmith. Seeking to learn more, he both went to night school and took private lessons during his apprentice training. In 1872, at the age of 16, he moved westward, securing a job as a fireman on an Iron Mountain railroad in Missouri. Eventually he moved up to engineer. In his spare time from his railroad job, he studied electricity.

Near the end of 1874, he moved to Springfield, Ill., and worked in a rolling mill. Early in 1876, he moved to the East, where he worked part time in a machine shop and spent his afternoons and evenings in further study. As a special student, he took college courses in electrical and mechanical engineering for two years. He then went to sea early in 1878 as engineer on a British steamer, *Ironsides*. At sea for several years, he visited many parts of the world. Returning to America in 1880, he ran a locomotive on the Danville and Southern Railroad for a while.

Woods then settled in Cincinnati, Ohio, and took out his first patent (No. 299,894) on June 3, 1884, for a steam boiler furnace. He followed this up with a patent late in 1884 (No. 308,817) for a telephone transmitter and a patent on April 7, 1885 (No. 315,368) for an "Apparatus for Transmission of Messages by Telephone and Electricity." The American Bell Telephone Company eventually bought this patent from Woods. Meanwhile, he formed his own company in Cincinnati, the Woods Electric Company, to manufacture and sell telephone, telegraph, and electrical instruments.

His most important invention was the "Induction Telegraph System" (Patent No. 373,915, dated November 29, 1887), which made it possible for moving trains to communicate with one another and for station operators to communicate with moving trains. This Synchronous Multiplex Railway Telegraph system made rail travel much safer by permitting dispatchers to note at a glance the position of any rolling trains. Thus, collisions could be more easily averted. The Edison and Phelps Company challenged Woods in two court cases, claiming priority for Thomas Edison, who was working on a similar device. But Woods won both times, being certified by the U.S. Patent Office as the inventor.

The versatile inventor had a wide range of patents, including a polarized relay (1887), galvanic battery (1888), automatic safety cut-out for electric circuits (1889), amusement apparatus (1899), incubator (1900), and automatic air brake (1902). His incubator was a forerunner of modern devices that hatch as many as 100,000 eggs at once. Most of his inventions concerned railroad telegraphs, electrical brakes, and electric railway systems. He invented an "Electro-Mechanical Brake" in August, 1887, and an "Electro-Magnetic Brake Apparatus" that October. Two later railway brake devices (No. 775,825 of March 29, 1904, and No. 795,243 of July 18, 1905) were jointly patented by Woods and his brother, Lyates Woods, as co-inventors. They assigned these two patents to Westinghouse Electric Company. In 1891, Granville Woods took out a patent for an electric railway system and in 1893 he took out patents for an electric railway supply system and an electric railway conduit. He sold his patent No. 667,110 (January 29, 1901) for an electric railway to the General Electric Company of Thomas

Edison. Others of Woods patents were sold to the American Engineering Company.

Eventually, Woods closed his factory in Cincinnati and moved to New York City where he concentrated on inventing until the end. He took out more than fifty patents in his lifetime, exceeding the output of any other Afro-American inventor.

Woodson, Carter G. (1875–1950), Father of Negro History

Carter Godwin Woodson was the premier Afro-American historian. There were earlier black writers of history such as William C. Nell, William Wells Brown, Joseph T. Wilson, George W. Williams, who was the first to write history of scholarly merit, and W. E. B. Du Bois (q.v.), the first scientifically trained black historian. But Woodson deserves the title of Father of Negro History because he founded the main organizations and journals, systematically gathered the basic source materials, and wrote prolifically about the history of his people. Almost single-handedly, he rescued black history from neglect and made it an important, respected discipline, inspiring the many black historians who came after him.

He was born at New Canton in rural Buckingham County, Va. His parents were poor, former slaves who struggled to support their nine children by farming. Since Carter was needed to help them in the field, he could not attend regularly the five-month term of the district school for blacks. Through self-instruction, the ambitious lad was able to absorb the rudiments of elementary schooling by the time he was 17. Since Buckingham, like other Virginia counties, provided public high schools only for whites, Carter's thirst for secondary schooling had to be satisfied elsewhere. In 1892, he persuaded his brother Robert to move with him to Huntington, W.Va., so that they could go to Douglass High School. Their parents joined them a year later. For three years, Carter was able to attend school only part-time, a few months a year, having to work in distant Fayette County coal mines to support himself and help his family. Finally, early in 1895, he entered Douglass High full-time. The energetic youth completed high school in a year and a half, receiving his diploma in 1896.

He then studied for two years at Berea College, an integrated school in Berea, Ky., in which all students, white and black, paid their way by working on campus, producing things the college sold to maintain itself. In 1898, he became a teacher at Winona in Fayette County. His work was so impressive that in 1900 he was called to the principalship of Douglass High from which he had graduated four years before. During his three years as principal, Woodson continued studying at Berea summers, and received the Litt. B. degree in 1903. He then took a position as supervisor of schools in the Philippines, learning to speak Spanish fluently. During his three years in the Philippines, he continued studying summers, now at the University of Chicago, which awarded him a B.A. in 1907. He spent a year of study and travel, 1906–1907, in Asia and Europe, including a semester at the Sorbonne, the University of Paris, where he did graduate work in history and learned to speak fluent French. He then continued graduate work in history at the University of Chicago and received an M.A. in 1908. He next spent a year at Harvard University, studying for his Ph.D. degree under such eminent historians as W. B. Munro and Edward Channing.

In 1909, Woodson moved to Washington, D.C., as a teacher of history, English, Spanish, and French in Dunbar High School. He accepted the job to be near the Library of Congress where he did the research for his doctoral dissertation, "The Disruption of Virginia." In 1912, Harvard awarded him the Ph.D. in history. Only the second black to hold a Ph.D. in history, he concentrated on that field thereafter. The first black Ph.D. in history, W. E. B. Du Bois (Harvard, 1895), spread himself into many other fields, writing sociology, essays, and novels, and also becoming a major spokesman for his race, including serving a quarter-century (1910–1934) as an NAACP executive and editor of its *Crisis* magazine.

Woodson devoted his whole career to correcting misconceptions about the black man's past. He had a missionary zeal to tell about the achievements of Afro-Americans and their African ancestors so as to overcome the constant refrain dinned by newspapers, magazines, textbooks, and racist politicians on the theme that blacks were inferior people who had never accomplished anything worthwhile. In September, 1915, in Chicago, along with four men whose interest he had aroused, he founded The Association for the Study of Negro Life and History (ASNLH). On October 3, 1915, the ASNLH was incorporated under the laws of the District of Columbia and was based in the nation's capital thereafter. On January 1, 1916, Woodson brought out the first issue of the Association's quarterly publication, *The Journal of Negro History*, which reached a circulation of 4,000 within a year. Published continuously ever since, the *Journal* is an indispensable tool for all researchers on black history. As the only active, trained black historian in the early years (Du Bois was busy with the NAACP), Woodson ran the ASNLH and the *Journal* as virtually a one-man operation, serving as executive director of the former and editor of the latter until his passing in 1950. During those years, he contributed more articles and book reviews to the *Journal* than any other writer. He had to train research assistants, direct research projects, administer the ASNLH central office, raise money, keep in touch with the branches, and write books. For seven years, he did all this while teaching full-time, first at Dunbar High and then at Armstrong Manual Training High School, the other secondary school for blacks in Washington, D.C. In 1918, he became principal for one year at Armstrong, serving simultaneously as an instructor at Miner Normal School in Washington. For the 1919–1920 school year, he was Dean of the School of Liberal Arts and Head of the Graduate Faculty at Howard University in Washington, and also taught history. The strong-willed Woodson, who brooked no dissent in ASNLH operations, clashed with the university's president, refused to apologize in writing, and thus was dropped. He became the Dean of West Virginia Collegiate Institute (now West Virginia State College) for two years, reorganizing its college department.

In 1922, he retired from teaching, and devoted his remaining twenty-eight years to Negro history. In the early, precarious years, 1915–1918, he had to use his small income from teaching to help the Association and the *Journal* to weather financial storms, making up deficits out of his own pocket. Gradually, memberships and contributions were built up to make them self-sustaining. Philanthropist Julius Rosenwald early gave $400 a year. The Carnegie and Laura Spelman Rockefeller foundations each donated $5,000 a year for five years, beginning in 1921. This income enabled Woodson to stop teaching and to become full-time ASNLH executive director and to continue his research and writing.

His first book, *The Education of the Negro Prior to 1861*, was published in 1915, followed by *A Century of Negro Migration* (1918), and *The History of the Negro Church* (1922). Also in 1922, he published his important textbook, *The Negro in Our History*, which remained the standard work on black history until superseded by *From Slavery to Freedom* (1947), the outstanding textbook by John Hope Franklin (*q.v.*). Woodson's textbook was so popular and so widely adopted that it went through nine editions in his lifetime. He later adapted it for elementary grades under the title *Negro Makers of History* (1928) and for secondary school as *The Story of the Negro Retold* (1935). Meanwhile, he wrote *The Mis-Education of the Negro* (1933), edited such books as *Free Negro Owners of Slaves in 1830* (1924), compiled such works as *Negro Orators and their Orations* (1925), and collaborated with his research assistants on such books as *The Negro Wage Earner* (1930). He wrote such books on Africa as *The African Background*

Outlined (1936) and *African Heroes and Heroines* (1939). He edited a four-volume set, *The Works of Francis J. Grimke*, in 1942.

Most of his books were published by The Associated Publishers Inc., an independent, income-producing affiliate of the ASNLH that he founded in 1921 to publish works on blacks because most publishers showed little interest in publishing many scholarly, documented works on black history. In 1937, he founded *The Negro History Bulletin*, a monthly issued from October to June annually. The *Journal* was intended for scholars but the *Bulletin* was a popular magazine geared to public school teachers, pupils, and the interested, dedicated laymen who worked in the Association's many branches throughout America. Woodson edited the *Bulletin* as well as the *Journal*. In 1926, he launched the observance of Negro History Week, held annually in the second week of February to coincide with the birthdays of Abraham Lincoln (February 12) and Frederick Douglass (February 14).

Woodson never married, describing his work in Negro history as his wife and family. His spirit lives on in the things that resulted from his herculean labors, the institutions he founded that are still going strong—ASNLH, Associated Publishers, *Journal of Negro History*, Negro History Week, and *Negro History Bulletin*. For fifteen years after his passing, the ASNLH had to depend on a dedicated office staff and volunteer workers. In 1965, it received another full-time executive director, Charles H. Wesley, the third Afro-American with a Ph.D. in history (Harvard, 1925), who had written several important books on black history in the 1920s and 1930s under ASNLH auspices before serving twenty-three years as president of an Ohio college. Besides Wesley, other black historians contemporaneous with Woodson include such persons as A. A. Taylor, Luther P. Jackson, and Lorenzo Greene.

Wright, Richard (1908–1960), Novelist

Richard Wright was the first black novelist to be ranked among America's greatest fiction writers. His novel *Native Son* (1940) is a landmark in American literature, establishing the theme of the violent, brutalized, ghetto black created by a society that denies his humanity and controls him in a degraded, terrorized environment. Wright also wrote short stories, nonfiction, and a brilliant autobiography.

Older of two sons and grandson of slaves, he was born near Natchez, Miss.. His father was a sharecropper who never cleared anything because the books were kept by white planters whose word could not be questioned safely. His mother occasionally worked as a country schoolteacher. His discouraged father moved the family to Memphis, Tenn., where he worked as a drugstore porter until he deserted them. Six-year-old Richard learned hunger as his mother scratched out a living as a domestic worker. While she worked, he roamed the streets, begging pennies, learning profanity, and getting drunk on saloon handouts. Overburdened, his mother placed the boys in an orphanage. He began school in Memphis, but his mother moved away with her sons. Living with her sister in Elaine, Ark., they ate abundantly because her sister's husband was a prosperous saloon-keeper. But jealous whites, anxious to take over the business, murdered him, forcing the family to flee to West Helena, Ark. Richard knew hunger again and also a growing dread of white people who could so casually slap, kick, molest, and murder blacks. He resumed school in West Helena, but his mother suffered a paralytic stroke and was taken to her parents' home in Jackson, Miss. His brother was sent North but Richard stayed with an uncle in nearby Greenwood. He went to school there, but the unruly lad soon had to be returned to Jackson.

From 1920 to 1925, Richard lived at his grandparents' house with his invalid mother and other relatives, attending school but also becoming increasingly bitter and impatient. Ardent Seventh-Day Adventists, his grandmother and aunt made him go to an Adventist school and tried to force their faith on him, but he rebelled. Wielding knife or razor blade, he resisted whippings at home. He finally returned to public schools. Insensitive to the humble role he was expected to play, the bright, questioning skeptic became an outcast in the pious household. Relatives told him he was headed for the gallows. He found a refuge in reading pulp novels and magazines. In eighth grade, he wrote a story, "The Voodoo of Hell's Half-Acre," published in three installments by a black weekly newspaper, the Jackson *Southern Register*, but family, school-mates, and teachers all disparaged his dream of escaping from their circumscribed reality to become a writer. He was chosen valedictorian on finishing the ninth grade, the end of public schooling for Jackson blacks. By stubbornly refusing to read a speech his principal wrote, and delivering his own instead, he killed his chances of being aided to go to college and become a teacher in Jackson.

Beginning full-time work in 1925, the 16-year-old learned the reality of the black man's place in Southern society. As a porter in a clothing store that specialized in selling cheap goods to blacks on credit, he had to suffer silently, or else swiftly forfeit his life, while the proprietors abused their black customers, even viciously beating a woman who fell behind on payments. Eventually his eyes revealed his disgust and he was fired from that and a succession of jobs because he had not learned to play the servile, fawning, cringing role Mississippi whites expected of blacks. Hired to learn the optics trade by a kindly Yankee businessman new to the South, he was thwarted by the two white craftsmen. Determined to keep a black from ascending to their level, they forced him to quit in a brutal confrontation. Knowing they would kill him, he dared not tell the employer why he quit, but vowed to flee the South. At jobs in a hotel and then in a theater, he learned, like his fellow brutalized, cringing employees, to retaliate against the hateful white employers by stealing from them; petty thievery was often winked at by whites as part of the system of degrading blacks.

With the ill-gained money, the 17-year-old moved to Memphis late in 1925. Having learned to conceal outwardly his inability to feel the inferiority whites demanded he show in their presence, he got along. But he always had to be on his guard lest a chance expression, word, or movement betray to fear-ridden whites that he was not reconciled to accepting a servile status in life. He secured a job in an optical shop but this time stayed in his place as an errand boy and porter. He budgeted and saved so he could move on to Chicago. His mother and brother joined him in Memphis. A southern editorial severely criticizing H. L. Mencken made Mencken's works attractive to him. A friendly white craftsman at the shop let him use his card to check out books since blacks were barred from the Memphis public library. Richard had to write forged notes pretending he was getting the books for the white man. He read novelists mentioned by Mencken, including Conrad, Dostoyevsky, Tolstoy, Kafka, Twain, Norris, Lewis, and Dreiser. He determined to become a writer, to break out of the controlled niche in which Southern whites confined him.

Late in 1927, when he was 19, Wright moved to Chicago and got work first as a porter and errand boy in a delicatessen and then as a waiter and dishwasher in a tearoom. After taking a civil service examination, he became a substitute clerk in the post office in the fall of 1929. Freed from the long hours and taxing toil of menial labor, he could use his free time to study, read, think, and try to write. He observed the life of ghetto blacks, not as openly brutalized as blacks down South but still slapped back into their place in countless ways. Disillusioned with American democracy and the Northern "paradise" he drifted into leftist causes, meeting socialist and Communist writers, working in the Marxist John Reed Club, and writing poems and essays for radical journals. Refusing to submit to Communist Party discipline and to sacrificing time from writing to work in radical political activities, he quit the club but continued in sympathy with Communist ideals. As the Depression worsened and mail slackened, he was laid off. He saw the brutalities of rent riots, eviction, joblessness, and hunger. He went on relief but because he was classified as a writer was given a job on the W.P.A. Writers' Project in 1935. He learned much about the writing craft from his fellow workers and continued toiling on some stories he was preparing. He decided to move to the publishing capital, New York City, hoping to get on the Writers' Project there while trying to peddle his stories to major magazines. On the eve of his departure, he received notice of appointment to a permanent postal clerkship. Tempted only fleetingly to accept that secure post, he tore up the notice and hitchhiked to New York in the spring of 1937, determined to sink or swim as a writer.

He lived precariously for several months before getting on the Federal Writers' Project there. He also wrote for leftist periodicals such as *New Masses* and the *Daily Worker*. Magazines were lukewarm toward his stories, but Harper's Publishing Company bought four of them for publication as a book. This collection, *Uncle Tom's Children* (1938) was well received, and Wright's reputation was established. These stories told of alienated, brutalized black sharecroppers meeting violence as they contended with restrictions imposed by white America. Now Wright's works were eagerly sought by magazines.

In 1939, he received a Guggenheim Fellowship that enabled him to quit the Writers' Project and concentrate on finishing the novel that he had been working on for several years. Published in 1940, *Native Son* was the first novel by a black selected for the Book-of-the-Month Club or for a Modern Library edition. Set in Chicago and much more harsh and brutal than his first book, it tells of the dehumanizing ghetto life and murder trial of Bigger Thomas, a violent product of the ghetto who accidentally smothers his employer's drunken daughter. In 1941, Wright wrote the text to accompany a photographic essay of his people, *Twelve Million Black Voices*. His fourth book was his autobiography, *Black Boy* (1945), also a Book-of-the-Month Club selection. He bought his mother a home in Chicago, but otherwise cared little about the wealth rolling in from his writings.

Estranged from America's racist ways and materialistic outlook, Richard Wright left the country in 1947. While living abroad, mostly in France, the rest of his life, the expatriate wrote a number of other books. But *Native Son* and *Black Boy* are generally considered his best works. His other writings, some published posthumously, include four novels, *The Outsider* (1953), *The Long Dream* (1958), *Lawd Today* (1963), and *Savage Holiday* (1965); a collection of short stories, *Eight*

Men (1961); and four nonfiction works, *Black Power* (1954), *The Color Curtain* (1956), *Pagan Spain* (1957), and *White Man, Listen!* (1957). He collaborated with dramatist Paul Green on the 1941 play *Native Son*, based on his novel. Actor Canada Lee gave a powerful portrayal as Bigger.

Young, Charles (1864–1922), Army Officer

Charles Young was the first Afro-American to become a full colonel in the regular army. To avoid promoting him to combat general in World War I, the army retired him on grounds of health.

Son of former slaves, Young was born in a log cabin in the hamlet of Mays Lick, in northeastern Kentucky. When he was 9, his parents moved fifteen miles northward to the town of Ripley, Ohio, just across the Ohio River from Kentucky. Upon finishing high school there, he briefly taught school. In 1884, he was appointed to the U.S. Military Academy at West Point, fourteen years after the first black cadet, James W. Smith of South Carolina, was admitted. Young was the ninth black admitted but only the third to graduate because of the difficult studies and the pressure brought by prejudiced cadets to keep blacks from finishing. In 1877, Henry Flipper of Georgia became the first to graduate, but he was court-martialled and dismissed from the service four years later on what seemed trumped-up charges of misconduct in handling funds. In 1887, John Alexander of Arkansas became the second to graduate but he had a heart attack and passed away after only seven years of service.

Flipper and Alexander passed their courses easily but Young had problems. He was turned out of his original Class of 1888 because of deficiencies in mathematics. He was readmitted in the Class of 1889 after passing a make-up examination. He became discouraged because of his poor work in engineering and ordinance. His engineering instructor, Lieutenant George Goethals of Brooklyn, who later built the Panama Canal, helped Young prepare for a special re-examination in engineering. Young finally passed all of his courses and received his diploma on August 31, 1889, two months after the regular graduation exercises. Graduating 49th in a class of 49, he was the only black West Point graduate ever to rank lowest in his class. Like all black cadets, Young suffered indignities at West Point, being ostracized for the most part or being derisively labeled "load of coal." But he ignored the taunts and snubs.

Young began his military career as a second lieutenant in the Tenth Cavalry Regiment, one of the four black regular army units—24th and

25th Infantry and 9th and 10th Cavalry—most of those officers were white. After brief service with the 10th Cavalry and 25th Infantry, he spent three years with the Ninth Cavalry at Fort Robinson in Nebraska and Fort Du Chesne in Utah. In September, 1894, he was assigned to Wilberforce University, near Xenia, Ohio, as instructor of military science. While there, he was promoted to first lieutenant in December, 1896. A charming host, he entertained prominent blacks in his home and coached the school's glee club and drama group.

In May, 1898, at the outbreak of the Spanish-American War, Young was assigned with the brevet (temporary) rank of major to command a black volunteer unit of the Ohio National Guard, the Ninth Infantry Battalion. The 9th and 10th cavalry regiments in which he formerly served fought in Cuba rescuing Teddy Roosevelt's Rough Riders at San Juan Hill. But Young's Ohio volunteer battalion did not get into the fighting, serving at camps in Virginia, Pennsylvania, and South Carolina while Young drilled them to peak efficiency. When a group of white soldiers at Camp Alger, Va., refused to salute him because of his color, Young took off his coat and made them salute it, showing respect for the rank if not him.

After the war, Young was mustered out of the volunteer service, rejoining the Ninth Cavalry, back from Cuba, at Fort Du Chesne early in 1899. Soon they went to California on alert for overseas duty. Sent to the Philippines, 1901 to 1903, they helped to suppress the Filipino Insurrection. Young, who had reverted to the regular army rank of first lieutenant, was promoted to captain in February, 1901. From 1903 to 1904, he served as superintendent of two national parks in California. In 1904, he was appointed the U.S. Military attaché to Haiti, where, at great risk during Haitian civil warfare, he courageously made maps of the island that the United States desperately needed. From 1911 to 1912 he was a staff officer in Washington, D.C. In 1912 he was sent to Liberia as military attaché, and promoted to the rank of major in August of that year. Returning to America in 1915, he served with the Tenth Cavalry. In 1916, Major General John Pershing, soon to command American forces in World War I, led an expedition into Mexico to suppress Pancho Villa's border raids. A West Point cadet from Missouri (1882–1886) when Young was there, Pershing had served as lieutenant with the Tenth Cavalry in Indian Wars in the southwest and at Cuba, gaining the nickname "Black Jack" for leading Negro troops. The Tenth Cavalry, with Major Young commanding a squadron, served under Pershing in Mexico. Young's squadron rescued a white major and his men when Mexicans ambushed them near Parral. Newspapers noted this heroic exploit. Young became a lieutenant-colonel in June, 1916.

As the senior black officer in the regular army when the United States entered World War I in April, 1917, Young should have been promoted to brigadier-general and given command of a brigade (about three regiments) of black troops. Former president Theodore Roosevelt told NAACP executive James Weldon Johnson (*q.v.*) he favored that. But this apparently was distasteful to the Southern-oriented administration of Woodrow Wilson and to the regular Army, 75 percent of whose career officers were Southern whites. The War Department called Young up for a physical examination and ordered him retired with the rank of full colonel on June 22, 1917, because of "high blood pressure." Black newspapers made a big issue of this rebuff. Young returned to his home in Wilberforce, Ohio. In June, 1918, to prove his fitness, 54-year-old Colonel Young rode horseback from Wilberforce to Washington, D.C., covering the 500 miles in sixteen days, stopping at towns overnight to rest his horses. He rode to the War Department for a prearranged interview with Secretary of War Newton Baker, telling him that the ride, which newspapers covered, proved his fitness. When Baker asked if he wanted combat or noncombatant duty, Young requested combat. He then rode back to Ohio on horse.

But the Army did not recall him to duty until November 6, 1918, five days before the Armistice concluding hostilities. Colonel Young was sent to Camp Grant in Illinois to take charge of trainees there. When the camp was disbanded, he was sent to Monrovia late in 1919 to reorganize Liberia's Army. Black protesters demanded to know why he was sent to the arduous West African climate if his health had been too poor two years before to command troops in France. Early in 1922, while on a research expedition to Nigeria, he became ill and passed away. His body was returned to America early in 1923 for memorial services at City College New York and Arlington Amphitheater, with interment in the national cemetery.

Young knew German, Italian, Spanish, Latin, and Greek, and voraciously read literature in the original. He played the piano, violin, and cornet, and composed pieces for them, including a cradle song, an African suite, and a Caribbean suite. He composed music for lyrics his friend poet Paul Laurence Dunbar (*q.v.*) had written for a mutual friend to sing. Young arranged hymns and composed serenades for his church choir's performances. He wrote several poems and also wrote a pageant called "The Military Morale of Races." He wrote a book on Haiti's liberator, Toussaint L'Ouverture, and was gathering material for a book on Africa when he made the final trip to Kano in the interior of Nigeria from his post in Liberia.

Young, Whitney M., Jr. (1921–1971), Urban League Executive

Under the dynamic leadership of Whitney Moore Young, Jr., the National Urban League (NUL) has become a major force in the struggle to improve the black man's lot in America. Shunning violence and extremism, Young employs skillful persuasive negotiation to change the economic status of blacks by opening up positions heretofore closed and by upgrading black workers.

He was born at Lincoln Ridge, Ky., about twenty miles east of Louisville. He and his two sisters were brought up there on the campus of Lincoln Institute where their father served on the faculty. The institution was a private boarding high school for blacks, and drew students from throughout Kentucky and beyond. It was established in 1910 as a spin-off from formerly integrated Berea College after Kentucky passed a law in 1904 requiring Berea to expel its black students or remove them to a separate branch at least twenty-five miles away. Whitney M. Young, Sr., graduated from Lincoln in 1916 and immediately joined the faculty as a teacher, coach, and engineer. Whitney, Jr., and his two sisters attended the school where their father became president in 1935, retiring in 1966.

After graduating from Lincoln Institute, Whitney enrolled at a black school in Frankfort, Kentucky State College. A pre-medical major, he played on the basketball team and was president of the senior class. After graduation in 1941, he taught at the Rosenwald High School in Madisonville, Ky., for a year, also serving as coach and assistant principal. Young entered the Army in 1942, and was sent to Massachusetts Institute of Technology, 1942–1943, to study engineering. Subsequently, he served in Europe in a black outfit with white officers. As first sergeant of his company, he was intermediary between the Southern white captain who was company commander and the men who defied their fearful officers overseas.

By the time Young left the service, he had decided to go into social work. He enrolled at the University of Minnesota, and was awarded his M.A. degree in social work in 1947. For his master's thesis, he wrote a history of the Urban League in St. Paul, Minn. Upon graduation, he was hired by the St. Paul Urban League as director of industrial relations and vocational guidance. He helped to open up jobs for blacks as department store clerks, streetcar motormen, and taxi drivers. From 1950 to 1953, he was executive secretary of the Omaha Urban League. While there, he also taught at the School of Social Work of the University of Nebraska and at Creighton University in Omaha. In 1954, he became dean of the School of Social Work at Atlanta University. During his half-dozen years there, the school's enrollment and budget nearly doubled. Active also in the NAACP, he became local vice president. For 1960–1961, he took leave, with a Rockefeller Foundation special grant, to study at Harvard University as a visiting scholar.

On August 1, 1961, he became executive director of the National Urban League, chosen to succeed Lester Granger who retired after leading the NUL since 1941. Founded in 1910 as the National League on Urban Conditions, it had been headed by black sociologists George Haynes from 1911 to 1914 and Eugene Kinckle Jones from 1914 to 1941. When Young took over in 1961, the National League's annual budget was $325,000, its national office had a staff of 38, and the branches were only loosely coordinated. With his vigorous direction, the organization became much more cohesive. Five regional offices and a Washington office were set up. The budget increased to $6,100,000 and the League grew to 93 branches with 1,600 employees nationwide.

Young called for a Marshall Plan at home for blacks, a massive Federal expenditure of one hundred billion dollars in a crash program to overcome decades of deprivation and inequity. His column, "To Be Equal," appears in many newspapers, and his book, *To Be Equal* (1964), forcefully expounded the worsening economic plight of black Americans. At a time when polarization of the races is increasing, Young has been an important voice for national unity. Pushing for green power he has been the driving force behind the NUL's important National Skills Bank and has helped the League secure important job training contracts with the Labor Department for upgrading the urban poor. For years, he has argued that business must do more than simply passively announce the dropping of discrimination in employment. Instead, he calls for business to actively recruit understandably skeptical blacks, train them to overcome past neglect, and give the hardcore unemployed a chance to prove themselves by relaxing rules requiring high school diplomas and clean police records as prerequisites for hiring. Once deemed visionary, his ideas have now been applied by the National Alliance for Business, headed by Henry Ford II, and have been found to be practical, workable, and sensible.

Whitney Young moved the Urban League into an influential role in the civil rights movement from which it had previously held aloof. Along with the heads of SCLC, NAACP, CORE, and SNCC, he helped plan the 1963 March on Washington. Generally considered one of the half-dozen top black leaders, Young was consulted often by the President of the United States.

Index

Aaron, Henry (Hank), 197, 367
Abbott, Robert S., 160, 244–245
Abernathy, Ralph, 348
Abolitionists, 96–97, 98, 103, 104, 109, 116, 425
Abolition movements, 55, 57, 103, 117, 121, 135, 163
Acts of the Apostles, 6
Adams, Henry, 151
Adams, John Quincy, 76
Adams, Samuel, 48, 51
Adamwa language, 11
Afonso V, 19
Africa:
 agriculture in, 21
 archeological excavations in, 9
 civilizations of, 7, 20–21
 commerce of, 8, 21
 crafts of, 21
 culture of, 22
 early civilization of, 11
 early development in, 4–5
 early empires of, 11
 fossils found in, 4
 languages of, 7, 8, 10, 11, 12, 13–14, 22
 misconceptions about, 3, 4
 religions of, 21
 slavery in, 23
 slave traders, 17
 topography of, 3–4
 welfare system, 21
Africa and Africans, Bohannon, 4
African Methodist Episcopal (A.M.E.) church, 63, 247, 384–385
African Methodist Episcopal Zion (A.M.E.Z.), 103

Africans:
 in Bermuda, 36
Africanus, Leo, 15
Afro-American (newspaper), 160
Afro-Americans, *see* Blacks
After Slavery: The Negro in South Carolina during Reconstruction, 1861–1877, Williamson, 125
Akan, the, 29
Aksum, kingdom of, 6, 7
Aksumites, 7
Alabama, 133
Alaska, 141
Al-Bakri, 13
Aldridge, Ira, 102, 245
Alexander, Archie A., 246–247
Alexander, John, 192
Alexander VI, Pope, 27
Alexander the Great, 6
Al-Hasan ibn Muhammad, 15
Allen, Richard, 62, 103, 177, 247–248
American Baptist Home Mission Society, 165
American Colonization Society, the, 176
American Federation of Labor (A.F.L.), 154
American League, the, 188
American Missionary Association (Congregational), 165
American Negro Slavery, Phillips, 87
American Revolution, the, 49
 and blacks, 176
American Samoa, 141
American Theatre for Poets, the, 340

Amistad, the (slave ship), 76
Anderson, Marian, 191, 198, 248
Anderson, Osborn, 115
Andrew Johnson and Reconstruction, McKitrick, 125
Anglo-Saxon Clubs, the, 183
Angola, Portuguese, 9
Antislavery societies, 56
Arabian Peninsula, the, 6
Arab slave traders, 24
Arabs, the, 12
Arkansas, 133
Arkwright, Richard, 66
Armfield, John, 82
Armstrong, Louis, 249
Asbury, Francis, 62
Ashanti people, the, 24
Ashanti (kingdom), 29
Ashe, Arthur, 249–250
Ashley, William, 101
Askia Daud, 15
Askia dynasty, 14
Askia Ishak I, 15
Askia Muhammad Touré, 14, 15
Athanasius, Patriarch of Alexandria, 7
Atlanta Compromise speech, 145, 149–150, 161, 163, 164, 168, 440
Atlanta University, 166
Attles, Al, 197
Attucks, Crispus, 48, 49
Austin, Richard, 220
Aviles, Menendez de, 32
Ayllon, Lucas Vasquez de, 32
Azurara (chronicler of Portuguese exploration), 17, 19

Bain, Thomas, 122
Balboa, Vasco Núñez de, 31
Baldwin, James, 199, 250–251
Baltimore, Md., 152
Bancroft, Frederic, 83, 84
Banks, Nathaniel, 118
Banneker, Benjamin, 59–60, 203–204, 251
Bannister, Edward M., 252
Bantu, 9, 10

Bantu-Negro language group, 8
Barthé, Richmond, 253
Baylor, Elgin, 196, 407
Beattie, John, 283
Beckwourth, James P., 101–102, 253–254
Belafonte, Harry, 254–255
Benin (kingdom), 29
Benjamin, Judah P., 101
Berbers, the, 12
Bernard, Francis, 48
Bethune, Mary McLeod, 255–256, 445
Beveridge, Albert, 141
Bigard, Barney, 291
Biggs, Thornt, 157
Birmingham, Ala., 211
Birth of a Nation (film), 124, 173
Black Cargoes, Mannix and Cowley, 27, 28–29
Black codes, the, 129
Black Construction, Du Bois, 124
Black Laws (of Ohio), 99
Black, Julian, 355
Black Moses: The Story of Marcus Garvey and the Universal Negro Improvement Association, Cronon, 175
Black Muslims, the, 211, 215, 217–218, 360–362
Black Panther Party, the, 219, 376–379
Black Power, 218
Blacks:
  abolitionists, 425
  African heritage of, 22–24
  and American Revolution, 176
  architects, 467
  as capitalists, 100, 159–160, 297, 349, 409, 413, 435
  churchmen, 62–63, 102, 156, 247, 261, 279, 317, 384
  composers, 256, 271, 310, 331, 415
  as cowboys, 156–157
  denial of rights, 95, 129, 145–147, 152, 460
  disfranchisement of, 145
  early settlers of America, 36

as educators, 102, 138, 165–166, 255, 268, 322, 329, 448
economists, 313
employment census of 1890, 153
as explorers, 70, 158–159, 293, 320
as free men in early Virginia, 37
in government, 256, 260, 262, 313, 363, 444
as heroes, 52, 70, 118, 174, 411, 480
illiteracy of, 132
as indentured servants, 35, 37, 40–41
as inventors, 100–101, 371, 395, 471
journalists, 404, 410
leaders, 135–137, 162–165, 263, 282, 284, 294, 295, 309, 346, 358, 372, 376, 393, 422, 427, 431, 437, 447, 455, 459, 482
lynchings of, 144, 148, 179–180, 446–448, 457
in medicine, 103, 158, 278, 283, 464
middle class, 179
migration of, 149, 151, 177, 192
in military, 48, 51, 53–54, 70–71, 105–107, 116–119, 174, 192, 194, 264, 275, 479
organizations of, 175, 181
as painters, 102, 156, 252, 288, 420, 453, 468
photographers, 381
as pioneers, 101–102, 253, 279
playwrights, 312, 340
as poets, 154, 185–186, 258, 286, 326, 336, 367, 451
political movements, 171
in reconstruction politics, 124, 132
politics of, 144
in politics, 187, 219–220, 258, 259, 270, 277, 388, 418
population of, 41–42, 44, 45, 85–86, 94–95, 97, 151, 152, 153–154, 192, 213
prejudice against, 39, 93–94, 99, 131, 139, 214

prize fighters, 103, 159, 333, 354
publishers, 160, 244–245, 338, 433
early rights movements, 95–96, 98
rights of, 130, 143, 146–147, 208–213
scholars, 352, 472
scientists, 139, 158, 251, 266, 341
sculptors, 253, 351
in show business, 102, 160, 186, 190, 198–199, 245, 248, 249, 254, 262, 265, 267, 272, 274, 276, 287, 289, 290, 296, 301, 307, 308, 315, 324, 328, 369, 386, 397, 400, 441, 461
as slave owners, 85
as sociologists, 300
in sports, 159, 186, 188–190, 196–198, 249, 259, 266, 305, 365, 379, 401, 405
status in Colonial America, 36–37
writers, 103, 155, 157, 167, 250, 269, 292, 299, 475
Black Zionism, 176
Blackburn, Jack, 355
Blackman, Pomp, 51
Bland, James, 160, 256
Blanton, Jimmy, 291
Blow, Henry, 120
Bohannon, Paul, 4
Bond, Horace Mann, 125
Boston, Ralph, 380
Boston *Guardian*, the, 168
Boston, Mass., 152
Boston Massacre, the, 49–50
Bowler, Jack, 90
Bradley, Joseph P., 143
Bradley, Thomas, 220
Breckenridge, John, 115
Breed's Hill, 51
Bridgetower, George Augustus, 20
Brimmer, Andrew F., 256–257
Bronco Sam, 157
Brooke, Edward, 220, 257–258
Brooklyn Dodgers, the, 188
Brooks, Gwendolyn, 199, 258–259

Brooks, Preston, 113
Brown, Jim, 196, 259
Brown, John, 113, 115, 162, 163
Brown, Lawrence, 291
Brown, Moses, 45
Brown, Nicholas, 45
Brown, Rap, 218
Brown, Wesley, 195
Brown, William, 48
Bruce, Blanche Kelso, 132, 259–
260
Bullock, Rufus, 135
Bunche, Ralph, 212, 260
Bunker Hill, Battle of, 51
Burgess, John M., 261–262
Burleigh, Harry T., 160, 262
Burns, Anthony, 112
Burns, Tommy, 334
Burton, Mary, 47
Bushmen, 10
Butcher, Margaret, 345, 354
Butler, Andrew, 113
Butts, Fanny, 165
Byrd, Harry F., Sr., 208

Calhoun, John, 111
Campanella, Roy, 196
Camp, Walter, 159
Candace of Ethiopia, Queen, 6
Cardozo, Francis, 132, 262–263
Carmichael, Stokely, 218, 263–264
Carney, Harry, 291
Carney, William, 118, 264–265
Carpetbag governments, 132–133,
151
Carroll, Diahann, 199, 265
Carver, George Washington, 139,
266
Cartwright, Edmund, 66
Cartwright, Samuel, 91
Casor, John, 34
Castillo, Alonzo del, 31
Cato Conspiracy, the, 43
Chamberlain, Houston Stewart, 140
Chamberlain, Wilt, 196, 266–267
Channing, Edward, 108
Charles, Ezzard, 357
Charles I, King of Spain, 31
Charles II, King of England, 41, 42

Charles, Ray, 267–268
Charleston, S.C., 43, 152
Charlton, Cornelius, 194
Chase, Stephen A., 93
Chavis, John, 102, 268–269
Chesnutt, Charles Waddell, 155,
269–270
Chicago *Defender*, the (news-
paper) 160, 244
Chicago, Ill., 59, 152
Chisholm, Elizabeth, 391
Chisholm, Shirley, 220, 270–271
Choyinski, Joe, 333
Cibola, 32
Cincinnati, O., 152
Cinque, Joseph, 76
Civil Rights Act of 1875, 143
Civil Rights Act of 1957, the, 144
Civil Rights Act of 1968, the, 348
Civil Rights Act of 1964, the, 144,
211, 348
Civil Rights Act of 1965, 348
Civil War, the:
and blacks, 105–107, 116
causes of, 108–112, 113, 115
and revisionist historians, 107–
110
and slavery, 110
*Civil War and Reconstruction in
Alabama*, Fleming, 123
Clansman, The, Dixon, 124
Cleaver, Eldridge, 219, 378
Cleveland, Grover, 135
Clinton, Tenn., 208
Coffles, 82
Cole, Arthur C., 108
Cole, Bob, 161, 271–272
Cole, Nat, 272–273
Collins, Janet, 181, 273–274
Colonel's Dream, The, Chesnutt,
156
Colston, James A., 450
Columbus, O., 152
Compromise of 1850, the, 111–112
Confederate Congress, the, 119
Confederate States of America, the,
115, 120, 127, 129, 130
Congo, Republic of, 9
Congo River, 3, 18

Congress of Racial Equality (CORE), 208
Conjure Woman, The, Chesnutt, 155
Conkling, Roscoe, 120
Constitutional Convention of 1787, 71
Continental Congress, the, 57
Cook, Mercer, 272
Cook, Will Marion, 161
Cooper, Albert, 376
Copeland, John, 115
Cornish, James, 158
Cornish, Samuel, 103, 410
Coronado, Francisco, 32
Cortés, Hernán, 31
Corwin, E. H. L., 284
Cosby, Bill, 199, 274–275
Cotton, 64–65, 68–69
Cotton engine (gin), 66–68
Coulter, E. Merton, 123
Cowley, Malcolm, 27
Cox, La Wanda and John, 125
Crandall, Prudence, 98
Craven, Avery, 108, 109
Craven, Wesley Frank, 39
Creek Indians, 69–70, 71
Creelman, James, 134
Creole, the (slave ship), 76
Crompton, Samuel, 66
Cronon, E. David, 175
Curtin, Philip, 4
Cuba, 141
Cuffe, Paul, 100, 176

Dancer, Earl, 442–443
Dahomey, 18, 29
Daquin, Louis, 70
Darwin, Charles, 140
Davis, Asa, 10
Davis, Benjamin J., 314
Davis, Benjamin O., Jr., 192, 275–276
Davis, Benjamin O., Sr., 192
Davis, Jefferson, 119
Davis, John, 70
Davis, Sammy, Jr., 276–277
Davis, William W., 123
Dawes, Will, 51

Dawn of African History, The, Oliver, 8
Dawson, William L., 187, 277–278
Degler, Carl, 39
De Gobineau, Arthur, 140
Delaney, Martin R., 177
Delaware, colony of, 45–46
Democratic Party, the, 128
Dempsey, Jack, 355
DePriest, Oscar, 187
Derham, James, 58, 278
De Sable, Jean, 279
Description of North Africa, al-Bakri, 13
DeVoto, Bernard, 109
Dew, Thomas R., 84
Dias, Bartolomew, 18
Dickinson, John, 48
Diego el Negro, 31
Divine, Father, 279–280
Dixon, Dean, 281
Dixon, George, 159
Dixon, Thomas, 124
Dodd, William E., 108
Dom Affonso I, King, 9, 10
Dorantes, Andres, 31
Douglas, Stephen, 112–114
Douglass, Frederick, 80, 92–97, 98, 104, 116, 117, 130, 135–137, 142, 150, 163, 168, 177, 178, 183, 204, 282
Downing, Emanuel, 44
Drew, Charles R., 195, 283
Drew, Timothy, 185
Drower, Margaret S., 5
Du Bois, W. E. B., 124, 162, 163, 166, 167–171, 172, 173, 177, 199–200, 204, 284–286
Dumas, Alexander, 20
Dunbar, Paul Laurence, 155, 286–287
Duncanson, Robert, 102, 288
Duncan, Todd, 190, 287–288
Dunham, Katherine, 289–290
Dunlop, Alexander, 122
Dunning, William A., 123, 127
Duse Mohammed Ali, 181
Dusk of Dawn, Du Bois, 162, 166

East Africa, 3, 4
Eaton, Clement, 66, 81
Ebony (magazine), 339
Eckenrode, Hamilton J., 123
Egypt, 5, 6
Eisenhower, Dwight, 208
El Hage, 20
Ellicott, Andrew, III, 61
Ellington, Duke, 290–292
Ellison, Ralph, 199, 292–293
Elmina Castle, 24
Emancipation Proclamation, the, 117
Emerson, John, 113
Era of Reconstruction 1865–1877, The, Stampp, 125
Essay on the Inequality of Human Races, de Gobineau, 140
Esterbrooks, Prince, 50
Estevanico (black explorer), 31–32, 293–294
Ethiopia, 6
Ethiopian Church, 7
Everett, Edward, 52
Evers, Charles, 219, 294–295
Evers, Medgar, 211
Explorers Club, the, 322
Eyewitness: The Negro in American History, Katz, 71
Ezana, King, 7

Fair Employment Practices Committee (FEPC), 192, 194, 395
Falconbridge, Alexander, 29
Fanon, Frantz, 219
Fard, W. D., 185
Farmer, James, 208, 295–296
Father Henson's Story of His Own Life, Henson, 79
Faubus, Orval, 208
Ficklen, John R., 123
Fisk University Jubilee Singers, the, 160
Fitzgerald, Ella, 296–297
Fleming, Walter L., 123
Flipper, Henry, 192
Florida, 133
Fons, the, 29
Forbes, George W., 169

Forman, James, 221
Forten, Charlotte, 112
Forten, James, 100, 103, 297–299
Fort Jackson, Treaty of, 71
Fort Mims Massacre, the, 70
Fort Pillow, Tennessee, 118
Fort Sumter, 115
Fort Wagner, South Carolina, 118
Fourteenth Amendment, the, 131
Franklin, Benjamin, 53
Franklin, Isaac, 82
Franklin, John Hope, 2, 5, 125, 299–300
Franks, Leo, 180
Frazier, E. Franklin, 22, 300–301
Free African Society, the, 62, 247
Freedmen's Bureau, the, 131
From Slavery to Freedom, Franklin, 2
Frumentius (bishop), 7
Fuller, Meta Warrick, 352

Gabriel (slave), 90
Gama, Vasco da, 8, 18–19
Gao (old capital of Songhay), 15
Garner, Erroll, 301–302
Garner, James W., 123
Garnet, Henry Highland, 178
Garrison, William Lloyd, 103
Garvey, Marcus, 174, 175–176, 180–185, 204, 302–304, 373
Garvey's Watchman (periodical), 180
Georgia, 133
Georgia, colony of, 44
George III, King of England, 57
Geyl, Pieter, 109
Ghana, 11, 12, 13, 18
Gilliam, Jim, 197
Gilpin, Charles S., 308–309
Gibbs, Jonathan, 132
Gibson, Althea, 197, 305–307
Gibson, Kenneth, 219, 420
Gold Coast, the, 18, 25
Goldsby, "Cherokee Bill," 157
Gompers, Samuel, 154
Gonçalvez, Antam, 17
Gonga Musa, *see* Mansa Musa
Grain Coast, the, 18

Grant, Ulysses S., 107, 133
Greeks, the, 12
Green, Shields, 115
Greene, Catherine Littleton, 65
Greene, Nathanael, 64–65
Greer, Sonny, 291
Growth of Southern Civilization, 1790–1860, The, Eaton, 66, 81
Guam, 141
Guinea, 18

Hajj, the, 1
Hall, Prince, 58, 309–310
Hamilton, J. G. de Roulhac, 123
Hamilton, Thomas, 83
Hamito-Semitic (Afro-Asiatic) languages, 7
Hammond, James H., 67–68
Hammond, Jupiter, 58
Hancock, John, 51
Handlin, Mary, 39
Handlin, Oscar, 39
Handy, W. C., 310–311
Hansberry, Lorraine, 199, 312–313
Hardwick, Otto, 291
Hargreaves, James, 66
Harlan, John Marshall, 147
Harlem Renaissance, the, 179, 185, 327, 337, 367, 468
Harlem Shadows, McKay, 185
Harpers Ferry, W.Va., 115, 162
Hastie, William H., 193, 313–315
Hatcher, Richard, 219, 420
Haulti, 7
Hausa states, the, 11
Hawaiian Islands, the, 141
Hawile-Assaraw, 7
Hawkins, John, 27
Hayes, Roland, 186, 315–317
Haynes, Lemuel, 51
Healy, James A., 317–319
Henry, Andrew, 101
Henry, Patrick, 48
Henry the Navigator, Prince, 17, 18
Henson, Josiah, 79–80, 87
Henson, Matthew, 158–159, 320–322
Herodotus, 7

Herskovits, Melville, 22–23
Higginson, Thomas Wentworth, 105
Hill, Richard, 122
History and Description of Africa, Africanus, 15
History of Negro Slavery in New York, A, McManus, 46
Hodges, Johnny, 291
Holmes, Hodgen, 67
Hoover, Herbert, 193
Hope, John, 165, 322–324
Hope of Liberty, The, Horton, 103
Horne, Lena, 324–326
Hornsby, Rogers, 189
Horseshoe Bend, the Battle of, 71
Horton, George Moses, 103
House Behind the Cedars, The, Chesnutt, 156
Houston, Charles H., 364
Howard, Jacob, 120, 121
Howell, Clark, 135
How Peary Reached the Pole, Mac-Millan, 321
Hudson River School, 289
Hughes, John, 116
Hughes, Langston, 186, 326–328
Hughson, John, 47
Hutchinson, Thomas, 49
Hutton, Bobby, 378
Hyksos, 5

Ibn-Batuta, 1, 8, 14
Ife, the, 29
Ife art, 22
Image of Africa, The, Curtin, 4
Independent Magazine, The, 148
Indianapolis, Ind., 152
Industrial Revolution, the, 66
Innis, Roy, 218
Invisible Man, Ellison, 292
Iowa, 112
Irvis, Charlie, 291
Ishak II, 15
Islamic faith, 12, 29

Jackson, Andrew, 70, 71, 111
Jackson, Mahalia, 328–329
Jackson, May Howard, 352
Jackson, Maynard, 219

Jacksonville, Fla., 152
Jay, John, 56
Jefferson, Thomas, 57, 61, 110
Jersey City Giants, 188
Jim Crow, 146, 147, 183
Joel, Lawrence, 194
Jones, Absalom, 62, 247
Jones, Edward, 410
Johnson, Andrew, 122, 128–131
Johnson, Anthony, 34
Johnson, Campbell, 193
Johnson, Charles S., 329–331
Johnson, Hall, 331–333
Johnson, Henry, 174
Johnson, Jack, 159, 333–325
Johnson, James Weldon, 172, 336–338
Johnson, John H., 338–339
Johnson, J. Rosamond, 161, 336
Johnson, Lyndon B., 209, 211–212, 220, 365
Johnston, Joshua, 58
John III (King of Portugal), 10
Jordan, Winthrop, 39, 95
Journal of Negro History, The, 473–474
Judar Pasha, 15
Julian, Percy, 341, 344
Just, Ernest E., 158, 344–345

Kanem-Bornu (kingdom), 11
Kaniaga, 13
Kansas, 112
Kansas-Nebraska Act of 1854, the, 112, 113, 114
Karina, battle of, 13
Karnak, temple at, 5
Kashta (founded kingdom of Kush), 6
Katz, William L., 71
Kennedy, John F., 209, 364
Kennedy, Robert F., 209
Kenworthy, E. W., 202
Kilwa, 7, 8
King, Coretta Scott, 348
King, Martin Luther, Jr., 202–208, 219, 220, 346–349
King, Yolande, 205
Kongo, 8, 9

Ku Klux Klan, the, 133, 180, 183, 447
Kush, 5, 6

Lacoste, Pierre, 70
Lafon, Thomy, 100
Lake Tanganyika, 4
Lançarote (slave trader), 19
Larkin, Thomas, 349, 350
Las Casas, Bartholomew, 31
Leakey, Louis S. B., 4
Leakey, Mary, 4
Leary, Lewis, 115
Leidesdorff, William, 100, 349–350
Lemmons, Bob, 157
L'Enfant, Pierre-Charles, 61
Leslie, Lew, 370
Lewis, Edmonia, 351–352
Lewis, John, 210
Lewis, Oliver, 376
Lewis, William Henry, 159
Liberator, The (newspaper), 103
Liberia, 176
Libyans, the, 12
Lillard, Joe, 196
Limpopo River, 8
Lincoln, Abraham, 115, 116, 118–119, 125, 126, 127, 128
Lions of Judah, dynasty of, 7
Little, Malcolm, *see* Malcolm X
Little Rock, Ark., 208
Locke, Alain, 352–353
Locke, John, 42
Long, Thomas, 105
Lonn, Ella, 123
Lossing, Benson J., 60
Louis, Joe, 186, 306, 354–358
Louisiana, 125, 133, 145
Louisiana Purchase, the, 110, 111, 112
Love, Nat, 157
Luthuli, Albert, 212
Lynch, John R., 124
Lynchings, 148, 179–180, 446–448, 457
Lyrics of Lowly Life, Dunbar, 155

McDaniel, Hattie, 387
McKay, Claude, 185, 367–369

McKissick, Floyd, 218
McKitrick, Eric, 125
McLendon, Johnny, 197
McManus, Edgar, 45
McMaster, John Bach, 108
McPherson, James M., 105
Malcolm X, 211, 216–218, 358–363, 375
Mali, 2, 11, 13, 14
Malindi, 8
Mande language, 11, 13
Mangum, Willie P., 269
Manly, Charles, 269
Mannix, Daniel, 27
Mansa Musa, 1–3, 14
Marciano, Rocky, 357
Marcos, Friar, 32
Marichal, Juan, 196
Marion, Francis, 65
Marrow of Tradition, The, Chesnutt, 156
Marshall, Thurgood, 200, 220, 363–365
Martin, Richard B., 261
Maryland:
  black population of, 42
Maryland, colony of, 41–42
Massachusetts Bay Colony, the, 44
Matthew, Gervase, 8
Matzeliger, Jan, 158
Mays, Willie, 197, 365–367
Mbznza, Congo, 9
Meade, George P., 101
Mecca, 1
Medal of Honor, the Congressional, 118, 174, 194
Meet General Grant, Woodward, 106–107
Melaso, 7
Menelik, 7
Mennonites, 55
Meredith, James, 209
Meroe (in Kush), 6, 7
Merrick, John, 413–414
Metcalfe, Ralph, 380
Miley, Bubber, 291
Miller, Dorie, 194
Miller, Kelly, 162
Miller, Phineas, 64, 66

Mills, Florence, 369–371
Mills, Irving, 291
Minnesota, territory of, 112
Minutemen, black, 51
Mississippi, 133, 145
Missouri, 110, 112
Missouri Compromise of 1820, the, 110, 113, 114
Mitchell, Arthur, 187
Mogadishu, 8
Molineaux, Tom, 103
Mombasa, 8
Monroe, James, 90
Monrovia, Liberia, 176
Montgomery, Ala., 152, 202, 204
Montreal Royals, 188
Moore, Aaron McDuffie, 413–414
Morgan, Garrett A., 371–372
Moslem religion, 7
Moslems, 1
Mossi states, the, 11
Motley, Constance Baker, 271
Muhammad, Elijah, 185, 215–216, 217, 360–362, 372–375
Muhammad, Elijah, Jr., 375
Muhammad, Herbert, 375
Muhammad, Wallace D., 375
Murphy, Carl, 160
Murphy, Isaac, 159, 375–376
Murray, John, 53
Myers, Isaac, 395
Myth of the Negro Past, The, Herskovits, 22–23

Naga:
  temple of, 6
Nanton, Joe, 291
Napata (in Kush), 5, 6
National Association for the Advancement of Colored People, the (NAACP), 163, 172, 174, 183, 200, 207, 285, 457–459, 460–461
National League, the, 188
National Negro Business League, the, 177
National Urban League, 180, 483
Native Son, Wright, 475, 478
Nebraska, territory of, 112

Negro Convention Movement, the, 177

Negro Education in Alabama: A Study in Cotton and Steel, Bond, 125

Negroes with Guns, Williams, 216

Negro Explorer at the North Pole, A, Henson, 320

Negro Family in the United States, The, Frazier, 22

Negro in Chicago, The, Johnson, 330

Negro in Mississippi, The, Wharton, 125

Negro in South Carolina During Reconstruction, The, Taylor, 124

Negro's Civil War, The, McPherson, 105–106

Negro World (newspaper), 182

Newby, Dangerfield, 115

Newby, Madison, 121

New Orleans, La., 125, 152

New Orleans, Battle of, 70

Newton, Huey, 219, 376–379

Newton, John, 28

New York City, 47

New York, colony of, 45

New York *Herald,* the, 252

New York, state of, 152

Niagara Movement, the, 162–163, 165, 170, 172–173, 285

Nigeria, 18

Niger River, 4, 13

Niger River valley, 4, 5

Nile River, 5, 6

Nixon, John, 54

Nixon, Richard, 100, 292

Nobel Peace Prize, the, 212, 261, 348

Noble Drew Ali, 185

Nok, the, 29

Nok culture period, 22

North Carolina, 42, 133

North Carolina, colony of, 42

North Carolina Mutual Life Insurance Company, the, 159–160, 414

North Star, The (newspaper), 97–98

Northwest Ordinance, the, 57, 141

Norton, Daniel, 120, 121

Notes on Virginia, Jefferson, 61

Nubians, 5, 7

Nuflo de Olano, 31

Oberlin College, Ohio, 163

Oglethorpe, James E., 44

Oil River, 25, 29

Olduvai Gorge, 4

Olive, Milton, 194

Oliver, Roland, 8, 9

Olmstead, Frederick Law, 83, 91

Origin of Species, The, Darwin, 140

Organization for Afro-American Unity (OAAU), 217, 362

Otis, James, 48

Overton, Monk, 376

Ovington, Mary White, 172

Owen, Chandler, 393

Owens, Jesse, 186, 379–381

Oyo (kingdom), 29

Pace, Harry, 338

Page, Thomas Nelson, 140

Pakenham, Edward, 70

Paleolithic Age, 4

Pan-African Congress, 178

Parker, George, 34

Parker, Jonas, 50

Parker, Robert, 34

Parks, Gordon, 381–384

Parks, Rosa, 204, 347

Parsons, Edmund, 122

Patriarch of Alexandria (Athanasius), 7

Patrick, Rembert, 125

Payne, Daniel A., 384–385

Peace and Freedom Party, the, 379

Peace Mission Movement, 280

Peary, Robert, 159, 320

Peculiar Institution, The, Stampp, 87–90

Penn, William, 46

Pennsylvania, colony of, 46

runaways, 33, 92, 428–430
  as soldiers, 117
  status of, in colonies, 38
  trade of, 17–19, 45, 81
  transport of, 28, 82–83, 84
  treatment of, 19–20
Slave trade:
  in America, 19
  prohibition of, 73–74
  Southern viewpoint, 77–78
Slave Trading in the Old South,
    Bancroft, 83
Sleeping Car Porters, Brotherhood
    of, 394
Smith, Francis, 50
Smith, Harry, 168
Smith, James McCune, 103
Smith-Lever Act of 1914, the, 139
Social Darwinists, 140
Sofala, 8
Solomon, King, 6
Somalia, 6
*Some Historical Errors of James
    Ford Rhodes*, Lynch, 124
Songhay, 11, 14, 24
Soninke people, 12
Southern Regional Council, the,
    324
Soul on Ice, Cleaver, 219
Souls of Black Folk, The, Du Bois,
    169, 170, 177
South Carolina, 115, 133, 145
South Carolina, colony of, 42
Southern Christian Leadership Con-
    ference (SCLC), 208, 347
Southern Manifesto, the, 207
Spanish-American War, the, 141
Spaulding, Charles Clinton, 159,
    413–415
Spingarn, Arthur, 173
Spinning jenny, the, 66
Spinning mule, the, 66
Springfield, Ill., 148, 172
Stampp, Kenneth, 39, 125
Staples, Thomas, 123
Stephens, Alexander, 115
Stevens, Thaddeus, 120, 127
Still, William, 104, 415–418, 429
Stokes, Carl, 219, 418–420

Stokes, Louis, 420
Storey, Moorfield, 173
Strayhorn, Billy, 291
*Stride Toward Freedom: The Mont-
    gomery Story*, King, 205
Student Nonviolent Coordinating
    Committee (SNCC), 209, 347
Sudan, 6, 12, 14
Sudanic blacks, 12
Sumanguru, King of Kaniaga, 13
Sumner, Charles, 98, 113, 127
Sumner, William Graham, 140
Sundiata Keita, 13
Sunni Ali Ber, King, 14
Sunni dynasty, 14
*Suppression of the African Slave-
    Trade to the United States of
    America, 1638–1870, The,* Du
    Bois, 167, 285
Supreme Court, the, 113, 143, 146,
    200–201, 207, 208
Swahili, 8
Swett, Samuel, 52

Taney, Roger B., 114
Tanner, Benjamin Tucker, 156
Tanner, Henry O., 156, 420–422
Tanutamon (Kusite ruler), 5
Tanzania, 8
Tappan, Arthur, 96
Tarhaga (Kusite ruler), 5
Taylor, Alrutheus A., 124
Taylor, Marshall W., 159
Tecumseh, 69–70
Tenkhamenin, King of Ghana, 13
Tennessee, 133
Terrell, Mary Church, 422–425
Terry, Lucy, 58
Texas, 133
Thebes, temple of, 5
Thirteenth Amendment, the, 128
Thompson, C. Mildred, 123
Thompson, William, 194
Timbuctoo and Hausa, El Hage, 20,
    21
Timbuktu, 14
Tocqueville, Alexis de, 94
Togo, 18
Tordesillas, the Treaty of, 27

Townsend, Willard, 395
Travels in Asia and Africa, Ibn-Batuta, 1, 14
Tristam, Nuño, 17
Trotter, William Monroe, 168, 169, 173
Truman, Benjamin, 122–123
Truman, Harry S., 195, 459
Truth, Sojourner, 104, 425–427
Tubman, Harriet, 104, 427–431
Turner, Charles Henry, 345
Turner, Frederick Jackson, 108
Turner, Nat, 91, 431–433
Tuskegee Institute, 134, 139, 439
Tuskegee Machine, the, 167, 168
Tuskegee News Bureau, the, 167
Tweed Ring, the, 133
Twenty-fifth Dynasty, 6
Tyler, John, 77

Underground Railroad, the, 104, 427–430
Union Party, the, 128
United States, the, 141–142
    attitude of, toward slave trade, 77–78
    westward expansion of, 69–70
Universal Negro Improvement Association (UNIA), 175, 181, 303
Up from Slavery, Washington, 135, 164, 181
Upper Guinea, 25

Vaca, Cabeza de, 31, 32
Van Buren, Martin, 76
Vann, Robert, 160, 433–435
Vesey, Denmark, 91
Vicksburg, Miss., 152
Virginia, 208, 133
    enslavement laws of, 38–39
    population of blacks in, 41
    slavery in, 37–38, 40–41
Virginia, colony of, 36
Virgin Islands, the, 141
Voting Rights Act of 1965, the, 212

Wade-Davis Bill, the, 127
Wadsworth, James S., 126

Wake Island, 141
Walcott, Joe, 333
Walker, David, 103–104, 177, 204
Walker, George Nash, 462
Walker, Madame C. J., 160, 435–436
Walker, Maggie Lena, 160, 436–437
Walker, Moses F., 188
Wallace, George, 209, 211
Walling, William English, 148, 149
Wangara, 12
Warbourg, Eugene, 352
Ward, Artemas, 51
Warfield, William, 392
War of 1812, the, 70
Warren, Earl, 200
Washington, Booker T., 134–139, 145, 149, 150, 154, 161, 163, 164, 173, 177, 181, 204, 437–440
Washington, George, 53–54, 60, 452
Washington, Kenny, 402
Washington, Walter E., 420
Washington, D.C., 152
Water frame, the, 66
Waters, Ethel, 441–444
Weary Blues, Hughes, 186
Weaver, Robert C., 220, 444–446
Weld, Theodore, 163
Wells, Ida B., 446–448
Wesley, Charles H., 475
West Africa, 2, 10, 15, 17
    empires in, 20
    trade with Europe, 24
Western Sudan, 11
Western Sudanic language, 11
Wharton, Clifton R., Jr., 448–450
Wharton, Vernon Lane, 125
Wheatley, Phillis, 59–60, 155, 451–453
Whetsol, Arthur, 291
Whig Party, the, 112
White, Bill, 197–198
White, Charles, 453–455
White, Walter, 172, 200, 204, 455–459
White Citizens' Councils, 208

White Over Black, Jordan, 39, 95
Whites:
  attitudes to blacks, 164
  as indentured servants, 37, 40–41
  in race riots, 152
Whitney, Eli, 65, 67
Whittemore, Cuff, 51
Wife of His Youth and Other Stories, The, Chesnutt, 155
Wilkins, Len, 197
Wilkins, Roy, 172, 219, 459–461
Willard, Jess, 335
Williams, Alfred Daniel, 346
Williams, Bert, 161, 461–464
Williams, Camilla, 190
Williams, Cootie, 291
Williams, Daniel Hale, 157–158, 195, 464–466
Williamson, Joel, 125
Williams, Paul R., 467–468
Williams, Robert F., 216
Wilmot Proviso, the, 111

Wilson, Woodrow, 108, 173
Winkfield, Jimmy, 376
Winthrop, John, 44
Wood, Cato, 51
Woodruff, Hale, 468–470
Woods, Granville, 158, 470–472
Woodson, Carter G., 472–475
Woodward, W. E., 106
Wretched of the Earth, The, Fanon, 219
Wright, Jonathan J., 132
Wright, Richard, 475–478

Yemen, 6
Yorubas, the, 29
Young, Charles, 174, 192, 479–481
Young, Whitney, Jr., 219, 482–483

Zambesi River, 8
Zanj, land of, 8
Zanzibar, 8
Zimbabwe, 7, 8, 9
Zinjanthropus, 4